Compiled for the Georgia Institute of Technology

Languages and Translation

Second Edition

CS 2130

Taken from

Efficient C Programming by Mark Allan Weiss and
Advanced UNIX Programming by Warren W. Gay

Cover Art: "Abstract #1," by Dave Taylor.

Excerpts taken from:

Efficient C Programming: A Practical Approach
by Mark Allen Weiss
Copyright © 1995 by Prentice-Hall, Inc.
A Pearson Education Company
Upper Saddle River, New Jersey 07458

Advanced UNIX Programming
by Warren W. Gay
Copyright © 2000 by Sams Publishing
A Pearson Education Company
Indianapolis, Indiana 46290

This special edition published in cooperation with Pearson Custom Publishing.

Printed in the United States of America

10 9 8 7 6 5 4 3 2 1

Please visit our web site at www.pearsoncustom.com

ISBN 0–536–67990–8

BA 995109

 PEARSON CUSTOM PUBLISHING
75 Arlington Street, Suite 300, Boston, MA 02116
A Pearson Education Company

Contents

Section

One

Taken from
Efficient C Programming
by Mark A. Weiss

1

C: A General Overview

Most people who are learning a new language want to write programs immediately. We provide a quick tour of C to get you started.

1.1 History

In the beginning, there was *BCPL*, developed in 1967 for use in operating systems and compiler design. Ken Thompson developed the *B* programming language, using many of the ideas in BCPL, and in 1970 used it to implement the first version of UNIX at Bell Laboratories.

In 1972, Dennis Ritchie designed C and implemented it on a PDP-11. UNIX was rewritten in C in 1974. *B* and *BCPL* were typeless languages: every object occupied a machine byte. Thus they could be viewed as fancy assembly languages. By contrast, C provided a rich set of types, thereby making high-level programming easier.

C's popularity exploded with the distribution to universities of free UNIX systems and C compilers, and the publication of the classic book by Kernighan and Ritchie [Kernighan 78]. For many years, the reference manual provided in its appendix was the defacto language document. The version of C described there is popularly known as *K&R C*.

K&R C set an early standard for portability when its compiler and the UNIX system were moved, relatively effortlessly, to other platforms. Researchers at Bell Laboratories used UNIX and developed many exciting tools, including a typesetting system. As UNIX spread to more and more universities, and students graduated from these universities, C became more and more popular.

The initial design of C reflected the fact that it was used to implement an operating system. Until then, all operating systems were written in an assembly language because compiler technology did not generate sufficiently efficient code from higher-level languages. K&R C provided constructs, such as pointer arithmetic, direct memory access, increment operators, bitwise operations, and octal and hexadecimal constants, that mimicked the PDP-11's instruction set, while at the same time keeping the language small but high level. Consequently, the compiler was able to generate reasonably efficient code.

K&R C, and also UNIX, were presumed to be used by experts. It is worth remembering that in the early 1970s screen editors did not exist. Instead, editing was done a line at a time, and terminal output was exceptionally slow. C thus provided rather terse syntax to minimize typing. Many symbols have various meanings, depending on context: * can mean multiplication or pointer dereferencing and is part of the commenting conventions. The language syntax allows a wide range of constructs. Some of these constructs are very useful, but unfortunately, are sometimes used unintentionally. When that happens, the compiler cannot report a syntax error.

The growth of personal computers also made the small and powerful UNIX and C systems attractive. C was quickly adopted as a more general-purpose language whose users included nonexperts. A host of software vendors started producing C compilers, adding their own extra features.

In the early 1980s, it became clear that C was emerging as a major programming language. However, competing compiler vendors had made C less portable. One reason was that K&R C was ambiguous in some of the language description and was thus interpreted differently by various compilers. Also, a host of clever but nonetheless unacceptable and nonportable programming tricks had emerged; it became clear that they should be disallowed. Since compiler technology became better and computers became faster, it also became feasible to add helpful features to the language, in the hopes of enhancing portability, and reducing the chances of undetected errors.

Thus began an effort to develop a standard C. The result is ANSI C, which is described in the document [ANSI 90].[1] Kernighan and Ritchie's book was revised to reflect ANSI C [Kernighan 88].[2] This is the language we will describe. ANSI C cleans up ambiguities in K&R C and, as much as possible, defines the language precisely. It incorporates changes that help eliminate silly errors (e.g., 9 is no longer an octal digit). As much as possible, it remains compatible with most of K&R C. Most important, it introduces the notion of the *function prototype* to allow strict type checking. Judging by the size of their respective compilers, ANSI C is about twice as complex as K&R C.

By no means is C perfect. For instance, there is no way to treat strings in the same manner as integers. However, major changes are unlikely to be made to C because of the large investment that has already been made. This investment, in fact, suggests that C will be around for quite some time, even as new languages are developed. One such language is C++.

C++ should be viewed as a completely new language, based largely on C. It includes modern constructs and may emerge as a dominant language later in the decade. Everybody, it seems, wants to learn C++.

C++ is perhaps the most demanding language to come into popular use. Some argue that it might be too difficult to be generally useful. Only time will tell if that is the case. Even if C is eventually replaced by C++, we think that a firm knowledge of C is essential to take full advantage of C++. We provide an introductory chapter to let you decide if C++ is worth learning. [Ellis 90] gives a complete C++ description.

---

[1] Material in Appendix B is reprinted from ISO/IEC 9899:1990 with permission of the American National Standards Institute (ANSI) under an exclusive licensing agreement with the International Organization for Standardization (ISO). No part of ISO/IEC 9899 may be reproduced in any form, electronic retrieval system or otherwise, without the prior written consent of the American National Standards Institute, 11 West 42nd Street, New York, N.Y., 10036. The standard is a required document for anyone interested in the nuances of C.

[2] The first edition is still in print. Besides providing historical perspective, it is useful for those who have to work with old code.

1.2   The Environment

How are C programs entered, compiled, and run? The answer, of course, depends on the particular platform that hosts the C compiler.

On personal computers that run windowing systems, *integrated environments* are available. These user-friendly systems provide editors that allow automatic compilation, linking, and running of programs; when compiler errors are detected, the editor is restarted at the offending line in the source code. Consequently, on these systems, each step is as simple as a click of a button.

The other common platform is, of course, UNIX. In the simplest scenario, a program is entered into a source file whose name ends with a *.c*, using an editor such as *vi* or *emacs*. The local compiler, typically *cc* or *gcc*, compiles the program and generates an executable file named *a.out*.

For C programs, input can come from one of three general places. These sources are:

1.   The terminal, which we denote as the *standard input*.

2.   Additional parameters in the invocation of the executable programs. These are known as *command line arguments*.

3.   A file.

Command line arguments are particularly important for specifying program options. They are discussed in Chapter 12.

C provides mechanisms to read and write files portably (usually). We discuss this in Chapter 12. Many operating systems provide an alternative known as *file redirection*. On UNIX, for instance, the command

a.out < inputfile > outputfile

automatically arranges things so that any terminal reads are redirected to come from *inputfile*, and terminal writes are redirected to go to *outputfile*.

For most of the book, we assume that input and output come directly from and to the terminal and defer treatment of files until late in the book. We do this for two reasons. First, it allows us to concentrate on the language syntax without worrying about peripheral issues. Second, because files requires some (limited) knowledge of strings, it is difficult to place them early.

1.3   Basic C

Let us begin by examining the simplistic C program shown in Figure 1.1. A C program consists of a collection of interacting functions. When the program is run, the special function `main` is invoked. Line 2 signifies that the function `main` is invoked with no parameters. The keyword `void` is optional: we could have just placed nothing between the parentheses. We use `void` to reiterate to the reader that we have deliberately, rather than accidentally, decided to have no parameters. In Section 12.7 we will see that access to command line arguments can be obtained by declaring `main` with parameters. Like other functions, the body of `main` is enclosed by braces.

```
/* 1*/    #include <stdio.h>

/* 2*/    main( void )
/* 3*/    {
/* 4*/        printf( "Is there anybody out there?\n" );
/* 5*/        return 0;
/* 6*/    }
```

Figure 1.1:   Simple C program.

Line 4 shows a simple use of the output routine `printf`. Constant strings are enclosed by a pair of double quotes ("). The string is printed to the standard output. Because newlines are not supplied automatically, we specify, via the special sequence \n, that one should be provided. The `return` at line 5 signifies the end of the `main` function, and consequently, the end of the program. The return code of 0, signifying no errors, is communicated back to the caller (which is typically some sort of a command interpreter).

The line numbers that are shown on the left are a pedagogical feature supplied by us to ease identification of source code features. Any text surrounded by a /* and a */ is a comment. A comment is treated as white space by the compiler. Comments do not nest.

The #include statement at line 1 instructs the compiler to replace that line logically with the contents of the file stdio.h, which is in a system-dependent directory. That file contains some information that is needed for the `printf` routine. Thus any program that performs output (or input) will contain this statement.

ANSI C specifies that the # that begins the #include statement must be the first non-white-space character on the line. Because ANSI C also clearly specifies that the comment is interpreted as white space *before* the # is seen, the #include should be recognized. Some pre-ANSI compilers, however, fail to recognize this #include directive. This is one example of the language ambiguities that were resolved by ANSI C .

Figure 1.2 shows a second program that illustrates more complex output, input, looping, and arithmetic. It prompts the user repeatedly for numbers and outputs their average. Lines 5 and 6 declare three variables. `double` represents the basic floating-point type; the alternative `float` has less precision on some machines. The declaration shows that objects may be initialized when they are declared. At lines 7 and 8 we prompt the user for input. The EOF marker on a UNIX system is the *control-d* character. On other machines it may be *control-z*. The `printf` statement at lines 14 and 15 is used to give the final answer. The string is output with the value of `ItemsRead` substituted for the %d and the average (`Sum/ItemsRead`) substituted for the %f. Sequences in the `printf` *control string* are called conversion specifiers. They are always replaced by sequentially scanning for addition `printf` parameters. The %d and %f correspond to `int` and `double` parameters. However, no type checking is performed, so if an incorrect type is used, you can count on a run-time error. Note that division of a `double` by an `int` results in a temporary conversion of the `int` to a `double`; the result of the division is a `double`. Note also that white space can be used to split long lines. However, you may not arbitrarily split a line in the middle of a token (this includes string constants).

The reading of input and the arithmetic computations are performed by the `while` loop at lines 9 to 13. `scanf` reads the next `double` (specified by the %1f conversion) into `ThisItem`. Note the slight difference between formats for `printf` and `scanf`. The

```
/* 1*/    #include <stdio.h>

/* 2*/    /* Read Items, Compute Their Average */

/* 3*/    main( void )
/* 4*/    {
/* 5*/        int ItemsRead = 0;
/* 6*/        double ThisItem, Sum = 0.0;

/* 7*/        printf( "Enter as many items as you want\n" );
/* 8*/        printf( "Terminate with non-double or EOF marker\n" );

/* 9*/        while( scanf( "%lf", &ThisItem ) == 1 )
/*10*/        {
/*11*/            ItemsRead++;
/*12*/            Sum += ThisItem;
/*13*/        }

/*14*/        printf( "The average of %d items was %f\n",
/*15*/                ItemsRead, Sum / ItemsRead );

/*16*/        return 0;
/*17*/    }
```

Figure 1.2:   Read numbers and output their average.

& is an important technical requirement. In this context it is the *address-of operator*. It is used because scanf wants to know *where* to place the input. &ThisItem represents the memory location where the object ThisItem is stored. If scanf is successful, it evaluates to 1. While this is the case, we execute the body of the while loop. Line 11 adds one to ItemsRead, and line 12 increments Sum by ThisItem. The while loop will terminate when scanf evaluates to −1 because the end of input is reached, or 0, which occurs when a format error is detected.

This example illustrates that C provides a host of operators to supplement the traditional +, −, *, and / operators. In many cases, their use results in more compact code. Of course, C provides the traditional if/else constructs, as well as the logical *AND*, *OR*, and *NOT* operators (in the form &&, ||, and !). As we'll see, C also provides convenient looping mechanisms with the general purpose for loop.

1.4   Functions

As we have already mentioned, a C program consists of a set of functions that interact. Figure 1.3 illustrates a program with two functions. It prints out the first few values of *N*! (the product of the first *N* positive integers). Notice that unlike other languages, C functions do not nest. Also, C functions can be recursive.

The function Factorial is written in lines 2 to 10. Lines 2 and 3 indicate that it takes one parameter, which is an unsigned long int and returns an unsigned

```
/* 1*/    #include <stdio.h>

/* 2*/    unsigned long int
/* 3*/    Factorial( unsigned long int N )
/* 4*/    {
/* 5*/        int i;
/* 6*/        unsigned long int Answer = 1;

/* 7*/        for( i = 1; i <= N; i++ )
/* 8*/            Answer *= i;

/* 9*/        return Answer;
/*10*/    }

/*11*/    main( void )
/*12*/    {
/*13*/        int i;
/*14*/        const int MaxNum = 12;

/*15*/        printf( " N        N!\n" );
/*16*/        for( i = 0; i <= MaxNum; i++ )
/*17*/            printf( "%2d %10lu\n", i, Factorial( i ) );

/*18*/        return 0;
/*19*/    }
```

Figure 1.3:   Print table of factorials.

long int; this type is nonnegative and is at least 32 bits (although the size is clearly machine dependent). N is the (only) *formal parameter* to the Factorial function.

This function declares two variables whose scope is limited to the invocation of the function, computes the factorial using a for loop, and returns the result. Both i and Answer are destroyed when the function returns; each function invocation begins with new local variables.

The for loop is a generalization of the looping mechanism made popular by earlier languages. The form we have used here is completely equivalent to the Pascal

```
for i:=1 to N do
```

The *= operator is much like the += operator, with multiplication used instead of addition.

In the main routine we declare two variables. The variable i, which is local to main, is completely unrelated to the identically named variable in Factorial. The variable MaxNum is assigned the value 12; because it is a const, it cannot be reassigned (without going through considerable effort). Constants are also commonly represented using #define statements. There are important differences between these two mechanisms. The const directive is an important ANSI C addition.

At line 15 we print a header for our table of factorials. Then at lines 16 and 17 we loop from 0 to MaxNum and print out i following by *i*!. The numbers in the conversion specifiers indicate field widths and are used to guarantee that the output shown in Figure 1.4 lines up nicely.

N	N!
0	1
1	1
2	2
3	6
4	24
5	120
6	720
7	5040
8	40320
9	362880
10	3628800
11	39916800
12	479001600

Figure 1.4:   Output for Figure 1.3.

In C, parameters are passed to functions by value. This means that the actual argument i is copied to the formal parameter N. Parameters cannot be passed directly by reference; this has important ramifications for C programmers. Functions that do not return values are declared to return void.

ANSI C provides type checking of function calls. This means that the actual argument types must match the formal parameter types. To provide this checking, the signature of the function (i.e., the list of parameter types) must be available prior to the function call. Thus we have written Factorial before main. If Factorial were to follow main, the compiler might complain. By providing the prototype (i.e., a declaration that indicates the function's signature and return type), we can provide enough information to allow complete type checking. This is perhaps the most important feature added by ANSI C.

We point out that the type checking is not completely strict. Notice that i is an int, but N is an unsigned long int. Although these are not identical types, ANSI C provides that they are *compatible* and defines a conversion mechanism that makes sense as long as i assumes values in the range covered by an unsigned long int. If not, unexpected results will occur at run time, because ANSI C does not check that arithmetic is within the bounds specified by the type; it is expected that the programmer would not rely on the conversion if he or she could not guarantee (as we have) that i was in the proper range. Further, Factorial will silently generate meaningless answers for 15! because the arithmetic overflow will be ignored. main does not have a type specified for the return value. This is because in C, types default to int.

1.5   Arrays

Like other languages, C supports arrays. For basic uses, the syntax is simple. However, there are several differences between arrays in C and many other languages. First, arrays are always indexed starting with 0. Second, index range checking is not performed. Third, arrays cannot be copied by =.

Figure 1.5 shows a simple program that reads in the winning lottery numbers and outputs a table showing how often each number has appeared. In our state, numbers 1 to

```
/* 1*/    #include <stdio.h>

/* 2*/    /* Compute Frequency Of Lottery Numbers */

/* 3*/    #define MaxNum 49        /* Numbers Range From 1 To 49 */

/* 4*/    main( void )
/* 5*/    {
/* 6*/        int Count[ MaxNum + 1 ];   /* Frequency Of Each Number */
/* 7*/        int Number;
/* 8*/        int i;

/* 9*/        for( i = 0; i <= MaxNum; i++ )
/*10*/            Count[ i ] = 0;

/*11*/            /* Note: No Prompting For Input */
/*12*/        while( scanf( "%d", &Number ) == 1 )
/*13*/            if( Number < 1 || Number > MaxNum )
/*14*/                printf( "Out of range number ignored\n" );
/*15*/            else
/*16*/                Count[ Number ]++;

/*17*/            /* Output The Data, Seven Numbers Per Line */
/*18*/        for( i = 1; i <= MaxNum; i++ )
/*19*/        {
/*20*/            printf( "%3d:%4d", i, Count[ i ] );
/*21*/            if( i % 7 == 0 )
/*22*/                printf( "\n" );
/*23*/            else
/*24*/                printf( "    " );
/*25*/        }

/*26*/        return 0;
/*27*/    }
```

Figure 1.5:   Compute frequency of occurrence for lottery numbers.

49 are in play. Since we would like this program to work for any lottery, we #define a symbolic constant to replace 49. For technical reasons, we cannot use a const int.

Line 6 declares an array Count that stores 50 ints (indexed from 0 to 49, inclusive). The array could be initialized in the declaration, but instead, we use a for loop. Lines 12 to 16 read numbers one at a time using scanf. At line 13 we test if Number is less than 1 *OR* greater than MaxNum, and if so, we print a warning message. Otherwise, we increment the corresponding counter. Because the if/else construction that spans lines 13 to 16 is considered one statement, it does not have to be surrounded by braces. At lines 18 to 25 we print the answers. % is the *MOD* operator; when i is divisible by 7, we print a newline; otherwise, we print some blank space.

```
/* 1*/    /* Return 1 if Str1 And Str2 Are Equal */

/* 2*/    int
/* 3*/    IsEqual( char Str1[ ], char Str2[ ] )
/* 4*/    {
/* 5*/        int i;

/* 6*/        for( i = 0; Str1[ i ] == Str2[ i ]; i++ )
/* 7*/            if( Str1[ i ] == '\0' )
/* 8*/                return 1;        /* Equal Strings */

/* 9*/        return 0;                       /* Not Equal */
/*10*/    }
```

Figure 1.6:   Routine to compare two strings.

Printing a string	Use `%s` conversion
Reading a string	Use `%s` conversion; do not use & however!
Copying	Use `strcpy( To, From );`
Compare	Use `strcmp( Str1, Str2 );` return is negative, zero, or positive

Figure 1.7:   String operations.

1.6   Strings

Arrays are used to implement *strings*: a string is just an array of characters. In C, characters are stored in objects of type `char`; character constants are enclosed by single quotes. We have already seen that string constants are enclosed by double quotes. However, string variables are not part of the ANSI C language proper. Instead, library routines are used to implement the string. The special character \0, known as the *null terminator*, signals the end of the string. Note carefully that in the library implementation, the end of the array does not signal the end of the string, even if no null terminator is present.

Because strings are arrays, the normal == and = operators do not work as they would if strings were basic types. Thus, everything from comparison to copy must be implemented by a function. As an example, the routine in Figure 1.6 returns 1 if two strings `Str1` and `Str2` are equal, and zero otherwise. In the `for` loop, the middle expression is the continuation test: the `for` loop continues as long as the test is true. As a practical matter, we would normally not implement `IsEqual` ourselves, but instead we would use the library routines. Figure 1.7 summarizes the basic string operations. Figure 1.8 illustrates the `%s` conversion for strings. It repeatedly reads a string, and writes it out. The `scanf` does not require an & because, as we will see, `Str` already represents an address. However, to guard against an array overflow, the `%s` conversion should have a number that indicates the maximum allowable string length. In Chapter 8 we discuss these issues in more detail.

```
/* 1*/    #include <stdio.h>

/* 2*/    /* Read And Write Strings */

/* 3*/    #define MaxLen 512

/* 4*/    main( void )
/* 5*/    {
/* 6*/        char Str[ MaxLen + 1 ];

/* 7*/        while( scanf( "%s", Str ) == 1 )
/* 8*/            printf( "I read %s\n", Str );

/* 9*/        return 0;
/*10*/    }
```

Figure 1.8:   **Read strings, and write them.**

1.7   Structures

The *structure* is used to store a collection of objects as a unit. Other languages refer to the construct as a *record*. The declaration

```
struct Complex
{
    double Real;
    double Imag;
};
```

declares that the new type struct Complex has two *fields*, Real and Imag. Objects of this type can then be declared, and the objects can be assigned, passed as parameters, or returned as a group. Alternatively, individual members can be accessed by the . operator:

```
struct Complex A, B, C;

A.Real = 2; A.Imag = 3;
B = A;                      /* Copy is allowed */
C = AddComplex( A, B );   /* Structures can be passed and returned */
```

The AddComplex routine could be written as shown in Figure 1.9. Because structures might be large objects, and call by value requires a copy, structures are generally not used as parameters to functions, nor returned by functions. The alternative is discussed in the next section.

1.8   Pointers

Recall that a *pointer* is a variable that is used to store an address where another object resides. That object is accessed by *dereferencing* the pointer. C uses pointers much more

```
/* 1*/    struct Complex
/* 2*/    AddComplex( struct Complex X, struct Complex Y )
/* 3*/    {
/* 4*/        struct Complex Sum;

/* 5*/        Sum.Real = X.Real + Y.Real;
/* 6*/        Sum.Imag = X.Imag + Y.Imag;

/* 7*/        return Sum;
/* 8*/    }
```

Figure 1.9:   Simple routine to add complex numbers passed by value.

than any other language. It differs from most other languages by allowing pointers to be involved in address arithmetic. It is impossible to write any meaningful C program without making use of pointers.

The three basic parts of the pointer syntax are the declaration, changing (or examining) *where* a pointer points, and dereferencing. Declaring that a variable is a pointer is simple. For instance, to declare that P is a pointer to an int, we write

```
int *P;                /* P is a pointer to an int */
```

If an initial value is supplied, it must be an address; then P is assigned that address. An address may be another pointer or can be obtained by using the address-of operator &. Thus

```
int X = 5;
int *P = &X;           /* P points at X */
```

To dereference a pointer, we use the * operator. Thus the value of *P is 5; ++*P changes X to 6. However, *P++ involves a precedence issue. It turns out that the ++ is applied to P and not *P. Since pointer arithmetic is allowed, a result of this is that P no longer points at X.

Three of the common uses of pointers are as follows:

1. Call by reference semantics (i.e., *var* in Pascal) for basic types are achieved by passing pointers as parameters. We have already seen this in scanf. Figure 1.10 (which is identical to Figure 6.11) illustrates a Swap routine. Notice that since Swap expects addresses, main must use the & operator to get the addresses of the objects that are to be swapped. The use of the const directives in this context is discussed in Chapter 6.

2. Pointers are used to pass structures, thereby avoiding the overhead of a structure copy that would be incurred if the structure were passed as a parameter. The -> operator is used to access fields of a pointed-at structure. As an example, Figure 1.11 shows the routine AddComplex rewritten to accept pointers to structures. We also see that *typedef* creates synonyms for existing types. Here we have used it as a shorthand. The const directives indicate that the first two structures should not be altered, but that the third may.

3. Array names are actually pointers to the block of memory that stores the array. Consequently, when an array name is used as a parameter, call by reference is in effect for the array aggregate. The relationship between arrays and pointers pro-

```
/* 1*/     #include <stdio.h>


/* 1*/     void
/* 2*/     Swap( int * const X, int * const Y )
/* 3*/     {
/* 4*/         int Tmp;

/* 5*/         Tmp = *X;
/* 6*/         *X  = *Y;
/* 7*/         *Y  = Tmp;
/* 8*/     }


/* 1*/     main( void )
/* 2*/     {
/* 3*/         int A = 5, B = 7;

/* 4*/         Swap( &A, &B );              /* Must Pass The Address */
/* 5*/         printf( "%d %d\n", A, B );

/* 6*/         return 0;
/* 7*/     }
```

Figure 1.10: **Using pointers to simulate call by reference.**

```
/* 1*/     typedef struct Complex Complex;

/* 2*/     void
/* 3*/     AddComplex( const Complex *X, const Complex *Y, Complex *Sum )
/* 4*/     {
/* 5*/         Sum->Real = X->Real + Y->Real;
/* 6*/         Sum->Imag = X->Imag + Y->Imag;
/* 7*/     }
```

Figure 1.11: AddComplex **using pointers to structures.**

vides a mechanism to allocate and expand arrays dynamically. Because strings are arrays, pointers are an essential mechanism in the implementation and use of strings.

1.9 Files

ANSI C specifies a set of library routines that must be present in conforming implementations. One part of the library deals with files. Figure 1.12 modifies Figure 1.2 to prompt the user for a file that contains the input items.

```
/* 1*/    #include <stdio.h>

/* 2*/    /* Read Items, Compute Their Average */

/* 3*/    main( void )
/* 4*/    {
/* 5*/        FILE *Fp;                      /* File Pointer */
/* 6*/        char FileName[ 256 ];          /* File Name */
/* 7*/        int ItemsRead = 0;
/* 8*/        double ThisItem, Sum = 0.0;

/* 9*/        printf( "Enter input file: " );
/*10*/        if( scanf( "%s", FileName ) != 1 ||
/*11*/                ( Fp = fopen( FileName, "r" ) ) == NULL )
/*12*/        {
/*13*/            fprintf( stderr, "Cannot open input file\n" );
/*14*/            return 1;
/*15*/        }

/*16*/        while( fscanf( Fp, "%lf", &ThisItem ) == 1 )
/*17*/        {
/*18*/            ItemsRead++;
/*19*/            Sum += ThisItem;
/*20*/        }

/*21*/        printf( "The average of %d items was %f\n",
/*22*/                ItemsRead, Sum / ItemsRead );

/*23*/        return 0;
/*24*/    }
```

Figure 1.12: **Figure 1.2 modified to read an arbitrary file.**

A variable of type FILE * is declared for each file that we want to deal with. The function fopen, called at line 11, is used to assign each file a *stream*. That stream is used for subsequent I/O operations. The fscanf at line 16 is identical to scanf except that input comes from the stream that is passed by reference as the first parameter. Line 13, by the way, illustrates the best way to report error messages, especially when error messages are common and likely to be interleaved with actual output: they are written to the predefined error stream stderr.

1.10 Summary and Book Organization

This chapter is intended to provide a very brief description of basic C features. We have not attempted to be specific about anything, or to warn you about possible errors. In subsequent chapters, we fill in all the details. In Chapter 2 we discuss "straightline C." This is C without looping or conditionals. You will find detailed information on the basic integer and floating-point types, rules for naming variables, and operators. Some topics that are covered in great detail in later chapters are also covered in less detail there. In Chapter 3 we discuss flow of control features, including `if` statements and looping constructs. In Chapter 4 we discuss functions. The preprocessor, which is the part of the language that handles `#include` and `#define` statements, is discussed in Chapter 5. The combination of these four chapters provides complete details (except for fancy I/O syntax) on the language features that would be considered simple.

The aggregate types, namely, arrays, strings, and structures, are covered in Chapters 7 to 9. But first, we discuss the pointer variable, because as we have seen, any serious implementation of an aggregate type requires a thorough understanding of pointers.

The syntax of C is completed by the end of Chapter 9. So why does the text not end there? The answer is that programming is much more than syntax. In Chapter 10 we study the use of pointers and structures to implement *data structures*. A thorough understanding of data structures can make for more readable and more efficient programs.

An entire chapter is then devoted to the study of *recursion*. We have tried to pick practical examples from a wide spectrum of applications that greatly benefit from the use of recursion. This is hardly a C topic: there is no single line of code that could not be directly translated to another language that supports recursion, such as Pascal.

In Chapter 12 we examine input and output in detail. We discuss all the `printf` and `scanf` options, files, and command line arguments. Chapter 13 is an introduction to UNIX systems programming. In Chapter 14 we examine C++. As the C++ juggernaut continues to grow, it seems likely that more and more C programmers will be asked to step up to C++. Chapter 14 provides a gentle introduction to show what C++ is all about.

EXERCISES

1. Compile, link, and run the program in Figure 1.1.

2. When you run the following program, it should echo back the command line arguments, each on a separate line. Check that it works on your system.

   ```
   #include <stdio.h>

   main( int argc, char **argv )
   {
       while( --argc )
           puts( *++argv );
   }
   ```

3. The following program copies from the standard input to the standard output. Use redirection to copy from one file to another file. What happens if the output and input files are the same?

   ```
   #include <stdio.h>

   main( void )
   {
       int Ch;

       while( ( Ch = getchar( ) ) != EOF )
           putchar( Ch );
       return 0;
   }
   ```

4. Grab the most recent tax table. Write a function that takes an *adjusted gross income* and *filing status* (married, single, etc.) and returns the amount of tax owed.

5. Write a function to compute X^N for nonnegative integers N. Assume that $X^0 = 1$.

6. *Note: This exercise requires no knowledge of sports.* The National Football League has a complicated formula for rating its quarterbacks. The five basic parameters are:

   (a) Passing attempts (A)

   (b) Completions (C)

   (c) Yards (Y)

   (d) Touchdowns (T)

   (e) Interceptions (I)

   From these parameters we compute:

   (a) Completion percentage (CMP) = C / A * 100.0

   (b) Yards per attempt (YD) = Y / A

   (c) Touchdowns per attempt (TD) = T / A * 100.0

   (d) Interceptions per attempt (INT) = I / A * 100.0

   We then *normalize* each of these quantities as follows:

   (a) NCMP = (CMP - 30.0) / 20.0

   (b) NYD = (YD - 3.0) / 4.0

   (c) NTD = (TD) / 5.0

   (d) NINT = (9.5 - INT) / 4.0

   The minimum normalized value for any category is 0.0, and the maximum is 2.375. The quarterback rating is

   $$\text{Rating} = 100.0 * (\text{NCMP} + \text{NYD} + \text{NTD} + \text{NINT}) / 6.0$$

   Write a program that reads lines containing a quarterback name and the five basic quantities and outputs the corresponding quarterback ratings.

7. Continuing Exercise 6, write the routine

   ```
   void ComputeRating( struct QB *Player );
   ```

   A `struct QB` contains fields storing a `Name` (as a string), attempts, completions, yards, touchdowns, interceptions, and the rating. `ComputeRating` fills the rating field on the basis of the other fields.

8. Write a program that reads lines containing the name and basic quarterback statistics into an array of `struct QB`, and then outputs the data with the rating included.

9. Write a program that reads a sequence of `doubles` into an array and outputs them in sorted order.

10. Write a function that returns nonzero if string `Str1` is a prefix of string `Str2`. Do not use any library routines.

2

Simple Straightline C

In this chapter we begin our examination of C by showing the basic lexical elements, types, and operations. *Straightline C* describes C code, which has no conditional statements, loops, or user-defined functions. These additional topics are discussed in the next two chapters. Because this is only an introductory chapter, in many places reference to a later chapter in the book is provided for more details.

2.1 The First Program

Our first program is shown in Figure 2.1. It is an extremely simple program that merely prints out the phrase *Testing 123* to the terminal. Before we even begin to discuss the details of C, it is important to type the program on your system and make it run. How this is done is system dependent.

If you are running in a UNIX environment, you need to place the code in Figure 2.1 in a file whose name ends in *.c*. For example, *sample.c* would be an appropriate name. This would be done using a text editor; the two likely choices are *vi* or *emacs*.

You should type the program in exactly as it is written in Figure 2.1, except that the beginning numbers, such as /* 1*/, on each line are unnecessary. We have numbered

```
        /*
         * A Simple First Program.
         * MW, 10/13/95
         */

/* 1*/    #include <stdio.h>

/* 2*/    main( void )
/* 3*/    {
/* 4*/        printf( "Testing 123\n" );
/* 5*/    }
```

Figure 2.1: Program to print "Testing 123."

18

lines, so they are easily referenced. Notice that programs in this book are printed in a fixed-width font, so you can easily see blank spaces. Also, be careful to type everything in the same case (upper or lower, as appropriate), as shown.

If you have done everything correctly, the command

cc sample.c

should run smoothly. It will generate a file called *a.out*, and the subsequent command *a.out* will then run the program. Note that in this scenario, whenever you compile a program, an *a.out* file is generated. This is not a meaningful name. The command

cc sample.c -o sample

will generate a file called *sample* instead of *a.out*.

The *cc* command translates the source file into an equivalent assembly language program. If your C code is illegal, the compiler will complain and give error messages. The messages may seem a bit cryptic at first, but with experience, it rarely takes long to get the compiler to agree that your program is legal. Of course, legal programs do not necessarily do what you intend. On a UNIX system, the debugger *dbx*, discussed in Section 13.3.1, can help track down the coding error.

Once an equivalent assembly language program is generated, another program called the *assembler* converts the program into binary files. Finally, a program called the *linker* is called, which combines binary files and library units together into an executable program and removes the temporary files that were created. You can see all this excitement by specifying the *-v* (verbose) option:

cc -v sample.c

Some systems have more than one compiler. For example, many university environments use the GNU C compiler, which is typically accessed by using *gcc* instead of *cc*. The GNU compiler is free of charge, whereas some ANSI C compilers are quite expensive. On the other hand, it is public domain, and comes as is and unsupported. Thus you may need to use the command *gcc* instead of *cc*. If you are using a personal computer, the details are similar (see the appendix for additional information). Compiling a file named *sample.c* will usually generate a file *sample.exe*, which can be run by the command *sample*.

Virtually all of the compilers allow you to specify options (such as the *-v* option that we have already seen). One such option allows you to invoke an optimizer. The compiler will spend some extra time attempting to generate faster and/or smaller code for you. Some compilers come with several levels of optimization. You can also combine options (as long as they do not conflict):

cc -O -v sample.c -o sample

compiles *sample.c*, invokes an optimizer, shows you all the work the compiler is doing, and places the end product in *sample*. Check your manual pages for more detailed information.

2.2   Tokens and White Space

The basic unit of a C program is a character. Virtually every character that appears on a standard keyboard can be used in a C program. This includes the lowercase characters a–z,

```
#include<stdio.h>
main(void){printf("Testing 123\n");}
```

Figure 2.2:   First program rewritten without unnecessary white space.

the uppercase characters A–Z, the digits 0–9, *white space*: blanks, newlines, tabs (both horizontal and vertical), the form feed character, and the following 29 symbols:

! # % ^ & * ( ) _ \ - | + = { } [ ] : ; " ' ~ < , > . ? /

In C, the basic characters are combined into *tokens*, which are the logical equivalent of words. These tokens then form *statements*, which in turn form *functions*. Many functions can be combined into a single C source file, and one or more C source files can be combined into a program.

In English, white space is needed to separate words, because otherwise ambiguity results. For example, the sequence Theneatfish needs white space to distinguish between The neat fish and Then eat fish. Space does not need to be present between all words for this purpose if there is punctuation; however, it is customary to place one space after a comma, and two after a period because it looks nice.

Similarly, in C, white space is essential to enhance readability and also, occasionally, to distinguish tokens. It is important to note that white space is any nonzero amount of blanks, newlines, form feeds, or tabs; the amount or type of space is unimportant (except for preprocessor commands). The typical uses of white space are:

1. Blank lines to show logical separation between different parts of the code
2. Indenting of lines to show logic
3. Spaces around tokens to give them clear visibility
4. Form feeds to force page breaks when printing code listings.

We discuss the popular styles of using white space later in the book, as appropriate. Figure 2.2 shows the routine in Figure 2.1 written without comments or unecessary white space. Note that the newline at the end of the first line is needed (because the leading # signals a preprocessor command), and the space is needed between Testing and 123. Although some programmers are quite proud of their ability to minimize source code size, the lack of readability of that approach should be apparent. The few extra keystrokes are more than worth the effort.

2.3   Comments

The first four (unnumbered) lines of Figure 2.1 constitute a comment. A comment is text that is meant to help the reader understand what the program is doing or to issue disclaimers. Comments are ignored completely by the compiler and in ANSI C are logically replaced by white space. The program in Figure 2.1 also has comments indicating the line numbers for lines 1 through 5.

```
/* 1*/    /* This comment ends early on the next line.
/* 2*/     * This is not in the comment!
/* 3*/     * Neither is this; the next line is also an error.
/* 4*/     */

/* 5*/    #include <stdio.h>

/* 6*/    main( void )
/* 7*/    {
/* 8*/        printf( "Testing 123\n" );
/* 9*/    }
```

Figure 2.3: Incorrect program: comments do not nest.

      In C, comments begin with the *comment start token*, which is a slash (/) and asterisk (∗) placed consecutively (/∗), and end with the *comment end token*, namely an asterisk and

slash placed consecutively (∗/). Note that this means that there can be no space between the asterisk and slash.

      Because text following the comment start token is ignored until a comment end token is seen, it follows that comments do not nest: the code in Figure 2.3 is incorrect. In that example, the first comment on line 1, namely /∗ 1 ∗/, is correct. The second comment starts immediately afterward but is terminated by the comment end token on line 2. The part of lines 2 and 3 that was obviously meant to be a continuation of line 1's comment is no longer a comment, and represents illegal C syntax. Line 4 now contains a comment end token, but it is not matched to a comment start token, and thus another syntax error would be reported.

      As mentioned earlier, comments exist to make the code easier for humans to read. These humans include other programmers who may have to modify or use your code, as well as yourself. It is important to provide useful comments. A general rule of thumb is that each program should have a comment providing its author, date of origin (and dates of modification), and a description of what the program does. The description should in particular list any assumptions, limitations, and deficiencies that are important for a user to know. (Such features are occasionally known as *bugs*.) It is also important to comment individual lines or blocks of code that are tricky and not obvious to a casual but experienced reader of the code. You can assume an experience level equal to your own. We have more to say about comments as warranted later in the book.

2.4 #include **Statements**

Returning to Figure 2.1, we see on (commented line) 1 the first actual C statement. The *include* statement has the effect of logically reading in another file. In our example the contents of a file named stdio.h are processed as if they had been on line 1 of our input file. The < and > that surround stdio.h, sometimes known as *angle brackets*, indicate that the file stdio.h does not reside in the current directory but rather, in a system directory. On UNIX, for example, it resides in the publicly readable directory */usr/include*.

Surrounding the file name by quotes instead of angle brackets would indicate that the current directory should be searched for the file to include (and then system directories, if the search fails).

The names of included files typically end in *.h*, although this is not required. These files typically contain constants and type declarations (we define these terms shortly) that programs need to know about. The included files may themselves have *include* statements, so *include* statements, unlike comments, do nest. For obvious reasons, however, it is almost always an error for a file to include itself either directly or indirectly.

 The *include* statement is part of the language known as the *preprocessor*. Lines whose first non-white-space character is a # are preprocessor lines and are treated somewhat differently from other lines. One might say that the preprocessor is not part of C but is a required supplement. In Chapter 5 we provide a complete discussion of the preprocessor.

2.5 Identifiers

 One type of token is an *identifier*. An identifier is typically used to provide a name for an object. When it comes to choosing identifiers, there are several important rules. First, the name may only consist of letters (in either lower or upper case), digits, or the underscore (_) character. All other characters are forbidden. The identifier may not start with a digit. The compiler will interpret an illegal character to be the start of a new token, and all prior characters will be considered as the name of the identifier. Needless to say, this will probably result in lots of error messages. Although identifiers may be as long as you like, the compiler might only look at the first 31 characters. Relying on longer identifiers is a nonportable practice. We will see in Chapter 4 that for certain identifiers, as few as six characters might be examined.

C is case sensitive, which means that there is a difference between upper and lower case. Thus becky and Becky are different identifiers. Additionally, there are a special set of words, known as keywords, which you may not use as identifiers. The list of C keywords is

auto	break	case	char
const	continue	default	do
double	else	enum	extern
float	for	goto	if
int	long	register	return
short	signed	sizeof	static
struct	switch	typedef	union
unsigned	void	volatile	while

The list of keywords provided is the minimum specified by the ANSI standard. Some compilers have more keywords, such as asm and fortran. Notice that goto1 is a valid identifier and is not a keyword. On the other hand, 1goto represents two tokens: 1 and the keyword goto.

2.6   `#define` **Statements**

Another important preprocessor command is the `#define` statement. A typical use of this statement is to associate a symbol to a constant. As an example,

```
#define MinimumWage 4.50
```

causes all occurrences of the token `MinimumWage` to be replaced by `4.50`. The use of symbolic constants is considered good programming practice, since it makes programs more readable and more easily modifiable. For example, if the minimum wage is raised from $4.50 to $4.75, only one change is needed in a program that uses the above `#define` statement. If `#define` is not used, all occurrences of `4.50` that correspond to the minimum wage must be changed to `4.75`; this must be done manually on a case-by-case basis (rather than through a global editor change) because some occurrences of `4.50` might not represent a minimum wage and thus should not be altered. Advanced uses of the `#define` statement are discussed in Chapter 5.

2.7   **Objects and Declarations**

Figure 2.4 shows a second trivial C program. Line 4 declares three objects and *initializes* two of them. We commonly use the term *variable*, which reflects the fact that the values stored in these objects can be changed as well as examined. The declarative part of a function (i.e., the place where the declarations are made) always immediately follows the first brace. Once a nondeclarative statement is made (such as at line 5), it is illegal to issue any more declarations within the function.[1] It is customary to put a blank line after the last declaration to separate declarations visually from the rest of the function.

A declaration does what it sounds like: it declares your intention to use certain variables and instructs the compiler to set aside memory for that purpose. It is illegal to reference an object without declaring your intention to do so. The declaration of each object consists essentially of three parts, one of which is optional. First we must say what kind of an object we are asking for. In our case the objects will hold integer values (discussed later in this section). Next, the object must be named by using an identifier. Optionally, we may also assign an initial value to the object.

In our example, at line 4, the object named `First` can hold an integer, and initially it is holding a 12. Similarly, `Third` can hold an integer, which initially is 6. Also, `Second` can hold an integer, but no initial value is assigned. The value of an uninitialized variable in this context is not defined, although zero is not uncommon (and occasionally gives the incorrect perception of a correct program). However, this is system dependent, and if you want to initialize a variable to zero, you must do it explicitly. Reading from an uninitialized variable is likely to cause an error when the program is run.

Keywords may not be used to name objects. Each identifier declared in a function must have a different name (subject to the 31-character rule above). Moreover, it is almost

[1]Unless a block is declared—see Chapter 3.

```
/* 1*/    #include <stdio.h>

/* 2*/    main( void )
/* 3*/    {
/* 4*/         int First = 12, Second, Third = 6;

/* 5*/         Second = 8;
/* 6*/         printf( "The ints: %d %d %d\n", First, Second, Third );
/* 7*/         First = Third;
/* 8*/         printf( "The ints: %d %d %d\n", First, Second, Third );
/* 9*/         Third += Second;
/*10*/         printf( "The ints: %d %d %d\n", First, Second, Third );
/*11*/         First = Second + Third;
/*12*/         printf( "The ints: %d %d %d\n", First, Second, Third );
/*13*/         First++;
/*14*/         ++Second;
/*15*/         printf( "The ints: %d %d %d\n", First, Second, Third );
/*16*/         Third = First++ + ++Second;
/*17*/         printf( "The ints: %d %d %d\n", First, Second, Third );
/*18*/    }
```

Figure 2.4:   Simple program to show operators.

always a bad idea to name an object with an identifier that has been set aside for other purposes. An example would be naming an identifier `printf` (which, as we will see later, is a library routine used for formatted output). A convention that you can generally count on is that the names of library routines do not use both upper- and lowercase letters. When we write our programs, identifiers will be in a mixed case, with the first character guaranteed to be upper case. Examples of this style are `Number`, `MyName`, and `PrintAnInt`. Our only exceptions will be the identifiers `i`, `j`, and `k`. That way, we can be sure not to conflict with system names, and also, it will be apparent whether or not we are referring to a system library. Choosing meaningful identifier names is the most important technique for maintaining readable code. We will discuss this issue where appropriate.

2.8   Integer Types and Integer Constants

The most common type is probably the integer. The keyword `int` is used to specify that an object is an integer. The disadvantage of using integers is that only a relatively small number of integers can be represented, and of course a real number such as 3.14 cannot be represented. In this case a floating-point type, which is an abstraction used to approximate real numbers, would be needed. On the other hand, operations on integers have the big advantage that they are exact, and in many cases, the number of representable integers is sufficient. Operations on integers are almost always significantly faster than floating-point operations.

Modern computers provide 32-bit integers. On these machines, the integers typically range from -2^{31} to $2^{31} - 1$, inclusive. Thus integers from -2,147,483,648 to 2,147,483,647 can be represented. Many personal computers still use 16-bit integers. For those machines, the integers typically range from -65,536 to 65,535. In addition to the number of bits, the range of representable integers depends on the internal representation used by the supporting hardware. The values that we have provided are obtained by the popular *two's-complement* representation. An alternative representation is *one's complement*. In that representation, the most negative integer representable by *two's complement* is not representable (because zero is representable in two distinct ways). A detailed discussion of binary codes can be found in [Aho 92]. You can find out the minimum and maximum integers on your system by examining the values of INT_MIN and INT_MAX in the standard header file <limits.h>.

 Independent of what the actual range of integers is, multiplying two integers that are in range, but whose product is out of range, is problematic. In other languages, such as Pascal, an integer overflow is detected, and the program would terminate immediately with a run-time error. In C, the multiplication is legal, and the answer will probably contain the least significant 32 (or 16) bits of the product, which is hardly a desirable feature. The same problem can occur with addition or subtraction, but is much less likely.

2.8.1   Octal and Hexadecimal Constants

In addition to the normally used decimal integer constants,[2] octal and hexadecimal integers are supported. Because octal and hexadecimal merely represent a different way of inputting and outputting an integer, no special type declaration is required. The only difference is that octal constants begin with a 0, and hexadecimal constants begin with a 0x. Thus 255, 0377, and 0xff all represent the same constant value. The reason this is important to know is that a leading 0 in a number alters its meaning from decimal to octal. Thus it is important that a leading 0 not be put in unless you really mean it.

Integers can be printed in decimal by specifying a %d in printf. Each %d is replaced by an appropriate integer, as specified in a comma separated list following the control string. Thus in line 6 of Figure 2.4, the three %ds are replaced by the values of First, Second, and Third. Octal and hexadecimal integers can be printed using %o and %x, respectively. We will have more to say on printf later in this chapter; a complete description is provided in Chapter 12.

2.8.2   Long and Short Integers

ANSI C specifies that int may be qualified with either the keyword short or long. Unfortunately, it does not require that short integers are any shorter than integers or that long integers are longer than integers. The only guarantee is that short int and long int are at least as short and long, respectively, as int. Typically, however, you can expect that short integers are 16 bits and long integers are 32 bits.[3] The size of unqualified integers, as we have said before, is generally dependent on the architecture.

 Long integers may help if integer operations are resulting in overflow. If a long integer is actually longer than an integer, it is good style, and in some older compilers imperative, to write long integer constants with either an upper- or a lowercase L. It should be evident that

---

[2]Note that −1 is not an integer constant but rather, is an integer constant expression in which the operator − is applied to the integer constant 1.

[3]They will never be less. See Appendix C.

using an uppercase L is more readable than its lowercase counterpart, because it is not easily confused with a 1. For this reason you should always use an uppercase L. Lowercase 1s can cause incredible problems. Never use it as an identifier, and be alert for the possibility that the last digit of an integer might accidentally not be the 1 that you expect.

Short integers are useful if you need to allocate many integers that are small in magnitude. Be alert that manipulation of several short integers could produce nonshort intermediate results and thus cause silent errors. It is safer to avoid short unless a significant memory savings can be realized.

Short and long integers can be printed by using %hd and %ld, respectively. It is obvious that l stands for *long*; because s is used for other purposes, the second letter of *short* is used.[4] The h is technically unnecessary here but is widely used because it is required for a similar input routine. For long ints, however, if you use just %d, you may get errors.

If you need to store a very small integer, you can use the type char, which usually takes 8 bits. This type is generally used for other purposes (see Chapter 8). If you do this, you should carefully heed the warning in the next section.

2.8.3 Unsigned Types

The binary representation of integers (normal, short, or long) requires that one bit be used to indicate the sign (negative or nonnegative). If we know that our integers are not negative, that extra bit can be used to extend (by a factor of 2) the positive range. Thus instead of a range of -2^{31} to $2^{31} - 1$ for 32-bit integers, we obtain a range of 0 to $2^{32} - 1$. A similar range extension applies for 16-bit integers.

By default, int, short int, and long int are signed quantities. They can be made unsigned by saying unsigned int, unsigned short int, unsigned long int, respectively.

Integer constants may be suffixed with u or U to indicate that it is unsigned. If no suffixes are present, then the type of the constant is the first of int, long int, unsigned long int that can hold it.

The default signed status of the 8-bit char is unspecified in the standard. Thus if you are using this type for very short integers, you should explicitly qualify it as either signed char or unsigned char, for ranges of -128 to 127 or 0 to 255, respectively.

Note that for the purposes of symmetry, the type signed int, as well as its long and short counterparts, are legal even though the qualifier is redundant. To print out an unsigned integer, use %u instead of %d. Unsigned short and long integers are printed by %hu and %lu, respectively. To print out a char that is being used to represent a small integer, you should use %d.

As an aside, we point out that unsigned integers are treated differently in C than many other languages. In Pascal, for example, an unsigned integer is merely a subset of the integer, thus ranging over only the nonnegative values of integer. Their main use in Pascal is not to extend the range of integers but to achieve tighter overflow (and underflow) checking.

---

[4]Actually, h stands for *half*.

```
/* 1*/    #include <stdio.h>

/* 2*/    main( void )
/* 3*/    {
/* 4*/        double A = 373737.0;
/* 5*/        double B;

/* 6*/        B = A*A*A + 0.37/A - A*A*A - 0.37/A;
/* 7*/        printf( "The value of B is %f.\n", B );
/* 8*/    }
```

Figure 2.5:   Program that should print 0.000000, but does not.

2.9   Floating-Point Types and Constants

One of the important uses of computers is number crunching: solving or simulating engineering and physics problems. Another important use, banking, requires computations in an noninteger domain. In the number-crunching world, real numbers rather than integers dominate. Thus we need floating-point types.

One problem that affects floating-point computations is that there are too many floating-point numbers. Specifically, while there are only 10 integers in the closed interval between 1 and 10, there are an infinite number of floating-point numbers in the same interval. Thus only some of these numbers can be represented exactly, and the rest must be approximated by one of the representables.

Figure 2.5 illustrates a very simple use of floating-point numbers which immediately exposes their limitations. In that program we declare two variables, A and B, of type double. A is initialized to have the value 373,737; double refers to double-precision floating point, because typically, doubles are stored in eight bytes, whereas the old-style floating-point numbers were stored in only four.

Note that when representing floating-point constants, we include a decimal point and both an integer and fractional part. One can also provide an exponential part: $1.2e-34$ represents $1.2 * 10^{-34}$. A floating-point constant may not contain any blanks or other funny characters, and it *must* contain either a decimal point or an exponential part (or else it is interpreted as an integer). If it contains a decimal point, it *must* contain either an integer or a fractional part; as mentioned above, good style would include both. When the exponential notation is used, it is good practice to have the magnitude of the preexponential part be at least 1.0 and strictly less than 10.0, as is common in scientific notation. This is, however, not a requirement. There are, of course, limits on how large and small floating-point numbers can be. This is discussed below.

Returning to our example, we see that B is then assigned a value that is mathematically zero. It is then printed on line 7 using the %f converter. On most machines, this value will not be zero, showing that even double precision is not sufficient. In this example, when a very small number is added to a very large number, the result is not exactly the mathematical sum, but an approximation. The closest representable number, not surprisingly, is the very large number that we started with. Thus the subtraction gets a result down to zero, and the final value assigned to B is just $-0.37/A$. This effect, known as *roundoff error*, accumulates as floating-point numbers are operated on. After thousands of successive operations, the total roundoff error can be ridiculously high if care is not taken. Of course, this limitation is present in all programming languages.

Because of this, and the fact that floating-point operations are typically more expensive than integer operations, floating-point types should be used only when integer types are not suitable. C provides three types of floating-point representations. In nondecreasing order of precision they are: `float`, `double`, and `long double`. As is the case with integers, a `long double` is not necessarily more precise than a `double`, and a `double` is not necessarily more precise than a `float`. The default working type in C is `double`, and all standard library routines expect `double`s to be passed. Since even double-precision arithmetic is prone to roundoff errors quickly, it is a very bad idea to use `float` unless you are certain that it provides enough precision.

Originally, C specified that all floating-point arithmetic was performed in double precision. This is no longer the case. However, compilers may perform arithmetic on `float` operands using double precision. `long double` can be used if more precision is needed, but `long double`s are not guaranteed to provide more precision, and if they do, there will be a performance penalty for floating-point operations.

On our machine, a `double` is implemented using 64 bits (i.e., eight bytes). For 64-bit double-precision floating-point numbers, one possible implementation is the following: one bit stores the sign S, 52 bits store an unsigned integer M, and 11 bits store an unsigned integer E, and represent, roughly speaking, $(-1)^S (0.M)(2^{(E-1023)})$. For instance, a typical representation might be $-0.101 * 2^{011}$, which represents $-\frac{5}{8}2^3 = -5.0$ (exactly). Some consequences are that under this scheme, 52-bit integers can be exactly represented, but the division 1.0/3.0 cannot be represented exactly, since

$$\frac{1}{3} \equiv \sum_{i=1}^{\infty} 2^{-2i}.$$

Although the exact method of representing floating-point numbers varies, some conclusions can be drawn. The largest representable double-precision number under this scheme is slightly less than 2^{1024}, which is almost $1.8 * 10^{308}$. The magnitude of the smallest representable double-precision number is about 2^{-1075}, which is about $2.4 * 10^{-324}$. By providing 52 bits, which represent all 15-bit integers and some 16-bit integers, we can be sure that we have 15 significant digits. Further details can be found in [Aho 92]. As we have explained before, the `%f` option can be used to print floating-point numbers. However, `%lf`, which reflects the fact that historically, a `double` was a `long float`, is necessary for a similar input routine. This incongruety is unfortunate and leads to a common error.

You may find when printing out floating-point numbers that the output format is not exactly how you would like. In Chapter 12 we show the plethora of `printf` options that will allow you to print out floating-point quantities using a wide range of formatting options. Keep in mind that although only a few digits are shown by default when printing out small floating-point numbers, it is always possible that when you see `1.00000`, what is really being represented is `1.00000000000001`; thus sometimes you really do want to see what is being represented. Most of the time the few decimal places that `printf` provides are sufficient.

2.10   The `typedef` Statement

The `typedef` statement is provided by C to allow the programmer to assign meaningful names to existing types. As an example, suppose that we need to declare objects of type *32-bit unsigned integer*. On some machines this might be an `unsigned long int`, while on others, perhaps an `unsigned int` is the most appropriate type. Just as we used `#define` to localize constants, a `typedef` is used to localize types. The first of the following statements:

```
typedef unsigned long int Int32;
```

```
Int32    X, Y, Z;            /* Declare 3 Int32 objects */
```

declares that `Int32` is a **synonym** for the type `unsigned long int` that can then be used in declarations. The `typedef` syntax rule is easy to remember: the synonym is placed in the same location in which an object would be placed.

The `typedef` statment appears to duplicate the functionality of the `#define`. Why not use the following statement?

```
#define Int32 unsigned long int
```

The answer is that in addition to the basic object types, we will see in later chapters that complex types can also be created in C. For the most complex types, the `typedef` provides more functionality than the simple `#define`. As a result, it is better to use a `typedef`. We will revisit the `typedef` later in the book when we discuss more complex types.

2.11   The `sizeof` Operator

C provides the `sizeof` operator that can be used to determine the number of bytes that are used to store an object. There are two forms. First,

```
sizeof( Type )
```

provides the number of bytes needed to store an object of type `Type`. Thus `sizeof(Int32)` will evaluate to the number of bytes used to store an `Int32`, namely 4.

The second form is

```
sizeof Object
```

and provides the number of bytes needed to store `Object`. Typically, parentheses are included even though they are optional. We discuss the `sizeof` operator in more detail in Section 7.8.

2.12   String Constants

Roughly speaking, a sequence of characters surrounded by a pair of double quotes (`"`) is a string constant. Thus `"Testing 123"` is a string constant. Special sequences are also recognized. The most common sequence is `\n`, which represents the newline character inside a string constant. The   \n is needed instead of an explicit carriage return because if a carriage return is detected before the closing double quote, a syntax error is generated.

A string constant is considered to be one token. Thus any symbols inside the string constant that would otherwise be tokens are not recognized as such. For example, if the sequence /* appears inside a string constant, it is not interpreted as the comment starter token. ANSI C has introduced concatenation of string constants. Thus

```
"abc" "def"
"ghi"
```

is equivalent to the single token "abcdefghi".

Our limited discussion reflects the fact that for now, we use string constants only in conjunction with the input and output routines scanf and printf. String constants are discussed in more detail in Chapter 8.

2.13   main

The body of the function main is illustrated on lines 3 through 5 in Figure 2.1. As shown on line 2, a function has a name (which is an identifier), followed by a parenthesized list of parameters. We call this the function declaration. The keyword void specifies that this particular function takes no parameters. If we were writing a function to compute cube roots, we would presumably pass one parameter that would be the number whose cube root would be extracted. Following the declaration of the function are statements that are to be performed by the function. The collection of statements is surrounded by braces (see lines 3 and 18).

As we will see in Chapter 4, all functions are written essentially this way, although obviously most functions will be somewhat more complicated. It is good programming practice, however, to ensure that functions are not too complicated by breaking them up into smaller fragments as appropriate.

main is a special function because every program must have one. A program is started by executing the statements in main. If the main function is not present, the linker will generate an error. This would happen, for instance, if you used Main instead of main, because C is *case sensitive* (upper- and lowercase characters are different).

As we will see later, main can be extended in two ways. First, normally when a program is run, additional parameters are supplied on the command line, besides just the name of the command. For instance, one says

vi sample.c   or   *cc -O -v sample.c -o sample*

rather than just *vi* or *cc*. In Section 12.7 we'll see how main can be extended to support this. We will also see in Chapter 4 that main can be extended to communicate error codes to its invoker.

2.14   printf

Unlike main, which is a function that we must provide, printf is a function that is provided for us in the standard library and is quite powerful (there are lots of options). This

```
The ints: 12 8 6
The ints: 6 8 6
The ints: 6 8 14
The ints: 22 8 14
The ints: 23 9 14
The ints: 24 10 33
```

Figure 2.6:   Output of the second program.

is discussed in detail in Chapter 12, and also in other places, where appropriate. The form we have used in Figure 2.1 is the most simple: a string constant is output to the screen. A newline is never supplied automatically by printf, since otherwise all the output for a line would have to be specified at once. Generally, it is more convenient to print out a line in parts.

The sequence \n must be used explicitly to specify that a new line is to be printed. Since this sequence can appear anywhere and more than once in the string constant, one printf statement could print out several lines of complex text. We will see more examples of this later in the chapter.

Inside the string constant, known as the *control string*, we can specify that additional variables are output by using the % conversion sequences. We have already shown the appropriate sequences for each of the basic data types that have been discussed, and in Chapter 12, all the options for printf are fully discussed.

2.15   Expressions and Simple Statements

A basic unit in C is the expression: a constant or variable by itself is an expression, as are combinations of constants and variables with operators. An expression followed by a semicolon is a simple statement. In Chapter 3 we examine other types of statements.

2.16   Assignment Operators

A simple C program is shown in Figure 2.4. That program does nothing in particular except demonstrate a few basics. The output of the program is shown in Figure 2.6. C uses = for assignment. On line 5 the variable Second is assigned the value 8, while on line 7 the variable First is assigned the value of the variable Third (which at that point is 6). As is common with virtually all programming languages, subsequent changes to the value of Third do not affect First.

Besides the basic assignment operator, several other assignment operators are available, as indicated on line 9. The += operator adds the value on the right-hand side (of the += operator) to the variable on the left-hand side. Thus Third is incremented from its value of 6 before line 9, to a value of 14. C provides various other assignment operators, such as -=, *=, and /=, which alter the variable on the left-hand side of the operator.

Note carefully that the left-hand side of any assignment operator must contain an expression that refers to an object: thus 2 += X makes no sense.[5] Also, these operators are two-character tokens, and thus you cannot put a space in between. As we mentioned before, these operations (in particular *=) could result in an overflow. In that case, you will silently be getting wrong answers. The one exception is that an attempt to divide by (an integer) zero generally results in a program crash.

A feature of C is that assignment operators not only assign to a variable, but also form an expression that itself has a value. Thus the expression X = 5 (with no semicolon) not only assigns X the value of 5, but also evaluates to 5. Note that an expression followed by a semicolon is a basic statement, and recall that C functions consist of statements. Accordingly, most lines in Figure 2.4 end in semicolons.

A direct consequence of this is that

```
X += (Y = 5);
```

is a statement that assigns to the variable Y the value of 5 and then increments the variable X by 5. As a second example, if X has the value of 5 and Y has the value of 6, then

```
X += (Y += 2);
```

increments Y to 8 and then increments X by 8 to the value of 13.

In these examples, parentheses are not necessary: assignment operators are processed strictly right to left. The reason for this is that since the left-hand side of the operator is adjusted by the right-hand side, going from right to left is the only order that makes sense.

As a direct consequence, the statement

```
A = B = C = 0;
```

assigns the value of 0 to C, B, and A, in that order.

As this example shows, the combination of several assignment operators in one expression can be a powerful tool. It is also perilous, if abused. For instance, consider the result of the (legal but silly) statement

```
X += X += X;
```

when X is initially 1. The rightmost += alters X to 2. It is now unclear, however, whether the leftmost += increments the original value of X (1) or the new value of X (2), so should the answer be 3 or 4? ANSI C specifies that this statement is ambiguous, so neither answer is guaranteed. Therefore, it is best to avoid altering any variable more than once in an expression. ANSI C has made the rules more precise by the introduction of the *sequence point* abstraction. We discuss this in Section 3.2.2.

2.17   Binary Arithmetic Operators

Line 11 in Figure 2.4 illustrates a binary operator that is typical of all programming languages. The value of Second and Third is added, and the resulting value is assigned to

---

[5]The term *expression that refers to an object* specifically allows the expression (X) += 2 but does not allow, for example, X++ += 2. An expression that may appear on the left-hand side of an assignment operator is known as a *modifiable lvalue*. For the most part, an lvalue is either the name of an object or a parenthesized lvalue. Specifics are provided in Appendix A6.

First. Second and Third remain unchanged. Besides the addition operator +, there are a host of other operators in C. The ones found in typical use are -, *, /, and %, which are used for subtraction, multiplication, division, and remainder.

As in many languages, when applied to integers, division returns only the integral part and discards any remainder. The % operator can be used to find out what the remainder is—in many applications it is more important than the quotient. As before, division by zero is, of course, not allowed.

 A major headache for C and many other languages is dealing with negative numbers in the context of division and remainder. For instance, 8/3 is always 2, because integer division rounds down, but 8/-3 can be either -2 or -3, depending on your interpretation of "rounding down." In C, this value is unspecified, and since it is guaranteed that X % Y ≡ X - (X / Y) * Y, the remainder is also unspecified.

If there is only one binary operator, the meaning of an expression is clear. But what does 4 * 5 - 6 - 6 mean? Mathematically trained people know that multiplication has a higher *precedence* than subtraction, so that the multiplication operator is operating on 4 and 5. They also know that subtractions are processed from left to right, meaning that the evaluation is

(((4 * 5) - 6) - 6)

as opposed to

((4 * 5) - (6 - 6)).

Thus subtraction *associates* from left to right.

C follows the usual mathematical convention that the + and - binary operators have the same precedence and that this precedence is lower than the * and / binary operators. Furthermore, all of these operators associate from left to right. We use the term *binary operators* because some of these one-character tokens can be used in a different context.

Once we have settled on assigning precedence and associativity to these operators, we immediately realize that all, and not just some, operators must have precedence and associativity rules.

Being similar to the / operator, the % binary operator is assigned the same precedence and associativity as multiplication and division.

Assignment operators are also operators. We have already decided previously that they associate from right to left. All assignment operators have the same priority as each other, and this priority is lower than that of the binary arithmetic operators. The reason for this is that

B = A *= 1 + 1;

should clearly double A and assign this value to B, rather than multiply A by 1 and then assign to B the value of A + 1. Note also that there is a %= operator, which does what you would expect. In general, any binary mathematical operator can be extended into an assignment operator.

 Since there are many operators in C, there are a host of precedence rules that occasionally combine in a funny way. Every so often, when we introduce new operators, we provide a table that indicates the precedence rules for all operators that have thus far been discussed. If you are not sure how an expression will be evaluated, or even if the meaning looks complicated, then parenthesize. Parentheses evaluate left to right and have the highest precedence of any operator.

Note that since an expression followed by a semicolon is a statement,

```
X;
X + Y;
```

are two statements that do not really do anything. Thus some coding mistakes that are obvious errors in other languages are legal. In many instances, including this one, some compilers will warn you that although legal, your code is probably erroneous.

2.18   Unary Operators

In addition to binary operators, which require two operands, C provides *unary* operators, which require only one operand. The most familiar unary operator is the *unary minus*. The unary minus operator allows us to write negative constants and variables just as is done algebraically. Thus if A has the value of 2, -2 and -A both have the value -2.

Because -2 + 8 is expected to produce (-2) + 8 and not -(2 + 8), the unary minus operator has high precedence. Indeed, it has higher precedence than multiplication (and its equivalents). Also, because - - A means A, it is clear that the unary minus operator associates from right to left. As we will see in a few paragraphs, --A means something entirely different.

In the interest of fair play and equality, ANSI C provides the rarely used *unary plus* operator.

In addition to the unary minus and plus operators, C provides operators to add and subtract 1 to and from a variable. A reason for this is that these are two of the most common operations performed on a computer, and many machines architectures have single instructions for them. Thus, on early compilers, using this operation translated not only into shorter, but also into faster code. Note that this applies to variables only; if you want to add 1 to an expression that is not a variable, you have to use + 1.

The most benign use of the feature is shown in lines 13 and 14 of Figure 2.4. In both cases, the *autoincrement* operator, ++, adds 1 to the value of its variable. In C, however, an operator applied to a variable always yields an expression that has a value. Although we are guaranteed that X will be incremented before the execution of the next statement, the question arises: If an autoincrement is part of a larger expression, what is the value of that autoincrement expression?

In this case, the placement of the ++ is crucial. The semantics of ++X is that the value of the expression is X+1, while the semantics of X++ is that the value of the expression is X. This feature is shown in line 16 of Figure 2.4 (and the last two lines of output in Figure 2.6. First and Second are both incremented by 1, and Third is obtained by adding the original (i.e., line 15) value of First with the incremented (i.e., line 17) value of Second.

As you may suspect, several warnings are in order. First, both ++ and -- are two-character tokens, so you cannot put space between them. If you do, they will look like consecutive unary plus or minus tokens, which will either make sense, or (if you are lucky) be detected as a syntax error. It is also customary to put no space between the autoincrement token and the variable on which it is operating.

Second, applying an autoincrement or autodecrement to the same variable more than once in a statement is a terrible idea, because the consequences are undefined. Do not do this under any circumstances. Altering a variable in the middle of a statement is known as a *side effect*. Actually, an even more restrictive rule applies: except as noted later, a variable may be altered at most once per statement, and if it is altered, the prior value may only be used to determine the value to be stored.[6]

As an example, if A has the value of 1, the expression A + ++A could evaluate to 3 or 4, depending on the compiler. To define precisely when this rule applies, ANSI C introduced the notion of a *sequence point*. This is discussed in Section 3.2.2.

For technical reasons, although autoincrement and autodecrement are treated together, when it comes to precedence and associativity, the X++ case (known as postfix) is treated differently from the ++X case (known as prefix). In particular, and perhaps not surprisingly, the postfix increment operators associate left to right, while the prefix increment operators associate right to left.

Prefix increment operators look like unary minus operators, and indeed have the same precedence as the unary plus and minus, while postfix operators have higher precedence. This is necessary to give Y = -X++; its intended meaning of incrementing X and setting Y equal to the negative of the old value of X, rather than binding the unary minus to X and making the autoincrement illegal (because it is not operating on a variable but on the expression -X). If the prefix notation was used, the normal right-to-left evaluation would make sense. A commonly used postfix operator is the function call operator ( ), which differs from parentheses.

2.19 Type Conversions

When an operator is applied to two variables of the same type, the result is clear. However, if the two variables have different types, unexpected results can occur. In fact, many languages do not allow this. C has a clear set of rules that governs most cases. In general, when we have two different types, the "most restrictive" type is converted to the "least restrictive" type. As an example of what this means, if D is a double and I is an int, then in D + I, I is converted temporarily to a double for use in the addition.

The most simplest conversion is the *integer promotion*. A char or short, either signed or unsigned, may be used in an expression wherever an integer may be used. If an int can represent all the values of the original type, the value is converted to int; otherwise, it is converted to unsigned int.

This integer promotion rule is fairly simple to understand. However, bad things start happening, for instance, when an integer is converted to an unsigned integer, because the conversion does not make much sense for negative integers. Also, if an unsigned integer is converted to a signed integer, it is possible that the conversion does not make sense because the largest unsigned integer is larger than the largest signed integer.

Similar problems occur for floating-point types. When a floating-point type is converted to a less precise floating-point type, the value is changed to either the next-higher or next-lower representable value. It may also be possible that the original value is out of range for the new type, in which case the behavior is undefined.

---

[6]The "prior value" clause allows

```
A = A + 1;
```

to be defined, but not

```
A = ++A + 1;
```

- First, if either operand is a `long double`, the other is converted to a `long double`.
- Otherwise, if either operand is `double`, the other is converted to a `double`.
- Otherwise, if either operand is `float`, the other is converted to a `float`.
- Otherwise, the integral promotions are performed on both operands; then if either operand is `unsigned long int`, the other is converted to `unsigned long int`.
- Otherwise, if one operand is `long int` and the other is `unsigned int`, the effect depends on whether a `long int` can represent all the values of an `unsigned int`; if so, the `unsigned int` operand is converted to `long int`; if not, both are converted to `unsigned long int`.
- Otherwise, if one operand is `long int`, the other is converted to `long int`.
- Otherwise, if either operand is `unsigned int`, the other is converted to `unsigned int`.
- Otherwise, both operands have type `int`.

Figure 2.7:   Arithmetic conversion rules.

When all integers are representable by doubles (because, for example, a double is stored in twice as many bits), a conversion from an integer to a double is safe. However, a conversion of a double that is in between two integer values to an integer discards the fractional part. Figure 2.7 describes the official rules for converting two types. It pretty much does what you would expect.

The main problem with the type conversion rules is that they are applied on an operator-by-operator basis. This means that an expression with six operators and seven variables, only one of which is double and the rest of which are integers, may be done in mostly integer math, with a type conversion at the end. Consider, for example, the variables `D`, which is a `double`, and `I1` and `I2`, which are integers 8 and 5. The expression `D = I1/I2` is evaluated as 1.00000, because `I1/I2` is an integer division, whose result is converted to a double.

In this case, what is needed is an implicit type conversion, which in C is known as a *type cast*. The syntax would be `D = (double) I1/I2`. Here `I1` is implicitly temporarily converted to a `double`. To perform the division, the automatic conversion rules convert `I2` to a `double`, and then the result is as intended.

Note that the type cast was effective on `I1`, rather than the quotient, which implies that the type cast, which is an operator, has higher precedence than division. Indeed, it is very much like a unary operator and has precedence just below the other prefix unary operators, such as `-`, `--`, and `++`. Figure 2.8 shows the precedence rules for the operators that we have discussed so far.

Figure 2.9 illustrates the type conversion rules between integer and floating-point types. Line 2 shows that fractional parts are discarded in a conversion from floating-point to integral types. On line 3, the entire right-hand side of the assignment is evaluated using integer math. The result of line 4 is unchanged because the division is still an integer division. The explicit type conversion at line 5 forces all computations to be done in floating-point math. On line 6, the subtraction of `Z` from `Y` is logically 3. However, roundoff error could give an answer of 2.99999999999..., and if this happened, the resulting conversion to an `int` would remove the fractional part, and thus assign `A` the value of 2. The type conversion rules can cause so much trouble that it is best to avoid mixing types, and if you must, always use an explicit type conversion.

Category	Examples	Associativity
Primary expression	*identifiers* *constants*	None
Postfix	Function ( ) ++ --	Left to right
Prefix and unary	+ - ++ --	Right to left
Type cast	(TypeName)	Right to left
Multiplicative	* / %	Left to right
Additive	+ -	Left to right
Assignment	= *= /= %= += -=	Right to left

Figure 2.8:   Precedence and associativity of operators.

```
          int A, B = 4, C = 5;
          double X, Y = 6.8, Z = 3.8;

/* 1*/        A = Y;                        /* Result: A is 6 */
/* 2*/        A = -Y;                       /* Result: A is -6 */
/* 3*/        X = A / B + C;                /* Result: X is 4.0 */
/* 4*/        X = A / B + ( double ) C;     /* Result: X is 4.0 */
/* 5*/        X = ( double ) A / B + C;     /* Result: X is 3.5 */
/* 6*/        A = Y - Z;                    /* Result: A is 2 or 3 */
```

Figure 2.9:   Examples of implicit and explicit type conversions.

2.20   Bitwise Operators

In addition to the high-level operations such as addition and multiplication, ANSI C provides for the manipulation of integers on a bit-by-bit basis. This allows us to pack several boolean variables into an integral type. To make our examples shorter, we assume that an `int` is represented in 16 bits.

2.20.1   Shift Operators

C provides two shift operators, $<<$ and $>>$, which implement a left shift and a right shift, respectively. An expression of the form

```
Expr1 << Expr2
```

evaluates to the result of shifting the bit pattern in `Expr1` to the left by `Expr2` places. In the result the lowest `Expr2` bits have zero. Similarly,

```
Expr1 >> Expr2
```

evaluates to the result of shifting the bit pattern in `Expr1` to the right by `Expr2` places. If `Expr1` is an `unsigned` type, or is signed but happens to be nonnegative, the highest

```
unsigned int A = 3737;        /* 0000111010011001 */
unsigned int B = A << 1;      /* 0001110100110010 */
unsigned int C = A >> 2;      /* 0000001110100110 */
unsigned int D = C << 2 << 3; /* 0111010011000000 */
unsigned int E = 1 << 15;     /* 1000000000000000 */

        int F = 3737;         /* 0000111010011001 */
        int G = F << 4;       /* 1110100110010000 */
        int H = G >> 4;       /* ????111010011001 */
```

Figure 2.10:   Examples of the shift operators.

 Expr2 bits in the result are guaranteed to be filled with zeros. Otherwise, what gets filled in is machine dependent. Although shifting is the only bitwise operator whose result could be different for `signed` and `unsigned` types, it is nonetheless customary to use `unsigned` types when dealing with bit operators. Our examples will assume that this is the case.

 For the shift operators, if Expr2 is negative, or is greater than or equal to the number of bits in an `int`, the result is undefined. Also, in evaluating the shift operations, Expr1 is promoted to an `int` type. Figure 2.10 shows the result of applying some shift operations. Notice that for unsigned types, a left shift by one place is equivalent to multiplication by 2, and a right shift by one place is equivalent to division by 2. Similarly, a left shift or right shift by i places is equivalent to a multiplication or division, respectively, by 2^i. Historically, programmers have used these tricks to replace expensive multiplication and division with cheap bit shifts. Virtually all modern compilers will implement this optimization, thus rendering this practice obsolete.

The computation of D in the example illustrates that the shift operators associate from left to right: the interpretation is

```
unsigned int D = ( C << 2 ) << 3; /* 0111010011000000 */
```

 One final word: as we will see in Chapter 3, both < and > are relational operators. Thus if you accidentally type only half of the shift operator token, the compiler will not complain and you will have an expression that does not evaluate to what you expect.

2.20.2   Bit Complement

$\sim$ is the unary one's-complement operator. The result of

```
~Expr
```

is an expression with all of Expr's bits flipped to the other value. As an example,

```
unsigned int A = 3737;        /* 0000111010011001 */
unsigned int B = ~A;          /* 1111000101100110 */
```

2.20.3   Bitwise *AND, OR,* and *XOR*

The *AND* of two bits is 1 if and only if both bits are 1. The *OR* of two bits is 1 if and only if either bit is 1. The *exclusive or, XOR,* of two bits is 1 if and only if the bits are different (i.e, one bit is 1 and the other is 0). The three bitwise binary operators &, |, and ^ apply *AND, OR,* and *XOR,* respectively, to two integral expressions, bit by bit. Figure 2.11 shows some examples.

```
unsigned int A = 3737;        /* 0000111010011001 */
unsigned int B = 7474;        /* 0001110100110010 */
unsigned int C = A | B;       /* 0001111110111011 */
unsigned int D = B & C;       /* 0001110100110010 */
unsigned int E = C ^ D;       /* 0000001010001001 */
```

Figure 2.11: **Examples of the** *AND*, *OR*, **and** *XOR* **shift operators.**

2.20.4 Bitwise Assignment Operators

With the exception of the unary complement operator, all the bitwise operators we have discussed require two expressions and are thus binary operators. Logically, then, the shorthand A &= B should make sense. Indeed, this is the case: all of the binary bitwise operators have a corresponding assignment operator. The earlier warning for shift operators applies here, too, because both <= and >= are relational operators.

2.20.5 Precedence of the Bitwise Operators

Like all operators, the bitwise operators have precedence and associativity. Because these operators are not as standard as +, *, and so on, the assignment of precedence and associativity is not at all obvious. Indeed, for some operators, it is easy to decide on precedences, while for others, it is difficult. First we will settle on the relative precedences and associativities of the bitwise operators and then place them in their proper places among all the other operators.

Based on the fact that the complement operator is *unary*, we will give it high precedence, have it associate from right to left, and eventually group it with all of the other unary operators. Similarly, the bitwise assignment operators will be lumped in with all assignment operators. This leaves only the binary bitwise operators. All of these operators will have lower precedence than addition and subtraction, so that A << 2 + 3 shifts by 5. Of course, they must have higher precedence than the assignment operators, or else we will have to parenthesize A = B & C. Based on the fact that the shift operators are similar to multiplication and division, and thus closest to the normal mathematical operations, they will have the highest precedence of the bitwise binary operators.

Because bitwise *AND* is a boolean multiply, while *OR* is a boolean addition, & will have higher precedence than |. Because *XOR* is a combination of *AND* and *OR*, we place ^ between & and | in the precedence table. All of the bitwise binary operators associate from left to right, as is the case with the other binary operators. Figure 2.12 summarizes the precedence and associativity rules for the bitwise operators. Figure 2.15, shown toward the end of this chapter, gives the precedence and associativity for all the operators we have discussed.

2.20.6 An Example of Bit Packing

Figure 2.13 shows how the bitwise operators are used to pack information into a 16-bit integer. This information is maintained by a typical university for a wide variety of reasons, including state and federal mandates. Many of the items require simple yes/no answers and are thus logically representable by a single bit. As Figure 2.13 shows, 10 bits are used to represent 10 categories. A faculty member can have one of four possible ranks (assistant,

Category	Examples	Associativity
Unary complement	~	Right to left
Shift	<< >>	Left to right
Boolean AND	&	Left to right
Boolean XOR	^	Left to right
Boolean OR	|	Left to right
Assignment	&= |= ^= <<= >>=	Right to left

Figure 2.12:   **Precedence and associativity of bitwise operators.**

associate, and full professor as well as nontenured earning), and thus two bits are required. The remaining four bits are used to represent one of 16 possible colleges in the university.

Lines 21 and 22 show how *Tim* is represented. Tim is a tenured associate professor in the College of Arts and Science. He holds a Ph.D., is a U.S. citizen, and works on the university's main campus. He is not a member of a minority group, disabled, or a veteran. He is on a nine-month contract. Tim's bit pattern is given by

$$0011\ 10\ 1\ 0\ 0\ 1\ 1\ 1\ 0\ 0\ 0\ 0$$

or 0x3a70. This bit pattern is formed by applying the *OR* operator on the appropriate fields.

Lines 24 and 25 show the logic used when Tim is deservedly promoted to the rank of full professor. Rank has all of the rank bits set to 1 and all the other bits zero:

$$0000\ 11\ 0\ 0\ 0\ 0\ 0\ 0\ 0\ 0\ 0\ 0$$

The complement, ~Rank, is thus

$$1111\ 00\ 1\ 1\ 1\ 1\ 1\ 1\ 1\ 1\ 1\ 1$$

Applying a logical *AND* of this and Tim's current setting turns off Tim's rank bits:

$$0011\ 00\ 1\ 0\ 0\ 1\ 1\ 1\ 0\ 0\ 0\ 0$$

The result of the logical *OR* operator at line 25 thus makes Tim a full professor without altering any of the other bits:

$$0011\ 11\ 1\ 0\ 0\ 1\ 1\ 1\ 0\ 0\ 0\ 0$$

Lines 27 and 28 illustrate extraction. Here we have *Bob*:

$$0011\ 10\ 1\ 0\ 1\ 1\ 1\ 1\ 0\ 0\ 0\ 0$$

We can find out that Bob is tenured, because Bob & Tenured is a nonzero result. We can also find out that Bob is in College #3 by shifting right 12 bits and then looking at the resulting low four bits. Notice that the parentheses are required.

```
/* 1*/    /* Faculty Profile Fields */   /* On If */

/* 2*/    #define Sex          0x0001    /* Female */
/* 3*/    #define Minority     0x0002    /* In A Minority Group */
/* 4*/    #define Veteran      0x0004    /* Veteran */
/* 5*/    #define Disabled     0x0008    /* Disabled */
/* 6*/    #define UScitizen    0x0010    /* Citizen */
/* 7*/    #define Doctorate    0x0020    /* Holds A Doctorate */
/* 8*/    #define Tenured      0x0040    /* Tenured */
/* 9*/    #define TwelveMonth  0x0080    /* On 12 Month Contract */
/*10*/    #define Visitor      0x0100    /* Not Permanent Faculty */
/*11*/    #define Campus       0x0200    /* Works At Main Campus */

/*12*/    #define Rank         0xc00     /* Two Bits For Rank */
/*13*/    #define Assistant    0x0400     /* Assistant Professor */
/*14*/    #define Associate    0x0800    /* Associate Professor */
/*15*/    #define Full         0xc00     /* Full Professor */

/*16*/    #define College      0xf000    /* Represents 16 Colleges */
/*17*/        ...
/*18*/    #define ArtsScience  0x3000    /* College #3 */
/*19*/        ...


/*20*/        /* Initialize Appropriate Fields */
/*21*/    Tim = ArtsScience | Associate | Campus | Tenured |
/*22*/                Doctorate | UScitizen;

/*23*/        /* Promote Tim To Full Professor */
/*24*/    Tim &= ~Rank;         /* Turn All Rank Fields Off */
/*25*/    Tim |= Full;          /* Turn Rank Fields On */

/*26*/        /* Find Bob's Tenure And College */
/*27*/    BobsTenured = Bob & Tenured;    /* Zero If Untenured */
/*28*/    BobsCollege = ( Bob >> 12 ) & 0x000f;
```

Figure 2.13:   Packing bits for faculty profiles.

2.21   scanf

Just as printf can be used for formatted output, the library routine scanf can be used for input. scanf is a complex routine and is treated fully in Chapter 12. Figure 2.14 shows how it is used. Much like printf, %d is used to specify an int. However %lf, not %f, is needed for the double. This illustrates that for advanced applications, the printf and scanf options are drastically different.

The most important difference is that in scanf, the parameters that follow the control string are preceded by an &. In this context, the & represents the *address-of* operator. This unary operator provides the memory location where an object is stored. Thus scanf wants

```
/* 1*/    #include <stdio.h>

/* 2*/    main( void )
/* 3*/    {
/* 4*/        int X;
/* 5*/        double Y;

/* 6*/        printf( "Enter an integer and a real: " );
/* 7*/        scanf( "%d %lf", &X, &Y );
/* 8*/        printf( "You entered %d and %f\n", X, Y );
/* 9*/    }
```

Figure 2.14: **Using** `scanf` **to read an** `int` **and a** `double`.

to know *where* to place values that it reads. Forgetting the & is a common mistake, as is forgetting the l in %lf.

Note carefully that the bitwise *AND* operator, which is binary, and the address-of operator, which is unary, are completely different, even though they are represented by the same token &. The compiler can tell which operator is implied by examining the context in which it is used. Several other tokens, most notably *, +, and -, represent both a binary and a unary operator.

2.22   Summary

In this chapter we saw how to construct a minimal C program. In the next two chapters we discuss conditional expressions, loops, and functions.

A short list of the concepts that were covered is provided in Section 2.22.1. One of the important points is that the expressive power of C, which is one of its great advantages, can also lead to silly errors. Some of the things that bear watching are listed in Section 2.22.2.

2.22.1   What Was Covered

- To test a C program on UNIX, give it a name that ends in *.c*, and use the *cc* command. You can run it by typing *a.out*. There are various options and the procedure is different on other systems.

- It is important to use *white space* to make your programs easier to read.

- Comments are used to help convey information to the reader of the program. They are treated as white space by the compiler.

- The #include statement is used to read the contents of another file. Our use was for system files, such as <stdio.h>.

- C is case sensitive.

- Execution begins in the main function, which must be provided by the user.

- The printf function is used for output. The first parameter, which is the control string, is printed, and conversion sequences that begin with the % character are replaced by

Category	Examples		Associativity
Primary expression	*identifiers* *constants*		None
Postfix	Function ( ) ++ --		Left to right
Prefix and unary	+ - ++ -- ~		Right to left
Type cast	(TypeName)		Right to left
Multiplicative	* / %		Left to right
Additive	+ -		Left to right
Shift	<< >>		Left to right
Boolean AND	&		Left to right
Boolean XOR	^		Left to right
Boolean OR	|		Left to right
Assignment	= *= /= %= += -= &= |= ^= <<= >>=		Right to left

Figure 2.15:   Precedence and associativity of operators.

subsequent parameters. The \n sequence prints a newline, which is never supplied automatically.

- All variables must be declared in the declaration section before use. A type and name must be provided, and an initial value may be specified. It is important to choose meaningful names.

- C provides many integer types: short, int, long, which may be signed (by default) or unsigned. A short is not longer than an int, and an int is not longer than a long. A char can be used for 8-bit integers.

- C provides a host of operators. All have precedence and associativity. The state of affairs at this point in the book is shown in Figure 2.15.

- Floating-point arithmetic is discussed in this chapter. C provides float, double, and long double. Stick with double for now, and beware of roundoff errors.

- A complicated sequence of rules is used to convert one type to another type when operations are performed on different types. In general, the computation is done using the least restrictive type. A type cast can be used to force a conversion.

- There is still lots of C to learn!

2.22.2   Friendly Reminders

Here are some of the things you should be on the lookout for. (Many of these items apply to other programming languages as well.)

- Comments do not nest.
- C is case sensitive.
- Remember to initialize variables before using their values. Many systems assign default values of zero. If your program no longer works when you move from one machine to another, this is a possible source of the difficulty.
- Keywords cannot be used as identifier names. Library routines should not be used either. Also, try not to have identifier names that begin with the underscore character _.
- Mixing integer types can produce unexpected, and in some cases unspecified, results.
- Constant integers that start with a 0 are octal numbers. Unless this is your intention, start an integer with a nonzero digit.
- Arithmetic overflow on integers is silent in C.
- Variables that are subjected to side effects such as an intermediate assignment or autoincrement/autodecrement operator should be used only once in a statement. Otherwise, the result may be undefined.
- The result of division and remainder when one number is negative is not defined precisely by the standard.
- When using long integer constants, put an L as the last character. Do not use a lowercase replacement l.
- Be careful if you are using `char` to store 8-bit integers. Always use either `signed` or `unsigned`, because the default is unspecified.
- When printing unsigned integers, always use `%u`.
- Floating-point computations are not exact. Beware!
- A type cast must be used if integer operations are to be assigned to a floating-point value. Otherwise, the operations are done using integers, and the integer result is all that gets converted.
- Converting a floating-point number that does not represent an integer value to an integer discards the fractional part. However, because of roundoff error, this could result in the wrong answer (e.g., 6.8–3.8 could be 2.99999..., and be converted to 2).
- Apply shift operators on unsigned types to ensure portability.
- Forgetting a < or > in a shift operator will give a relational operator.
- `printf` does not check that the parameters you pass are the same type as expected by the `%` converter.
- Parameters that follow the control string must be preceded by an & because `scanf` expects addresses of objects. Also, do not forget that the scanning conversion for `double` is `%lf`, not just `%f`.
- On UNIX, *-lm* needs to be placed at the end of the *cc* command if math libraries are used.

EXERCISES

1. Enter, compile, link, and run the program in Figure 2.1.
2. Adjust the program in Figure 2.1 to obtain errors. Show that comments do not nest, strings must be on one line, and that C is case sensitive.

3. Write a program that prints out *Testing 123* but omits the newline.

4. Write a program that prints out the following numbers in decimal, octal, and hexadecimal: 37, 037, 0x37.

5. Assuming that a float uses 23 bits for *M* and 8 bits for *E*, what are the largest and smallest representable numbers?

6. Show that all 52-bit integers are representable as doubles, assuming the representation in the text.

7. Let B have the value of 5 and C have the value of 8. What is the value of A, B, and C after each line of the following program fragment?

```
A = B++ + C++;
A = B++ + ++C;
A = ++B + C++;
A = ++B + ++C;
```

8. Suppose that A has the value of 1. On your computer, what is the value of A++ + ++A, and what is A after the operation? How about A += A += A?

9. In the first expression of Exercise 8, suppose that there were no blank spaces (i.e., there were five plusses in a row). Can you think of another legal interpretation of the plusses, obtained by adding appropriate blanks? What would the compiler do if there were no blanks?

10. Write a program to print out the values of the largest and smallest int on your system by printing the appropriate values in the include file <limits.h>.

11. What are the values of (int)3.1, (int)3.5, and (int)3.9? What are the values of (int)-3.1, (int)-3.5, and (int)-3.9?

12. What are the values assigned on lines 1 through 6?

```
int A, B = 5, C = 7;
double X, Y = 2.8, Z = 16.8;
```

```
/* 1*/    A = Y;
/* 2*/    A = -Y;
/* 3*/    X = A / B + C;
/* 4*/    X = A / B + ( double ) C;
/* 5*/    X = ( double ) A / B + C;
/* 6*/    A = Y - Z;
```

13. What is 8/-5 on your system? What are all the possible values? What are the possible values of 8%-5 for each of the possible values of 8/-5?

14. C originally used =- instead of -=. Why do you think the change was made?

15. Although type conversions work for operators, they cannot work for printf parameters. Why? We discuss this more in Chapter 4. What gets printed by the following?

```
printf( "%d %f\n", 8.0, 8 );
```

16. What does the following code intend to do, and what might go wrong? Using an extra variable, what is the sensible way to achieve the same effect?

```
A -= B;
B += A;
A = B - A;
```

17. For 16-bit integers, suppose that A=0xC0B3 and B=0x2435. Determine the following values, assuming that A and B are both unsigned, and indicate which answers would be affected if A were signed.

(a) ~A

(b) A | B

(c) A & B

(d) A ^ B

(e) A >> 2

(f) A << 2

(g) A << -2

18. (a) What does the following code do?

```
A ^= B;
B ^= A;
A ^= B;
```

(b) Is the statement

```
A ^= B ^= A ^= B;
```

equivalent?

3

Decisions, Decisions, Decisions

In Chapter 2 we looked at computations in which a sequence of statements is executed one by one, from the first statement to the last statement. In this chapter we examine statements that affect the flow of control: namely, conditional statements and loops. As a consequence, new operators are also introduced.

3.1   Relational and Equality Operators

The most basic test that we can perform on numbers is the comparison. Mathematically, the six possibilities are $<$, $\leq$, $>$, $\geq$, $\neq$, and $=$. These possibilities are represented in C by the six operators $<$, $<=$, $>$, $>=$, $!=$, and $==$. The relational and equality operators are binary, meaning that they require two expressions, *LeftExpr* and *RightExpr*. The result of applying the operator on the two expressions always evaluates to either 0 (representing *false*) or 1 (representing *not false*), depending on whether the implied mathematical relationship between the left and right operands is false or true. Unlike many other languages, C does not provide a boolean type, but rather, uses integers to represent them implicitly.

Figure 3.1 shows the values that result from applying the relational and equality operators. X<Y is 1 only if X is strictly less than Y; if they are equal, X<Y is 0. X<=Y is 1 if X is strictly less than Y or if X and Y have identical values. Although this seems simple enough, the richness of C's operator set makes it likely that eventually you will make a simple mistake, such as a typographical error, which will not be caught by the compiler. Thus it is important to keep in mind what can go wrong.

Possibly the most common error is using an assignment statement instead of an equality comparison. As Figure 3.1 shows, X=Y assigns the value of Y to X and evaluates to that value. Thus, using an assignment statement instead of an equality comparison is generally perfectly legal, and almost certain to do the wrong thing by yielding an incorrect value and altering a variable.

One way to protect yourself is to note that the left-hand side of an assignment cannot be an arbitrary expression but must be a variable. Thus 1==X is a legal comparison of X

47

X	Y	Relational and Equality Operators						Possible Mistakes		
		X<Y	X<=Y	X>Y	X>=Y	X!=Y	X==Y	X=Y	X<<Y	X>>Y
3	3	0	1	0	1	0	1	3	24	0
3	4	1	1	0	0	1	0	4	48	0
4	3	0	0	1	1	1	0	3	32	0

Figure 3.1:   Relational and equality operators (and some nonrelational mistakes).

and 1, but 1=X is not a legal assignment. In this case the compiler will complain and you will notice that you have forgotten an =. Although many people like to use this trick, it does not read quite as nicely as X==1, so its use is strictly a matter of personal taste.

C also provides operators << and >>. Although it is not a common error, it is possible to mistype the shift operators <<, <<=, >>, >>=, which were discussed in Section 2.20.1, as relational operators (and vice versa). In either case, the result is legal code but incorrect results. Because the relational and equality operators are, by definition, operators, they have precedence and associativity rules. The associativity of all the operators is left to right, but all that does is tempt you to make elementary mistakes. As an example the expression 2<X<7 always evaluates to 1, because 2<X evaluates to either 0 or 1, and both of those values are less than 7. Thus C syntax is not quite as mathematical as you might like.

Since we would like the expression X<Y+5 to be evaluated as X<(Y+5), the relational operators have lower precedence than the additive operators. When it comes to precedence, the equality operators are treated differently from the relational operators. This is because we would like the expression A<B == C<D (deliberately written with prejudicial spacing) to be true exactly when the A<B and C<D have the same truth value. Therefore, the equality operators have slightly lower precedence than the relational operators. They have higher precedence than the assignment operator, so that A=B==C assigns to A the truth value of B==C.

Thus the relational and equality operators have precedence lower than the additive operators and higher than the assignment operators. Because this is exactly where the precedences of the binary bitwise operators lie, we see that the language designers had to determine (somewhat arbitrarily) the relative precedences of the relational, equality, and bitwise operators. A summary of the additions to the precedence and associativity table is shown in Figure 3.2.

The result, at first glance, appears inconsistent. The relational and equality operators are placed lower than the shift operators but higher than all the other binary bitwise operators. It would seem that a reasonable ordering would have given either all of the bitwise binary operators higher precedence than the relational operators, or lower precedence than the equality operators, rather than put some higher and some lower. What has happened is that the binary bitwise operators should have been placed higher than the relational operators, but for consistency with the operators discussed in the next section, the & and | operators, and thus the ^ operator, are placed below the equality operators. Consequently, the expression (A&B)==C requires parentheses.

For the relational and equality operators, if the two operands are not of the same type, the type conversion rules discussed in Section 2.8.2 are applied. Unexpected results can

Category	Examples	Associativity
Primary expression	*identifiers* *constants*	None
Postfix	Function( ) ++ --	Left to right
Prefix and unary	~ + - ++ --	Right to left
Type cast	(TypeName)	Right to left
Multiplicative	* / %	Left to right
Additive	+ -	Left to right
Shift	<< >>	Left to right
Relational	< <= > >=	Left to right
Equality	== !=	Left to right
Boolean AND	&	Left to right
Boolean XOR	^	Left to right
Boolean OR	|	Left to right
Assignment	= *= /= %= += -= &= |= ^= <<= >>=	Right to left

Figure 3.2:   Precedence and associativity of operators.

occur if the types are incompatible. Also, be careful about comparing two floating-point quantities. Because of roundoff errors, after several successive operations, a floating-point number might not be exactly what you expect. In that case, an equality test will fail. For instance, you may be surprised to find that the value of

```
0.1 + 0.1 + 0.1 + 0.1 + 0.1 + 0.1 + 0.1 + 0.1 == 0.8
```

is generally zero.[1] To get around this, you may need to rewrite some expressions. As an example, instead of X==Y, you may need

```
fabs( X - Y ) <= Epsilon
```

where `fabs` is the floating-point absolute value function[2] and `Epsilon` is a symbolic constant given by a #define statement.

3.2   Logical Operators

In addition to the relational and equality operators, C provides *logical* operators that are used to simulate the boolean algebra concepts of *AND*, *OR*, and *NOT*. These are sometimes

---

[1]Of course, as is the case for many of the warnings in the book, this is true for all programming languages.

[2]You'll need to #include <math.h>.

		Logical Operators				Possible Mistakes	
X	Y	X && Y	X || Y	!X	!!X	X & Y	X | Y
0	0	0	0	1	0	0	0
0	7	0	1	1	0	0	7
5	0	0	1	0	1	0	5
5	7	1	1	0	1	5	7
8	7	1	1	0	1	0	15

Figure 3.3: **Logical operators (and some nonlogical mistakes).**

known as *conjunction*, *disjunction*, and *negation*. These operations are represented in C by &&, ||, and !. Like a relational or equality operator, the result of a logical operator is either 0, representing *false*, or 1, representing *true*. There is no such restriction on the value of the operands. An operand of 0 is interpreted to represent *false*, while any nonzero value is interpreted to represent *true*. Note carefully that -1 is thus considered *true*.

Figure 3.3 shows the values that result from applying the logical operators. Note that !!X is not the same as X, because if X is nonzero, the result of the second negation will be 1, as opposed to X. Recall that since both & and | are bit manipulation operators, the *AND* and *OR* logical and bit operators have the same problem as the equality operator: it is easy to mistype a different token. For these operators, the result is semantics, which in many cases appears equivalent but is actually never equivalent.

Although A&B will always evaluate to A&&B when either A or B is zero, as Figure 3.3 shows, it is possible for A&B to evaluate to zero even if A and B are both nonzero. The | operator does not seem to suffer from the same problem, since although the exact value is not the same, A|B evaluates to zero exactly when A||B does. There is an extremely subtle problem here, too, however, because | and || are different operators and thus have different precedences. We will see another difference in the next few pages. Consequently, do not use | instead of ||.

As is customary, we now provide the precedence and associativity rules. First, negation is a unary operator and is treated the same as unary minus. Thus it associates right to left and has fairly high precedence. The logical *AND* and *OR* operators both associate left to right. The associativity makes sense in that

```
X != 0 && Y != 0 && Z != 0
```

evaluates to what you would expect. Based on the fact that in boolean algebra an *AND* is similar to a multiply, while an *OR* is similar to an addition, the logical *AND* has higher precedence than the logical *OR*. On the other hand, since the intent is to combine relational expressions such as

```
X != 0 && Y != 0
```

&& has lower precedence than the equality operators.[3] The same reasoning tells us that the logical operators should have lower precedence than the bitwise operators, and this is what the language designers decided, too.

---

[3]This is why the binary bitwise operators, which are similar to the logical operators, were given precedence below the equality operators.

Category	Examples	Associativity
Primary expression	*identifiers constants*	None
Postfix	Function( ) ++ --	Left to right
Prefix and unary	! ~ + - ++ --	Right to left
Type cast	(TypeName)	Right to left
Multiplicative	* / %	Left to right
Additive	+ -	Left to right
Shift	<< >>	Left to right
Relational	< <= > >=	Left to right
Equality	== !=	Left to right
Boolean AND	&	Left to right
Boolean XOR	^	Left to right
Boolean OR	|	Left to right
Logical AND	&&	Left to right
Logical OR	||	Left to right
Assignment	= *= /= %= += -= &= |= ^= <<= >>=	Right to left

Figure 3.4:   Precedence and associativity of operators.

Using the same reasoning as for the equality operator, we see that the logical operators should have higher precedence than the assignment operators. Note that the logical operators are special in that the two operands do not have to be of the same type. Figure 3.4 shows the up-to-date precedence and associativity rules.

3.2.1   Short-Circuit Evaluation

During the evaluation of the expression X&&Y, if X is zero, C saves time by not evaluating Y, since the expression will evaluate to zero no matter what Y is. The same observation holds true when evaluating X||Y and X is nonzero. Performing this optimization is known as *short-circuiting*.

Although this seems simple enough, a direct consequence is that X&&Y is not the same as Y&&X. As an example, when X is 0, the expression

```
X != 0 && 1/X != 3
```

evaluates to zero, while

```
1/X != 3 && X != 0
```

causes an illegal division by zero. This example illustrates one of the real benefits of short-circuit evaluation: problematic cases can be handled easily.

On the other hand, one has to be careful about incorporating side effects into the second part of the short-circuit expression: when X is 1 in

```
--X == 0 || --Y == 0
```

Y does not get decremented.

A very interesting, although perhaps technical point is that the logical operators are unusual in that they define the order of evaluation of their operands. Thus the logical operators guarantee the left-to-right evaluation of its operands and will not evaluate the second operand if the first can determine the result of the operator.

Because logical operators associate left to right,

```
--X == 0 || --Y == 0 || --Z == 0
```

decrements X. If the result is 0, the expression evaluates to 1. Otherwise, it decrements Y. If that result evaluates to 0, the expression evaluates to 1. Otherwise, it decrements Z. If that result evaluates to 0, the expression evaluates to 1; otherwise, it evaluates to 0. An equivalent expression is

```
!--X || !--Y || !--Z
```

which is not equivalent to

```
!--X | !--Y | !--Z
```

(because the bitwise operator guarantees that X, Y, and Z are all decremented). This is another very technical difference between the | and || operators. The former guarantees evaluation of both operands.

 As you might imagine, it can be quite hard to read some of this. It is a good idea to use parentheses for complicated boolean constructs even if they are not required by the precedence rules:

```
(--X == 0) || (--Y == 0) || (--Z == 0)
```

This is especially true when mixing logical *AND* and logical *OR*.

3.2.2   Sequence Points and Order of Evaluation

In addition to short-circuiting, the binary logical operators are different from most other operators for two reasons:

1. Left-to-right evaluation of the operands is guaranteed.

2. Side effects in the first operand are **guaranteed** to be complete before the second operand is evaluated.

Let us explain what all this means. Like other languages, C does not specify the order of evaluation of operands. This is because among the several equivalent orders, the best ordering can be significantly better than the worst, and depends strongly on the machine's architecture. Thus in the expression

```
( Expr1 ) - ( Expr2 )
```

Expr2 could be evaluated before Expr1. If the result depends on Expr1 being evaluated before Expr2 is evaluated, the entire result is undefined. For instance, if both Expr1 and Expr2 represent functions that read an integer from a terminal, the first integer read could go to either Expr1 or Expr2, depending on how the compiler has sequenced the evaluations.

```
if( expression )
    statement
```

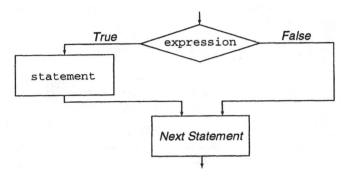

Figure 3.5:   Syntax and flow diagram for the if statement.

We have also seen the *general rule* that a variable which is subjected to a side effect should appear only once in a statement, except that it may appear so that its original value can be used to obtain the new value (pg. 35) because the exact timing of when the side effect takes place is not specified (and again depends on the machine's architecture). General rules are fine, but a language needs precise rules to avoid ambiguity. Thus ANSI C defines the *sequence point*.

A *sequence point* is a point in the execution of a program at which all previous side effects are guaranteed to be completed and no new side effects have started. Thus the disposition of all side effects is known. Sequence points exist:

1.   At the ; that terminates an expression

2.   Immediately after the first operand in a && or || expression

3.   A few other places, discussed in this chapter

4.   After evaluation of function arguments (discussed in Chapter 4)

Notice that when an operator defines a sequence point, it automatically guarantees left-to-right evaluation of its operands. Conversely, when the order of evaluation is guaranteed, it makes sense that a sequence point be generated. Appendix A.4 provides a list of all places where sequence points occur.

3.3   Conditional Statements

3.3.1   The if Statement

The if statement is the fundamental decision maker. The basic form is shown in Figure 3.5. If expression evaluates to *true*, then statement is executed; otherwise, it is not. As usual, true means nonzero. When the if statement is completed, control passes to the next statement. After expression is evaluated, a sequence point is generated. Thus any side effects are guaranteed to be completed. Figure 3.5 illustrates the flow of control.

Optionally, we can use an if-else statement, which is shown in Figure 3.6. In this case, if expression evaluates to *true*, then statement1 is executed; otherwise,

```
if( expression )
    statement1
else
    statement2
```

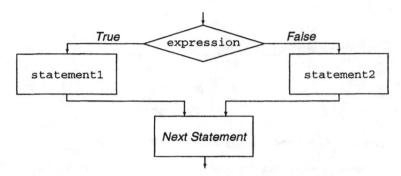

Figure 3.6:   Syntax and flow diagram for the if-else statement.

```
printf( "1/X is ");
if( X != 0.0 )
    printf( "%f\n", 1 / X );
else
    printf( "undefined\n" );
```

Figure 3.7:   Example of if-else.

```
printf( "1/X is ");
if( X )
    printf( "%f\n", 1 / X );
else
    printf( "undefined\n");
```

Figure 3.8:   Example of C conciseness.

statement2 is executed. In either case, control then passes to the next statement. Figure 3.7 shows an example. As shown in Figure 3.8, the code fragment in Figure 3.7 can be written with fewer keystrokes because the equality operator is redundant. This is a two-edged sword. It can make for more compact code but can also make for harder-to-read code. Additionally, the fact that any expression can be used to drive the if, rather than the strict boolean types used in most other languages means, once again, that the penalty for expressive power is that some typographical errors are not detected by the compiler as illegal statements, even though compilers for other languages would catch equivalent mistakes.

        For increased readability it is very important to indent the statement that is the target of the if or if-else conditions, as we have done. Otherwise, it can be hard to see which statements are being executed. Also remember, that only one statement is allowed to be subjected to each of the if and else clauses, no matter how you indent. If you put an extra statement, your code is not doing what you think it is. This can be very hard to spot because the indentation will mislead you. Figure 3.9 shows a simple example.

```
if( X == 5 )
    printf( "X is " ); printf( "5\n" );
```

Figure 3.9:   Silly example: Second `printf` is not part of the `if`.

```
if( X < 0 );
    printf( "X is negative\n" );
```

Figure 3.10:   Extra semicolon leads to a bug.

3.3.2   What Counts as a Statement?

There are several constructs that qualify as statements. We already know that any expression followed by a semicolon is a statement. We now discuss three other forms.

The Null Statement

Although an expression followed by a semicolon is a statement, the expression is itself optional. In some cases, most notably the beginning of a `for` loop, which we describe in Section 3.4.2, this can be a useful feature. A semicolon by itself is the *null statement*. Unfortunately, as Figure 3.10 shows, the null statement can also lead to many problems. In this case, the statement that is meant to be executed when X is negative is always executed, because the null statement finishes the `if`. If you use a null statement, always put in on a line by itself so it is clear that the use is intentional.

The Compound Statement

The syntax of the `if` statement tells us that only one statement can be executed as a result of an `if` test. In most cases we would like to execute a sequence of statements when a condition is true. The *compound statement* allows us to get by this restriction. A compound statement consists of a sequence of any number of statements surrounded by a pair of braces. As an example, the body of `main` is itself a compound statement. Note that there is no semicolon after the closing brace.

The `if` Statement

Since the `if` statement is itself a statement, one can use a second `if` statement as the action of an `if` statement. Indeed, one can use any of the statements that are described later in this chapter. One particularly popular construction is the `if else if ...` sequence. As an example of this, the code fragment in Figure 3.11 computes the 1992 federal income tax owed by a single person.

If the general indenting style is followed literally, the code would look like Figure 3.12. Because the `if else if ...` processes alternative choices for the same variable, the style in Figure 3.11 conveys more meaning and is preferable. As an aside, the code in Figure 3.11 suffers from an obvious style problem. Constants such as `21450.0` appear several times, and typing any one of them wrong will result in an incorrect calculation. This is a classic example of why failing to use a `#define` is considered poor style. It makes more sense to use a meaningful name and define that name as a synonym for the constant than to type the constant in repeatedly. An extra benefit is that when tax rates change, fewer changes are required of the code. Exercise 2 asks you to implement a complete program, which includes using symbolic constants.

```
if( TaxableIncome < 0.0 )
    TaxOwed = 0.0;
else if( TaxableIncome <= 21450.0 )        /* && >= 0.0 */
    TaxOwed = 0.15 * TaxableIncome;
else if( TaxableIncome <= 51900.0 )        /* && > 21450.0 */
    TaxOwed = 0.28 * ( TaxableIncome - 21450.0 ) + 3217.50;
else   /* TaxableIncome > 51900.0 */
    TaxOwed = 0.31 * ( TaxableIncome - 51900.0 ) + 11743.50;
```

Figure 3.11:   Example of `if else if ...` **.**

```
if( E1 )
    S1
else
    if( E2 )
        S2
    else
        if( E3 )
            S3
        else
            S4
```

Figure 3.12:   Literal, but not always preferable style for `if else if ...` **.**

```
if( X >= 0 )
    if( X <= 5 )
        printf( "0 <= X <= 5\n" );
    else
        printf( "X > 5\n" );
else
    printf( "X < 0\n" );
```

Figure 3.13:   Nested `if else`.

```
if( X >= 0 )
    if( Y < Z )
        Y += sqrt( X );
    else
        Z += sqrt( X );
```

Figure 3.14:   The dangling `else`: **indentation reflects correct interpretation.**

3.3.3   Nested `if` Statements

In Section 3.3.2 we saw that an `if` statment can be part of the `else` clause. It can also
be part of the `if` clause. As an example, the code in Figure 3.13 shows several `if`s. One
problem with nesting `if` statements is illustrated in Figures 3.14 and 3.15. Although the
`else` statement is indented at its intended spot in both cases, since the amount of white
space is meaningless, we know that for consistency, the `else` must associate with either
the innermost or outermost `if` in both cases.

```
if( X >= 0 )
    if( Y < 0 )
        Y += sqrt( X );
else
    Y += sqrt( -X );
```

Figure 3.15:   The dangling else: indentation reflects incorrect interpretation.

```
if( X >= 0 )
{
    if( Y < 0 )
        Y += sqrt( X );
}
else
    Y += sqrt( -X );
```

Figure 3.16:   Undangling the else indentation reflects correct interpretation.

In the absence of mind-reading capabilities, there is no obvious correct interpretation, so the most reasonable rule is applied: an else matches the innermost dangling if.[4] Thus Figure 3.14 is interpreted by the compiler in a manner consistent with its indentation, while Figure 3.15 is not. Figure 3.16 shows that to force the intended meaning, we must make sure that the else matches the outermost if. This can be done by placing the inner if inside braces. Be careful when nesting if statements. Even experienced C programmers occasionally forget braces, and it can be hard to spot the error, because the indentation is misleading.

3.4   Loops

In any language, the basic form of repetition is the *loop*. C provides three loop structures: the while statement, the for statement, and the do while statement.

3.4.1   The while **Statement**

The syntax of the while statement is shown in Figure 3.17. As long as expression evaluates to true, which as we recall means nonzero, statement is executed and expression is reevaluated. When expression evaluates to zero, the while statement is terminated and flow passes to the next statement. Note that this is not the only way to terminate the loop, as we will see below.

Note that if expression is initially zero, statement is never executed. To guarantee that statement is executed at least once, you need the do while statement, which is discussed later. As with the if statement, a sequence point is generated after the evaluation of expression. A further similarity is that statement can be a null statement, a compound statement, or any of the statements discussed in this chapter (including if and

---

[4]Exercise 3 asks you to explain why this is the most reasonable.

```
while( expression )
    statement
```

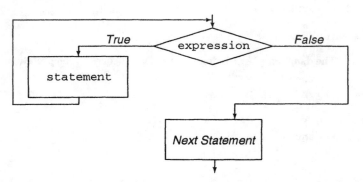

Figure 3.17:   Syntax and flow diagram for the `while` **loop.**

`while`). Generally, `statement` does something that can potentially alter the value of `expression`, since otherwise, the loop could be infinite. Note that there is no semicolon after

```
while( expression )
```

Accidentally putting one in is sure to cause an infinite loop, unless `expression` has some side effect, because the semicolon is interpreted as a null statement.

As an example of the use of the `while` statement, in Figure 3.18 we show a program that prompts the user for a number and then prints its prime factorization. For now we make the (unwarranted) assumption that the input is error free, and later we show how to add the appropriate checks.

Recall that a prime number is a number that has no factors, except itself and 1. The prime factorization of `1234567890` is `2 * 3 * 3 * 5 * 3607 * 3803`. The algorithm we use to determine a prime factorization is *trial division*. Let N be a number. We try continually dividing N by numbers that are smaller than N but larger than 1. If we find a number X such that X divides N exactly, we have a factor and can continue the process on the quotient N/X. Otherwise, we try the next number, X. Since X may be a multiple prime factor (as is 3, above), we do not advance X when we find an exact division; otherwise, we miss subsequent occurrences of X in the factorization. If we begin the process with $X = 2$ and stop with $X = N$, we are guaranteed that all the numbers that are output are prime, since if X is output and were not prime, we would have outputted X's factors earlier.

We provide two improvements to this algorithm that lessen the number of operations it performs. Most significant is the observation that if N is not prime, it must have a factor that is less than or equal to $\sqrt{N}$. Second, since 2 is the only even prime number, there is no point in trying larger even numbers as factors. Thus in Figure 3.18, we declare three variables: `PossibleFactor` is the current value of X, and `UnfactoredPart` represents the part of N that has not been factored. Initially, `PossibleFactor` is 2, and `UnfactoredPart` is N, namely `NumberToFactor`. This is shown on lines 8 and 9. Note that the initialization of `PossibleFactor` could have been done as part of its declaration.

The `while` statement that encompasses lines 10 to 24 searches for factors. The expression at line 10 incorporates the previous observation that we only need to try factors

```
/* 1*/    /* Print Prime Factorization Of A Number */

/* 2*/    #include <stdio.h>

/* 3*/    main( void )
/* 4*/    {
/* 5*/        unsigned long NumberToFactor, PossibleFactor,
                                               UnfactoredPart;

/* 6*/        printf( "Enter a number to factor: " );
/* 7*/        scanf( "%lu", &NumberToFactor );

/* 8*/        PossibleFactor = 2;
/* 9*/        UnfactoredPart = NumberToFactor;
/*10*/        while( PossibleFactor * PossibleFactor <= UnfactoredPart )
/*11*/        {
/*12*/            if( UnfactoredPart % PossibleFactor == 0 )
/*13*/            { /* Found A Factor */
/*14*/                printf( "%lu ", PossibleFactor );
/*15*/                UnfactoredPart /= PossibleFactor;
/*16*/            }
/*17*/            else
/*18*/            { /* No Factor; Try Next Factor */
/*19*/                if( PossibleFactor == 2 )
/*20*/                    PossibleFactor = 3;
/*21*/                else
/*22*/                    PossibleFactor += 2;
/*23*/            }
/*24*/        }

/*25*/        /* Print Last Factor */
/*26*/        printf( "%lu\n", UnfactoredPart );
/*27*/    }
```

Figure 3.18: Print prime factorization of a number.

up to and including the square root of the portion we are attempting to factor. It has been written to avoid the square-root computation (see the exercises for an improvement). If the division is exact, we have found a factor, and act accordingly, as shown in lines 13 to 16. Otherwise, we set PossibleFactor to the next odd number, at lines 18 to 23.

When the loop terminates, at line 25, we know that UnfactoredPart represents a prime number, and it can be printed as the largest factor of NumberToFactor. In the special case where NumberToFactor is prime, this is the only thing that is printed. Let us examine the program more closely to see what kind of errors might occur. The braces at lines 13 and 16 are necessary, because otherwise line 14 is the statement attached to the if, and line 15 is treated as the statement following the if. Fortunately, the compiler would give a syntax error, because the else is now misplaced.

Because the if else statement counts as one statement, the braces at lines 11 and 24 are unnecessary. Similarly, the braces at lines 18 and 23 are unnecessary. In both cases,

```
for( initialization; test; adjustment )
     statement
```

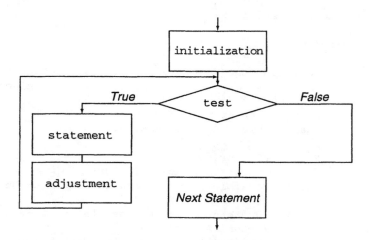

Figure 3.19:   Syntax and flow diagram for `for` **statement.**

 however, their presence makes the code easier to read. Note that although we have an `if else if else` construct, we have not lined up the second `if` with the first, as was done in Figure 3.11. This is because here the `if else if else` does not really represent a three-way choice, and thus our style of indenting is in keeping with our logic.

On line 12, if = was used instead of ==, the compiler would give a syntax error. This is because the precedence rules interpret the expression as

```
( UnfactoredPart % PossibleFactor ) = 0
```

 and only variables can be assigned to it. On line 19, however, the use of = would be legal. In this case, `PossibleFactor` would be assigned 2, the `if` would evaluate to true, thus executing line 20, and the result would be an infinite loop in most cases. Even experienced programmers do this, so be on the lookout, especially when debugging.

3.4.2   The `for` Statement

The `while` statement is sufficient to express all repetition. Even so, C provides two other forms. The `for` statement is provided in most languages in part because it appeared (in a different form) in FORTRAN. The typical use of the `for` statement is to loop with a counter. However, the C `for` statement encompasses the `while` statement as a special case, thus allowing for much more than simple iteration.

The syntax of the `for` statement is shown in Figure 3.19. `initialization`, `test`, and `adjustment` are all expressions, and all three are optional. If `test` is not present, it defaults to the expression 1, which is obviously always true. Note that just like 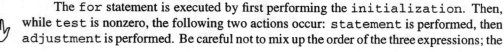 the `if` and `while` statements, there is no semicolon after the closing parenthesis. Also, not surprisingly, a sequence point is generated after each of the three expressions.

The `for` statement is executed by first performing the `initialization`. Then, while `test` is nonzero, the following two actions occur: `statement` is performed, then `adjustment` is performed. Be careful not to mix up the order of the three expressions; the

```
/* 1*/    /* Find Numbers Equal To Sum Of The Cubes Of Their Digits */

/* 2*/    #include <stdio.h>

/* 3*/    main( void )
/* 4*/    {
/* 5*/        int Hund, Tens, Ones;

/* 6*/        for( Hund = 1; Hund <= 9; Hund++ )
/* 7*/            for( Tens = 0; Tens <= 9; Tens++ )
/* 8*/                for( Ones = 0; Ones <= 9; Ones++ )
/* 9*/                    if( Hund * Hund * Hund + Tens * Tens * Tens
/*10*/                        + Ones * Ones * Ones
/*11*/                            == 100 * Hund + 10 * Tens + Ones )
/*12*/                        printf( "%d%d%d\n", Hund, Tens, Ones );
/*13*/    }
```

Figure 3.20:   **Program to find all three-digit numbers that equal the sum of the cubes of their digits.**

compiler will never complain, and you will have a program that is probably an infinite loop. Clearly, if `initialization` and `adjustment` are omitted, then the `for` statement behaves exactly as a `while` statement. The advantage of a `for` statement is clarity: it is much easier to see what the range of the counter is.

Just as `if` statements can be nested, loops can also be nested. As an example, the program in Figure 3.20 can be used to find all three-digit integers, N, which have the property that the sum of the cubes of their digits is equal to N. As an example,

$$1^3 + 5^3 + 3^3 \equiv 153.$$

 An unrelated point: when a line of code becomes excessively long, you should break it between tokens.[5] The text after which the line is broken should be aligned so as not to be confusing. Thus we have indented lines 10 and 11 more than line 12 so that it is obvious that line 12 is the result of the `if`.

The triple `for` loop tests each possible three-digit number, in sequence, to see if it satisfies the test. The most striking part of the code is the fact that not a single brace is needed in the loops, because the `statement` part for each of the three `for` loops is either another `for` statement or an `if` statement. Thus lines 6 to 12 are actually just one statement! We see the advantage of placing `adjustment` as an expression on the same line as `for`. Which loop form is used is mostly a matter of personal preference. If you have no preference, use the `for` statement for simple counting and the `while` or `do while` statement otherwise.

 In any case, when nesting loops as we have done in Figure 3.20, you have to be careful that you do not overwhelm the computer with too many calculations. In our example, three loops which count 9, 10, and 10 numbers, respectively, combine to iterate 900 times. Three nested loops, each of which count from 1 to 1000, perform 1 billion iterations! Even on a

---

[5]An alternative is to use the \ character to enable line continuation. This is best in preprocessor lines but is not recommended elsewhere (see Section 5.1).

```
Prompt User
Read Value
while( Value Is No Good )
{
     Prompt User
     Read Value
}
```

Figure 3.21:   A while **statement looks awkward.**

```
do
     statement
while( expression );
```

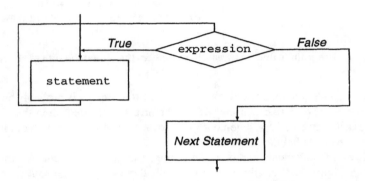

Figure 3.22:   Syntax and flow diagram for do while **statement.**

computer that runs at 10 MIPS (million instructions per second), one can see that 1 billion iterations of several instructions will take some time. We will have lots more to say about efficiency later in the book.

3.4.3   The do while **Statement**

The while statement repeatedly performs a test, and if the test is true, executes an embedded statement. One problem is that it if the initial test is false, the embedded statement is never executed, and in some cases we would like to guarantee that the embedded statement is executed at least once. As an example, when requesting input from the user, we repeatedly prompt the user and read input until we determine that the input is valid. Figure 3.21 shows how this is done with a while statement, using pseudocode.

The syntax of the do while loop is shown in Figure 3.22. Here the test is done at the bottom of the loop rather than at the top, so we are guaranteed that the body of the loop is executed at least once. The flow diagram indicates that the loop is identical to a while loop except that statement is always performed at least once. Figure 3.23 modifies Figure 3.22 by using the do while statement. We use pseudocode because of the intricacies of scanf.

 There are important points to make about the do while statement. First, the semicolon really is required at the end of the statement. Second, it is good practice to put braces around statement, even if they are not necessary, because otherwise the

```
do
{
    Prompt User
    Read Value
} while( Value Is No Good );
```

Figure 3.23:   A good use of the `do while` **statement.**

reader can be confused and think you are starting a `while` statement. The `do while` statement is by far the least frequently used of the three looping constructs. However, when you have to do something repeatedly, and it has to be done at least once, the `do while` is the method of choice.

3.4.4   The `break` and `continue` Statements

The `for` and `while` statements provide for termination before the start of a repeated statement. The `do while` statement allows termination after execution of a repeated statement. Occasionally, we would like to terminate execution in the middle of a repeated (compound) statement. The `break` statement, which is the keyword `break` followed by a semicolon, can be used to achieve this. Typically, an `if` statement would precede the `break`.

Figure 3.24 shows a multiple use of the `break` statement in a program which finds a prime number that is at least as large as some number input by the user. `PossiblePrime` represents a possible candidate for a prime number. After it is read, it is incremented if necessary to make it odd (lines 15 and 16). Our routine treats numbers less than or equal to 3 as special cases. We then search continually, via the `for` statement at line 17 for a prime, adding two to our candidate in each successive attempt. The test condition is absent, and thus always true, so the `break` statement at line 28 is the only way to exit. In the body of the outer `for` loop, we do a trial division. The `for` loop at line 20 exits either when a factor is found (in the test portion), or we obtain a sufficiently large `Divisor`, implying that our candidate is prime. In the latter case, the exit is forced by a `break` statement at line 24, after a variable is set indicating the successful search for a prime. Two points: first, a `break` statement applies to the innermost loop only. If you have too many nested loops, you may find it difficult to `break` out of the innermost loop past the outermost loop. Indeed, the `break` at line 24 is awkward. Second, the immediate termination of the loop implies that the `adjustment` part of the `for` statement is not executed. Thus the value of `PossiblePrime` at line 31 is the same as it was when the `break` at line 28 was performed.

A second problem we would like to handle is that occasionally there are cases where we would like to give up on the current iteration of a repeated statement for the current value and go to the next iteration. This can be handled by a `continue` statement. Like the `break` statement, the `continue` statement includes a semicolon. The most typical use is to avoid complicated `if else` patterns inside loops. As an example, we have rewritten the code in Figure 3.18 to use a `continue` statement. The result is shown in Figure 3.25. As with the `break` statement, the `continue` statement is applicable only to the innermost loop. A `continue` that is not inside a loop is illegal. The same applies to the `break` statement, except when used in a `switch` statement, as described in the next section. When used with a `for` statement, the `continue` causes the `adjustment` to be executed, thus providing the effect of advancing to the next iteration.

```
/* 1*/    /* Find Next Prime After Some Starting Number */

/* 2*/    #include <stdio.h>
/* 3*/    #define TRUE 1

/* 4*/    main( void )
/* 5*/    {
/* 6*/        unsigned long int Divisor, PossiblePrime;
/* 7*/        int FoundPrime;

/* 8*/        printf( "Enter the starting number: " );
/* 9*/        scanf( "%lu", &PossiblePrime );

/*10*/        if( PossiblePrime <= 2 )
/*11*/            PossiblePrime = 2;
/*12*/        else
/*13*/        if( PossiblePrime != 3 )
/*14*/        {
/*15*/            if( PossiblePrime % 2 == 0 )
/*16*/                PossiblePrime++; /* Need An Odd Number */

/*17*/            for( ; ; PossiblePrime += 2 )
/*18*/            {
/*19*/                FoundPrime = !TRUE;
/*20*/                for( Divisor = 3; PossiblePrime % Divisor;
                                              Divisor += 2 )
/*21*/                    if( Divisor * Divisor > PossiblePrime )
/*22*/                    {
/*23*/                        FoundPrime = TRUE;
/*24*/                        break;
/*25*/                    }
/*26*/
/*27*/                if( FoundPrime )
/*28*/                    break;
/*29*/            }
/*30*/        }

/*31*/        printf( "Next largest prime is %lu\n", PossiblePrime );
/*32*/    }
```

Figure 3.24:   Program to find a prime number; illustrates the break **statement.**

3.5 The switch Statement

 The if else if ... construct is so common that a few standard tricks are available to make it more efficient. If the cases are all mutually exclusive, then by arranging them in order of most likely occurrence, some time can be saved, because fewer expressions are evaluated on average to determine which part of the construct is executed.

```
/* 1*/     /* Print Prime Factorization Of A Number */

/* 2*/     #include <stdio.h>

/* 3*/     main( void )
/* 4*/     {
/* 5*/         unsigned long NumberToFactor, PossibleFactor,
                                              UnfactoredPart;

/* 6*/         printf( "Enter a number to factor: " );
/* 7*/         scanf( "%lu", &NumberToFactor );

/* 8*/         PossibleFactor = 2;
/* 9*/         UnfactoredPart = NumberToFactor;
/*10*/         while( PossibleFactor * PossibleFactor <= UnfactoredPart )
/*11*/         {
/*12*/             if( UnfactoredPart % PossibleFactor == 0 )
/*13*/             { /* Found A Factor */
/*14*/                 printf( "%lu ", PossibleFactor );
/*15*/                 UnfactoredPart /= PossibleFactor;
/*16*/                 continue;
/*17*/             }

/*18*/             /* No Factor; Try Next Factor */
/*19*/             if( PossibleFactor == 2 )
/*20*/                 PossibleFactor = 3;
/*21*/             else
/*22*/                 PossibleFactor += 2;
/*23*/         }

/*24*/         /* Print Last Factor */
/*25*/         printf( "%lu\n", UnfactoredPart );
/*26*/     }
```

Figure 3.25: **Print prime factorization, and use the** continue **statement.**

An extremely common situation in which even more improvement is possible is an if else if ... chain in which each if test is an equality test between an expression and a small integral value. An example of where this applies is parsing: we perform a different action depending on which of the many characters (which are typically 8-bit integers) we see. Although an if else if ... chain can be used, it is clumsy for two reasons. First, some cases require the same action, so the if tests may involve many logical or (||) operations. Second, for any case, all the previous cases have been tested and found to be not applicable. This can be expensive.

It turns out that in this special case, in which we need to choose among several small integer values, the compiler can do the test efficiently by using a lookup table to implement a multiway (instead of a two-way) branch. In C, we must list each individual case separately. Thus to specify all cases from 1 to 5, the five cases 1, 2, 3, 4, and 5 must be listed. The cases that are listed must represent constant values, and of course a case can be listed only once. Also, only integer values (or shorter) can be supported: floating-point values and strings are specifically excluded, but enumerated types, which we discuss in Section 7.7,

```
/* 1*/    /* Print Distribution Of Last Digit Of Random Numbers */

/* 2*/    #include <stdio.h>
/* 3*/    #include <stdlib.h>                      /* For rand( ) */

/* 4*/    main( void )
/* 5*/    {
/* 6*/        int i;
/* 7*/        int Zeros = 0, Odds = 0, Others = 0;


/* 8*/        for( i = 0; i < 10000; i++ )
/* 9*/            switch( rand( ) % 10 )
/*10*/            {
/*11*/              case 0:
/*12*/                 Zeros++;
/*13*/                 break;

/*14*/              case 2:
/*15*/              case 4:
/*16*/              case 6:
/*17*/              case 8:
/*18*/                 Others++;
/*19*/                 break;

/*20*/              default:
/*21*/                 Odds++;
/*22*/                 break;
/*23*/            }

/*24*/        printf( "Zeros: %d, odds: %d, others: %d\n",
/*25*/                           Zeros, Odds, Others );
/*26*/    }
```

Figure 3.26: Frequency count for last digits of random numbers.

are acceptable. As an example, the code in Figure 3.26 generates 10,000 random numbers and keeps a frequency count of the number of zeros, odd digits, and other types of their last digit. It uses the random number generator `rand`, which is discussed in Appendix D.

The `switch` statement consists of an expression (shown at line 9) and a statement, which is almost always a compound statement. The (generally compound) statement contains a sequence of statements and a collection of *labels*, which represent possible values of the expression. A sequence point is generated after the expression. Note that the labels are not themselves statements, just place marks. All the labels must be distinct, and the optional `default` label, if present, matches any unrepresented label. If there is no applicable case for the switch expression, the switch statement is over; otherwise, control passes to the appropriate label, and all the statements from that point on are executed. A `break` may be used to force early termination of the `switch`.

A very common error is forgetting to include a `break` statement. You can avoid this problem by practicing safe programming. Separate the cases into logical groups, put

```
for( i = 0, j = 1; i < 5; i++, j += i++ )
    printf( "i = %d, j = %d, i + j = %d\n", i, j, i + j );
```

Figure 3.27:   Contrived example of , operator.

plenty of white space between the cases, and always use a `break` after a group is processed. Although there are cases where you really do want to fall from one logical group into another logical group, they are rare and probably indicate that an `if else if` construct is more appropriate.

You should always use a `default`, if for no other reason than to catch an unexpected case. Make the `default` case either the first or the last case, and even though it is not necessary, use a `break` even after the last case. This will save you in the event that you add a new last case.

3.6   Occasionally Useful Stuff

C provides three constructs which are, in very special cases, useful. They should, however, be used only in the situations described, because they can be dangerous, or at the very least lead to unreadable code when overused.

3.6.1   The , Operator

The first operator we examine is the *comma* operator, `,`. Although commas separate parameters in declaration statements and function calls, those commas are not the comma operator. The comma operator was designed because in some cases more than one variable needs to be initialized or adjusted in the parenthesized trio of expressions that begins the `for` statement. `LeftExpr,RightExpr` evaluates `LeftExpr` and then evaluates and assumes the value (and type) of `RightExpr`. For instance, a typical usage is:

```
for( i = 0, Sum = 0; i <= N; i++ )
    Sum += N;
```

Note that the order of evaluation is defined, which is unusual. This is because the comma operator generates a sequence point. Also note that use of the comma token in a function call does not guarantee left-to-right evaluation because in that context it is not the *comma operator*. Thus the following is not guaranteed to print out 1 followed by 2.

```
i = 0;
printf( "%d %d\n", ++i, ++i );    /* ; is the only sequence point */
```

The result of the comma operator is that `LeftExpr,RightExpr` is an expression that can be used wherever an expression is appropriate.

The code in Figure 3.27 shows a contrived example. Initially, `i` has the value of 0 and `j` has the value of 1, and the printed values are 0, 1, and 1. The adjustment increments `i` to 1, then `j` by the value of `i`, which being 1, sets `j` to 2, and then `i` is incremented again. The multiple use of side effects is guaranteed to be correct here, because the comma

operator generates a sequence point. The second adjustment sets `i` to 4 and `j` to 5. The third adjustment sets `i` to 6 and `j` to 10.

Since the comma operator is generally used to separate assignment statements, it has lower priority than the assignment statement. Indeed, the comma operator has the lowest precedence of all operators. As you would expect, it associates left to right. As mentioned before, the commas that appear in procedure calls such as the `printf` in Figure 3.27 are not comma operators. If you use the comma operator inside a parameter list or a declaration

list, you must parenthesize the entire comma expression. Because it is easy to forget the parentheses, and in some cases (most notably `printf` and `scanf`) the compiler will not generate an error, it is a good idea to avoid using the comma operator in those contexts.

A tempting use of the comma operator is to use it to separate expressions instead of using a semicolon. The idea is that the aggregate would only be a single expression, which when followed by a semicolon could be used as the single repetitive statement of a loop,

thus avoiding the braces that otherwise would be required. It is a bad idea because it makes the code more oblique but saves only two keystrokes plus indentation.

3.6.2 The `?` `:` Operator

Occasionally, we want to assign a value to a variable that depends on the result of a simple test. For instance, suppose that we want to assign to `X` the maximum of `Y` and `Z`. The normal `if` statement would require four lines of code. C provides the *conditional operator* `?` `:` for this.

The conditional operator requires three expressions and is written as

```
TestExpr ? YesExpr : NoExpr
```

The `?` generates a sequence point. Thus `TestExpr` is evaluated first, including evaluation of side effects. Then either `YesExpr` or `NoExpr` is evaluated, and this is the result of the entire expression. If `TestExpr` is true, `YesExpr` is evaluated; otherwise, `NoExpr` is evaluated. Thus

```
X = ( Y > Z ) ? Y : Z;
```

solves our problem. Although this is a nice shorthand, anything more complicated really ought to use an `if` statement, because overuse of the conditional operator can lead to code that is more difficult to read, does not save a significant number of keystrokes, and is no more efficient. Occasionally, the conditional operator is used in `#define` macros in the case when an expression is preferable to a statement (see Chapter 5).

To be useful in the example above, the conditional operator needs to have higher

precedence than assignment. Indeed, that is exactly where it falls: it is just above assignment. The conditional operator can be nested, thus leading to truly bizarre code. It associates right to left.

If `YesExpr` and `NoExpr` have different types, one might expect that the type of the conditional would depend on which expression gets executed. This is not the case because

the type must be determined when the program is compiled, not when it is run. Thus the resultant type is obtained by applying the usual type conversion rules on `YesExpr` and `NoExpr`. This, however, violates our suggestion of using only the conditional operator for trivial purposes; this kind of stuff is best avoided.

3.6.3 The Dreaded `goto` Statement

When we are at a point inside a nested loop and would like to break out of the entire loop, we have a problem because the `break` statement only exits the innermost loop. The `goto` statement provides unconditional transfer to any point (in the current function). Figure 3.28

```
/* 1*/    /* Find Next Prime After StartingNumber */

/* 2*/    #include <stdio.h>

/* 3*/    main( void )
/* 4*/    {
/* 5*/         unsigned long int Divisor, PossiblePrime;

/* 6*/         printf( "Enter the starting number: " );
/* 7*/         scanf( "%lu", &PossiblePrime );

/* 8*/         if( PossiblePrime <= 2 )
/* 9*/             PossiblePrime = 2;
/*10*/         else
/*11*/         if( PossiblePrime != 3 )
/*12*/         {
/*13*/             if( PossiblePrime % 2 == 0 )
/*14*/                 PossiblePrime++; /* Need An Odd Number */
/*15*/
/*16*/             for( ; ; PossiblePrime += 2 )
/*17*/                 for( Divisor = 3; PossiblePrime % Divisor;
                                                    Divisor += 2 )
/*18*/                     if( Divisor * Divisor > PossiblePrime )
/*19*/                         goto FoundPrime;
/*20*/         }

/*21*/    FoundPrime:
/*22*/         printf( "Next largest prime is %lu\n", PossiblePrime );
/*23*/    }
```

Figure 3.28:   Example of a `goto`**.**

modifies Figure 3.24 and shows how the `goto` can occasionally simplify code. Line 19 contains the jump to the *labeled statement*, which is at lines 21 and 22. A labeled statement consists of any statement (including the null statement) preceded by an identifier and a :. The identifier that names the label could be the same as a variable name, but this is poor style. (Of course many people think that any use of a `goto` is poor style in itself.)

Using a `goto` to break out of a deeply nested loop is the most justifiable use of a `goto` in C. In that case we are generally talking about handling unusual error cases, not the typical control flow shown in our example.

Although the `goto` looks like an improvement in Figure 3.28, the proper course would be to define a function that tests a number for primality, and loop until the function returns success. We show this at the start of Chapter 4.

Intuitively, the reason the `goto` is bad is that if gotos are used, then when you arrive at a labeled statement, you cannot determine how you arrived there by examination of the previous statement in the source code. In general, this makes programs harder to debug and understand. Obviously, there are exceptions, since otherwise the `goto` would be removed from C. However in the large majority of applications, the `goto` statement is considered bad style.

One beneficial application of the `goto` is when you are writing a program that converts another language into C. By applying the C compiler on the result, you have implemented a portable compiler for the original language. The C code produced as output by these programs is filled with `goto` statements, because they are easiest to generate and are not meant to be read or modified by humans.

C provides so many flow of control features that the use of a `goto` is almost always an indication of poor (or mechanical) programming. Figure 3.28 represents the only use of the `goto` in this book.

3.7   Recurring Case Study: Part 1

We close with a complete program that illustrates some of the constructs described in this chapter. Sections 4.7, 7.11, 8.15, and 9.9 extend this example to use more advanced features (in a manner described below). Our starting program repeatedly prompts the user to enter one of three shapes (circle, rectangle, or square) and its dimensions. The program prints the shape entered, its dimensions, and its area. On input, we use 1 to represent a circle, 2 for a rectangle, and 3 for a square. The program terminates if bad input is encountered at any point.

Figure 3.29 represents an implementation. The meaningful variable names (in particular, the `#define` statements at lines 2 to 5) make comments redundant. The `while` clause at line 10 is used to drive an infinite loop that stops only when a `break` statement is reached as a result of bad (or end of) input. An equivalent alternative to line 10 is `for(;;)`. Lines 17 to 43 process each of the possible values of shapes, including an illegal shape. For each recognized shape, we perform some input and then output.

One important note is that to rewrite lines 17 to 43 as a `switch` statement, some logic needs to be reworked. This is because the `break` statements that correspond to bad inputs would be part of the `switch`, not the `while` loop.

In future sections we will examine some extensions of this program:

1. As new shapes are added to the repertoire of known shapes, the `if/else` statement in lines 17 to 43 starts getting excessively long. It would be better to break things up by using *functions*. Additionally, the format used in lines 23, 31, and 40 is meant to be identical but would not be if the programmer accidentally typed something slightly inconsistent (e.g., forgetting the `.2` in the conversion specifier for `scanf`). It would be better to have the printing of the area be performed in one place rather than many. This is discussed in Section 4.7.

2. The current implementation allows storage of only one (the current) shape. If we wanted to read all the input shapes and then group similar shapes together by printing out the circles, followed by rectangles, followed by squares, we would need to limit the number of shapes to be small and alter our logic drastically. In Section 7.11 we use an alternative method (*arrays*).

3. Entering 1 for circle, 2 for rectangle, and 3 for square is not meaningful. It would be better to enter `circle` for circle, and so on. After we discuss strings, we implement this improvement in Section 8.15.

4. In Section 9.9 we implement an extension that prints the input shapes in groups, with each group sorted by area. The code there uses some of the most advanced

```
/* 1*/    #include <stdio.h>

/* 2*/    #define Pi 3.1416
/* 3*/    #define Circle 1
/* 4*/    #define Rectangle 2
/* 5*/    #define Square 3

/* 6*/    main( void )
/* 7*/    {
/* 8*/        int Choice;
/* 9*/        double Dim1, Dim2;

/*10*/        while( 1 )
/*11*/        {
/*12*/            printf( "Enter %d for circle, ", Circle );
/*13*/            printf( "Enter %d for rectangle, ", Rectangle );
/*14*/            printf( "Enter %d for square: ", Square );

/*15*/            if( scanf( "%d", &Choice ) != 1 )
/*16*/                break;

/*17*/            if( Choice == Circle )
/*18*/            {
/*19*/                printf( "Enter radius: " );
/*20*/                if( scanf( "%lf", &Dim1 ) != 1 )
/*21*/                    break;
/*22*/                printf( "Shape is circle radius %.2f; ", Dim1 );
/*23*/                printf( "the area is %.2f\n", Dim1 * Dim1 * Pi );
/*24*/            }
/*25*/            else if( Choice == Square )
/*26*/            {
/*27*/                printf( "Enter side: " );
/*28*/                if( scanf( "%lf", &Dim1 ) != 1 )
/*29*/                    break;
/*30*/                printf( "Shape is square side %.2f; ", Dim1 );
/*31*/                printf( "the area is %.2f\n", Dim1 * Dim1 );
/*32*/            }
/*33*/            else if( Choice == Rectangle )
/*34*/            {
/*35*/                printf( "Enter length and width: " );
/*36*/                if( scanf( "%lf %lf", &Dim1, &Dim2 ) != 2 )
/*37*/                    break;
/*38*/                printf( "Shape is rectangle " );
/*39*/                printf( "length %.2f width %.2f; ", Dim1, Dim2 );
/*40*/                printf( "the area is %.2f\n", Dim1 * Dim2 );
/*41*/            }
/*42*/            else        /* Illegal Choice */
/*43*/                break;
/*44*/        }
/*45*/    }
```

Figure 3.29:   Program to read shapes and output areas.

Category	*Examples*	*Associativity*
Primary expression	*identifiers* *constants*	None
Postfix	Function ( ) ++ --	Left to right
Prefix and unary	! ~ + - ++ --	Right to left
Type cast	(TypeName)	Right to left
Multiplicative	* / %	Left to right
Additive	+ -	Left to right
Shift	<< >>	Left to right
Relational	< <= > >=	Left to right
Equality	== !=	Left to right
Boolean AND	&	Left to right
Boolean XOR	^	Left to right
Boolean OR	|	Left to right
Logical AND	&&	Left to right
Logical OR	||	Left to right
Conditional	? :	Right to left
Assignment	= *= /= %= += -= &= |= ^= <<= >>=	Right to left
Comma	,	Left to right

Figure 3.30:   Precedence and associativity of operators.

C features (e.g., arrays of structures with pointers to functions) to implement extensibility: it becomes very easy to add new shapes.

3.8   Summary

In this chapter we examined new statements that allow the conditional, and if necessary, repetitive processing of statements. This led to new categories of operators: namely, the relational, equality, and logical operators. We also discussed the null and compound statements, the comma and conditional operator, and the `goto` statement.

The current status of the precedence and associativity table is shown in Figure 3.30. In Chapter 4 we examine the use of *functions*, which further simplifies our code.

3.8.1   What Was Covered

- In C, anything nonzero (including negative values) is *true*, while zero is *false*.

- The *relational* operators are <, <=, >, and >=.

- The *equality* operators are == and !=, and they have lower precedence than the relational operators.

- The *logical* operators are &&, ||, and !. Their precedences and associativities are all different and are shown in Figure 3.30. The binary operators *short circuit*.

- The if statement is the fundamental decision maker. An else clause is optional. The switch statement can be used to choose among several small integral values.

- Loops can be performed via the for, while, and do while statements. The do while is useful when you want to guarantee at least one iteration.

- The break statement exits a loop statement or a switch statement. The continue statement is used to advance to the next iteration immediately. These apply only to the innermost loop or switch statement.

- The comma and conditional operator and the goto exist. Although occasionally important, be careful not to overuse them.

- A *sequence point* is a point in the execution of a program at which all previous side effects are guaranteed to be completed and no new side effects have started. Sequence points exist:

  1. At the ; that terminates an expression
  2. Immediately after the first operand in a &&, ||, ? :, or comma operator
  3. After the control expressions in an if, while, do while, or switch statement, and the three expressions in a for loop
  4. After evaluation of function arguments (discussed in Chapter 4)

3.8.2   Friendly Reminders

- A<B<C does not have the usual mathematical interpretation.

- Watch out for the common programming error of using = instead of ==. Also, look out for & and | instead of && and ||, respectively. A less common but equally damaging error is << or >> instead of < or >, respectively.

- The relational and equality operators have higher precedence than the bitwise binary operators. Thus

  `if( A & B == C )`

  is interpreted as

  `if( A & ( B == C ) )`

  which is probably unintended.

- On many terminals, the + is located on the same key as the =. This means that one can occasionally type <+, or >+ unintentionally. Because of the unary plus operator, these are all legal, and will give you an off-by-one error. (In other words,< will be used instead of <=.) =+ will also be interpreted legally.

- Equality comparisons that involve floating-point numbers are very dangerous because of roundoff errors. You may need to introduce a fudge factor. If you do, place a prominent comment explaining the justification.

- The syntax for the if, for, and while statements does not include a semicolon after the parenthesized expression(s). If you put one there accidentally, it will be interpreted as a null statement to be performed if the parenthesized expression is true. You must use a semicolon to finish a do while statement, however.

- The conditional and loop statements allow execution of exactly one statement. If you want to execute more, you have to combine the statements into a *compound statement* by surrounding them with braces. If you forget to do this, statements after the first are considered to be outside the construct.

- The else associates with the nearest unmatched if, regardless of any intended indentation. If the nesting gets complicated, use braces to disambiguate, or, preferably, use functions, as described in Chapter 4.

- Make sure that you have the *correct* order of the three for expressions. Any order is sure to be legal.

- When using a switch, do not forget the break statement between logical groups, because otherwise you will fall to the next group, which is likely to be unintended.

- Use the comma operator sparingly, and preferably only in the trio of expressions that starts the for statement.

- Deeply nested loops can make very small programs operating on very small numbers consume very large amounts of computer time.

EXERCISES

1. What are the values of A, X, Y, and Z after the following code is executed?

   ```
   A = X = Y = Z = 1;
   A = ++X || ++Y && ++Z;
   ```

2. Write a program that prompts the user for an (adjusted gross) income and prints out the amount of tax owed, using this year's tax rate. Make sure that you include plenty of #defines.

3. Why does an else match the most recently seen if? *Hint: Consider how many subsequent lines the compiler would need to examine for other strategies.*

4. Write a while statement that is equivalent to the for fragment below. Why would this be useful?

   ```
   for( ; ; )
       statement
   ```

5. Suppose that the == on line 19 of Figure 3.18 is typed mistakenly as =. For which values of UnfactoredPart is the mistake not noticeable?

6. Line 10 of Figure 3.18 rewrites the square-root test because the expression

   ```
   while( PossibleFactor <= sqrt( ( double ) UnfactoredPart ) )
   ```

   requires an expensive square-root computation at every iteration. Modify the program so that the square-root computation is performed only when UnfactoredPart is initialized, and subsequently altered at line 15. To prevent roundoff errors, add one to the value returned by sqrt.

7. Rewrite Figure 3.18 by using a `for` loop.

8. Rewrite Figure 3.24 by using `FoundPrime` in the trio of expressions at line 17. Compare your rewrite with the original.

9. Write a program to generate the addition and multiplication tables for single-digit numbers that elementary school students are accustomed to seeing.

10. Rewrite Figure 3.13 using two `? :` operators.

11. The basic loan has three parameters: the *annual interest rate*, *monthly payment*, and *loan balance*. As an example, consider a $300 loan at 12% annual (i.e., 1% monthly) interest, which is being paid off at $100 per month.

    After the first month, the balance is $200, but after interest, it increases to $202.

    After the second month, the balance is $102, but after interest, it increases to $103.02.

    After the third month it is $3.02, which after interest increases to $3.05.

    The remainder is paid off in the fourth month.

    The total payment is $303.05, of which $3.05 is interest.

    Write a program that prompts for the three parameters and conveys this information in a nice table. Assume that the three parameters have been provided by a `#define` statement. For example:

Month	Starting Balance	Payment	Middle Balance	Interest	Ending Balance
1.	300.00	100.00	200.00	2.00	202.00
2.	202.00	100.00	102.00	1.02	103.02
3.	103.02	100.00	3.02	0.03	3.05
4.	3.05	3.05	0.00	0.00	0.00

12. Write a program to determine all pairs of positive integers, (A, B) such that $A < B < 1000$ and $(A^2 + B^2 + 1)/AB$ is an integer. Can you see a general way to express all possible solutions?

13. The equation $A^5 + B^5 + C^5 + D^5 + E^5 = F^5$ has exactly one integral solution that satisfies $0 < A \le B \le C \le D \le E < F \le 75$. Write a program to find the solution. Your program will probably use an excessive amount of time. Does the hint that B, C, and D are all in the 40s help much?

14. Recall that the left-hand side of an assignment statement must generally be an object, but a parenthesized lvalue is still an lvalue. With that in mind, is either of the following statements legal? Are the parentheses necessary?

    ```
    ( Z ? X : Y ) = 5;
    ( Z ? X : X + Y ) = 5;
    ```

15. Write a program to play the passive side of a *Hi-Lo* game. The program will randomly generate a secret positive number. The user will repeatedly guess the number, and for each guess, the program responds either HIGHER, LOWER, or YOU WIN. When the correct number is guessed, the program will output the total number of guesses and then exit.

16. Write a program to play the active side of *Hi-Lo*. Have the user type 1 if the program's guess is too high, 2 if it is too low, and 3 if it is correct. Try to come up with a strategy that minimizes the worst-case number of guess and make sure that you can detect when the user has given inconsistent responses to the program's guesses.

17. The *Monty Hall* problem, based on the popular game show *Let's Make a Deal!*,[6] causes quite a spirited discussion because its solution is counterintuitive and depends strongly on the wording

---

[6]This is a registered trademark of Hatos-Hall Productions.

of the problem. Monty shows you three doors numbered 1, 2, and 3. One door contains the grand prize, and the other two doors contain prizes worth significantly less. Only Monty knows where the grand prize is. Moreover, to make things interesting, **Monty will never reveal your door or the grand prize first.**

Monty lets you pick any door. Then Monty shows you a door that is not yours, and as we have mentioned, it does not have the grand prize. Suppose that Monty offers you a chance to switch to the other unopened door. Should you?

Write a program that plays the game 1000 times and employs the strategy of always switching doors. You should win two-thirds of the time.

18. Let N be an `unsigned` integral type. What is the value of i (as a function of N) when the following loop terminates? *Hint: Consider the binary representation of* N.

```
for( i = 0; N &= N - 1; i++ )
    ;
```

19. In the following decimal arithmetic puzzle, each of the 10 different letters is assigned a unique digit. Write a program that finds all possible solutions (one of which is shown).

```
   BECKY          M=1 B=2 I=3 R=4 Y=5        20785
 - MARIA          O=6 C=7 K=8 A=9 E=0      - 19439
   -----                                     -----
    MIRO                                       1346
```

20. Write a program that prompts the user for three numbers and outputs them in sorted order. Your sorting algorithm should perform no more than three comparisons for any input (although the source code may contain many more than three comparisons).

21. Write a program that prompts the user for four numbers and outputs them in sorted order. Try to perform the sort in five comparisons.

22. Write a program that prompts the user for five numbers and outputs them in sorted order. Try to perform the sort in eight comparisons. It can be done in seven.

23. The *median* of N numbers (where N is odd) is the $[(N+1)/2]$th largest number. For instance, the median of the group 5, 7, 1, 4, 2 is 4.

   (a)   Write a program that prompts the user for three numbers and outputs the median. When the program is run, it should never use more than three comparisons.

   (b)   Write a program that prompts the user for five numbers and outputs the median:
   i.   Using at most eight comparisons
   ii. Using at most seven comparisons
   iii. Using at most six comparisons

4

Functions

High-quality stereo systems do not come in one piece but rather, consist of many separate components, such as the speakers, tape deck, compact disk player, amplifier, and tuner. These items communicate via simple connections, where necessary. By making the system *modular*, we simplify the process of changing it: for instance, an improved tape deck is easily installed, without change to any of the other components. Each component in turn consists of many other smaller components, which consist of smaller components, and so on. Another example of this idea is the automobile, which consists of many separate systems, each using modular parts. Indeed, as a trip to the automotive section of a discount store will show, many cars, even those from different manufacturers, use very similar parts that do not have to be reinvented all of the time.

In both cases we design a product *top-down* by determining what the specifications of the main pieces are. Then we design these pieces, applying the same strategy. Eventually, we have designed many trivial pieces, and in some cases, the same trivial piece can be used several times (such as a tire or a pushbutton). Top-down modular design of computer programs is implemented via the *function*. A function should be used to perform one basic operation. A C program consists of a collection of functions that interact by calling each other and passing information back and forth. For all but trivial programs, this is a much better strategy than attempting to throw everything into `main`, because it simplifies the debugging, maintenance, and upgrading processes.

We begin by rewriting the program in Figure 3.28. The resulting program is shown in Figure 4.1. In the next section we examine this new program to illustrate the basic principles relating to functions. Although the new program is longer than the original, the primary reason for this is that the program is relatively trivial. Even so, the new version is slightly more flexible and provides a routine that will be used later in the book.

4.1   The Parts of a Function

Figure 4.1 shows three functions. Each function contains a *name*, a (possibly empty) *list of parameters*, and a *return type*. Collectively, this defines the *interface*. The actual code

```
/* 1*/    #include <stdio.h>

/* 2*/    /* Return True Iff N Is Prime */
/* 3*/    int
/* 4*/    IsPrime( unsigned long int N )
/* 5*/    {
/* 6*/        unsigned long int Divisor;

/* 7*/        if( N % 2 )
/* 8*/            for( Divisor = 3; N % Divisor; Divisor += 2 )
/* 9*/                if( Divisor * Divisor > N )
/*10*/                    return 1;

/*11*/        return N == 2 || N == 3;
/*12*/    }


/*13*/    /* Return An Odd Starting Number */
/*14*/    unsigned long int
/*15*/    FirstTrial( void )
/*16*/    {
/*17*/        unsigned long int StartingNum;

/*18*/        printf( "Enter a starting number: " );
/*19*/        if( scanf( "%lu", &StartingNum ) == 1 )
/*20*/            return StartingNum % 2 ? StartingNum : ++StartingNum;

/*21*/        printf( "Bad number entered\n" );
/*22*/        return 0;
/*23*/    }


/*24*/    /* Find Next Prime After Some Starting Point */
/*25*/    main( void )
/*26*/    {
/*27*/        unsigned long int PossiblePrime = FirstTrial( );

/*28*/        for( ; !IsPrime( PossiblePrime ); PossiblePrime += 2 )
/*29*/            ;

/*30*/        printf( "Next largest prime is %lu\n", PossiblePrime );
/*31*/    }
```

Figure 4.1: **Program to find a prime number, using functions.**

to implement the function, sometimes known as the *function body*, is formally a compound statement. The *return* statement is an important new construct. We now describe the rules for each of these parts.

4.1.1 Function Name

A function name is an identifier, and thus all of the usual rules apply. Meaningful function names should be used, and predefined system names should be avoided. By capitalizing appropriately, you can be more certain of avoiding naming conflicts. In our example the three functions are `IsPrime`, `FirstTrial`, and of course, `main`. We place the name of the function on a separate line to facilitate searching for it via a text editor. Many editors have special mechanisms for restricting searches to the beginning of a line. For instance, using the UNIX editor *vi*, the pattern `^FirstTrial` matches only line 15 (assuming that our line number comments are not present).

4.1.2   The Parameter List

When the math library function `sqrt` is called, the user must provide a `double`-precision floating-point number. When `printf` is called, several parameters are also passed. The *parameter list* specifies what the arguments to the function are. When these arguments are specified in the description of the function, they are called *formal parameters*. Thus, for instance, `IsPrime` has one formal parameter, `N`, which is of type `unsigned long int`. `FirstTrial`, on the other hand, has no formal parameters. When defining the interface, the keyword `void` should be used when there are no formal parameters. This makes it clear that you have not simply forgotten to specify the parameter list. Both `void` and the parameter list syntax are new in ANSI C . In Section 4.2.1 we discuss this in more detail.

Each formal parameter is accompanied by a type. An identifier is used to name each formal parameter. Identifiers may be reused in different functions.

When calling a function, the *actual arguments* that you supply must be of the same number and type as the formal parameters. The compiler is willing to convert types to satisfy this requirement, if such a conversion is feasible. An important caveat is that during compilation, when a function call is detected, the compiler needs to know the type and number of formal parameters so that this check can be performed. One way to do this is to order the functions so that this is always true (however, this is not always possible). Another way is to use *function prototypes*, which are discussed in Section 4.2.1.

If no parameters are required, the actual argument list is empty, as shown on line 27. You cannot use `void` here, even though it would make sense. In some languages (e.g., Pascal and Ada), functions with no parameters are written without parentheses. If you do that, you will either get a (sometimes hard to understand) syntax error, or legal code which does something quite different.

As we will see below, a function guarantees that the actual arguments themselves are unchanged as a result of a function call, even if the corresponding formal parameters are altered in the function body. This rule has important ramifications and can cause problems for the uninitiated.

4.1.3   The Return Value

Each function is allowed to send directly back to its caller one piece of information. This is achieved by the `return` statement (which we discuss below), and the piece of information returned is called the *return value*. The effect of calling a function with its actual arguments is that the function call evaluates, as an expression, to the return value. The general rule is that you can return to any object that can be assigned. The returned type is provided in the interface prior to the function name. Some functions have no need to return values; in this case, `void` is used. Functions that have no return values are typically called *procedures* in other languages. We may occasionally use that term.

If a return type is not specified, an `int` is assumed by default. For example, we see that `main` returns an `int`. The ANSI C standard requires this, and attempting to change `main` to return a `void` is, strictly speaking, illegal. Some compilers will complain. This is discussed in Section 4.5. The reason that `main` returns an `int` is that some systems provide additional support to send back an error code to the user of the program.

Because actual arguments cannot be altered by a function call, the return value is the only direct form of communication from the function to its caller.

4.1.4   The Function Body

The function body is delimited by braces, and consists of a sequence of declaration statements, followed by nondeclaration statements. Recall that `main` is a function, so that the structure that we have become used to extends to general functions. The variables that are declared in the function body are called *local* variables, because they exist only inside the function and only when the function is active. Thus, unless arrangements are made (Section 4.4), they are destroyed when a function terminates, and re-created when a function is reactivated. A direct consequence of this rule is that generally local variables need to be reinitialized on each invocation of the function. This occurs naturally unless poor style is used.

Local variables follow the identifier rules, which we described in Section 2.7, but their names may not conflict with a formal parameter of the function in which they are declared. Some more details about these variables are discussed in Section 4.4. Formally, the function body is a compound statement. As we saw in Section 3.3.2, a compound statement is a collection of statements enclosed by braces. It would then seem logical that it should be possible to declare variables inside the compound statement of a loop, which would only be active inside the loop. Indeed, this is possible. However, we will avoid using this feature because our functions will be sufficiently compact to justify the declaration of all its variables in one place.

4.1.5   The `return` Statement

The `return` statement is one of only two mechanisms by which a function terminates normally. The other way to terminate is by completing the last statement of the function. The form of the `return` statement is

```
return Expr;
```

where `Expr` is any expression. `Expr` is converted, if possible, to the return type; if this is not possible, an error is reported.

A null expression is possible; thus

```
return;
```

merely terminates the function but does not send back a return value. The effect is the same as reaching the end of the function. If the function has a `void` return value, this is the correct form of action; otherwise, it results in undefined behavior. Some compilers will disallow a `return` with no expression for nonvoid functions, while others will merely chastise you. Returning a value in a `void` function is illegal.

Parentheses are not required around the return expression, although some consider their use to be good style. Others dislike it, especially in simple cases, because it gives the illusion of making a call to a function named `return`. We will not use parentheses, because of the latter reason. Exercise 1 asks you to provide an additional benefit of not using parentheses for the `return` statement.

Let us analyze the three functions in Figure 4.1. It is important that each function begin with a comment that states its purpose briefly and that the routines be robust in the sense that their correctness is independent of other routines. First, `IsPrime` is a function that returns 1 if the formal parameter `N` is a prime number, and 0 otherwise. We use `unsigned long int` because we are writing general routines, which should not be operating on negative numbers. The code in lines 7 to 10 represents the fact that (except for the special cases of 2 and 3) a number is prime if it is odd, and it is not divisible by any odd number between 3 and its square root. Line 11 is reached only if `N` is even, or divisible by a (relatively) small odd number. Thus line 11 returns zero unless a special case is detected. Otherwise, line 10 will be executed when `Divisor` is large enough, and 1 will be returned.

An important point is that as the program stands now, line 7 is unnecessary, since `N` is always odd. But this fact is dependent on other routines, and we cannot be sure that this will be true in general. Thus we write the routine without any assumptions, with confidence that minor tinkering of other parts of the program will not affect the correctness of `IsPrime`.

`FirstTrial` is a simple function that prompts the user for an input number and adds one if necessary to make it odd. Line 20 illustrates the intended use of the `?:` operator: namely to provide simple one-line expressions. `scanf` returns the number of parameters that were successfully read, and thus if the user does not enter an `unsigned long int`, `scanf` will not `return` 1. When that occurs, the error message at line 21 is produced. This approach is passive because it merely detects an error and gives up. In later chapters we will see how to recover from input errors.

`main` loops on `PossiblePrime`, continuing while `IsPrime` indicates that `PossiblePrime` is not prime. When the loop terminates, we know that we have found a prime number, and it is printed. Note that `PossiblePrime` could have been initialized as part of the `for` statement. Also note the placement of the semicolon on line 29. It is hard to miss, and thus does not look unintentional.

4.1.6 Call by Value

In any language, when a function is called, there are two arrangements that can be made for the parameters. It is important to have a good understanding of which method is being used. In one arrangement, the formal parameters become a synonym for the actual arguments, and all references to the formal parameters are really references to the actual arguments. Not surprisingly, this is known as *call by reference*.

The alternative form is *call by value*. In this arrangement, the actual arguments are copied into the formal parameters. Thus the values of the actual arguments are used by the functions. However, any changes made in the function to the formal parameters cannot possibly affect the actual arguments.

As an abstract example, suppose that you are working on a research paper and FAX a copy to a friend for review. Any scribbling that your friend does on the FAX may alter their copy of the research paper, but your copy remains unchanged no matter what. In C, all parameters are passed by value.[1] Figure 4.2 illustrates that actual arguments are not

---

[1]Call by reference can be simulated by pointers. This is discussed in Section 6.5. In some cases, a preprocessor macro is used to achieve this effect. In Section 5.3 we discuss this in detail.

```
/* Swapping routine that doesn't work */

void
Swap( int Left, int Right )
{
    int Temp;

    Temp = Left;
    Left = Right;
    Right = Temp;
}

main( void )
{
    int Left, Right;

    Left = 5; Right = 7;
    Swap( Left, Right );
    printf( "Left = %d, Right = %d\n", Left, Right );
}
```

Figure 4.2:   Example that shows the effect of call by value.

affected by function calls. Because Left is 5 and Right is 7 prior to the function call, we are guaranteed that they retain these values after the function call. This holds even though the formal parameters and actual arguments have the same names.

This is because the compiler internally maps each name into some memory location. Thus two pieces of memory, which we denote as *M1* and *M2*, are set aside for main's Left and Right. When a call to Swap is made, three more pieces of memory, *M3*, *M4*, and *M5*, are set aside for Temp, Left, and Right, which are variables that are local to Swap. Note that each call to Swap will set aside three pieces of memory, which may be different from the previous three pieces.

On function invocation, *M1* and *M2* are copied to *M4* and *M5*, respectively. All references inside Swap refer to *M3*, *M4*, and *M5*. When the function terminates, *M3*, *M4*, and *M5* are unmapped (i.e., these memory locations are available for future use), and we see that *M1* and *M2* were never touched. Figure 4.3 illustrates the memory assignments made by the compiler for these five objects. The : : symbol is used in the diagram to illustrate the function in which each variable is visible. It is not part of C. We also number the functions to illustrate that subsequent calls to Swap need not use the same parts of memory to store the local variables.

Keeping track of which memory location represents which variable is straightforward bookkeeping, although it is something the programmer would not want to do. If you want to be nosey, you can see for yourself where the compiler is storing items. This is discussed in Chapter 6.

Since a change in a formal parameter is not reflected in the actual argument, we can wonder if assignment to a formal parameter should even be allowed, since it is likely to be misleading. At least one language (*Ada*) outlaws assignment to formal parameters that are called by value. In most cases this is probably a wise decision, but occasionally, assigning

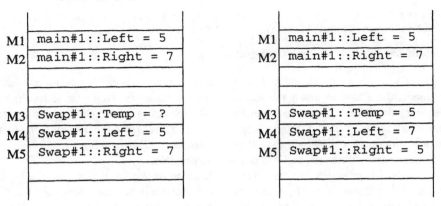

Figure 4.3:   Call by value illustrated. First diagram is memory prior to first statement in Swap. **Second picture is memory prior to return of** Swap.

to formal parameters makes the code easier to follow. An example of this is shown in Figure 4.13. Generally, though, we will not alter a formal parameter.

4.2   Splitting It Up

When a program gets to be large, compiling it becomes time consuming. This is especially annoying in the development stage, because most recompilations reflect very minor changes. Thus it is advantageous to split the program up into several smaller files, compile each file separately, and then link the result. This way a recompilation of a trivial change takes less time.

4.2.1   Function Prototypes

Originally, C suffered from the problem that no checking was done to ensure that actual arguments and formal parameters were the same type. This made it more likely that programming errors would go unnoticed. This is because, as shown in Figure 4.4, the old-style declaration did not include parameter types in the parameter list.[2] Thus when a call to Max is attempted, more effort is required to decide that its formal parameters are integers, and this is impossible if Max is defined in another file.

```
int
Max( A, B )
int A;
int B;
{
    return A > B ? A : B;
}
```

Figure 4.4:   Old-style function declarations.

---

[2]By the way, the old-style declaration is still legal to ease the transition but will soon be extinct. Do not use it.

```
/*2a*/    int                IsPrime( unsigned long int N );
/*2b*/    unsigned long int FirstTrial( void );
```

Figure 4.5:   Prototypes for first program.

As we have mentioned before, the compiler will check that when a function call is made, the actual arguments match the formal parameters. However, it does not want to examine future lines of code, so whenever a function call is attempted, the formal parameters must have already been declared. One way to do this is to arrange the functions in an order that if function F calls function G, then G precedes F. This is tedious to do by hand when there are many functions, and it is not always possible.

ANSI C provides an alternative, the *function prototype*, which lists the types of the return value and the formal parameters. If a prototype is provided for every function, and placed before the first function, we can be guaranteed that complete type checking will be performed. As an example, Figure 4.5 shows the prototypes for the program in Figure 4.1. Note that main does not need to be included, and we have lined up the function names to make it look nice.

Although we have provided the names of the formal parameters, this is unnecessary, since the purpose of function prototypes is strictly type checking. It is a good idea to include them anyway, since in some cases it helps the user of the function remember the order and roles of the parameters (some of which may have the same type).

If a prototype is missing, then when a function call is encountered before the body of the function is seen, inconsistencies between the actual arguments and formal parameters are not detected. With prototypes, if the actual argument and formal parameter types do not match, an appropriate type conversion will be coerced, if possible. Some compilers will warn you that this is being done. Some will warn you if you ask to be warned by specifying an appropriate option. Some compilers are very quiet.

As an example of the type conversions, the header file <math.h> includes the prototype

```
double sqrt( double );
```

Figure 4.6 shows that if the prototype is not included, an int 5 is passed to sqrt. This is interpreted as a zero, probably because on our machine, a double is represented by 64 bits and an int is represented by 32 bits. When the include file is present, as shown in Figure 4.7, the int 5 is automatically type-converted to a double 5, to match the formal parameter.

A very important point is that the prototype

```
double sqrt( );
```

indicates that the sqrt function returns a double, but the parameter types are unknown. We have seen earlier that this is the old style. If this form is used, the type conversion described in Figure 4.7 will not be applied. Unfortunately, many system administrators have installed *gcc* but not the new header files. The old header files have the old-style prototypes, resulting in the erroneous behavior described.

From our discussion we also see that

```
int F( );
int F( void );
```

have different meanings. Always use void when parameter lists are empty.

```
/* 1*/    #include <stdio.h>

/* 2*/    main( void )
/* 3*/    {
/* 4*/          /* Prints 5 0.000000 */
/* 5*/          printf( "%d %f\n", 5, sqrt( 5 ) );
/* 6*/    }
```

Figure 4.6:   Forgetting to include <math.h> **gives erroneous results.**

```
/* 1*/    #include <stdio.h>
/* 2*/    #include <math.h>

/* 3*/    main( void )
/* 4*/    {
/* 5*/          /* Prints 5 2.236068 */
/* 6*/          printf( "%d %f\n", 5, sqrt( 5 ) );
/* 7*/    }
```

Figure 4.7:   Automatic conversion of int **to** double **when** <math.h> **is included.**

4.2.2   How to Split Programs into Modules

Figures 4.8, 4.9, and 4.10 show how we split up our prime-finding program. The file *prime.c*, shown in Figure 4.8, contains two routines that deal with prime numbers. One tests primality, and the other searches for a prime number. We will have occasion later in the book to use both of these routines. The prototypes for these routines are contained in *prime.h*, which is shown in Figure 4.9. Figure 4.10 shows main and a supporting routine. The statement

```
#include "prime.h"
```

makes the prototypes available for stricter type checking, and possibly type conversion.

To compile this on a UNIX system, *prime.c* and *main.c* are separately compiled and then linked with either

cc prime.c main.c -lm

or

cc -c prime.c main.c
cc prime.o main.o -lm

However, if we change only *main.c*, the program can be recompiled by

cc -c main.c
cc prime.o main.o -lm

Thus we save the time that it takes to compile *prime.c*. The only difficult part is deciding, when a change is made, which routines need recompilation. For instance, if *prime.h* changes, both *main.c* and *prime.c* need to be recompiled.

Not surprisingly, this process can be automated. An early popular program to do this was called *make*, and this is now widely available in various forms where a C compiler is present. The UNIX version of this is discussed in Chapter 13. In that chapter we also

```
/* 1*/    #include "prime.h"

/* 2*/    /* Return True Iff N Is Prime */
/* 3*/    int
/* 4*/    IsPrime( unsigned long int N )
/* 5*/    {
/* 6*/        unsigned long int Divisor;

/* 7*/        if( N % 2 )
/* 8*/            for( Divisor = 3; N % Divisor; Divisor += 2 )
/* 9*/                if( Divisor * Divisor > N )
/*10*/                    return 1;

/*11*/        return N == 2 || N == 3;
/*12*/    }



/*13*/    /* Return Smallest Prime >= N */
/*14*/    unsigned long int
/*15*/    FindPrime( unsigned long int N )
/*16*/    {
/*17*/        unsigned long int TestPrime;

/*18*/        TestPrime = N % 2 ? N : N + 1;
/*19*/        for( ; ! IsPrime( TestPrime ); TestPrime += 2 )
/*20*/            ;

/*21*/        return TestPrime;
/*22*/    }
```

Figure 4.8:   Primality finding routines: *prime.c*.

```
/* 1*/    int               IsPrime( unsigned long int N );
/* 2*/    unsigned long int FindPrime( unsigned long int N );
```

Figure 4.9:   Header file for primality finding routines: *prime.h*.

discuss how to create our own libraries, where object code of our favorite routines can be saved. This is important since we do not want a long list of *.o* files to be required for each compilation, especially when they are likely to be scattered around our directories.

4.3   Functions as Parameters

Suppose that we want to write a general routine that solves $F(x) = 0$ for an arbitrary function $F(x)$. One way to do this is to write a routine Solve and presume the existence of a function

```
double F( double X );
```

The problem with this approach is that we are limited to solving one equation per program unless we take some drastic steps.

```
/* 1*/     #include <stdio.h>
/* 2*/     #include "prime.h"

/* 3*/     /* Return An Odd Starting Number */
/* 4*/     unsigned long int
/* 5*/     FirstTrial( void )
/* 6*/     {
/* 7*/         unsigned long int StartingNum;

/* 8*/         printf( "Enter a starting number: " );
/* 9*/         if( scanf( "%lu", &StartingNum ) == 1 )
/*10*/             return StartingNum % 2 ? StartingNum : ++ StartingNum;

/*11*/         printf( "Bad number entered\n" );
/*12*/         return 0;
/*13*/     }


/*14*/     /* Find Next Prime After Some Starting Point */
/*15*/     main( void )
/*16*/     {
/*17*/         printf( "Next largest prime is %lu\n",
/*18*/                        FindPrime( FirstTrial( ) ) );
/*19*/     }
```

Figure 4.10:   main **routine that generates next largest prime:** *main.c.*

The alternative is to make F a parameter to Solve. Since a formal function parameter consists of a name and its type, we can use

```
double F( double X )
```

as a formal parameter. Then any function with this prototype can be used as an actual argument.

4.3.1   Example: The Bisection Method for Finding Zeros

As an example of passing a function as a parameter, we show how to find an approximate solution to the general equation $F(x) = 0$. It is important to understand that this is a difficult problem, and our solution is not applicable for serious work. Although it works reasonably well for many applications, more accurate methods are known.

The basic idea of the algorithm is that if the sign of a continuous function changes between two points, zero must lie between them. For example, let $F(x) = x^3 - 5$. Since $F(1) = -4$ and $F(2) = 3$, we can be sure that a root of the equation lies between 1 and 2 (see Figure 4.11).

We can evaluate $F(x)$ further at the midpoint of the two known points, and since $F(1.5) = -1.625$, we see that the root is between 1.5 and 2. We can continue this way until we eventually find a zero of the equation. Unfortunately, as Figure 4.12 shows, there are some practical problems. First, we cannot expect ever to find an X that evaluates to exactly 0 since such an X is irrational and thus clearly unrepresentable in double-precision math. Thus an attempt to do that would result in an infinite loop.

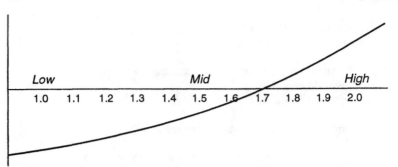

Figure 4.11:   Graph of $F(x) = x^3 - 5$ in the interval $1 \leq x \leq 2$.

Low Point	*High Point*	*Mid Point*	*Function at Mid Point*
1.000000000000	2.000000000000	1.500000000000	-1.625000000000
1.500000000000	2.000000000000	1.750000000000	0.359375000000
1.500000000000	1.750000000000	1.625000000000	-0.708984375000
1.625000000000	1.750000000000	1.687500000000	-0.194580078125
1.687500000000	1.750000000000	1.718750000000	0.077362060547
1.687500000000	1.718750000000	1.703125000000	-0.059856414795
1.703125000000	1.718750000000	1.710937500000	0.008439540863
1.703125000000	1.710937500000	1.707031250000	-0.025786578655
1.707031250000	1.710937500000	1.708984375000	-0.008693076670
1.708984375000	1.710937500000	1.709960937500	-0.000131660141
1.709960937500	1.710937500000	1.710449218750	0.004152716952
1.709960937500	1.710449218750	1.710205078125	0.002010222597
1.709960937500	1.710205078125	1.710083007812	0.000939204781
1.709960937500	1.710083007812	1.710021972656	0.000403753209
1.709960937500	1.710021972656	1.709991455078	0.000136041756

Figure 4.12:   Bisection algorithm with starting points 1.0 and 2.0 and $F(x) = x^3 - 5$.

Worse, although we generally make progress toward our goal of $F(x) = 0$, as we can see, the progress is not uniform. For example, the tenth estimate 1.7099609375 is better than any of the subsequent five. We will adopt a simple strategy: when the interval we are searching (in our case, initially 1.0 to 2.0) shrinks to only $\epsilon = 10^{-10}$ of its original size, we will stop the algorithm and return the last evaluated midpoint if an exact zero has not already been found. In our case this means that we evaluate 34 midpoints in the worst case, since this is exactly equal to $\lceil - \log_2 \epsilon \rceil$.[3] We can generally expect a better answer at the cost of more time as ϵ is decreased, but if ϵ is too small, roundoff errors could result in an infinite loop.

---

[3] $- \log_2 \epsilon$ is the solution of $2^n = 1/\epsilon$.

```
/* 1*/     #include "root.h"

/* 2*/     int
/* 3*/     DifferentSign( double F( double ), double Pt1, double Pt2 )
/* 4*/     {
/* 5*/         return ( F( Pt1 ) < 0 ) != ( F( Pt2 ) < 0 );
/* 6*/     }

/* 7*/     double
/* 8*/     Solve( double F( double ), double Low, double High )
/* 9*/     {
/*10*/         double Mid = ( Low + High ) / 2.0;
/*11*/         double SmallInterval = ( High - Low ) * Epsilon;

/*12*/         if( ! F( Low ) )
/*13*/             return Low;
/*14*/         else
/*15*/         if( ! F( High ) )
/*16*/             return High;
/*17*/         else
/*18*/         if( ! DifferentSign( F, Low, High ) )
/*19*/         {
/*20*/             printf( "Suggested points have same sign!\n" );
/*21*/             return SolveError;
/*22*/         }

/*23*/         while( F( Mid ) && ( High - Low ) > SmallInterval )
/*24*/         {
/*25*/             if( DifferentSign( F, Low, Mid ) )
/*26*/                 High = Mid;
/*27*/             else
/*28*/                 Low = Mid;

/*29*/             Mid = ( Low + High ) / 2.0;
/*30*/         }

/*31*/         return Mid;
/*32*/     }
```

Figure 4.13:   Bisection method to find roots of an equation.

Figure 4.13 shows an implementation of the bisection algorithm. The file `root.h`, which is specified at line 1, contains the prototype for `Solve` as well as `#define`s for `Epsilon` and `SolveError`. It is shown later in this chapter in Figure 4.16. The function `DifferentSign` requires a function, `F`, and two points, `Pt1` and `Pt2`. It returns true if `F(Pt1)` and `F(Pt2)` evaluate to a different sign (note that zero is considered positive for the purpose of this test). Note that the parentheses are not required because the equality operator has lower precedence than the relational operator.

`Solve` operates exactly as we described above. It requires two points, `Low` and `High`, for which `F` evaluates to different signs. If `Low` and `High` do not satisfy this requirement, an error is printed at line 20 and the value `SolveError` is returned. A possible return value would be the largest representable `double` and is specified in `root.h`. If by chance either of these points is a zero of `F`, an answer is returned at line 13 or 15.

Otherwise, we iterate as long as we have not found a zero and our interval is not too small. As mentioned earlier, an interesting aspect of the code is that we alter the formal parameters `Low` and `High`. This seems like the natural thing to do, since after all, in our description of the algorithm we refer to a shrinking interval. Of course, the actual arguments are unchanged.

Notice by the way that (mathematically) the root of $F(x)$ is exactly the cube root of 5, so solving equations is a more general problem than extracting roots. We will use this later in the chapter to provide a cube-root routine.

4.4   Storage Classes

4.4.1   `register` **Variables**

Although most data are stored in main memory, a few memory cells known as *machine registers* are also available. These registers provide faster access because they are built into the computer's central processing unit, while the rest of main memory is attached separately. Most of the registers are reserved for system use, but a few are available.

When allocating the space for each function's variables, a compiler will attempt to put the variables that it thinks are most commonly used in registers. It does this by taking an educated guess. If you would like to add your opinion to its guess, you can augment a local variable (including a formal parameter) with the keyword `register`. Keep in mind that the compiler may think that it is smarter than you and thus can ignore your opinion.

Most compilers do a pretty good job of allocating frequently used variables, so you will generally find that no speed improvement results from using `register`. However, occasionally, you run across a compiler that can really use the advice (and does).

There are two schools of thought on whether or not `register` is a good idea. On the one hand, protecting yourself from a stupid compiler is probably a good idea. On the other hand, it is something that in a perfect world, the programmer should not worry about. And, of course, you might be giving bad advice.

There is one important restriction that `register` variables carry: one cannot find their main memory location (i.e., address), since technically they are not located in main memory but in CPU memory. An important ramification of this is discussed in Chapter 12.

4.4.2   `static` **Local Variables**

Local variables are created when a function is called and are destroyed when a function terminates. In a sense, then, functions have no memory of their previous incarnations. Although this is generally a good idea, occasionally it is too restrictive.

A `static` local variable provides continuity: although it is local to the function, it is created when the program is run and exists until the program ends, without being destroyed in the interim. As an illustration, the following routine prints a message that tells how many times it has been called.

```
void
CountCalls( void )
{
    static int CallNumber = 0;

    printf( "This is call number %d.\n", ++CallNumber );
}
```

Because a `static` local variable is created only once, the initialization is performed only once. By default, `static` variables are initialized to zero. However, it is best to do this explicitly anyway. Although it seems like a good idea, you cannot have a `static` `register` variable. For reasons that are discussed below, the initialization value must be a constant. `register` and `static` specify *storage classes* because they instruct the compiler how to store variables. A third storage class, `auto`, also exists. That is what you get if you do not use any other qualifiers.

One common use of `static` is in conjunction with large arrays (and strings and structures). The benefit is that by using `static`, we avoid reallocating and deleting a local copy each time a procedure is run. We shall see that we can also return references to these copies (which is a rather complicated topic in itself). Other than those uses that we discuss later in text, `static` local variables should be avoided, precisely because they tend to destroy the independence of the function. Specifically, the action of a function may now depend on the results of its previous incarnations. Thus unless this knowledge is essential, it is best that a function compute values based only on the information specified in the parameter list, rather than attempting to incorporate history.

4.4.3   Global Variables Confined to a Single File

Although we have restricted our attention to local variables, which are only available inside the function in which they are declared, we can also declare variables that have global visibility. Global variables are a two-edged sword. Allowing many routines to access one commonly shared variable directly can occasionally simplify the code. However, once we allow all of these routines the privilege of altering the variable, we are likely to complicate the code. Consider, for example, the following code:

```
static int Global = 5;

main( void )
{
    AnotherFunction( );
    printf( "%d\n", Global );
}
```

In this example, `Global` is declared as an external variable. The keyword `static` indicates that `Global` is visible to all functions in the source file below the point in which it is declared. Note that an identically named local variable would *hide* rather than refer to the global variable. This is illustrated in Figure 4.14. The output would be the same even if the local variable was not `static`. Hiding variables in this manner is usually a bad idea.

The problem with global variables is illustrated in the earlier example: we do not know what value is printed, because `Global` might have been altered by `AnotherFunction`. One possible way to restrict this is to use the qualifier `const`:

```
static const int X = 5;

void
HideFunction( void )
{
    static int X = 3;          /* Local X Hides Global X */

    printf( "%d\n", X );       /* Prints 3 */
}

main( void )
{
    HideFunction( );
    printf( "%d\n", X );       /* Prints 5 */
}
```

Figure 4.14:   Local variable hides global variable.

```
static const int Global = 5;
```

sets `Global` to 5, and then disallows any future changes to it.

Although it is more common to use a `#define` for this purpose, there are some advantages to using a variable. Most notably, using a `#define` does not define a new variable but merely replaces text with other text during compilation. Thus

```
#define Global 5
```

just replaces all occurrences of `Global` with 5. Because of this, a debugger will not be able to find any reference to `Global`. If it is a variable, a debugger can print its value.

Other than using `const`, however, there is little that can be done to restrict access to a global variable. Anybody who can read it can write to it. We adopt the following general rule: except in rare cases, *a global variable will never be assigned to by more than one routine*. We use the term *write-once variable* to describe this. This is strictly our convention, and thus there is no way to enforce it.

Here are a couple of examples of the use of a write-once variable.

1. When writing a full-screen text editor, we need to know the size of the screen (rows and columns). This can be determined only when the program is run, but once the variables are set, they are never changed.

2. When processing a command that includes options, we need to set flags indicating which options have been selected. Once this is done, they never change.

3. A program may request the user to provide the name of a file that can be used to log errors. Once this name is provided, it need never change.

Just as `static` local variables are initialized to zero by default, so are global variables. The reason is that space for variables of both storage classes is allocated when the program is compiled, while space for automatic variables is allocated as the program executes. Therefore, if you specify an initial value for a global variable, it must evaluate to a compile-time computable constant.

```
/* 1*/     static double Radicand;

/* 2*/     static
/* 3*/     double
/* 4*/     CubeRootEqn( double X )
/* 5*/     {
/* 6*/          return X * X * X - Radicand;
/* 7*/     }

/* 8*/     double
/* 9*/     Cbrt( double N )
/*10*/     {
/*11*/          Radicand = N;
/*12*/          if( N > 0 )
/*13*/              if( N > 1.0 )
/*14*/                  return Solve( CubeRootEqn, 1, N );
/*15*/              else
/*16*/                  return Solve( CubeRootEqn, N, 1 );
/*17*/          else
/*18*/              if( N > -1.0 )
/*19*/                  return Solve( CubeRootEqn, -1, N );
/*20*/              else
/*21*/                  return Solve( CubeRootEqn, N, -1 );
/*22*/     }
```

Figure 4.15:   **Additional routines in** *root.c*.

```
/* 1*/     #include <float.h>

/* 2*/     #define Epsilon         1E-10
/* 3*/     #define SolveError      DBL_MAX

/* 4*/     double Solve( double F( double ), double Low, double High );
/* 5*/     double Cbrt( double N );
```

Figure 4.16:   **Header file** *root.h*.

Let us provide an example where the use of global variables seems unavoidable but in which we can attempt to hide its use. We will write a function

```
double Cbrt( double N );
```

that returns the cube root of N. Recall that this is the real solution of $X^3 - N = 0$, so we would like to use the routine `Solve`, which we wrote in Figure 4.13. Indeed, we ought to place it in the same file (*root.c*), and add the prototype for `Cbrt` to the header file *root.h* (in Figure 4.16).

The problem is that we need an equation to pass to `Solve`, and since N is not known at compile time, and the equation can only take one parameter X, we seem to be stuck. Our solution is to keep a global variable `Radicand`. As Figure 4.15 shows, `Cbrt` sets this variable so that `CubeRootEqn` can use it. Once we have the `CubeRootEqn` function set up, we just need to call `Solve`. The `if else` chains reflect the following properties of the cube-root function:

$1 < N$	$1 < \sqrt[3]{N} < N$
$0 \le N \le 1$	$N \le \sqrt[3]{N} \le 1$
$-1 \le N < 0$	$-1 \le \sqrt[3]{N} < N$
$N < -1$	$N < \sqrt[3]{N} < -1$

 Inside *root.c*, `Radicand` is visible only below its declaration. Thus we would attach Figure 4.15 to the end of Figure 4.13 to reduce its visibility. When applied to global variables, the keyword `static`, specifies that the scope of the variable is limited to the file in which it appears. Thus it cannot be altered by a routine, such as `main`, which appears in any other file. To some extent, this mitigates the danger of using a global variable.

`static` is also used to hide the visibility of `CubeRootEqn`. Under normal circumstances, the absence of its prototype in the header file would only defeat automatic type conversion. Other routines could still call `CubeRootEqn`, just as `sqrt` can be called without including `<math.h>`. Making the function *static* completely hides it from other files. Thus nobody else can call it.

4.4.4 Global Variables across Several Files: `extern`

The previous example uses a global variable whose scope is limited to a single source file. Equally important is the case in which we want a global variable to be shared across several source files. Each file that accesses the object must declare it. There are four types of declarations.

1. A *defining declaration* is used to allocate and initialize the object. An example is

    `int Global = 0;`   `/* Defining Declaration */`

2. A *referencing declaration* containing the reserved word `extern` is used to specify that a defining declaration is specified elsewhere. An example is

    `extern int Global;`   `/* Referencing Declaration */`

3. The third form is the *semireferencing* declaration. An example is

    `int Global;`   `/* Semi-Referencing Declaration */`

    This declaration is a defining declaration in ANSI C. However, some compilers (most notably those running under UNIX) allow the *semireferencing* declaration to be used as a referencing declaration also.

4. The declaration

    `extern int Global = 0; /* Do not use this */`

    is illegal in original C, and legal but discouraged in ANSI C. Some compilers (most notably those running under UNIX) will not accept it, and most others will issue a warning.

extern int Global1;	int Global1 = 5;	extern int Global1;
int Global2;	extern int Global2;	extern int Global2;
extern int Global3;	extern int Global3;	extern int Global3;
extern int Global4;	int Global4;	int Global4;
int Global5 = 2;	int Global5 = 3;	extern int Global5;
extern int Global6 = 2;	extern int Global6;	extern int Global6;
(file1.c)	*(file2.c)*	*(file3.c)*

Figure 4.17:   Different methods of declaring `extern` objects.

Among all the files being linked, there may be only one defining declaration per object. If there are no defining declarations, the symbol will be reported as undefined by the linker. UNIX compilers allow a semireferencing declaration to be used if no defining declaration is given. This is an accepted extension to ANSI C whose use is not portable. If there is more than one defining declaration, the appropriate symbol is reported as multiply defined. To ensure portability it is advisable to use only the first two types of declarations.

As an example, Figure 4.17 shows three files. `Global1` is declared using the preferred method. The defining declaration is in *file2.c*; the other files provide referencing declarations. `Global2` is declared using the most popular alternative scheme. It is initialized to zero by default. The declaration for `Global3` will generate a linker error because there is no defining definition. According to ANSI C, `Global4` is multiply defined because there are two defining declarations. Under UNIX, one of these will be considered a referencing declaration and `Global4` will not be reported as multiply defined. `Global5` is multiply defined under all implementations. Finally, `Global6` is defined and initialized to 2 in *file1.c*, so according to ANSI C, the linkage rules are satisfied. However, some compilers will not accept the declaration in *file1.c*.

 Files that are the target of `#include` statements should use only referencing declarations. Otherwise, multiply defined symbols will result when each source code file applies an `#include` directive. An appropriate source file would then supply the defining declaration. As an example, the global variable `errno` is declared in the *errno.h* header file as

```
extern int errno;
```

The library source file *errno.c* provides the defining declaration.

A loose analogy, which is not far from the truth, is that function names are essentially external variables. The prototype represents a referencing declaration, and the defining declaration is provided when the function body is specified. Knowledge of this fact unifies many concepts, such as the fact that we can pass their names as parameters. Also, because function names are essentially global variables, they do not nest as is customary in other languages, such as Pascal. The keyword `extern` can precede any function prototype or declaration. By default a function has `extern` scope (instead of `static` scope discussed in Section 4.4.3).

 There is an important technical point that one needs to be aware of, although it crops up only occasionally. Although local variables that are different in their first 31 characters are guaranteed to be distinct, to be compatible with some old-style linkers that are still in use, ANSI C specifies that it is possible for global variables that agree in only the first six

```
/* 1*/    void
/* 2*/    PrintBinary( unsigned int N )
/* 3*/    {
/* 4*/        if( N >= 2 )
/* 5*/            PrintBinary( N >> 1 );     /* All The Other Bits */
/* 6*/        printf( "%d", N & 01 );       /* Least Significant Bit */
/* 7*/    }
```

Figure 4.18:   **Recursive routine to print** N **in binary.**

characters to be considered the same. Since functions are in the same namespace, you could have problems on some older machines if you are not careful.

4.5   The Return Value of `main`

As we have mentioned before, `main` is a function that returns an `int`. Because there is no value returned in the programs we have written, some compilers will justly complain. There is a tendency to change `main` to return `void` to remove the warnings. This is illegal in ANSI C but might not elicit a compiler warning.

The correct approach is to `return` zero if all is well in the program, and a nonzero value otherwise. Some systems have particular error codes, which should be used instead of arbitrary numbers. From now on, we will end `main` with a `return` statement. Frequently, it is obvious in the middle of a program that something is terribly wrong, and we would then like to terminate and send back an error code to the user. The `exit` library routine can be used for this purpose.

```
exit( Code );
```

causes the program to terminate and send back `Code` as the return value of `main`. It can be called from anywhere. Note that unlike `return`, `exit` really is a function, so parentheses are required. Also, it is bad style to have scattered `exit` calls. Good style requires a more streamlined approach, such as a call to an error routine which then calls `exit`.

4.6   Recursion

We have seen a general style where we write functions that call other functions. One might wonder if a function can call itself. Alternatively, can function A call function B if function B also calls function A? The answer to both questions is yes, and when a function calls itself, either directly or indirectly, we say that it is recursively defined. In most cases this is either a powerful technique or a horrendous mistake. Figure 4.18 shows a recursive function that prints N in binary. It is difficult (perhaps impossible) to achieve the same result with fewer lines of nonrecursive code. In Chapter 11 we discuss recursion in detail, providing many good examples of its power and a couple of examples of disaster.

```
/* 1*/    #include <stdio.h>

/* 2*/    #define Pi 3.1416
/* 3*/    #define Circle 1
/* 4*/    #define Rectangle 2
/* 5*/    #define Square 3

/* 6*/    #define NoArea ( -1.0 )

/* 7*/    double
/* 8*/    ProcessCircle( void )
/* 9*/    {
/*10*/        double Dim1;

/*11*/        printf( "Enter radius: " );
/*12*/        if( scanf( "%lf", &Dim1 ) != 1 )
/*13*/            return NoArea;
/*14*/        printf( "Shape is circle radius %.2f; ", Dim1 );
/*15*/        return Dim1 * Dim1 * Pi;
/*16*/    }
```

Figure 4.19:   **Function to process circles for case study (square and rectangles are left to the reader).**

4.7   Recurring Case Study: Part 2

In Section 3.7 we wrote a program to read a series of shapes and write them back out, along with their areas. In this section we fix two problems:

1. The lack of functions yields a long (27 lines) `if`/`else` sequence; that sequence gets even longer as new types of shapes are added.

2. The output of the area is given in three separate `printf` statements. For consistency it would be better to do it in one place so that all the output statements are guaranteed to appear in the same format.

To do this we define a function for each type of shape that is recognized. The function prompts for and reads the dimensions, prints a brief message, and returns the area. If something goes wrong, we return a negative number to differentiate it from a possible area. Figure 4.19 shows the function for the circle. The corresponding functions for the rectangle and square are trivial to fill in. The `if`/`else` sequence in `main` consists of a call to the appropriate function. If all goes well (as evidenced by a nonnegative area), the area is printed. The resulting main is shown in Figure 4.20.

The entire program, as shown, is placed in a single file, for two reasons. First, the program is rather short; additional features require more knowledge of the language for a convenient implementation. Second, the `main` routine explicitly references the different

```
/* 1*/    main( void )
/* 2*/    {
/* 3*/        int Choice;
/* 4*/        double Area;

/* 5*/        while( 1 )
/* 6*/        {
/* 7*/            printf( "Enter %d for circle, ", Circle );
/* 8*/            printf( "Enter %d for rectangle, ", Rectangle );
/* 9*/            printf( "Enter %d for square: ", Square );

/*10*/            if( scanf( "%d", &Choice ) != 1 )
/*11*/                break;

/*12*/            if( Choice == Circle )
/*13*/                Area = ProcessCircle( );
/*14*/            else if( Choice == Square )
/*15*/                Area = ProcessSquare( );
/*16*/            else if( Choice == Rectangle )
/*17*/                Area = ProcessRectangle( );
/*18*/            else        /* Illegal Choice */
/*19*/                break;

/*20*/            if( Area < 0 )
/*21*/                break;
/*22*/            printf( "the area is %.2f\n", Area );
/*23*/        }
/*24*/    }
```

Figure 4.20: `main` **routine for case study.**

types of shapes. Consequently, it does not make sense to try to place code for each type of shape in a separate file; this will be done in Section 9.9.

4.8 Summary

In this chapter we have shown the basics of constructing and using functions. Top-down design of a program dictates that a problem is decomposed repeatedly into smaller problems, resulting in a collection of short, well-connected functions.

A good function does exactly one thing, makes as few assumptions about its environment as possible, and should never exceed one page of code. Most functions take less than half a page.

As we learn more about the language, and programming in general, we will be able to show the top-down design of larger programs. The advantage of this approach will be more obvious at that time.

In the remainder of this section, we list some specific points that were covered in this chapter.

4.8.1 What Was Covered

- A *top-down* design consists of repeatedly splitting a problem into smaller problems until the problems become simple.

- Functions help implement a top-down design. A function performs a computation based on a list of parameters. It is generally a good idea for the function always to perform the same computation when presented with the same parameters, although occasionally the history of previous function invocations influence the calculation. The function may return a value back to the caller via the `return` statement.

- We provide a simple primality testing routine, which will be important in Chapter 10.

- A simple routine to find the zeros of an equation is shown. More sophisticated routines are possible and are needed for serious applications.

- All parameter passing is done using *call by value*.

- The keyword `void` is used to specify a function that has no return value or an empty formal parameter list.

- The function prototype, introduced in ANSI C, allows strong type checking. It provides the return and parameter types for functions.

- Local variables are visible only inside the functions that they are declared in. Unless they are `static`, they are by default uninitialized and exist only while the function is active. They do not retain memory from function call to function call. `static` variables are initialized to zero by default and are not destroyed when the function ends.

- `register` variables are used to suggest fast storage. The compiler may ignore the advice.

- A compound statement may include declarations.

- Header files are used to define constants and function prototypes. This allows separate compilation, which can speed up program development. In Chapter 13 we discuss *make* and user-defined libraries.

- A function can be passed as a parameter. The formal parameter must include the prototype of an acceptable function.

- C allows global variables, but they should be used sparingly. If they are used, consider using `static` global variables, to limit their visibility to the file in which they reside. Technically, a function is a global variable.

- `main` returns an `int`, which can be used to communicate errors to the user. The `exit` function forces the program to end and sends an `int` back to the user.

4.8.2 Friendly Reminders

- Changes made to formal parameters do not affect the actual arguments because formal parameters are merely a copy of the actual arguments.

- A function call with no actual arguments still requires parentheses.

- Always remember to return a value in a nonvoid function. Many compilers will warn you if it believes you have forgotten to do it. Listen to the warning!

- The compiler may decide to ignore your advice when you declare a variable `register`. The memory location of a `register` variable is undefined, whether or not the compiler decides to use a machine register. This is an important point for `scanf`, which is discussed in Chapter 12.

- Avoid global variables unless they are constants or you agree to allow only one routine to assign to them. Otherwise, a logistic nightmare can result.

- Unlike Pascal functions, C functions do not nest.

EXERCISES

1. What diagnostics are produced for the following mistyped `return` statements?

    ```
    retrun 0;
    retrun( 0 );
    ```

2. A program keeps crashing when calling the function `write`, defined as

    ```
    void
    write( int x )
    {
        printf( "Write: %d\n", x );
    }
    ```

    What is the problem?

3. Show that if `Solve` terminates, it must terminate within $\lceil -\log_2 \epsilon \rceil$ iterations. If we want to guarantee termination in 20 iterations, what is a good choice for ϵ?

4. On your machine, how small can ϵ be and still guarantee termination?

5. As shown in Figure 4.13, what does `Solve`, do when `High < Low`? Adjust the routine so that it is more robust.

6. What is the effect of declaring a `static` variable in a header file?

7. Write the following routines:

    ```
    int Max ( int A, int B );
    int Max3( int A, int B, int C );
    int Max4( int A, int B, int C, int D );
    ```

    These routines return the maximum of two, three, and four integers.

8. Suppose that we want to print out numbers in brackets, as follows: `[1] [2] [3]`, and so on. Write a routine that takes two parameters: `HowMany` and `LineLength`. You should print out line numbers from 1 to `HowMany` in the format above, but do not output more than `LineLength` characters on any one line. Do not start a `[` unless you can fit the corresponding `]`.

9. Write a function with prototype

    ```
    int IsLeap( int Year );
    ```

    which returns 1 if `Year` is a leap year and 0 otherwise. A year Y is a leap year if Y is divisible by 4, but not divisible by 100 unless it is also divisible by 400.

10. Write a function with prototype

    ```
    int IsActualDate( int Month, int Day, int Year );
    ```

    which returns 1 if Month, Day, and Year represent an actual date (e.g., June 31, 1994 is not an actual date). Month is an integer between 1 and 12, Day is an integer between 1 and 31, and Year is an integer between 1600 and 2500.

11. Write a function with prototype

    ```
    int ElapsedDays( int Month, int Day, int Year );
    ```

    ElapsedDays should return the number of days since December 31, 1599. If any of the parameters are out of range, or don't make sense (e.g., February 31), return -1. Do not forget leap years.

12. Write a program that prompts the user for two dates and prints the number of days between them (by subtracting the result of two calls to ElapsedDays, above).

13. Write a function that takes an amount of money and outputs a representation using the minimum number of coins and bills. For instance, in U.S. currency, assuming no half-dollars, the output for 6.37 would be
    ```
    1  five-dollar bill
    1  one-dollar bill
    1  quarter
    1  dime
    2  pennies
    ```

14. Write a function that prints the representation of its integer parameter as a roman numeral. Thus if the parameter is 1994, the output is MCMLXLIV.

15. Write a routine with prototype

    ```
    double function Pow( double X, unsigned int N );
    ```

    that returns X^N.

16. Using the previous routine and Solve, write a routine with prototype

    ```
    double function Root( double X, unsigned int N );
    ```

    that returns $X^{1/N}$.

17. Write the routine Root by applying a direct bisection method.

18. For any positive N, let

    $$x_0 = 1 \quad \text{and} \quad x_i = \frac{1}{3}\left(2x_{i-1} + \frac{N}{x_{i-1}^2}\right).$$

    It can be shown that this sequence converges to $\sqrt[3]{N}$. Write a routine to extract cube roots based on this method and compare its accuracy with the method show in the chapter. *Note: This algorithm is based on the Newton–Raphson method, which is described below.*

19. The derivative, $F'(x)$, is defined as

    $$F'(x) = \lim_{\Delta \to 0} \frac{F(x + \Delta) - F(x)}{\Delta}.$$

    Write a routine with prototype

    ```
    double Derivative( double F ( double ), double X );
    ```

    that computes the derivative. To do this you will need to define an appropriate value of Δ. Choose $\Delta = \epsilon x$ for some ϵ. (When $x = 0$, use $\Delta = \epsilon$.) Try $\epsilon = 10^{-10}$.

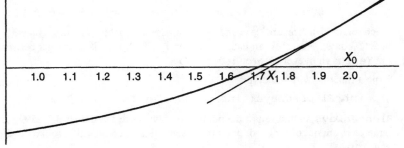

Figure 4.21:   Mathematical illustration of Newton–Raphson method. $F'(x)$ is the slope of the tangent at x.

20.   The *Newton–Raphson* method is another algorithm used to find a root of $F(x) = 0$. Starting with an initial guess x_0, we compute $x_i = x_{i-1} - F(x_{i-1})/F'(x_{i-1})$. Mathematically trained readers can try to derive this formula from Figure 4.21. It can be shown that in many cases, this sequence converges to a root. Using the function `Derivative` from Exercise 19, write another version of `Solve`. What happens if $F'(x)$ is 0 at some point? Can you tell which algorithm is better?

21.   In Section 4.7 all floating-point quantities are output using `%.2f`. Write a function that prints a `double` in this format, and rewrite Figures 4.19 and 4.20 to use that function.

5

The Preprocessor

The original C language included a phase that was executed prior to the compilation. This phase, known as the *preprocessor*, conceptually applied simple textual alterations to the input file, passing the result along to the compiler. The two most popular alterations were (and still are) the inclusion of header files, via #include, and the macro replacement of tokens via #define. The #define statement can also be used to implement parameterized macros, which look like, but are quite different from, functions.

Original C considered preprocessing and compilation as entirely separate entities, in part because older computers had much more limited memory and computation power than we are now accustomed to. By separating the preprocessor, the compilation became somewhat simpler and less memory intensive. However, different compilers had preprocessors with various rules, some of which were not entirely consistent.

The ANSI C committee attempted to codify the most popular and logical rules into official practices. It is no longer guaranteed, for instance, that the preprocessor and compiler are actually separate entities, although most implementations allow examination of the result of logically applying only the preprocessor. In this chapter we examine the C preprocessor in detail.

5.1 Overview

Figure 5.1 lists the preprocessor commands. Preprocessor lines start with #. ANSI C allows white space to precede and follow the #, although not all compilers are quite as liberal. The judicious use of white space before and after the leading # serves to increase readability. A line with only a # and white space is a *null directive* and is treated as a blank line.

When a preprocessor directive is identified, the entire line (and only that line) is treated as a preprocessor command. This is fundamentally different from the compiler proper, which generally treats newlines no differently than other white space. In part this explains why preprocessing is sometimes performed in a separate pass.

Long lines can be broken by a   \. If the last character on a preprocessor line is a   \, the next line is interpreted as a continuation of that line. For example, if the next line begins

Unconditional Compilation	
`#include`	Insert text from another file
`#define`	Define a preprocessor macro
`#undef`	Undefine a preprocessor macro
Macro Operators (not commands)	
`#`	Stringization: replace a **macro parameter** with a string constant
`##`	Token Merge: create a single token from two adjacent tokens
Conditional Compilation	
`#ifdef`	Test if a preprocessor macro name is defined
`#ifndef`	Test if a preprocessor macro name is undefined
`#if`	Test if a compile-time condition is true
`#else`	Indicate alternative if a preprocessor test fails
`#elif`	Combines `#if` and `#else`
`#endif`	End a preprocessor conditional
Communicating with Compiler	
`#line`	Supply a line number for compiler messages
`#error`	Produce a compilation error
`#pragma`	Provide implementation specific directive(s) to the compiler

Figure 5.1:   C preprocessor commands.

with a #, it will not be interpreted as a new preprocessor command. Note carefully that if white space follows the   \, the last character is not a   \, and thus line continuation is not in effect.

The   \ is not restricted to the preprocessor and can be used to continue any line of source code. This extension to all source code is new in ANSI C and was adopted because many compilers were allowing it. The use of the   \ to continue nonpreprocessor lines is always avoidable and almost never enhances readability. Thus it should be avoided.

Finally, a technical point is in order. Because the contents of a comment are ignored and the comment is treated as white space, any line breaks that occur inside a comment do not count as the end of a line (see Exercise 2).

5.2   Simple Textual Substitution via `#define`

We have already seen one use of `#define`. The directive

`#define Identifier ReplacementText`

causes the substitution of all occurrences of the token `Identifier` with the sequence of tokens given in `ReplacementText`.[1] This form is commonly used to give symbolic meanings to constants. `ReplacementText` can be essentially anything, although poor choices will lead to errors during the compilation phase. Besides using the `#define` for symbolic constants, popular uses include variations of the following:

---

[1]Thus, occurrences inside string constants are not replaced.

```
#define Max 50;                 /* The semicolon is inappropriate */
if( X == Max )                  /* if ( X == 50; ) */

#define Max = 50                /* The = is inappropriate */
if( X == Max )                  /* if ( X == = 50 ) */
```

Figure 5.2:   Typical macro mistakes which generate syntax errors.

```
#define C A + B                 /* Incorrect: See next line */
D = C * C;                      /* D = A + B * A + B */

#define C ( A + B )             /* The correct way ... */
D = C * C;                      /* D = ( A + B ) * ( A + B ) */
```

Figure 5.3:   Typical precedence error generated by macros.

```
#define FOREVER for( ; ; )
#define True    1
#define False   0
```

Some common mistakes are illustrated in Figure 5.2. In the first example, an extra semicolon is included on the preprocessor line. When the textual substitution is made, in the subsequent `if` statement, the result is to place an illegal semicolon inside the parentheses. A similar mistake is to include an extra = in the replacement text. In both cases, the compiler error may be difficult to detect because the error will be at the `if` statement, which may be many lines away from the `#define` statement.

Figure 5.3 illustrates a common error that will not evoke any complaints from the compiler. The direct substitution of the text `A + B` for `C` means that the value that is computed for `D` is not as expected, because of the higher precedence of * over +. The correct way to use the `#define` is to parenthesize any replacement text that involves an operator, thus eliminating the potential for unexpected interaction due to precedence rules. Make sure that white space separates the identifier and the first parenthesis; otherwise, you get a parameterized macro (discussed in the next section).

Note that `ReplacementText` is optional, and if it is not present, white space is used. Thus, in the following sequence, the value printed is 3 - - 4 (i.e., 7), which makes sense, rather than (the illegal) 3 -- 4.

```
#define M
printf( "%d\n", 3-M-4 );
```

Borrowing from C++, some compilers are now using // as a comment starter. Text following // until the end of line is treated as a comment; the end of line serves as a comment-ending token. Note that this is not ANSI C. If you use this type of comment, do not put it on a preprocessor `#define` line (because the expansion may include the comment, and comment more than you expect).

5.3   Parameterized Macros

Good software engineering technique demands that a program be broken down into functions, each of which performs a single task. As a direct consequence, we are virtually assured that some of these functions will be short and trivial. For example, the following routine, which returns an absolute value, is basically a simple one-line routine:

```
int
AbsoluteValue( int X )
{
    return X >= 0 ? X : -X;
}
```

This routine, although simple to code, illustrates a problem. The time to perform the function call, which involves copying parameters, and also returning back to the caller, is likely to exceed the cost of the actual absolute value computation. Of course, since these costs are only on the order of microseconds, it is acceptable unless there are thousands (or more) of calls to `AbsoluteValue`. If there are, the overhead of performing the function call can become significant.

The programmer might then be tempted to avoid the function call by explicitly performing identical actions. For instance, all calls

```
Y = AbsoluteValue( X );
```

could be replaced by the semantically equivalent

```
Y = X >= 0 ? X : -X;
```

This alternative is faster than calling the function because it performs an identical computation without the overhead of a function call. However, it is poor programming practice, because it destroys the modularity of the program.

The best solution is to ask the compiler to expand the function call *inline* to a semantically equivalent expression, thus avoiding the overhead of a function call. The only penalty for performing an inline expansion is that it increases the size of the program. Thus we are implementing a classic time/space tradeoff. As we will see later, some compilers can do this if requested to by a `#pragma inline` directive.

C provides a simple alternative through macro expansion. The macro expansion is a good alternative when a simple, short, function is frequently called. As we will see, however, special care is required in all but the most trivial uses, because the expansion is not guaranteed to be semantically equivalent to the function call.

5.3.1   Basic Ideas

The macro expansion in our case is given by

```
#define AbsoluteValue(X) ( (X) >= 0 ? (X) : -(X) )
```

 The parameterized macro consists of the name that is followed immediately by an opening parenthesis. If white space separates the name and opening parenthesis, the preprocessor will interpret the line as a simple (unparameterized) macro.

A comma-separated list of typeless parameters follow, and then a closing parenthesis. A parameterized macro can have zero parameters. Everything that follows the closing parenthesis is interpreted as the replacement text. When the parameterized macro is called, textual substitution occurs in the same manner as a simple (unparameterized) macro, and the actual arguments are directly substituted for every occurrence of a corresponding formal parameter.

Thus the statement

```
Y = AbsoluteValue( A - 3 );
```

expands to

```
Y = ( ( A - 3 ) >= 0 ? ( A - 3 ) : - ( A - 3 ) );
```

 The white space in the result reflects the fact that the preprocessor scans for, and also outputs, token sequences. ANSI C is careful to make this distinction, which on older compilers was not clearly specified (see Section 5.3.2). Note that in the macro definition, we have diligently parenthesized. We can see that this is necessary to ensure that precedence rules do not produce an unintended answer. If, in the definition, we use `-X` instead of `- (X)`, the corresponding substitution `-A  -  3` would produce an incorrect answer.

Even when we have all the required parentheses, because a parameterized macro is not a pure function call, one must be careful to remember that the parameters may be evaluated more than once. In particular, the function call `AbsoluteValue( A++ )` is not semantically equivalent to the corresponding macro call, because the macro call is expanded to

```
A++ >= 0 ? A++ : - ( A++ )
```

Here, since the `?` is a sequence point, we actually evaluate the absolute value of `A+1`. Also, the final value of `A` will not be `A+1`, because two increments are performed. Similar expressions that do not have sequence points would give undefined results.

As a second example, consider the sequence

```
#define Min( X, Y ) ( ( (X) < (Y) ) ? (X) : (Y) )
```

```
printf( "%f\n", Min( sin( Theta ), cos( Theta ) ) );
```

Although the correct answer is produced, the macro expands and three rather than two calls to trigonometric functions are performed. If this is the dominant action, the macro has made the program slower, not faster.

Although our examples may indicate that macros are dangerous, in addition to the potential time savings that they can produce, they have at least two other important uses. First, as we have indicated, the parameters to the macros are typeless. Thus the `Min` macro can be used to find the minimum of two variables of any type. If a function was used, we would have to write a separate `Min` function for each possible type, and annoyingly, we would have to provide a different name for each.

Macros are also useful because the direct textual substitution of parameters can be used to get around the call by value mechanism of functions. As an example, we can write the `Swap` routine as a macro. We will assume that we are working with integers.

```
#define Swap( X, Y ) { int Tmp = X; X = Y; Y = Tmp; }
```

To declare the extra variable, we need to introduce a block. There is no need to parenthesize `X`, `Y`, or `Tmp` since by virtue of appearing as an lvalue, we can reasonably expect that `X` and `Y` are primary expressions. Of course, we have already seen that it is best to make sure that the actual macro arguments are simple and without side effects.

Unlike the function call, the call to the macro `Swap( A, B )` expands into a block statement and thus does not need a semicolon. Should one be provided, it would be interpreted as a null statement, which is generally innocuous. Occasionally, it would lead to a syntax error, as in

```
if( A > B )
    Swap( A, B );
else
    printf( "No swap\n" );
```

Here the extraneous semicolon makes the `else` statement illegal. An additional problem is that the call `Swap(Tmp, New)` will cause a run-time error because the block variable `Tmp`, introduced in the macro, hides the actual argument `Tmp`. Alternatives include requiring the macro caller to declare a temporary variable for use in the macro, or having the macro use, for the temporary variable, a name that is less likely to clash (perhaps by incorporating addition underscore characters).

A final technical point. Recall that only lines beginning with a # (not counting initial white space) are preprocessor commands. Lines that *expand* to begin with a # are not preprocessor commands. As an example, the following code, which attempts to include `"header.h"`, does not work. Instead, the resultant `#include` statement is passed to the compiler proper, where it is flagged as a syntax error.

```
#define Include #include "header.h"
Include
```

5.3.2 Macro Operators

The preprocessor provides two operators that can be used in the replacement text of a parameterized macro. The first is the *stringization* operator, #. If X is a preprocessor macro formal parameter, #X is the actual corresponding argument, represented as a string. As an example, if we define

```
#define Stringize(X) #X
```

then `Stringize(3)` is `"3"`, and `Stringize(A - B)` is `"A - B"`. The stringization operator works correctly if the actual argument is a string constant, so `Stringize("3")` generates the string `"\"3\""`.

The stringization operator is useful for debugging because typically we want to print out not only the value of some expression, but also the actual expression. For instance, we would want printing statements that look like

```
printf( "(i): %d\n", i );
printf( "(A - B): %d\n", A - B );
```

so that the values that are printed can be identified meaningfully.

Since ANSI C collapses consecutive string constants, these two statements can be written equivalently as

```
printf( "("     "i"        "): %d\n", i );
printf( "("     "A - B"     "): %d\n", A - B );
```

(We have exaggerated the white space to make things a bit easier to see.) Here we have split up the `printf` control string into three parts, and only the second part is different. Thus we see that to perform a debugging print for any integer, we can write the `PrintIntDebug` macro shown in Figure 5.4. In that macro we see that the result of `#Expr` is a string that is used as the second part of the control string. Figure 5.4 shows a small sample program, and corresponding output.

The second useful macro operator is the *token merging* operator ##. The ## operator is applied when a macro call is processed, and the formal parameters are replaced by the actual argument. At that point, if a ## is encountered, the two tokens that surround it are combined by eliminating the ## and surrounding white space. Thus `A + B ## C` becomes `A + BC`. The token merging operator may not start or finish the replacement text.

```
/* 1*/    #define PrintIntDebug( Expr ) \
/* 2*/         printf( "(" #Expr "): %d\n", ( Expr ) )

/* 3*/    int
/* 4*/    main( void )
/* 5*/    {
/* 6*/        int X = 5, Y = 7;

/* 7*/        PrintIntDebug( X + Y );

/* 8*/        return 0;
/* 9*/    }

(X + Y): 12
```

Figure 5.4:   **Using the # operator for debugging prints.**

```
/* 1*/    #define PrintDebug( Expr, Type ) \
/* 2*/         printf( "(" #Expr "): %" Type##Conv "\n", ( Expr ) )
/* 3*/    #define intConv        "d"
/* 4*/    #define doubleConv     "f"

/* 5*/    main( void )
/* 6*/    {
/* 7*/        int X = 5, Y = 7;
/* 8*/        double A = 5.0, B = 7.0;

/* 9*/        PrintDebug( X + Y, int  );
/*10*/        PrintDebug( A + B, double  );
/*11*/        return 0;
/*12*/    }

(X + Y): 12
(A + B): 12.000000
```

Figure 5.5:   **Extending the debugging prints with ##.**

The token merging operator is new in ANSI C. It replaces the old hack of using a comment (e.g., A + B/**/C) to achieve the same result. In ANSI C the comment is replaced by white space, and the trick does not work.

Figure 5.5 illustrates a use of the token merging operator. Here we define PrintDebug to accept a type. The printf thus needs %d for ints, %f for doubles, and so on. On line 2, Type##Conv expands to intConv when Type is int and doubleConv when Type is double. The appropriate conversion is then used in the printf statement.

5.3.3   Rescanning of Macros

The last example illustrates a feature of macros that we have not explained precisely. Macros are never expanded when defined; they are expanded only upon invocation. When a macro is invoked, a direct textual substitution is performed, and actual arguments replace formal parameters. Then the # and ## operators are applied.[2] The result of these steps expands line 9 in Figure 5.5 to

```
printf( "(" "X + Y" ")" : %" intConv "\n", ( X + Y ) );
```

At this point, *rescanning* for macros is performed, from the beginning of the macro, using the same strategies. Thus the macro substitution of "d" for intConv is applied. This strategy is repeatedly applied as necessary to expand the macro. Concatenation of string constants is performed after preprocessing is complete. (See Appendix A1.)

As an example of rescanning, consider the sequence

```
#define TWO 2
#define Double(X) ((X)*TWO)
#define Quadruple(X) (Double(Double(X)))

Z = Quadruple( A );
```

The replacement sequence is

```
Z = ( Double( Double( A ) ) );
Z = ( ( ( Double( A ) ) * TWO ) );
Z = ( ( ( ( ( A ) * TWO ) ) * TWO ) );
Z = ( ( ( ( ( A ) * 2 ) ) * TWO ) );
Z = ( ( ( ( ( A ) * 2 ) ) * 2 ) );
```

One problem that concerned the language designers is shown in the following sequence:

```
#define X Y
#define Y Z
#define Z X

A = X;
```

A possible scenario is that we substitute X with Y. Then, when rescanning, we substitute Y with Z, and then on another rescan, we substitute Z with X, and end up rescanning indefinitely. Some older compilers hang on this code.

To avoid this, ANSI C specifies that macros which appear in their own expansion, either directly or indirectly (as is the case here), are not subject to further rescanning. Thus here we obtain

```
A = X;
```

as the final result. This feature is occasionally useful. If we want to change the library sqrt routine to return zero for the square root of any negative number, we can do this quickly in our program via

```
#define sqrt(X) ( ( X ) > 0 ? sqrt( X ) : 0 )
```

5.3.4 Predefined Macros

ANSI C specifies that five macros must always be defined. These are shown in Figure 5.6. _FILE_ and _LINE_ can be used to determine the current file and line number, respectively, in the source code. As an example, in Figure 5.7 we use these macros in the PrintDebug routine, written previously in Figure 5.5. Our modification includes the file

---

[2]Note that the order in which # and ## are evaluated is undefined.

Macro	Value
__FILE__	A string storing the name of the current source file
__LINE__	The current line number of the current source file
__DATE__	The date of compilation stored as a string of the form "Mmm dd yyyy"
__TIME__	The time of compilation stored as a string of the form "hh:mm:ss"
__STDC__	If the compiler conforms to ANSI C , this macro is defined to be 1

Figure 5.6:   The five predefined macros.

```
/* 1*/    #define PrintDebug( Expr, Type )                                      \
/* 2*/        printf( __FILE__ "[%d](" #Expr "): %" Type##Conv "\n",  \
/* 3*/                    __LINE__, ( Expr ) )
/* 4*/    #define intConv        "d"
/* 5*/    #define doubleConv     "f"

/* 6*/    main( void )
/* 7*/    {
/* 8*/        int X = 5, Y = 7;
/* 9*/        double A = 5.0, B = 7.0;

/*10*/        PrintDebug( X + Y, int  );          /* Really Line 12 */
/*11*/        PrintDebug( A + B, double  );       /* Really Line 13 */
/*12*/        return 0;
/*13*/    }
```

```
fig5.7.c[12](X + Y): 12
fig5.7.c[13](A + B): 12.000000
```

Figure 5.7:   Debugging prints with file and line number included.

name and line number in the debugging print statement. In the output, we see that the calls
to PrintDebug occur at lines 12 and 13 (the line numbers indicated by the comments
fail to include two blank lines). Notice that because __LINE__ evaluates to an integer, we
use a %d in the printf at line 2, and supply __LINE__ as the corresponding parameter.
Stringization via #__LINE__ does not work because __LINE__ is not a formal parameter.
__DATE__ and __TIME__ can be used to access the date and time of the compilation. This is
useful for programs that print a version number and the compilation time at startup.

5.3.5 Forcing a Real Function Call

Sometimes we would like to have the best of both worlds. We may have a situation where
we would like to invoke a real function most of the time, but at a crucial juncture in the
code, we would like to invoke a macro. We can achieve this by putting parentheses around
the name of the routine when a function call is intended, and not using parentheses when
the macro is intended. An example that illustrates the syntax is shown in Figure 5.8. Note
that in the function declaration, the parentheses are necessary to avoid a macro substitution.
Without them, line 3 is expanded to

```
( ( double X ) * ( double X ) )
```

```
/* 1*/    #define Square( X ) ( ( X ) * ( X ) )

/* 2*/    double
/* 3*/    ( Square )( double X )    /* Parentheses Are Required */
/* 4*/    {
/* 5*/        return X * X;
/* 6*/    }

/* 7*/    main( void )
/* 8*/    {
/* 9*/        double A = 5.0;

/*10*/        printf( "%f\n", Square( A ) );        /* Macro Call */
/*11*/        printf( "%f\n", ( Square )( A++ ) );  /* Function Call */
/*12*/        return 0;
/*13*/    }
```

Figure 5.8:   **Mixing functions and macros.**

5.4   #undef **and Redefinition of Macros**

The #undef command is used to undefine a preprocessor macro. If the macro was already undefined, the #undef is ignored. The primary use of the #undef command is to undefine a macro so that it can be given a new definition without generating a compiler error. A typical sequence is thus

```
#undef Max
#define Max 100
```

The redefinition of a macro is not allowed in ANSI C unless the new definition is the same, token for token, as the existing definition. Both the new and old definitions must have white space in the same locations, although the amount and type of white space may vary. Figure 5.9 shows some examples. The redefinition of Five is illegal because 05 is not the same as 5. The first redefinition of Six is legal because the previous definition has been removed via the #undef. The two subsequent redefinitions are also legal because all the tokens match, as do the locations of white space.

The first redefinition of Max is illegal because here the location of white space is not identical in the redefinition. The second redefinition is also illegal because the tokens A and B are different from the original (even though the intent is identical). Some older compilers do not allow any redefinitions without an #undef. That is probably the best strategy.

5.5   **The** #include **Statement**

As we have already seen, a line that contains an #include command is logically replaced with the contents of a file. There are three forms of the #include command. Two of these forms are given by

```
#define Five 5
#define Five 05                /* Illegal: 05 is not identical to 5 */

#define Six 6
#undef Six
#define Six 06                 /* Legal: Six was not already defined */
#define Six      06            /* Legal: White space is white space */
#define Six 06  /**/  /* Legal: Comments are white space */

#define Max(X,Y) ( (X) > (Y) ? (X) : (Y) )
#define Max(X,Y) ((X)>(Y)?(X):(Y))                /* Illegal */
#define Max(A,B) ( (A) > (B) ? (A) : (B) ) /* Illegal */
```

Figure 5.9: **Examples of legal and illegal macro redefinitions.**

```
#include <FileName>
#include "FileName"
```

The first form is typically used to search for `FileName` in "standard system" directories, while the second form searches first in "local" directories and then the "standard" directory.

The ANSI C standard is very ambiguous on this matter because some systems allow the user to specify a specific search path for both possibilities. On UNIX systems, for example, the "standard system" search begins in the directory `/usr/include`, and the "local" search begins in the current directory.

In the first form, `FileName` may not contain a > or newline; `FileName` may not contain " or newline in the second form. In both forms, single quotes, backslashes, and the comment start sequence give implementation-dependent results. On MS-DOS systems, `FileName` may need sequences of \\ to separate directory names.

`#include` files may be nested; the maximum allowed depth is implementation dependent, but ANSI C guarantees at least eight. `#include` files may `#include` themselves, although it is hard to imagine why this would be desirable, and further, without care, the nesting limitation is certain to be reached.

An ambiguity that ANSI C leaves unsettled is the case where file *A* includes file *B*, which is in another directory. If *B* then includes a file named *C* which appears in both *A* and *B*'s directory, it is undefined which file is included by *B*. This ambiguity is avoided by keeping all (nonsystem) source files in the same directory.

A third form of the `#include` is given by

```
#include TokenSequence
```

Here, `TokenSequence`, which does not begin with a < or ", is expanded as normal. The result must be one of the two legal `#include` forms above, in which case the `#include` is applied. Note however that `"Filename"` is not a string constant and that even if it were, string concatenation is performed after the preprocessing phase. Thus the following attempt generates a compiler error:

```
#define MyDirectory     "/usr1/nina"
#define MyFile          "header.h"

#include MyDirectory "/" MyFile        /* WRONG! */
```

```
#ifdef UNIX
    UNIX specific code goes here
#endif

#ifdef MSDOS
    MS-DOS specific code goes here
#endif

#ifdef VMS
    VMS specific code goes here
#endif
```

Figure 5.10:   **Conditional compilation via** #ifdef.

5.6   Conditional Compilation

For most applications, ANSI C programs can be written portably, meaning that they can be compiled and executed on any platform. However, there are always some applications that are inherently system dependent. For these applications, we expect that some (generally small) part of the code is not portable and must change significantly from system to system.

One way of making a system-dependent program easy to compile is to write versions of the nonportable code for each platform. We can then direct the compiler to choose the appropriate code fragments and ignore the inappropriate ones. Figure 5.10 shows how the #ifdef command can be used for this. Here we write code for each supported operating system. Exactly one of UNIX, MSDOS, or VMS is defined prior to the first #ifdef. Then one of the code fragments is included; the others are ignored.

On most systems it is possible to define a prepreprocessor symbol at compile time. On UNIX, for instance, the command

```
cc -DUNIX program.c
```

makes UNIX a defined macro, just as a first source line of

```
#define UNIX
```

would. Another common use of #ifdef centers around debugging. Typically, we add many printing statements in the course of program development. When a program appears to work, we would like those statements to go away, but if we eliminate them completely and a bug reappears, we will have to retype the debugging statements. Thus the typical solution is to comment out the debugging statements.

One problem with this is that comments do not nest. Thus if the debugging statements already contain a comment, our strategy will not work. The other problem is that it can be annoying to have to go and uncomment the code: it can require altering many lines. A simple solution is to define a symbol DEBUG. Then debugging code can be conditional on DEBUG being defined:

```
#ifdef DEBUG
    debugging statements
#endif
```

This works because #ifdef statements nest.

```
#ifndef _HEADER
    #define _HEADER
    #ifndef Max
        #define Max 100
    #endif

    Other stuff like function prototypes
#endif
```

Figure 5.11:   Use of #ifndef **in header files.**

```
#if defined( VMS ) || defined( UNIX )
    Code which is usable by both VMS and UNIX
#else
    Code which is usable by MSDOS
#endif
```

Figure 5.12:   #if **and** #else.

Several other preprocessing directives are available for conditional compilation.

```
#ifndef SYMBOL
```

includes code if SYMBOL is not defined. Two typical uses are shown in Figure 5.11, which represents a typical .h header file. The symbol _HEADER is defined when the header file is first included. The #ifndef guarantees that if this file is included a second time, we do not waste time reprocessing it. We also #define the symbol Max as 100; however, if Max was already defined, perhaps to some other value, we do not attempt to redefine it.

In addition to the commands that we have already seen, ANSI C also provides more general conditional processing. The #if command causes the inclusion of text if an integral compile-time constant condition is true. The condition may include any operator except sizeof and type cast, and may not include an enumeration constant. It may include the defined operator, which is illustrated in Figure 5.12. #else and #elif can be used to generate chains of conditionals. The former is shown in Figure 5.12.

5.7   Miscellaneous Directives

Three additional preprocessor commands are specified by ANSI C. The first, #error, causes the compiler to terminate with an error message. The error message is provided by the preprocessor tokens which follow the command; this message is generated after normal macro expansion. As an example, Figure 5.13 makes Figure 5.12 more robust by guaranteeing that at least one of VMS, UNIX, and MSDOS is defined. Note that the second # in the body of the #else is treated normally because it is inside a string constant.

The #line directive is used to alter the current line number and file name. This is useful for designing languages. Suppose that we have developed a language called MW. Our MW compiler works by translating MW code into C code and then calling the C compiler. Presumably, legal MW code will generate legal C code. If the translation generates illegal C code, we may assume an error in the MW source code. When the illegal C code is flagged by the C compiler, we would like to have the error message point back at the original bad

```
#if defined( VMS ) || defined( UNIX )
    Code which is usable by both VMS and UNIX
#elif defined( MSDOS )
    Code which is usable by MSDOS
#else
    #error "Need to #define VMS, UNIX, or MSDOS"
#endif
```

Figure 5.13: `#error` **directive.**

line of `MW` code. If our `MW` compiler writes out `#line` directives during the translation, the resulting C compiler error message can be made to correspond to the actual errors in the `MW` code.

The common form of the `#line` command is

```
#line LineNum "filename"
```

 `LineNum` must be a constant integral expression, and `"filename"` is optional. An alternative syntax is similar to the third form of the `#include` command. The preprocessor tokens that follow `#line` are expanded in the usual manner, and the result must match the first form for `#line`.

The final preprocessor command is `#pragma`. The `#pragma` executes compiler-specific options, which generally have no semantic meaning. Typical uses of the `#pragma` are directives to request optimization (perhaps for either time or space) and to request inline expansion.

Note that not all preprocessors are ANSI compliant. You may find, for example, that `#error` is unsupported on your system.

5.8 Summary

In this chapter we have described the C preprocessor. Historically, preprocessor commands, which begin with #, have been used to aid program readability, portability, and debugging.

Simple macros are useful for defining symbolic constants, and file inclusion and conditional compilation aid in software maintenance and general portability. These should be used as much as possible.

On the other hand, parameterized macros can be viewed as a simple measure designed for instances where the overhead of a function call or the call by value restriction is overly burdensome. Overuse of parameterized macros is best avoided.

Some of the other preprocessor features, such as stringization, token merging, and the predefined macros, are useful debugging aids.

5.8.1 What Was Covered

- Lines that begin with a # (not counting initial white space) are preprocessor commands. (Note that lines that *expand* to begin with a # are not preprocessor commands.) As an example, the following code, which attempts to include `"file3"`, does not work. Instead, the resultant `#include` statement is passed to the compiler proper, where it is flagged as a syntax error.

```
#define Include( FileNum )   #include "file" #FileNum
Include( 3 );
```

- Lines may be extended by using a \ as the last character. The next line is then considered part of the current line, even if it begins with a #.

- The # on a line by itself is the *null directive*.

- The preprocessor performs textual substitution via #define. Except for its understanding of tokens, it knows very little C syntax and does not check that the result of the substitution makes sense.

- Parameterized macros are useful for avoiding the overhead of a function call. However, they are dangerous, precisely because a textual substitution of actual arguments for formal parameters is performed in the body of the macro.

- The stringization operator # can be used to convert an actual *macro argument* to a string.

- The token merging operator ## combines two tokens into a new token. No check is made to see if this new token makes sense.

- After an initial macro expansion and application of the stringization and token merging operators, the result is rescanned for further macro expansions. This process perpetuates until there are no unexpanded macros. However, when a macro appears in its own expansion, rescanning for that macro terminates.

- Five macros are predefined. They are __FILE__, __LINE__, __DATE__, __TIME__, and __STDC__.

- A function call, rather than a macro expansion, can be forced by parenthesizing the name of the function.

- On some systems, macros can be defined at compile time by using a compiler option. On UNIX, the option is -D.

- #undef causes the preprocessor to undefine a macro. If the macro was not already defined, the #undef has no effect. #undef is useful because macros may only be redefined to the same sequence, token for token, including placement of white space.

- The #include statement is logically replaced by the contents of a file. These statements may nest.

- Conditional compilation is governed by the directives #ifdef, #ifndef, #if, #else, #elif, and #endif. This is useful for maintaining program portability, debugging, and avoiding repetitive rescanning of header files.

- The #error directive causes termination of the compilation with an error message.

- The #line directive is used to change the compiler's notion of the current line number and source file.

- The #pragma directive is used to communicate system-dependent options, such as requesting optimization or in-line functions, to the compiler.

5.8.2 Friendly Reminders

- Although white space that precedes the initial # in a preprocessor directive is ignored, white space that follows a terminating \ is not ignored. If the last character on a line is not a   \, line continuation will not be in effect. Obviously, this can be difficult to spot visually.

- Because the #define is a direct textual substitution, parentheses should be used liberally to help ensure that the semantics of an expansion are not altered due to precedence rules. When defining symbolic numeric constants, do not use an = or ; in the #define command.

- A parenthesis that immediately follows the macro name in a #define indicates a parameterized macro. Otherwise, the macro is not parameterized, and the parenthesis is part of the replacement text. Be careful not to mix up the two forms.

- Because macro parameters may be evaluated more than once, do not pass a complicated expression as an actual argument. In particular, do not pass an expression that includes a function call or a side effect.

- When a parameterized macro expands to a block, it should be called without a trailing semicolon.

- On MS-DOS systems, full pathnames for files contain backslashes. You must use an escape sequence.

- Some compilers are now using / / as a comment starter. Text following / / until the end of line is treated as a comment; the end of line serves as a comment-ending token. Note that this is not ANSI C. If you use this type of comment, do not put it on a preprocessor #define line (because the expansion may include the comment, and comment more than you expect).

- Order of evaluation of the # and ## operators is undefined.

- Remember that errors which result from poor substitution text will generally not be reported until the compilation phase. Thus the error messages are not likely to point to the macro definition, but instead, to the macro expansion.

EXERCISES

1. What happens on your system when the   \ that is intended to end a line has some white space after it?

2. According to ANSI C, the comment in the fragment below serves the same purpose as a   \. Does your compiler agree?

   ```
   #define Add( X, Y ) /*
       This should be part of the previous line */ ( (X) + (Y) )
   ```

3. The macro assert(Expr) tests Expr, and if it is zero, prints a diagnostic that includes Expr, along with the current line number and source file. If NDEBUG is defined, assert prints nothing. Write the assert macro.

4. The *majority* function for booleans returns true if more than half of the parameters are true, and false otherwise. Write the macro

   ```
   #define Majority( X, Y, Z )
   ```

   which returns zero if at least two of X, Y, and Z are zero, and 1 otherwise.

5. Using one / and one % operator, implement the macro

   ```
   #define Divide( Numerator, Denominator, Quotient, Remainder )
   ```

6. Write an iteration macro:

   ```
   #define ITER( i, Low, High )
   ```

   which generates the clause that directs a `for` loop, using `i` as a counter running from `Low` to `High`, inclusive.

7. Write a macro to find the maximum of four numbers.

8. A *safe macro* can be implemented by declaring a block and copying the macro parameters into block variables. Parameters thus become implicitly typed. Write the `Max` macro for integers as a safe macro.

9. Implement the macro

   ```
   #define main
   ```

   The macro will print out the compilation date and time of the program and then start execution of the program.

10. On your system, is it legal for a file to `#include` itself? If so, write a program that prints out the maximum nesting depth for the `#include` statement.

11. Write a macro that generates a compile time error if `MaxLinesPerFunction` lines have been processed since the last call to that macro. This macro can thus be placed at the start of every function to ensure that all functions are reasonably small.

12. Write a macro

    ```
    #define IsLeap( Year )
    ```

    which tests if `Year` is a leap year.

13. Some systems accept `#` as an alternative to `#line`. Does yours?

14. What does the following code do?

    ```
    #define INC #include <stdio.h>
    INC
    ```

Part II

Efficient C: Data Structures and Algorithms

6

Pointers

In this chapter we discuss *pointer* variables, which are also known as *pointers*. A pointer is a variable that can be used to access another variable. Thus rather than *direct* access of a variable, a pointer provides *indirect* access. As we will see in the coming chapters, this is a very powerful utility, which can allow us to save incredible amounts of processing time. On the other hand, it is very easy to get into lots of trouble when using pointers, particularly if you have only a partial understanding of the concept. In this chapter we introduce basic syntax and the use of pointers to achieve call by reference semantics. In the next three chapters we illustrate more complex uses of the pointer variable.

6.1   The Pointer Variable

People use pointers in real-life situations all the time. Let us look at some examples:

- Suppose that a stranger in town comes up to you and asks for directions. If you do not know the answer, you may give the indirect answer: *Go to the gas station and ask them for directions.*

- If someone asks you for a phone number, rather than giving an immediate, direct reply, you may say: *Let me look it up in the phone book.*

- When a professor says *Do Problem 7.1 in the textbook*, the actual homework assignment is stated only indirectly. This illustrates another nice point: even if the actual problem changes in a subsequent edition of the book, the professor's directive still makes sense (although the homework assignment might no longer be meaningful).

- A classic example of indirect access is looking up a topic in the index of a book. The index tells you where a full description can be found.

In all these cases, rather than providing information directly, we are giving out information indirectly by providing a pointer to the information.

In C, a pointer is a variable that stores an address where other data is. Since an address is expected to be an integer, a pointer variable can usually be represented internally as just an `unsigned int` or `long int`, depending on the particular machine. What makes a pointer variable more than just a plain integer is that we can access the datum that is being pointed at. This is known as *dereferencing* the pointer.

As we have seen, when you tell the stranger to go to the gas station to get further information, you are giving an indirect answer. Even so, you are still responsible for guaranteeing that you have actually provided a gas station. Thus if you provide the stranger a location that is not really a gas station, your indirect answer (i.e., pointer) is no good. This is an *illegal indirection*. Sometimes an illegal indirection is immediately obvious (you tell the stranger to drive 50,000 miles), while other times it is not obvious until you actually go to the location and find out it is not a gas station. On the other hand, you might yourself be a stranger in town, and need to answer *I don't even know where a gas station is*. This is sort of a nothing answer, which is guaranteed not to lead anywhere.

Finally, if the professor wants to change the programming assignment, there are two ways to do it. One way is to keep the book but change to Problem 7.2. The other way is to change the book, so that Problem 7.1 becomes a new problem. The difference here is that in the first case we are changing where the pointer points at, while in the second case we are still pointing at Problem 7.1 but have changed the datum that is being pointed at.

Summarizing our observations, to implement the concept of a pointer, we need to address (pardon the pun!) several issues:

1. How do we declare that a variable can be used as a pointer?
2. How, using a pointer, do we access another variable indirectly?
3. How do we represent a pointer that leads to nowhere?
4. How do we redirect a pointer to a new location?
5. How do we change the data that the pointer is pointing at?
6. What does the keyword `const` (Section 4.4.3) mean with pointers?

6.2   The Address-of Operator &

In Section 2.21 we discussed `scanf` and the & operator. Let us explain more formally what is going on. Because of call by value, `scanf` cannot possibly place a scanned input value in an actual argument supplied by the caller. Consequently, it requests different information from the user. What `scanf` needs is the memory location in which it should place its scanned value. As we mentioned earlier, every object has memory set aside for it by the compiler. By applying the *unary* & operator, known as the *address-of* operator, we can usually find out where in memory an object is being stored.

Another way of looking at this is that while `printf` requires parameters of the form **what?**, `scanf` wants parameters of the form **where?**. A **where?** parameter is a *pointer variable*, and thus `scanf` expects pointers as its parameters. Along with its output in Figure 6.2 and the diagram in Figure 6.3, Figure 6.1 illustrates the *address-of* operator. At lines 8 to 11 we print out the memory locations of several variables. As we can see from the output, the `static` and `extern` (i.e., global) variables are treated very similarly when the compiler assigns memory locations. Actually, on our system, had Z not been initialized, X, Y, and Z would have been assigned memory locations 0x40e8, 0x40f0, and 0x40f8. Our system distinguishes between initialized data and uninitialized data.

```
/* 1*/    /* A Very Flawed Program */

/* 2*/    #include <stdio.h>

/* 3*/    int Global;

/* 4*/    main( void )
/* 5*/    {
/* 6*/        static int X, Y, Z = 1;
/* 7*/        int Local;

/* 8*/            /* First, We Will Be Nosey */
/* 9*/        printf( "X, Y, and Z are at %x, %x, %x\n", &X, &Y, &Z );
/*10*/        printf( "Global is at: %x\n", &Global );
/*11*/        printf( "Local is at: %x\n\n", &Local );

/*12*/        printf( "X, Y, and Z are at %u, %u, %u\n", &X, &Y, &Z );
/*13*/        printf( "Values of X, Y, and Z: %d %d %d\n", X, Y, Z );

/*14*/            /* Now Show Some Typical scanf Errors */
/*15*/        printf( "Enter 1 to read into Y, 2 for Z\n" );
/*16*/        scanf( "%d", &X );
/*17*/        if( X == 1 )
/*18*/        {
/*19*/            printf( "Enter Y: " );
/*20*/            scanf( "%d", Y ); /* Wrong! */
/*21*/            printf( "Y = %d\n", Y );
/*22*/        }
/*23*/        else
/*24*/        if( X == 2 )
/*25*/        {
/*26*/            printf( "Enter Z: " );
/*27*/            scanf( "%d", Z ); /* Wrong! */
/*28*/            printf( "Z = %d\n", Z );
/*29*/        }
/*30*/        return 0;
/*31*/    }
```

Figure 6.1: Program that illustrates address-of operator and `scanf` errors.

```
X, Y, and Z are at 40f0, 40f8, 40c0
Global is at: 40d8
Local is at: f7fffafc

X, Y, and Z are at 16624, 16632, 16576
Values of X, Y, and Z: 0 0 1
Enter 1 to read into Y, 2 for Z
```

Figure 6.2: Output of Figure 6.1 program.

On the other hand, `Local` is assigned a rather bizarre-looking memory location. It is bizarre because the address, treated as either a signed or unsigned 32-bit integer, has a

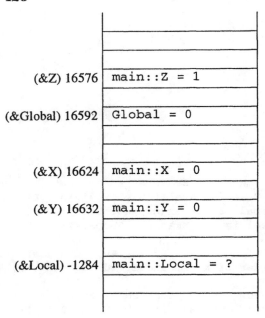

(&Z) 16576	`main::Z = 1`
(&Global) 16592	`Global = 0`
(&X) 16624	`main::X = 0`
(&Y) 16632	`main::Y = 0`
(&Local) -1284	`main::Local = ?`

Figure 6.3:   Memory corresponding to Figures 6.1 and 6.2.

larger magnitude than the amount of memory on our system. The correct interpretation is probably a 24-bit signed integer, which in this case is -1284. This reflects the fact that on our system, local variables are allocated on the fly, as function calls are made, from the high end of memory downward (until the global and static data are encountered). 1284 may represent the offset from the starting point of the high end.

The address returned by the & operator, as we can thus see, is not something that is meant to be printed. All the address-of operator is used for is to obtain an address of an object so that a pointer can point at that object. The & has one important restriction: you cannot apply it to a variable that is declared `register`, because a machine register is not a main memory location. The compiler will complain if you attempt this.

The rest of the program, from line 14 downward, illustrates the correct and incorrect use of `scanf`. On line 16, an integer value is read from the terminal. Here the use is correct because we are telling `scanf` to place the result in the memory location that is where X is stored.

If the user does not type an integer, nothing is read, X is unaltered, and the effect is that the program ends.[1] If the user has typed 1, line 19 prompts the user to change Y at line 20. However, line 20 is wrong. Because Y has a current value of 0, the request to `scanf` is to read a value from the terminal and place it in memory location 0. This is not the memory location where Y is to be stored.

In fact, 0 is guaranteed to be an illegal memory location. On any machine, your program should crash here. UNIX will give you a *segmentation violation*; other machines will be less cryptic.

If the user has set X to 2, the `scanf` at line 27 crashes. Once again, the request is to place the input in a weird memory location, in this case 1. On most machines, you'll get the

---

[1]Recall that `static` variables are initialized to zero by default.

same error message as before. On some UNIX machines, you may get a *bus error*, which is really cryptic. `ints`, which are typically four bytes on machines running UNIX, must be stored in a memory location that is divisible by 4. Thus attempting to write an integer to an odd memory location is illegal. The bus error message means that an illegal address was detected on the address bus before it became obvious that the address was out of range. But it is the same problem.

Forgetting the & when using `scanf` is certainly one of the most common errors and one that even experienced C programmers do all the time. There is virtually no chance that it will never happen to you. The trick is to recognize the error quickly and not waste too much time and effort tracking down the mistake. Because the & is an operator, we need to consider its precedence and associativity. The unary address-of operator is on an equal footing with other unary operators.

An additional warning is in order about the *address-of* operator. You cannot just send the address of a variable to any function and expect it to be alterable. The formal parameter of the receiving function has to have a type declaration indicating that a **where?** parameter is being sent instead of the usual **what?** parameter. We discuss this in Section 6.5.

6.3 Pointer Syntax

We can declare that a variable `Ptr` points at an object of type `int` by saying

```
int *Ptr;
```

The value represented by `Ptr` is an address. Like other variables, this declaration does not initialize `Ptr` to any particular value, so using `Ptr` before assigning to it will produce bad results.

Suppose that we also have the following declarations:

```
int X = 5, Y = 7;
```

We can make `Ptr` point at `X` by assigning to `Ptr` the memory location where `X` is stored. We already know how to do that, since the unary address-of operator & provides this information. Thus

```
Ptr = &X;                 /* LEGAL */
```

sets `Ptr` to point at `X`. Figure 6.4 illustrates this in two ways. On the left, we see the model of memory shown in Figure 6.3. The figure on the right uses an arrow to show "pointing."

The value of the data being pointed at is obtained by the dereferencing operator *. In our case `*Ptr` will evaluate to 5, which is the value of the pointed-at variable, `X`. It is illegal to dereference something that is not a pointer. In some sense the * is the opposite of &, and for the purposes of precedence and associativity, they are equals. As we will see later, this has important ramifications. Figure 6.5 shows the resulting precedence and associativity table.

Dereferencing works not only for reading values from a variable but also for writing new values to the variable. Thus if we say

```
*Ptr = 10;                /* LEGAL */
```

we have changed the value of `X` to 10. Figure 6.6 shows the changes that result. By the way, this shows the problem with pointers: unrestricted alterations are possible, and a runaway pointer can overwrite all sorts of variables unintentionally.

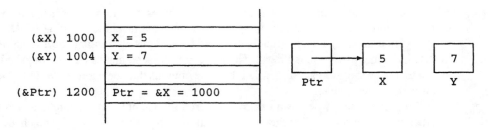

Figure 6.4:   Pointer illustration.

Category	Examples	Associativity
Primary expression	*identifiers constants*	None
Postfix	Function( ) ++ --	Left to right
Prefix and unary	* & ! ~ + - ++ --	Right to left
Type cast	(TypeName)	Right to left
Multiplicative	* / %	Left to right
Additive	+ -	Left to right
Shift	<< >>	Left to right
Relational	< <= > >=	Left to right
Equality	== !=	Left to right
Boolean AND	&	Left to right
Boolean XOR	^	Left to right
Boolean OR	|	Left to right
Logical AND	&&	Left to right
Logical OR	||	Left to right
Conditional	?:	Right to left
Assignment	= *= /= %= += -= &= |= ^= <<= >>=	Right to left
Comma		Left to right

Figure 6.5:   Precedence and associativity of operators.

We could also have initialized `Ptr` at declaration time, by having it point to `X`:

```
int X = 5, Y = 7, *Ptr = &X;     /* LEGAL */
```

The declaration says that `X` is an `int` initialized to 5, `Y` is an `int`, initialized to 7, and `Ptr` is a pointer to an `int`, initialized to point at `X`. Let's look at what could have gone wrong and how this can be confusing if you do not quite understand what is going on. The following two initializations are both incorrect:

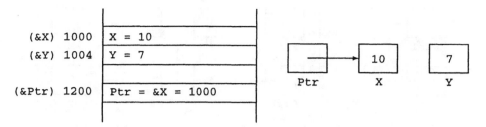

Figure 6.6:   **Result of** `*Ptr=10` **in Figure 6.4.**

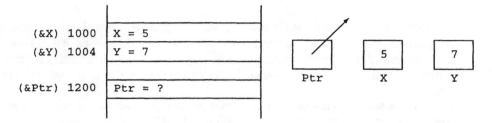

Figure 6.7:   **Uninitialized pointer.**

```
int *Ptr = &X, X = 5, Y = 7;      /* ILLEGAL */
int X = 5, Y = 7, *Ptr = X;       /* ILLEGAL */
```

In the first case, we are using X before it has been declared, so the compiler will complain. In the second case, we are trying to have Ptr point at X, but we have forgotten that a pointer holds an address. Thus we need an address on the right-hand side of the assignment. Generally, the compiler will warn you that you have forgotten the &, although it may do it somewhat cryptically.

Now suppose that we have the correct declaration, but with Ptr uninitialized:

```
int X = 5, Y = 7, *Ptr;           /* LEGAL */
```

What is the value of Ptr? As Figure 6.7 shows, the value is undefined, because it was never initialized. Because of this the value of *Ptr is also undefined. However, in some sense it is more undefined, because Ptr could hold an address that makes absolutely no sense at all, thus causing a program crash if it is dereferenced.

We have already seen the correct syntax for an assignment:

```
Ptr = &X;        /* LEGAL */
```

Suppose that we forget the address-of operator. Then the assignment

```
Ptr = X;         /* ILLEGAL: RHS NOT AN ADDRESS */
```

rightly generates a compiler error. There are two ways to make the compiler shut up. One is to take the address on the right-hand side, as is done in the correct syntax. The other method is erroneous:

```
*Ptr = X;        /* WRONG WAY TO INITIALIZE!! */
```

The compiler is quiet because the statement says that the `int` to which Ptr is pointing should get the value of X. For instance, if Ptr is &Y, then Y is assigned the value of X. So this is perfectly legal. However, it does not make Ptr point at X. Moreover, since Ptr is uninitialized, dereferencing it is likely to cause a run-time error. In hindsight, this is obvious from the picture. The moral is always to draw pictures at the first sign of pointer trouble.

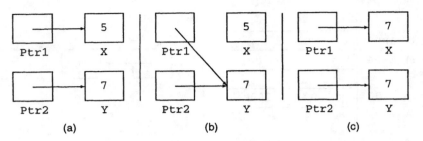

Figure 6.8: **(a) Initial state; (b)** `Ptr1 = Ptr2` **starting from initial state;**
(c) `*Ptr1 = *Ptr2` **starting from initial state.**

This is a common error for two reasons. First, since it makes the compiler quiet, programmers feel comfortable about using the incorrect syntax. Second, it looks somewhat like the syntax that is used for initialization at declaration time. The difference is that the `*` at declaration time is not a dereferencing `*`, just an indication that the variable is a pointer type.

As we saw earlier, sometimes we want to state explicitly that a pointer is pointing nowhere, as opposed to an undefined location. The NULL pointer does this: it points at a memory location (0) that is guaranteed to be incapable of holding anything. Consequently, a NULL pointer cannot be dereferenced. The symbolic constant NULL is defined in `<stdio.h>` and some other header files.

A dereferenced pointer behaves just like the object it is pointing at. Thus after the following three statements, the value stored in X is 15.

```
X = 5;
Ptr = &X;
*Ptr += 10;
```

However, we must be cognizant of precedence rules because it is possible to perform arithmetic not only on the dereferenced values, but also on the (un-dereferenced) pointers themselves. As an example, the following two statements are very different:

```
*Ptr += 1;
*Ptr++;
```

In these statements, the `+=` operator is applied to `*Ptr`, while the `++` operator is applied to `Ptr`. The result of applying the `++` operator to `Ptr` is that `Ptr` will be changed to point at a memory location one "memory unit" larger than it used to. We will discuss this in Section 7.10.

Finally, if `Ptr1` and `Ptr2` are pointers to the same type, then

```
Ptr1 = Ptr2;
```

sets `Ptr1` to point to the same location as `Ptr2`, while

```
*Ptr1 = *Ptr2;
```

assigns the dereferenced `Ptr1` the value of the dereferenced `Ptr2`. As Figure 6.8 illustrates, these statements are quite different. Moreover, when the wrong form is used mistakenly, the consequences might not be obvious immediately. In the example, after the assignment, `*Ptr1` and `*Ptr2` are both 7 in both cases. Similarly, the expression

```
Ptr1 == Ptr2
```

is true if the two pointers are pointing at the same memory location, while

```
*Ptr1 == *Ptr2
```

is true if the values stored at the two indicated addresses are equal. It is common to use the wrong form.

The requirement that `Ptr1` and `Ptr2` point to the same type is a consequence of the fact that C is strongly typed: we cannot mix different types of pointers, without using a type conversion. This is discussed further in Section 6.6.

6.4   The `const` Qualifier with Pointers

When we declare

```
const int X;
```

the meaning is pretty clear: the variable `X` is not modifiable. What does

```
const int *Ptr;
```

mean?

One can imagine one of several possible meanings. Perhaps it means that `Ptr` cannot be changed to point at another memory location. It could mean that `Ptr` can change, but the data that it points at can never be changed. Or it could mean both. In C, the issue is settled by allowing two possible placements of `const`. Figure 6.9 shows the possibilities. When the keyword `const` appears before the `*` in the type declaration, it means that the dereferenced value is unmodifiable and thus, among other restrictions, can never appear on the left side of an assignment. Thus in the first two cases,

```
*Ptr = 10;
```

is illegal. When the `const` appears after the `*` in the declaration, it means that the (un-dereferenced) pointer is not modifiable. Thus in the first and third cases,

```
Ptr = &X
```

is illegal.

Sometimes, the compiler is quite good at preventing you from doing bad things. For example, the second declaration below is illegal:

```
const int X = 5;        /* Perhaps a global */
int *Ptr = &X;          /* Ptr points at X */
```

Our compiler will not allow this because it is concerned that by placing `*Ptr` on the left side of an assignment, `X` can be altered later, despite the `const` directive. Even if `Ptr` is declared without an initialization, and assigned later (hopefully), the compiler will complain. However, declaring

```
const int X = 5;        /* Perhaps a global */
const int *Ptr = &X;    /* Ptr points at X */
```

is acceptable. Although `Ptr` can be reassigned to point anywhere, it will never change the variable at which it is pointing. Thus it could never try to change `X`. It is possible to defeat this mechanism by an explicit type conversion, but doing so is a bad idea. Figure 6.10 shows how. By using `const` directives carefully, you can have the compiler catch lots of errors that result from forgetting a `*`.

```
const int * const Ptr;    /* *Ptr and Ptr   are unmodifiable */
const int *       Ptr;    /* *Ptr           is unmodifiable */
      int * const Ptr;    /*           Ptr  is unmodifiable */
      int *       Ptr;    /* Nothing        is unmodifiable */
```

Figure 6.9: `const` **with pointers.**

```
/* 1*/    #include <stdio.h>

/* 2*/    main( void )
/* 3*/    {
/* 4*/        const int X = 5;                /* X Should Not Change  */
/* 5*/        const int *PtrC = &X;      /* A Constant Pointer To It */
/* 6*/        int *PtrNC = ( int * ) PtrC; /* PtrNC Is Not Constant */

/* 7*/        *PtrNC = 10;                    /* So This Changes X!   */
/* 8*/        printf( "%d\n", X );

/* 9*/        return 0;
/*10*/    }
```

Figure 6.10:   Type conversions defeat the `const` **directive.**

6.5   Call by Reference

An important, although sometimes overused application of pointers is achieving *call by reference* semantics. As we know, parameters to functions are passed by value and thus cannot be altered directly. As we saw in Figure 4.2, this makes it impossible to write a function that swaps the values of its two parameters. However, by introducing a level of indirection we can get around this restriction. The idea, which is also used by `scanf`, is to pass pointers. We can then swap their dereferenced values. This is implemented in Figure 6.11.

The `Swap` routine at line 2 expects two pointers, X and Y. Thus X and Y will store the addresses of the two integers that are to be swapped. Thus, the `main` routine, at line 4 passes the addresses of A and B. Figure 6.12 shows, pictorially, what is going on. When dealing with pointers, it is a good idea to draw a picture at the first sign of confusion. Here we see that A initially has the value of 5, B initially has the value of 7, X points at A, and Y points at B. Tmp is just a local integer to `Swap`. Lines 5, 6, and 7 implement the standard swapping algorithm by moving around *X, *Y, and Tmp, all three of which represent plain integers. Thus at the end of the algorithm, the values pointed at by X and Y have been swapped. Tmp has the value 5, but since it is a local variable, it disappears after the `Swap` terminates.

Line 2 of the `Swap` function shows the less common placement of `const`. Here we are saying that where X and Y point at will not change during the `Swap` routine. One reason that we use the `const` directive is that sometimes it helps the compiler detect erroneous code. In Figure 6.13, `WrongSwap1` shows an example of code that compiles but does not do what we think. Here, as Figure 6.14 illustrates, we are swapping where X and Y point at, not their dereferenced values. Since X, Y, and Tmp all vanish after `Swap` ends, all we

```
/* 1*/    #include <stdio.h>


/* 1*/    void
/* 2*/    Swap( int * const X, int * const Y )
/* 3*/    {
/* 4*/        int Tmp;

/* 5*/        Tmp = *X;
/* 6*/        *X  = *Y;
/* 7*/        *Y  = Tmp;
/* 8*/    }


/* 1*/    main( void )
/* 2*/    {
/* 3*/        int A = 5, B = 7;

/* 4*/        Swap( &A, &B );              /* Must Pass The Address */
/* 5*/        printf( "%d %d\n", A, B );

/* 6*/        return 0;
/* 7*/    }
```

Figure 6.11: **Swapping two values by reference.**

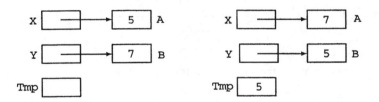

Figure 6.12: **Pictorial view of swapping: before and after.** X, Y, **and** Tmp **are local variables that vanish after** Swap **returns.**

have achieved is a shuffling of copied values: A and B are unchanged. The correct use of const would have caught the error by dissallowing the alteration of X and Y.

WrongSwap2 shows another common error: because X and Y are pointers, many beginners think that Tmp ought to be one, too. Figure 6.14 also shows why this does not work. Since Tmp is pointing nowhere, the assignment at line 5 is undefined. This can be tricky because if Tmp happens to be pointing at a legal address for an integer, that address will be used for a temporary variable, and the Swap will succeed! Of course, some variable may be overwritten in the process.

On the other hand, a common initial value is 0, so Tmp is more likely to be a NULL pointer, thus resulting in a run-time crash. If you are lucky, you will get this alternative, because silently overwriting a variable can be very hard to track down. Thus you should always make sure that your pointers point somewhere, perhaps by initializing them to NULL if necessary.

```
/* 1*/    void     /* Swaps Where X And Y Point, Not Their Value */
/* 2*/    WrongSwap1( const int *X, const int *Y )
/* 3*/    {
/* 4*/        const int *Tmp;

/* 5*/        Tmp = X;
/* 6*/        X   = Y;       /* Would Be Caught By Compiler if The */
/* 7*/        Y   = Tmp;     /* const Directive Was Used Correctly */
/* 8*/    }
```

```
/* 1*/    void     /* Can Lead To A Difficult To Track Down Bug */
/* 2*/    WrongSwap2( int * const X, int * const Y )
/* 3*/    {
/* 4*/        int *Tmp;      /* Pointer Not Needed To Store The int */

/* 5*/        *Tmp = *X;     /* Major Error: Tmp Is Undefined */
/* 6*/        *X   = *Y;
/* 7*/        *Y   = *Tmp;
/* 8*/    }
```

Figure 6.13: Possible errors when implementing Swap.

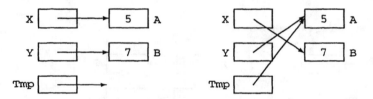

Figure 6.14: Pictorial view of WrongSwap1: before and after.

6.6   The Generic Pointer void *

Earlier we said that one cannot just mix and match pointers, because pointers must be of the same type. Thus a short int * cannot be assigned to an int * without at least generating a compiler warning. Note that their dereferenced values are compatible under the normal type conversion rules. This is shown in Figure 6.15. This brings up a question: How does scanf get around this, since it does not know what kind of pointers it is receiving? The answer is the generic pointer void *. Suppose that VoidPtr is declared:

void *VoidPtr;

Then VoidPtr can be assigned or assigned to any pointer value. However, it cannot be dereferenced, since it is not a pointer to any type. Figure 6.15 shows some legal and illegal uses of void *. The last legal assignment shows up a technical point. On many machines, quantities such as ints are stored over several bytes and can start only in certain places. On our machine, for instance, 32-bit integers must be aligned to start on a byte boundary that is divisible by 4. This means that interpreting a short int * pointer as an int *

```
int   X = 5;
short int  S = 6;
int  *IntPtr;
short int *ShortPtr;
void *VoidPtr;
```

```
/* Statements which are legal at compile time */
IntPtr = &X;              /* IntPtr points at X */
ShortPtr = &S;            /* ShortPtr points at S */
*IntPtr = *ShortPtr;      /* X gets integer value 6 */

VoidPtr = ShortPtr;       /* VoidPtr points at S */
IntPtr = VoidPtr;         /* Dangerous: IntPtr points at S */
*IntPtr = 2;              /* Could be an alignment error */

/* Illegal statements detected by the compiler */
*VoidPtr = 7;             /* Can't dereference a void * */
IntPtr = ShortPtr;        /* Can't mix pointers without a cast */
```

Figure 6.15: Possible sequence of statements, some of which are illegal.

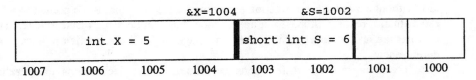

Figure 6.16: Memory layout with four-byte `ints` and two-byte `shorts`.

pointer is allowable by the hardware only half of the time (and although allowed the other half of the time, might not make sense). In our case, if S is not stored in an address that is divisible by 4, dereferencing `IntPtr` is illegal. On UNIX, you get the cryptic *bus error* message, which, as we have seen, means that the address the computer used to fetch an integer was misaligned. Figure 6.16 gives an example where this might occur. If S was stored at memory location 1000, the hardware fault would not occur.

The primary use of `void *` is for routines such as `scanf` that need a pointer, but do not immediately know what type the pointer is. Once `scanf` reads the conversion string, it can use a `switch` statement to convert the `void *` to the appropriate pointer. `scanf` uses another feature: the number of parameters it takes is variable. The mechanism for achieving this is described in Section D.10 of Appendix D.

6.7 Pointers to Functions

In Section 4.3.1 we saw how functions can be passed as parameters. Technically speaking, what is passed is a pointer to a function. The pointer represents the address where the object code for the function is stored. Because of this, an alternative syntax is frequently used. The declaration

```
double ( *PtrFunc )( double );
```

says that `PtrFunc` is a pointer to a function that takes a `double` as parameter and returns a `double`. The parentheses are necessary because

```
double *PtrFunc( double );
```

says that `PtrFunc` is a function that takes a `double` and returns a pointer to a `double`, which is quite different.

For the first declaration, consider the following code:

```
PtrFunc = sqrt;
printf( "Square root of 5 is %f\n", ( *PtrFunc )( 5.0 ) );
printf( "Square root of 5 is %f\n", PtrFunc( 5.0 ) );
```

First we have `PtrFunc` point at the `sqrt` function. The implication is that a function name, such as `sqrt`, is essentially a constant pointer. The first `printf` dereferences `Ptr`, thus calling `sqrt` indirectly. The parentheses are once again necessary. The second `printf` statement is equivalent in ANSI C, but not in older versions of C. The logic is that since `sqrt(5.0)` makes sense and `sqrt` is basically a pointer, `PtrFunc(5.0)` should make sense too. This is why the code in Figure 6.17, which uses explicit pointers to functions, is equivalent in ANSI C to the code in Figure 4.13.

When implicit pointers to functions are used, as in Figure 4.13, we save keystrokes and get code that is generally more readable. However, in Figure 4.13, it is difficult to tell, without examining the function prototype for `Solve`, that `F` is a pointer to a function, rather than a real function. In complex code, this can be a big disadvantage. Since our routines are always short enough to fit on a page, we will use implicit pointer to function dereferencing.

Overusing pointers to functions can lead to bizarre declarations and puzzling code loaded with parentheses and asterisks. For example, how does one declare a pointer to a function that accepts a pointer to a function that accepts a `double`, returns a pointer to a `double`, and returns a pointer to a function that accepts an `int` and returns an `int`? See the appendix for answers. In Section 9.7 we will see an excellent use of pointers to functions.

6.8   Summary

C relies on pointers more than most high-level programming languages. In this chapter we have seen the basic syntax and how pointers are used to implement call by reference semantics. In Chapter 7, we examine the *array*, which in C is strongly related to pointers.

6.8.1   What Was Covered

- The *pointer* variable emulates the real-life indirect answer. In C it is just a variable that stores the address where some other data reside. Although any sufficiently large integer could do this, a pointer is special because it can be dereferenced, thus allowing access to those other data.

- An *illegal indirection* refers to the attempted dereferencing of a variable that is not a pointer, or a pointer that is not pointing at valid data.

```
/* 1*/      #include "root.h"

/* 2*/      int
/* 3*/      DifferentSign( double ( *F )( double ),
                                        double Pt1, double Pt2 )
/* 4*/      {
/* 5*/          return  ( ( *F )( Pt1 ) < 0 ) != ( ( *F )( Pt2 ) < 0 );
/* 6*/      }


/* 7*/      double
/* 8*/      Solve( double ( *F )( double ), double Low, double High )
/* 9*/      {
/*10*/          double Mid = ( Low + High ) / 2.0;
/*11*/          double SmallInterval = ( High - Low ) * Epsilon;

/*12*/          if( ! ( *F )( Low ) )
/*13*/              return Low;
/*14*/          else
/*15*/          if( ! ( *F )( High ) )
/*16*/              return High;
/*17*/          else
/*18*/          if( ! DifferentSign( F, Low, High ) )
/*19*/          {
/*20*/              printf( "Suggested points have same sign!\n" );
/*21*/              return SolveError;
/*22*/          }

/*23*/          while( ( *F )( Mid ) && ( High - Low ) > SmallInterval )
/*24*/          {
/*25*/              if( DifferentSign( F, Low, Mid ) )
/*26*/                  High = Mid;
/*27*/              else
/*28*/                  Low = Mid;

/*29*/              Mid = ( Low + High ) / 2.0;
/*30*/          }

/*31*/          return Mid;
/*32*/      }
```

Figure 6.17: **Bisection algorithm with explicit pointers to functions.**

- The NULL pointer is guaranteed to point at memory that cannot be accessed. It is also used to indicate error conditions for routines that return a pointer.

- For pointers, the const directive can be used to specify that the pointer or the dereferenced value is unmodifiable. To get both, you need to use const twice.

- Pointers can be used to implement call by reference.

- Pointers to different types cannot be mixed, without a type conversion, except for void *. A pointer of type void * cannot be dereferenced.

- A function name that is passed as a parameter is treated as a pointer. For convenience, the pointer is implicitly dereferenced when appropriate.

6.8.2   Friendly Reminders

- Always make sure that a pointer is pointing at valid data before attempting to dereference the data. If `Ptr` is uninitialized, the assignment

  ```
  *Ptr = X;
  ```

  is likely to cause a program crash.

- In a declaration,

  ```
  *Ptr = &X;
  ```

  makes `Ptr` point at `X`. As an assignment statement,

  ```
  *Ptr = &X;
  ```

  is wrong (unless `Ptr` is a pointer to a pointer) because the left-hand side is the dereferenced value rather than the pointer. The * in the declaration is not a dereferencing operator but rather, a type declaration.

- Be careful not to mix up a pointer and the value being pointed at.

  ```
  Ptr1 == Ptr2
  ```

  is true if both pointers are pointing at the same memory location, while

  ```
  *Ptr1 == *Ptr2
  ```

  is true if the values stored at the two indicated addresses are equal.

- Type casting a `short int *` to an `int *` is dangerous, because the address may not be aligned correctly. An attempt to access an `int` using a misaligned address will generally cause a crash. On UNIX, the error is a *bus error*.

- Although `const` can be defeated by a type conversion to a non-const variable, do not do it. The protection afforded by the directive is valuable.

- `*Ptr++` increments `Ptr`, not `*Ptr`, because of the precedence rules.

- Do not forget to parenthesize when declaring and using pointers to functions.

EXERCISES

1. Write the routine `Sort3`, with prototype provided below. `Sort3` rearranges the dereferenced parameters in nondecreasing order.

   ```
   void Sort3( int *A, int *B, int *C );
   ```

2. Write several different programs to see if the value of `main` is always the same on your machine. If you know enough assembly language for your machine, call `Peek` to try and determine the first instruction.

3. If you know enough assembly language for your machine, write into some memory location `M` code that executes a jump statement to itself. Then declare `P` to be a pointer to a function, set `P` to `M`, and execute

   ```
   ( *P )( );
   ```

   See if you can get an infinite loop.

4. Does the code in Figure 6.10 defeat the `const` mechanism on your machine?

5. Consider

```
int A, B;
int *Ptr;           /* A pointer */
int **PtrPtr;       /* A pointer to a pointer */

Ptr = &A;
PtrPtr = &Ptr;
```

   (a) Is this legal?

   (b) What are the values of `*Ptr` and `**PtrPtr`?

   (c) How can we alter `PtrPtr` so that it points at a pointer to B without directly touching `Ptr`?

   (d) Is the following legal?

```
PtrPtr = Ptr;
```

6. **(a)** Is `*&X` always equal to `X`? If not give an example.

   (b) Is `&*X` always equal to `X`? If not give an example.

7. On your machine, is `*0` detected at compile time as an error?

8. For the declarations

```
int A = 5;
int *Ptr = &A;
```

   What are the values of the following?

   (a) `Ptr`

   (b) `*Ptr`

   (c) `Ptr == A`

   (d) `Ptr == &A`

   (e) `&Ptr`

   (f) `*A`

   (g) `*&A`

   (h) `**&Ptr`

7

Arrays

Suppose we have three numbers that we want to print out, avoiding duplicates. Thus only 8 5 is printed if the three numbers are 8 5 8. Figure 7.1 shows a program that does this. It works by declaring three variables Num1, Num2, and Num3, and performing checks to avoid printing of duplicates. The program, which seems simple and efficient, has a fundamental problem: it does not nicely extend in the event that we want to handle more numbers. For instance, four numbers would severely complicate the code.

To handle four elements, we could use an alternative algorithm: arrange Num1, Num2, Num3, and Num4 in nondecreasing order (i.e., sort them), after which it is easy to print out the nonduplicates. Figure 7.2 shows an implementation. Lines 15 to 19 rearrange the four numbers so that Num1 $\leq$ Num2 $\leq$ Num3 $\leq$ Num4. The ith number is printed only if it differs from the previous number.

This improved algorithm has merit in that it extends easily to larger amounts of data: we just need to sort more items and then apply the same sequential scan. The problem now is that if we have 10 numbers, we need to declare 10 variables and incur a drastic increase in the number of lines of code. Although it is reasonable to expect that more instructions have to be executed when more data are processed, it is not reasonable to expect to write more code to do it; rather, we expect some shorthand that will allow the use of loops.

In this chapter we examine the *array*, which is the basic mechanism for storing similar variables. In C, arrays are implemented by pointers; consequently, the material in Chapter 6 should be well understood before proceeding with this chapter. We also look more closely at the sorting problem, producing a short algorithm that is very efficient and we examine *multidimensional* arrays. Finally, we see how arrays can be allocated and expanded as the program runs.

7.1   Basics

An array is a collection of identically typed variables. Just as a variable must be declared before it appears in an expression and initialized before its value is used, so must an array. An array is declared by giving it a name, in accordance with the usual identifier rules, and by telling the compiler what type the elements should be. If we are declaring a new array

140

```
/* 1*/    #include <stdio.h>

/* 2*/    /* Print Three Integers, But Avoid Duplicates */

/* 3*/    main( void )
/* 4*/    {
/* 5*/        int Num1, Num2, Num3;

/* 6*/        printf( "Enter three integers: " );
/* 7*/        if( scanf( "%d %d %d", &Num1, &Num2, &Num3 ) != 3 )
/* 8*/        {
/* 9*/            printf( "Expected three integers -- exiting...\n" );
/*10*/            return 1;
/*11*/        }

/*12*/        if( Num1 == Num2 )
/*13*/            if(  Num2 == Num3 )
/*14*/                printf( "%d\n", Num1 );
/*15*/            else
/*16*/                printf( "%d %d\n", Num1, Num3 );
/*17*/        else /* Num1 != Num2 */
/*18*/            if( Num1 == Num3 || Num2 == Num3 )
/*19*/                printf( "%d %d\n", Num1, Num2 );
/*20*/            else
/*21*/                printf( "%d %d %d\n", Num1, Num2, Num3 );

/*22*/        return 0; /* Normal Exit */
/*23*/    }
```

Figure 7.1: **Poor program to print three integers without duplicates.**

(rather than a parameter to a function), a size must also be provided, either explicitly or implicitly. For now, we use the most direct method of specifying an integer as the size.

Figure 7.3 shows that at line 7, an array named Num is declared and contains four integers. The four variables that are declared can then be accessed by *indexing* the array appropriately. Specifically, four consecutive integers **beginning from zero** are used to access the four variables. Thus in Figure 7.3, the variables Num[0], Num[1], Num[2], and Num[3] are used instead of the corresponding Figure 7.2 variables Num1, Num2, Num3, and Num4.

The use of arrays allows code simplification. As one example, lines 21 to 26 in Figure 7.3 can be collapsed as shown in Figure 7.4. By using arrays we can easily extend the program to handle large amounts of data. The result is shown in Figure 7.5. First, at line 6, we define an array to hold the input; we are prepared for up to MaxN integers. In the example, MaxN is 10. Line 6 also defines a variable Tmp, which is used in the sorting phase (to hold an array item temporarily). Line 7 declares two counting variables and the variable ItemsRead that keeps track of the number of input items.

```
/* 1*/     #include <stdio.h>

/* 2*/     #define CompExch( X, Y ) \
/* 3*/         if( X > Y ){ int _Tmp; _Tmp = X; X = Y; Y = _Tmp; }

/* 4*/     /* Print Four Integers, But Avoid Duplicates */

/* 5*/     main( void )
/* 6*/     {
/* 7*/         int Num1, Num2, Num3, Num4;

/* 8*/         printf( "Enter four integers: " );
/* 9*/         if( scanf( "%d %d %d %d",
/*10*/                  &Num1, &Num2, &Num3, &Num4 ) != 4 )
/*11*/         {
/*12*/             printf( "Expected four integers -- exiting...\n" );
/*13*/             return 1;
/*14*/         }

/*15*/         CompExch( Num1, Num2 );
/*16*/         CompExch( Num3, Num4 );
/*17*/         CompExch( Num1, Num3 );
/*18*/         CompExch( Num2, Num4 );
/*19*/         CompExch( Num2, Num3 );

/*20*/         printf( "%d", Num1 );
/*21*/         if( Num2 != Num1 )
/*22*/             printf( " %d", Num2 );
/*23*/         if( Num3 != Num2 )
/*24*/             printf( " %d", Num3 );
/*25*/         if( Num4 != Num3 )
/*26*/             printf( " %d", Num4 );
/*27*/         printf( "\n" );

/*28*/         return 0;   /* Normal Exit */
/*29*/     }
```

Figure 7.2:   Poor program to print four integers without duplicates.

The program in Figure 7.5 consists of three phases, which we will eventually break into functions. First, we read up to MaxN integers from the input. The third phase mimics Figure 7.4 to output nonduplicates once the first element is printed. The second phase is the sorting part. It is estimated that computers spend over 80% of their time sorting. Thus sorting is a well-studied problem, with a host of good (and bad) solutions. The algorithm that we have implemented here is *insertion sort*. Insertion sort is generally considered a good solution if only a few elements need sorting, because it is such a short algorithm. If we are dealing with a large amount of data, however, insertion sort is a poor choice because it is too time consuming. In that case, better algorithms are known, such as *Shellsort* (Section 7.5) and *quicksort* (Section 11.4.2).

```
/* 1*/    #include <stdio.h>

/* 2*/    /* Print Four Integers, But Avoid Duplicates */

/* 3*/    #define CompExch( X, Y ) \
/* 4*/        if( X > Y ) { int _Tmp; _Tmp = X; X = Y; Y = _Tmp; }

/* 5*/    main( void )
/* 6*/    {
/* 7*/        int Num[ 4 ];   /* Num[ 0 ] Num[ 1 ] Num[ 2 ] Num[ 3 ] */

/* 8*/        printf( "Enter four integers: " );
/* 9*/        if( scanf( "%d %d %d %d",
/*10*/                &Num[ 0 ],&Num[ 1 ],&Num[ 2 ],&Num[ 3 ] ) != 4 )
/*11*/        {
/*12*/            printf( "Expected four integers -- exiting...\n" );
/*13*/            return 1;
/*14*/        }

/*15*/        CompExch( Num[ 0 ], Num[ 1 ] );
/*16*/        CompExch( Num[ 2 ], Num[ 3 ] );
/*17*/        CompExch( Num[ 0 ], Num[ 2 ] );
/*18*/        CompExch( Num[ 1 ], Num[ 3 ] );
/*19*/        CompExch( Num[ 1 ], Num[ 2 ] );

/*20*/        printf( "%d", Num[ 0 ] );
/*21*/        if( Num[ 1 ] != Num[ 0 ] )
/*22*/            printf( " %d", Num[ 1 ] );
/*23*/        if( Num[ 2 ] != Num[ 1 ] )
/*24*/            printf( " %d", Num[ 2 ] );
/*25*/        if( Num[ 3 ] != Num[ 2 ] )
/*26*/            printf( " %d", Num[ 3 ] );
/*27*/        printf( "\n" );

/*28*/        return 0;  /* Normal Exit */
/*29*/    }
```

Figure 7.3: **Previous program using arrays but no loops.**

```
/*21*/    for( i = 1; i < 4; i++ )
/*22*/        if( Num[ i ] != Num[ i - 1 ] )
/*23*/            printf( " %d", Num[ i ] );
```

Figure 7.4: **Array used to simplify code in Figure 7.3.**

The initial state is that the first element, considered by itself, is sorted. The final state which we need to attain is that all the elements, considered as a group, are sorted. Figure 7.6 shows that the basic action of insertion sort is to arrange that the first i elements are sorted, where i increases by one in each stage. This is what the outer loop at line 13 of Figure 7.5 is controlling.

```
/* 1*/    #include <stdio.h>

/* 2*/    /* Print Up To MaxN Integers, But Avoid Duplicates */

/* 3*/    #define MaxN 10

/* 4*/    main( void )
/* 5*/    {
/* 6*/        int Num[ MaxN ], Tmp;
/* 7*/        int j, Counter, ItemsRead = 0;

/* 8*/            /* Read Input */
/* 9*/        printf( "Enter up to %d integers: ", MaxN );
/*10*/        while( ItemsRead < MaxN
                        && scanf( "%d", &Num[ ItemsRead ] ) > 0 )
/*11*/            ItemsRead++;
/*12*/            /* Sort Input, Using Insertion Sort */
/*13*/        for( Counter = 1; Counter < ItemsRead; Counter++ )
/*14*/        {
/*15*/            Tmp = Num[ Counter ];
/*16*/            for( j = Counter; j > 0 && Tmp < Num[ j - 1 ]; j-- )
/*17*/                Num[ j ] = Num[ j - 1 ];
/*18*/            Num[ j ] = Tmp;
/*19*/        }

/*20*/            /* Output Non-Duplicates */
/*21*/        printf( "%d", Num[ 0 ] );
/*22*/        for( Counter = 1; Counter < ItemsRead; Counter++ )
/*23*/            if( Num[ Counter ] != Num[ Counter - 1 ] )
/*24*/                printf( " %d", Num[ Counter ] );
/*25*/        printf( "\n" );

/*26*/        return 0;  /* Normal Exit */
/*27*/    }
```

Figure 7.5: **Duplicate routine extended to handle larger amounts of data.**

Array Position	*0*	*1*	*2*	*3*	*4*	*5*
Initial state:	8	5	9	2	6	3
First 2 elements sorted:	5	8	9	2	6	3
First 3 elements sorted:	5	8	9	2	6	3
First 4 elements sorted:	2	5	8	9	6	3
First 5 elements sorted:	2	5	6	8	9	3
First 6 elements sorted:	2	3	5	6	8	9

Figure 7.6: **Basic action of insertion sort.**

Array Position	0	1	2	3	4	5
Initial state:	8	5				
First 2 elements sorted:	5	8	9			
First 3 elements sorted:	5	8	9	2		
First 4 elements sorted:	2	5	8	9	6	
First 5 elements sorted:	2	5	6	8	9	3
First 6 elements sorted:	2	3	5	6	8	9

Figure 7.7:   Closer look at action of insertion sort.

When the body of the `for` loop is entered, at line 14, we are guaranteed that the elements in array positions 0 to `Counter-1` are already sorted, and we need to extend this for positions 0 to `Counter`. Figure 7.7 shows a closer look at what has to be done, showing only the relevant part of the array. At each step, the element in boldfaced type needs to be added to the sorted previous part of the array. This is easily done by placing it in a temporary variable and sliding all the elements that are larger than it over one place to the right. After that is done, we can copy the temporary variable into the former position of the leftmost relocated element (this is shown in italics on the following line). We keep a counter `j`, which is the position where the temporary variable should be written back to. `j` decreases by one every time an element is slid over. Lines 15 to 18 implement this.

 It is important to check that this works in two boundary cases. First, if the boldfaced element is the largest in the group, it is copied out to the temporary variable, and then back immediately, and is thus correct. If the boldfaced element is the smallest in the group, the entire group moves over and the temporary is copied back into array position 0. We just need to be careful that we do not run past the end of the array. Thus we can be sure that when the outer `for` loop terminates, the `Num` array is sorted.

7.2   Limitations and Technicalities of Arrays

 The use of arrays shown in Section 7.1 is deceptive because it hides several details, which if forgotten, can make for difficult debugging. When a new array is allocated, the compiler checks the type declaration to decide how much memory it needs to set aside. This is essentially the only thing that the size component of the array declaration is used for. In fact, after the array is allocated, with minor exceptions, the size is pretty much irrelevant. **The name of the array represents a pointer to the beginning of allocated memory for that array.** Many of the following rules are a direct consequence of this fact.

7.2.1   No Index Range Checking

 The most important problem a C programmer is likely to run into is the fact that no index range checking is ever performed. That means that if you index an array out of its bounds, you will not necessarily get any error messages, either at compile time or at run time. What you are likely to do is to stray into other parts of memory, reading and perhaps writing over some other variables. The reason for this is that an array name is little more than a pointer. Index checking would require that the array bounds be somehow encoded into the pointer.[1] Although this is certainly possible, ANSI C does not require it. Since most other languages, including C++, provide a reasonable mechanism for index range checking, the lack of it may be viewed as a deficiency of C.

This problem is compounded by the fact that in C, an array of N elements is inalterably indexed from 0 to $N - 1$. It is an incredibly common error to attempt to index an N-element array with N, but this is one spot past the end of the array. This *off-by-one* error is so frequent that some compilers will allocate the Nth spot for you, in effect providing an array of $N + 1$ elements indexed from 0 to N. Although well intentioned, this just hides difficult-to-spot errors, which will appear if the program is moved to another compiler that strictly follows the ANSI C standard.

Figure 7.8 illustrates how arrays are handled in C. Line 6 declares a small array of integers, which is named Num. Because this declaration is surrounded by declarations of other integers, we expect that the memory locations that are assigned to Num are surrounded by the memory locations that are assigned to First, Second, Third, and Fourth. Of course, the method that the compiler uses to determine memory assignments varies from machine to machine.

Lines 13 to 18 print out (in hexadecimal) these memory assignments, and for our machine, the output is shown at the bottom of Figure 7.8. Note that Num[1] is placed four memory locations after Num[0], which reflects the fact that on our machine, an integer consumes four bytes. Indeed, in our machine, Num[i] can be found at memory location f7fffae8 + 4i.[2]

The good news is that it is easy to access an element given the starting point of the array and its index. The memory location of the start of the array is stored in Num (and cannot be changed). Thus Num and &Num[0] are equivalent, and Num can be viewed as a constant pointer. Later in this chapter we examine a commonly used equivalence between arrays and pointers. The bad news is that forgetting an index is meaningful even when it should not be:

```
Num[0]  +  Num  +  Num[2];
```

is legal, even though we forgot [1]. Many compilers will warn you if you do this, but the warning (that you are mixing pointers and nonpointers) can be confusing. More bad news is the fact that the formula for computing &Num[i] makes sense even when i is out of the declared array bounds.

In our case &Num[4] and &Second are the same, meaning that the illegal references to Num[4] go to Second. Thus when Num[4] is printed, at line 21, the value output is the value of Second. When Num[4] is changed to zero at line 23, the value of Second is changed to zero. This can obviously lead to some difficult-to-spot bugs. As an example, on our machine, if the condition at line 11 was

```
i  <  Len  +  2
```

---

[1]Note that such an implementation would incur space overhead. In the most common application (short strings) the overhead could be significant.

[2]Recall from Section 6.2 that this is not an actual memory address, but more likely represents a small negative offset from some fixed memory location.

```
/* 1*/    #include <stdio.h>

/* 2*/    #define Len 3

/* 3*/    main( void )
/* 4*/    {
/* 5*/          int First, Second;
/* 6*/          int Num[ Len ];
/* 7*/          int Third, Fourth;
/* 8*/          int i;

/* 9*/          /* Initialize Array To Zero, Other Variables To Five */
/*10*/          First = Second = Third = Fourth = 5;
/*11*/          for( i = 0; i < Len; i++ )
/*12*/              Num[ i ] = 0;

/*13*/          printf( "Addresses are:\n" );
/*14*/          printf( "&First = %x, &Second = %x\n", &First, &Second );
/*15*/          printf( "&Third = %x, &Fourth = %x\n", &Third, &Fourth );
/*16*/          for( i = 0; i < Len + 2; i++ )
/*17*/              printf( "&Num[%d] = %x\n", i, &Num[ i ] );
/*18*/          printf( "\n" );

                /* Print Array Starting Point */
/*19*/          printf( "Num = %x\n", Num );
/*20*/          /* This Will Usually Print One Of Other Variables */
/*21*/          printf( "Num[%d] = %d\n", Len + 1, Num[ Len + 1 ] );

/*22*/          /* This Will Usually Overwrite One Of Other Variables */
/*23*/          Num[ Len + 1 ] = 0;
/*24*/          printf( "First = %d, Second = %d\n", First, Second );
/*25*/          printf( "Third = %d, Fourth = %d\n", Third, Fourth );
/*26*/    }
```

```
Addresses are:
&First = f7fffafc, &Second = f7fffaf8
&Third = f7fffae4, &Fourth = f7fffae0
&Num[0] = f7fffae8
&Num[1] = f7fffaec
&Num[2] = f7fffaf0
&Num[3] = f7fffaf4
&Num[4] = f7fffaf8

Num = f7fffae8
Num[4] = 5
First = 5, Second = 0
Third = 5, Fourth = 5
```

Figure 7.8:   **Effect of out-of-bounds array indices.**

```
void
Junk( int ArraySize )
{
    int Array[ ArraySize ];  /* Illegal declaration */

    ...
}

main( void )
{
    int HowMany;

    if( scanf( "%d", &HowMany ) == 1 )
        Junk( HowMany );
    ...
}
```

Figure 7.9:   Illegal program: array size must be a constant expression.

and the declarations for i and Second were interchanged, the for loop at line 11 would be infinite, because when i was Len+1, the array assignment at line 12 would reset it to zero.

Close examination of the memory assignments show that on our compiler, Num[3], which is illegal, does not conflict with any of the other variables. Thus we essentially get an extra array spot. But as we have mentioned, this just hides potential bugs. On machines where no extra spot is allocated for the array, you may find that First gets altered instead of Second. On other machines you may find that it is Third or Fourth, or possibly i, or none of the above. It does not really matter: indexing out of bounds is a major error, which is likely to cause difficult-to-spot bugs.

Because an array name is a pointer, it turns out that X[3] can be written as *(X+3). Historically, this equivalence between arrays and pointers has been used to traverse arrays using pointers, resulting in faster programs. Modern optimizing compilers have made many of these techniques unnecessary, but even so the idiom is still widely prevalent in many C programs. In Section 7.10.2 we discuss the use of pointer math and array traversals in more detail.

7.2.2   Array Size Must Be a Constant

 As the title of this section indicates, when an array is declared, its size must be a compile-time computable *integral constant expression*. Thus the declaration in Figure 7.9 is illegal. The ANSI C standard precisely defines a compile-time computable expression. Generally speaking, any constants appearing with normal operators such as addition and multiplication qualify. Even if they are applied to a constant, function calls, and expressions with variables are out. One important technical restriction is that variables declared with the const qualifier, although essentially constants, are still considered variables for the purpose of this rule. Therefore, they cannot be used in the size specification of an array. You have to use #define instead.

```
int Squares[ 5 ] = { 0, 1, 4, 9, 16 };
int Squares[ 5 ] = { 0, 1, 4 };
int Squares[   ] = { 0, 1, 4, 9, 16 };
int Squares[   ];
```

Figure 7.10:   Three forms of array declaration with initialization.

7.2.3   Arrays Cannot Be Copied or Compared

Suppose that A and B are arrays of the same type. In many languages, if they are also the same size, the statement A=B would perform an element-by-element copy of the array B into the array A. In C, this statement is illegal because A and B represent pointers to the start of their respective arrays, specifically, &A[0] and &B[0]. Thus A=B is an attempt to change where A points, rather than copying the contents of array B into array A. What makes the statement illegal rather than legal, but wrong, is that A is a const pointer and cannot be reassigned to. In fact, the only way to copy two arrays is to do it element by element: there is no shorthand.

A similar argument shows that the expression A==B does not evaluate to 1 if and only if each element of A matches the corresponding element of B. Instead, this expression is legal. It evaluates to 1 if and only if A and B represent the same memory location (i.e., they refer to the same array).

7.2.4   Aggregate Initialization and Global Arrays

Like other variables, arrays can be declared with initial values. Figure 7.10 shows three scenarios. In the first declaration, a complete list of initial values is provided. Any expression that can be used to initialize the type T may be used to initialize a component of an array of type T. Thus if the array is static or extern, the initializers must be compile-time computable constants, while if it is automatic, they may be more general expressions.[3]

In the second declaration, only some array elements are initialized to specified values. Specifically, only Squares[0], Squares[1], and Squares[2] have initial values. The other array members are automatically initialized to zero. Thus specifying { 0 } is a simple way to initialize an entire array to zeros.

In the third case, the compiler will presume that the array size is 5, based on the presence of five initial values. If the size of the array is meant to be equal to the number of initializers (i.e., you do not plan to extend past the initial list), it is a good idea to use this form since the computer can count at least as well as you.

The fourth form does not allocate an array. This is because the compiler cannot possibly deduce how large it should be. Thus if it appears as an attempt to declare a local variable, the compiler will complain.

On the other hand, if it appears outside a function, by default it is an extern variable name. Thus it symbolizes that the actual array is declared and allocated (i.e., defined), using one of the first three forms, somewhere else. The typical scenario is similar to the use of extern that we saw in Section 4.4.3. A program that is split into several files, each of

---

[3]Initialization of automatic arrays is new in ANSI C. It is not allowed in older versions of C.

which must share an array, will use a defining declaration in one file and a referencing declaration in other files.

7.2.5   A Precedence Rule

 An important point, which is especially useful in conjunction with scanf, is that expressions such as &Num[i] are legal and are interpreted as &(Num[i]). Thus it follows that the array indexing operator [ ] has a higher precedence than the address-of operator &. Otherwise, the interpretation would be (&Num)[i], which would be illegal. Additionally, array indexing associates from left to right. Therefore, it is equivalent to other postfix operators. Figure 7.29 shows an updated precedence and associativity table.

7.2.6   Index Type Must Be Integral

Not surprisingly, the index of an array must be an integral type. This means int, possibly augmented with short or long. The 8-bit char type is also acceptable. The index does not have to be an unsigned integer, and a negative index is legal, and as we will see in Section 7.10.2, can in some cases make sense. But more often than not, using a negative index is wrong.

7.3   Passing Arrays as Parameters

An array can be used as a parameter to a function, and although the rules follow logically from our previous discussion, it is important to state them explicitly. Remember that the array name is little more than a pointer. Thus suppose that we have a function FunctionCall which accepts one array of int as its parameter. The caller/callee views are

```
FunctionCall( ActualArray );              /* function call */

FunctionCall( int FormalArray[ ] )        /* function declaration */
```

First note that in the function declaration, the brackets only serve as a type declaration, in the same way that int does. In accordance with the call by value conventions of C, the value of ActualArray is copied into FormalArray. Because ActualArray represents the memory location where the entire array ActualArray is stored, FormalArray[i] accesses ActualArray[i]. This means that the variables represented by the indexed array are modifiable. Thus an array, when considered as an aggregate, is passed *by reference*, in the same way that pointers used in Section 6.5 simulate call by reference.

Furthermore, because a new array is not defined, the compiler has no need for a size component. If one is provided to make the code more readable, it is ignored by the compiler and present only for human readers. Because of this, it is impossible to determine the number of elements in an array when it is a formal parameter, even by using the sizeof operator (as we see in Section 7.8). In most cases this means that the array size has to be passed as an additional parameter. It is may be helpful to realize that since `FormalArray` is just a pointer, an equivalent declaration would be

```
FunctionCall( int * FormalArray )        /* function declaration */
```

From this declaration, it is more obvious that the size of the actual array is unknown.

A third important restriction is that arrays cannot be used as return values, since the assignment operator is not defined for them. Thus `int[]` is not a legal return type. Of course, pointers can be returned. As an example of array parameters, we rewrite in Figures 7.11 and 7.12 the duplicate removal program shown in Figure 7.5. The function `GetInts`, declared at line 5, will fill the array `Array` with up to `MaxItems` integers, returning the actual number of integers matched. It is called by `main` at line 28 with `main`'s local array `Num`. `PrintNondup`, declared at line 15, scans the first `N` positions of `Array`, which is presumed sorted, and uses the same algorithm that we have seen before to print nonduplicates.

An interesting feature is that we have passed the array using the type qualifier `const`. Because of this, elements of the array `Array` cannot be easily changed by an assignment operator, or autoincrement or autodecrement. Attempts to do that would cause the compiler to issue an error. This idea is that we can achieve an effect similar to call by value and protect elements of an array parameter from being altered. Unfortunately, it is far from foolproof. As an example, if `Array` is similarly declared to be a `const int` at line 5, our compiler does not complain, because it does not notice the assignment. Even so, if you intend to pass an array but not modify it, you should use the `const` qualifier because every now and then the compiler catches an error for you.

Some programmers like to pass all parameters of basic types, such as `MaxItems` at line 5, as `const`. This officially disallows assignment to a formal parameter. Since the formal parameter is only a copy of the actual argument and thus its changes do not affect the actual argument, and since we generally do not alter it anyway, it is unclear if this is a good idea. In most cases we will not bother using redundant `const`s.

The rules for arrays and functions can thus be summarized as follows:

1. Because the array name is little more than a pointer, array aggregates are passed by reference, and thus the formal array is the actual array. Changes in the actual array are reflected by changes in the formal array.

2. The `const` qualifier can be used to attempt to restrict changes in the formal, and thus the actual array.

3. The number of elements in a formal array is indeterminable. If a number is supplied in the formal array declaration, it is ignored.

4. An array cannot be returned as the value of a function.

7.4 The `typedef` Statement Revisited

The insertion sort routine shown in Figure 7.12 is a straightforward implementation of the algorithm described previously. The new twist is the `typedef` statement at line 2.

```
/* 1*/    #include <stdio.h>
/* 2*/    #define MaxN 10

/* 3*/    /* Read Up To MaxItems Ints; No Attempts At Error Recovery */
/* 4*/    int
/* 5*/    GetInts( int Array[ ], int MaxItems )
/* 6*/    {
/* 7*/        int i = 0;

/* 8*/        printf( "Enter up to %d integers: ", MaxItems );
/* 9*/        while( i < MaxItems && scanf( "%d", &Array[ i ] ) == 1 )
/*10*/            i++;

/*11*/        return i;
/*12*/    }

/*13*/    /* Print Non-Duplicates: Sorted Array Array With N Items */
/*14*/    void
/*15*/    PrintNondup( const int Array[ ], unsigned int N )
/*16*/    {
/*17*/        int i;

/*18*/        printf( "%d", Array[ 0 ] );
/*19*/        for( i = 1; i < N; i++ )
/*20*/            if( Array[ i ] != Array[ i - 1 ] )
/*21*/                printf( " %d", Array[ i ] );
/*22*/        printf( "\n" );
/*23*/    }

/*24*/    main( void )
/*25*/    {
/*26*/        int Num[ MaxN ];
/*27*/        int ItemsRead;

/*28*/        ItemsRead = GetInts( Num, MaxN );
/*29*/        printf( "Processing %d items\n", ItemsRead );
/*30*/        if( ItemsRead > 0 )
/*31*/        {
/*32*/            InsertSort( Num, ItemsRead );
/*33*/            PrintNondup( Num, ItemsRead );
/*34*/        }

/*35*/        return !ItemsRead;
/*36*/    }
```

Figure 7.11: **Using functions to implement duplicate removal.**

The obvious intent is that rather than specify in multiple places the type of element that is being sorted, it is specified only in line 2. For very elementary uses, such as those shown in Section 2.10, the typedef seems redundant because a #define could be used.

```
/* 1*/    /* Insertion Sort: Array A With N Items */

/* 2*/    typedef int ElementType;

/* 3*/    void
/* 4*/    InsertSort( ElementType A[ ], unsigned int N )
/* 5*/    {
/* 6*/        ElementType Tmp;
/* 7*/        int i, j;

/* 8*/        for( i = 1; i < N; i++ )
/* 9*/        {
/*10*/            Tmp = A[ i ];
/*11*/            for( j = i; j > 0 && Tmp < A[ j - 1 ]; j-- )
/*12*/                A[ j ] = A[ j - 1 ];
/*13*/            A[ j ] = Tmp;
/*14*/        }
/*15*/    }
```

Figure 7.12:   Insertion sort.

The `typedef` is not redundant because it records a synonym during compilation rather than performing a textual substitution during the preprocessing stage.

As an example, the routine in Figure 7.13 shows how we can adjust the previous program to avoid altering the input array. We adjust `PrintNondup` to make a call to insertion sort on a *copy* of the array. The main problem we run into is the declaration of the temporary array in `PrintNondup`. The problem is that we must provide a size for it, and we need a constant rather than N.[4] Although `MaxN` could be used for this purpose, we define a new type at line 3 instead. This type, reminiscent of Pascal, declares that an `IntArray` is an array of 10 integers. Note carefully that absolutely no range checking is performed even here. We use `IntArray` at lines 7, 9, and 22. Lines 9 and 22 declare local arrays of 10 integers; the size component of the type is ignored at line 7, just as it is normally done. This kind of use of `typedef` can be helpful if several different-sized array types are present. By using symbolic names, it can be easier to avoid accidentally declaring an inappropriate size for one of them.

 We reiterate the simple rule for the `typedef` syntax: place the word `typedef` first, and then write a normal variable declaration, replacing the variable with the new type name.

7.5   Shellsort: A Simple, but Faster Sorting Algorithm

As we have shown in Figure 7.12, insertion sort is an easily implemented sorting algorithm. Unfortunately, when there are many items to sort, it is inefficient. We can quantify this by measuring the number of times that lines 12 and 13 in Figure 7.12 are executed, because this is exactly the number of times that array items are reassigned values during the course

---

[4]We will see later how to allocate arrays of nonconstant size.

```
/* 1*/    #include <stdio.h>
/* 2*/    #define MaxN 10
/* 3*/    typedef int IntArray[ MaxN ];

/* 4*/    /* Print Non-Duplicates: Array Array With N Items */
/* 5*/    /* Do Not Alter The Array */

/* 6*/    void
/* 7*/    PrintNondup( const IntArray Array, unsigned int N )
/* 8*/    {
/* 9*/        IntArray Tmp; /* A Temporary Array */
/*10*/        int i;

/*11*/        for( i = 0; i < N; i++ ) /* Copy Into Tmp */
/*12*/            Tmp[ i ] = Array[ i ];
/*13*/        InsertSort( Tmp, N ); /* Sort Tmp */

/*14*/        printf( "%d", Tmp[ 0 ] );
/*15*/        for( i = 1; i < N; i++ )
/*16*/            if( Tmp[ i ] != Tmp[ i - 1 ] )
/*17*/                printf( " %d", Tmp[ i ] );
/*18*/        printf( "\n" );
/*19*/    }

/*20*/    main( void )
/*21*/    {
/*22*/        IntArray Num;
/*23*/        int ItemsRead;

/*24*/        ItemsRead = GetInts( Num, MaxN );
/*25*/        printf( "Processing %d items\n", ItemsRead );
/*26*/        if( ItemsRead > 0 )
/*27*/            PrintNondup( Num, ItemsRead );

/*28*/        return !ItemsRead;
/*29*/    }
```

Figure 7.13: **Use of** typedef **to declare local arrays.**

of the algorithm. To do this we look at the state of the array after each iteration of the outer
for loop is complete.

∞   Figure 7.14 shows what happens when the input is presented in reverse order. It
happens that this is the worst thing that can happen. What is clear from the picture is that
there are many changes being made to the array. Specifically, except for the single entry on
the *initial state* line, all the elements have been moved. This accounts for roughly half of the
"boxes" in the figure, which tells us that the number of data movements that are performed
to insertion sort N elements which are initially in reversed order is roughly $N^2/2$. If N is
10,000, we are looking at roughly 50,000,000 data movements.

          Since each data movement is accompanied by some additional computation, such
as comparisons and subtractions, it is reasonable to expect that perhaps 250,000,000 in-

Array Position	0	1	2	3	4	5	6	7
Initial Input:	8	7	6	5	4	3	2	1
Initial state:	8							
First 2 elements sorted:	7	8						
First 3 elements sorted:	6	7	8					
First 4 elements sorted:	5	6	7	8				
First 5 elements sorted:	4	5	6	7	8			
First 6 elements sorted:	3	4	5	6	7	8		
First 7 elements sorted:	2	3	4	5	6	7	8	
First 8 elements sorted:	1	2	3	4	5	6	7	8

Figure 7.14:   Worst-case data moves for insertion sort.

structions will have to be executed. On a 5-MIPS machine, which executes 5,000,000 instructions per second (according to a salesperson), this works out to about 50 seconds. Of course, these are only ballpark estimates, but for instance if we double N, we can expect a fourfold increase in worst-case running time, because there will be roughly four times as many data movements. Although specific constants are always difficult to deal with, the fundamental characteristic of the algorithm is that the running time is basically some constant times N^2, regardless of the speed of the machine or how many instructions are executed per data movement. To give this some mathematical backup, we say that insertion sort is an $O(N^2)$ algorithm. Although the worst case does not always happen, it turns out that a typical case requires half as many data movements as the worst case, so insertion sort runs in $O(N^2)$ time on average.

The first algorithm to improve substantially on insertion sort was *Shellsort*. Shellsort was discovered in 1959 by Donald Shell. Although it is not the fastest algorithm known, it is only two lines longer than insertion sort (one of which is a declaration), thus making it the simplest of the faster algorithms.

Shell's idea was to avoid the large amount of data movement by first comparing elements that were far apart, then elements that were less far apart, until gradually shrinking toward the basic insertion sort. Thus in Figure 7.15, lines 8 to 14 represent a *gap insertion sort*: after the loop is executed, we can be sure that elements separated by a distance of Gap in the array are sorted. For instance, when Gap is 1, the loop is identical, statement by statement, to insertion sort.

It is easy to show several facts. First, as we have shown, if Gap is ever 1, the inner loop is guaranteed to sort the array A. If Gap is never 1, there is always some input for which the array cannot be sorted. Thus Shellsort always sorts as long as we eventually have Gap equal to 1, and at that point we can stop. Shell suggested starting the Gap at N/2, and halving it until it eventually reached 1, after which the program could terminate. This is implemented by the for loop at line 7 of Figure 7.15.

As shown in Figure 7.17, this algorithm represents a substantial improvement over insertion sort, despite the fact that it nests three for loops instead of two, which is usually

```
/* 1*/    void
/* 2*/    Shellsort( ElementType A[ ], const unsigned int N )
/* 3*/    {
/* 4*/        unsigned int Gap;
/* 5*/        ElementType Tmp;
/* 6*/        unsigned int i, j; /* Loop Counters */

/* 7*/        for( Gap = N/2; Gap > 0; Gap /= 2 )
/* 8*/            for( i = Gap; i < N; i++ )
/* 9*/            {
/*10*/                Tmp = A[ i ];
/*11*/                for( j = i; j >= Gap && Tmp < A[ j - Gap ];
                                                        j -= Gap )
/*12*/                    A[ j ] = A[ j - Gap ];

/*13*/                A[ j ] = Tmp;
/*14*/            }
/*15*/    }
```

Figure 7.15:   Simple Shellsort.

```
/* 1*/    void
/* 2*/    Shellsort( ElementType A[ ], const unsigned int N )
/* 3*/    {
/* 4*/        unsigned int Gap;
/* 5*/        ElementType Tmp;
/* 6*/        unsigned int i, j; /* Loop Counters */

/* 7*/        for( Gap = N/2; Gap > 0; Gap = Gap == 2 ? 1 : Gap / 2.2 )
/* 8*/            for( i = Gap; i < N; i++ )
/* 9*/            {
/*10*/                Tmp = A[ i ];
/*11*/                for( j = i; j >= Gap && Tmp < A[ j - Gap ];
                                                        j -= Gap )
/*12*/                    A[ j ] = A[ j - Gap ];

/*13*/                A[ j ] = Tmp;
/*14*/            }
/*15*/    }
```

Figure 7.16:   Improved Shellsort.

bad. By altering the sequence of gaps, one can further improve the algorithm's performance. Figure 7.16 is almost the same as Figure 7.15, except that Gap is divided by 2.2. This typically improves performance by about 25 to 35%, although nobody knows why. The complication at line 7 is necessary because it is a bad idea to have Gap equal to 2. If that happens, Gap/2.2 goes below 1, breaking the algorithm. Thus if Gap is about to be set to 2, we reset it to 1.

The table in Figure 7.17 compares the sorting algorithms. It includes a third set of gaps, described below. Despite the fact that Shellsort is so old, its analysis is very difficult.

N	Insertion Sort	Shellsort		
		Figure 7.15	Odd Gaps Only	Figure 7.16
1000	122	11	11	9
2000	483	26	21	23
4000	1936	61	59	54
8000	7950	153	141	114
16000	32560	358	322	269
32000	131911	869	752	575
64000	520000	2091	1705	1249

Figure 7.17:   Comparison of running time (in milliseconds) for sorting integers.

∞   The results below can give a flavor of the complications. For the program in Figure 7.15, the worst case can be proven to be $O(N^2)$, which happens if N is an exact power of 2, and all of the large elements are in even-indexed array positions, and all of the small elements are in odd-indexed array positions. In fact, when N is an exact power of 2, the average running time can be shown to be $O(N^{3/2})$. This is because when N is a power of 2, each large gap is an exact multiple of the smaller gap that directly follows.

If the program in Figure 7.15 is adjusted so that whenever Gap is even we add one to make it odd, this can never happen. We leave this trivial modification as an exercise for the reader. When that is done, it can be proven that the worst case is $O(N^{3/2})$. The average performance of the algorithm is unknown but seems to be $O(N^{5/4})$ based on simulations.

The program in Figure 7.16 is analytically no different from the program in Figure 7.15. For instance, there are values of N (such as 80,520) that force Gap always to be even until it finally becomes 1, resulting in $O(N^2)$ worst-case running time. Therefore, there is no justifiable reason for it to perform better, but in spite of that, it typically performs very well.

The table in Figure 7.17 compares the performance of insertion sort and Shellsort, with various gap sequences. These results were obtained on a fast machine. The test is clearly biased against the original gap sequence because N is chosen to be 125 times an exact power of 2. Rounding up to an odd number is thus beneficial here, especially as N gets large.

The easily drawn conclusion is that Shellsort, even with the simplest gap sequence provides a significant improvement over insertion sort at a cost of only two lines of code. A slight change to the gap sequence can improve performance further. However, although slight improvements are possible and some of these improvements have theoretical backing, there are no sequences known that markedly improve on the sequence shown in Figure 7.16.

7.6   Multidimensional Arrays

In some cases, arrays need to be accessed based on more than one index. A common example of this is a matrix. Another example would be the storage of a multiplication table or any function of two variables. A multidimensional array is allocated by specifying the range of its indices, and each element of the array is accessed by placing each index in its own pair of brackets. As an example, we implement the basic routines used to represent a tic-tac-toe game. A board is defined in Figure 7.18 as a two-dimensional array; each index ranges from 0 to 2. The declarations in lines 1 to 8 represent an *enumerated type*, which we discuss in the next section. Lines 18 and 26 show how the two-dimensional array is accessed. More examples are shown in Figure 7.19. We will use these routines in Section 11.5.

To see how two-dimensional arrays are implemented, suppose that we declare an array `X[2][3]`, which consists of two rows and three columns. Thus six memory locations are set aside. The compiler will treat this as a single-dimensional array by allocating consecutive portions of memory to represent

`X[0][0], X[0][1], X[0][2], X[1][0], X[1][1], and X[1][2].`

Thus `X[Row][Column]` references position `Row * 3 + Column` relative to the location of `X[0][0]`.

`X[0]` contains the memory location where the first row is stored. In general, `X[i]` contains the memory location where the *i*th row is stored. Consequently, each `X[i]` represents pointer to memory that represents the *i*th row. `X` contains the memory location where the sequence of memory locations `X[i]` are stored. Consequently, `X` represents a pointer to an array of pointers.

Because of this, when passing a multidimensional array as a parameter, in order to be able to compute the mapping, the formal parameter type must include all but the first index size. In the case of a two-dimensional array, this means, as we have seen, that the number of columns is needed; the number of rows is not. When declaring a multidimensional array, all but the first index size must be provided.

Figure 7.20 illustrates six possibilities for two-dimensional arrays. The first declaration provides a complete list of values, which are nicely separated to illustrate each row. Typically, the initialization would span several lines so that the matrix form can be arranged visually. The fourth declaration is equivalent, because two rows have been provided.

As the second declaration shows, the braces are optional. In this case, the array is initialized in the mapped one-dimensional order. When all the initializers are present, the lack of braces does not alter the meaning. The fifth declaration, however, initializes the first two columns of the first row and then the first column of the second row. Other entries are set to zero, just as in the one-dimensional case. If braces were not used, the initialization would be interpreted as three columns of the first row, and the number of rows would be assumed to be 1.

The third declaration, in accordance with our rules, initializes the first row and the second row is set to all zeros. The last declaration is illegal as an automatic variable but can be used to indicate that an `extern` variable of three columns is declared and allocated elsewhere.

One important warning is in order for Pascal programmers who accidentally use the syntax `A[i,j]` instead of `A[i][j]`. If you make the mistake, you may be in for some trouble because the comma operator will essentially make the reference `A[j]`, which, as we have seen, has meaning. In most contexts, you will get an error message.

```
/* 1*/      enum Piece { Human, Computer, Empty  };
/* 2*/      enum Side { You, Me };
/* 3*/      enum Color { X, O };
/* 4*/      enum Score { HumanWin, Draw, ComputerWin, Unclear };

/* 5*/      typedef enum Piece Piece;
/* 6*/      typedef enum Side Side;
/* 7*/      typedef enum Score Score;
/* 8*/      typedef enum Color Color;

/* 9*/      #define Bsize 3              /* 3 By 3 Tic Tac Toe */
/*10*/      typedef Piece BoardType[ Bsize ][ Bsize ];


/*11*/      /* Prototypes For Two Unwritten Routines */
/*12*/      void GetMove( BoardType B, Side S );
/*13*/      int IsWon( BoardType B, Side S );


/*14*/      /* Place Piece P ( Possibly Empty ) */
/*15*/      void
/*16*/      Place( BoardType Board, int Row, int Column, Piece P )
/*17*/      {
/*18*/          Board[ Row ][ Column ] = P;
/*19*/      }

/*20*/      int
/*21*/      IsFull( BoardType Board )
/*22*/      {
/*23*/          int Row, Column;

/*24*/          for( Row = 0; Row < Bsize; Row++ )
/*25*/              for( Column = 0; Column < Bsize; Column++ )
/*26*/                  if( Board[ Row ][ Column ] == Empty )
/*27*/                      return 0;

/*28*/          return 1;
/*29*/      }
```

Figure 7.18:   **Routines for tic-tac-toe, part 1.**

7.7   **Enumerated Types:** enum

In Figure 7.18, lines 1 to 8 show some of the syntax for *enumerated types*. An enumerated type declares a set of symbolic constants. Line 2, for example, declares that variables of type enum Side should have the names You and Me. Internally, You and Me are represented as zero and 1, which is important because it means that these values can index an array or

```
/* 1*/    int
/* 2*/    IsEmpty( BoardType Board, int Row, int Column )
/* 3*/    {
/* 4*/        return Board[ Row ][ Column ] == Empty;
/* 5*/    }

/* 6*/    void
/* 7*/    MakeEmpty( BoardType Board )
/* 8*/    {
/* 9*/        register int Row, Column;

/*10*/        for( Row = 0; Row < Bsize; Row++ )
/*11*/            for( Column = 0; Column < Bsize; Column++ )
/*12*/                Board[ Row ][ Column ] = Empty;
/*13*/    }

/*14*/    void
/*15*/    PrintBoard( BoardType Board )
/*16*/    {
/*17*/        int Row, Column;

/*18*/        printf( "---\n" );
/*19*/        for( Row = 0; Row < Bsize; Row++ )
/*20*/        {
/*21*/            for( Column = 0; Column < Bsize; Column++ )
/*22*/                if( Board[ Row ][ Column ] == Empty )
/*23*/                    printf( " " );
/*24*/                else if( Board[ Row ][ Column ] == Computer )
/*25*/                    printf( CompColor == X ? "X" : "O" );
/*26*/                else
/*27*/                    printf( CompColor != X ? "X" : "O" );
/*28*/            printf( "\n" );
/*29*/        }
/*30*/        printf( "---\n" );
/*31*/    }
```

Figure 7.19:   Routines for tic-tac-toe, part 2.

```
int SumSquares[ 2 ][ 3 ] = { { 0, 1, 4 }, { 1, 2, 5 } };
int SumSquares[ 2 ][ 3 ] = { 0, 1, 4, 1, 2, 5 };
int SumSquares[ 2 ][ 3 ] = { { 0, 1, 4 } };
int SumSquares[   ][ 3 ] = { { 0, 1, 4 }, { 1, 2, 5} };
int SumSquares[   ][ 3 ] = { { 0, 1, }, { 1 } };
int SumSquares[   ][ 3 ];
```

Figure 7.20:   Six forms of two-dimensional array declaration.

be used in a case statement. You can specify a representation:

```
enum Side { You = -1, Me = 1 };
```

uses nondefault values.

Ideally, however, we should not make use of these values. A variable of this enumerated type can be declared by

```
enum Side S;
```

to avoid having to use enum over and over again, we have used the `typedef` facility. In this case line 6 states that `Side` can be used wherever the type enum `Side` was used. Figure 7.19 shows the use of both the enumerated type `Color` and `Piece`.

Since enumerated types are basically just constants, one might wonder if they have any use. The real use of an enumerated type would be checking by the compiler that only `You` and `Me` get assigned to type `Side`, while only `X` and `O` get assigned to type `Color`. If we use `#defines`, we have no guarantee that we might not mix up the `X` and `You` accidentally. Unfortunately, this kind of type checking, although highly desirable, is not required, so many compilers do not do it. Some do, so if your does, you should definitely consider using enumerated types. Because so many compilers do not perform the type checking, the enumerated type is used much less in C than in other languages.

7.8   The `sizeof` **Operator Revisited**

An apparent limitation of arrays is that if the number of elements is determined by an initializer list rather than an explicit declaration, it seems hard to figure out directly how many elements there are. Recall from Section 2.11 that the `sizeof` operator applied to any object tells how many bytes have been allocated for it. Thus by dividing the size of an entire array by the size of one element, we can arrive at the number of elements.

 It is important to realize that this does not apply to formal array parameters. As we have said before, there is no way to know how large such an array is. Figure 7.21 illustrates the `sizeof` operator. The parentheses that surround the object are not necessary but are included because it makes the code easier to read. An alternative form is

```
sizeof( type name );
```

Here the parentheses are required. Figure 7.21 shows that on our machine, an `int` is four bytes.

Three technical points. First, `sizeof` applied to a type name is evaluated at compile time, so its value can be used as a `case` label or to declare an array size. Second, `sizeof` yields an unsigned integer constant of type `size_t`, which is defined in `<stddef.h>`. Third, it has the same precedence and associativity as the other unary operators. We defer rewriting the precedence table until the end of the chapter.

7.9   **Dynamic Allocation of Arrays**

We now look at an interesting equivalence that allows us to allocate arrays, even when their size is not known at compilation time. When we declare an array A, we know that we

```
/* 1*/    #include <stdio.h>

/* 2*/    void
/* 3*/    PrintSize( int A[ ] )
/* 4*/    {
/* 5*/         printf( "Size of formal A[ ] is %u\n", sizeof( A ) );
/* 6*/    }

/* 7*/    main( void )
/* 8*/    {
/* 9*/        int A[ ] = { 1, 2, 3, 4, 5 };

/*10*/        printf( "Size of actual A[ ] is %u\n", sizeof( A ) );
/*11*/        printf( "A has %u elements\n",
                                 sizeof( A )/sizeof( A[ 0 ] ) );
/*12*/        printf( "Ints are %u bytes\n\n", sizeof( int ) );
/*13*/        PrintSize( A );

/*14*/        return 0;
/*15*/    }
```

```
Size of actual A[] is 20
A has 5 elements
Ints are 4 bytes

Size of formal A[] is 4
```

Figure 7.21:   Example of the `sizeof` **operator.**

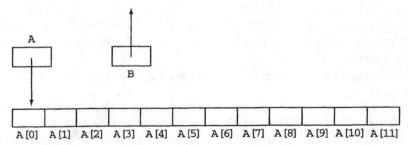

Figure 7.22:   What an array looks like.

obtain variables A[0], A[1], and so on. The actual number of variables that are allocated
is determined at the point of its definition. A stores the location of the array, and thus
as we have already mentioned, and as Figure 7.22 shows, A can be viewed as a pointer.
Recall that A[i] is meaningful as long as i is an integral value, even though it might refer
to something that is not part of the allocated array: the compiler computes, via a simple
formula, the memory location where A[i] ought to be stored.

      This observation has important ramifications, some of which we discuss in the next
section. For now, suppose that A is an array of 12 integers, and we have declared B, of type

`int *`. Initially, B is pointing nowhere. Suppose that we then have B point where A is pointing via the assignment B=A. Since B and A are otherwise indistinguishable, we would expect that A[i] and B[i] are identical. Indeed, this is true!

Thus a pointer can be used wherever an array name is used because an array name really is just a pointer. There are really only two basic differences:

1. A pointer is modifiable, while an array name is not. (However, since an array is converted to a pointer for parameter passing, this restriction does not apply to function parameters:

```
int A[ ];
int * A;
```

are identical parameters to a function.)

2. When defined, arrays get the additional memory allocated. Pointers do not. Thus the situation in Figure 7.22 is representative of the declaration

```
int A[12], *B;
```

In this section we address the second item by showing how C allows us to obtain memory from the system as the program runs. By requesting 12 `int`s worth of memory, and assigning B to point to the start of that block of memory, B can mimic an array.

7.9.1 Dynamic Allocation: `malloc` and `calloc`

The basic routine for dynamically allocating memory is `malloc`. `malloc` takes an unsigned integer HowManyBytes as a parameter and returns a pointer to HowManyBytes bytes of contiguous memory. Although we use `malloc` in the context of arrays, dynamic memory allocation is important in many other contexts. Examples are provided in Sections 10.5 and 11.4.1. A more technical description is given by the prototype in `<stdlib.h>`:

```
void *malloc( size_t HowManyBytes );
```

As we mentioned in Section 7.8, `size_t` is defined in several leader files and is the type returned by the `sizeof` operator. It is some sort of an `unsigned int` (possibly a `long`). Because `malloc` returns `void *`, the location of the allocated memory can be assigned to any typed pointer. If the compiler complains about mismatched pointer types, either it is not an ANSI C compiler, or you have forgotten the `#include` statement required.

By the way, before the generic pointer `void *` was introduced in ANSI C, `malloc` returned a `char *` pointer, which meant that generally a type conversion would be needed. Occasionally, you still see the type conversion, although it is no longer required. Old habits die hard.

Figure 7.23 shows how we can dynamically allocate an array whose size is specified by the user. We set a limit of MaxN, which is a global constant, defined elsewhere. At line 5 we declare the pointer NumArray. After the value of ItemsRead is read, the array is allocated at line 11. The amount of memory requested is exactly equal to the size of one integer times the number of integers we expect to read. Merely asking for ItemsRead bytes is not enough and is a common programming error. We check to make sure that the `malloc` succeeded at line 12.

```
/* 1*/    #include <stdio.h>
/* 2*/    #include <stdlib.h>

/* 3*/    main( void )
/* 4*/    {
/* 5*/        int *NumArray;          /* A Dynamically Allocated Array */
/* 6*/        int ItemsRead = 0;

/* 7*/        printf( "How many items? " );
/* 8*/        scanf( "%d", &ItemsRead );
/* 9*/        if( ItemsRead <= 0 || ItemsRead > MaxN )
/*10*/            Error( "ItemsRead is out of range" );

/*11*/        NumArray = malloc( sizeof( int ) * ItemsRead );
/*12*/        if( NumArray == NULL )
/*13*/            Error( "Out of memory" );

/*14*/        if( GetInts( NumArray, ItemsRead ) != ItemsRead )
/*15*/            Error( "Not enough input" );

/*16*/        PrintNondup( NumArray, ItemsRead );

/*17*/        return !ItemsRead;
/*18*/    }
```

Figure 7.23:   Example of dynamic memory allocation.

A similar routine is `calloc`, which requires two parameters: the size of an object and the number of objects. As you would expect, the amount of allocated memory is exactly equal to the product of these two numbers. Besides the obvious replacement of multiplication with a comma, the difference between `malloc` and `calloc` is that `calloc` initializes allocated memory to zeros, while `malloc` leaves the memory uninitialized.[5] We use `malloc` because we are initializing the memory ourselves and do not want to pay the extra cost of initializing to values that will be overwritten immediately.

7.9.2 Memory Leaks: `free`

Once we allow the user to specify how many elements there are, and thus how large `NumArray` is, we have a second problem. Recall that the routine `PrintNondup` makes a copy of the array so that the copy can be sorted and processed without affecting the original. Using the same strategy, we can implement `TmpArray` dynamically by declaring it as a pointer and having it point at a dynamically allocated chunk of `N` integers. Although this is simple enough to do, there is a problem that is shown in Figure 7.24.

---

[5]`calloc` initializes to all-bits zero, which is guaranteed to be the same as `(int)` 0 or other integer types' 0; however, this equivalence is not guaranteed for non-integer types. Consequently, code that relies on `calloc` initializing an array of pointers or `double`s to all zero is nonportable and should use additional preprocessor conditional compilation statements.

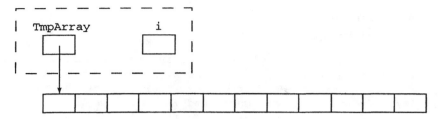

Figure 7.24:   Example of a memory leak.

Local variables disappear when a routine terminates. Thus the memory associated with the local variable i is made available for other purposes after PrintNondup returns. Had TmpArray been a true array, the entire local array would be returned to the system, so that the memory it occupied could be reused. Since TmpArray is just a pointer, the pointer variable is returned to the system, but the dynamically allocated chunk of memory to which it points is not. Thus in Figure 7.24 only the memory cells inside the dashed box are free to be reused, while the dynamically allocated memory, which is now unreferenced, and thus totally useless, can never be recycled.

This loss of usable memory is known as a *memory leak*. If we were to call PrintNondup often enough, we would find that eventually we have used up all the memory that the system has available. Some languages implement *garbage collection*: occasionally, the system looks for dynamically allocated memory which is no longer being referenced. This is a nontrivial chore that could take lots of time. C does not do garbage collection, but instead expects that you explicitly inform the system that it is free to recycle dynamically allocated memory when it is no longer needed.

The routine to do this is free. The only parameter to free is the pointer to memory, which is to be freed for reuse. Figure 7.25 shows the entire PrintNondup routine and how easy it is to use free (at line 23). An easy-to-remember rule to avoid memory leaks is the following: every dynamic allocation should have a corresponding free, although if the free would be the last line of main, it is not really necessary, since when a program terminates, the memory it uses is presumably freed automatically.

Since free is written to accept void *, any pointer suffices, without need for a type conversion. ANSI C specifies that calling free with a NULL pointer is legal and does nothing. Not all compilers handle this case correctly, however. On the other hand, free is easily confused. It wants memory that has been dynamically allocated but has not yet been freed. If you pass a pointer to memory that was never allocated by malloc or one of the other memory allocation functions, or to allocated memory that has been already freed, a great catastrophe is likely to result. Also, you should never dereference a pointer that is pointing at already freed memory.

7.9.3 Array Doubling: realloc

malloc and calloc allow us to allocate arrays dynamically when we do not know their size at compile time. The technique we have used is still a bit restrictive, because we have to know how large the array is before we start reading the data that will go into the array. Sometimes the number of elements in the input is not available until after the input has been read. In this case we need to assume a default size for the array and then enlarge the array whenever it gets full.

```
/* 1*/      #include <stdio.h>
/* 2*/      #include <stdlib.h>

/* 3*/      /* Print Non-Duplicates: Array Has N Items. Since */
/* 4*/      /* We Do Not Know N, TmpArray Is Dynamically Allocated */
/* 5*/      /* However, We Must Now Remember To free The Memory! */
/* 6*/      /* Array Is Left Untouched */

/* 7*/      void
/* 8*/      PrintNondup( const int Array[ ], const unsigned int N )
/* 9*/      {
/*10*/          int *TmpArray;                      /* A Temporary Array */
/*11*/          int i;

/*12*/          TmpArray = malloc( sizeof( int ) * N );
/*13*/          if( TmpArray == NULL )
/*14*/              Error( "No memory for temporary array" );

/*15*/          for( i = 0; i < N; i++ )         /* Copy Into TmpArray */
/*16*/              TmpArray[ i ] = Array[ i ];
/*17*/          Shellsort( TmpArray, N );            /* Sort TmpArray */

/*18*/          printf( "%d", TmpArray[ 0 ] );
/*19*/          for( i = 1; i < N; i++ )
/*20*/              if( TmpArray[ i ] != TmpArray[ i - 1 ] )
/*21*/                  printf( " %d", TmpArray[ i ] );
/*22*/          printf( "\n" );

/*23*/          free( TmpArray );                 /* Must free The Array Now */
/*24*/      }
```

Figure 7.25: Using `free` **to plug a memory leak.**

Suppose that A points to N dynamically allocated ints. We can enlarge A to N+1 dynamically allocated ints by using the following strategy:

```
int *Original = A;
int i;

A = malloc( sizeof( int ) * ( N + 1 ) );
for( i = 0; i < N; i++ )
    A[ i ] = Original[ i ];
free( Original );
```

What we have done is to have Original point at the N ints and then have A point at newly allocated memory for N+1 ints. The N ints are copied over and then the original block of memory is freed. Now A has room for the new element.

A moment's thought will convince you that this is an expensive operation, since we copy N elements from Original to A. Moreover, after the new element is added, we are full again, we would have to repeat this expensive process to add a second new element. Therefore, when we enlarge A we really enlarge it by doubling the size. The cost of performing the realloc, which is proportional to N data copies, is paid by the next N array insertions. This accounting view means that dynamic allocation adds only constant work per insertion.

The function realloc is available to enlarge (or shorten) a dynamically allocated array. The prototype, defined in <stdlib.h>, is

```
void *realloc( void *Original, size_t NewBytes );
```

 realloc expects a pointer to some previously dynamically allocated memory, and an unsigned integer, which, as in malloc, states the number of bytes that the new structure should hold. ANSI C specifies that Original can be NULL, although some nonconforming implementations handle this case incorrectly.

 A pointer to newly allocated memory, or NULL on error, is returned. The newly allocated memory is initialized by using the original memory. You should always use realloc, instead of the malloc and free combination described above, because occasionally realloc can extend the size of memory without changing where it begins, thus avoiding the expensive element-by-element copy.

Figure 7.26 shows how realloc can be used to read integers until the end of input is detected. The routine GetInts needs to pass two items back to the caller: the number of items read, and a pointer to the block of memory where they are. This is achieved by returning the latter, and passing the number of items read by reference, using a pointer.

Thus line 5 of the main routine shows that NumArray is dynamically allocated and initialized by GetInts, and the variable ItemsRead, passed indirectly by reference, is set by GetInts. In GetInts, line 13 dynamically allocates an array of five elements. We continually read integers until the end of input (or a noninteger is detected). If the array is full, lines 21 to 24 double the array size. Note that at line 22, the number of bytes, not just the number of elements, is used as a parameter to realloc; just as with malloc, it is a common error to forget the multiplication.

When the reading is finished, we set *ItemsRead to equal NumRead. Technically speaking, NumRead is unnecessary because we could have used *ItemsRead everywhere. Doing that is a bad idea, however, and in fact will cause an error if you are not careful. In our case we could set

```
*ItemsRead = 0;
```

initially, and change the condition at line 19 to

```
*ItemsRead == ArraySize
```

The left-hand side of line 26 could then change to

```
Array[ (*ItemsRead)++ ]
```

The parentheses are needed, as we will see in the next section. Otherwise, the ++ would be applied to ItemsRead instead of the dereferenced pointer. The compiler would catch this mistake because line 7 says that ItemsRead cannot be modified (only the data it points at can). This example shows that when working with a parameter passed by reference, it is a good idea to use a temporary variable. Line 29 returns the pointer to the dynamically allocated memory, after shrinking it to an exact fit. Shrinking always works, so we do not need to test against NULL.

A common error, shown in Figure 7.27, is to attempt to write GetInts with prototype

```
int GetInts( int *Array )
```

```
/* 1*/    /* Read An Unlimited Number Of Ints */
/* 2*/    /* With No Attempts At Error Recovery */
/* 3*/    /* Correct Implementation */
/* 4*/    /* Returns A Pointer To The Data */
/* 5*/    /* ItemsRead Is Set By Reference To #Items Read */

/* 6*/    int *
/* 7*/    GetInts( int * const ItemsRead )
/* 8*/    {
/* 9*/        int NumRead = 0;
/*10*/        int ArraySize = 5;
/*11*/        int InputVal, *Array;
/*12*/
/*13*/        Array = malloc( sizeof( int ) * ArraySize );
/*14*/        if( Array == NULL )
/*15*/            Error( "Out of memory" );

/*16*/        printf( "Enter any number of integers: " );
/*17*/        while( scanf( "%d", &InputVal ) == 1 )
/*18*/        {
/*19*/            if( NumRead == ArraySize )
/*20*/            { /* Array Doubling Code */
/*21*/                ArraySize *= 2;
/*22*/                Array = realloc( Array,
                                      sizeof( int ) * ArraySize );
/*23*/                if( Array == NULL )
/*24*/                    Error( "Out of memory" );
/*25*/            }
/*26*/            Array[ NumRead++ ] = InputVal;
/*27*/        }

/*28*/        *ItemsRead = NumRead;
/*29*/        return realloc( Array, sizeof( int ) * NumRead );
/*30*/    }

/* 1*/    main( void )
/* 2*/    {
/* 3*/        int *NumArray;
/* 4*/        int ItemsRead;

/* 5*/        NumArray = GetInts( &ItemsRead );
/* 6*/        PrintNondup( NumArray, ItemsRead );
/* 7*/        return !ItemsRead;
/* 8*/    }
```

Figure 7.26:   Correct implementation of memory doubling.

```
/* 1*/     /* Read An Umlimited Number Of Ints */
/* 2*/     /* With No Attempts At Error Recovery */
/* 3*/     /* Returns #Items Read */
/* 4*/     /* Will Fail Because Array Is A Copy Of NumArray And So */
/* 5*/     /* Changes In Where It Points Are Not Seen In NumArray */

/* 6*/     int
/* 7*/     GetIntsWrong( int *Array )
/* 8*/     {
/* 9*/         int NumRead = 0;
/*10*/         int ArraySize = 5;
/*11*/         int InputVal;
/*12*/
/*13*/         Array = malloc( sizeof( int ) * ArraySize );
/*14*/         if( Array == NULL )
/*15*/             Error( "Out of memory" );

/*16*/         printf( "Enter any number of integers: " );
/*17*/         while( scanf( "%d", &InputVal ) == 1 )
/*18*/         {
/*19*/             if( NumRead == ArraySize )
/*20*/             { /* Array Doubling Code */
/*21*/                 ArraySize *= 2;
/*22*/                 Array = realloc( Array,
                                        sizeof( int ) * ArraySize );
/*23*/                 if( Array == NULL )
/*24*/                     Error( "Out of memory" );
/*25*/             }
/*26*/             Array[ NumRead++ ] = InputVal;
/*27*/         }

/*28*/         return NumRead;
/*29*/     }
```

Figure 7.27:   **Incorrect implementation of memory doubling.**

with the intention of filling Array, expanded if necessary, and returning the number of items read. This could work only as long as Array is not repositioned to another part of memory by any of the alloc routines. Figure 7.28 shows what happens when this is not the case.

Array represents a copy of NumArray, so initially it points somewhere. If malloc or realloc is called, Array points to the new memory. But this has no effect on NumArray, which still points where it used to. When GetInts terminates, NumArray still points at its original value, and the newly allocated memory is unreferenced.

The reason this error is so common is that many C programmers think that passing a pointer means that call by value is no longer in effect. Call by value is in effect for the pointer; it is just not in effect for the data being pointed at. The difference is very significant. This explains, for instance, why realloc must return the pointer to the new memory rather than just reflecting this change in the pointer parameter it is passed.

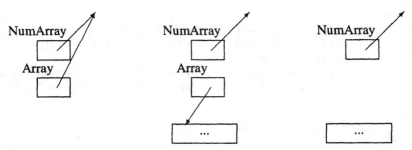

Figure 7.28:   Why previous implementation was incorrect.

One way to achieve call by reference on the actual pointer is to pass a pointer to the pointer. If this seems messy, you are right. Except for the situation we will discuss in Chapter 8 (i.e., arrays of strings), it is a good idea to avoid pointers to pointers until you have lots of experience.

7.10   Pointer Arithmetic

In this section we look at how arithmetic applies to pointers. We have two issues to consider. First, in an expression such as *X+10 or *X++, is the operator (+ or ++) being applied to X or *X? The answer to this question is determined by normal precedence rules. In the first case, 10 is added to *X, while in the second case, the increment is applied to X. The second issue, then, is to decide what it means to increment or apply various operations to a pointer.

7.10.1   Implications of the Precedence of * and []

The dereferencing operator * and the address-of operator &, as we have already mentioned, have the same precedence and associativity as those of the other prefix operators. Because of this, the only arithmetic operator of higher precedence is the postfix autoincrement or autodecrement. Thus, in all of the following expressions, the operator is applied to the dereferenced value:

```
*X + 5          /* Adds 5 to *X */
*X == 0         /* True if *X is 0 */
*X / *Y         /* Divide *X by *Y */
```

The last example divides two dereferenced pointers. It is tricky because the space between the / and * is necessary to avoid interpretation of the comment start token. Notice carefully that because of precedence rules, *X++ is interpreted as *(X++), not (*X)++.

The array access operator [] has the same precedence as the postfix operators. (We will see the two remaining postfix operators in the Chapter 9.) Therefore, if X is a pointer, all of the following operators are applied to the indexed value of X:

```
5 + X[0];       /* Add X[0] and 5 */
0 == X[0]       /* True if X[0] is 0 */
++X[0];         /* Increment X[0] */
X == &X[0]      /* Always true */
```

Category	Examples	Associativity
Primary expression	*identifiers* *constants*	None
Postfix	Function( ) [ ] ++ --	Left to right
Prefix and unary	sizeof * & ! ~ + - ++ --	Right to left
Type cast	(TypeName)	Right to left
Multiplicative	* / %	Left to right
Additive	+ -	Left to right
Shift	<< >>	Left to right
Relational	< <= > >=	Left to right
Equality	== !=	Left to right
Boolean AND	&	Left to right
Boolean XOR	^	Left to right
Boolean OR	|	Left to right
Logical AND	&&	Left to right
Logical Or	||	Left to right
Conditional	? :	Right to left
Assignment	= *= /= %= += -= &= |= ^= <<= >>=	Right to left
Comma	,	Left to right

Figure 7.29:   Precedence and associativity of operators.

X++[0] is interpreted as (X++)[0], which, as we have seen, is the same as *X++. The fourth example is a tautology (i.e., always true) because X always stores the memory location of X[0]. An important technical point that we use in Chapter 8 is that [ ] has higher precedence than *. Figure 7.29 shows an up-to-date precedence table.

7.10.2   What Pointer Math Means

Suppose that X and Y are pointer variables. Now that we have decided on precedence rules, we need to know what the interpretation is for arithmetic performed on pointers. For instance, what does it mean to multiply X by 2? The answer in most cases is that arithmetic on pointers would be totally meaningless and is therefore illegal.

Looking at the various operators, we see that none of the multiplicative operators make sense. Therefore, a pointer may not be involved in a multiplication. Note carefully that the dereferenced value can, of course, be multiplied, and that what we are restricting is computations involving addresses.

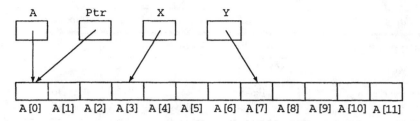

Figure 7.30:   Pointer arithmetic: `X = &A[3]; Y = X + 4.`

Equality and logical operators all make sense for pointers, so they are also allowed and have obvious meanings. Assignment by = is allowed of course, but `*=`, `/=`, and `%=` are obviously disallowed. Therefore, the questionable operators are the additive operators (including `+=`, `-=`, `++`, `--`), and the relational operators (`<=`, `>=`, `<`, and `>`). To make sense, all these operators need to be viewed in the context of an array.

Figure 7.30 shows an array `A` of `ElementType`, a pointer `Ptr` to `ElementType`, and the assignment `Ptr=A`. The picture reinforces the idea that the value stored in `A` is just the memory location where the zeroth element of the array is stored and that elements of an array are guaranteed to be stored in consecutive and increasing memory locations. If the array `A` is an array of characters, `A[1]` is stored in memory location `A+1`, because characters use one byte. Thus the expression `++Ptr` would increase `Ptr` by one, which would be equal to the memory location of `A[1]`.

We see from this example that adding a constant to a pointer variable can make sense in an array of characters. If `A` was an array of four-byte integers, adding one to `Ptr` would make only partial sense under our current interpretation. This is because `Ptr` would not really be pointing at an integer, but somewhere in the middle, and as we have seen before, it would be misaligned. Since that interpretation would give erroneous results, C uses the following interpretation: `++Ptr` adds the size of the pointed at object to the address stored in `Ptr`.

This carries over to other pointer operations. The statement `X=&A[3]` will make `X` point at `A[3]`. Parentheses are not needed, as we have already seen several times. The statement `Y=X+4` will have `Y` point at `A[7]`. In Chapter 8, we will see why pointers can be useful for traversing through arrays.

Because pointers and array names represent addresses, `A[3]` and `X[0]` are identical. So are `A[0]` and `X[-3]`! A consequence of this is a very technical rule. For the most part we view pointers as plain integers. However, some machines place additional hardware restrictions on pointers, attempting to provide checks against runaway pointers. All of the following are out-of-range array accesses: `A[12]`, `A[13]`, and `A[-1]`. Therefore, all cause undefined behavior and should never occur in a "correct program."

The technical rule concerns the corresponding pointers `A+12`, `A+13`, and `A-1` that point at those undefined memory locations on the fringe of the array. Strictly speaking, only the first pointer is guaranteed to be a legal pointer. This is because ANSI C specifies that a pointer may point to one past the end of an array (but may not be dereferenced). In Section 8.8 we will see why this is allowed. However, a pointer may not point to the memory just before the start of the array, or more than one past the end of the array. There are some machines whose hardware may generate a run-time error if you attempt to generate such a pointer, even if it is never dereferenced.

```
/* 1*/    #include <stdio.h>
/* 2*/    #define MaxN 10

/* 3*/    /* Read Up To MaxItems Ints; No Attempts At Error Recovery */
/* 4*/    int
/* 5*/    GetInts( int *Array, int MaxItems )
/* 6*/    {
/* 7*/        int i = 0;

/* 8*/        printf( "Enter up to %d integers: ", MaxItems );
/* 9*/        while( i < MaxItems && scanf( "%d", Array++ ) == 1 )
/*10*/            i++;

/*11*/        return i;
/*12*/    }
```

Figure 7.31:   Pointer implementation of GetInts.

Thus in Figure 7.30, Y=X-3 would be legal but Y=X-4 would not. Y=X+9 would be legal (pointing one after the end of an array), but neither would a subsequent *Y or a subsequent ++Y. Even if your machine has no such checking (and most do not), a strictly conforming ANSI C program should not attempt these assignments.

Although it makes sense to add or subtract an integer type from a pointer type, it does not make sense to add two pointers. It does, however, make sense to subtract two pointers: Y-X evaluates to 4. Thus pointers can be subtracted but not added. The average of two pointers X and Y is obtained by X+(Y-X)/2. This works because Y-X evaluates to an integer, and then an integer is added to X.

Given two pointers X and Y, X<Y is true if the object X is pointing at is at a lower address than the object Y is pointing at. Assuming that neither is pointing at NULL, this expression is almost always meaningless unless both are pointing at elements in the same array. In that case, X<Y is true if X is pointing at a lower-indexed element than Y, because as we have seen, the elements of an array are guaranteed to be stored in increasing and contiguous parts of memory. This is the only legitimate use of the relational operator on pointers, and all other uses should be avoided. Figure 7.31 rewrites GetInts from Figure 7.11 to use pointers. In Section 8.8 we discuss the use of pointers for array traversal in more detail.

7.11   Recurring Case Study: Part 3

In this section we extend the program (fragment) in Section 4.7 to read up to 1000 geometric objects and then output them in groups. First the circles are printed, then the rectangles, and then the squares. We use two arrays to store the objects that are read. One array stores the type of shapes encountered, and a second array stores their area. An obvious limitation, especially for rectangles, is that we do not keep track of the dimensions. In Section 9.9 we will.

The entire program is a straightforward exercise in using arrays. We still use the code from Figure 4.19. Figure 7.32 is a short routine to print out the shape name given its

```
/* 1*/    void
/* 2*/    PrintShapeName( int i )
/* 3*/    {
/* 4*/        if( i == Circle )
/* 5*/            printf( "circle" );
/* 6*/        else if( i == Rectangle )
/* 7*/            printf( "rectangle" );
/* 8*/        else if( i == Square )
/* 9*/            printf( "square" );
/*10*/        else
/*11*/            printf( "unrecognized shape" );
/*12*/    }
```

Figure 7.32: `PrintShapeName` **from case study.**

```
/* 1*/    #define MaxShapes 1000

/* 2*/    void
/* 3*/    OutputShapes( const double ShapeType[ ],
/* 4*/                        const double Areas[ ], double HowMany )
/* 5*/    {
/* 6*/        int i, j;

/* 7*/        printf( "\n" );
/* 8*/        for( i = Circle; i <= Square; i++ )
/* 9*/        {
/*10*/            for( j = 0; j < HowMany; j++ )
/*11*/                if( ShapeType[ j ] == i )
/*12*/                {
/*13*/                    PrintShapeName( i );
/*14*/                    printf( " area %.2f\n", Areas[ j ] );
/*15*/                }
/*16*/        }
/*17*/    }
```

Figure 7.33: **Routine to output shapes in groups.**

type. Figure 7.33 prints the shape types and areas for each object, and ensures that circles precede rectangles which in turn precede squares. The main routine shown in Figure 7.34 completes the implementation.

7.12 Summary

In this chapter we have begun looking at arrays, which are used to represent a collection of similar variables. We have examined the strong connection between arrays and pointers. In the next chapter we continue this discussion by examining strings.

```
/* 1*/   main( void )
/* 2*/   {
/* 3*/       int i, j, ShapesRead, Choice;
/* 4*/       double Areas[ MaxShapes ];
/* 5*/       double ShapeType[ MaxShapes ];

/* 6*/       for( i = 0; i < MaxShapes; i++ )
/* 7*/       {
/* 8*/           printf( "Enter %d for circle, ", Circle );
/* 9*/           printf( "Enter %d for rectangle, ", Rectangle );
/*10*/           printf( "Enter %d for square: ", Square );

/*11*/           if( scanf( "%d", &Choice ) != 1 )
/*12*/               break;

/*13*/           if( Choice == Circle )
/*14*/               Areas[ i ] = ReadCircle( );
/*15*/           else if( Choice == Square )
/*16*/               Areas[ i ] = ReadSquare( );
/*17*/           else if( Choice == Rectangle )
/*18*/               Areas[ i ] = ReadRectangle( );
/*19*/           else        /* Illegal Choice */
/*20*/               break;

/*21*/           ShapeType[ i ] = Choice;
/*22*/       }

/*23*/       OutputShapes( ShapeType, Areas, i );

/*24*/       return 0;
/*25*/   }
```

Figure 7.34: Revised main procedure for outputting shapes in groups.

7.12.1 What Was Covered

- To declare an array, we need to provide a name, the base type, and if the array is not already existing, either a direct or an indirect idea of how large it is.

- When an array is created, the collection of variables can be accessed by indexing the array with a number from zero up to *but not including* the number of elements in the array.

- In C, an array is just a pointer that represents the main memory location where the elements of the array are stored. A compile-time constant amount of memory can be set aside.

- C does not provide range checking on array indexes. If you use an inappropriate index, you'll access some other part of memory, and you could be colliding with another object.

- The size of an array must be a constant, and only integral expressions can be used as an index.

- Arrays cannot be copied using the assignment operator. Instead, they must be copied element by element.

- Arrays can be initialized when they are allocated by specifying a (possibly partial) list of values, surrounded by braces.

- Array aggregates are passed *by reference* in C. They cannot be returned.

- Insertion sort is a slow algorithm for large amounts of data. It takes $O(N^2)$ time on average. Shellsort is much faster.

- Multidimensional arrays are implemented by an internal mapping to single-dimensional arrays. The compiler must always know the range of all the indices, except possibly the first.

- The `sizeof` operator can be used to find out how many bytes a data type or specific object uses. A `char` always uses one byte, by definition.

- `malloc` and `calloc` are the basic memory allocation routines. Each returns a pointer to a specified amount of newly found memory, or `NULL` if none is available.

- Dynamically allocated memory that is no longer needed can be recycled by `free`.

- Memory can be extended or shrunk by calling `realloc`. Expand by doubling the current size.

- Array access has highest priority. Dereferencing has higher priority than all but the postfix operators.

- Pointers may be compared, assigned, and subtracted. None of the multiplicative operators are valid, and two pointers may not be added. An integer I may be added or subtracted from a pointer, which advances (or retracts) it by I objects (of the type being pointed at).

- Using pointers to traverse an array can be faster than using an index on some machines (but do Exercise 17 to find out about yours). In Chapter 8 we will see examples of where its use might be justified.

7.12.2 Friendly Reminders

- No range checking is ever performed for array indices.

- Remember that for an array of N elements, N should not be used to index the array, because it is out of bounds. Some compilers will cut you some slack, but they should not; this can cause problems when you move the program to another machine.

- Because the name of an array represents a memory location, forgetting to index it may not be detected by the compiler. As a direct consequence, if A and B are arrays, A==B does not compare the contents of the two arrays.

- A function that is receiving an array cannot determine its size, even by using `sizeof`.

- Using `const` to try to make an array parameter unalterable is not foolproof, so do not assume that it is.

- Use braces to indicate each dimension when initializing a multidimensional array.

- The declaration

  ```
  int A[ 100 ][ 100 ][ 100 ];
  ```

  allocates a million integers. Multidimensional arrays are very good at eating up all of your memory. Be careful about how large you make them.

- The Pascal syntax `A[i,j]` is wrong for C. The compiler might not even warn you because the comma operator will be applied, creating a single index which could be meaningful.

- The parameter to `malloc` is the number of bytes requested. Thus, when dynamically allocating an array, you must multiply the basic element size by the number of elements to get `malloc`'s parameter. Using the number of elements usually will not allocate sufficient memory. The same comment applies to `realloc`.

- Memory provided by `malloc` is uninitialized. `calloc` does initialize memory to all bits zero.

- `free` wants a pointer to dynamically allocated memory, which has not yet been recycled. If you pass a pointer (besides `NULL`) that does not satisfy this requirement, chaos results. It is legal to pass a `NULL` pointer to `free`, but some compilers do not behave correctly when that happens.

- Do not dereference a pointer `Ptr` after `free(Ptr)`, until `Ptr` points at some other memory. After the `free`, `*Ptr` is undefined.

- Although ANSI C specifies that `Original` (which represents a pointer to memory being expanded) may be `NULL` when calling `realloc`, not all implementations behave correctly.

- `realloc` returns a pointer to the new array. Do not forget to use this return value: expecting an update of the formal parameter is wrong, because of call by value.

- Although pointers can be used to achieve call by reference, remember that the value of a formal pointer parameter cannot be changed. It is only the dereferenced pointer (i.e., the value of what is being pointed at) that can change. This restates the previous warning.

- Do not use the relational operators on pointers unless they are pointing to parts of the same array.

- You should never need to use `malloc` when you declare a pointer to traverse an already existing array.

EXERCISES

1. The *Sieve of Eratosthenes* is a method used to determine all primes less than a given number N. It is very fast. Initially, we write down all the integers from 2 to N. Begin P at 2. Cross out all multiples of P starting with 2*P; this is easily done by crossing out every Pth entry. Then increment P to the next non-crossed-out integer. Again, cross out all multiples of P. Repeat these steps until P is greater than the square root of N. The numbers that have not been crossed out represent all of the prime numbers smaller than or equal to N. Write a program that implements the sieve for N = 100,000.

2. *Goldbach's conjecture* states that every even number greater than 2 can be represented as a sum of two primes. Using the Sieve of Eratosthenes, write a program that accepts any even integer N less than 100,000 and prints two prime numbers that verify the conjecture.

3. Redo Exercise 3.13 by precomputing all values of X^5 and storing them in an array. Make the algorithm more efficient by using the following observation: *For each tuple (A, B, C, D, E), we only need to check that there exists some F that is in the array. Thus we can scan the array sequentially and terminate the search (unsuccessfully) if $F^5 > A^5 + B^5 + C^5 + D^5 + E^5$. Moreover, the last tuple processed (with one exception) was $(A, B, C, D, E-1)$. Therefore, we can begin the current search for F starting with one less than the point where F terminated in the previous search.*

4. A polynomial such as $3x^2 + 5x + 2$ of small degree can be represented by storing the coefficients in an array. For instance, the array `PolyArray` would have

   ```
   PolyArray[2]  =  3,
   PolyArray[1]  =  5,
   PolyArray[0]  =  2,
   ```

   and all other entries zero. Define the new type `Polynomial`, with `MaxDegree` equal to 100:

   ```
   typedef double Polynomial[ MaxDegree ];
   ```

   Write the following functions:

   ```
   void Add( Polynomial Left, Polynomial Right,
                                   Polynomial Sum );
   void Sub( Polynomial Left, Polynomial Right,
                                   Polynomial Diff );
   void Mult( Polynomial Left, Polynomial Right,
                                   Polynomial Prod );
   void Print( Polynomial Left );
   void GetPoly( Polynomial Left );
   ```

   Be sure to handle overflow for `Mult` correctly.

5. Assuming that enough memory is available, how long do you think it would take to insertion sort 1,000,000 elements? How long would the various Shellsort algorithms take?

6. Verify the data in Figure 7.17 by implementing all the sorting methods, including the adjustment to avoid even gaps in Shellsort.

7. A slightly better increment sequence is given by using gaps that are either of the following types:
   $$9 * 4^i - 9 * 2^i + 1 \quad \text{or} \quad 4^i - 3 * 2^i + 1.$$

   The first type includes 1, 19, 109, 505, while the second type includes 5, 41, 209. Thus the last few gaps are 505, 209, 109, 41, 19, 5, 1. Modify the Shellsort routine to use these gaps, by storing, in an array `GapArray`, a sorted list of all gaps up to 100,000,000, and then appropriately indexing the array to find each successive gap.

8. Write routines to perform matrix addition and multiplication. This exercise requires only basic knowledge of linear algebra.

9. Write the function `Reverse`, whose prototype is shown below, that reverses the items in array A.

   ```
   void Reverse( int *A, unsigned int N );
   ```

10. What do you expect, and what does your system actually do when the call to

```
New = realloc( void *Original, size_t NewBytes );
```

occurs with:

(a) `Original` equal to NULL?

(b) `NewBytes` equal to zero?

11. Write the function `DoubleArray` to implement the array doubling strategy shown in Section 7.9.3. Write a companion function for integer arrays. The prototypes are

```
void *DoubleVoid( void *Original, size_t OldBytes );
int  *DoubleInt(  int *Original, size_t OldSize );
```

12. In an array A of N items, the majority element, if one exists, is an element that appears at least $\lfloor N/2 \rfloor + 1$ times. For integers, a prototype would be

```
int Majority( const int A[ ], unsigned int N );
```

If a majority element exists, `Majority` returns any index i such that A[i] is the majority element. Otherwise, −1 is returned.

(a) One solution is to sort a copy of A and then perform a sequential scan. Write a program that implements this method.

(b) Can you think of a significantly faster way to solve the problem?

13. Write a program that prompts the user for a sequence $A_1, A_2, \ldots, A_N$ of numbers and finds a contiguous subsequence of maximum sum. For example, the contiguous subsequence of maximum sum for the following input is shown in boldface type.

$$-2 \quad \mathbf{5} \quad \mathbf{-4} \quad \mathbf{3} \quad \mathbf{8} \quad -1 \quad -5 \quad 2 \quad -4 \quad 6$$

How does the running time of your program vary with N? *There are several solutions to this problem, with drastically different running times. The best algorithm takes only $O(N)$ time.*

14. Extend the previous program to find a subrectangle in a two-dimensional array of maximum sum.

15. Write the routine `Peek`, with prototype provided below, to output the value stored in the `Bytes` bytes beginning at memory location `Address`.

```
void Peek( const void *Address, unsigned int Bytes );
```

16. Using preprocessor macros, write a set of routines to support bit arrays. Provide

```
Allocate( M, HowMany ) /* Have M point to HowMany Bits */
ClearAll( M )          /* Set All Bits to 0 */
SetBit( M, i )         /* Set Bit i to 1 */
OffBit( M, i )         /* Set Bit i to 0 */
IsTrue( M, i )         /* Return Bit i */
```

17. Write the procedures

```
int Max1( const int A[ ], unsigned int N );
int Max2( const int *A  , unsigned int N );
```

which return the maximum element in an array of integers. `Max1` uses a loop with an `int` counter, while `Max2` does a pointer traversal, as in Figure 7.31. Run for large N on identical inputs and with the compiler's highest optimization setting enabled. Which method is faster?

8

Characters and Strings

Although computers were originally used to perform mathematical and engineering calculations, bookkeeping and word-processing applications are probably much more prevalent currently. These applications require dealing with words rather than numbers. The character is the fundamental data type used for this purpose. In this chapter we will see how characters are handled in C and how they are combined to form easily manipulated *strings*.

8.1 The `char` Type

A variable of type `char` can be used to store a single character. We have already seen most of the allowed characters. Besides the 26 lowercase and 26 uppercase characters, we have 10 digits, the blank space, and an additional group of "printable" characters such as:

`!  "  #  $  %  &  '  (  )  *  +  ,  -  .  /  :  ;  <  =  >  ?  @  [  \  ]  ^  _  {  |  }  ~`

for a total of roughly 94 printable characters (the actual group of printing characters is implementation specific). We also have some "unprintable," or at the very least, hard-to-spot characters, such as *tab*, *alert* (bell), *newline*, and *formfeed*, among others.

8.2 A `char` Is a Small Integer

Internally, each of these characters is represented by a small binary number; the entire mapping is known as the *character set*. To represent roughly 100 numbers, a 7-bit binary number is needed. This will provide room for $2^7 = 128$ different characters. In C, a `char` is used for this purpose. It defines a *byte*, which is the quantum storage unit and is almost always an 8-bit quantity. The eighth bit can be used for one of two purposes.

One possibility is to extend the character set to include fancy symbols, such as musical notes. This is popular among personal computers. Another alternative is to use it as a check, in which case the eighth bit represents the *parity bit*. One possibility is *even parity*: the parity bit is chosen so that an even number of bits (including the parity bit) are 1s. In this

```
/* 1*/    #include <stdio.h>

/* 2*/    main( void )
/* 3*/    {
/* 4*/        char Ch;

/* 5*/        while( scanf( "%c", &Ch ) != EOF )
/* 6*/            printf( "Read a *%c*, internal number %d\n", Ch, Ch );

/* 7*/        return 0;
/* 8*/    }
```

```
Read a *A*, internal number 65
Read a *b*, internal number 98
Read a *c*, internal number 99
Read a * *, internal number 32
Read a *d*, internal number 100
Read a *e*, internal number 101
Read a *f*, internal number 102
Read a *
*, internal number 10
```

Figure 8.1:   **Program to show internal representation of** char.

case, a one-bit error can be detected. This is useful when bit errors occur as isolated events, as is the case with storage on magnetic tapes. Noisy phone lines and cables introduce "bursts" of errors, in which case the simple parity bit has limited usefulness. Thus many machines do not make use of the parity bit.

The most popular representation scheme, at least for C programs, is the ASCII character set. The ASCII character set is shown in Appendix B. But other representations are allowable, such as EBCDIC, which is popular among IBM mainframes. Because most C programs have been developed on ASCII character set machines with no parity (i.e., the eighth bit is always 0), some unfortunate coding practices have developed, which break when parity bits or other character sets are allowed. We will discuss this as appropriate.

Figure 8.1 will read from the terminal until the end-of-file marker, printing out each character and its internal representation. The output corresponds to Abc def, followed by a *newline* and end of file. The %c conversion is used to read characters, but as we see later, there are faster ways. We have surrounded the output character by two asterisks, so that blanks and newlines are more obvious.

8.2.1   Character Constants

Most character constants can be represented by enclosing them in single quotes. Thus

char Ch = 'a';

declares Ch and assigns it an initial value that represents the letter a. The quotes are clearly necessary, since otherwise the compiler will look for a variable named a. Unfortunately, this mechanism does not work for all the printable characters and is very ugly for the nonprintable characters.

Special Printable Constants

If we scan our list of printable constants, we can see that a few will be problematic. First, a single quote would be represented as ' ' ', which turns out to be very confusing to the compiler. To express this, an *escape sequence* is used. Escape sequences always begin

with the backslash character; in our case ' \ ' ' represents the single-quote character. It is a common error to use a / instead of a \. Sometimes the compiler will catch this for you.

Also, although ' " ' is legal and not confusing to the compiler, ' \ " ' can also be used to represent the double-quote characters. This escape sequence for double quotes is important when using string constants.

By solving one problem we have created another: How does one represent the *backslash*? Not surprisingly, its escape sequence is \\.

It is important to realize that escape sequences are only recognized at compile time

by the compiler inside a (single)-quoted character constant or a (double)-quoted string constant. For example,

```
printf( "%c%c", '\\', '\\' );
```

prints out a backslash, followed by another backslash; the resulting sequence of two backslashes is not an escape sequence.

Special Unprintable Constants

Since *unprintable* characters are, by definition, hard to print, special escape sequences are provided for them also. We have already seen the *newline* escape sequence \n. Two other important nonprintable characters represent the alert symbol (i.e., bell) and the tab symbol. They are \a and \t, respectively. It is bad practice to type either of these symbols in directly from the keyboard using a *control-g* or *tab* key because the direct form does not print and thus is not seen by a reader of your program.

Another special character is the *null character*, \0, which is used for strings. The null character is always represented internally as a zero. This is a special case of using any one-, two-, or three-digit octal number, or a one- or two-digit hexadecimal number (which must be preceded by a lowercase x) as escape sequences. For example, as we saw in Figure 8.1, in ASCII, a newline character is represented by a decimal 10, which is 012 in octal, or 0a in hexadecimal. All of the following escape sequences would work for the newline, although only the first is guaranteed on all character sets: \n, \12, \012, \xa, and \x0a.

Forgetting the x in a hex conversion is certain to produce unexpected results. In our example, \a will ring the bell and \0a will produce a warning message. The table in Figure 8.2 summarizes the escape codes.

8.2.2   `char` **Arithmetic and Type Conversions**

If Ch is a char, Ch+1 is the next character in the machine's character set. In ASCII, the lowercase letters are assigned consecutive integers, as are the uppercase letters and the digits. Thus for an ASCII machine that does not use a parity bit, the expression

```
Ch - 'a' + 1
```

maps a lowercase a to 1 and a lowercase z to 26. On this machine

a	alert (bell)
b	backspace
f	form feed
n	newline
r	carriage return
t	horizontal tab
v	vertical tab
\	backslash
'	single quote
"	double quote
?	question mark

Figure 8.2:   Escape sequences.

```
int
IsLower( char C )
{
    return C >= 'a' && C <= 'z';
}
```

Figure 8.3:   Nonportable implementation of `IsLower`.

```
Ch >= 'a' && Ch <= 'z'
```

evaluates to true exactly when Ch is a lowercase letter. Because this code does not work if
the character set changes, it is a bad idea to use it. The routines in the next section have been
designed exactly for this purpose and are guaranteed to work regardless of the character set.

　　　The type conversion rules for `char` are the same as for `short`: a `char` can be
assigned to any `int`, but going the other way, though defined, is dangerous if the `int`
represents a number that is too large for a `char`. Moreover, by default, it is unspecified
whether a `char` is considered a `signed` or an `unsigned` quantity.

8.3   Special Character Routines and `ctype.h`

As we mentioned above, on many machines the routine in Figure 8.3 can be used to test
if C is a lowercase character. However, since this test is character-set dependent, ANSI C
specifies that a collection of routines must be provided with the compiler to perform these
types of tests.

 　　　Figure 8.4 shows the routines that are guaranteed to be available, and when they return
true. Note that true is guaranteed to be nonzero and is generally not 1. The last column

Macro	*Evaluates nonzero if:*	*Symbolic Representation*
isprint(Ch)	Ch is one of the printables	P = implementation dependent[1]
isupper(Ch)	Ch is an uppercase letter	U = [A-Z]
islower(Ch)	Ch is a lowercase letter	L = [a-z]
isalpha(Ch)	Ch is a letter	$A = U \cup L$
isdigit(Ch)	Ch is a digit	D = [0-9]
isxdigit(Ch)	Ch is a hexadecimal digit	X = [0-9a-fA-F]
isspace(Ch)	Ch is a spacing character	S = [\t\n\b\v\r]
isalnum(Ch)	Ch is a letter or a digit	$AN = A \cup D$
ispunct(Ch)	Ch is a punctuation character	$PN = P - AN - [\ ]$
isgraph(Ch)	Ch is printable, but not a space	$G = P - [\ ]$
iscntrl(Ch)	Ch is a control character	$C = \overline{P}$

Figure 8.4:   Character testing functions in <ctype.h>.

attempts to give a symbolic meaning to the groups. For the most part it is obvious what these routines test for.[2]

An efficient and machine-independent way to implement a test such as isupper would be to store an array, indexed from 0 to 255. We could precompute the value of this array and store ones in the array positions corresponding to the values 'A', 'B', ..., 'Z', and zeros elsewhere. Then the test is a simple array access (slightly modified if a char is signed). This is almost exactly how these routines work. Since each attribute is represented by a bit, bit operators are used to pack eight attributes into a char. Figure 8.5 shows a typical implementation of this strategy. Note that the array _ctype_, which is defined (i.e., initialized) elsewhere, is offset by one to allow the case where Ch is EOF. On many systems, EOF is -1.

Some implementations provide the routine isascii(Ch), which returns true if Ch is in the character set. This could be important because all of these routines can work with ints, and thus you can tell if a type conversion would be successful. Figure 8.6 shows a simple program that prints out the various characteristics of each char, along with its decimal, octal, and hexadecimal representation. We also make extensive use of the escape sequences.

The routine PrintBool prints either a single T or F (with five leading spaces), depending on whether or not Val is nonzero. Testing if Val is 1 does not work because these routines do not always return 1 for true. They do always return nonzero for true and zero for false. The main loop is a do while loop instead of the most customary for loop. The for loop cannot be used because the test in

---

[1]For implementations that use a seven-bit ASCII character set, P represents the 95 characters between '\0x20' (space) and '\0x7e' (tilde).

[2]We show the return values for the default locales. See Section D.6 for further details.

```
#define    _U       01           /* Upper Case */
#define    _L       02           /* Lower Case */
#define    _N       04           /* Digit */
#define    _S       010          /* White Space */
#define    _P       020          /* Punctuation */
#define    _C       040          /* Control Character */
#define    _X       0100         /* Hexadecimal Digit */
#define    _B       0200         /* Blank Space */

extern     char     _ctype_[];

                /* Some routines */
#define    isprint(Ch)   ( (_ctype_+1)[Ch] & (_P|_U|_L|_N|_B) )
#define    isupper(Ch)   ( (_ctype_+1)[Ch] & _U )
#define    islower(Ch)   ( (_ctype_+1)[Ch] & _L )
#define    isalpha(Ch)   ( (_ctype_+1)[Ch] & (_U|_L) )
#define    isdigit(Ch)   ( (_ctype_+1)[Ch] & _N )
```

Figure 8.5: **Implementation of some** `<ctype.h>` **routines.**

```
for( Ch = 0; Ch < 128; Ch++ )
```

is always true if an unsigned character ranges from -128 to 127. The alternatives are to test against 127 at the bottom of the loop as we have done, or declare `Ch` to be an `int` and allow the automatic type conversions to do the rest.

To access these character routines, you generally must `#include` the standard header `<ctype.h>`, as we have done on line 2. As Figure 8.5 shows, these routines are not functions but instead are preprocessor macros that reside entirely in the include file. We mention this for three reasons. First, an advantage of using a macro is that it is faster because it avoids the overhead of a function call. The overhead is usually insignificant, but since in our case these tests can be performed in one statement, the function call would take more time than the actual test. In some applications, the difference in running time might be noticeable. Some compilers also provide true functions that are used if you do not include `<ctype.h>`. On other machines, you may just find that you have an undefined routine. Second, an occasionally important technical point is that because these routines are not functions, you cannot pass them to a routine that expects a function. Third, because these routines are implemented by an array access and are not really functions, passing a large positive or negative number will index the array out of bounds, and can produce bizarre results or even a program crash.

ANSI C also specifies that two other functions must be provided: `toupper` and `tolower`. `toupper(Ch)` returns the upper case version of `Ch` if `Ch` is a lowercase character. If `Ch` is not a lowercase character, `toupper` returns `Ch`. `tolower(Ch)` performs the similar function of returning a lowercase equivalent, if this makes sense. In both cases, `Ch` is untouched. On ANSI C compilers, both `toupper` and `tolower` are generally implemented as functions because the error checks require two accesses of `Ch`. As we saw in Section 5.3, two accesses would make a macro unsafe if `Ch` is involved in side effects. Many systems provide `_toupper` and `_tolower`, which are unsafe macros: they are fast but fail if the parameter is not a lower- or uppercase character, respectively. In some cases this is acceptable, because a test has already been done; however, its limited

```
/* 1*/    #include <stdio.h>
/* 2*/    #include <ctype.h>

/* 3*/    void
/* 4*/    PrintBool( int Val )
/* 5*/    {
/* 6*/        printf( "%6c", Val ? 'T' : 'F' );
/* 7*/    }

/* 8*/    main( void )
/* 9*/    {
/*10*/        char Ch = 0;

/*11*/        printf( "DEC OCT HEX CHAR ALPHA UPPER LOWER " );
/*12*/        printf( "DIGIT ALNUM  HEX   SPACE PUNCT\n" );
/*13*/        do
/*14*/        {
/*15*/            printf( "%3d %3o %3x ", Ch, Ch, Ch );

/*16*/            if( isgraph( Ch ) )
/*17*/                printf( "%4c", Ch );
/*18*/            else if( isprint( Ch ) )
/*19*/                printf( "  sp" );
/*20*/            else switch( Ch )
/*21*/            {
/*22*/                case '\a': printf( "bell" ); break;
/*23*/                case '\n': printf( "  nl" ); break;
/*24*/                case '\0': printf( "null" ); break;
/*25*/                case '\t': printf( " tab" ); break;
/*26*/                default  : printf( "\\%03o", Ch ); break;
/*27*/            }

/*28*/            PrintBool( isalpha( Ch ) );
/*29*/            PrintBool( isupper( Ch ) );
/*30*/            PrintBool( islower( Ch ) );
/*31*/            PrintBool( isdigit( Ch ) );
/*32*/            PrintBool( isalnum( Ch ) );
/*33*/            PrintBool( isxdigit( Ch ) );
/*34*/            PrintBool( isspace( Ch ) );
/*35*/            PrintBool( ispunct( Ch ) );

/*36*/            printf( "\n" );
/*37*/        } while( Ch++ != 127 );

/*38*/        return 0;
/*39*/    }
```

Figure 8.6: **Program to print out characteristics of the** chars.

```
/* 1*/     int
/* 2*/     ToUpper( char Ch )
/* 3*/     {
/* 4*/         switch( Ch )
/* 5*/         {
/* 6*/             case 'a': return 'A';
/* 7*/             case 'b': return 'B';
/* 8*/             case 'c': return 'C';
/* 9*/             case 'd': return 'D';
/*10*/             case 'e': return 'E';
/*11*/             case 'f': return 'F';
/*12*/             case 'g': return 'G';
/*13*/             case 'h': return 'H';
/*14*/             case 'i': return 'I';
/*15*/             case 'j': return 'J';
/*16*/             case 'k': return 'K';
/*17*/             case 'l': return 'L';
/*18*/             case 'm': return 'M';
/*19*/             case 'n': return 'N';
/*20*/             case 'o': return 'O';
/*21*/             case 'p': return 'P';
/*22*/             case 'q': return 'Q';
/*23*/             case 'r': return 'R';
/*24*/             case 's': return 'S';
/*25*/             case 't': return 'T';
/*26*/             case 'u': return 'U';
/*27*/             case 'v': return 'V';
/*28*/             case 'w': return 'W';
/*29*/             case 'x': return 'X';
/*30*/             case 'y': return 'Y';
/*31*/             case 'z': return 'Z';

/*32*/             default : return Ch;
/*33*/         }
/*34*/     }
```

Figure 8.7: **Portable** `ToUpper`.

 availability destroys portability. Some older systems implement `toupper` and `tolower` as unsafe macros. Until these systems become more rare, it might be better to write your own routine. This can be done portably by the code in Figure 8.7.

Perhaps this seems like a lot of work to do in the name of portability, especially if you are already on an ASCII machine. However, if you are on an ASCII machine, you can use the program in Figure 8.8 to generate, line for line, the routine in Figure 8.7. Note that Figure 8.8 uses the ASCII assumption that both lower- and uppercase characters are represented sequentially. Thus the loop at line 10 is over all lowercase characters, and the addition at line 11 by the constant `'A'-'a'` converts from lower to upper case. This is an example of writing a program to generate a program. We compile Figure 8.8, run it and

```
/* 1*/    /* Generate Routine In Previous Figure. */
/* 2*/    /* This Program Works Only An ASCII Machine */
/* 3*/    /* But Code That Is Generated Is Portable To Any Machine */

/* 4*/    #include <stdio.h>

/* 5*/    main( void )
/* 6*/    {
/* 7*/        char C;

/* 8*/        printf( "int\nToUpper( char Ch )\n{\n" );   /* ToUpper */

/* 9*/        printf( "\tswitch( Ch )\n\t{\n" );      /* Start switch */

/*10*/        for( C = 'a'; C <= 'z'; C++ )            /* Print Cases */
/*11*/            printf( "\t\tcase '%c': return '%c';\n",
                                       C, C + 'A'-'a' );
/*12*/        printf( "\t\tdefault : return Ch;\n" );

/*13*/        printf( "\t}\n}\n" );                    /* Closing Braces */

/*14*/        return 0;
/*15*/    }
```

Figure 8.8: **Generation of** ToUpper; **works only on an ASCII machine.**

save the output in *toupper.c*, and then compile *toupper.c*. In addition to saving some typing effort, we also avoid the possibility of a silly error, such as forgetting to type in the case label for 't'.

Because white space is needed only for human readers, we could remove all of the \n, \t, and blanks spaces from the output statements and still have a legal ToUpper routine as output.

8.4 Single-Character I/O

Although scanf can be used to read a character at a time, it takes a fair amount of time. One reason for this is that scanf is a very general purpose routine, so it has to take time to figure out what is being asked of it, even if it is only a simple %c. The other reason is that scanf is a true function, and thus some overhead is incurred.

If scanf is called for just one character of input several thousand times in a program the overhead could start adding up. On our fast machine, each call requires roughly 13 microseconds. Thus 1000 calls takes 13 milliseconds, which is a lot compared to the 9 milliseconds required to Shellsort 1000 integers. The same argument holds for printf. Because of this, two fast routines, which are usually implemented as macros, are provided in <stdio.h>. They are called getchar and putchar.

8.4.1 putchar

putchar(Ch) prints the character Ch onto the standard output. Thus

putchar('\n');

```
/* 1*/    #include <stdio.h>

/* 2*/    main( void )
/* 3*/    {
/* 4*/        int Ch;          /* Must Be An int!! */

/* 5*/        while( ( Ch = getchar( ) ) != EOF )   /* ( ) Needed!! */
/* 6*/        {
/* 7*/            putchar( Ch );
/* 8*/            if( Ch == '\n' )
/* 9*/                putchar( '\n' );
/*10*/        }

/*11*/        return 0;
/*12*/    }
```

Figure 8.9:   **Program to output a double-spaced version of the input.**

 outputs a newline character. Because there is always a possibility that the write might fail, `putchar` returns `EOF` if a character is not output. Otherwise, it returns that output character as an integer. Although `putchar` is a macro, its parameter is evaluated only once, so it is a safe macro.

8.4.2 `getchar`

The routine `getchar` takes no parameters and returns the next character from the input. If the end of input has been reached, `EOF` is returned. This automatically raises an annoying problem: If `getchar` has to return every possible character, plus the special symbol `EOF`, the number of possible return values is larger than the number of different values that can be held by a character. Therefore, we have perhaps the ugliest part of C: `getchar` returns an `int`.

 The value that is returned is either `EOF`, which must be a negative number, but is typically -1, or a quantity that fits in 8 bits. Failing to assign `getchar`'s return value to an `int` (by using the more natural `char`) is an extremely common error. All the calls to `getchar` will work except, of course, the one that occurs after the end of input is reached. If the `char` is `unsigned`, it will never equal `EOF`, so the end of input can never be detected. A good compiler will warn you of this, but not all compilers are so nice.

Figure 8.9 shows how `getchar` and `putchar` can be used to double space the input. Besides the requirement that `Ch` be an `int`, the other tricky part is the term in parentheses at line 5. Because `!=` has higher precedence than `=`, if the parentheses are omitted, the result of `getchar` is compared with `EOF`, and then either a 0 or 1 is assigned to `Ch`. This is another common programming error.

On our system, `getchar` is about 10 times faster than the corresponding `scanf`. Of course, this is noticeable only when the input has been redirected to come from a disk file. `putchar` is not that much faster, because even when the output is redirected to a disk file, on our system, disk writes are much slower than the reads, and thus the bottleneck is not in the `printf` to start with.

8.5   The String Abstraction

In C, a *string* is merely an array of characters. At first glance this would mean that the string `Becky` would be an array of five characters: `'B'`, `'e'`, `'c'`, `'k'`, and `'y'`. The problem with this strategy is that if this array is passed to any routine, such as `printf`, that routine would not know how many characters are in the array, because as we have seen, a function that receives an array has no idea how large the array is. The solution to this problem is either to require a major alteration of the language, which would somehow pass a size component (this is done in Pascal and Ada), or to use a slightly larger array with an *end marker*.

For instance, if we declared an array of six elements, we could place a blank in the last spot to signal that only the first five positions represent significant characters. If all routines are written to reflect this convention, we have a solution to our problem that requires little alteration to the language. Because we might actually want to use a blank in a string (e.g., to store a street address), we need to pick an endmarker that is not likely to otherwise appear in the string. In C, this special character is the *null* character, `'\0'`. The escape sequence indicates that the null character is always represented internally as zero. A common error is to forget the `\`. This leaves `'0'`, which of course is the character representation for the digit zero. Therefore, if an array of six characters has `'B'`, `'e'`, `'c'`, `'k'`, `'y'`, and `'\0'`, it represents the string *Becky*.

Because receiving routines have no concept of array size, the *null* character signifies an immediate termination of the string, even if it is not at the end of the array. Thus we call `\0` the *null terminator*. If the array contains `'B'`, `'e'`, `'\0'`, `'c'`, `'k'`, and `'y'`, the string implied is *Be*. If the array contains `'B'`, `'\0'`, `'e'`, `'c'`, `'k'`, and `'y'`, the string implied is *B*. A common mistake is assuming that a string of length 1 can be represented by a character. You cannot use `'B'` when you mean `"B"`, and vice versa. This is an incredibly frequent error, which is often not noticed by the compiler but will crash your program.

 On the other hand, if you want to read the next character from input but skip over leading white space, neither `getchar` or `scanf` with `%c` works. However, `scanf` with `%1s` will work if a string is provided: the character will then reside in array spot zero. If the array contains `'\0'`, `'B'`, `'e'`, `'c'`, `'k'`, and `'y'`, an empty string (of length 0) is represented. Empty strings are sometimes useful but can also signal that something is wrong with your program (just as stray zeros do).

8.5.1   Declaration of Strings

A string is declared as an array of characters. Figure 8.10 shows a few possibilities, some of which are incorrect. The first three statements declare `Name` to be an array of six characters, and specify their initial values. The second declaration is equivalent to the first because zeros are used to complete the initialization and zero is exactly the value of `\0`. The fourth declaration declares the array without an initial value, and the fifth declaration is illegal for local variables, but specifies, for a nonlocal variable, the existence of an `extern` string that is allocated elsewhere. This is a straightforward application of the array declaration rules seen in Figure 7.10. The sixth declaration is wrong because the size of `Name` will be taken to be five characters and thus there is no room to tack on a null terminator.

If you think this is a lot of work just to declare a string, you are not alone. Therefore, C provides *string constants*. String constants provide a shorthand method of specifying a

```
char Name[ 6 ] = { 'B', 'e', 'c', 'k', 'y', '\0' };
char Name[ 6 ] = { 'B', 'e', 'c', 'k', 'y' };
char Name[   ] = { 'B', 'e', 'c', 'k', 'y', '\0' };
char Name[ 6 ];              /* Declares, does not initialize */
char Name[   ];                        /* Illegal for automatics */

char Name[   ] = { 'B', 'e', 'c', 'k', 'y' };   /* Wrong!! */
char Name[   ] = "Becky";
char Name[ 5 ] = "Becky";                        /* Wrong!! */
char Name[ 9 ] = "Becky";          /* Allows longer name later */
```

Figure 8.10:   Some correct and incorrect string declarations.

sequence of characters. They automatically include the null terminator as an invisible last character. Any character may appear in the string constant except the ", which must be escaped. Note that the ' does not need to be escaped inside a string constant. Generally speaking, a string constant may appear anywhere that both a string and a constant may appear. We have already used string constants extensively in the printf and scanf statements. Like an array name, the string constant is treated by the compiler as a pointer.

In Figure 8.10, the seventh declaration allocates an array of six characters and initializes it to the appropriate null terminated string. The eighth declaration is an error in our context but will not be caught by the compiler because it is (unfortunately) legal. The ninth declaration allocates a larger array than what is currently needed. This is required if we wish later to assign Name a longer string. Even though Name represents a string, the declaration

```
char Name1[ ] = Name;
```

is illegal: only constant strings (or a list of characters) are allowed.

Figure 8.11 shows an example of how strings are used. The program is another portable implementation of ToUpper. Although it is shorter than Figure 8.7, it is less efficient: nearly 100 operations are performed in the event that Ch is not a lowercase character, and for an average lowercase character, roughly half that amount, or almost 50 operations, are performed. The switch statement is implemented much more efficiently by the compiler (see Exercise 2).

The algorithm itself is quite simple: two arrays Lower and Upper are declared. A search for Ch in Lower is performed. If a match is found, the corresponding character in Upper is returned, otherwise, we eventually reach the null terminator, exit the loop, and return the original character. Because the null terminator has value zero, the test at line 7 can be written simply as Lower[i]. There is no gain in speed by doing this, since the compiler does it internally. A few keystrokes are saved at the expense of clarity. Although we generally will not use too many shorthand methods, it is still important to understand them because you may have to modify code that others have written.

8.5.2   String Constant Concatenation

A string constant must appear entirely on one line. For very long strings this can make for hard-to-read code. For instance, some printers will not print anything that is past the eightieth column. To alleviate this problem, ANSI C specifies that consecutive string constants, separated by zero or more white space, are treated as one. Thus "ABC" "DEF"

```
/* 1*/    int
/* 2*/    ToUpper( char Ch )
/* 3*/    {
/* 4*/        static const char Lower[ ] = "abcdefghijklmnopqrstuvwxyz";
/* 5*/        static const char Upper[ ] = "ABCDEFGHIJKLMNOPQRSTUVWXYZ";

/* 6*/        int i;

/* 7*/        for( i = 0; Lower[ i ] != '\0'; i++ )
/* 8*/            if( Lower[ i ] == Ch )
/* 9*/                return Upper[ i ];

/*10*/        return Ch;
/*11*/    }
```

Figure 8.11:   Slower, but shorter portable `ToUpper`.

is the same as `"ABCDEF"`, even if the two original string constants appear on different lines.

8.6 `printf` **and** `scanf`

Both `printf` and `scanf` use the `%s` conversion for strings. There are two things to be aware of, and both apply to `scanf`. First, because a string is an array, the name of a string is a memory address, which indicates where the characters are stored. Therefore, an address-of operator is not needed, and in fact using one will give the wrong result.[3] Second, the statement

```
scanf( "%s", Name );
```

which is intended to read a string and place it in Name can fail badly if a long string is typed. This is because the lack of range checking in arrays means that characters will be faithfully copied into successive memory locations. If Name is declared to hold nine characters, then the statement should read

```
scanf( "%8s", Name );
```

to prevent trashing adjacent variables.

For `scanf`, ANSI C has added the `%[` conversion. This matches strings whose character sets are restricted. As an example, `%[a-zA-Z]` matches strings consisting only of letters. In Section 12.2.3 we discuss fancy `scanf` features in detail. We use shorthand later in this chapter to simplify code. As is the case for `%s`, the `%[` conversion should also include a limit on the number of characters to be read, to avoid overrunning of memory. Indeed, `scanf` warnings that we specify for `%s` will also apply for the `%[` conversion.

If you do not supply a string for the `%s` conversion, you expect to get the wrong answer. Typically, however, the problem will be more drastic: your program may crash if a string is not supplied for a `%s` converter because `printf` expects the memory location where a sequence of characters is present. As an example,

----

[3]Some pre-ANSI compilers will give the intended result, but this is wrong.

??<	{	??>	}	??/	\
??(	[	??)	]	??=	#
??!	|	??'	^	??-	~

Figure 8.12:   Trigraph sequences.

```
/* 1*/    ??=include <stdio.h>

/* 2*/    main( void )
/* 3*/    ??<
/* 4*/        printf( "Hello world??/n" );
/* 5*/    ??>
```

Figure 8.13:   Trigraph usage to replace #, {, \, }.

```
printf( "%s %d\n", 25, "Hello" );
```

causes `printf` to search memory location 25 for a null terminated string, which is likely to cause a crash.

8.6.1   Trigraphs

Not all terminals and character sets contain braces. Obviously, this can make compiling a C program somewhat difficult. In an effort to alleviate this problem, nine special sequences have been defined for ANSI C. These are known as *trigraph* sequences and are summarized in Figure 8.12. As a result, the program in Figure 8.13 is completely equivalent to that in Figure 2.3. The four trigraph sequences replace #, {, \, and }. Trigraphs are processed prior to escape sequences and before the scanning for tokens.

At first glance it seems like trigraphs are useful for those programmers who are operating on a restricted character set and is a feature that can be totally ignored by everyone else. This is not entirely true because a *constant* string such is What??!! cannot be printed directly: The trigraph sequence is interpreted first, resulting in What|!. Figure 8.14 shows two alternatives that give the desired result. The first option, at line 5, uses the fact that constant strings separated by white space are concatenated together. Since the trigraph is no longer present, we get the intended output. The second option, at line 6, uses the escape sequence for ?, which exists specifically for this purpose. If there are multiple ?s, you only need to escape the last one.

 Since few C programmers need to use trigraphs, the feature has by and large become a nuisance to many. So many people have been upset that some compilers do not implement it, and others (such as *gcc*) process them only if requested. The *gcc* option is *-trigraphs*. This stubbornness, however, can lead to some difficulties when code is ported. If you have two consecutive ?s in your code, you should use the trigraph option just to make sure that there are no any unintended effects.

A sometimes confusing point about both trigraphs and escape sequences is how they are interpreted. Like escape sequences, trigraphs are meaningful only when read as sequences of characters in a source program. If the string Name with characters '?', '?', '>', *bsl*, 'n', and *null* is printed, the output is ??>\n. If the program has the con-

```
/* 1*/    #include <stdio.h>

/* 2*/    main( void )
/* 3*/    {
/* 4*/         printf( "What??!!\n" );        /* What|! */
/* 5*/         printf( "What??" "!!\n" );     /* What??!! */
/* 6*/         printf( "What?\?!!\n" );       /* What??!! */
/* 7*/    }
```

Figure 8.14:   Trigraphs and how to get around them.

stant string `"??>\n"` specifically declared in it, it represents a string with characters `'}'`, *newline*, and *null*.

8.7   String Operations

One limitation of the string implementation in C is that strings cannot be copied by the = operator, or compared meaningfully by any of <, >, or ==. This follows directly from the fact that a string is just a (null terminated) array of characters, and these operations are not available to arrays. Also, for a given string such as `"1234"`, there is no built-in method to assign the corresponding value 1234 to an integer.

Although this seems like a limitation, it is only a minor inconvenience because it is easy enough to write routines to perform all these functions. In the interest of uniformity, ANSI C specifies that certain routines must be available, and it is good programming practice to use them. We now discuss these routines, showing how some *might* be implemented. The actual implementations may be faster.

The prototypes for all these routines can be found in `<string.h>`. You should `#include` that file whenever you use these string functions. Also, all these routines work for empty strings (`""` of zero length) but generally fail if a NULL pointer is passed as a string parameter.

8.7.1 `strlen`

The routine

```
size_t strlen( const char *Str );
```

returns the length of the null-terminated string `Str`. Figure 8.15 shows a simple implementation. By following our usual capitalization convention, we avoid conflict with the library routine. The prototype in Figure 8.15 is equivalent to the prototype above because of the equivalence of arrays and pointers discussed in Section 7.9.

In Figure 8.15 when the `for` loop ends, the value of `i` is the index of the null terminator. But since the array starts at zero, this is exactly equal to the length of the string. Figure 8.16 shows an implementation of `strlen` that saves keystrokes. Because the null terminator evaluates to zero, the test against it is redundant (although arguably more readable). We also increment `i` prior to using it to index `Str`. Thus we initialize it to -1.

```
/* 1*/    unsigned int
/* 2*/    Strlen( const char Str[ ] )
/* 3*/    {
/* 4*/        int i;

/* 5*/        for( i = 0; Str[ i ] != '\0'; i++ )
/* 6*/            ;

/* 7*/        return i;
/* 8*/    }
```

Figure 8.15:   Simple implementation of strlen.

```
/* 1*/    unsigned int
/* 2*/    Strlen( const char Str[ ] )
/* 3*/    {
/* 4*/        int i = -1;

/* 5*/        while( Str[ ++i ] )
/* 6*/            ;

/* 7*/        return i;
/* 8*/    }
```

Figure 8.16:   Alternative implementation of strlen.

8.7.2 strcpy

The routine

```
char *strcpy( char *Lhs, const char *Rhs );
```

is used to copy the string Rhs into Lhs. If Lhs is not long enough to hold all the characters in Rhs plus the null terminator, somebody else's memory gets overwritten, and tragedy may result. We use Lhs and Rhs for *left-hand side* and *right-hand side*, respectively.

The order of parameters is easy to remember if you keep in mind that

```
strcpy( Lhs, Rhs );
```

is meant to mimic the statement

```
Lhs = Rhs;
```

To mimic the fact that assignments nest (i.e., A=B=C makes sense), the library routine strcpy returns Lhs. The return value is generally ignored. Because of it, however,

```
strcpy( A, strcpy( B, C ) );
```

does for strings A, B, and C what A=B=C; would do for ints. Figure 8.17 shows an implementation. Each character of Rhs is copied to Lhs, and when the null terminator is copied, the value of the test at line 6 is zero, finishing the loop.

```
/* 1*/    char *
/* 2*/    Strcpy( char Lhs[ ], const char Rhs[ ] )
/* 3*/    {
/* 4*/        int i;

/* 5*/        if( Lhs != Rhs )
/* 6*/            for( i = 0; Lhs[ i ] = Rhs[ i ]; i++ )
/* 7*/                ;

/* 8*/        return Lhs;
/* 9*/    }
```

Figure 8.17: Simple implementation of strcpy.

8.7.3   strcat

The routine

```
char *strcat( char *Lhs, const char *Rhs );
```

appends the string Lhs to the end of Lhs and returns Lhs. The usual disclaimer applies: Lhs needs to be large enough to hold the result, or else the usual overwriting of memory results.

8.7.4   strcmp

The routine

```
int strcmp( const char *Lhs, const char *Rhs );
```

 returns a negative number, zero, or a positive number, depending on whether Lhs is less than, equal, or greater than Rhs. The ordering is based on the local character set. If the strings consists entirely of single-case letters, the ordering is alphabetical. An examination of the ASCII character set shows that all uppercase characters appear before lowercase characters, so

```
strcmp( "ZZ", "aa" )
```

returns a negative number. Thus, when alphabetizing strings, one usually converts everything to a common case.

Figure 8.18 shows an implementation. If the statement at line 8 is reached, Lhs and Rhs are different and i is the index of the first mismatch. Thus a simple subtraction returns the correct answer. If the two strings are identical, eventually we reach their null terminator simultaneously and the condition at line 6 is true, forcing a return. Note that if Lhs and Rhs have unequal lengths, the null terminator (which is zero) of the shorter string will be reached if the shorter string is a prefix of the longer string, causing a return at line 8. Thus "then" is greater than "the\0".

8.7.5   atoi, atof, atol

The routines atoi, atof, and atol convert strings to numbers. They have been used for many years and are included for compatibility with older programs. The more advanced routines, strtol, strtod, and strtul, are discussed in Appendix D; they are better at dealing with errors, and are thus preferable, but are more complicated.

```
/* 1*/    int
/* 2*/    Strcmp( const char Lhs[ ], const char Rhs[ ] )
/* 3*/    {
/* 4*/        int i;

/* 5*/        for( i = 0; Lhs[ i ] == Rhs[ i ]; i++ )
/* 6*/            if( Lhs[ i ] == '\0' )
/* 7*/                return 0;

/* 8*/        return Lhs[ i ] - Rhs[ i ];
/* 9*/    }
```

Figure 8.18: **Simple implementation of** `strcmp`.

```
/* 1*/    int
/* 2*/    IsPrefix( const char Little[ ], const char Big[ ] )
/* 3*/    {
/* 4*/        return !strncmp( Little, Big, strlen( Little ) );
/* 5*/    }
```

Figure 8.19: `IsPrefix`: **test if the first string is a prefix of the second.**

`atoi(Str)` returns the integer value represented in `Str`. Only the leading characters prior to a nondigit are examined, so `atoi("3x4")` and `atoi("3 4")` both return 3, and `atoi("junk")` returns 0. `atof(Str)` and `atol(Str)` are the `double` and `long int` equivalents. These conversion routines are found in `<stdlib.h>`.

8.7.6 `strncmp`, `strncpy`, **and** `strncat`

Sometimes it is necessary to perform a partial comparison on two strings. The routine

`int strncmp( const char *Lhs, const char *Rhs, int N );`

is like `strcmp` except that only the first `N` characters are used. Thus

`strncmp( "this", "that", 2 )`

returns 0. If `N` is zero or negative, the return value is automatically zero, which makes sense.

Figure 8.19 shows the routine `IsPrefix`, which can be used to test if one string is a prefix of another. This is useful for parsing commands, where abbreviations are considered acceptable. The routine `strncpy` takes a third parameter, `N`, and copies exactly `N` characters into `Lhs`. This means that if `strlen(Rhs)` is less than `N`, an appropriate number of null terminators are copied until a total of `N` characters have been copied. Otherwise, the first `N` characters of `Rhs` are copied without a null terminator.

One would expect that `strncat` would have similar behavior, but it does not. The result of `strncat` is that one null terminator is always written, so at most `N+1` characters are appended to `Lhs`.

8.7.7 `puts`

The routine

`int puts( const char *Str );`

```
/* 1*/      unsigned int
/* 2*/      Strlen( const char * const Str )
/* 3*/      {
/* 4*/          const char *Sp = Str;

/* 5*/          while( *Sp++ )
/* 6*/              ;

/* 7*/          return Sp - Str - 1;
/* 8*/      }
```

Figure 8.20: `strlen` **using pointers.**

is used to output the string `Str`, which is presumed null terminated, followed by a newline. It is thus a simple shorthand for a `printf` statement and is somewhat faster because of the lack of fancy options. `EOF` is returned if there is an error.

If you do not want the newline, you have to use

```
printf( "%s", Str );
```

 Do not try to be fancy and use

```
printf( Str );
```

It is not the same! (See Exercise 9.)

There used to be a `gets` routine to read one line of input into a string passed as a parameter. However, the routine was unsafe because there was no parameter passed to indicate the maximum array size. This resulted in programs crashing and created a well-known security leak that was eventually exploited, resulting in the infamous internet worm. Consequently, `gets` is considered taboo. Many system administrators have removed it from the library; even if it is present in yours, do not use it.

8.8 Pointers and Strings

A common use of pointer arithmetic is quick array access for string routines. Figures 8.20 to 8.22 show revised versions of the string routines that mimic `strlen`, `strcpy`, and `strcmp`. These routines were written previously using arrays in Figures 8.15 to 8.18. `Strlen` is passed a string `Str` in the form of a `char *`. Recall that the two `const`s mean that the string cannot be modified, nor can `Str` be reset to point at another string. The second `const` is present as a reminder that we do not intend to alter `Str`. At line 4, we declare a second pointer `Sp` that is initialized to point to the start of the string. We use `const` to signify that `Sp` will not alter any of the characters in the string. This is not merely good programming practice, but a requirement, since we are having `Sp` point at a string `Str`, which is itself a `const`. We continually advance `Sp`, breaking the loop only after it is pointing at the null terminator. This is written concisely at line 5: the value of the expression is what `Sp` points at, and immediately after the test is completed, `Sp` is advanced to point at the next character in the string.

When the `while` loop terminates, `Sp` is pointing at the position after the null terminator. Recall from Chapter 7 that ANSI C specifies that it is legal to point there. The length

```
/* 1*/    /* Incorrect Routine That Works On Almost All Machines */

/* 2*/    unsigned int
/* 3*/    WrongStrlen( const char * const Str )
/* 4*/    {
/* 5*/        const char *Sp = Str - 1;    /* Illegal Pointer */

/* 6*/        while( *++Sp )
/* 7*/            ;

/* 8*/        return Sp - Str;
/* 9*/    }
```

Figure 8.21: Incorrect `strlen` **using pointers.**

```
/* 1*/    char *
/* 2*/    Strcpy( char * const Lhs, const char *Rhs )
/* 3*/    {
/* 4*/        char *Lhp = Lhs;

/* 5*/        if( Lhs != Rhs )
/* 6*/            while( ( *Lhp++ = *Rhs++ ) != '\0' )
/* 7*/                ;

/* 8*/        return Lhs;
/* 9*/    }
```

Figure 8.22: `strcpy` **using pointers.**

of the string is thus given by the formula at line 7 as one less than the difference between the final and initial positions of `Sp`. Figure 8.21 shows an incorrect implementation that mimics Figure 8.15 directly. It is wrong because `Sp` is initialized to point prior to the start of the array, which is a technical violation of the ANSI C rules. Although this code will run without error on the vast majority of platforms, it is nevertheless incorrect and may fail on some machines.

Why might a pointer implementation be faster than an array implementation? Let's consider a string of length 3. In the array implementation, we access the array via `S[0]`, `S[1]`, `S[2]`, and `S[3]`. `S[i]` is accessed by adding one to the previous value $i-1$, and then an addition of `S` and `i`, to get the required memory location. In our pointer implementation, `S[i]` is accessed by adding 1 to `Sp`, and we never keep a counter `i`. Thus we save an addition for each character, paying only an extra two subtractions during the `return` statement.

The next question is whether or not the trickier code is worth the time savings. The answer is that in most programs, a few routines dominate the total running time. Historically, the use of trickier code for speed has been justified only in those routines that actually account for a significant portion of the program's total running time, or which are used in enough different programs to make the optimization effort worthwhile. However, good modern compilers can perform this optimization anyway. Thus, like the `register` variable, the use of pointers to traverse arrays will help some compilers, will be neutral for others, and

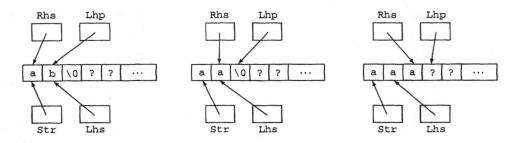

Figure 8.23:   Copying a string to part of itself bombs.

may even generate slower code than the typical index addressing mechanism. Even so, the idiom is so widely used that it is worth examining a few more examples.

Figure 8.22 shows our pointer version of `Strcpy`. Recall that Lhs is returned to allow nested `Strcpy` calls. Because we are returning Lhs, we need a second pointer, Lhp, to traverse the left-hand-side array. The basic copying loop is executed at line 6. We assign the character pointed at by Lhp with the character pointed at by Rhs, and automatically advance both after the condition is complete. The loop is continued until the null terminator is copied. Thus Lhs is automatically null terminated. Since the null terminator is represented as a zero, the comparison against it is redundant. Thus we could have written

```
/* 6*/               while( *Lhp++ = *Rhs++ )
```

That alternative is a bit more cryptic, and some compilers will warn you that you may have made a mistake. Thus we write the test explicitly.

Line 5 tests for a condition known as *aliasing*. If we call `Strcpy(A,A)`, we should not perform the copy. In this case, the copying would do the correct thing even if we did not have the test, but even so, it is good to get in the habit. Our routine is by no means bullet proof. Figure 8.23 shows how the following fragment bombs horribly. There we see the first three stages of `Strcpy` for the following input:

```
char Str[ 100 ] = "ab";
Strcpy( Str + 1, Str );
```

At the beginning of the algorithm, Rhs points at the first element of the `Str` array, and both `const` Lhs and Lhp point at the second element. In the first iteration, we copy the character pointed at by Rhs into the character pointed at by Lhp, and then advance both pointers. The second picture shows that the second element of the array is thus changed to an `'a'`. This causes an immediate problem: we have unknowingly overwritten part of what is supposed to be treated as a `const` input string. The extent of the problem is made clear in the third picture. The next copy overwrites the null terminator before advancing the two pointers. Thus, regardless of how long `Str` is, we will keep on writing the character `'a'` until we have gone past the computer's limit of memory. At that point we will crash with a memory violation.

This error can be avoided by testing if Lhs lies between Rhs and Rhs + Strlen(Rhs) + 1. If this is the case, the string can be safely copied by going backward from the end of Rhs to the beginning. Unfortunately, this adds overhead to the routine, just to guard against a relatively rare occurrence. Thus the library `strcpy` is likely to exhibit behavior

```
/* 1*/    int
/* 2*/    Strcmp( const char *Lhs, const char *Rhs )
/* 3*/    {
/* 4*/        for( ; *Lhs == *Rhs && *Lhs != '\0';  Lhs++, Rhs++ )
/* 5*/            ;

/* 6*/        return *Lhs - *Rhs;
/* 7*/    }
```

Figure 8.24: `strcmp` **using pointers.**

similar to our example (see Exercise 17). The ANSI C standard specifically states that the behavior of `strcpy` is undefined if the two strings overlap.

A common error for beginners is to think that whenever a pointer is declared, it must be initialized by calling `malloc`. In addition to showing a limitation of `strcpy`, the pictures and the code show that this is not necessary. Allocating unneeded memory in an attempt to initialize pointers that traverse already allocated objects will only result in wasted time and memory leaks.

A pointer implementation of `strcmp` is shown in Figure 8.24. As in `strcpy`, two pointers traverse their respective strings. When the `for` loop terminates, either `Lhs` and `Rhs` are either both pointing at their respective null terminators, or they have detected a mismatch. Thus we only need to subtract their dereferenced values to obtain the negative, zero, or positive number that indicates the result of the string comparison.

Notice that there is a huge difference between an empty string `" "` and a `NULL` string. Passing a `NULL` pointer to any of our routines causes an error, while passing a pointer to a null terminator is handled correctly. The library routines generally behave in the same manner, although some compilers will accept the `NULL` pointer.

8.9 Additional String Routines

ANSI C provides many additional routines in `<string.h>`. Three routines that we have not discussed yet are very useful. First, the routine `strchr` can be used to scan a string for a specific character. The prototype is

```
char *strchr( const char *Str, int SearchChar );
```

`strchr` returns a pointer to the first occurrence of `SearchChar` in `Str`, or `NULL` if the character is not found. The routine `strrchr` is similar, returning, instead, a pointer to the last occurrence of `SearchChar`.

These routines have no memory, so successive calls with the same parameters yield the same pointer. However, the pointer that is returned can be used as `Str` in a subsequent call. Thus the routine in Figure 8.25 can be used to count the number of times `SearchChar` appears in string `Str`.

The third routine of interest is `strstr`. The prototype, which is also provided in `<string.h>`, is

```
char *strstr( const char *Str, const char *Pattern );
```

`strstr` returns a pointer to the first occurrence of `Pattern` in `Str`, or `NULL` if the string is not found. Subsequent calls using the returned value as the new `Str` can get all

```
/* 1*/    int
/* 2*/    CountChars( const char *Str, char SearchChar )
/* 3*/    {
/* 4*/        unsigned int Matches = 0;

/* 5*/        if( Str != NULL )
/* 6*/            while( ( Str = strchr( Str, SearchChar ) ) != NULL )
/* 7*/            {
/* 8*/                Str++;
/* 9*/                Matches++;
/*10*/            }

/*11*/        return Matches;
/*12*/    }
```

Figure 8.25: **Example of** `strchr`**: count number of occurrences of** `SearchChar`**.**

occurrences. In Appendix D we look at some of the trickier routines, such as `strtok`, which can be used somewhat like `scanf` to do quick parsing of tokens.

8.10   A Common Pointer Error

Recall that a fundamental difference between arrays and pointers is that an array definition allocates enough memory to store the array, while a pointer points to memory that is allocated elsewhere. Because strings are arrays of characters, this distinction applies to strings. A common error is declaring a pointer when an array is needed. As an example, consider the following declarations:

```
char Name[ ] = "Becky";
char *Name1 = "Becky";
char *Name2;
```

The first declaration allocates six bytes for `Name`, initializing it to a copy of the constant string `"Becky"` (including the null terminator). The second declaration states merely that `Name1` points at the zeroth character of the string constant `"Becky"`. Many compilers will not accept the declaration of `Name1`. This is because the statement

```
Name[1] = 'u';
```

is an attempt to alter the string constant. If the string constant is stored in read-only memory, the attempt to alter it would generate a hardware fault. Thus many compilers will insist on the declaration

```
const char *Name1 = "Becky";
```

to disallow the assignment to `Name[1]`. An example where this is useful is

```
const char *Message = "Please log in: ";
```

Another common consequence of declaring a pointer instead of an array object is the following statement (in which we assume that `Name2` is not a `const` pointer):

```
strcpy( Name2, Name );
```

```
/* 1*/    int
/* 2*/    Itoa( char Str[ ], int N )
/* 3*/    {
/* 4*/        return sprintf( Str, "%d", N );
/* 5*/    }
```

Figure 8.26: `itoa`: **Convert an integer to a string.**

Here the programmer expects to copy Name into Name2 but is fooled because the prototype for strcpy indicates that two pointers are to be passed. The call fails, of course, because Name2 is just a pointer, rather than a pointer to sufficient memory to hold a copy of Name. If Name2 is a NULL pointer or points at a string constant stored in read-only memory, or points at a random illegal location, strcpy is certain to attempt to dereference it, generating an error. If Name2 points at a modifiable array, however, there is no problem.

8.11   sscanf **and** sprintf

The sscanf and sprintf routines are similar to scanf and printf except that their input/output comes from an extra first parameter, which is a string. As an example, the routine in Figure 8.26 will write in the parameter string Str the null-terminated string representation of N. If N is 40, Str represents "40". Of course, no check is made to ensure that Str points at sufficient memory to store the result. The name of the routine indicates that it goes in the direction opposite atoi.

sscanf is similar to scanf except that there is no concept of input digestion between calls. That is, successive calls to scanf with the same string always start reading from the beginning, even if previous matches have occurred. It is hard to do anything else. sscanf is useful when exactly one line of input must be read, but the line can take several forms. An example is Exercise 13.

8.12   Case Study: A Simple Word Processor

As an example of how strings are manipulated, we will write a simple program that performs right justification of an input stream. We will use a simple model: any sequence of characters except the blank, tab, and newline characters defines a word. One or more blank lines signify the end of a paragraph and the beginning of a new paragraph. The number of characters that will be output on a line, and the number of blanks spaces that are used to indent, are defined as constants in Figure 8.27.

Employing a top-down design, we look at the main routine next. As shown in Figure 8.28, until EOF is read, we read the next group of input repeatedly. We use scanf and the %[option extensively to simplify the code. It is probably more efficient to use only getchar; we leave that implementation as an exercise. At line 6 we scan for a sequence of non-white-space characters, and if we find them, we call a routine Justify to handle it and then continue to read more input. Otherwise, we check to see if the pending characters are a sequence of blanks and/or tabs, in which case we skip them, by continuing to read more input.

```
/* 1*/    #include <stdio.h>
/* 2*/    #include <string.h>

/* 3*/    #define LineLen        72
/* 4*/    #define IndentLen       5
/* 5*/    #define FLUSH          " "
```

Figure 8.27:   Constants for word processor.

```
/* 1*/    main ( void )
/* 2*/    {
/* 3*/         char Str[ 1000 ];

/* 4*/         for( ; ; )
/* 5*/         {
/* 6*/             if( scanf( "%[^ \t\n]", Str ) == 1 )
/* 7*/             {
/* 8*/                 Justify( Str );        /* Get A Word And Justify */
/* 9*/                 continue;
/*10*/             }
/*11*/             else                       /* Get White Space */
/*12*/             if( scanf( "%[ \t]", Str ) == 1 )
/*13*/                 continue;
/*14*/             else                       /* Must Be A Newline Or EOF */
/*15*/             {
/*16*/                 if( getchar( ) == EOF ) /* Should Be A Newline */
/*17*/                     break;
/*18*/             /* If There's another newline, then new paragraph */
/*19*/                 if( scanf( "%[\n]", Str ) == 1 )
/*20*/                     Justify( FLUSH );
/*21*/             }

/*22*/         }
/*23*/         Justify( FLUSH );                      /* Finish Off Last Line */
/*24*/         return 0;
/*25*/    }
```

Figure 8.28:   Driver routine for word processor.

Otherwise, the next character is a newline, or we have reached the end of input. In the latter case, we exit the loop and call Justify with the parameter FLUSH to signify that any unwritten words be written as a last line (unjustified). If we have not reached the end of input, we check at line 19 if any blank lines are present, and if so, we tell Justify to FLUSH unwritten output. We have declared Str to hold a huge number of characters, as an alternative to adding a maximum field width to scanf.

Having written main, we proceed to write Justify. This is shown in Figure 8.29. CurrentLine stores the unwritten output, and CharsHeld keeps track of how much unwritten output there is. Note that LineLen+1 characters are allocated, because of the null terminator. Forgetting that is easy to do and can break the program. Indent represents

```
/* 1*/     /* If Word Is FLUSH, Then Output The Current Line. */
/* 2*/     /* Otherwise, Add Word To End Of Line; if It Doesn't Fit */
/* 3*/     /* Then Output The Current Line ( Padded ) */

/* 4*/     void
/* 5*/     Justify( const char Word[ ] )
/* 6*/     {
/* 7*/          static char CurrentLine[ LineLen + 1 ] = "";
/* 8*/          static int CharsHeld = 0;
/* 9*/          static int Indent = IndentLen;      /* Amount To Indent */
/*10*/          static int LineLimit = LineLen - IndentLen;
/*11*/          int WordLen = strlen( Word );

/*12*/          if( strcmp( Word, FLUSH ) == 0 )
/*13*/          {
/*14*/                  /* Print The Pending Line. */
/*15*/              PrintSpaces( Indent );
/*16*/              puts( CurrentLine );                        /* No Padding */
/*17*/              Indent = IndentLen;                 /* For Next Line */
/*18*/          }
/*19*/          else
/*20*/          if( CharsHeld + WordLen < LineLimit )
/*21*/          {
/*22*/                  /* Word Fits On The Line */
/*23*/              if( CharsHeld ) /* Toss In Blank if Not First Word */
/*24*/              {
/*25*/                  strcat( CurrentLine, " " );
/*26*/                  CharsHeld++;
/*27*/              }
/*28*/              strcat( CurrentLine, Word );
/*29*/              CharsHeld += WordLen;
/*30*/              return;
/*31*/          }
/*32*/          else
/*33*/          {     /* Print The Pending Line With Padding */
/*34*/              PrintSpaces( Indent );
/*35*/              PutOut( CurrentLine, LineLimit );
/*36*/              Indent = 0;                 /* Next Line Is Not Indented */
/*37*/          }

/*38*/                  /* Start Up The Next Line */
/*39*/          strcpy( CurrentLine, Word );
/*40*/          CharsHeld = WordLen;
/*41*/          LineLimit = LineLen - Indent;
/*42*/     }
```

Figure 8.29: `Justify` **routine: keep track of pending words.**

the amount of indenting that is performed for the current line, and `LineLimit` represents the number of characters that can be absorbed until the line must be output. Lines 12 to 18 handle the flushing of the last line. Appropriate indenting, followed by the current line

```
/* 1*/    void
/* 2*/    PrintSpaces( int HowMany )
/* 3*/    {
/* 4*/        while( HowMany-- > 0 )
/* 5*/            putchar( ' ' );
/* 6*/    }

/* 7*/    void
/* 8*/    PutOut( const char Line[ ], int Length )
/* 9*/    {
/*10*/        int SmallGapLen;
/*11*/        int NumGaps = 0;
/*12*/        int NumSmallGaps;
/*13*/        int LineLen = strlen( Line );
/*14*/        int TotalSpaces;
/*15*/        int i;

/*16*/        for( i = 0; Line[ i ]; i++ )
/*17*/            if( Line[ i ] == ' ' )
/*18*/                NumGaps++;

/*19*/        if( !NumGaps )
/*20*/        {
/*21*/            puts( Line );
/*22*/            return;
/*23*/        }

/*24*/        TotalSpaces = Length - LineLen + NumGaps;
/*25*/        SmallGapLen = TotalSpaces / NumGaps;
/*26*/        NumSmallGaps = NumGaps - TotalSpaces % NumGaps;

/*27*/        for( i = 0; Line[ i ]; i++ )
/*28*/            if( Line[ i ] == ' ' )
/*29*/                PrintSpaces( SmallGapLen +
                                  ( NumSmallGaps-- <= 0 ) );
/*30*/            else
/*31*/                putchar( Line[ i ] );
/*32*/        putchar( '\n' );
/*33*/    }
```

Figure 8.30: `PrintSpaces` **and** `PutOut`: **output routines.**

(without padding), is output, and we set up Indent for a new paragraph. Lines 39 to 41 are then executed to initialize the next line.

Lines 34 to 36 are executed when Word does not fit in the current line. In this case we print the appropriate amount of indentation and then call PutOut to right-justify the line. The next line is not indented, so we set Indent to zero, and as before, make arrangements for the next line. The last case to handle is when the word fits. The test for this is done at line 20; the < is used instead of <= because of the space that has to be placed between words. If the word fits, we tack on a blank (if it is not the first word on the line) and then the word to the current line.

The two remaining routines are shown in Figure 8.30. PrintSpaces is a simple loop that prints HowMany blanks. Note the use of the postfix autodecrement. The value

The two remaining routines are shown in Figure 8.30. `PrintSpaces` is a simple loop that prints `HowMany` blanks. Note the use of the postfix autodecrement. The value of `HowMany` is used in the test, and then it is decremented. Using the prefix form results in one too few spaces. The `PutOut` algorithm is straightforward. First, we compute the number of gaps between words by counting the number of blanks. Since we have ensured that exactly one blank separates a word, this works. If there are no gaps because there is only one word, the word is output (but cannot be justified), and we give up.

Otherwise, we compute the total number of blank spaces that will be present on the line. Then we compute the size of a small gap and the number of each of those. The remaining gaps will require one more space. As an example, if we have to distribute 14 spaces among nine gaps, four gaps will get one space, and the remaining five will get two. This calculation is done at lines 24 to 26. We then write the line out, replacing a blank with an appropriate number of blanks. On line 29, when the number of small gaps that remain to be output becomes zero, the comparison evaluates to 1, causing the output of an extra space.

8.13   Dangerous Stuff: Routines That Return ∗

We have seen that routines such as `strcpy`, `strchr`, and `strstr` can return a string via a `char *` return type. In all these cases, however, we return a pointer to some part of an already existing array. In this section we examine routines that return a pointer to a local variable. As we will see, there are three basic cases that can occur, and all methods can be potentially dangerous for the uninitiated.

8.13.1   Returning a Pointer to a Static Variable

A date in ANSI C is represented by a variable of type `time_t`. On many UNIX systems, `time_t` is a `long int` that measures the number of seconds since the beginning of January 1, 1970. Although this is a reasonable representation, it is hardly something that is meaningful to the average user. Thus ANSI C provides `ctime`. Its prototype, defined in `<time.h>`, is

```
char *ctime( const time_t *T );
```

`ctime` expects the *address* of a `time_t` variable and returns a pointer to 26 bytes of memory representing the time in the format

```
"Tue Nov 13 20:32:00 1973\n\0"
```

Where do the 26 bytes of memory come from? The fine print of `ctime` says that it returns a pointer to *static* data. This means that each call to `ctime` uses the same part of memory to store the 26-byte time.

Figure 8.31 illustrates an important consequence of returning a pointer to static data. At line 9 we get the current time of day using the routine `time`. This is another routine, defined in `time.h`, and it expects the address of a `time_t` variable in which it will place a representation of the current time. At line 10 this time is converted. We then suspend execution for 5 seconds, meaning that we do nothing. (`sleep` is a UNIX-specific routine.) At lines 12 and 13 we get the current time again. When we print out the two times at lines 14 and 15, we expect them to be 5 seconds apart, but as the output shows, they are identical. This is because `Bct` and `Act` are pointing at the `static` memory used by `ctime`. Thus they have to be representing the same string.

```
/* 1*/    /* Print Out Starting And Ending Time. */
/* 2*/    /* Incorrect: ctime Returns A Pointer To static Data */

/* 3*/    #include <time.h>
/* 4*/    #include <stdio.h>

/* 5*/    main( void )
/* 6*/    {
/* 7*/        time_t Before, After;
/* 8*/        char *Bct, *Act;

/* 9*/        time( &Before );
/*10*/        Bct = ctime( &Before );

/*11*/        sleep( 5 );

/*12*/        time( &After );
/*13*/        Act = ctime( &After );

/*14*/        printf( "Before: %s", Bct );
/*15*/        printf( "After:  %s", Act );

/*16*/        return 0;
/*17*/    }
```

```
Before: Mon Oct 16 22:59:11 1995
After:  Mon Oct 16 22:59:11 1995
```

Figure 8.31:   Incorrect use of `ctime`: **static data is overwritten.**

 The moral of the story is that if a routine returns a pointer to static data, you must be done using the return value before the next call to the routine. Otherwise, the static data gets overwritten. If this is not possible, you must make a copy of the static data.

8.13.2   Returning a Pointer to an Automatic Variable

 Although returning a pointer to a `static` variable requires the user to be alert, returning a pointer to an automatic variable is a truly stupid idea. Some compilers will stop you from doing it because it cannot possibly be safe. The reason is that the variable being pointed at is deallocated when the routine returns. Thus you are pointing at a variable that potentially no longer exists. Therefore, never return a pointer to an automatic variable.

8.13.3   Returning a Pointer to a Dynamically Allocated Variable

 A third option is to have a routine dynamically allocate new storage via `malloc` and return a pointer to it. We have seen this already in `GetInts`. You still need to be careful to document this, because it could result in memory leakage if the caller of the routine does not eventually `free` the allocated memory.

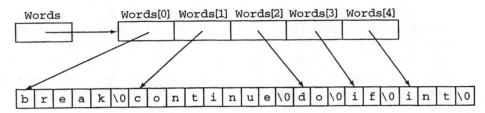

Figure 8.32: `char *Words[ ] = { "break", "continue", "do", "if", "int" };.`

8.14 Arrays of Strings: `char * []`

In this section we consider the efficient representation of an array of strings. Because some strings are short and some are long, we want to use the `char *` representation of a string rather than constraining ourselves to some fixed length. Thus an array of strings is an array of `char *` variables.

Figure 8.32 illustrates the consequence of the following declaration:

```
char *Words[ ] = { "break", "continue", "do", "if", "int" };
```

The declaration states that `Words` is an array of `char *`, and the initialization tells us that the array holds five pointers. `Word[0]` is initialized to point at `"break"`, `Word[1]` points at `"continue"`, and so on. `Words[1][3]` is the character `'n'`.[4]

Each individual string must be stored in contiguous memory. It is likely, but not required, that the compiler will store the entire collection of strings in consecutive memory locations. Notice that the declaration is interpreted as an array of pointers rather than a pointer to an array. This is because `[ ]` has higher precedence than `*`, and thus the array type sticks to `Word`.

```
char *(Words[ ]);
```

would declare a pointer to an array, which would be drastically different. Actually, it would be illegal, because an array size would be required to perform the initialization. The declaration

```
char **Words;
```

would be identical to the declaration shown in Figure 8.32, although it is a bit more confusing. It would be needed if you planned to expand the array of strings dynamically. On the other hand, the declaration

```
char Words[ ][ ];
```

is wrong, even if array bounds are provided, because it declares a two-dimensional array of characters.

---

[4]Strictly speaking, we should declare `const char *Words[ ] ....`

A common mistake when specifying the initialization list is forgetting a comma. Because the comma separates two strings, when it is forgotten, string concatenation takes over. In our example, if the comma between `"if"` and `"int"` is omitted, `Words` is an array of four pointers, the last of which points at `"ifint"`. Watch out for this one, as it happens all the time, especially to the typing deficient. In the remainder of this section we look at how arrays of strings are manipulated by showing three sample programs.

8.14.1   Application: Error Messages

Our first application is a simple mechanism to handle error messages. By having one routine do this, we can assure consistency in the reporting of errors. Moreover, we can avoid the repetitive typing of long error messages by calling our routine with the name of a short error code. Figure 8.33 shows how this is done. The error codes are listed in lines 6 to 10, and the corresponding error messages are listed in lines 15 to 19. The use of an (anonymous) enumerated type guarantees that the error codes are assigned consecutive integers starting from zero. This is perfect, because it means that the error codes can be used as an index into the `ErrorMessages` array. Thus the basic implementation of `PrintError` becomes trivial.

8.14.2   Application: Sorting an Array of Strings

Our second example shows how to sort an array of strings. We use the basic Shellsort algorithm from Section 7.5. To sort an array of strings, we need to adjust the type declarations at lines 4 and 7 to reflect `char *`. Two strings are compared by `strcmp` at line 14 (Figure 8.34). The only remaining detail is how the array is rearranged. The phrasing of the last sentence provides a hint: the strings never change, but rather, the pointers in the array A of pointers move. This is reflected in two ways. First, A is declared to be an array of `const char *` (i.e., strings that do not change value). Second, we use the same assignment statements that were present in our original Shellsort rather than replacing them with `strcpy`. The assignment statements just rearrange the pointers. Figure 8.35 shows how `Words` is sorted if it is declared as

```
const char *Words[ ] = { "break", "continue", "if", "do", "int" };
```

A `strcpy` would not work for three reasons. First, because of the `const` declaration, the compiler will not allow it. Second, though `Tmp` is a pointer, it is not pointing at anything in particular, so a `strcpy` at line 12 would be catastrophic. Even if `Tmp` were a large array, line 15 would show the third problem. We can never be certain that the string `A[j]` is large enough to hold the string `A[j - Gap]`. All of this comes back to the basic abstract point: when we sort an array, the items in the array move. In our case, the items are pointers to chunks of memory, so it is the pointers, not the chunks, that need to move.

8.14.3   Application: Binary Search for Strings

Our final application concerns searching. Here we have a collection of items, and we would like to know if an arbitrary item X is in the collection. In Figure 8.36 the items are strings that represent the names of states. We use our now standard method of declaring and initializing an array of strings. Presumably, a routine would convert the input from the user to lowercase, and strip out blanks.

```
/* 1*/    #include <stdio.h>

/* 2*/    /* The Error Codes. */
/* 3*/    /* Automatically Assigned Starting From 0 */

/* 4*/    enum
/* 5*/    {
/* 6*/        ErNoMem,
/* 7*/        ErOutOfRange,
/* 8*/        ErFormat,
/* 9*/        ErEOF,
/*10*/        ErError
/*11*/    };

/*12*/    /* The Corresponding Error Messages */

/*13*/    const char *ErrorMessages[ ] =
/*14*/    {
/*15*/        "Out of memory",
/*16*/        "Input value out of range",
/*17*/        "Format error",
/*18*/        "Premature end of input",
/*19*/        "Bad argument to PrintError"
/*20*/    };

/*21*/    static const NumErr =
/*22*/                    sizeof( ErrorMessages ) / sizeof( char * );

/* 1*/    void
/* 2*/    PrintError( int ErrorNum )
/* 3*/    {
/* 4*/        if( ErrorNum < 0 || ErrorNum >= NumErr )
/* 5*/            ErrorNum = ErError;
/* 6*/        printf( "Error: %s.\n", ErrorMessages[ ErrorNum ] );
/* 7*/    }
```

Figure 8.33:   Routines to print out errors by code.

We could now use a simple sequential scan to perform the search. However, this is inefficient: on average, we would examine 25 strings before finding a match, and an unsuccessful search would require that we examine all of the strings. To make the search more efficient, we will *preprocess* the data by arranging the items in sorted order. This could be done either by hand or by calling Shellsort once before the first search.

Once we have done that, a much more efficient algorithm is achieved by performing the searches in the middle of the array rather than at an end. This is known as a *binary search* and is implemented in Figure 8.36.

At any point in time we keep track of Low and High, which delimit the portion of the array where an item, if present, must reside. Initially, the range is from 0 to ArrayLen-1. If Low is larger than High, we know that the item is not present, and we return -1, which

```
/* 1*/    /* Shellsort An Array Of Strings */
/* 2*/    /* Do Not Move Strings, But Just Pointers */

/* 3*/    void
/* 4*/    Shellsort( const char *A[ ], const unsigned int N )
/* 5*/    {
/* 6*/        unsigned int Gap;
/* 7*/        const char *Tmp;
/* 8*/        unsigned int i, j; /* Loop Counters */

/* 9*/        for( Gap = N/2; Gap > 0; Gap = Gap == 2 ? 1 : Gap / 2.2 )
/*10*/            for( i = Gap; i < N; i++ )
/*11*/            {
/*12*/                Tmp = A[ i ];
/*13*/                for( j = i; j >= Gap &&
/*14*/                      strcmp( Tmp,  A[ j - Gap ] ) < 0; j -= Gap )
/*15*/                    A[ j ] = A[ j - Gap ];

/*16*/                A[ j ] = Tmp;
/*17*/            }
/*18*/    }
```

Figure 8.34:   Shellsort an array of strings. `string.h` **is already included.**

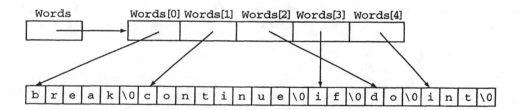

Figure 8.35:   Result of sorting `const char *Words[ ] = { "break",`
`"continue", "if", "do", "int" };`.

cannot be confused with the return value of a successful search. Otherwise, we let `Mid` be the halfway point of the range (rounding down if the range has an even number of elements) and compare the item we are searching for with the item in position `Mid`. As Figure 8.37 shows, if the item we are looking for is less than the item in position `Mid`, it must reside in the range `Low` to `Mid-1`, while if it greater, it must reside in `Mid+1` to `High`. Thus lines 14 to 17 of `BinarySearch` alter the possible range, essentially cutting it in half. In our case, this limits the number of possible calls to `strcmp` to six.

    If we are lucky and find a match, we can immediately return to the position where the match occurred. Since we are only lucky once per `BinarySearch`, we do not test for that case first, but instead, arrange the tests so that the mostly likely successes come early. This minimizes the total number of tests. By the way, this routine is trickier than it seems. Exercise 31 shows some common errors.

```
/* 1*/      const char *States[ ] =
/* 2*/      {
/* 3*/          "alabama","alaska","arizona","arkansas","california",
/* 4*/          "colorado","connecticut","delaware","florida","georgia",
/* 5*/          "hawaii","idaho","illinois","indiana","iowa",
/* 6*/          "kansas","kentucky","louisiana","maine","maryland",
/* 7*/          "massachusetts","michigan","minnesota","mississippi",
/* 8*/          "missouri","montana","nebraska","nevada","newhampshire",
/* 9*/          "newjersey","newmexico","newyork","northcarolina",
/*10*/          "northdakota","ohio","oklahoma","oregon","pennsylvania",
/*11*/          "rhodeisland","southcarolina","southdakota","tennessee",
/*12*/          "texas","utah","vermont","virginia","washington",
/*13*/          "westvirginia","wisconsin","wyoming"
/*14*/      };

/*15*/      static const NumStates = sizeof States / sizeof( char * );



/* 1*/      /* Return Position Of A String In An Array Of Strings */
/* 2*/      /* Array Must Be Sorted; return -1 if Not Found */

/* 3*/      int
/* 4*/      BinarySearch( const char *Str, const char *StrArray[ ],
/* 5*/                      const unsigned int ArrayLen )
/* 6*/      {
/* 7*/          int Low = 0, High = ArrayLen - 1;
/* 8*/          int Mid;
/* 9*/          int Cmp;

/*10*/          while( Low <= High )
/*11*/          {
/*12*/              Mid = ( Low + High ) / 2;
/*13*/              Cmp = strcmp( Str, StrArray[ Mid ] );
/*14*/              if( Cmp < 0 )
/*15*/                  High = Mid - 1;
/*16*/              else if( Cmp > 0 )
/*17*/                  Low = Mid + 1;
/*18*/              else
/*19*/                  return Mid;
/*20*/          }

/*21*/          return -1; /* Item Not Found */
/*22*/      }
```

Figure 8.36: **Binary search on an array of strings.**

Low		Mid		High
< StrArray[Mid]			> StrArray[Mid]	

Figure 8.37: **Binary search illustrated.**

```
/* 1*/     #include <stdio.h>

/* 2*/     #define Pi 3.1416
/* 3*/     #define NoArea ( -1.0 )

/* 4*/     enum { Circle, Rectangle, Square };

/* 5*/     /* Names Must Be in The Same Order As enum List */
/* 6*/     static char *ShapeNames[ ] =
/* 7*/     {
/* 8*/         "circle",
/* 9*/         "rectangle",
/*10*/         "square",
/*11*/     };

/*12*/     #define DiffShapes ( sizeof ShapeNames / sizeof( char * ) )
```

Figure 8.38:   Beginning of case study revision; includes list of shape names.

8.15   Recurring Case Study: Part 4

User friendliness is an important component of any program. Prompting for a number (e.g., 1) instead of a name (e.g., `circle`) can make a program more difficult to use initially. In this section we adjust the previous implementation so that it accepts names instead of numbers. A side benefit is that it will be easier to add new types of shapes. Figure 8.38 shows three constructs that are added since Section 7.11. The enum is used instead of a sequence of `#define` statements. A consequence is that `Circle` is assigned the value 0, `Rectangle` is 1, and `Square` is 2. The only reason for using the enumerated type is to guarantee this assignment; consequently, there is no type name associated with the enum. Next we provide an array of strings. Note that the value `Circle` represents the position of `"circle"` in the `ShapeName` array. Finally, `DiffShapes` represents the number of currently known shapes.

To add a new shape, we need to add an entry to the enum declaration, add a new string at the end of `ShapeName`, provide a corresponding `Process` function, and add a case to the `if/else` statement in `main`. In Chapter 9 we will see how to make additions of new types of shapes slightly easier. Figure 8.39 replaces Figure 7.32. The routine `GetChoice` shown in Figure 8.40 is called in place of the `scanf` at lines 11 and 12 in `main` (Figure 7.34). In addition, lines 8 to 10 are now obsolete. These are the only changes needed in `main`. `GetChoice` reads a string and then scans the `ShapeNames` array until it finds a match. It returns the index where the match occurs, or -1 if no match is found. A binary search is not used because the number of items in the array is so small.

The preprocessor macro `StrConv` is used to generate the string field conversion for `printf`. Since `MaxStringLen` is 80, we want `"%80s"`. The macro at line 2 does not quite work because

`StrConv1( MaxStringLen )`

expands to

```
/* 1*/    void
/* 2*/    PrintShapeName( int i )
/* 3*/    {

/* 4*/        if( i < 0 || i >= DiffShapes )
/* 5*/            printf( "unrecognized shape" );
/* 6*/        else
/* 7*/            printf( "%s", ShapeNames[ i ] );
/* 8*/    }
```

Figure 8.39: Revised `PrintShapeName`.

```
/* 1*/    #define MaxStringLen 80
/* 2*/    #define StrConv1( Len ) ( "%" #Len "s" )
/* 3*/    #define StrConv( Len ) ( StrConv1( Len ) )

/* 4*/    int
/* 5*/    GetChoice( void )
/* 6*/    {
/* 7*/        int i;
/* 8*/        char Str[ MaxStringLen + 1 ];

/* 9*/        if( scanf( StrConv( MaxStringLen ), Str ) == 1 )
/*10*/            for( i = 0; i < DiffShapes; i++ )
/*11*/                if( strcmp( Str, ShapeNames[ i ] ) == 0 )
/*12*/                    return i;

/*13*/        return -1;
/*14*/    }
```

Figure 8.40: Parse an input string and return number corresponding to type of shape.

`"%MaxStringLens"`

Consequently, we use an extra level of macros. The macro call at line 9 expands to

`StrConv1( 80 )`

and then we get the desired result when the macro is rescanned. See Chapter 5 for more details.

8.16   Summary

In this chapter we have discussed the string, which in C is implemented as a null-terminated array of characters. Because of the relationship between pointers and arrays, the basic string type is `char *`. We saw some more of the library string routines, and in Section 8.14 we saw how to initialize, sort, and search an array of strings.

The routines in Section 8.14 were a bit limited, however. Suppose that given a state, we want to know the capital, population, and so on? Although we could keep parallel arrays representing each of these pieces of information, it is a messy approach. We would have to pass all the arrays as parameters to avoid using large numbers of global variables, and in addition, sorting the collection would be messy, since we would have to make sure that all the arrays were consistent with each other (i.e., the ith capital refers to the ith state). In Chapter 9 we will examine the *structure*, which is a way to collect all the information into one variable.

8.16.1 What Was Covered

- A char is used to store a single character. Internally it is a small (usually 8-bit) integer.

- A character constant is surrounded by single quotes. Special escape sequences are used for unprintable characters and a few printable characters, such as quotes and the backslash.

- The routines in <ctype.h> can be used to test the properties of a character. These routines are generally fast macros. Their use guarantees portability.

- <ctype.h> also provides toupper and tolower, but some older systems have different, unsafe forms. Beware of these.

- Single-character I/O can be performed by getchar and putchar.

- A *string* is a null-terminated array of characters. Always leave room in the array declaration for a null terminator.

- Two string constants separated by white space are concatenated automatically.

- The trigraph feature is provided for limited character sets. It can occasionally lead to unexpected output.

- Trigraphs and escape sequences apply only to the source code. If we output the string Name, which has the characters *backslash* followed by 'n', we get \n.

- Strings can be copied and compared by strcpy and strcmp. The = and == operations do not work, even though the latter is legal. The string operations mimic the corresponding operations for integers, so the first parameter represents the left side of the operator. Other operations are also available.

- puts can be used to output a null-terminated string. A newline is printed automatically afterward. gets should not be used for input because it does not guard against overflow.

- sscanf and sprintf can be used to read and write from strings. They have the same syntax as scanf and printf except that an additional string is used as the leading parameter.

- Using pointers to traverse an array has historically been faster than using an index. However, the code is trickier, and the speed advantage has been largely negated by modern optimizing compilers.

- strchr and strrchr return a pointer to the first and last occurrences, respectively, of a given character in a given string. strstr can be used to search for a fixed pattern in a string.

- An array of strings is declared using char *Str[ ].

- The binary search can be used to search a sorted array quickly.

- A simple word processor is implemented in only about 100 lines of code. The exercises ask you to improve it.

8.16.2   Friendly Reminders

- A char is not necessarily unsigned.

- The ASCII character set, although widely used, is not universal. Use the library routines when possible, and avoid nonportable constructs.

- Do not forget the x when using a hexadecimal escape sequence, and do not forget the \ when using an escape sequence—particularly when using the tab, newline, or null terminator escapes. Also, remember that a / is not a \.

- The is... routines in <ctype.h> return nonzero, but generally not 1, for true.

- Although an int can be sent to the is... macros in <ctype.h>, if it is large, an out-of-bounds array access will result, possibly crashing the program.

- Do not test a char for being less than 128. It may be a tautology (i.e., always true).

- <ctype.h> also provides toupper and tolower, but some older systems have different, unsafe forms. Beware of these.

- getchar returns an int because EOF needs representation. Storing the return value in a char is wrong and on some machines can lead to a nonterminating input scan.

- When using getchar, remember that != has higher precedence than =, so an assignment of the return value of getchar must be parenthesized.

- Do not interchange 'x' and "x". The former is a single character; the latter is an array of two characters, the second of which is the null terminator.

- An array large enough to hold a string of length L must have size $L + 1$ so that a null terminator can be stored.

- The declaration

  ```
  char *Str2 = "Constant string";
  ```

  does not allocate memory to store a copy of the constant string. Instead, it just has Str2 point at the zeroth character of the constant string. Section 8.10 contains more common errors.

- Never use the & operator on a string for scanf. The string name already represents a memory address.

- For scanf, use a maximum-field-width specifier with the %s and %[conversions unless you can declare a huge array. If you are writing a critical program, you should use the specifier even if the array is huge. Otherwise, a large input string may corrupt memory.

- Specifying a nonstring for the %s converter will probably cause your program to crash.

- Watch out for trigraph sequences. They start with ??.

- Do not use any relational or equality operators on strings because what you will be comparing are their memory locations.

- strncpy and strncat have different behavior for overflow.

- Do not use

  ```
  printf( Str );
  ```

but instead use

```
printf( "%s", Str );
```

- The NULL pointer is not equivalent to the empty string " ". Most of the string routines will fail on NULL pointers.

- When a pointer to static data is returned from a routine, the dereferenced value is valid only until the next call to the routine. At that point it is overwritten.

- Never return a pointer to an automatic local variable.

- If a routine returns a pointer to dynamically allocated memory, the user of the routine must eventually call free to avoid memory leakage.

- Be careful not to forget the comma that separates the strings in an array of string initialization. If you do, string concatenation will be performed silently.

EXERCISES

1. Write a portable implementation of ToLower.

2. Compare the time required to execute the following code, using the two implementations of ToUpper in the text, as well as your library routine:

```
main( void )
{
    int i, Ign;

    for( i = 0; i < 10000; i++ )
    {
        Ign = ToUpper( 'm' );
        Ign = ToUpper( 'M' );
    }
    return 0;
}
```

3. Use an array to implement ToUpper and ToLower portably and efficiently. You may write a program to generate these routines.

4. Write a program that counts and outputs the total number of each of the following types of characters: *upper, lower, numeric, blank, tab, newline,* and *all other.* The program should read the input until the end of file and print all six totals.

5. Write a program that counts and outputs the total number of each of the 26 lower- and uppercase letters.

6. The following code compiles but generates an error when run. What is the problem?

```
# include <stdio.h>

main( void )
{
    char *Name;

    printf( "Enter a name: " );
    if( scanf( "%s", Name ) == 1 )
        printf( "Read %s\n", Name );
    return 0;
}
```

7. What's wrong with the following code fragment?

```
char *Str1 = "abc";
char *Str2 = "def";

printf( "%s\n", strcat( Str1, Str2 ) );
```

8. Write routines to implement (without using pointer arithmetic):

   (a) `strcat`

   (b) `strncpy`

   (c) `strncmp`

   (d) `strtol`

   (e) `strtod`

   (f) `StrUpper`, which changes its parameter to upper case. You may assume the existence of `ToUpper`, which operates on a single character.

   (g) `StrLower`, which changes its parameter to lower case. You may assume the existence of `ToLower`, which operates on a single character.

   (h) `puts`

9. Why are the following statements not equivalent?

```
printf( "%s", Str );
printf( Str );
```

10. Write the routine

```
int ReadLine( char *Str, unsigned int N );
```

that reads up to N characters from one line, discards the terminating newline, and tacks on a null terminator. If N-1 characters are read prior to the newline, the rest of the line is discarded. Return a value that indicates if input characters were ignored.

11. Write the routine

```
int GetWord( char *Word, unsigned int MaxLen );
```

that skips white space and reads the next word from input. A word is any sequence of non-white-space characters. If this word would have string length greater than MaxLen, return an error.

12. Write the routine

```
void SkipLine( void );
```

that reads and discards all characters up to and including a newline.

13. The UNIX editor command for delete is d, but can be preceded by either zero, one, or two comma-separated numbers. The following are all legal: d; 2d; 13,15d. However, the command must be entirely on one line. Write a routine that prints the word `deletion` when one of these forms is detected. *Hint: Read the line and then use* `sscanf` *by trying to match the longest command first.*

14. Implement the following routines, using pointer traversals. Remember that `strcat`, `strncpy`, and `puts` return pointers.

   (a) `strcat`

   (b) `strncpy`

   (c) `strncmp`

     (d) `strchr`

     (e) `strrchr`

     (f) `strstr`

     (g) `puts`

15. Type in both the pointer and array versions of `Strlen`, `Strcpy`, and `Strcmp`. Write a driver program that generates strings of various lengths and performs many of these string operations. On your machine, with all optimization options enabled, are the pointer versions significantly faster than the array versions? *Depending on your system, you may be surprised by the answer.*

16. Although `strcat` returns a pointer to the resultant string, for consecutive `strcat` operations, it would be more efficient to return a pointer to the null terminator of the resultant string. Modify `strcat` to do this.

17. A library routine might improve on our `strcpy` by optimizing the copying of characters. On some 16-bit machines, for instance, copying two bytes at a time is just as efficient as copying one byte. These kinds of optimizations are inherently nonportable.

     (a) Rewrite `Strcpy` for your machine. If both `Rhs` and `Lhs` are aligned on an `int` boundary, do a type conversion to `(int *)`. You'll need an algorithm to determine if any of the bytes that form the copied `int` represent the null terminator.

     (b) How does this affect the example in Figure 8.23?

     (c) On your machine, show how to achieve a similar effect.

18. Using the algorithm suggested in the text and not a temporary array, write `strcpy` so that it safely copies even if the two strings overlap.

19. Many systems have the routine `strdup`

```
char *strdup( const char *Str );
```

     `strdup` dynamically allocates enough memory to store a copy of `Str`, performs the copy, and returns a pointer to that memory. It is not part of ANSI C. Write `strdup`.

20. Suppose that `Ch` is a `char`. Which of the following statements are legal, and what do the legal statements do? Test these statements on your machine.

```
Ch = "Silly"[ 1 ];
Ch = 1[ "Silly" ];
"Silly"[ 1 ] = 'a';
1[ "Silly" ] = 'a';
```

21. Suppose that `Str1` and `Str2` are both of type `char *`. On your machine, what gets printed, and what logic is the compiler using to arrive at its answer?

```
Str1 = "Silly";
Str2 = "Silly";
puts( Str1 == Str2 ? "Equal" : "Not Equal" );
```

22. Rewrite the `main` procedure in Figure 8.28 to use `getchar` exclusively.

23. Suppose in the `Justify` routine shown in Figure 8.29 that the first parameter to both `strcat` routines is `CurrentLine + CharsHeld`. What happens?

24. Modify the justification algorithm so that N blank lines terminate the previous paragraph, output $N - 1$ blank lines, and begin a new paragraph. (The current algorithm always prints no blank lines.)

25. Modify the justification algorithm so that the sequence ## at the end of a line forces all pending text to be output, flush right, with no blank padding.

26. Modify the justification algorithm so that the sequence @@ at the end of a line forces all pending text to be centered, with no blank padding.

27. When a period ends a sentence, two spaces are generally required to follow.

    (a) Modify the justification algorithm so that two spaces always follow a period unless the period ends an output line.

    (b) Modify the justification algorithm so that two spaces follow the period if the period ends an input line. As in part (a), no spaces are required if the period ends an output line.

28. The justification algorithm always prints the larger gaps toward the right side and the small gaps toward the left side. A prettier method is to alternate, so that if one line has its large gaps on the left, the next line has its large gaps on the right. Add this improvement to the PutOut routine.

29. Modify PrintError to take a char * second parameter. Print that parameter after the sequence Error: but before the remainder of the error message. Handle the case where NULL is passed.

30. Write a program that reads, sorts, and then outputs a sequence of strings read from the terminal. You may assume a maximum string length of 256, but the number of strings is unknown until the end of input is reached. Since you will need array doubling, the type declaration is char **Str.

31. For the binary search routine in Figure 8.36, show the consequences of the following replacement code fragments:

    (a) Line 10: Using the test Low < High

    (b) Line 12: Assigning Mid = Low + High / 2

    (c) Line 15: Assigning High = Mid

    (d) Line 17: Assigning Low = Mid

    (e) Line 21: Returning 0 instead of -1 when the item is not found

32. Rewrite the binary search routine to use pointers LowPtr, MidPtr, and HighPtr. Recall that average of pointers can be achieved by subtraction. Thus the computation of MidPtr is obtained via

    ```
    MidPtr = LowPtr + ( HighPtr - LowPtr ) / 2;
    ```

33. The 11-letter word MISSISSIPPI has only four different letters. Its ratio of string length to unique characters is thus 2.75. Write a program that reads a sequence of words and outputs all words whose ratio is larger than 2. If you have a sufficiently complete dictionary, you should find at least one word with ratio 3, namely *deeded*.

34. Write the routine

    ```
    int RomanToInt( const char *RomanStr );
    ```

    that returns the integer represented by the roman number RomanStr. Return -1 on error.

35. The *word search game* consists of a square array of characters (the *puzzle*) and a sequence of hidden words (the *word list*) that appear in the puzzle in any of the eight horizontal, vertical, or diagonal orientations. The puzzle in Figure 8.41 contains the following words: char (fourth column going down), do (third column going down), float (top left going diagonally),

`icons` (top right going diagonally), `if` (top right going left), `int` (top right going down), `main` (last column, going left), `scanf` (bottom left going up), and `short` (bottom left going right). An instance of the word search game is input by specifying the puzzle, then a blank line, and then the word list. Write a program that solves the word search game.

```
f  c  r  f  i
n  l  d  c  n
a  n  o  h  t
c  n  i  a  m
s  h  o  r  t
```

Figure 8.41:   Puzzle for word search exercise.

9

Structures

As we have seen, an array is a collection of identically typed objects. The array has two major benefits. First, we can index, and thus loop over, each item in the array. Second, when using functions, we can pass the name of the array instead of passing each object as a parameter. In this chapter we examine the *structure*. The structure is used to store a collection of objects that need not be of the same type. Because the objects in the collection are not constrained to be of the same type, we cannot simply loop over them as we would for an array. Consequently, we need to provide an alternative to the array index to access individual variables in a structure. The major benefit of the structure is limited to the ability to treat related variables as a unit, which is important when passing it between functions. In this chapter we examine the syntax and simple uses of the structure.

9.1 Syntax for Structures

We begin by showing the simplest use of structures, as well as the more advanced, but seldom used, *bit fields* and `union` declaration.

9.1.1 Declaration and Initialization

The declaration in Figure 9.1 creates the new type `struct Student`. The syntax is that the keyword `struct` is followed (optionally) by a *tag name* and then a brace-enclosed list of *fields*, with their types. Because it is a declaration statement, you must make sure to supply a semicolon.

    A common error is to forget the semicolon. If the structure declaration, for example, appears on the lines directly preceding `main`, your program may crash on exit. This is because the missing semicolon tells the compiler that the function `main` returns a variable of the type `struct ...`!! In our example, `Student` is called the *structure tag name*. Note carefully that `Student` is not a type. To make it a type, we can use the *typedef*, shown later in Figure 9.1. We are allowed to reuse `Student` because tag names and types

```
struct Student
{
    char *FirstName;
    char *LastName;
    int SocialSecurityNum;
    double GradePointAvg;
};

typedef struct Student Student;

struct Student Valedictorian;
Student Salutatorian;
Student SchoolRoll[ MaxStudents ];
Student X = { "John", "Doe", 123456789, 3.12 };
Student Y = Salutatorian;
```

Figure 9.1:   Declaration of `struct Student`.

```
typedef struct
{
    char *FirstName;
    char *LastName;
    int SocialSecurityNum;
    double GradePointAvg;
} Student;
```

Figure 9.2:   `typedef` declaration of `Student`.

```
struct Student
{
    char *FirstName;
    char *LastName;
    int SocialSecurityNum;
    double GradePointAvg;
} Valedictorian, Salutatorian, SchoolRoll[ MaxStudents ],
        X = { "John", "Doe", 123456789 }, Y = Salutatorian;
```

Figure 9.3:   Declaration of `struct Student`.

have a different namespace: they are stored separately by the compiler.[1] We can combine the `typedef` and `struct` declaration by placing the word `typedef` before `struct` and the word `Student` before the last semicolon in the original `struct` declaration. Moreover, since the tag name is optional, we can remove it. Figure 9.2 shows this style.

Once we have a type declaration, we can declare variables of that type. One way is to provide a comma-separated list of variables following the } and preceding the semicolon. This makes for difficult-to-read code, as shown in Figure 9.3. In Figure 9.1 we show some more readable alternatives. There `Valedictorian` is declared using the basic structure declaration, while the declaration of `Salutatorian` uses the name created by the `typedef`. We can also declare an array of structures, as is done for `SchoolRoll`.

_____

[1]Making the tag name and type name identical is a widely adopted practice. This is perhaps the only instance in C where duplication of names is commonly accepted.

Finally, the last two declarations shows how structures can be initialized. As with arrays, we provide a brace-enclosed list of initial values for each structure field, in order. If there are too many initial values it is an error, and if there are too few, the remaining fields are initialized to zero. A structure can also be initialized to have the same value as another structure of the same type. As with other types, a structure that is uninitialized will be set to all zeros if it is `static` or `external`, and will be undefined if it is `automatic`.

9.1.2   Operations on Structures

The most important operation allowed on a structure is the member operation. The `.` operator allows access to any field of the structure. Thus, in our example, `X.GradePointAvg` has the value of `3.12`, and `X.GradePointAvg` behaves as any variable of type `double` would. Like the `[ ]` operator, the `.` operator is a postfix operator, because it follows the name of a structure. Therefore, it has the same precedence and associativity rules as other postfix operators, such as `[ ]` and the postfix autoincrement and autodecrement. In the next section, we will see an important consequence of this, that leads, at least indirectly, to the establishment of another operator. A further consequence is that the statement

```
scanf( "%d %lf", &Y.SocialSecurityNum, &Y.GradePointAvg );
```

performs as intended, because the member access has higher precedence than the address-of operator (which is a prefix operator).

Besides accessing members, what can be done on structures as a unit? The answer is not much. In fact, before ANSI C, the answer was virtually nothing, except to take its address via the `&` operator, and figure out how much storage it uses, with the `sizeof` operator.[2] All other operations on a structure were forbidden, including equality comparison, assignment, and use as a function parameter. Notice that if assignment is not allowed, returning a structure makes little sense, and is thus also disallowed.

ANSI C has slightly relaxed these rules, although in many cases it is a good idea not to take advantage of them. It is still illegal to compare two structures, even for equality, because all of the reasonable methods give the logically correct answer only part of the time. It is now legal to copy a structure, and consequently, it is also legal to pass a structure as a parameter and to return a structure. However, it is a bad idea in many cases. Looking at our example, let's consider the consequence of `Y=X`. First, note that unlike arrays, structure variables do not represent main memory addresses but rather, the entire structure unit. The assignment is a byte-by-byte copy of `X` into `Y`. As a result, `Y.SocialSecurityNum` gets the value `123456789`, and `Y.GradePointAvg` gets the value `3.12`. In fact, if all the fields are numbers, copying a structure seems like a good idea.

In our case, however, we have two strings in the structure. As a result of the copy, `Y.FirstName` points at the same five bytes of memory as `X.FirstName`, and `Y.LastName` points at the same four bytes of memory as `X.LastName`. The good news is that copying the value of a memory address is cheap, but the cost is that two variables are sharing information. If the string represented by `X.LastName` changes, it will also change the string represented by `Y.LastName`, which is probably not what was intended. Thus in many applications where copying is prevalent, it might be better to declare `FirstName`

---

[2]Note that the size of a structure may be more than the sum of the sizes of its fields. This is because holes in the structures may be necessary to achieve proper alignment of each field. See the discussion in Section 6.6, and in particular, Figure 6.16.

and LastName as arrays, thus setting aside memory. But now we have to set aside lots of memory, say 20 bytes per string. In addition to the wasting of space that will occur in a large array of such structures, we have the problem that a byte-to-byte copying of the structures implies that all 20 bytes of each string are copied, even if the null terminator appears much earlier. After all, the compiler has no way to know that the array of characters is to be treated as a string. The result is that copying structures that have arrays in them, which is quite common, is very expensive, because entire arrays are copied. Thus, if you must copy structures, it is usually better to do it member by member if strings are involved.

Because copying a structure can be expensive, and because call by value entails an automatic copy, it is generally a bad idea to pass a structure as a parameter when speed is a primary criterion. Instead, a pointer to the structure (preceded by const if we do not intend modification) is generally passed. Similarly, structures are rarely returned. Either a pointer to a structure is returned, or the return is simulated by adjusting a structure passed by reference.[3] Requiring the explicit intervention of the user in this manner is one of the biggest shortcomings of C, not to mention a confusing part of the language.

To summarize: you can only take the address of a structure, access its members, and compute its size in traditional C. ANSI C also allows assignment, passing by value, and returning, but in many cases, these new features are not worth using because of the significant overhead they involve.

9.1.3   Example: Dates

As an example of how structures are typically used, we consider the tm structure, defined in <time.h>. Figure 9.4 shows the fields specified by ANSI C .[4] Your system may have more, but these must be present. The fields are self-explanatory, except for the last one, which deals with whether or not daylight savings time is in effect; this is important for determining elapsed login time when the login session includes a time change. We will discuss this more in Appendix D.

As an example, November 13, 1973 at 8:32 PM would be represented by

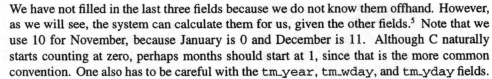

```
struct tm TheDay = { 0, 32, 20, 13, 10, 73 };
```

We have not filled in the last three fields because we do not know them offhand. However, as we will see, the system can calculate them for us, given the other fields.[5] Note that we use 10 for November, because January is 0 and December is 11. Although C naturally starts counting at zero, perhaps months should start at 1, since that is the more common convention. One also has to be careful with the tm_year, tm_wday, and tm_yday fields.

A person born on Nov. 13, 1973 will naturally have a few birthdays fall on Friday the 13th. Figure 9.5 shows a simple program to calculate when this occurs. Note that the

---

[3]Recall the warnings in Section 8.13. Returning a pointer to a structure requires care.

[4]A relatively unknown fact is that leap seconds are added to minutes in the same way that a leap day is added to some Februarys. The ANSI C committee mistakenly thought that 2 seconds could be added to some minutes, and thus allowed the tm_sec field to range from 0 to 61. In reality, any given minute may have at most one leap second added.

[5]Calculating the last field also requires knowledge of the location of the computer, because daylight savings time is not uniformly applied.

```
struct tm
{
    int     tm_sec;     /* seconds after the minute (0- 61)  */
    int     tm_min;     /* minutes after the hour   (0- 59)  */
    int     tm_hour;    /* hours after midnight     (0- 23)  */
    int     tm_mday;    /* day of the month         (1- 31)  */
    int     tm_mon;     /* month since January      (0- 11)  */
    int     tm_year;    /* years since 1900         (0-   )  */
    int     tm_wday;    /* days since Sunday        (0-  6)  */
    int     tm_yday;    /* days since January 1     (0-365)  */
    int     tm_isdst;   /* daylight savings time flag        */
};
```

Figure 9.4: `struct tm` **as defined in** `<time.h>`.

```
/* 1*/    /* Find All Friday The 13th Birthdays */
/* 2*/    /* For Person Born On Nov. 13, 1973 */

/* 3*/    #include <time.h>
/* 4*/    #include <stdio.h>

/* 5*/    main( void )
/* 6*/    {
/* 7*/        const Friday = 6 - 1;       /* Sunday Is 0, ... */
/* 8*/        struct tm TheTime = { 0 };  /* Set All Fields To 0 */
/* 9*/        int Year;

/*10*/        TheTime.tm_mon = 11 - 1;    /* January Is 0, ... */
/*11*/        TheTime.tm_mday = 13;       /* 13th Day Of The Month */

/*12*/        for( Year = 1973; Year < 2073; Year++ )
/*13*/        {
/*14*/            TheTime.tm_year = Year - 1900; /* 1900 Is 0, ... */
/*15*/            if( mktime( &TheTime ) == -1 )
/*16*/            {
/*17*/                printf( "mktime failed in %d\n", Year );
/*18*/                break;
/*19*/            }
/*20*/            if( TheTime.tm_wday == Friday )
/*21*/                printf( "%s", asctime( &TheTime ) );
/*22*/        }

/*23*/        return 0;
/*24*/    }
```

Figure 9.5:   Program to find all Friday the 13th birthdays for a friend.

program is simple because the system provides a routine to figure out what day of the week
a particular date falls on. That in itself is a tricky function because of leap years.

Line 8 declares a variable of type `struct tm`, which we initialize to all zeros. This
is important, because if, for example, tm_hour happens to have a value such as 48, the

routines we will use will add 2 days, to make the time and date "normal." We set the month and day fields at lines 10 and 11, and then iterate over at most 101 years. For each year we set the year field in the structure and then call mktime. The library routine mktime expects the *address* of a structure and will normalize it. The normalization guarantees that there are 0 to 59 seconds, 0 to 59 minutes, and so on, by adding to the next-largest quantum unit field as needed. It also calculates the day of the week and year, as well as if daylight savings time is in effect (under certain conditions).

If something goes wrong, it returns -1. The typical reason for failure is that the year is either too large or small. When that happens, we give up. On a successful return from mktime, we check if the tm_wday field represents a Friday, and print out the complete date using asctime. Notice that asctime also expects the address of the structure.

9.2 Arrays of Structures

Just as we can have arrays of int, double, and char, we can have arrays of any type, including a structure. Indeed, there is nothing that is particularly special about it. As an example, Figures 9.6 and 9.7 show some routines that can be used to simulate a card game. Lines 1 to 6 show the representation of a playing card. The first structure member represents the face value (1 to 13), where the *jack*, *queen*, and *king* are 11, 12, and 13, respectively, and the *ace* is a 1. The second structure member represents the suit, as defined by the enumerated type at line 1.

In friendly card games, one usually plays with a single deck, but casinos use several (usually, eight) decks at once, and usually only deal about 75% of those cards, at which point new cards are used. The parameters at lines 8, 9, and 11 can thus be altered to reflect casino rules. We have used the #define instead of const because these numbers represent the size of an array in a declaration. As we have seen before, const will not work.

The one routine in Figure 9.6 fills and then shuffles an array of cards with the requisite number of decks. The loop at lines 6 to 13 places the cards in a nonrandom order. Lines 15 to 21 perform the shuffling. The algorithm we use is that each card (except the first) is swapped with a randomly chosen card. The declaration and assignment at line 17 states that each time through the loop, RandCard is assigned the value of a "random" number. This number is obtained by calling the library routine rand and then making it small enough to be used as an array index by applying %(i+1). The effect of this is that in each iteration of the loop, SomeCards[i] is swapped with one of SomeCards[0], SomeCards[1],..., SomeCards[i], thus rearranging the cards in some nonobvious manner. It turns out that this is a better method than swapping with a totally random card via %TotalCards (see Exercises 3 and 4).

Let us explain in more detail what is going on. The routine rand returns an int that is obtained by calling a *random* number generator. Actually, what you get is not random at all but is supposed to look random to the untrained eye. Successive calls to rand give different numbers, but the ANSI C implementation of rand is not really very good for serious applications. More time consuming, but statistically better random number generators are available on many systems, and these should be used instead of rand if good statistical properties are needed. Unfortunately, only rand is specified by ANSI C, so using something else makes your program nonportable.

```
/* 1*/      typedef enum { Heart, Diamond, Club, Space } SuitType;

/* 2*/      typedef struct Card
/* 3*/      {
/* 4*/          unsigned int FaceVal;
/* 5*/          SuitType Suit;
/* 6*/      } Card;

/* 7*/          /* Constants To Allow Multiple Decks */
/* 8*/      #define Decks           1
/* 9*/      #define CardsPerDeck    52
/*10*/      #define TotalCards      ( Decks * CardsPerDeck )
/*11*/      #define MinCards        20 /* # Cards Till Need New Decks */

/*12*/      #include <stdlib.h>

/* 1*/      /* Discard Old Stack Of Cards And get New Cards */
/* 2*/      void
/* 3*/      NewDeck( Card SomeCards[ ], const int NumDecks )
/* 4*/      {
/* 5*/          int i, j, k;

/* 6*/              /* Load Up All The Cards */
/* 7*/          for( i = 0; i < NumDecks; i++ )
/* 8*/            for( j = 0; j < 13; j++ )
/* 9*/              for( k = 0; k < 4; k++ )
/*10*/              {
/*11*/                  SomeCards[ 52*i + 4*j + k ].Suit = k;
/*12*/                  SomeCards[ 52*i + 4*j + k ].FaceVal = j + 1;
/*13*/              }

/*14*/              /* Shuffle */
/*15*/          for( i = 1; i < TotalCards; i++ )
/*16*/          {       /* Choose Random Card And Swap */
/*17*/              int RandCard = rand( ) % ( i + 1 );
/*18*/              Card TmpCard = SomeCards[ i ];

/*19*/              SomeCards[ i ] = SomeCards[ RandCard ];
/*20*/              SomeCards[ RandCard ] = TmpCard;
/*21*/          }
/*22*/      }
```

Figure 9.6:   Some routines to simulate cards.

An important point is that you'll get the same random sequence every time you run the program. This is good for debugging, but bad once the program works. `srand` should be used once at the start of the program to add more randomness. We will say much more about the random number routines in Appendix D. The exercises ask you to look more closely at this algorithm and the properties of `rand`.

Figure 9.7 shows some additional routines. `Deal` assigns the next card from the dealer's undealt stack of cards to a `Card` passed by reference. It keeps the decks in a local

```
/* 1*/    /* Return The Next Card */
/* 2*/    void
/* 3*/    Deal( Card *OneCard )
/* 4*/    {
/* 5*/        static Card TheCards[ TotalCards ];
/* 6*/        static int CardsUndealt = 0;

/* 7*/        if( CardsUndealt < MinCards )
/* 8*/        {
/* 9*/            NewDeck( TheCards, Decks );
/*10*/            CardsUndealt = TotalCards;
/*11*/        }

/*12*/        *OneCard = TheCards[ --CardsUndealt ];
/*13*/    }

/* 1*/    /* Get Five Cards */
/* 2*/    void
/* 3*/    DealHand( Card Hand[ ] )
/* 4*/    {
/* 5*/        int i;

/* 6*/        for( i = 0; i < 5; i++ )
/* 7*/            Deal( &Hand[ i ] );
/* 8*/    }

/* 1*/    /* Returns Non Zero If All Cards Have Same Suit */
/* 2*/    int
/* 3*/    IsFlush( const Card Hand[ ] )
/* 4*/    {
/* 5*/        int i;

/* 6*/        for( i = 1; i < 5; i++ )
/* 7*/            if( Hand[ i ].Suit != Hand[ 0 ].Suit )
/* 8*/                return 0;

/* 9*/        return 1;
/*10*/    }
```

Figure 9.7:   Some more routines to simulate cards.

`static` variable. If the number of undealt cards is below the minimum, an entirely new deck is constructed. Note that if 20 cards are undealt, the remaining cards are in array positions 0 to 19; thus the prefix autodecrement is used. Thus the top card is copied to the structure `OneCard`, passed by reference, at the same time that the `static` variable `CardsUndealt` is decremented.

The routine `DealHand` fills a five-card hand by calling `Deal`. The routine `IsFlush` tests if the five cards have identical suits, by checking the last four cards against the first. Of course, in both routines, the indices begin at zero, in keeping with C conventions.

```
/* 1*/    int
/* 2*/    IsLeap( int Year )
/* 3*/    {
/* 4*/        if( Year % 4 )        /* Not Divisible By 4 */
/* 5*/            return 0;
/* 6*/        if( Year % 100 )      /* Divisible By 4, But Not 100 */
/* 7*/            return 1;
/* 8*/        if( Year % 400 )      /* Divisible By 100, But Not 400 */
/* 9*/            return 0;
/*10*/        return 1;             /* Divisible By 400 */
/*11*/    }
```

Figure 9.8: Routine `IsLeap`, which determines if `Year` is a leap year.

9.3 Pointers to Structures

The `Deal` routine in Section 9.2 assigns to a structure passed by reference. This is typical because passing a structure by value would force a potentially expensive copy. In this section we examine in detail how structures are passed by reference. As an example, suppose that we have a `struct tm` structure seen earlier and would like to fill in the `tm_yday` (days since Jan. 1) field. As we have seen, `mktime` does this for us, but handles only a certain range of years, because it deals with seconds also. Specifically, only 136 years' worth of seconds fit in a 32-bit unsigned integer. Thus, on many systems, the limit for `mktime` is generally not much more than 136 years.

Algorithmically, the tricky part is determining when a year is a leap year. This is shown in Figure 9.8. The rule is that years divisible by 4 are leap years, except that those divisible by 100 are not, except that those divisible by 400 are. Thus in any 400-year period, there are 97 leap years, making the average year have 365.2425 days.

Figure 9.9 shows the routine `MkYear`. As we can see, it expects a pointer to a `struct tm`. Lines 5 to 8 declare two arrays that contain the number of days in each month. The pointer at line 9 will be set to point to the start of one of these arrays as soon as the leap year calculation is done (at line 16). You can see now why the `tm_mon` field uses zero for January.

Assuming that we have not been passed a `NULL` pointer, we copy the relevant fields into temporary variables. As we have mentioned before, it is a good idea to avoid dereferencing pointers as much as possible because it could take extra time, and also because it is more error-prone. At lines 17 and 18, we check that the date is reasonable. Note that the `mktime` routine would adjust the other fields to obtain a normal form of time. Thus if the month was 14, the day 52, and the year 1910, it would be converted to March 24, 1911. It is actually a very tricky conversion, especially when leap years intrude. Thus we just return -1 if the fields do not make sense. Otherwise, the simple loop at lines 20 and 21 increments `Days` by the number of days in months preceding `Month`.

We see from this example that a pointer to a structure behaves no differently than any other pointer. However, we see a technical point. Because the dereferencing oper-

```
/* 1*/    /* Fill In The tm_yday Field, As In mktime */

/* 2*/    int
/* 3*/    MkYear( struct tm *TmStruct )
/* 4*/    {
/* 5*/        static const int MonthDays[ ] =
/* 6*/            { 31, 28, 31, 30, 31, 30, 31, 31, 30, 31, 30, 31 };
/* 7*/        static const int LeapMonthDays[ ] =
/* 8*/            { 31, 29, 31, 30, 31, 30, 31, 31, 30, 31, 30, 31 };
/* 9*/        const int *MyMonthDays;
/*10*/        int i;

/*11*/        if( TmStruct != NULL )
/*12*/        {
/*13*/                int Days  = ( *TmStruct ).tm_mday;
/*14*/            const int Month = ( *TmStruct ).tm_mon;
/*15*/            const int Year  = ( *TmStruct ).tm_year + 1900;

/*16*/            MyMonthDays = IsLeap( Year ) ?
/*                                  LeapMonthDays : MonthDays;
/*17*/            if( Month < 0 || Month > 11 || Days < 0 ||
/*18*/                    Days > MyMonthDays[ Month ] )
/*19*/                return -1;

/*20*/            for( i = 0; i < Month; i++ )
/*21*/                Days += MyMonthDays[ i ];

/*22*/            ( *TmStruct ).tm_yday = Days;
/*23*/            return 0;
/*24*/        }
/*25*/        return -1;
/*26*/    }
```

Figure 9.9:   **Routine** `MkYear`, **which emulates** `mktime` **by expecting a pointer to a** `struct tm`.

ator * is a prefix operator, and the field member operator . is a postfix operator, the field member operator has higher priority. Thus the parentheses are needed, since otherwise the interpretation is *(TmStruct.tm_mday). The compiler would then complain, since TmStruct is not a structure and thus cannot have the . applied to it. It is thus unlikely that you would have an undetected error result from forgetting the parentheses.

On the other hand, it is incredibly annoying to have to use the parentheses over and over again, so C provides a postfix operator that accesses a member of a pointed-at structure. This is the -> operator. Since it is a token, you cannot have space between these two characters. Thus TmStruct->tm_mday represents the tm_mday field of the structure pointed at by TmStruct. Because -> is a postfix operator, it has the same precedence and associativity as array access, structure member, and postfix autoincrement

Category	*Examples*	*Associativity*
Primary expression	*identifiers* *constants*	None
Postfix	Function( ) . -> [] ++ --	Left to right
Prefix and unary	sizeof * & ! ~ + - ++ --	Right to left
Type cast	(TypeName)	Right to left
Multiplicative	* / %	Left to right
Additive	+ -	Left to right
Shift	<< >>	Left to right
Relational	< <= > >=	Left to right
Equality	== !=	Left to right
Boolean AND	&	Left to right
Boolean XOR	^	Left to right
Boolean OR	|	Left to right
Logical AND	&&	Left to right
Logical OR	||	Left to right
Conditional	?:	Right to left
Assignment	= *= /= %= += -= &= |= ^= <<= >>=	Right to left
Comma	,	Left to right

Figure 9.10:   Precedence and associativity of operators.

and autodecrement. The statement

```
scanf( "%d", &TmStruct->tm_mday );
```

thus reads an integer into TmStruct->tm_mday. Figure 9.10 summarizes the precedence
and associativity rules, including the structure member operators.

Figure 9.11 shows how this new operator is used. It is such a nice shorthand that
it is considered bad style not to use it. Moreover there is really no reason ever to pass a
structure directly unless it happens to take up only one or two integers worth of space. If
 not, you should always pass structures by reference, and use a const qualifier if you want
to indicate that it will not be changed.

```
/* 1*/      /* Fill In The tm_yday Field, As In mktime */

/* 2*/      int
/* 3*/      MkYear( struct tm *TmStruct )
/* 4*/      {
/* 5*/          static const int MonthDays[ ] =
/* 6*/              { 31, 28, 31, 30, 31, 30, 31, 31, 30, 31, 30, 31 };
/* 7*/          static const int LeapMonthDays[ ] =
/* 8*/              { 31, 29, 31, 30, 31, 30, 31, 31, 30, 31, 30, 31 };
/* 9*/          const int *MyMonthDays;
/*10*/          int i;

/*11*/          if( TmStruct != NULL )
/*12*/          {
/*13*/                  int Days  = TmStruct->tm_mday;
/*14*/              const int Month = TmStruct->tm_mon;
/*15*/              const int Year  = TmStruct->tm_year + 1900;

/*16*/              MyMonthDays = IsLeap( Year ) ?
/*                                  LeapMonthDays : MonthDays;
/*17*/              if( Month < 0 || Month > 11 || Days < 0 ||
/*18*/                      Days > MyMonthDays[ Month ] )
/*19*/                  return -1;

/*20*/              for( i = 0; i < Month; i++ )
/*21*/                  Days += MyMonthDays[ i ];

/*22*/              TmStruct->tm_yday = Days;
/*23*/              return 0;
/*24*/          }
/*25*/          return -1;
/*26*/      }
```

Figure 9.11:   Previous routine using the -> operator.

9.4   Case Study: Indirect Sorting

Thus far we have used pointers to achieve call by reference (e.g., scanf), and in conjunction with arrays and dynamic allocation. In this section we will examine another use of pointers. As we have seen, large structures are expensive to copy, because a simple one-line assignment statement translates into a copy of one chunk of memory to another, which is done sequentially. Although sorting large structures is algorithmically identical to sorting integers, the data movement is extremely expensive, so we want to make adjustments to the algorithm to avoid it as much as possible. In Chapter 8 we saw that sorting strings does not incur the overhead of data movement because what we were sorting was an array of pointers. We generalize this strategy to arbitrary structures in this and the next sections. Figure 9.12 shows the basic object we are working with. On our machine, where integers

```
/* 1*/    typedef struct Block
/* 2*/    {
/* 3*/         char Junk[ 508 ];
/* 4*/         int Key;
/* 5*/    } Block;


/* 6*/    struct Block P[ 2000 ];
```

Figure 9.12: Basic objects being sorted.

```
/* 1*/    /* Shellsort An Array Of Blocks. */
/* 2*/    /* Very Slow Because Of Block Copies. */

/* 3*/    void
/* 4*/    Shellsort( Block A[ ], const unsigned int N )
/* 5*/    {
/* 6*/         unsigned int Gap;
/* 7*/         Block Tmp;
/* 8*/         unsigned int i, j; /* Loop Counters */

/* 9*/         for( Gap = N/2; Gap > 0; Gap = Gap == 2 ? 1 : Gap / 2.2 )
/*10*/             for( i = Gap; i < N; i++ )
/*11*/             {
/*12*/                 Tmp = A[ i ];
/*13*/                 for( j = i; j >= Gap &&
/*14*/                             Tmp.Key < A[ j - Gap ].Key; j -= Gap )
/*15*/                     A[ j ] = A[ j - Gap ];

/*16*/                 A[ j ] = Tmp;
/*17*/             }
/*18*/    }
```

Figure 9.13: Simple Shellsort implementation: lots of copies.

are four bytes, it is a 512-byte block of data, and since we have about 2000 of them, we are sorting a total of 1 megabyte of data.[6]

9.4.1 Shellsort with Lots of Block Copies

The basic Shellsort algorithm is used once again and is shown in Figure 9.13. This algorithm is an expensive implementation: it takes only 23 milliseconds to Shellsort 2000 integers, but now it takes roughly 725 milliseconds to Shellsort 2000 blocks. The entire increase in running time is due to the block copies.[7] It turns out that there are roughly 47,000 block

---

[6]The resulting 1 megabyte object may be too large for direct use on personal computers. Consult the compiler manual to examine your options.

[7]In Chapter 13 we will see how the *prof* utility on UNIX can be used to obtain this information effortlessly.

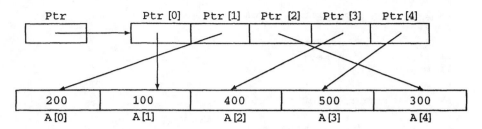

Figure 9.14:   Using `Block **Ptr`.

copies for an average run of Shellsort. Of course, since elements have to be rearranged, there must be some copies, but since there are only 2000 elements, we should expect to get by with much less than 47,000 copies. Thus if we can reduce the number of block copies significantly, we would expect a significant improvement in the running time.

9.4.2   Using Pointers to Reduce the Copying

In Section 8.14.2 we saw that sorting strings does not require any movement of the strings themselves, but rather, only the pointers move. Thus we know that using pointers can help us avoid large amounts of data movements. However, whereas for strings the input is represented as an array of pointers, here we have an array of blocks, which must be rearranged. Thus we cannot hope to get by with no block movements.

Let's talk tactics. The input is in an array A. We will need a second array `Ptr`, which will contain pointers to the blocks. Initially, `Ptr[i]` will point at `A[i]`. Then, as in Section 8.14.2, we will perform a sort by accesses on `Ptr` only. Figure 9.14 shows the result. `Ptr[0]` points at the smallest element in A, `Ptr[1]` at the next smallest element, and so on. Once this is done, the final phase consists of rearranging A to reflect the correct ordering. The easiest way to do this is to declare a third array, `ACopy`. We can write out the correct sorted order to `ACopy`, and then copy `ACopy` back to A.

Now that we have described the logic, let's examine how this is implemented in C. We have done the complete `Shellsort` routine in Figure 9.15. Actually, it is all relatively straightforward, although misplacing a * anywhere is guaranteed to drive you crazy. Line 7 declares the variable `Tmp`. Since now the basic action of Shellsort is to rearrange pointers, `Tmp` is a pointer to a block, just like any `Ptr[i]`. Lines 9 and 10 declare `Ptr` and `ACopy`, respectively. We would like `Ptr` to be an array of pointer to `Block`, and `ACopy` to be an array of `Block`. The natural declarations would be `Block *Ptr[N]` and `Block ACopy[N]`, but we cannot do this since N is not a compile-type constant. Thus they have to be allocated dynamically. Therefore, in the declaration we use a * instead of a [ ] and then allocate these arrays dynamically at lines 12 to 15. This is exactly what we did in Chapter 7. Notice that `ACopy` points at enough memory to hold N `Block`s, while `Ptr` points at enough memory to hold N pointers to `Block`. Make sure that you understand the distinction. We have also shown the commonly used method of doing the allocation and testing for failure in one expression. The parentheses are necessary because of precedence rules.

The rest of the algorithm follows our description almost verbatim. At lines 16 and 17, we initialize the *i*th pointer to point at the *i*th block. Lines 18 to 27 perform Shellsort using `Ptr` instead of A. At line 24 we see the use of -> to access the `Key` of the `Block`

```
/* 1*/     /* Shellsort An Array Of Blocks. */
/* 2*/     /* Uses Only 2N Block Copies. */

/* 3*/     void
/* 4*/     Shellsort( Block A[ ], const unsigned int N )
/* 5*/     {
/* 6*/         unsigned int Gap;
/* 7*/         Block *Tmp;
/* 8*/         unsigned int i, j;                    /* Loop Counters */
/* 9*/         Block **Ptr;                /* Array Of Pointers To Block */
/*10*/         Block *ACopy;                         /* Sorted Array */

/*11*/         /* Allocate And Initialize Pointers for Indirect Sort */
/*12*/         if( ! ( Ptr = malloc( N * sizeof( struct Block * ) ) ) )
/*13*/             Error( "Out of memory" );
/*14*/         if( ! ( ACopy = malloc( N * sizeof( struct Block ) ) ) )
/*15*/             Error( "Out of memory" );
/*16*/         for( i = 0; i < N; i++ )
/*17*/             Ptr[ i ] = &A[ i ];

/*18*/         /* Indirect Shellsort */
/*19*/         for( Gap = N/2; Gap > 0; Gap = Gap == 2 ? 1 : Gap / 2.2 )
/*20*/             for( i = Gap; i < N; i++ )
/*21*/             {
/*22*/                 Tmp = Ptr[ i ];
/*23*/                 for( j = i; j >= Gap &&
/*24*/                         Tmp->Key < Ptr[ j - Gap ]->Key; j -= Gap )
/*25*/                     Ptr[ j ] = Ptr[ j - Gap ];
/*26*/                 Ptr[ j ] = Tmp;
/*27*/             }

/*28*/         for( i = 0; i < N; i++ )            /* Make Sorted Array */
/*29*/             ACopy[ i ] = *Ptr[ i ];

/*30*/         for( i = 0; i < N; i++ )            /* Copy It Back */
/*31*/             A[ i ] = ACopy[ i ];

/*32*/         free( ACopy ); free( Ptr );        /* Clean Up */
/*33*/     }
```

Figure 9.15: Shellsort with pointers: only 2*N* block copies.

being pointed at. When we come to line 28, we have the situation shown in Figure 9.14. We can thus form a sorted array in ACopy, by copying the Block that is referenced by Ptr[i]. We can then copy this array back into A, as shown at lines 30 and 31. At line 32 we recycle Ptr and ACopy, which are no longer needed.

On our machine, this algorithm runs in roughly 150 milliseconds, which is a large reduction from the previous case. The reason is that all block copies are now performed at lines 29 and 31 instead of during the actual Shellsort. It is very easy to see that this means that a total of only 2*N* block copies are done, which in our case is only 4000.

9.4.3   Avoiding the Extra Array

The algorithm in Figure 9.15, although improved from the nonpointer implementation in Figure 9.13, has a potentially important problem. By using the array ACopy, we have doubled the total space requirement. Since by assumption N is relatively large (or else we would use insertion sort), and the size of a Block is large (or else we would use Figure 9.13), we can reasonably expect that we are operating near the memory limits of our machine. Thus while we can expect to use an extra array of integers, we cannot necessarily expect an extra array of Blocks to be available.

A second consequence of our decision to use ACopy is that a total of $2N$ block copies are used. Although this is an improvement on the original algorithm, we will show how to do better by avoiding the extra copy. In particular, we will never use more than $3N/2$ block copies, and on almost all inputs, we will use only a few more than N. Thus not only will we save space, but we will use fewer copies. Our modified routine is shown in Figure 9.16. The Shellsort algorithm is identical and is omitted to save space. The difference in this algorithm is that A is rearranged without using an extra array. Before we step through the code, let's get a general idea of what needs to be done. Surprisingly, we have already done it before.

Figure 9.17 shows the same input as in Figure 9.14. Instead of showing the Ptr array, we are showing what we shall denote as the Rank array. Rank[i] tells the index where the element that should be in A[i] can be found. Thus Rank[2] is 4, because the element that *should* be in A[2] is currently in A[4]. When Rank[i]==i, the ith element is correctly placed. Otherwise, the Rank array tells us exactly what elements need to be moved where. To get an idea of what we have to do, let us start with $i = 2$. Since Rank[2] is 4, we know we need to move A[4] to A[2]. But first, we have to save A[2], or we will not be able to place it correctly. So first, we have Tmp=A[2], and then A[2]=A[4]. Now that A[4] has been moved to A[2], it is a good time to move something into A[4], which is essentially vacant. By examining Rank[4], we see that the correct statement is A[4]=A[3]. Now we need to move something into A[3]. Since Rank[3] is 2, we know that we want to move A[2] there. But A[2] has been overwritten at the start of this rearrangement; since its original value is in Tmp, we finish with Rank[3]=Tmp. What we saw is that starting with i equal to 2, and following the Rank array, we form a cyclic sequence 2,4,3,2, which corresponds to

```
Tmp  = A[2];
A[2] = A[4];
A[4] = A[3];
A[3] = Tmp;
```

Thus we have rearranged three elements using only four Block copies and one extra Block of storage. Actually, we have already seen this method before. The innermost loop of insertion sort saves the current element A[i] in a Tmp variable. We then assign A[j]=A[j-1], to move lots of elements over one to the right. Finally, we assign A[j]=Tmp to place the original element. We are doing exactly the same thing here, except that instead of sliding over by one, we are using Rank to guide how the rearrangement is performed.

This algorithm is easily translated into C code. At lines 21 and 22 of Figure 9.16, we compute the Rank array. At line 24 we search sequentially for a position i that contains

```
/* 1*/    /* Shellsort An Array Of Blocks. */
/* 2*/    /* Avoid Excessive Copying And Extra Array Of Blocks */

/* 3*/    void
/* 4*/    Shellsort( Block A[ ], const unsigned int N )
/* 5*/    {
/* 6*/         unsigned int Gap;
/* 7*/         Block *Tmp;
/* 8*/         unsigned int i, j, NextJ;              /* Loop Counters */
/* 9*/         Block **Ptr;              /* Array Of Pointers To Block */
/*10*/         int *Rank;      /* Array Listing Correct Final Position */
/*11*/         Block ShuffleTmp; /* Temp for The Final Rearrangement */

/*12*/         /* Allocate And Initialize Pointers for Indirect Sort */
/*13*/         if( ! ( Ptr = malloc( N * sizeof( struct Block * ) ) ) )
/*14*/            Error( "Out of memory" );
/*15*/         if( ( Rank = malloc( N * sizeof( int ) ) ) == NULL )
/*16*/            Error( "Out of memory" );
/*17*/         for( i = 0; i < N; i++ )
/*18*/             Ptr[ i ] = &A[ i ];

/*19*/         /* Indirect Shellsort (Omitted: Figure 9.15, 19-27) */
/*20*/             /* Determine Correct Positions */
/*21*/         for( i = 0; i < N; i++ )
/*22*/             Rank[ i ] = Ptr[ i ] - &A[ 0 ];

/*23*/             /* Shuffle It Back */
/*24*/         for( i = 0; i < N; i++ )
/*25*/             if( Rank[ i ] != i )
/*26*/             {
/*27*/                 ShuffleTmp = A[ i ];
/*28*/                 for( j = i; Rank[ j ] != i; j = NextJ )
/*29*/                 {
/*30*/                     A[ j ] = A[ Rank[ j ] ];
/*31*/                     NextJ = Rank[ j ];
/*32*/                     Rank[ j ] = j;
/*33*/                 }
/*34*/                 A[ j ] = ShuffleTmp;
/*35*/                 Rank[ j ] = j;
/*36*/             }

/*37*/         free( Rank ); free( Ptr ); /* Clean Up */
/*38*/    }
```

Figure 9.16:   Shellsort with pointers, but no extra array.

the wrong element. When we find such an i, we do the sequence of assignments that we described above. We also update the Rank array when we assign to A[j]. The order of lines 31, 32, and the update to the for loop are crucial, since the value in Rank[j] indicates the location of the next position to examine. We have to save it before updating it.

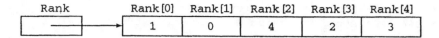

Rank	Rank [0]	Rank [1]	Rank [2]	Rank [3]	Rank [4]
→	1	0	4	2	3

200	100	400	500	300
A [0]	A [1]	A [2]	A [3]	A [4]

Figure 9.17:   Data structures used for rearrangement.

In general, what happens is that we have a collection of cycles that are rearranged. In Figure 9.16 there are two cycles: one involves two elements, and the other involves three. Rearranging a cycle of length L uses $L + 1$ block copies, as we have seen. Cycles of length 1 merely represent elements that are already correctly placed, and thus use no copies. This improves nicely on the previous algorithm, because now an array that is already sorted does not incur any block copies.

∞   Let C_1 be the number of cycles of length 1, and $C_{L>1}$ be the number of longer cycles. Then the total number of block copies is $N + C_{L>1} - C_1$. The worst thing that can happen is that we have $N/2$ cycles of length 2, in which case $3N/2$ block copies are performed. This can happen if the input is 2 1 4 3 6 5 .... However, this is not likely to happen randomly. One can prove (Exercise 8) that on average,

$$C_{L>1} = \sum_{i=2}^{N} \frac{1}{i} \approx \ln N - 0.423,$$

while C_1 is on average 1. Thus a random arrangement of the input yields only a very small number of cycles. In our case we observed 2006 block copies averaged over 10 trials, which is in strong agreement with the theoretical answer. The sorting time was thus reduced to only 80 milliseconds, which is only a few times more than the ideal of sorting integers.

9.5   Generic Functions

We have seen that large structures can be sorted efficiently using pointers and writing a few extra lines of code. Unfortunately, every time we have a different structure, we will have to modify our Shellsort algorithm, even though not much is actually changing. In this section we show how to write a generic version of Shellsort, which will work with any type.

The generic Shellsort, based on Figure 9.15, is shown in Figure 9.18. We have used the more inefficient routine only because of space limitations, not because it is any more complex. Probably the most striking feature of the generic routine is that every line corresponds to the Shellsort used for the `Block` type in Section 9.4. (We have placed the opening { at the end of line 5 to make the correspondence direct.)

The type declaration for the generic sort is somewhat different. First, we have declared A to be of type `void *`. It still represents the memory address where the array is stored and is thus a pointer, but since we do not know the type, we use `void *`, which matches any pointer type. Note that `void A[ ]` does not make sense and is thus illegal.

```
/* 1*/    /* Shellsort An Array Of Unknowns. */
/* 2*/    /* Uses Only 2N Block Copies. */

/* 3*/    void
/* 4*/    Shellsort( void *A, const unsigned int N, const size_t Size,
/* 5*/               int Cmp( const void *, const void * ) ) {

/* 6*/        unsigned int Gap;
/* 7*/        void *Tmp;
/* 8*/        unsigned int i, j;                        /* Loop Counters */
/* 9*/        void **Ptr;             /* Array Of Pointers To Unknowns */
/*10*/        void *ACopy;                              /* Sorted Array */

/*11*/        /* Allocate And Initialize Pointers for Indirect Sort */
/*12*/        if( ( Ptr = malloc( N * sizeof( void * ) ) ) == NULL )
/*13*/            Error( "Out of memory" );
/*14*/        if( ( ACopy = malloc( N * Size ) ) == NULL )
/*15*/            Error( "Out of memory" );
/*16*/        for( i = 0; i < N; i++ )
/*17*/            Ptr[ i ] = A + i * Size;

/*18*/            /* Indirect Shellsort */
/*19*/        for( Gap = N/2; Gap > 0; Gap = Gap == 2 ? 1 : Gap / 2.2 )
/*20*/            for( i = Gap; i < N; i++ )
/*21*/            {
/*22*/                Tmp = Ptr[ i ];
/*23*/                for( j = i; j >= Gap &&
/*24*/                        Cmp( Tmp, Ptr[ j - Gap ] ) < 0; j -= Gap )
/*25*/                    Ptr[ j ] = Ptr[ j - Gap ];
/*26*/                Ptr[ j ] = Tmp;
/*27*/            }

/*28*/        for( i = 0; i < N; i++ )          /* Make Sorted Array */
/*29*/            memcpy( ACopy + i * Size, Ptr[ i ], Size );

/*30*/            /* Copy It Back */
/*31*/        memcpy( A, ACopy,  N * Size );

/*32*/        free( ACopy ); free( Ptr );      /* Clean Up */
/*33*/    }
```

Figure 9.18: Generic Shellsort, using extra array.

The number of elements is still passed as before. However, we also need two more pieces
of information to perform the sort. We need to know how large each element is; otherwise,
we cannot correctly index the array. We also need a function that takes a pointer to two
elements and, like strcmp, returns a negative, zero, or positive, depending on whether the
first element is smaller than, equal to, or larger than the second.

Lines 7, 9, and 10 use void * instead of Block *. Lines 12 to 15 allocate Ptr
and ACopy just as was done in Figure 9.15. The assignment

```
Ptr[ i ] = &A[ i ];
```

```
/* 1*/    int
/* 2*/    Comp( const void *Lhs, const void *Rhs )
/* 3*/    {
/* 4*/        int Leftkey  =  ( ( Block * ) Lhs )->Key;
/* 5*/        int Rightkey =  ( ( Block * ) Rhs )->Key;

/* 6*/         return Leftkey < Rightkey ? -1 : Leftkey != Rightkey;
/* 7*/    }


/* 8*/        /* ... */
/* 9*/        Shellsort( P, 2000, sizeof( Block ), Comp );
/*108*/       /* ... */
```

Figure 9.19:   Using the generic Shellsort.

however, cannot be performed directly. Since A is a pointer to void, the compiler cannot possibly know where A[i] is stored. We need to figure it out ourselves, but as line 17 shows, it is an easy calculation. The actual Shellsort is identical, except that the comparison at line 24 is rewritten to use Cmp.

Finally, we have to deal with copying to ACopy and then back to A. Of course, the assignment statements in the original program will not work, because void * variables represent only memory addresses and cannot be dereferenced. Thus we call the routine memcpy. The prototype for memcpy, which is found in <stddef.h>, is:

```
void *memcpy( void *To, void *From, size_t HowManyBytes );
```

memcpy copies HowManyBytes from From, placing the result in To. It returns To, thus allowing nested calls. On our system, this is the routine that is called to implement the Block copy anyway, so we do not lose any speed here. Thus lines 29 in both programs are completely equivalent. We implement lines 30 and 31 as one huge memcpy, thus saving the overhead of repeated function calls.

Figure 9.19 shows how the generic sorting routine is used. The commonly used trick of subtracting the two Key fields doesn't work because of the possibility of overflow. Comp is required to take two void * parameters, and rewriting it to accept two Block * parameters would be erroneous.

9.6   Incomplete struct **Declarations and Information Hiding**

In Section 9.1.3 we saw that a structure can be used to store, in one object, a time and date that consists of many components. The tm structure is unusual because it allows (and even encourages) the programmer to tinker with the individual components. In general, this is a bad design principle. A better method is to require the user to view an object as an atomic unit whose internal workings are unknown. All changes to the object would be made by routines that are provided in a library. This way the designer of the object can guarantee that the user can never place the object in an inconsistent or illegal state.

```
/* 1*/          /* Header File With Incomplete struct Declaration   */
/* 2*/      typedef struct Complex *Complex;

/* 3*/      Complex InitComplex( double Real, double Imag );
/* 4*/      void AddComplex( const Complex A, const Complex B,
                                                Complex Sum );
/* 5*/      void PrintComplex( const Complex A );
```

Figure 9.20:   Header file for complex number routines (File: *complex.h*).

An example of this principle is the implementation of the double type. No user would ever dream of attempting to adjust the individual bits that comprise a double. Rather, the normal arithmetic operators are always used.

As an example, we consider the implementation of a group of routines to support complex numbers. Recall that a complex number consists of a real part and an imaginary part. Thus a complex number is likely to be represented as a structure consisting of two fields. Because structures should be passed by reference, the actual Complex type is a pointer to a structure. The natural way to declare this type would be

```
struct Complex
{
    double Real;
    double Imag;
};
```

```
typedef struct Complex *Complex;
```

If this type declaration is placed in a header file that is included by the caller of the routines that manipulate Complex objects, the caller will also have access to the individual fields of the Complex structure.

The most sensible-looking solution would seem to be not to include the complete struct declaration in the header file, but instead, to place it in the file that contains the implementation of the Complex routines. Figure 9.20 illustrates the resulting header file, and Figure 9.21 illustrates the implementation file (which #includes the header file).[8] Note carefully that struct Complex is an incomplete type outside of *complex.c* (of course in *complex.c* it is complete).

As shown in Figure 9.22, main would declare Complex objects and manipulate them using the routines specified in the header file. However, because only an incomplete struct type is visible to main, expressions such as A->Real will not compile. *main.c* would need to provide the equivalent of lines 3 to 7 in Figure 9.21 to escape the information-hiding restrictions. If source code for the Complex struct were not available (e.g., if it was proprietary), it would be impossible for main to access individual fields directly.

 The incomplete type has additional restrictions: because its size is unknown, an incomplete type cannot be the target of an assignment, cannot be used as a parameter to sizeof, cannot be passed to (call by value implies a copy) a function, and cannot be returned from a function (implies a copy). Consequently, if we attempted to implement information hiding with

---

[8]We provide only the minimal subset of Complex routines needed to illustrate the incomplete type method.

```
/* 1*/    #include <stdio.h>
/* 2*/    #include "complex.h"

/* 3*/    struct Complex
/* 4*/    {
/* 5*/        double Real;
/* 6*/        double Imag;
/* 7*/    };

/* 8*/    void
/* 9*/    PrintComplex( const Complex A )
/*10*/    {
/*11*/        if( A != NULL )
/*12*/            printf( "%f+%fi", A->Real, A->Imag );
/*13*/        else
/*14*/            printf( "Uninitialized complex number detected\n" );
/*15*/    }

/*16*/    /* InitComplex And AddComplex Are Similar */
```

Figure 9.21:   **Implementation file for complex number routines (File:** *complex.c*).

```
/* 1*/    #include <stdio.h>
/* 2*/    #include "complex.h"

/* 3*/    main( void )
/* 4*/    {
/* 5*/        Complex A, B;

/* 6*/        A = InitComplex( 2.0, 4.0 );
/* 7*/        B = InitComplex( 0.0, 0.0 );

/* 8*/        AddComplex( A, A, B );
/* 9*/        printf( "B is: " ); PrintComplex( B ); printf( "\n" );

/*10*/        return 0;
/*11*/    }
```

Figure 9.22:   `main` **program that uses complex number package (File:** *main.c*)

```
typedef struct Complex Complex;
```

and pass `Complex` types, the compiler would complain. This restriction does not apply to a pointer to an incomplete type because the size of a pointer is known.

Finally, we mention that an incomplete type declaration can, of course, be specified without using a `typedef` declaration. For instance,

```
struct Complex;
```

specifies the incomplete type `struct Complex`.

9.7   Arrays of Structures with Pointers to Functions

In this section we discuss a useful C idiom that makes use of several C features. We illustrate the technique with a very simple example. Suppose that we want to execute one of several functions, depending on an input string. This is typical of a parsing phase in an interactive program in which input commands are processed. Of course, a sequence of if/else clauses can be used, but as new options are added, that method would require modification of a function. When there are many options, this can lead to an excessively long function. The method we illustrate is table driven: as new options are added, we need only to add an entry to a table. Figure 9.23 shows the relevant portion of code.

Each entry in the table is given by a CommStruct object, declared at lines 6 to 10. That object contains a string and a pointer to the corresponding function. The table is then provided at lines 11 to 19. Notice that the names of the functions must already be known; consequently, prototypes are specified prior to the table. For convenience we end the table with a pair of NULL pointers.

Executing the appropriate command is then a matter of performing a simple scan of the table until a match is found or the NULL pointer at the end is reached.[9] Line 24 uses the pointer method of stepping through an array. If the test fails, the NULL command has been reached. Otherwise, if a match is detected at line 25, the corresponding function is called at line 27. When there are many options, this technique requires considerably less lines of code and is more easily maintainable than the if/else alternative. It is a nice illustration of the power of C.

9.8   Occasionally Useful Stuff

C provides two constructs that are useful, although not widely encountered.

9.8.1   Bit Fields

On a 32-bit machine, using an int to represent a variable that can hold only seven values, and is thus representable in three bits, is wasteful. Although short int and even char are available, we might need something even shorter. Because of machine restrictions, this is generally not possible. However, inside a structure it is. In Figure 9.24 we show a new construction known as the *bit field*. A colon followed by a small constant integer is added to the field declaration. With a couple of exceptions, a bit field behaves like a normal integer except that the compiler will attempt to pack several consecutive bit fields into one integer. On a 16-bit machine, for instance, the two bit fields can share the storage of one integer.

---

[9]If the table is sorted, a binary search can also be used. In that case the NULL entry is unneeded and the high point of the array can be determined by using the sizeof operator twice. We leave this as Exercise 13.

```
/* 1*/    #include <stdio.h>

/* 2*/    void Help( void );
/* 3*/    void Quit( void );
/* 4*/    void Reset( void );
/* 5*/    void Undo( void );

/* 6*/    typedef struct
/* 7*/    {
/* 8*/        char *Command;
/* 9*/        void ( *Func )( void );
/*10*/    } CommStruct;

/*11*/    static const CommStruct TheCommands[ ] =
/*12*/    {
/*13*/        "exit", Quit,
/*14*/        "help", Help,
/*15*/        "quit", Quit,
/*16*/        "reset", Reset,
/*17*/        "undo", Undo,
/*18*/        NULL, NULL                  /* Place Last; No Match */
/*19*/    };

/*20*/    void
/*21*/    DoCommand( const char *Comm )
/*22*/    {
/*23*/        const CommStruct *Ptr;

/*24*/        for( Ptr = TheCommands; Ptr->Command != NULL; Ptr++ )
/*25*/            if( strcmp( Comm, Ptr->Command ) == 0 )
/*26*/            {
/*27*/                ( *Ptr->Func )( );
/*28*/                return;
/*29*/            }

/*30*/        printf( "Error: unrecognized command\n" );
/*31*/    }
```

Figure 9.23:   Example of an array of structures that contain pointers to functions as fields.

         Bit fields have several limitations. First, because the bit field might not align on a word boundary, you cannot take its address, and thus you cannot point at it. This means that we could not use scanf to read a bit field directly. Second, you cannot have an array of bit fields. Finally, you have to be careful:

```
int field : 2;
```

 allows the field member to take on the values -2 through 1, inclusive, on most machines. If you intend to allow 0 to 3, you must declare an unsigned int. Because of this and the fact that 8-bit chars are available, bit fields are rarely worth the effort unless we have a

```
struct tm
{
    int             tm_sec;       /* seconds after the minute  (0- 61)  */
    int             tm_min;       /* minutes after the hour    (0- 59)  */
    int             tm_hour;      /* hours after midnight      (0- 23)  */
    int             tm_mday;      /* day of the month          (1- 31)  */
    int             tm_mon;       /* month since January       (0- 11)  */
    int             tm_year;      /* years since 1900          (0-   )  */
    unsigned int tm_wday : 3;     /* days since Sunday         (0-  6)  */
    unsigned int tm_yday : 9;     /* days since January 1      (0-365)  */
    int             tm_isdst;     /* daylight savings time flag         */
};
```

Figure 9.24: `struct tm`, **using bit fields.**

```
struct Weather
{
    int Temp : 8;
    unsigned int Humidity : 7;
    unsigned int WindSpeed : 8;
    int WindChillFactor : 8;
    int TempHumidityIndex : 8;
};
```

Figure 9.25:   Example where four integers of memory suffice.

 large array of structures and space is at a premium. Even then, using the bitwise operators as we have seen in the `<ctype.h>` macros implementations (Figure 8.5) is a more popular alternative.

9.8.2   Unions

Our last look at syntax is the `union`. Sometimes we have a structure in which two or more fields can never be simultaneously active. In that case we would like to use the same memory to hold these variables. Let's look at the declaration in Figure 9.25, where everything fits in 8 bits.

The wind-chill factor is computed on cold days, while the temperature humidity index is computed on hot days. Thus these two fields are never active simultaneously. The `union`, which is declared like a structure, can be used to lower the space requirement. The amount of space used by the `union` is equal to the maximum space needed for any one of its fields. In Figure 9.26 the wind-chill factor for object `W` is obtained by accessing `W.FeelsLike.WindChillFactor`. By the way, since unions behave like structures, this shows how structures nest.

In this example we could have just used the less descriptive field `FeelsLike` rather than explicitly stating the other two fields. The real power of the `union` is that the members of the `union` do not have to have the same type. This is the most common and probably only justifiable use of the `union` (we shall see this in the next section).

```
struct Weather
{
    int Temp : 8;
    unsigned int Humidity : 7;
    unsigned int WindSpeed : 8;
    union
    {
        int WindChillFactor : 8;
        int TempHumidityIndex : 8;
    } FeelsLike;
};
```

Figure 9.26:   union **example.**

An important warning: if you assign to W.FeelsLike.WindChillFactor and then access W.FeelsLike.TempHumidityIndex, you get the value assigned for the wind-chill factor. This can be particularly damaging when the union fields do not have the same type. It is up to you to keep track of what the union is actually storing. This could be done by adding a one-bit field to struct Weather that keeps track of this.

The union can save some space, but generally it is not much, so it is worthwhile only if we have a large array of structures.

9.9   Recurring Case Study: Part 5

In this section we use an object-oriented approach to process the various shapes. We also extend the program specifications so that the objects in each group (of similar shape types) are printed in increasing area. Our program will consist of 10 files. Each type of shape will have a source file and a header file. We also define a ShapeType as a union of the various types of shapes; we then have various routines that work on an abstract shape. These routines will decide which of the possible shapes it has, and call an appropriate function. We also have an extra header file and a source file containing the main function.

We start by examining *shape.h*, shown in Figure 9.27. Lines 1, 2, and 25 are used to guarantee that the typedef at line 7 is encountered only once per source file compilation. The abstract shape consists of TheShape (similar to the enum in Section 8.15), the Area (needed only to avoid recomputation during the sorting phase), and a union that stores the appropriate dimensions. The name of that field is Dimension. Thus for a circle S, the radius is given by S.Dimension.Radius. For rectangles we need another struct. The width would be given by S.Dimension.Rect.Width. In both cases we are using *anonymous* types because no tag name or typedef is provided. This is a common practice when nesting structures and unions. We also provide three prototypes for reading, writing, and computing the areas of an abstract shape.

Each type of shape, as we have mentioned, requires a specialized routine to perform reading, writing, and an area calculation. The prototypes are in Figure 9.28; the implementation is shown in Figure 9.29. The implementation of these routines is straightforward given the type declarations, as are the (omitted) routines corresponding to rectangles and

```
/* 1*/    #ifndef _Shape
/* 2*/    #define _Shape

/* 3*/    #include <stdio.h>
/* 4*/    #include <stdlib.h>

/* 5*/    #define Pi 3.1416
/* 6*/    #define MaxStringLen 80

/* 7*/    typedef struct
/* 8*/    {
/* 9*/        int TheShape;
/*10*/        double Area;

/*11*/        union        /* Stores The Dimensions Of The Object */
/*12*/        {
/*13*/            double Radius;        /* Circle */
/*14*/            double Side;          /* Square */
/*15*/            struct                /* Rectangle */
/*16*/            {
/*17*/                double Length;
/*18*/                double Width;
/*19*/            } Rect;
/*20*/        } Dimension;
/*21*/    } ShapeType;

/*22*/    void WriteShape( const ShapeType *Shape );
/*23*/    void AreaShape( ShapeType *Shape );
/*24*/    ShapeType *ReadShape( void );

/*25*/    #endif
```

Figure 9.27: Source file *shape.h*.

```
/* 1*/    #include "shape.h"

/* 2*/    ShapeType *ReadCircle( void );
/* 3*/    void AreaCircle( ShapeType *Shape );
/* 4*/    void WriteCircle( const ShapeType *Shape );
```

Figure 9.28: Source file *circle.h*.

squares. Next we write the routines that select the appropriate `Read`, `Write`, and `Area` functions, based on the `TheShape` field of an abstract shape. Figure 9.30 illustrates the strategy. For each type of shape, we store its name (a string) and a pointer to the appropriate functions that should be called. We use a `NULL` entry to simplify the resulting code slightly.

Figure 9.31 gives the abstract reading, writing, and area functions. `AreaShape`, shown at lines 29 to 33, merely calls the corresponding area calculation function to fill in the `Area` field. Similarly, `WriteShape` consults the array of structures to find the name

```
/* 1*/    #include "circle.h"

/* 2*/    ShapeType *
/* 3*/    ReadCircle( void )
/* 4*/    {
/* 5*/        ShapeType *S;

/* 6*/        if ( S = malloc( sizeof ( ShapeType ) ) )
/* 7*/        {
/* 8*/            printf( "Enter radius: " );
/* 9*/            if( scanf( "%lf", &S->Dimension.Radius ) == 1 )
/*10*/                return S;
/*11*/        }

/*12*/        return NULL;
/*13*/    }

/*14*/    void
/*15*/    WriteCircle( const ShapeType *Shape )
/*16*/    {
/*17*/        printf( "radius %.2f", Shape->Dimension.Radius );
/*18*/    }

/*19*/    void
/*20*/    AreaCircle( ShapeType *Shape )
/*21*/    {
/*22*/        Shape->Area = Pi *Shape->Dimension.Radius
/*23*/                         *Shape->Dimension.Radius;
/*24*/    }
```

Figure 9.29:   Source file *circle.c*.

of Shape and to call the appropriate Write function. ReadShape gets a string from the input. It then scans ShapeTable looking for a match. We use a pointer to iterate over the table at line 12; the loop terminates if it reaches the NULL pointer at the end of ShapeTable. If a match is found at line 13, the corresponding Read function is called at line 15. If the reading is successful (i.e., a NULL pointer is not returned), the index in ShapeTable where the match occurred gives the current shape type. Thus the enumerated type used in Section 8.15 is not needed.

Finally, we give the main routine. In Figure 9.32, lines 28 to 32 read the shapes and calculate the areas. We then sort the shapes using the library routine qsort. qsort has the same interface as generic Shellsort. We could use Shellsort instead, but because our version is optimized to avoid block copies, and in this case we are already sorting pointers, we would want to modify generic Shellsort to do a direct rather than an indirect sort. The comparison function requires two pointers to the basic object being sorted and returns negative, positive, or zero, depending on whether the object pointed at by the first parameter is less than, greater than, or equal to the object pointed at by the second parameter. However the parameters must be declared as void * and converted in the routine.

```
/* 1*/    /* To Add A New Shape
/* 2*/     * 1. Create Appropriate Header And Source
/* 3*/     *         Read, Write, And Area Functions;
/* 4*/     * 2. Update #include Statements Below;
/* 5*/     * 3. Adjust typedef Shape
/* 6*/     */

/* 7*/    #include "circle.h"
/* 8*/    #include "square.h"
/* 9*/    #include "rectangle.h"

/*10*/    typedef struct
/*11*/    {
/*12*/        char *ShapeName;
/*13*/        ShapeType * ( *ReadShape )( void );
/*14*/        void ( *WriteShape )( const ShapeType *Shape );
/*15*/        void ( *Area )( ShapeType *Shape );
/*16*/    } ShapeSwitch;


/*17*/    static ShapeSwitch ShapeTable[ ] =
/*18*/    {
/*19*/        { "circle", ReadCircle, WriteCircle, AreaCircle },
/*20*/        { "rectangle", ReadRectangle, WriteRectangle,
                                            AreaRectangle },
/*21*/        { "square", ReadSquare, WriteSquare, AreaSquare },
/*22*/        { NULL, NULL, NULL, NULL }
/*23*/    };

/*24*/    #include <string.h>
```

Figure 9.30: Source file *table.h*.

Since the basic object is a pointer to a ShapeType, the comparison function is actually receiving two pointers to pointer to ShapeType. We dereference once to obtain pointer to ShapeType objects. The sort is done first by shape, and if the shapes are the same, then by area. This is shown at lines 3 to 21.

The technique we have used in this section is commonly employed by C programmers. As we will see in Chapter 14, C++ provides mechanisms for implementing abstract objects. That method can be viewed as automating the function selection process that we have described in this section.

```
/* 1*/    #include "table.h"

/* 2*/    #define StrConv1( Len ) ( "%" #Len "s" )
/* 3*/    #define StrConv( Len ) ( StrConv1( Len ) )

/* 4*/    ShapeType *
/* 5*/    ReadShape( void )
/* 6*/    {
/* 7*/        static char InputString[ MaxStringLen + 1 ];
/* 8*/        ShapeSwitch *Ptr;
/* 9*/        ShapeType *Shape;

/*10*/        printf( "Enter shape type: " );
/*11*/        if( scanf( StrConv( MaxStringLen ), InputString ) == 1 )
/*12*/            for( Ptr = ShapeTable; Ptr->ShapeName; Ptr++ )
/*13*/                if( strcmp( Ptr->ShapeName, InputString ) == 0 )
/*14*/                {        /* Found The Type */
/*15*/                    if( Shape = ( *Ptr->ReadShape )( ) )
/*16*/                        Shape->TheShape = Ptr - ShapeTable;
/*17*/                    return Shape;
/*18*/                }

/*19*/        return NULL;        /* No Match */
/*20*/    }

/*21*/    void
/*22*/    WriteShape( const ShapeType *Shape )
/*23*/    {
/*24*/        printf( "Shape is a %s ",
/*25*/                    ShapeTable[ Shape->TheShape ].ShapeName );
/*26*/        ( *ShapeTable[ Shape->TheShape ].WriteShape )( Shape );
/*27*/        printf( "; the area is %.2f\n", Shape->Area );
/*28*/    }

/*29*/    void
/*30*/    AreaShape( ShapeType *Shape )
/*31*/    {
/*32*/        ( *ShapeTable[ Shape->TheShape ].Area )( Shape );
/*33*/    }
```

Figure 9.31: Source file *shape.c.*

```
/* 1*/    #include "shape.h"

/* 2*/    /* Comparison Function for qsort */

/* 3*/    int
/* 4*/    Cmp( const void *Left, const void *Right )
/* 5*/    {
/* 6*/        ShapeType *LeftShape  = * ( ShapeType ** ) Left;
/* 7*/        ShapeType *RightShape = * ( ShapeType ** ) Right;

/* 8*/        if( LeftShape->TheShape < RightShape->TheShape )
/* 9*/            return -1;
/*10*/        else
/*11*/        if( LeftShape->TheShape > RightShape->TheShape )
/*12*/            return 1;

/*13*/            /* Same Shape */
/*14*/        if( LeftShape->Area < RightShape->Area )
/*15*/            return -1;
/*16*/        else
/*17*/        if( LeftShape->Area > RightShape->Area )
/*18*/            return 1;
/*19*/        else
/*20*/            return 0;
/*21*/    }

/*22*/    /* Read Some Shapes, Sort Them By Area, And Write Them Out */

/*23*/    #define MaxShapes 1000

/*24*/    main( void )
/*25*/    {
/*26*/        ShapeType *Shapes[ MaxShapes ];
/*27*/        int ItemsRead, i;

/*28*/        for( ItemsRead = 0; ItemsRead < MaxShapes; ItemsRead++ )
/*29*/            if( ( Shapes[ ItemsRead ] = ReadShape( ) ) == NULL )
/*30*/                break;
/*31*/            else
/*32*/                AreaShape( Shapes[ ItemsRead ] );

/*33*/        printf( "\n" );
/*34*/        qsort( Shapes, ItemsRead, sizeof( ShapeType * ), Cmp );
/*35*/        for( i = 0; i < ItemsRead; i++ )
/*36*/            WriteShape( Shapes[ i ] );

/*37*/        return 0;
/*38*/    }
```

Figure 9.32:   Source file *main.c.*

9.10   Summary

In this chapter we examined the *structure*. Structures are useful because they allow us to combine basic types into more abstract types, which can then be used atomically. We saw, for instance, how the components of a date and time can be combined into a single structure. In Chapter 10 we investigate the fundamental abstract types that can be implemented by structures.

9.10.1   What Was Covered

- A structure is used to store a collection of different typed variables. Access to the basic *fields* of a structure is provided by the `.` operator.

- Structures may be copied, passed as a parameter, and returned from a function. However, we usually avoid these operations because they can be very inefficient. In particular, we almost always pass and return structures by reference, using a pointer.

- The `->` operator is used to access a field of a pointed at structure. Because it is a postfix operator, both it and the `.` (field member access) operator associate from left to right and have higher precedence than the prefix operators such as `&` and `*`.

- Indirect sorting can be used to avoid a large number of block moves. It adds relatively few lines of code considering the amount of time it can save.

- The `void *` generic pointer can be used to implement generic functions. We must add two parameters in the case of our sorting routine: one to tell us how large a basic object is, and another that can be used to compare two objects. We can use `memcpy` to copy chunks of memory.

- The *bit field* is a little-used feature that can occasionally save space. A colon followed by a small constant integer is added to the normal field declaration. The `&` operator may not be applied to bit fields.

- The *union* is used to share memory among several variables when only one variable is active at any time.

9.10.2   Friendly Reminders

- Do not forget the semicolon after the brace in a structure declaration. If your program crashes on exit, this is a likely cause.

- Copying structures that have strings in them is a bad idea. If the string is represented by an array, the copy will be inefficient, because it will include characters past the null terminator. If the string field is only a pointer, two structures will be sharing the string.

- `rand` is not a good implementation. If you are doing serious statistical work, use something better.

- Remember that a bit field will be a signed type unless you use the `unsigned` qualifier.

- When using a `union`, you must remember to keep track of what is actually being stored. The compiler will not remember, and you will be in trouble if you interpret a `union` field in a different way than it was assigned.

EXERCISES

1. Implement `mktime`.

2. In Figure 9.7, instead of returning a `void`, we could have `Deal` return a pointer to a card. If so, what is wrong with the following statement?

   ```
   return &TheCards[ --CardsUndealt ];
   ```

3. Suppose that we implement the shuffle by swapping the ith element with a randomly chosen element, instead of using the text's strategy of swapping with a randomly chosen element **of index i or smaller**. Show that even for three elements, this new method cannot possibly generate each permutation with equal probability. *Hint: Compute the number of possible outcomes of the shuffle using this strategy, and compare with the number of possible permutations.*

4. Show that assuming true randomness, using the text's algorithm, there is exactly one way to generate each permutation, and thus each permutation is equally likely.

5. Suppose that you want to select a permutation of M items randomly from the sequence $1, 2, \ldots, N$. Show how to adapt the text's algorithm to do this in a statistically unbiased way.

6. The ANSI C random number generator is not statistically wonderful. How many different random numbers can a single call to `rand` yield? (Note: Your system may have a different implementation.)

7. The program in Figure 9.33 computes random numbers using the linear congruential method. It is similar to what is used by `rand` but has somewhat better properties. The $(i + 1)$th random number is obtained from the ith random number by applying the formula $x_{i+1} = Ax_i \pmod{M}$.

   (a) Why is the calculation so fancy?

   (b) Compare the random numbers obtained by `BetterRand` and `rand`.

8. Consider the improved rearrangement procedure in Figure 9.16. The analysis requires showing the average number of cycles of each length L. As usual, N is the number of elements being sorted. Let p be any position.

   (a) Show that the probability that p is in a cycle of length 1 is $1/N$.

   (b) Show that the probability that p is in a cycle of length 2 is also $1/N$.

   (c) Show that the probability that p is in a cycle of any length L is $1/N$.

   (d) Based on part (c), deduce that the expected number of cycles of length L is $1/L$. *Hint: Each element contributes $1/N$ to the number of cycles of length L, but a simple addition overcounts cycles.*

9. (a) Write the generic Shellsort without using the extra array, `ACopy`.

   (b) Write the generic Shellsort for small blocks. This implementation need not use any pointers.

   (c) Write a generic Shellsort that selects one of the above, depending on the size of a block. When does it become advantageous to use the indirect sort?

10. One would expect that the time required to `memcpy` one `Block` would depend only on the size of `Block`. This is not true, because computer performance is enhanced when memory accesses are sequential and adversely affected when memory accesses are random. Compare the time used for `memcpy` in Figures 9.15 and 9.16.

```
/* 1*/    static const long int A = 48271;
/* 2*/    static const long int M = 2147483647;    /* 2^31 - 1.  */
/* 3*/    static const long int Q = 44488;         /* M / A.     */
/* 4*/    static const long int R = 3399;          /* M % A.     */
/* 5*/    unsigned long int Seed;

/* 6*/    unsigned long int
/* 7*/    BetterRand( void )
/* 8*/    {
/* 9*/        long int TmpSeed;

/*10*/        TmpSeed = A * ( Seed % Q ) - R * ( Seed / Q );
/*11*/        if( TmpSeed >= 0 )
/*12*/            Seed = TmpSeed;
/*13*/        else
/*14*/            Seed = TmpSeed + M;

/*15*/        return Seed;
/*16*/    }
```

Figure 9.33:   Improved random number generator.

11.   Multiplication by 512 is sometimes much easier than multiplication by 510, because 512 is an exact power of 2. Indexing an array of structures involves an implicit multiplication by the structure size. Thus a 510-byte record will sometimes be padded with two characters. On your system, is there any significant difference between accessing 510-byte structures and 512-byte structures?

12.   Are the parentheses on line 4 in Figure 9.19 really necessary?

13.   Modify Figure 9.23 to use a binary search algorithm.

14.   Add the triangle and ellipse to the shape case study.

10

Data Structures

This chapter is an introduction to *data structures*, which can be viewed as the beginning of the advanced portion of the book. It consists of a collection of standard methods that use structures in conjunction with pointers to greatly increase the execution speed of a program. We build components that are combined at the end of the chapter to solve a nontrivial problem efficiently.

10.1   Stacks

We have seen that a structure, such as the `tm` structure, can be used to combine several components of a logical unit. The `tm` structure is poorly designed, however, because the user is encouraged to set its fields to values that might not make sense. For instance, one can set a date of January 50. As we mentioned in Section 9.6, we would like a more atomic type, which can be passed back and forth as a unit but whose parts are not meant to be accessed individually by the user.

Two examples of this come to mind. First, the `time_t` type, which represents in some mysterious manner the time of day, can be obtained by calls to `time` and passed to other routines. However, the fact that it is an `unsigned long int` on most machines is irrelevant: the documentation specifically warns users not to assume any representation of `time_t` and not to attempt to fiddle with it. Second, the `double` type is just a collection of bits, but we would generally not even try to do anything but apply the standard operations on the `double`.

These two examples illustrate the concept of an *abstract data type*. The basic idea is to define a new type and some operations. In an ideal situation, the user of the abstract data type (ADT) would only need to know how to interface to these routines, and does not have to know anything about the implementation. Ideally, the type should be treated as an aggregate whose components are not individually examined, except by the routines that implement the basic operations. This is known as *information hiding*. In C, the compiler

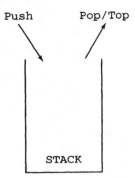

Figure 10.1:   Abstract stack operations.

cannot quite enforce information hiding, although a professor can.[1] We see in Chapter 14 that the more modern C++ has additional features that do support information hiding.

The rest of this chapter illustrates three basic abstract data types, beginning with the *stack*. A stack restricts access to the most recently inserted elements. It thus behaves very much like the common stack of bills, stack of plates, or stack of newspapers. The last item added to the stack is placed on the top and is easily accessible, while items that have been in the stack for awhile are more difficult to access; thus a stack is appropriate if we expect to access only the top item.

In a stack abstract data type, all other items are inaccessible. The three natural operations of Insert, Delete, and Find are named Push, Pop, and Top. These basic operations are illustrated in Figure 10.1. We also provide supporting functions to create an empty stack and to test for emptiness.

10.1.1   Application: Balancing Symbols

Before describing the detailed implementation of the stack, let us see one application. Looking at an application first emphasizes the fact that once the interface to the stack abstract data type is defined, we can write a program without worrying about how the stack is actually implemented.

A C program consists of many one-character symbols, and in some cases, the absence of just one symbol can create an incredibly long stream of error messages. One example of this is an unmatched brace ({). This is particularly troubling on terminals that do not have complete character sets. Thus it would be handy to have a program that would check to make sure that all of the opening symbols, such as parentheses, brackets, and braces, have a corresponding closing symbol.

A stack is useful here because we know that when a closing symbol such as) is seen, it matches the most recently seen unclosed (. Therefore, by placing opening symbols on a stack, we can easily check that a closing symbol makes sense. Specifically, we can check that a program is legitimate by starting with an empty stack and applying a Push whenever an opening symbol is seen. When the closing symbol is seen, the top symbol on the stack

---

[1]The use of incomplete struct types, discussed in Secion 9.6, can aid but not guarantee information hiding. Adding incomplete types and header files to the basic outlines provided in this chapter is simple and left as an exercise.

```
/* 1*/     #include <stdio.h>

/* 2*/     typedef struct
/* 3*/     {
/* 4*/         int Sym;              /* Not A char Because Of getchar */
/* 5*/         int Line;
/* 6*/     } Symbol;
```

Figure 10.2:   **Type declarations for balanced symbol checker.**

```
/* 1*/     int
/* 2*/     CheckMatch( const Symbol *OpSym, const Symbol *ClSym )
/* 3*/     {
/* 4*/         if( OpSym->Sym == '(' && ClSym->Sym == ')'
/* 5*/          || OpSym->Sym == '[' && ClSym->Sym == ']'
/* 6*/          || OpSym->Sym == '{' && ClSym->Sym == '}' )
/* 7*/             return 0;

/* 8*/         printf( "Found %c on line %d;"
/* 9*/                 " does not match %c at line %d\n",
/*10*/             ClSym->Sym, ClSym->Line, OpSym->Sym, OpSym->Line );
/*11*/         return 1;
/*12*/     }
```

Figure 10.3:   **Simple routine to check if two symbols are complementary.**

should be the corresponding open symbol. Assuming a match, it can be discarded from the stack, by a Pop. At the end of the input, we expect an empty stack, signifying that all open symbols have been closed. To allow us to indicate the line containing apparent mismatches, the stack stores structures consisting of the opening symbol and its line number. This is shown in Figure 10.2.[2]

Figure 10.3 prints an error message and returns 1 if the opening and closing structures do not contain matching symbols, and returns 0 otherwise. As usual, the structures are passed by reference. Recall that && has higher precedence than ||, so additional parentheses inside the if conditional are unnecessary.

Figure 10.4 shows the routine CheckBalance, which reads from the input, prints out error messages when mismatches are detected, and returns the number of mismatches it detected. Line 4 initializes the local stack S. As we will see when we discuss the stack implementation, this involves dynamic allocation of memory, and thus the routine StRecycle is called at line 40 to prevent memory leakage. The current symbol and line number is always in Last; the initialization sets the current line number to 1; this is incremented at line 11 when a newline is seen. Opening symbols are Pushed onto the stack at line 14. When a closing symbol is seen, we check that it corresponds to the symbol returned by Top. Notice that we first check that the stack is not empty, at line 17. At lines 33 to 39, we check for unmatched symbols.

---

[2]Because the structure is small, it is acceptable to avoid using pointers. Storing pointers to the structure on the stack would incur additional overhead of dynamic memory allocation (Exercise 2).

```
/* 1*/    int
/* 2*/    CheckBalance( void )
/* 3*/    {
/* 4*/         Stack S = StMakeEmpty( NULL );
/* 5*/         Symbol Last = { 0, 1 }, Match;
/* 6*/         int Errors = 0;

/* 7*/         while( ( Last.Sym = getchar( ) ) != EOF )
/* 8*/             switch( Last.Sym )
/* 9*/             {
/*10*/               case '\n':
/*11*/                 Last.Line++;
/*12*/                 break;
/*13*/               case '(': case '[': case '{':
/*14*/                 Push( Last, S );
/*15*/                 break;
/*16*/               case ')': case ']': case '}':
/*17*/                 if( StIsEmpty( S ) )
/*18*/                 {
/*19*/                     Errors++;
/*20*/                     printf( "Extraneous %c at line %d\n",
/*21*/                         Last.Sym, Last.Line );
/*22*/                 }
/*23*/                 else
/*24*/                 {
/*25*/                     Match = Top( S ); Pop( S );
/*26*/                     if( CheckMatch( &Match, &Last ) )
/*27*/                         Errors++;
/*28*/                 }
/*29*/                 break;
/*30*/               default:
/*31*/                 break;
/*32*/             }

/*33*/         while( !StIsEmpty( S ) )        /* Unmatched Symbols */
/*34*/         {
/*35*/             Errors++;
/*36*/             Match = Top( S ); Pop( S );
/*37*/             printf( "Unmatched %c at line %d\n",
/*38*/                     Match.Sym, Match.Line );
/*39*/         }
/*40*/         StRecycle( S );
/*41*/         return Errors;
/*42*/    }
```

Figure 10.4: Balanced symbol checking routine.

Note that the routine does not quite work because it does not understand C syntax. Thus it expects symbols to match even inside comments and does not know about character and string constants. Also, even if there is only one error, our program may print several messages after the first. The exercises ask you to improve these facets.

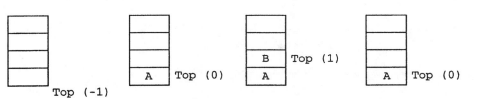

Figure 10.5: How the stack routines work: Empty stack, Push(A), Push(B), Pop.

10.1.2 Implementation of the Stack

As Figure 10.5 shows, a stack can be implemented with an array and an integer. The integer Top provides the array index of the top element of the stack, and thus when Top is -1, the stack is empty. To Push, we increment Top and place the new element in the array position Top. Finding the top element via Top is thus trivial, and the Pop can be performed by decrementing Top. To make the stack flexible, however, we add a few wrinkles. First, the array and Top are stored as members of a structure. Next, rather than using a fixed-size array, we allocate it dynamically, and double if necessary, using the techniques that we have seen in Chapter 7. Third, the Stack type is defined as a pointer to a structure, because for a general routine, passing a structure is unacceptable.

The result of all this is shown in Figure 10.6. At lines 4 to 9, we declare that a Stack is a pointer to a structure that has an array of elements (represented as a pointer), the current top of the stack (represented as an integer), and the maximum number of elements that can be represented in the stack until a realloc is needed. Initially, the latter value is 5, as shown at line 10. We also use the type StEtype; in our case, line 3 tells us that StEtype is Symbol. If we want to reuse the stack for another type, we have only to change line 3.

The routine to make an empty stack is shown next. There are two cases. If the stack already exists, we need only to set the top of the stack to -1. Otherwise, because the Stack type is a pointer to a structure, and one of the structure's members is a pointer, we will need to allocate some memory. At line 6 we allocate the structure, and at line 8, we allocate the array dynamically. We then set the maximum size field. After this memory allocation is complete, we can initialize the stack to its empty configuration. Notice that we must return S because S is passed call by value. Thus, as we have said in Chapter 7, having S point at newly allocated memory does not affect the actual argument.

If the user of the stack forgets to call StMakeEmpty, there is certain to be trouble. StInsistGood attempts to catch one possibility: our stack routines call it, and if S turns out to be NULL (which is probably the most common uninitialized value), an error message will be sent and the program will terminate. Of course, if S is uninitialized but not NULL, the program will probably crash silently.

Since StMakeEmpty allocates memory dynamically, it must be reclaimed, or else we will have a memory leak. StRecycle, shown in Figure 10.7, does this. Notice that memory is freed in the opposite order that it was allocated. The basic routines are implemented in Figure 10.8. They all follow the simple strategy outlined in Figure 10.5, except that error checks are added and Push implements array doubling. It is important to note that except when array doubling is performed, each of the basic operations is not only easily implemented but takes time that does not depend on the actual size of the stack. Using the notation in Chapter 7, we say that the time to execute a basic operation is thus $O(1)$, or a constant that is independent of the number of elements that are in the stack.

```
/* 1*/    #include <stdio.h>
/* 2*/    #include <stdlib.h>

/* 3*/    typedef Symbol StEtype;
/* 4*/    typedef struct StackStr
/* 5*/    {
/* 6*/        StEtype *Array;          /* The Array Of Elements */
/* 7*/        int TopOfStack;          /* Index Of Top Element */
/* 8*/        int MaxSize;             /* Maximum Stack Size */
/* 9*/    } *Stack;

/*10*/    static const StInitSize = 5;

/* 1*/    Stack
/* 2*/    StMakeEmpty( Stack S )
/* 3*/    {
/* 4*/        if( S == NULL )
/* 5*/        {
/* 6*/            if( !( S = malloc( sizeof( struct StackStr ) ) ) )
/* 7*/                return NULL;
/* 8*/            S->Array = malloc( sizeof( StEtype ) * StInitSize );
/* 9*/            if( S->Array == NULL )
/*10*/                return NULL;
/*11*/            S->MaxSize = StInitSize;
/*12*/        }
/*13*/        S->TopOfStack = -1;
/*14*/        return S;
/*15*/    }

/* 1*/    void
/* 2*/    StInsistGood( const Stack S )
/* 3*/    {
/* 4*/        if( S == NULL )
/* 5*/        {
/* 6*/            printf( "Stack routine received bad Stack\n" );
/* 7*/            exit( 1 );
/* 8*/        }
/* 9*/    }
```

Figure 10.6: Type declarations and `MakeEmpty` for stacks.

```
/* 1*/    void
/* 2*/    StRecycle( Stack S )
/* 3*/    {
/* 4*/        StInsistGood( S );
/* 5*/        free( S->Array );
/* 6*/        free( S );
/* 7*/    }
```

Figure 10.7: Recycling of stack's memory, after no longer needed.

```
/* 1*/    int
/* 2*/    StIsEmpty( const Stack S )
/* 3*/    {
/* 4*/        StInsistGood( S );
/* 5*/        return S->TopOfStack == -1;
/* 6*/    }


/* 1*/    void
/* 2*/    Push( StEtype X, Stack S )
/* 3*/    {
/* 4*/        StInsistGood( S );
/* 5*/        if( ++S->TopOfStack == S->MaxSize )
/* 6*/        {
/* 7*/            S->MaxSize *= 2;
/* 8*/            S->Array = realloc( S->Array,
/* 9*/                            sizeof( StEtype ) * S->MaxSize );
/*10*/            if( S->Array == NULL )
/*11*/            {
/*12*/                printf( "Can not extend the stack\n" );
/*13*/                exit( -1 );
/*14*/            }
/*15*/        }
/*16*/        S->Array[ S->TopOfStack ] = X;
/*17*/    }


/* 1*/    void
/* 2*/    Pop( Stack S )
/* 3*/    {
/* 4*/        if( StIsEmpty( S ) )
/* 5*/            printf( "Error: can not Pop an empty stack\n" );
/* 6*/        else
/* 7*/            S->TopOfStack--;
/* 8*/    }


/* 1*/    StEtype
/* 2*/    Top( const Stack S )
/* 3*/    {
/* 4*/        if( StIsEmpty( S ) )
/* 5*/            printf( "Error: can not Top an empty stack\n" );
/* 6*/        else
/* 7*/            return S->Array[ S->TopOfStack ];
/* 8*/    }
```

Figure 10.8:   Basic stack routines.

The time to perform a Push is likewise $O(1)$, as long as an array doubling is not involved. When an array doubling is involved, the time balloons to $O(N)$, because all N elements in the stack may need to be copied to a new array. Although this seems expensive, by virtue of the fact that since the previous array doubling at least $N/2$ constant-time Pushs must have preceded this expensive push, we can *amortize* this cost over all these operations and conclude that each Push is essentially a constant time operation.

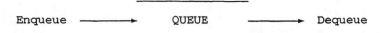

Figure 10.9:   Abstract queue operations.

Note that routines such as `MakeEmpty`, `IsEmpty`, and `Recycle` will be required for many of our abstract data types. To avoid name conflicts, we have included an `St` in these names for the stack ADT. The reason we have not used names like `MakeEmptyStack` is that on some older compilers, only the first six characters are significant for external names, which as we have seen includes function names.

10.2   Queues

In this section we look at another data structure, the *queue*. *Queue* is just a British word for *line*. Although there are many cases where it is important to be able to find and/or remove the most recently inserted item, there are equally many cases where this is not only not important, but actually the wrong thing to do. In a multiprocessing system, for example, when jobs are submitted to a printer, we expect the *least recent* or most senior job to be printed first. This is not only fair but is essentially required to guarantee that the first job does not wait forever. Thus printer queues can be expected to be found on all large systems.

The queue processes its items in *first come, first serve* behavior, which is typical of the normal waiting line. Like a stack, the insertion and deletion operations are given special names. For a queue, these names are `Enqueue` and `Dequeue`, respectively. It is common to implement `Dequeue` to remove the front item from the queue and also let the caller know what that item is. Thus it combines the `Insert` and `Find` operations. Figure 10.9 illustrates these abstract operations.

As we did when discussing stacks, first we give an application of queues, and then we show how the queue can be implemented.

10.2.1   Application: Merging Sorted Lists

Suppose that you are directing a single-elimination tennis tournament among players whose relative strengths are unknown. You have only one tennis court, and M players, and thus you need to come up with a schedule. If M is an exact power of 2, this is a simple enough matter, as Figure 10.10 shows. Here we have $M/2$ first-round games, played one after each other. Then the winners advance to the second round and play $M/4$ second-round games, again, one after each other, and so on. Since $M = 2^k$ for some k, to win the tournament, someone must win exactly k matches.

When M is not an exact power of 2, the problem seems more difficult, since we must introduce an element of unfairness, namely the *bye*. A *bye* means that someone gets to skip a match, and thus some players need k wins while others need $k - 1$ wins. Thus if only seven players are present, we might allow player 7 to advance to the second round without playing a match, thus retaining the basic structure of Figure 10.10. We must be careful that nobody gets more than one bye, since that would be terribly unfair. Thus if $M = 5$, we

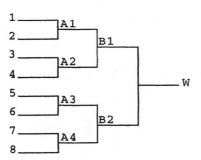

Figure 10.10:   Single-elimination tournament.

cannot just remove players 6 to 8 and leave the schedule unchanged, because then player 5 could win the tournament after winning only one match.

We can guarantee that nobody gets more than one bye by assigning only first-round byes. However, there is another extremely simple approach that is very appropriate for computers and which we will see can be used for other purposes. We can just simply place all the players in a queue. We remove two players from the queue, and after a match, the winner goes to the back of the queue, while the loser is eliminated. After $M - 1$ matches, the remaining player is the winner.

It is easy to see that at any point, nobody plays his or her ith match while someone else is waiting to play his or her $(i - 1)$th match. Thus we have some form of equity. This idea is commonly used in algorithm design to extend operations that are normally applied on only two operands to an unlimited number of operands. We consider as an example the merging of a bunch of groups of items, where each group is sorted. It is simple enough to merge two groups of sorted items, and thus by applying the same strategy we can immediately extend this to M groups. The generalization is not only simple but is efficient: it is impossible to improve substantially on the number of comparisons that are used.

Figure 10.11 shows three arrays, A, B, and C. A and B are sorted in increasing order and have three elements each; we would like to merge them and store the sorted result in C, which holds six elements. Obviously, we can just throw all the elements of A and B into C and call a sorting routine, such as Shellsort, but since we are given so much ordering information already, we expect to be able to do better.

The basic merging algorithm starts with three counters, ACtr, BCtr, and CCtr, which initially are at the start of their respective arrays. We then repeatedly compare A[ACtr] and B[BCtr]: the smaller of the two is then copied to C[CCtr], and then the appropriate counters are advanced.

Thus in Figure 10.11 we first copy the 2 from B into C. Once we do that we advance BCtr and CCtr, obtaining the second line. To focus on the algorithm, for both A and B, the blank cells indicate cells that have been copied over to C: they still contain their original values, however. For C, the blank cells indicate cells that have not yet been written to. Next we copy the 3 from A over to C, and advance ACtr and CCtr, obtaining line 3. The next two copies are from elements in B over to C, after which we obtain line 5. At this point, all elements in B have been copied, so we finish the merge by copying over all elements in A. The time required to do all this is linear in the total number of elements merged.

Figure 10.12 implements the merging of two sorted arrays. The trickiest part is the fact that we dynamically allocate C, and thus we have mallocs, frees, and also a structure

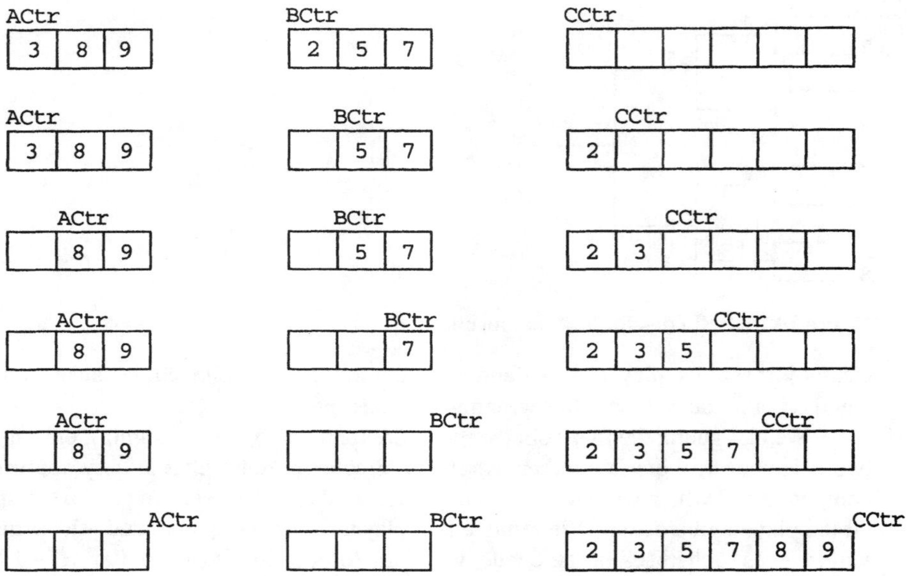

ACtr | 3 | 8 | 9   BCtr | 2 | 5 | 7   CCtr | | | | |

ACtr | 3 | 8 | 9   BCtr | | 5 | 7   CCtr | 2 | | | |

ACtr | | 8 | 9   BCtr | | 5 | 7   CCtr | 2 | 3 | | |

ACtr | | 8 | 9   BCtr | | | 7   CCtr | 2 | 3 | 5 | |

ACtr | | 8 | 9   BCtr | | | CCtr | 2 | 3 | 5 | 7 |

ACtr | | | BCtr | | | CCtr | 2 | 3 | 5 | 7 | 8 | 9

Figure 10.11: Merging of two sorted arrays.

that holds a dynamically allocated array and an integer reflecting its size. To avoid further complications, we pass and return this structure rather than using a pointer to it. If we ignore all of that overhead, the entire merging algorithm is contained in lines 15 through 23. Notice that the body of exactly one of the `while` loops at lines 20 and 22 is not executed, and exactly one is executed.

Once we have written the routine to merge two sorted arrays, merging M sorted arrays becomes simple. Figure 10.13 reflects the same algorithm that we described for tournament scheduling. On line 8 we Enqueue each sorted array. Then on lines 9 to 14, we repeatedly Dequeue two sorted arrays and Enqueue the result of merging them. At the end, the one remaining sorted array is the answer.

As we will see, it is easy to implement the queue so that all the operations take constant time. Consequently, the running time of the entire algorithm is $O(N \log M)$, where M is the number of sorted arrays that we start with and N is the total number of elements involved. The derivation of this bound is left as Exercise 4. Notice that we can always start with N sorted one-element lists. Thus this provides an $O(N \log N)$ sort: place each element in its own sorted array and run the merging algorithm. This is one implementation of an algorithm known as *bottom-up mergesort*.

10.2.2 Implementation of the Queue

The easiest way to implement the queue is to store the items in an array with the front item in the front (i.e., array index zero) position. If Back represents the position of the last item in the queue, to Enqueue we merely increment Back and place the item there. The problem is that the Dequeue operation is very expensive, because by requiring that the items be placed at the start of the array, we force the Dequeue to shift over all the items one position, after the front item is removed.

```
/* 1*/    #include <stdio.h>
/* 2*/    #include <stdlib.h>

/* 3*/    typedef struct
/* 4*/    {
/* 5*/        int *Array;
/* 6*/        int Size;
/* 7*/    } SortedInts;
```

```
/* 1*/    /* Merge Two Sorted Lists.  Since SortedInts Is */
/* 2*/    /* A Small Structure We Avoid Pointers */

/* 3*/    SortedInts
/* 4*/    MergeTwo( SortedInts struct1, SortedInts struct2 )
/* 5*/    {
/* 6*/        int *C;
/* 7*/        int *A = struct1.Array, *B = struct2.Array;
/* 8*/        int ACtr = 0, BCtr = 0, CCtr = 0;

/* 9*/        C = malloc( sizeof( int ) *
                              ( struct1.Size + struct2.Size ) );
/*10*/        if( C == NULL )
/*11*/        {
/*12*/            printf( "Can not allocate temporary array\n" );
/*13*/            return struct1;
/*14*/        }

/*15*/        while( ACtr < struct1.Size && BCtr < struct2.Size )
/*16*/            if( A[ ACtr ] <= B[ BCtr ] )
/*17*/                C[ CCtr++ ] = A[ ACtr++ ];
/*18*/            else
/*19*/                C[ CCtr++ ] = B[ BCtr++ ];

/*20*/        while( ACtr < struct1.Size )
/*21*/            C[ CCtr++ ] = A[ ACtr++ ];
/*22*/        while( BCtr < struct2.Size )
/*23*/            C[ CCtr++ ] = B[ BCtr++ ];

/*24*/        free( A ); free( B );
/*25*/        struct1.Size += struct2.Size;
/*26*/        struct1.Array = C;

/*27*/        return struct1;
/*28*/    }
```

Figure 10.12:   Code to merge two sorted arrays.

Figure 10.14 shows that to overcome this problem, when a Dequeue is performed, we increment Front rather than sliding over all the elements. When the queue has one element, both Front and Back represent the array index of that element. Thus for an

```
/* 1*/     SortedInts
/* 2*/     MergeM( const SortedInts A[ ], int M )
/* 3*/     {
/* 4*/         Queue Q = QuMakeEmpty( NULL );
/* 5*/         SortedInts One, Two, Merged;
/* 6*/         int i;

/* 7*/         for( i = 0; i < M; i++ )
/* 8*/             Enqueue( A[ i ], Q );

/* 9*/         for( i = 0; i < M-1; i++ )
/*10*/         {
/*11*/             Dequeue( &One, Q );
/*12*/             Dequeue( &Two, Q );
/*13*/             Enqueue( MergeTwo( One, Two ), Q );
/*14*/         }
/*15*/         Dequeue( &Merged, Q );

/*16*/         QuRecycle( Q );
/*17*/         return Merged;
/*18*/     }
```

Figure 10.13:   Code to merge *M* **sorted arrays.**

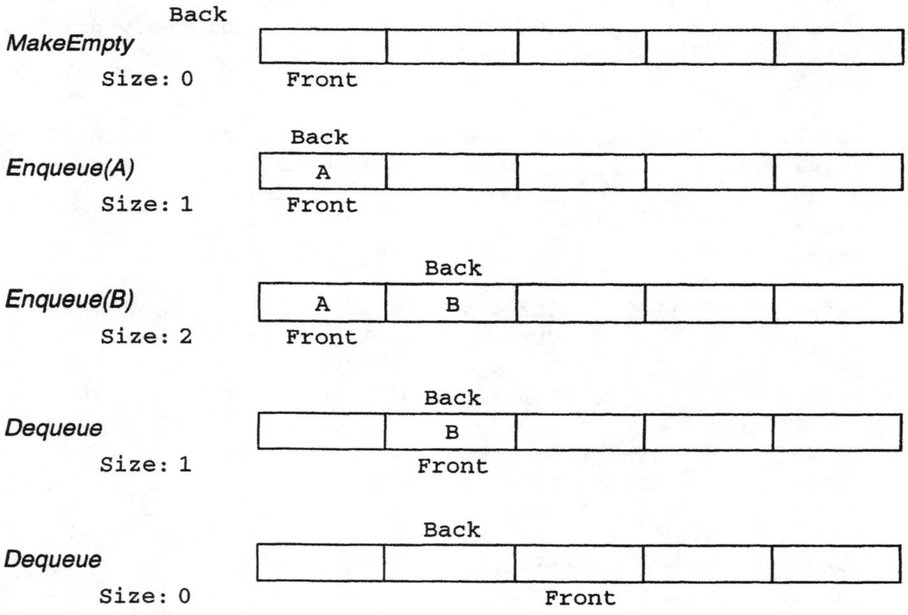

Figure 10.14:   Basic array implementation of the queue.

empty queue, Back must be initialized to Front-1.

This implementation assures us that both Enqueue and Dequeue can be performed in constant time. The fundamental problem with it is shown in the first line of

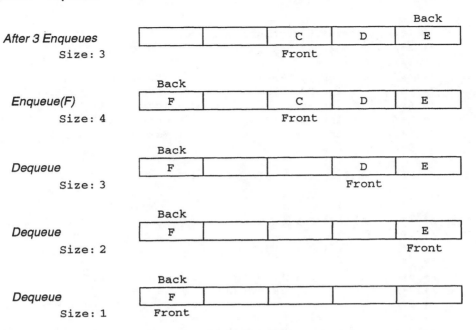

Figure 10.15:   Array implementation of the queue with wraparound.

Figure 10.15. After three more Enqueue operations, we cannot add any more items, even though the queue is not really full. Array doubling does not solve the problem, because even if the size of the array is 1000, after 1000 Enqueue operations, there is no room in the queue, regardless of its actual size. Even if 1000 Dequeue operations have been performed, thus abstractly making the queue empty, we cannot add to it.

As Figure 10.15 shows, however, there is plenty of extra space: all the positions before Front are unused and can thus be recycled. Thus we implement *wraparound*: when either Back or Front reaches the end of the array, we reset them to the beginning. We only need to double the array when Size becomes equal to the array size. To Enqueue(F), we therefore reset Back to the start of the array, and place F there. After three Dequeue operations, the Front is also reset to the start of the array.

Figure 10.16 shows the type declarations for the queue, and the routine to make an empty queue. It follows the same logic as the stack operations to allocate a queue structure and then the queue array. A recycling routine is also needed, but since it is virtually identical to the stack routine, we have not included it. Note carefully the initial values for both the front and back.

Figure 10.17 illustrates the Dequeue routine. Notice that the queue is empty if the size is 0. The Dequeue routine passes the front element back by reference, and increments (with wraparound if necessary) the Front position. It also decreases the current size by one. The Enqueue operation, shown in Figure 10.18, is conceptually simple, as lines 18 to 20 show. The rest of the routine deals with array doubling. Lines 7 to 14 are standard array doubling code. But the queue is trickier: if the elements in the queue are wrapped around in the original queue array, we must ensure that they are still wrapped around the larger array. Let OrigSz be the number of elements in the queue. If Q->Front is not

```
/* 1*/    typedef SortedInts QuEtype;
/* 2*/    typedef struct QueueStr
/* 3*/    {
/* 4*/        QuEtype *Array;        /* The Array Of Elements */
/* 5*/        int Front;             /* Index Of Front Element */
/* 6*/        int Back;              /* Index Of Back Element */
/* 7*/        int Size;              /* Current Number Of Elements */
/* 8*/        int MaxSize;           /* Maximum Queue Size */
/* 9*/    } *Queue;

/*10*/    static const QuInitSize = 5;

/* 1*/    Queue
/* 2*/    QuMakeEmpty( Queue Q )
/* 3*/    {
/* 4*/        if( Q == NULL )
/* 5*/        {
/* 6*/            if( !( Q = malloc( sizeof( struct QueueStr ) ) ) )
/* 7*/                return NULL;
/* 8*/            Q->Array = malloc( sizeof( QuEtype ) * QuInitSize );
/* 9*/            if( Q->Array == NULL )
/*10*/                return NULL;
/*11*/            Q->MaxSize = QuInitSize;
/*12*/        }
/*13*/        Q->Size = 0;
/*14*/        Q->Front = 0;
/*15*/        Q->Back = -1;
/*16*/        return Q;
/*17*/    }
```

Figure 10.16:   Code for type declarations and making an empty queue.

zero, the elements in the queue are represented by Q->Front to the end of the original array, and then the start of the original array to Q->Back. When we double the array, we have two ways to arrange the elements.

First, we can move the elements that were in positions 0 to Q->Back over to use the new array positions which begin at OrigSz. In this case the queue will now encompass positions Q->Front to Q->Back+OrigSz. An alternative possibility is to move the elements that were in Q->Front to the end of the original array over by OrigSz positions. This means that the queue will encompass positions Q->Front+OrigSz to the end of the new array, then wrapping around to the start of the new array, and over to Q->Back. Figure 10.19 shows these two rearrangement strategies.

Since both alternatives work, it is logical to choose the one that copies fewer elements. That is what the FixWraparound routine does. Note that in line 9 of FixWraparound, we could have used Q->Array as the second parameter to memcpy, since the array name is equal to the address of the zeroth element. We used the longer form to be consistent with the other three parameters (in the two memcpy calls). Note also that &Array is legal but is not the same at all.

```
/* 1*/    int
/* 2*/    QuIsEmpty( const Queue Q )
/* 3*/    {
/* 4*/         QuInsistGood( Q );
/* 5*/         return Q->Size == 0;
/* 6*/    }



/* 1*/    int
/* 2*/    Increment( int QParam, int QSize )
/* 3*/    {
/* 4*/         if( ++QParam == QSize )
/* 5*/             return 0;
/* 6*/         else
/* 7*/             return QParam;
/* 8*/    }



/* 1*/    void
/* 2*/    Dequeue( QuEtype *X, Queue Q )
/* 3*/    {
/* 4*/         if( QuIsEmpty( Q ) )
/* 5*/             printf( "Error: can not Dequeue an empty queue\n" );
/* 6*/         else
/* 7*/         {
/* 8*/             *X = Q->Array[ Q->Front ];
/* 9*/             Q->Front = Increment( Q->Front, Q->MaxSize );
/*10*/             Q->Size--;
/*11*/         }
/*12*/    }
```

Figure 10.17:   Dequeue **routine.**

10.3   Hash Tables

Stacks and queues are distinguished by three operations that implement Insert, Delete, and Find. For stacks, these are Push, Pop, and Top, while for queues, they are Enqueue and Dequeue (with the later combining the Delete and Find). In both cases the basic insertion and deletion operations are restricted to one element, which is either the most or least recently inserted item. In this section we look at unrestricted implementations, where we allow the retrieval or deletion of any item, as long as the name of the item is provided (Fig. 10.20). Thus, what we are implementing is essentially a *dictionary*. The difficult part is efficiency: we would like to maintain the $O(1)$ running time for the operations that the stack and queue provide.

To keep our dictionary as abstract as possible, we adopt the following convention. When an item is inserted into the dictionary, it is assigned a number (sequentially). This

Chapter 10.   Data Structures

```
/* 1*/    /* After Queue Is Doubled, Arrangement May Be Bad. */
/* 2*/    /* This Routine Fixes It, And Avoids Excessive Moves */

/* 3*/    void
/* 4*/    FixWraparound( Queue Q )
/* 5*/    {
/* 6*/        const int OrigSz = Q->MaxSize / 2;

/* 7*/        if( Q->Front < OrigSz / 2   )
/* 8*/        {
/* 9*/            memcpy( &Q->Array[ OrigSz ], &Q->Array[ 0 ],
/*10*/                    Q->Front * sizeof( QuEtype ) );
/*11*/            Q->Back += OrigSz;
/*12*/        }
/*13*/        else
/*14*/        {
/*15*/            memcpy( &Q->Array[  OrigSz + Q->Front ],
/*16*/                    &Q->Array[ Q->Front ],
/*17*/                    ( OrigSz - Q->Front ) * sizeof( QuEtype ) );
/*18*/            Q->Front += OrigSz;
/*19*/        }
/*20*/    }
/*21*/
```

```
/* 1*/    void
/* 2*/    Enqueue( QuEtype X, Queue Q )
/* 3*/    {
/* 4*/        QuInsistGood( Q );
/* 5*/        if( Q->Size == Q->MaxSize )
/* 6*/        {
/* 7*/            Q->MaxSize *= 2;
/* 8*/            Q->Array = realloc( Q->Array,
/* 9*/                    sizeof( QuEtype ) * Q->MaxSize );
/*10*/            if( Q->Array == NULL )
/*11*/            {
/*12*/                printf( "Can not extend the queue\n" );
/*13*/                exit( -1 );
/*14*/            }
/*15*/            if( Q->Front != 0 )
/*16*/                FixWraparound( Q );
/*17*/        }
/*18*/        Q->Back = Increment( Q->Back, Q->MaxSize );
/*19*/        Q->Array[ Q->Back ] = X;
/*20*/        Q->Size++;
/*21*/    }
```

Figure 10.18:   Enqueue **routine, including array doubling.**

number is presumably an index into another table, which will contain all the other information corresponding to that item. Although we could combine all this information into one structure, store the entire structure in the dictionary, and just use one field to perform

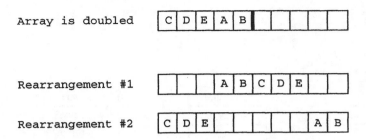

Figure 10.19: **Two possible rearrangement strategies for** FixWraparound. A **is at the front,** E **at the rear.**

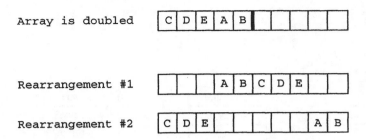

Figure 10.20: **Abstract hash table operations.**

the access, this is not as general a solution as the method we are proposing. Therefore, the first item that is inserted is assigned 0, the next item is assigned 1, and so on. To indicate an unsuccessful search we return -1, since that cannot be confused with a valid assigned number.

One use of this data structure is the symbol table, which the compiler uses to keep track of all the variables in your program. We will see an equivalent use in the next section.

10.3.1   Implementation by Linear Probing

Our basic givens are that each item in the dictionary is accessed by a *key* and that a successful Find operation will return a small positive integer that indexes into an array containing the complete item. The most common type of key is the string, so we will describe how dictionaries are implemented for the basic char * type.

Let us first consider a simple solution that works on an abstract computer, assuming only that the keys have some bounded length (such as eight characters). Just as the number 1234 is a collection of the digits 1, 2, 3, and 4, the string "junk" is a collection of characters 'j', 'u', 'n', and 'k'. Notice that the number 1234 is just $1 * 10^3 + 2 * 10^2 + 3 * 10^1 + 4 * 10^0$. Since a character is basically a small integer, we can interpret a string as an integer; one possible representation is $'j' * 128^3 + 'u' * 128^2 + 'n' * 128^1 + 'k' * 128^0$. This allows a simple implementation of the dictionary via an array. We set

```
Array[ i ] = -1;
```
for all i. To Insert a new item into the dictionary, we set

```
Array[ IntRep( Key ) ] = NextNumber;
```
where Key is the key of the item, IntRep returns the integer representation of Key, and NextNumber is the small positive integer that is returned by subsequent Finds.

```
Hash( "norman", 7 )  => 0
Hash( "mark", 7 )    => 6
Hash( "bill", 7 )    => 2
Hash( "becky", 7 )   => 6
Hash( "alicia", 7 )  => 1
```

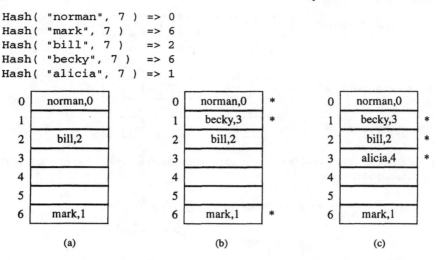

(a)   (b)   (c)

Figure 10.21: **Hash table after several insertions:** (a) inserting `norman`, `mark`, `bill`; (b) inserting `becky`: **wants spot 6; first vacancy is spot 1;** (c) inserting `alicia`: **wants spot 1; first vacancy is spot 3.**

The problem with this strategy is that the integer representation we have described generates huge integers: `IntRep("junk")` evaluates to 224229227 (on ASCII machines), and longer strings generate much larger integer representations. This makes direct application of this scheme impractical, because we do not have sufficient memory to declare the array. To make this scheme practical, we need to use a smaller array, and thus we need a function that generates smaller numbers. This method is known as *hashing*. Suppose that the array size is `TableSize`. Then by choosing

```
IntRep( Key ) % TableSize
```

we are guaranteed a number that can be used as an index into the array. This function, which maps the `Key` into an array position, is known as the *hash function*.

This new scheme introduces a complication, however: it is now possible for `Key1` and `Key2` to evaluate to the same array position, thus causing a *collision*. To resolve the collision, we adopt the simplest possible strategy and search sequentially until we find an empty cell. This strategy is known as *linear probing*. As with the queue, we implement wraparound, so that the sequential search tries array position 0 if position `TableSize-1` is occupied. Figure 10.21 illustrates linear probing. Here we assume a table with maximum size 7 and attempt to insert five strings. Their hash values are shown. `"norman"`, `"mark"`, and `"bill"` are easily inserted (along with an integer indicating their order of insertion) into the cell indicated by the hash function. Although `"becky"` hashes to position 6, it cannot be inserted there because that cell is already occupied. So position 0 (which immediately follows 6, when wraparound is considered) is attempted next, and when that fails, position 1, which is empty, is used. Finally, we insert `"alicia"` in position 3, because its hash position, 1, is taken, as is the first alternate.

Before we consider how to perform the `Find` operation, let us briefly describe the type declarations for the hash table. As Figure 10.22 shows, the basic cell consists of a string and an integer, representing an order of appearance. Since actual elements are numbered

```
/* 1*/    #include <stdio.h>
/* 2*/    #include <stdlib.h>

/* 3*/    #define NotFound  -1

/* 4*/    typedef struct HashEntry
/* 5*/    {
/* 6*/        char *Word;
/* 7*/        int Num;
/* 8*/    } Cell;

/* 9*/    typedef struct HashStr
/*10*/    {
/*11*/        Cell *Array;           /* The Array Of Cells */
/*12*/        int Size;              /* Current Number Of Elements */
/*13*/        int MaxSize;           /* Maximum Table Size */
/*14*/    } *HashTbl;

/*15*/    static const HaInitSize = 17;



/* 1*/    unsigned int
/* 2*/    Hash( const char *Key, const unsigned int TableSize )
/* 3*/    {
/* 4*/        unsigned int HashVal = 0;

/* 5*/        while( *Key != '\0' )
/* 6*/            HashVal = HashVal * 37 + *Key++;

/* 7*/        return HashVal % TableSize;
/* 8*/    }
```

Figure 10.22:   Hash table declarations and a hashing function.

starting at 0, we can take -1 to signify an empty cell. A #define is needed at line 3 in Figure 10.22 to allow initialization at line 5 in Figure 10.23. Note that since the basic cell represents Word as a char *, we expect that our insertions will allocate enough memory to store a copy of the inserted string.

The hash table, then, consists of an array of cells that we will allocate dynamically, as well as the current and maximum number of elements actually stored in the table. Figure 10.22 also shows the hash function. We have adjusted it slightly, using 37 instead of 128 as the multiplier. This is the hash function that was used in the example in Figure 10.21.

Figure 10.23 shows the MakeEmpty and Recycle routines that have become customary in our exposition of data structures. HaMakeEmpty frees the memory used to store the strings, if necessary, and then allocates a new hash table structure, followed by the actual array. It then makes all the cells empty by setting the Num field to NotFound and the Word field to NULL. Setting the Word field to NULL is important, because otherwise a subsequent free would crash. Of course, by careful coding we can ensure that Word is never accessed when Num is NotFound, but it can be tricky to get this correct in all places.

```
/* 1*/     HashTbl
/* 2*/     HaMakeEmpty( HashTbl H )
/* 3*/     {
/* 4*/         int i;
/* 5*/         const Cell InitCell = { NULL, NotFound };

/* 6*/         if( H != NULL )
/* 7*/         {
/* 8*/             for( i = 0; i < H->MaxSize; i++ )
/* 9*/             {
/*10*/                 free( H->Array[ i ].Word );
/*11*/                 H->Array[ i ].Num = NotFound;
/*12*/             }
/*13*/             H->Size = 0;
/*14*/             return H;
/*15*/         }

/*16*/         free( H ); /* Safe Even if H == NULL */
/*17*/         if( ( H = malloc( sizeof( struct HashStr ) ) ) == NULL )
/*18*/             return NULL;
/*19*/         H->Array = malloc( sizeof( Cell ) * HaInitSize );
/*20*/         if( H->Array == NULL )
/*21*/             return NULL;

/*22*/         H->Size = 0;
/*23*/         H->MaxSize = HaInitSize;
/*24*/         for( i = 0; i < H->MaxSize; i++ )
/*25*/             H->Array[ i ] = InitCell;

/*26*/         return H;
/*27*/     }


/* 1*/     void
/* 2*/     HaRecycle( HashTbl H )
/* 3*/     {
/* 4*/         int i;

/* 5*/         HaInsistGood( H );
/* 6*/         for( i = 0; i < H->MaxSize; i++ )
/* 7*/             free( H->Array[ i ].Word );
/* 8*/         free( H->Array );
/* 9*/         free( H );
/*10*/     }
```

Figure 10.23: `HaMakeEmpty` **and** `HaRecycle`.

Figure 10.24 shows the `Find` and `Insert` routines. Performing a `Find` is simple:
we follow the same path as the insertion. The `Find` is unsuccessful if we encounter an
empty cell. Thus both `Insert` and `Find` call the publicly invisible (via the `static`
declaration) `FindPos` routine. `FindPos` mimics the action of `Find` by computing the

```
/* 1*/    static int
/* 2*/    FindPos( const char *Key, const HashTbl H )
/* 3*/    {
/* 4*/        unsigned int Pos;

/* 5*/        Pos = Hash( Key, H->MaxSize );
/* 6*/        while( H->Array[ Pos ].Num != NotFound &&
/* 7*/                    strcmp( H->Array[ Pos ].Word, Key ) )
/* 8*/            if( ++Pos == H->MaxSize )
/* 9*/                Pos = 0;

/*10*/        return Pos;
/*11*/    }
```

```
/* 1*/    int
/* 2*/    Find( const char *Key, const HashTbl H )
/* 3*/    {
/* 4*/        return H->Array[ FindPos( Key, H ) ].Num;
/* 5*/    }
```

```
/* 1*/    /* Insert A new Key Into H, Making A Duplicate */

/* 2*/    int
/* 3*/    Insert( const char *Key, HashTbl H )
/* 4*/    {
/* 5*/        unsigned int Pos;

/* 6*/        if( H->Size > H->MaxSize / 2 )
/* 7*/            Rehash( H );

/* 8*/        Pos = FindPos( Key, H );
/* 9*/        if( H->Array[ Pos ].Num == NotFound )
/*10*/        {
/*11*/            H->Array[ Pos ].Word = Strdup( Key );
/*12*/            H->Array[ Pos ].Num = H->Size++;
/*13*/        }
/*14*/        return H->Array[ Pos ].Num;
/*15*/    }
```

Figure 10.24:   Find **and** Insert **routines.**

hash value at line 5 and then searching sequentially (with wraparound at lines 8 and 9) until either an empty cell or a match is found. At that point it returns the index of the cell that caused it to stop the search. Note that at line 6, the order of the tests is important. Thus the Find operation is just a trivial call to FindPos. To perform the Insert, we call FindPos at line 8. If the cell is empty, lines 11 and 12 place a copy of Key and the next assigned number in the cell. Insert returns this assigned number. If Key was already present, nothing is done and the number previously assigned to Key is returned.

Lines 6 and 7 are used to expand the hash table dynamically when it becomes full. Unlike the stack and queue, where the data structure is full if `Size == MaxSize`, we regard a hash table as being full when more than half of the table is occupied. This is because as the table becomes more crowded, it becomes harder to insert a new element.

∞   We can give a simple, though mathematically flawed explanation of this. Suppose that the table is half full. Then the probability of finding an empty cell at random is $\frac{1}{2}$. Thus the number of cells we expect to try until the insertion succeeds is 2. If the table is three-quarters full, the probability of finding an empty cell at random is $\frac{1}{4}$. Thus we expect to try about 4 cells, on average, until the insertion is successful. Now consider what happens when the table is 95% full: only one cell in 20 is empty, so we expect to try 20 cells until an insertion succeeds. Thus if λ is the fraction of the table that is full, then this analysis suggests that the insertion time is given by $1/(1 - \lambda)$.

Therefore, as the table approaches 100% capacity (i.e., λ tends toward 1), the insertion time seems to grow drastically. Thus we keep the table at least half empty at all times, doubling it when the 50% threshold is reached. This doubling is called *rehashing*, and the code to perform it is shown in Figure 10.25. It is very similar to the queue and stack doubling except that the technical details are somewhat more complicated. At line 7, instead of exact doubling, we double up to the nearest prime, because, in practice, we tend to get more uniform distribution from the hash function when the table size is prime.

The other important detail is that we cannot just blindly copy the old table to the new, because the positions in the old table are determined by the old hash function, while the positions in the new table are determined by the new hash function. Thus at lines 18 to 24, we reinsert each element in the old table into the new table.

The performance of hash tables, in practice, is very efficient, and as long as $\lambda < 0.5$, tends to be dominated mostly by the time required to compute the hash function. Thus improved efficiency could be obtained by using the fact that $37x = 32x + 4x + x$, because multiplication by 32 and 4 for a computer is as simple as multiplication by 100,000 or 100 is for humans. Some compilers already know this trick and will avoid the difficult multiplication by 37. Frequently, the multiplier is replaced by 32, for precisely this reason, although sometimes that tends to give a hash function which distributes poorly, thus causing more collisions than usual.[3]

∞   The formula given earlier for the number of cells that we expect to probe in an insertion is incorrect, although for $\lambda < 0.5$, the difference is not significant. The actual formula is $\frac{1}{2}[1 + 1/(1-\lambda)^2]$. The reason our analysis fails is that successive probes are not independent random events. This is somewhat similar to the airport parking garage analogy: even when a parking garage with many entrances is 5% empty, generally the empty spaces are far away, on the top level, because everybody is trying to park on the lower levels first. This formula implies that 2.5 rather than 2 cells are tried on average to insert an element into a table that is 50% full. To insert into an empty table, with $\lambda = 0$, the formula correctly says that 1 cell is tried on average. The formula can also be used to tell us how many probes are used, on average, for a `Find`. For an unsuccessful `Find`, the answer is easy: since an unsuccessful `Find` is just like an `Insert`, the average number of probes is identical.

For a successful `Find`, the answer is a bit more complicated. The time to perform `Find(Key)` is determined at the point that `Key` is inserted. For example, a `Find` on the

---

[3]A popular alternative to line `/*6*/` in the hash function is
```
/*6*/ HashVal = HashVal << 5 ^ *Key++;
```

```
/* 1*/      static void
/* 2*/      Rehash( HashTbl H )
/* 3*/      {
/* 4*/          unsigned int i, Pos, OldSize = H->MaxSize;
/* 5*/          Cell *OldArray = H->Array;
/* 6*/          const Cell InitCell = { NULL, NotFound };

/* 7*/          H->MaxSize = NextPrime( 2 * OldSize );
/* 8*/          H->Array = malloc( sizeof( Cell ) * H->MaxSize );
/* 9*/          if( H->Array == NULL )
/*10*/          {
/*11*/              printf( "Can not rehash\n" );
/*12*/              exit( -1 );
/*13*/          }
/*14*/          H->Size = 0;
/*15*/          for( i = 0; i < H->MaxSize; i++ )
/*16*/              H->Array[ i ] = InitCell;

/*17*/              /* Reinsert Old Elements Into new Table */
/*18*/          for( i = 0; i < OldSize; i++ )
/*19*/              if( OldArray[ i ].Num >= 0 )
/*20*/              {
/*21*/                  Pos = FindPos( OldArray[ i ].Word, H );
/*22*/                  H->Array[ Pos ] = OldArray[ i ];
/*23*/                  H->Size++;
/*24*/              }

/*25*/          free( OldArray );
/*26*/      }
```

Figure 10.25: Rehash **routine.**

first element inserted into the hash table always requires one cell probe. If the table is 50% full, a Find on the most recently inserted element takes 2.5 cell probes on average. So how long does an average successful Find take? The answer is obtained by averaging the cost of a successful Find over all the load values up to λ. This can be done by evaluating a definite integral, and the result is $\frac{1}{2}[1 + 1/(1 - \lambda)]$.

One last point about the hash table is the implementation of deletion. It is tempting to just free the word and set the Num field to NotFound. This does not quite work, because, for example, if we delete "norman" from the last hash table in Figure 10.21, most of the subsequent Find operations will fail. The alternative is *lazy deletion*: we mark the cell deleted by using a value of -2 for the Num field. Exercise 9 asks you to write the Delete routine and make any alterations to the other routines that might be necessary.

10.4   Case Study: Single-Source Shortest Paths

We will now write a program that brings together all the ideas that we have discussed in this chapter and introduce us briefly to a fundamental problem in a branch of mathematics

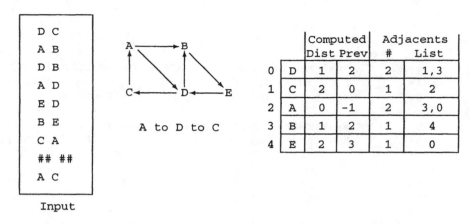

```
D C
A B
D B
A D
E D
B E
C A
## ##
A C
```

Input

A to D to C

		Computed		Adjacents	
		Dist	Prev	#	List
0	D	1	2	2	1,3
1	C	2	0	1	2
2	A	0	-1	2	3,0
3	B	1	2	1	4
4	E	2	3	1	0

Figure 10.26:   **Representation of a graph, and computed values when starting point is** A.

(and computer science) known as *graph theory*. The basic problem is as follows: we are given a set V of *vertices* that can represent cities or computers. Another commonly used word for vertex is *node*. We are also given a set E of *edges*: each edge tells us that we can get from some vertex v_i to some other vertex, v_j (but not necessarily from v_j to v_i). Thus an edge can represent a plane flight, or a unidirectional computer link.

The two sets V and E form a *graph G*. We would like to know, for any two s and t drawn from V, the minimum number of edges required to get from s to t (if, indeed, t is reachable from s). In practice, we expect the vertex set to be quite large. Since there could be an edge between each pair of vertices, it is possible for the number of edges to be proportional to the square of the number of vertices, but this is unusual for the kinds of graphs that are used to model transportation and communication problems. The middle picture in Figure 10.26 shows a typical visual representation of a graph. An edge from v_i to v_j, represented mathematically as (v_i, v_j), is drawn as a directed arrow from v_i to v_j. We can see that the shortest path from A to C has a length of two edges.

Even though we have not yet determined an algorithm to solve the shortest path problem efficiently, it is possible to write most of the program anyway. We do this step by step, and the last routine we write will solve for the shortest path. The first thing we need to do is to settle on the input format that we expect the user to provide. As Figure 10.26 shows, the user will represent the graph by providing a list of edges, one per line, terminating with ## ##. Then the user will specify a sequence of paths, again one per line, ending with an EOF marker. We will not restrict the names of the vertices in any way, except to limit them to 80 characters.

Now that we have decided what to expect from the user, we need to figure out how we will store the graph. As the middle picture of Figure 10.26 shows, the graph structure is determined by knowing, for each vertex, what other vertices are directly connected to it. For instance, B and D are connected directly to A. These are called *adjacent* vertices. Thus for each vertex we keep a list, known as an *adjacency list*, that tells us which vertices are adjacent to it, as well as a counter that tells us how big this list is.

Because some vertices may have many adjacent vertices, and others may have few, we implement the adjacency list as a dynamically expanding array. The structure, shown in Figure 10.27, is very much like a stack except that the access operations are not restricted

```
/* 1*/    typedef int ArEtype;

/* 2*/    typedef struct
/* 3*/    {
/* 4*/        int CurrentSize;
/* 5*/        int MaxSize;
/* 6*/        ArEtype *Array;
/* 7*/    } VarArray;


/* 1*/    void
/* 2*/    Add( ArEtype X, VarArray *A )
/* 3*/    {
/* 4*/        if( A->CurrentSize == A->MaxSize )
/* 5*/        {
/* 6*/            if( A->CurrentSize == 0 )
/* 7*/            {
/* 8*/                A->MaxSize = 2;
/* 9*/                A->Array = malloc( sizeof ( ArEtype )
                                            * A->MaxSize );
/*10*/            }
/*11*/            else
/*12*/            {
/*13*/                A->MaxSize *= 2;
/*14*/                A->Array = realloc( A->Array, sizeof( ArEtype )
/*15*/                                        * A->MaxSize );
/*16*/            }

/*17*/            if( A->Array == NULL )
/*18*/            {
/*19*/                printf( "Out of space\n" );
/*20*/                exit( -1 );
/*21*/            }
/*22*/        }
/*23*/        A->Array[ A->CurrentSize++ ] = X;
/*24*/    }
```

Figure 10.27:   Basic adjacency list routines.

to the top. The variable array structure, VarArray, contains a pointer to dynamically allocated memory, as well as both the current and maximum size of the adjacency list. We pass VarArray by reference, using a pointer.

The vertices themselves will be numbered sequentially as they first appear. Thus, in our input, D is vertex 0, C is vertex 1, A is vertex 2, B is vertex 3, and E is vertex 4. Thus we need a hash table to determine efficiently where the adjacency information for any vertex v is stored. All of this information will be available once the graph is read, which will be exactly when the ## ## sequence is seen.

We will also need to compute the shortest path information. In Figure 10.26 we have shown that for each vertex we have the length of the shortest path that starts at a designated starting vertex (in this case A). Thus the shortest path to C, starting from A, has length 2.

We will require that the shortest path algorithm compute this information given any starting vertex. In addition, to print the actual path, we require that the shortest path algorithm give us the next-to-last vertex on that shortest path. Thus the next-to-last vertex on the shortest path to C is D (indicated by the 0 in the Prev entry). The next-to-last vertex on the shortest path to D is A (indicated by the 2). By successively tracing back through this information, we have deduced the entire path.

Therefore, the basic graph structure consists of a hash table that is used to get an index into an array containing vertex information. For each vertex the four pieces of information are:

1. Its actual name (so paths can be output without using the internal array indices)

2. The computed shortest distance

3. The computed previous vertex on the shortest path

4. The adjacency list structure, VarArray

This is shown in the type declarations of Figure 10.28. We also provide two routines that we know we will need.

First we have AddNode. When we read a name from the user, we need to determine its corresponding array index or assign it the next available array index. Thus at line 6, we consult the hash table. If the Find is successful, we do nothing and return the array index. Otherwise, we Insert Name into the hash table and obtain from the hash table the next sequential number, which will be the array index. We then initialize that spot of the Graph array and make a copy of the name. Note that we cannot just have the NodeName field point at Name, because it would be pointing at a string that is constantly being overwritten. If space is at a premium, we could have it point at the same string that the hash table is pointing at, but that would involve altering and interfering with the hash table. The AddEdge routine just calls the Add routine in Figure 10.27 to place Dest in Source's adjacency list.

Once these routines are written, Figure 10.29 shows that it is easy to write the routine ReadGraph. Two parameters are passed: the Graph array and a hash table. We repeatedly read lines from the input, which we expect to have two strings, separated by blank space, and immediately terminated by a newline. We presume the routine GetTwoStrings, which returns 0 for a misformatted line or EOF when appropriate, has already been written (Exercise 11). If a line is misformed, lines 12 and 13 will cause it to be ignored, after printing a warning message. Line 15 checks to see if the ## ## sequence has been seen, and if so, ReadGraph returns. Otherwise, we call AddEdge, at lines 18 and 19, to insert the edge we have just read. As we have seen, AddNode will automatically insert newly seen vertices, and in any case, return an index into the Graph array.

Now that we have written all the code to read the graph, we need to write the functions to read the rest of the input, process each shortest path request, and output answers. As we mentioned earlier, after the shortest path algorithm has run and filled in the Distance and PreviousNode fields, we can determine the actual shortest path to any vertex by tracing back through the PreviousNode field. A direct application of this strategy, unfortunately, gives the path in reverse order, since it prints from the destination vertex back to the starting vertex.

To get the path in the correct order, we simply use a stack: as we trace the path from the destination back to the start, we stack all the vertices that we see on the path, and

```
/* 1*/      typedef int DisType;
/* 2*/      #define Infinity IntMax
/* 3*/      #define MaxNodes 3000

/* 4*/      typedef struct               /* Basic Vertex Structure */
/* 5*/      {
/* 6*/          char *NodeName;          /* Name */
/* 7*/          DisType Distance;        /* Distance From Start */
/* 8*/          int PreviousNode;        /* Previous Vertex On Path */
/* 9*/          VarArray Adj;            /* List Of Adjacent Vertices */
/*10*/      } Vertex;

/* 1*/      int
/* 2*/      AddNode( const char *Name, HashTbl H, Vertex Graph[ ] )
/* 3*/      {
/* 4*/          int NodeNum;
/* 5*/          const Vertex NewVert =
                              { NULL, Infinity, -1, { 0, 0, NULL } };

/* 6*/          if( ( NodeNum = Find( Name, H ) ) < 0 )
/* 7*/          {
/* 8*/              NodeNum = Insert( Name, H );
/* 9*/              if( NodeNum == MaxNodes )
/*10*/              {
/*11*/                  printf( "Graph is full. Increase MaxNodes\n" );
/*12*/                  exit( -1 );
/*13*/              }
/*14*/              Graph[ NodeNum ] = NewVert;
/*15*/              Graph[ NodeNum ].NodeName = Strdup( Name );
/*16*/          }
/*17*/          return NodeNum;
/*18*/      }


/* 1*/  void
/* 2*/  AddEdge( int Source, int Dest, Vertex Graph[ ] )
/* 3*/  {
/* 4*/      Add( Dest, &Graph[ Source ].Adj );
/* 5*/  }
```

Figure 10.28:   Basic graph structure, plus routines to add a node and an edge.

when we have reached the starting vertex, we can pop the stack repeatedly. This strategy is shown in Figure 10.30. At line 6 we handle the case where the destination is unreachable. Otherwise, at lines 11 to 15, we repeatedly Push previous nodes, including the starting vertex. Then at lines 16 to 20, we Pop these vertices. When the stack is finally empty, the loop terminates, and we can print the destination vertex (which was never pushed onto the stack).[4] Our previously written stack routines can be used if we make but one change: StEtype is now an int.

---

[4]This is done so that the word to appears one time fewer than the number of vertices on the path.

```
/* 1*/      #define MaxNodeLen 80
/* 2*/      typedef char NodeName[ MaxNodeLen + 1 ];
/* 3*/      const char *Term = "##";

/* 4*/      void
/* 5*/      ReadGraph( Vertex Graph[ ], HashTbl H )
/* 6*/      {
/* 7*/          NodeName Source, Dest;
/* 8*/          int RetVal;

/* 9*/          while( ( RetVal = GetTwoStrings(
/*10*/                          Source, Dest, MaxNodeLen ) ) >= 0 )
/*11*/          {
/*12*/              if( RetVal != 2 )
/*13*/                  printf( "Warning: skipped an input line\n" );
/*14*/              else
/*15*/              if( !strcmp( Source, Term ) && !strcmp( Dest, Term ) )
/*16*/                  return;
/*17*/              else
/*18*/                  AddEdge( AddNode( Source, H, Graph ),
/*19*/                           AddNode( Dest,   H, Graph ), Graph );
/*20*/          }
/*21*/          printf( "Input terminated early???\n" );
/*22*/      }
```

Figure 10.29: **Read a graph from the user.**

At this point, with the exception of the routine EvaluateShort, which actually figures out the shortest path, we are almost done. Figure 10.31 shows the two remaining supporting routines. The main routine merely declares and initializes the hash table and allocates the graph array. It then calls ReadGraph to read the graph and ProcessRequests. The main routine does not bother to call HaRecycle, since the program terminates immediately when the hash table is no longer needed. Any other routine besides main would be obligated to manage memory explicitly.

ProcessRequest works much like ReadGraph. It is passed both the Graph array and a hash table and repeatedly expects two strings per line until an EOF is reached. At lines 15 and 16, the source and destination vertex names are checked to make sure that they are graph vertices, and if so, the source index is used at line 21 to start EvaluateShort, while the destination index is used at line 22 by PrintPath. At this point all that remains is to write the shortest path routine. This turns out to be a relatively simple calculation. Let us start by concerning ourselves only with determining the shortest distance; later, we figure out how to set PreviousNode.

Recall that we have some source node; for the purposes of this discussion let us call it s. Let d_i be the length of the shortest path from s to i. The shortest path from s to itself is always zero, so we know immediately that $d_s = 0$. We do not know any other distances, so let us initially assign $d_i = \infty$ for all $i \neq s$.

Let us suppose that we have a roving eyeball that hops from vertex to vertex and is initially at s. The eyeball sees all vertices w adjacent to s, and thus we know for sure that we can set $d_w = 1$ if w is adjacent to s. Now let us move our eyeball to any vertex v such

```
/* 1*/    void
/* 2*/    PrintPath( int DestNode, const Vertex Graph[ ] )
/* 3*/    {
/* 4*/        Stack S = StMakeEmpty( NULL );
/* 5*/        int Intermediate;

/* 6*/        if( Graph[ DestNode ].Distance == Infinity )
/* 7*/            printf( "%s unreachable\n",
                                    Graph[ DestNode ].NodeName );
/* 8*/        else
/* 9*/        {
/*10*/            Intermediate = Graph[ DestNode ].PreviousNode;
/*11*/            while( Intermediate != -1 )
/*12*/            {
/*13*/                Push( Intermediate, S );
/*14*/                Intermediate = Graph[ Intermediate ].PreviousNode;
/*15*/            }
/*16*/            while( !StIsEmpty( S ) )
/*17*/            {
/*18*/                printf( "%s to ", Graph[ Top( S ) ].NodeName );
/*19*/                Pop( S );
/*20*/            }
/*21*/            printf( "%s\n", Graph[ DestNode ].NodeName );
/*22*/        }
/*23*/        StRecycle( S );
/*24*/    }
```

Figure 10.30:   Print shortest path from the table.

that $d_v \equiv 1$. As our eyeball looks out at vertices w that are adjacent to the current vertex v, it knows that if it sees $d_w \equiv \infty$, it can set $d_w = 2$, because if v is reachable in one edge, surely any vertex w that is adjacent to v is reachable in 2. After we have looked at all w adjacent to the current vertex v, we can move the eyeball to the next vertex v such that $d_v \equiv 1$, and continue the process of finding all vertices that are reachable in two edges.

When our eyeball has finished processing all vertices v that satisfy $d_v \equiv 1$, we move on to vertices satisfying $d_v \equiv 2$. For any w adjacent to such a v, if $d_w \equiv \infty$, we can set $d_w = 3$. Notice that when examining d_w, if it is not ∞, the distance already assigned to w is at least as short as 3 (because we have not assigned 4 or larger yet). Therefore, our strategy is very simple. At any point our eyeball is at some vertex v, which initially is s. For each w adjacent to v, if $d_w \equiv \infty$, we set $d_w = d_v + 1$. At this point we are also saying that we can get to w by following a path to v and then extending the path by the edge (v, w). This tells us that the PreviousNode field for w is v!

After we have processed all of v's adjacent vertices, we move the eyeball to another vertex u, such that $d_u \equiv d_v$; if this is not possible, we move to u, which satisfies $d_u \equiv d_v + 1$; if this is not possible, we are done. (Why?) We can figure out how to move the eyeball by scanning the Graph array looking for an appropriate vertex. There are problems with this strategy: first we must be careful not to let our eyeball visit a vertex v twice. Although that is easy enough to fix, the more pressing problem is that finding a vertex to relocate our eyeball can take lots of time, because it may degenerate into a linear scan of the Graph

```
/* 1*/    void
/* 2*/    ProcessRequests( Vertex Graph[ ], HashTbl H )
/* 3*/    {
/* 4*/        NodeName Source, Dest;
/* 5*/        int SourceNum, DestNum;
/* 6*/        int RetVal;

/* 7*/        while( ( RetVal = GetTwoStrings(
/* 8*/                        Source, Dest, MaxNodeLen ) ) >= 0 )
/* 9*/        {
/*10*/            if( RetVal != 2 )
/*11*/            {
/*12*/                printf( "Format error: skipping this line\n" );
/*13*/                continue;
/*14*/            }
/*15*/            SourceNum = Find( Source, H );
/*16*/            DestNum = Find( Dest, H );
/*17*/            if( SourceNum == -1 || DestNum == -1 )
/*18*/                printf( "Illegal vertex specified\n" );
/*19*/            else
/*20*/            {
/*21*/                EvaluateShort( SourceNum, Graph );
/*22*/                PrintPath( DestNum, Graph );
/*23*/            }
/*24*/        }
/*25*/    }


/* 1*/    main( void )
/* 2*/    {
/* 3*/        HashTbl H = HaMakeEmpty( NULL );
/* 4*/        Vertex G[ MaxNodes + 1 ];

/* 5*/        ReadGraph( G, H );
/* 6*/        ProcessRequests( G, H );
/* 7*/        return 0;
/* 8*/    }
```

Figure 10.31: `main` **routine, and routine to process connection requests.**

array. Since we have so many relocations, the total time spent could be quadratic in the number of vertices even if the number of edges is relatively small.

There is no need to do all that work because as we have seen, when a vertex w has its d_w lowered from ∞, it becomes a candidate for an eyeball visitation at some point in the future. This is because after the eyeball visits vertices that are in the current distance group, d_v, it will visit the next distance group, $d_v + 1$, which is the group containing w. Thus w just needs to wait on line for its turn, thus suggesting directly that we use a queue. Whenever we lower d_w from ∞, we will place it on a queue of vertices, waiting for an eyeball visitation. To select the next vertex v for the eyeball, we merely perform a Dequeue. We start with an empty queue, and then to get the algorithm rolling, we Enqueue the start vertex s. This method is known as a *breadth-first search*.

```
/* 1*/    void
/* 2*/    EvaluateShort( int StartNode, Vertex Graph[ ] )
/* 3*/    {
/* 4*/        int i, V, W;
/* 5*/        Queue Q = QuMakeEmpty( NULL );

/* 6*/        for( i = 0; Graph[ i ].NodeName != NULL; i++ )
/* 7*/        {
/* 8*/            Graph[ i ].Distance = Infinity;
/* 9*/            Graph[ i ].PreviousNode = -1;
/*10*/        }

/*11*/        Graph[ StartNode ].Distance = 0;
/*12*/        Enqueue( StartNode, Q );
/*13*/        while( !QuIsEmpty( Q ) )
/*14*/        {
/*15*/            Dequeue( &V, Q );
/*16*/            for( i = 0; i < Graph[ V ].Adj.CurrentSize; i++ )
/*17*/            {
/*18*/                W = Graph[ V ].Adj.Array[ i ];
/*19*/                if( Graph[ W ].Distance == Infinity )
/*20*/                {
/*21*/                    Graph[ W ].Distance = Graph[ V ].Distance + 1;
/*22*/                    Graph[ W ].PreviousNode = V;
/*23*/                    Enqueue( W, Q );
/*24*/                }
/*25*/            }
/*26*/        }
/*27*/        QuRecycle( Q );
/*28*/    }
```

Figure 10.32:   Shortest path calculation.

All of this is implemented in Figure 10.32. Line 5 declares an initially empty queue, and then lines 6 to 10 initialize the graph table entries so that all distances are ∞ and all previous node entries are -1. The queue is unchanged from our earlier implementation, except that QuEtype must be changed to be of type int. We set $d_s \equiv 0$ and Enqueue s at lines 11 and 12. We then repeatedly move the eyeball to a new vertex v by virtue of the Dequeue at line 15 and process all adjacent vertices by the loop at lines 16 to 25. Lines 19 to 24 represent a verbatim implementation of the basic algorithm.

This routine completes implementation of the shortest path algorithm. Because it is built on data structures that process each operation in constant time, it turns out that this is a very fast program. Most of the time is spent performing I/O, which is out of our control. On a graph with 3000 vertices and 50,000 edges, after the 10 seconds (of mostly disk I/O) required to read in the graph, each shortest path calculation is completed in 0.1 second. Had we used a quadratic algorithm for EvaluateShort, the running time would have increased dramatically to about 30 seconds. Had we not used a hash table, but instead implemented a linear scan for the table lookup, we would have used many minutes to read the input graph.

10.5   Linked Lists

In our implementations of stacks, we discovered that items can be efficiently inserted and removed from an array if these changes to the array are restricted to occur at the end of the list of items in the array. By careful interpretation of the "front" and "back" of the array, we can apply this strategy to implement queues. However, if we attempt to insert or delete an item that is in the middle of an array, we see that many items will have to move to maintain continuity among the array items. Therefore, if the order in which items appear in a list is important, an array is a poor choice.[5] Our last application of structures is the *linked list*. The linked list allows the insertion and deletion of items using only a constant number of data movements. There is a price to pay, however: we sacrifice the direct access that an array provides. In an array, the ith item is instantly accessible; this is no longer the case when we employ linked lists.

The basic idea of a linked list is to avoid the data movement problems of arrays by not storing elements contiguously. Therefore, every element is stored, along with a pointer to the next element. Thus we have a structure allocated (dynamically) for each element to hold both the element and a pointer to the next structure. As an example, we consider the *Josephus problem*. We start with N people sitting in a circle and one ball, initially in possession of player 1. At each turn the ball is passed p times, the person who last holds the ball is eliminated, the circle closes ranks, and the next person picks up the ball to repeat this process. The last player is the winner. Although p could be a random number that changes from turn to turn, it is common to imagine that it is fixed and perhaps much smaller than N. If N is 5 and p is 1, the players are eliminated in the order 2 4 1 5, and the winner is 3.

Figure 10.33 contains the routines and type declarations to solve the Josephus problem. At lines 1 to 5 we declare that the basic `Cell` structure consists of an integer representing a player, as well as a pointer to the next `Cell` structure. Line 4 seems like circular logic, but it is not: it only declares a pointer, not another `Cell` structure. The latter would indeed be illegal. The type that the `Next` field points at is a `struct Cell`, and although the declaration for `struct Cell` is not completed until line 5, the fact that it is a valid type is known at line 4.[6] In fact, this explains the main reasons that the structure tag name, which, because of the `typedef` facility, has hardly been used so far, is important.

Figure 10.34 shows three stages of the Josephus problem. The first thing we must do is construct our linked list, which will mimic the circle of players. The routine `GetCell` allocates a new `CellType` and sets the `Number` field to the passed parameter. Line 21 gets things started by creating a one-element list. To build our circular linked list, we repeatedly call `GetCell` and hook up each new cell to the end of the linked list; this is accomplished by lines 22 and 23. Figure 10.34 shows how this is done when `People` and `i` are both 5. Before we execute line 23 for the last time, we have the linked list depicted at the top of Figure 10.34. We then call `GetCell` to allocate a new cell (a); we set `Last->Next` to point at this new cell (b); then we reset `Last` to point at the new cell, which is now the last cell (c), and since this loop terminates, we execute line 24, which closes the linked list into a circle (d).

---

[5]If the order is not important and the number of items is large, a hash table is appropriate.

[6]Technically speaking, we say that at that point, `struct Cell` represents an incomplete structure declaration. See Section 9.6.

```
/* 1*/    typedef struct Cell
/* 2*/    {
/* 3*/        int Number;
/* 4*/        struct Cell *Next;
/* 5*/    } CellType;

/* 6*/    CellType *
/* 7*/    GetCell( int CellNo )
/* 8*/    {
/* 9*/        CellType *CellPtr = malloc( sizeof( CellType ) );

/*10*/        if( CellPtr == NULL )
/*11*/            Error( "Out of memory" );

/*12*/        CellPtr->Number = CellNo;
/*13*/        return CellPtr;
/*14*/    }

/*15*/    int
/*16*/    Jos( int People, int Passes )
/*17*/    {
/*18*/        CellType *BeforeBall, *Last, *First, *Loser;
/*19*/        int i;

/*20*/            /* Create The List */
/*21*/        First = Last = GetCell( 1 );
/*22*/        for( i = 2; i <= People; i++ )
/*23*/            Last = Last->Next = GetCell( i );

/*24*/        Last->Next = First;          /* Make List Circular */

/*25*/        for( BeforeBall = Last; People != 1; People-- )
/*26*/        {
/*27*/                /* Pass The Ball */
/*28*/            for( i = 0; i < Passes; i++ )
/*29*/                BeforeBall = BeforeBall->Next;

/*30*/                /* Remove A Player */
/*31*/            Loser = BeforeBall->Next;
/*32*/            BeforeBall->Next = Loser->Next;
/*33*/            free( Loser ); /* See Text Warning */
/*34*/        }
/*35*/        return BeforeBall->Number;
/*36*/    }
```

Figure 10.33:   Routine to solve the Josephus problem.

All that remains is to remove players repeatedly after skipping over Passes cells. The bottom of Figure 10.34 shows how player 2 would be eliminated. We merely reset the Next pointer of the cell prior to the cell containing player 2 to bypass player 2's cell. Thus the chain of links now skips past 2. The memory used for 2's cell is no longer needed, since

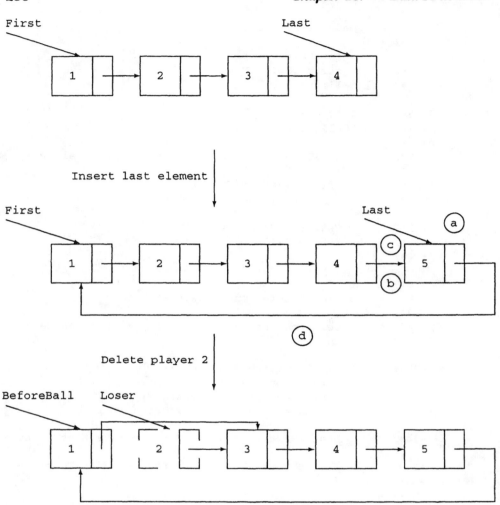

Figure 10.34: **Linked list insertion and deletion illustrated.**

that cell is now inaccessible in the list; it can be recycled by calling `free`. Lines 31 to 33 in Figure 10.33 implement this. We maintain `BeforeBall`, which will always point to the cell prior to player holding the ball. Thus the initialization at line 25 starts `BeforeBall` at the `Last` player.

When `People` has been decremented to only one, the sole remaining cell contains the winning player. An alternative test for this condition is that

```
BeforeBall == BeforeBall->Next
```

 will be true. There is an important performance issue dealing with the repeated calls to `free`. Under normal circumstances, the time spent by the calls to `free` should be insignificant. On our system, this is not always the case, particularly when `Passes` is 2. In this case the running time of the program increases by a factor of about 20 when we run the program with 10,000 players. You should always use the `free`, but beware that on some relatively rare occasions, you may need to comment it out for performance reasons.

10.6   Summary

In this chapter we investigated the general use of structures in implementing *abstract data types*, such as stacks, queues, and dictionaries. Because these are fundamental objects, it is worth developing efficient and general-purpose routines to support them. We saw how all of this can be melded to produce an efficient program to solve the shortest path problem.

Our discussion of abstract data types and the algorithms that use them can be considered a brief introduction to the theory of data structures and algorithms. A more detailed knowledge of this field is essential for any serious programmer. Three good books on the subject, well worth reading are [Cormen 90], [Sedgewick 90], and [Weiss 93]. This is the next logical step once you have mastered C.

In Chapter 11 we take one more look at fundamental algorithms when we discuss recursion. In Chapter 12 we discuss I/O in detail, and in Chapter 13 we examine how C is used to implement systems programming in UNIX. Finally in Chapter 14, we examine C++ and see how that language builds on C by providing support for abstract data types.

10.6.1   What Was Covered

- A stack is a last in, first out data structure. It is very useful for remembering things backward.

- A queue is a first in, first out data structure. It is good for forming waiting lines.

- A hash table can be used to implement a dictionary. For linear probing, make sure that the table is always at least half empty.

- By using all three of these data structures, we can solve the shortest path problem efficiently. The roving eyeball implements what is known as a *breadth-first search.*

- The linked list can be used when insertions and deletions are expected in the middle of a list rather than at an end. The price we pay is that the *i*th element in the list can no longer be accessed in constant time, as is the case with an array.

10.6.2   Friendly Reminders

- Our implementation of the queue is tricky, especially the parts to initialize and expand.

- The hash function should perform calculations using `unsigned ints`. Otherwise, because of overflow, a negative number could creep in.

- Although calls to `free` are generally quick, be aware that occasionally they can be very time consuming and might even need to be commented out.

EXERCISES

1. Pick any data structure in this chapter and implement it with a header file that contains the prototypes and an incomplete type declaration.

2. Modify Figure 10.4 to work if StEtype is declared as

```
typedef Symbol *StEtype;
```

3. For the symbol-matching program:

(a) Try to do better error recovery when a mismatch is detected, so that minimal error messages are printed.

(b) Give the program knowledge of C syntax. Symbols inside comments do not need matching, and neither do symbols inside character constants or constant strings. Symbols on a preprocessor line do not have to match either.

4. Show that the running time required to merge M sorted lists containing N total elements is $O(N \log M)$. *Hint: Every element involved in a two-way merge contributes one to the total number of comparisons.*

5. One popular brand of calculators implements computations via *reverse Polish notation.* A stack is used to hold operands, and when an operator is seen, two operands are popped from the stack, and the result of applying the operator to these is pushed back on the stack. As an example, 3 4 5 * + evaluates to 23 because multiplication is applied as 4 * 5, pushing 20, and then the addition is applied as 3 + 20, pushing 23. The top symbol on the stack is the printed answer. Write a program to implement reverse Polish arithmetic. Be careful to check for errors and note that for an operator such as -, the first element off the stack becomes the second of the two operands.

6. Use a linked list to implement a:

(a) Stack.

(b) Queue.

7. A popular alternative to linear probing is known as *separate chaining.* Here we maintain an array of (hopefully) very short linked lists. The hash function indicates which linked list stores the item. If the number of linked lists is roughly N (i.e., $\lambda = 1$), the expected insertion time is very small. Implement separate chaining hashing.

8. For linear probing, how many cell probes are performed on average in the new hash table when rehashing is implemented? *Hint: The average insert time is given by averaging over all insert times from $\lambda = 0$ to 0.25.*

9. Implement deletion in a hash table. Be careful to ensure that the other operations still work correctly. (This is much more tricky than it appears.)

10. Implement a Date abstract data type. Supply routines to initialize a date, compare two dates, subtract two dates, and add an integer (possibly negative) number of days to a date.

11. Implement a routine that reads a line of input and verifies that exactly two strings of bounded length are read. In the prototype below, EOF is returned on end of input, 0 is returned for error, and 2 is returned for success. The two strings are placed in Str1 and Str2.

```
int GetTwoStrings( char *Str1, char *Str2,
                                unsigned int MaxLen );
```

12. Remove the limitation of MaxNodes from the shortest path algorithm by expanding Graph dynamically.

13. A topological sort of graph is an arrangement of the vertices such that if there is an edge (u, v), then v must come after u. A topological sort exists (but is not necessarily unique) if and only if the graph has no cycles. The UNIX command *tsort* solves the topological sort problem, but is inefficient, requiring quadratic time in the worst case. Rewrite tsort so that it is more efficient. Your routine should detect a cycle if one exists. *Hint: For each vertex, maintain the number of incoming edges. Move the eyeball to a vertex v with no incoming edges, and output it. Then for each w adjacent to v, lower by one the count of incoming edges for w. Then repeat the process by moving the eyeball to another vertex with zero incoming edges.*

14. Write a program to implement the simple textual substitution performed by the preprocessor. Specifically, do not deal with parameterized macros. Thus, read the input; any input line containing

    ```
    #define SYMBOL REPLACEMENT_TEXT
    ```

    causes any appearance of SYMBOL on a subsequent line that does not begin with a # to be appropriately replaced. Implement rescanning for macros. Do not worry about comments or string constants.

15. A *double-ended queue*, or *deque*, supports both insertion and deletion at both the front and back. Implement a complete Deque abstract data type.

16. For sparse polynomials, such as $x^{1994} - 1$, the array representation suggested in Exercise 7.4 is inappropriate. Instead, a linked list can store each term of the polynomial (coefficient and exponent), sorted by exponent. Redo Exercise 7.4 to use the linked list representation. *Note: You may need to adjust the prototypes to* return *the resultant polynomial.*

17. Explain how each of the following problems can be solved by applying a shortest path algorithm. Then design a mechanism for representing an input, and write a program that solves the problem.

    (a) The input is a list of league game scores (and there are no ties). From this list, if all teams have at least a win and a loss, we can generally "prove," by a silly transitivity argument, that any team is better than any other. For instance, in the six-team league, where everyone plays three games, suppose that we have the following results:

    ```
    A beat B and C
    B beat C and F
    C beat D
    D beat E
    E beat A
    F beat D and E
    ```

    Then we can "prove" that A is better than F because A beat B, who in turn beat F. Of course, we can "prove" that F is better than A because F beat E and E beat A. Given a list of game scores and pairs of teams A and B, find a proof (if one exists) that A is better than B, or indicate that no proof of this form can be found.

    (b) A word can be changed to another word by a one-character substitution. Assume that a dictionary of five-letter words exists. Give an algorithm to determine if a word A can be transformed to a word B by a series of one-character substitutions, and if so, it outputs the corresponding sequence of words. As an example, bleed converts to blood by the sequence bleed, blend, blond, blood.

18. Write a program that reads the standard input and converts all labels (and their corresponding gotos) to integers. (Pascal requires that labels are integers rather than identifiers.)

11

Recursion

A function that is defined (partially) in terms of itself is called *recursive*. As we mentioned in Section 4.6, C supports recursive functions. Recursion, which is the use of recursive functions, is such a powerful (and sometimes misunderstood) tool that we feel that an entire chapter is needed to discuss it. Since no new syntax rules are required, this chapter is algorithm-oriented rather than language-oriented.

To discuss recursion, we will first examine the mathematical principle on which it is based, namely *mathematical induction*. Then we will give examples of simple recursive functions and prove that they generate correct answers. We also explore how recursion works, thus providing some insight into its limitations.

Once we have laid down the foundation, we examine some of the many uses of recursion by exploring three particular areas. First, we use recursion to perform some mathematical calculations. Next, we look at two classic uses of recursion when we implement searching and sorting via the *binary search tree* and *quicksort*, respectively. Finally, we see how recursion is used to program a computer to play two-person games, such as chess. In our case, using the supporting routines from Section 7.6, we give a routine that finds the optimal *tic-tac-toe* move.

11.1   Background: Proofs by Mathematical Induction

In this section we discuss *proof by mathematical induction*. Throughout this chapter we omit the word *mathematical* when describing this technique. Induction proofs are commonly used to establish theorems that hold for positive integers. We start by proving a simple theorem. It is easy to establish this particular theorem using other methods, but often it turns out that a proof by induction is the simplest mechanism.

Theorem 11.1: For any integer $N \geq 1$, the sum of the first N integers, given by $\sum_{i=1}^{N} i = 1 + 2 + \ldots + N$, is equal to $N(N + 1)/2$.

It is easy to see that the theorem is true for $N = 1$ because both the left- and right-hand sides evaluate to 1. Further checking shows that it is true for $2 \leq N \leq 10$. However, the fact that the theorem holds for all N that are easy to check by hand does not imply that it is true for all N. Consider, for instance, numbers of the form $2^{2^k} + 1$. The first five numbers corresponding to $0 \leq k \leq 4$ are 3, 5, 17, 257, and 65,537. These numbers are all prime, and indeed at one time it was conjectured that all numbers of this form are prime. This is not the case: it is easy to check by computer that $2^{2^5} + 1 = 641 * 6700417$. In fact, no other prime of the form $2^{2^k} + 1$ is known.

A proof by induction works in two steps. First, as above, we show that the theorem is true for the smallest case(s). We then show that if the theorem is true for the first few cases, it can be extended to include an additional case. For instance, we show that a theorem that is true for all $1 \leq N \leq k$ must be true for $1 \leq N \leq k + 1$. Once we show how to extend the range of true cases, we have shown that it is true for all cases, because we can extend the range of true cases indefinitely. Let us use this technique to prove Theorem 11.1.

Proof (of Theorem 11.1): Clearly, the theorem is true for $N = 1$. Suppose that the theorem is true for all $1 \leq N \leq k$. Then

$$\sum_{i=1}^{k+1} i = (k+1) + \sum_{i=1}^{k} i \qquad (11.1)$$

Since by assumption the theorem is true for k, we may replace the sum on the right-hand side of equation (11.1) with $k(k + 1)/2$, obtaining

$$\sum_{i=1}^{k+1} i = (k+1) + \frac{k(k+1)}{2} \qquad (11.2)$$

Algebraic manipulation of the right-hand side of equation (11.2) now yields

$$\sum_{i=1}^{k+1} i = \frac{(k+1)(k+2)}{2} \qquad (11.3)$$

This confirms the theorem for the case $k + 1$. Thus by induction, the theorem is true for all integers $N \geq 1$.

Let us explain why this constitutes a proof. First we showed that the theorem is true for $N = 1$. We call this the *basis*. One can view it as being the basis for our belief that the theorem is true in general. Once we have established the basis, we hypothesize that the theorem is true for some arbitrary k. We call this the *inductive hypothesis*. We show that if the theorem is true for k, it is true for $k + 1$. In our case since we know that the theorem is true for the basis $N = 1$, we now know that it is true for $N = 2$. Since it is true for $N = 2$, it must be true for $N = 3$. And since it is true for $N = 3$, it must be true for $N = 4$. Extending this logic, we see that the theorem is true for every positive integer beginning with $N = 1$.

Let us apply the proof by induction to a second problem, which is not quite as simple as the first. Let us examine the sequence of numbers $1^2, 2^2 - 1^2, 3^2 - 2^2 + 1^2, 4^2 - 3^2 + 2^2 - 1^2$, $5^2 - 4^2 + 3^2 - 2^2 + 1^2$, and so on. Each member represents the sum of the first N squares, with alternating signs. The sequence evaluates to 1, 3, 6, 10, and 15. It seems that in general the sum is exactly equal to the sum of the first N integers, which as we know from Theorem 11.1 would be $N(N + 1)/2$. Let us prove this:

Theorem 11.2: The sum $\sum_{i=N}^{1} (-1)^{N-i} i^2 = N^2 - (N-1)^2 + (N-2)^2 \ldots$ is $N(N+1)/2$.

Proof: The proof is by induction.

      Basis: Clearly, the theorem is true for $N = 1$.

      Inductive Hypothesis: Assume that the theorem is true for k. Then

$$\sum_{i=k+1}^{1} (-1)^{k+1-i} i^2 = (k+1)^2 - k^2 + (k-1)^2 \cdots \tag{11.4}$$

If we rewrite the right-hand side of equation (11.4), we obtain

$$\sum_{i=k+1}^{1} (-1)^{k+1-i} i^2 = (k+1)^2 - (k^2 - (k-1)^2 \cdots) \tag{11.5}$$

This allows a substitution to yield

$$\sum_{i=k+1}^{1} (-1)^{k+1-i} i^2 = (k+1)^2 - \sum_{i=k}^{1} (-1)^{k-i} i^2 \tag{11.6}$$

If we apply the inductive hypothesis, we can replace the summation on the right-hand side of equation (11.6), obtaining

$$\sum_{i=k+1}^{1} (-1)^{k+1-i} i^2 = (k+1)^2 - \frac{k(k+1)}{2} \tag{11.7}$$

Simple algebraic manipulation of the right-hand side of equation (11.7) then yields

$$\sum_{i=k+1}^{1} (-1)^{k+1-i} i^2 = \frac{(k+1)(k+2)}{2} \tag{11.8}$$

which establishes the theorem for $N = k + 1$. Thus, by induction, the theorem is true for all $N \geq 1$.

11.2 Basic Recursion

Proofs by induction show us that if we know that a theorem is true for one case and we can show that one case implies another, we know the theorem is true for all cases. Sometimes mathematical functions are defined recursively. For instance, let $S(N)$ be the sum of the first N integers. Then we have seen that $S(1) = 1$, and we can write $S(N) = S(N-1) + N$. Here we have defined the function S in terms of (a smaller instance of) itself. The recursive definition of $S(N)$ is identical to the *closed form* $S(N) = N(N+1)/2$, except that the recursive definition is defined only for positive integers and is less directly computable.

      Sometimes it is easier to write a formula recursively than in closed form. Even if it is not, we would expect that the recursive definition of the formula should be implementable

```
/* 1*/    /* Compute Sum Of The First N Integers Recursively */

/* 2*/    unsigned long int
/* 3*/    Sum( unsigned int N )
/* 4*/    {
/* 5*/        if( N == 1 )                    /* Base Case */
/* 6*/            return 1;
/* 7*/        else                            /* Recursive Call */
/* 8*/            return Sum( N - 1 ) + N;
/* 9*/    }
```

Figure 11.1:   Recursive evaluation of the sum of the first N integers. It is slightly flawed (see the text).

in C just as easily as the closed-form solution. Figure 11.1 shows a straightforward implementation of the recursive function. If $N = 1$, we have the basis, for which we know that $S(1) = 1$. We take care of this case at lines 5 and 6. Otherwise, we follow the recursive definition $S(N) = S(N - 1) + N$ precisely at line 8. It is hard to imagine that we could implement the recursive Sum function any more simply than this, so the natural question is: Does this actually work?

The answer to the question is "sort of." Except as noted below, this routine works. Let's see how Sum(4) is calculated. When the call to Sum(4) is made, the test at line 5 fails. Thus we execute line 8. At line 8 we evaluate Sum(3). Like any other function, this requires a call to Sum. In that call, we get to line 5, where the test fails, and thus we go to line 8. At this point we call Sum(2). Once again, we call Sum, and now N is 2. The test at line 5 still fails, so we call Sum(1) at line 8. Now we have N equal to 1, so Sum(1) returns 1. At this point, Sum(2) can continue, adding the return value from Sum(1) to 2, and thus Sum(2) returns 3. Now Sum(3) continues, adding the value of 3 that was returned by Sum(2) to N, which is 3. Thus Sum(3) returns 6. This enables the completion of the call to Sum(4), which finally returns 10.

If this seems like a lot of work, do not worry too much: it is the computer's job to handle all the bookkeeping, not yours. Of course, if there is too much bookkeeping even for the computer, it is time to worry. We will talk more about these details later. What we see is that if we have a base case, and if our recursive calls make progress towards reaching the base case, eventually we terminate. We thus have our first two fundamental rules of recursion:

1. *BASE CASES*: Always have at least one case that can be solved without using recursion.

2. *DON'T GET STUCK*: Any recursive call must make progress toward a base case.

We mentioned earlier that the routine does have a few problems. Let's discuss them quickly. One problem is that when $N = 0$, the function blows up.[1] This is natural, because the recursive definition of $S(N)$ does not allow for $N < 1$. We can fix this problem by extending the definition of $S(N)$ to include $N = 0$. Since there are no numbers to add in this case, a natural value for $S(0)$ would be 0. This makes sense because the recursive

---

[1] Actually at line 8, a call is made to Sum(-1), and -1 is converted to an unsigned int, and then strange things happen.

```
/* 1*/    /* Print N As A Decimal Number */

/* 2*/    void
/* 3*/    PrintDecimal( unsigned int N )
/* 4*/    {
/* 5*/        if( N >= 10 )
/* 6*/            PrintDecimal( N / 10 );
/* 7*/        putchar( '0' + N % 10 );
/* 8*/    }
```

Figure 11.2: Recursive routine to print *N* in decimal.

definition can apply for $S(1)$, since $S(0) + 1$ would then be 1. To implement this change, we just replace 1 with 0 on lines 5 and 6.

A second problem is that the return value may be too large to fit in an `unsigned long int`, but that is not an important issue here. A third problem, however, is: If *N* is large but not so large that the answer does not fit in an `unsigned long int`, it is possible for the program to crash or hang. On our system, for instance, $N \geq 74,754$ cannot be handled.

The reason is that as we have seen, the implementation of recursion requires some bookkeeping to keep track of the pending recursive calls, and for sufficiently long chains of recursion, the computer simply runs out of memory. We explain this in more detail later. If you implement this routine, you will also see that it is somewhat more time consuming than an equivalent `for` loop because the bookkeeping also uses up some time.

Suffice it to say that this particular example does not demonstrate the best use of recursion, since it is so easy to solve the problem without recursion. Most of the good uses of recursion will not exhaust the computer's memory and will be only slightly more time consuming than nonrecursive implementations. However, recursion will almost always lead to more compact code.

11.2.1 Printing Numbers in Any Base

A nice example of how recursion simplifies the coding of routines is number printing. Suppose that we would like to print out a nonnegative number *N* in decimal, but we can only print out one digit at a time. Consider, for instance, how we would print the number 1369. First we would need to print a '1', then '3', then '6', and then '9'. The problem is that obtaining the first digit is a bit sloppy: given a number *N*, we need a loop to determine the first digit of *N*. This is in contrast to the last digit, which is available immediately as $N\%10$.

Recursion provides a nifty solution. To print out 1369, we print out 136, followed by the last digit, 9. As we have mentioned, it is easy to print out the last digit using the mod operator. Printing out all but the number represented by eliminating the last digit is also easy, because it is the same problem as printing out $N/10$. Thus it can be done by a recursive call. The routine in Figure 11.2 implements this printing routine. If N is smaller than 10, line 6 is not executed and only $N\%10$ (which for N < 10 is N) is printed; otherwise, all but the last digit is printed recursively, and then the last digit is printed.

Notice how we have a base case (N is a one-digit integer) and that all recursive calls make progress toward the base case (because the recursive problem has one less digit). Thus

```
/* 1*/    /* Print N In Any Base */
/* 2*/    /* Assumes 2 <= Base <= 16 */

/* 3*/    void
/* 4*/    PrintInt( unsigned int N, unsigned int Base )
/* 5*/    {
/* 6*/        static char DigitTable[ ] = "0123456789abcdef";

/* 7*/        if( N >= Base )
/* 8*/            PrintInt( N / Base, Base  );
/* 9*/        putchar( DigitTable[ N % Base ] );
/*10*/    }
```

Figure 11.3: **Recursive routine to print** *N* **in any base.**

we have satisfied the first two fundamental rules of recursion. Since this printing routine is already provided, it may seem like a silly exercise. However, `printf` supplies only octal, decimal, and hexadecimal formats. To make the routine useful, we extend it to print in any base between 2 and 16. This trivial modification is shown in Figure 11.3.

We have introduced an array of characters to make the printing of `'a'` through `'f'` easier. Each digit is now output by indexing into the `DigitTable` array. The `PrintInt` routine is not robust. If `Base` is larger than 16, the index into `DigitTable` could be out of the `DigitTable` array.[2] If `Base` is zero, an arithmetic error will result when a division by zero is attempted at line 8. The most interesting error occurs when `Base` is 1. When that happens, the recursive call at line 8 fails to make progress, because the two parameters to the recursive call will be identical to the original call. Thus the system will make recursive calls until it eventually runs out of bookkeeping space (and perhaps exits less than gracefully).

We can make the routine more robust by adding an explicit test for `Base`. The problem with that strategy is that the test would be executed during each of the recursive calls to `PrintInt`, not just the first call. Once `Base` is valid in the first call, it is silly to retest it, since it does not change in the course of the recursion, and thus must still be valid. One way to avoid this inefficiency is to set up a driver routine that tests the validity of `Base` and then calls the recursive routine. This is shown in Figure 11.4. The use of driver routines for recursive programs is a common technique.

11.2.2 Why It Works

Let us show, somewhat rigorously, that the `PrintDecimal` algorithm works. Our "proof" will assume that we have made no syntax errors, and so on, because our goal is to verify that the algorithm is correct.

Theorem 11.3: The algorithm `PrintDecimal` shown in Figure 11.2 correctly prints N in base 10.

---

[2]Technically, since a null terminator is present, if `Base` is 17, the index is guaranteed to be into the array.

```
/* 1*/      /* Print N In Any Base */

/* 2*/      static char DigitTable[ ] = "0123456789abcdef";
/* 3*/      static const MaxBase = sizeof( DigitTable ) - 1;

/* 4*/      static void
/* 5*/      PrintInt1( unsigned int N, unsigned int Base )
/* 6*/      {
/* 7*/          if( N >= Base )
/* 8*/              PrintInt1( N / Base, Base  );
/* 9*/          putchar( DigitTable[ N % Base ] );
/*10*/      }

/*11*/      void
/*12*/      PrintInt( unsigned int N, unsigned int Base )
/*13*/      {
/*14*/          if( Base <= 1 || Base > MaxBase )
/*15*/              printf( "Can not print in base %u\n", Base );
/*16*/          else
/*17*/              PrintInt1( N, Base );
/*18*/      }
```

Figure 11.4:   Robust number printing program.

Proof: Let k be the number of digits in N. The proof is by induction on k.

Basis: If $k = 1$, no recursive call is made, and line 7 correctly outputs the one digit of N.

Inductive Hypothesis: Assume that PrintDecimal works correctly for all integers of $k \geq 1$ digits. We show that this assumption implies correctness for any $(k + 1)$-digit integer N. Because $k \geq 1$, the if statement at line 5 is satisfied for a $(k + 1)$-digit integer N. By the inductive hypothesis, the recursive call at line 6 prints the first k digits of N. Then the call at line 7 prints the final digit. Thus if any k-digit integer can be printed, so can a $(k + 1)$-digit integer. By induction, we conclude that PrintDecimal works for all N.

The proof of Theorem 11.3 illustrates an important principle. When designing a recursive algorithm, we can always assume that the recursive calls work, because when a proof is performed, this assumption will be used as the inductive hypothesis. At first glance, this seems strange. However, recall that we always assume that function calls work, and thus the assumption that the recursive call works is really no different. Just like any function, a recursive routine needs to combine solutions from calls to other functions to obtain a solution. It is just that "other functions" may include easier instances of the original function.

This observation leads us to the third fundamental rule of recursion:

3. *YOU GOTTA BELIEVE:* Always assume that the recursive call works.

Rule 3 tells us that when we design a recursive function, we do not have to attempt to trace the possibly long path of recursive calls. As we saw earlier, this can be a daunting task and tends to make the design and verification more difficult. A good use of recursion makes such a trace almost impossible to understand. Intuitively, we are letting the computer handle the bookkeeping, which were we to do it ourselves, would result in much longer code. This principle is so important that we state it again: **Always assume that the recursive call works.**

11.2.3   How It Works

We have already mentioned that the implementation of recursion requires additional bookkeeping on the part of the computer. This is not entirely true. A better statement is that the implementation of functions requires bookkeeping and that a recursive call is not particularly special (except that it can overload the computer's bookkeeping limitations). C, like other procedural languages, such as Pascal and Ada, implements functions using an internal stack of *activation records*. We can view an activation record as a piece of paper containing relevant information about the function. This includes, for instance, the values of the parameters and local variables. The actual contents of the activation record are system dependent.

When function F calls another function G, an activation record for F is allocated to save F's information. This is necessary, for instance, because G will typically use the same registers as F, so when G returns back to F, we need to be able to restore F's state to what it was prior to the function call. Also notice that G has no way of knowing where to return to, because G may be called from anywhere in the program. (Consider, for instance, all the calls to `printf` in a typical program.)

The *function calling sequence*, then, is implemented as follows: When a function F calls G, an activation record for F, which includes the (next instruction) address where G is to return, is pushed onto an internal stack. The *function return sequence* can then be implemented easily: When any function G returns, an activation record is popped from the internal stack; the variables (i.e., registers and memory locations) are restored, and control passes to the instruction indicated in the activation record.

The stack is used because functions return in reverse order of their invocation; recall that stacks are great for reversing things. The space overhead is the memory used by storing an activation record for each currently *active* function. Thus, in our earlier example where `Sum(74754)` crashes, we see that our system has room for roughly 74,754 activation records. (Note that `main` makes a call to `Sum` and thus generates an activation record itself.) The pushing and popping of the internal stack also represents the overhead of executing a function call. This is what is saved when a preprocessor macro is used to expand code inline.

The close relation between recursion and stacks tells us that recursive programs can always be implemented by using a stack. The result is slightly faster, but longer code. Since presumably our stack will store items that are smaller than an activation record, we can also reasonably expect to use less space. Conversely, many programs that use stacks can be implemented with less effort and only a minor time penalty using recursion. As an example, let us consider the routine `PrintPath`, implemented in Section 10.4. Recall that for any node `DestNode` in the graph, the shortest path from the starting node to `DestNode`, if defined, was obtained by iteratively tracing back via `Graph[DestNode].PreviousNode`. Since this gives the path in reverse order, we used a stack.

```
/* 1*/    /* PrintPath Is A Driver; PrintPath1 Does The Real Work */

/* 2*/    static void
/* 3*/    PrintPath1( int DestNode, const Vertex Graph[ ] )
/* 4*/    {
/* 5*/        if( Graph[ DestNode ].PreviousNode != -1 )
/* 6*/        {
/* 7*/            PrintPath1( Graph[ DestNode ].PreviousNode, Graph );
/* 8*/            printf( " to " );
/* 9*/        }
/*10*/        printf( "%s", Graph[ DestNode ].NodeName );
/*11*/    }


/* 1*/    void
/* 2*/    PrintPath( int DestNode, const Vertex Graph[ ] )
/* 3*/    {
/* 4*/        if( Graph[ DestNode ].Distance == Infinity )
/* 5*/            printf( "%s unreachable", Graph[ DestNode ].NodeName )
/* 6*/        else
/* 7*/            PrintPath1( DestNode, Graph );
/* 8*/        printf( "\n" );
/* 9*/    }
```

Figure 11.5:   Recursive printing of shortest paths.

A simple recursive solution is obtained with the following observation: The path to DestNode is exactly equal to the path to Graph[DestNode].PreviousNode, followed by DestNode. Thus we do not need to declare a stack, but rather, we implicitly use the internal stack. The simplified routine is shown in Figure 11.5. Note that we cannot print a newline in the recursive routine, since that would occur recursively after each node in the path. Also, we need to test that the path actually exists. Once the path to DestNode is known to exist, all the subpaths that are generated by the recursive calls are guaranteed to exist. Thus putting the test in the recursive call would be a waste. Therefore, we have a driver routine perform these two tasks.

11.2.4   Too Much Recursion Is Dangerous

In this chapter we see many examples that illustrate the power of recursion. However, before we do that, we must realize that recursion is not always appropriate. For instance, the use of recursion in Figure 11.1 is poor because a for loop would do just as well. A practical liability is that the overhead of the recursive call takes time and limits the value of N for which the program is correct. A good rule of thumb is that you should never use recursion as a substitute for a simple loop.

A much more serious problem is illustrated by an attempt to calculate the *Fibonacci numbers* recursively. The Fibonacci numbers F_0, F_1, ..., F_N, ... are defined as follows: $F_0 = 0$ and $F_1 = 1$. The ith Fibonacci number is equal to the sum of the $(i - 1)$th and $(i-2)$th Fibonacci numbers. Thus $F_i = F_{i-1} + F_{i-2}$. From this definition we can determine that the series of Fibonacci numbers continues: 1, 2, 3, 5, 8, 13, 21, 34, 55, 89, ...

The Fibonacci numbers have an incredible number of properties that always seem to crop up. In fact, one journal, *The Fibonacci Quarterly*, exists solely for the purpose of

```
/* 1*/    /* Compute The N th Fibonacci Number */
/* 2*/    /* Bad Algorithm */

/* 3*/    unsigned long int
/* 4*/    Fib( unsigned int N )
/* 5*/    {
/* 6*/        if( N <= 1 )
/* 7*/            return N;
/* 8*/        else
/* 9*/            return Fib( N - 1 ) + Fib( N - 2 );
/*10*/    }
```

Figure 11.6:   **Recursive routine for Fibonacci number—bad idea!**

publishing theorems involving the Fibonacci numbers. For instance, the sum of the squares of two consecutive Fibonacci numbers is another Fibonacci number. The sum of the first N Fibonacci numbers is 1 less than the $(N + 2)$nd Fibonacci number, and so on. (See the exercises for some other interesting identities.)

Because the Fibonacci numbers are defined recursively, it seems natural to write a recursive routine to determine F_N. This recursive routine, shown in Figure 11.6, works but has a serious problem. This routine, on our relatively fast machine, takes over 4 minutes to compute F_{40}. This is an absurd amount of time, considering that the basic calculation requires only 39 additions. The underlying problem is that this particular recursive routine performs redundant calculations. To compute Fib(N), we recursively compute Fib(N-1). When the recursive call returns, we then compute Fib(N-2) by using another recursive call. But we have already computed Fib(N-2) in the process of computing Fib(N-1), so that call to Fib(N-2) is a wasted, redundant calculation. In effect, we make two calls to Fib(N-2) instead of only one.

Normally, making two function calls instead of one would only double the running time of a program. However, it is worse than that, because each call to F(N-2) makes a call to F(N-3). That plus the call to F(N-3) that is directly made when evaluating F(N-1) means that there are actually three calls to F(N-3). In fact, it just keeps getting worse: each call to F(N-2) or F(N-3) results in a call to F(N-4), so there are five calls to F(N-4). Thus we get a compounding effect: each recursive call does more and more redundant work.

Let $C(N)$ be the number of calls to Fib made during the evaluation of Fib(N). Clearly, $C(0) = C(1) = 1$ call. For $N \geq 2$, we make the call for Fib(N), plus all the calls needed to evaluate Fib(N-1) and Fib(N-2) recursively (and independently). Thus,

$$C(N) = C(N - 1) + C(N - 2) + 1.$$

It is easily verified (by induction) that for $N \geq 3$, the solution to this recurrence is $C(N) = F_{N+2} + F_{N-1} - 1$. Thus the number of recursive calls is larger than the Fibonacci number we are trying to compute! For $N = 40$, $F_{40} = 102, 334, 155$, while the total number of recursive calls is over 300 million. No wonder the program takes forever.

This example illustrates the fourth and final basic rule of recursion.

4. *COMPOUND INTEREST RULE*: Never duplicate work by solving the same instance of a problem in separate recursive calls.

11.3   Numerical Applications

In this section we look at four problems drawn primarily from number theory. No attempt is made to review the prerequisite mathematics. Since these applications of recursion are not necessarily fundamental computer science topics, and we make no reference to them outside this section, they can be skipped.

However, for those well versed in mathematics, it provides some interesting examples that can be combined to implement an encryption algorithm.

Here are the four problems we examine:

1. *Modular Exponentiation*: Compute $X^N (\bmod\ P)$.

2. *Primality Testing*: Determine if N is prime.

3. *Greatest Common Divisor*: Compute $gcd(A, B)$.

4. *Multiplicative Inverse*: Solve $AX \equiv 1 (\bmod\ P)$ for X.

An important unstated fact is that the integers we expect to deal with are all large, requiring at least 100 digits each. Therefore, we must already have a way to represent the abstract data type `HugeInt`, along with a complete set of algorithms for basic operations such as addition, subtraction, multiplication, and division. Implementing the `HugeInt` efficiently is no trivial matter, and in fact there is an extensive literature on the subject.

The functions that we write will work with the basic `HugeInt` type, for which we assume that the normal arithmetic operations are defined. By using a `typedef` statement, we can make `HugeInt` equivalent to a `long int`, and thus the reader can test the basic algorithms. The routines that we describe will have the property that they can be extended to the `HugeInt` abstraction and still execute in a reasonable amount of time.

11.3.1   Modular Exponentiation

In this section we show how to compute $X^N (\bmod\ P)$ efficiently. This can be done by initializing `Result` to 1 and then repeatedly multiplying `Result` by X, applying the `%` operator after every multiply. Performing the `%` after every multiply instead of just the last multiply makes each multiplication easier because it keeps `Result` smaller.

After N multiplies, `Result` is the answer we are looking for. However, N multiplies is impractical if N is a 100-digit `HugeInt`. In fact, it is impractical on all but the fastest machines if N is 1 billion. A faster algorithm is based on the following observation: If N is even, $X^N = (X * X)^{N/2}$, while if N is odd, $X^N = X * X^{N-1} = X * (X * X)^{\lfloor N/2 \rfloor}$. As before, to perform modular exponentiation, we apply a `%` after every multiply.

The recursive algorithm in Figure 11.7 represents a direct implementation of this strategy. Lines 6 and 7 handle the base case: X^0 is 1, by definition.[3] At line 8 we make a recursive call based on the identity stated above. If N is even, this computes the desired answer, while if N is odd, we need to multiply by an extra X (and perform a `%`). This algorithm is faster than the simple algorithm proposed earlier. If $M(N)$ is the number of multiplies that are used by `Power`, we have

---

[3] We define $0^0 = 0$, for the purposes of this algorithm. We also assume that N is nonnegative, and P is positive.

```
/* 1*/    /* Compute X^N ( Mod P ) */

/* 2*/    HugeInt
/* 3*/    Power( const HugeInt X, const HugeInt N, const HugeInt P )
/* 4*/    {
/* 5*/        HugeInt Tmp;

/* 6*/        if( N == 0 )
/* 7*/            return 1;

/* 8*/        Tmp = Power( ( X * X ) % P, N / 2, P );
/* 9*/
/*10*/        if( N % 2 )
/*11*/            Tmp = ( Tmp * X ) % P;

/*12*/        return Tmp;
/*13*/    }
```

Figure 11.7:   Modular exponentiation routine.

$$M(N) \leq M\left(\left\lfloor \frac{N}{2} \right\rfloor\right) + 2.$$

This is because if N is even, we perform one multiplication, plus those done recursively, and if N is odd, we perform two multiplications, plus those done recursively. Since $M(0) = 0$, we can show that $M(N) < 2\log N$. Moreover, an average value of $M(N)$ is $\frac{3}{2}\log N$, because in each recursive step, N is equally likely to be even or odd. If N is a 100-digit number, then in the worst case, only about 665 multiplications (and typically only 500 on average) are needed.

11.3.2   Randomized Primality

Figure 4.8 described an algorithm known as *trial division* that tests a number for primality. Although it is reasonably fast for small (32-bit) numbers, it is unusable for larger numbers, because it could require the testing of roughly $\frac{1}{2}\sqrt{N}$ divisors, thus using $O(\sqrt{N})$ time.[4]

What we would like is a test whose running time is of the same order of magnitude as the Power routine above. A well-known theorem, in fact, looks very promising:

Theorem 11.4 *(Fermat's Little Theorem)*: If P is prime and $0 < A < P$, then

$$A^{P-1} \equiv 1(\bmod\ P).$$

A proof sketch is provided for completeness, although it is not needed to understand the algorithm.

Proof: Consider any $1 \leq k < P$. Clearly, $Ak \not\equiv 0(\bmod\ P)$ since P is prime and less than A and k. Now consider any $1 \leq i < j < P$. $Ai \equiv Aj(\bmod\ P)$ would imply that

---

[4]Although $\sqrt{N}$ may seem small, if N is a 100-digit number, $\sqrt{N}$ is still a 50-digit number; tests that take $O(\sqrt{N})$ time are thus out of the question for HugeInts.

$A(j-i) \equiv 0(\bmod P)$, which is impossible by the previous argument, since $1 \leq j-i < P$. Thus the sequence $A, 2A, ..., (P-1)A$, when considered $(\bmod P)$, is just a permutation of $1, 2, ..., P-1$. Thus the product of both sequences $(\bmod P)$ must be equivalent, yielding

$$A^{P-1}(P-1)! \equiv (P-1)!(\bmod P),$$

from which the theorem follows.

If the converse of Fermat's Little Theorem were true, we would have a primality testing algorithm that would be computationally equivalent to modular exponentiation [i.e., $O(\log N)$]. Unfortunately, it is not. It is easily verified that $2^{340} \equiv 1(\bmod 341)$, but 341 is composite $(11 * 31)$.

To do the primality test, we need an additional theorem:

Theorem 11.5: If P is prime and $X^2 \equiv 1(\bmod P)$, then $X \equiv \pm 1(\bmod P)$.

Proof: Since $X^2 - 1 \equiv 0(\bmod P)$ implies that $(X-1)(X+1) \equiv 0(\bmod P)$ and P is prime, either $X - 1$ or $X + 1 \equiv 0(\bmod P)$.

Now let us explain why a combination of these two theorems is useful. Let A be any integer between 2 and $N-2$. If we compute $A^{N-1}(\bmod N)$ and the result is not 1, we know that N cannot be prime, since otherwise we would contradict Fermat's Little Theorem. We say, then, that A is a *witness* to N's compositeness. Every composite number N has some witnesses A, but for some numbers, known as the *Carmichael numbers*, these witnesses are hard to find. To improve our chances, we use Theorem 11.5.

In the course of computing A^i, we compute $(A*A)^{\lfloor i/2 \rfloor}$. Let $X = A^{\lfloor i/2 \rfloor}$. Let $Y = X^2$. Notice that X and Y are computed automatically as part of the Power routine. If Y is 1 and if X is not $\pm 1(\bmod N)$, then by Theorem 11.5, N cannot be prime. We can return 0 for the value of A^i when this is detected. This will have the effect of making it appear as though N has failed the test of primality implied by Fermat's Little Theorem.

The routine Witness shown in Figure 11.8 computes $A^i(\bmod P)$, augmented to return 0 if a violation of Theorem 11.5 is detected. Thus if Witness does not return 1, then A is a witness to the fact that N cannot be prime. Lines 10 to 12 make a recursive call and produces X. We then compute X^2, as is normal for the Power computation.[5] We check if Theorem 11.5 is violated, returning 0 if it is. Otherwise, we complete the Power computation. The only remaining issue is correctness. If our algorithm declares that N is composite, N must be composite. If N is composite, is it true that all $2 \leq A \leq N-2$ are witnesses? The answer, unfortunately, is no. This means that there exist some choices of A that will trick our algorithm into declaring that N is a prime. In fact, if we choose A randomly, we have at most a $\frac{1}{4}$ chance of failing to detect a composite number, and thus making an error.[6]

This does not seem like very good odds, since a 25% error rate is considered very high. However, if we independently use 20 values of A, the chances that none of these will witness a composite number is $1/4^{20}$, which is about 1 in a million million. Those odds

---

[5]Note that in the power computation, N represents an exponent; here N represents the second operand of the % operator.

[6]This bound is typically pessimistic, and the analysis involves number theory that is much too involved for this book.

```
/* 1*/    /* If Witness Does Not return 1, N Is Definitely Composite */
/* 2*/    /* Do This By Computing A^i ( Mod N ) And Look For */
/* 3*/    /* Non-Trivial Square Roots Of 1 Along The Way */

/* 4*/    HugeInt
/* 5*/    Witness( const HugeInt A, const HugeInt i, const HugeInt N )
/* 6*/    {
/* 7*/        HugeInt X, Y;

/* 8*/        if( i == 0 )
/* 9*/            return 1;

/*10*/        X = Witness( A, i / 2, N );
/*11*/        if( X == 0 ) /* If N Is Recursively Composite, Stop */
/*12*/            return 0;

/*13*/        /* N Is Not Prime if We Find A Non-Trivial Root Of 1 */
/*14*/        Y = ( X * X ) % N;
/*15*/        if( Y == 1 && X != 1 && X != N - 1 )
/*16*/            return 0;

/*17*/        if( i % 2 )
/*18*/            Y = ( A * Y ) % N;

/*19*/        return Y;
/*20*/    }


/* 1*/    /* Make NumTrials Call To Witness To Check if N Is Prime */

/* 2*/    int
/* 3*/    IsPrime( const HugeInt N )
/* 4*/    {
/* 5*/        const int NumTrials = 5;
/* 6*/        int Counter;

/* 7*/        for( Counter = 0; Counter < NumTrials; Counter++ )
/* 8*/            if( Witness( RandInt( 2, N - 2 ), N - 1, N ) != 1 )
/* 9*/                return 0;

/*10*/        return 1;
/*11*/    }
```

Figure 11.8:   Randomized test for primality.

are much more reasonable and can be made even better by using more trials. The routine
IsPrime, which is also shown in Figure 11.8, uses five trials.

11.3.3   Greatest Common Divisor

Given two nonnegative integers A and B, their greatest common divisor $gcd(A, B)$ is the
largest integer D that divides both A and B. For instance, $gcd(45, 25)$ is 5. It is easy to

```
/* 1*/    HugeInt
/* 2*/    Gcd( const HugeInt A, const HugeInt B )
/* 3*/    {
/* 4*/        if( B == 0 )
/* 5*/            return A;
/* 6*/        else
/* 7*/            return Gcd( B, A % B );
/* 8*/    }
```

Figure 11.9:   Computation of greatest common divisor.

verify that $gcd(A, B) \equiv gcd(A - B, B)$. This is because if D divides both A and B, it must also divide $A - B$; and if D divides both $A - B$ and B, it must divide A also.

This observation leads to a simple algorithm in which we repeatedly subtract B from A, transforming the problem into a smaller one. Eventually, A becomes less than B, and then we can switch roles for A and B and continue from there. At some point B will become 0. At that point we know that $gcd(A, 0) \equiv A$, and since each transformation preserves the gcd of the original A and B, we have our answer. Known as *Euclid's Algorithm*, this was described over 2000 years ago. Although correct, it is unusable for HugeInts, because a huge number of subtractions are likely to be required.

A computationally efficient modification is that the repeated subtractions of B from A until A smaller than B is equivalent to the conversion of A to precisely A mod B. Thus $gcd(A, B) \equiv gcd(B, A \bmod B)$. This recursive definition, along with the base case where $B = 0$, are used directly to obtain the routine in Figure 11.9. The number of recursive calls that are used is proportional to the logarithm of A, which is the same order of magnitude as the other routines that we have seen in this section. The proof of this is left as an exercise. Oddly enough, the proof is by induction, and the Fibonacci numbers come into play.

11.3.4 Multiplicative Inverse

The solution $1 \leq X < N$ to the equation $AX \equiv 1 (\bmod N)$ is known as the *multiplicative inverse* of A, mod N. We also assume that $1 \leq A < N$. The ability to compute multiplicative inverses is important because equations such as $3i \equiv 7 (\bmod 13)$ are easily solved if we know the multiplicative inverse. In this example, if we multiply by 3's inverse (namely 9), we obtain $i \equiv 63 (\bmod 13)$, so $i = 11$ is a solution. If

$$AX \equiv 1 (\bmod N)$$

then

$$AX + NY \equiv 1 (\bmod N)$$

is true for any Y. For some Y, the equivalence must be true even without the congruence class. Thus the equation

$$AX + NY = 1$$

is solvable if (and only if) A has a multiplicative inverse.

Given A and B, we show how to find X and Y that satisfy

$$AX + BY = 1 \tag{11.9}$$

We assume that $0 \leq |B| < |A|$. To do this we extend the *gcd* algorithm to compute X and Y. First, consider the base case $B \equiv 0$. In this case we have to solve $AX = 1$, which implies that both A and X are 1. In fact, if A is not 1, there is no multiplicative inverse. A consequence of this fact is that A has a multiplicative inverse modulo N if and only if $gcd(A, N) = 1$.

Otherwise, B is not zero. Recall that $gcd(A, B) = gcd(B, A \bmod B)$. So let $A = BQ + R$. Here Q is the quotient and R is the remainder, and thus the recursive call is $gcd(B, R)$. Suppose that we can recursively solve

$$BX_1 + RY_1 = 1 \tag{11.10}$$

Since $R = A - BQ$, we have

$$BX_1 + (A - BQ)Y_1 = 1 \tag{11.11}$$

which means that

$$AY_1 + B(X_1 - QY_1) = 1 \tag{11.12}$$

Thus $X = Y_1$ and $Y = X_1 - \lfloor A/B \rfloor * Y_1$ is a solution. This is coded directly as `FullGcd` in Figure 11.10. `Inverse` just calls `FullGcd`, passing X and Y by reference. The only detail left is that the value given for X may be negative. If it is, line 8 of `Inverse` will make it positive. We leave a proof of that fact as an exercise for the reader. The proof can be done by induction.

11.3.5 Application: The RSA Cryptosystem

For centuries, number theory was thought to be a completely impractical branch of mathematics. Recently, however, number theory has emerged as an important field because of its applicability in cryptography. The problem we consider has two parts. Alice wants to send a message to Bob, but she is worried that the transmission may be compromised. For instance, if the transmission is over a phone line and the phone is tapped, somebody else may be reading the message. We assume that even if there is eavesdropping on the phone line, there is no maliciousness: Bob gets whatever Alice sends.

A solution to this problem is to use an encryption scheme, consisting of two parts. First Alice encrypts the message, and sends the result, which is no longer plainly readable. When Bob receives Alices transmission, he decrypts it, obtaining the original. One way for this to be done is for Bob to provide Alice with a method of encryption that only he knows how to reverse. We describe one method, known as the RSA cryptosystem (named after its authors), that seems to be a very elegant implementation of the strategy.

Our goal is to give only a high-level overview showing how the functions we have written in this section interact in a practical way. The references contain pointers to a more detailed description, as well as proofs of the key properties of the algorithm. Let us first remark that a message consists of a sequence of characters, and each character is just a sequence of bits. Thus a message is a sequences of bits. If we break up the message into blocks of B bits, we can interpret the message as a series of very large numbers. Thus the basic problem is reduced to encrypting a large number and then decrypting the result.

The RSA scheme begins by having the receiver determine some constants. First, two large primes p and q are randomly chosen. Typically, these would be 100 or so digits each. For the purposes of this example, suppose that $p = 127$ and $q = 211$. Note that Bob is the

```
/* 1*/     /* Given A And B, Assume Gcd( A, B ) = 1 */
/* 2*/     /* Find X And Y Such That A X + B Y = 1 */

/* 3*/     void
/* 4*/     FullGcd( const HugeInt A, const HugeInt B,
                                   HugeInt *X, HugeInt *Y )
/* 5*/     {
/* 6*/         HugeInt X1, Y1;

/* 7*/         if( B == 0 )
/* 8*/         {
/* 9*/             *X = 1;       /* If A != 1, There Is No Inverse */
/*10*/             *Y = 0;       /* We Omit this Check */
/*11*/         }
/*12*/         else
/*13*/         {
/*14*/             FullGcd( B, A % B, &X1, &Y1 );
/*15*/             *X = Y1;
/*16*/             *Y = X1 - ( A / B ) * Y1;
/*17*/         }
/*18*/     }

/* 1*/     /* Solve A X == 1 ( Mod N ) */
/* 2*/     /* Assume That Gcd( A, N ) = 1 */

/* 3*/     HugeInt
/* 4*/     Inverse( const HugeInt A, const HugeInt N )
/* 5*/     {
/* 6*/         HugeInt X, Y;

/* 7*/         FullGcd( A, N, &X, &Y );
/* 8*/         return X > 0 ? X : X + N;
/* 9*/     }
```

Figure 11.10:   **Routine to determine multiplicative inverse.**

receiver and thus is performing these computations. Let us remark that primes are plentiful. Bob can thus keep trying random numbers until two of them pass the primality test in Figure 11.8.

Next, Bob computes $N = pq$ and $N' = (p - 1)(q - 1)$. For our example this gives $N = 26,797$ and $N' = 26,460$. The receiver continues by choosing any $e > 1$ such that $gcd(e, N') = 1$. Bob can keep trying different values of e, by using Figure 11.9, until one is found that satisfies the property. Since any prime e would work, finding e is at least as easy as finding a prime number. In our case, $e = 13,379$ is one of many valid choices. Next, d, the multiplicative inverse of e, modulo N' is computed using the routine in Figure 11.10. In this example, $d = 11,099$.

Once Bob has computed all of these constants, he does the following. First, p, q, and N' are **destroyed**. The security of the system is compromised if any of these values are discovered. Bob then tells anybody who wants to send him an encrypted message what the values of e and N are, and keeps d secret. To encrypt an integer M, the sender computes $M^e (\text{mod } N)$, and sends it. In our case, if $M = 10,237$, the value sent is 8422. When an encrypted integer R is received, all Bob has to do is compute $R^d \pmod{N}$. For $R = 8422$ it can be verified that he gets back the original $M = 10,237$ (this is not accidental!). Both encryption and decryption can thus be carried out using the modular exponentiation routine in Figure 11.7.

Let us examine why the algorithm works. The choices of e, d, and N guarantee (via a number theory proof beyond the scope of this book) that $M^{ed} \equiv M \pmod{N}$, as long as M and N share no common factors. Since N's only factors are two 100-digit primes, it is virtually impossible for that to occur.[7] Thus decryption of the encrypted text gets the original back.

What makes the scheme seem secure is that knowledge of d is apparently required in order to decode. Now N and e uniquely determine d. For instance, if we factor N, we get p and q and can then reconstruct d. The caveat is that factoring is apparently very hard to do for large numbers. It has been shown, in fact, that if d can be computed, N can be factored easily. Thus the security of the RSA system is based on the fact that it seems hard to factor. So far, it has held up well.

This general scheme is known as *public key cryptography*. Anybody who wants to receive messages publishes encryption information for anybody else to use. In the RSA system, e and N would be computed once by each enrolled person, and listed in a publicly readable place. A problem with the system is that each person must safely hide a 200-digit key (d). Thus it must be saved somewhere (unlike a password, it is too long to be remembered). If the file where it is stored is compromised, so is the security of all incoming messages.

11.4   Searching and Sorting

In Section 8.14.3 we examined the binary search, which is used to access items efficiently by keeping them in sorted order. Unfortunately, it cannot handle insertions efficiently. Although the hash table structure in Section 10.3 can handle insertions, its contents are not kept sorted and thus cannot be directly viewed in order. We show how to use recursion to make the binary search dynamic. In Section 7.5 we saw an efficient sorting algorithm. Using recursion, we implement the *quicksort* algorithm, which is typically faster (although not as simple).

11.4.1   Binary Search Trees

In Section 8.14.3 we discussed the binary search. When performing a `Find` for an element X in an array, we maintain the current `Low` and `High` points, which delimit the range where X can be. Figure 11.11 illustrates the binary search strategy. If the delimited range is empty (i.e., `Low > High`), X is not found. Otherwise, if X is less than the element in the middle of the range, we only have to consider the subrange to the left of the middle; similarly, if X is greater than the element in the middle of the range, we only have to consider the subrange to the right of the middle. If X is equal to the element in the middle, then, of

---

[7]You are more likely to win a typical state lottery 13 weeks in a row. However, if this does happen, the system is compromised, because the greatest common divisor will be a factor of N.

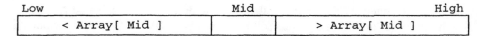

Figure 11.11:   Binary search.

```
/* 1*/    /* Return Position Of X In A */

/* 2*/    int
/* 3*/    BinarySearch1( const char *A[ ], const char *X,
                                          int Low, int High )
/* 4*/    {
/* 5*/        int Mid = ( Low + High ) / 2 ;
/* 6*/        int Cmp;

/* 7*/        if( Low > High )                        /* Not Found */
/* 8*/            return -1;
/* 9*/        if( ( Cmp = strcmp( X, A[ Mid ] ) ) < 0 )
/*10*/            return BinarySearch1( A, X, Low, Mid - 1 );
/*11*/        if( Cmp > 0 )                           /* X > A[ Mid ] */
/*12*/            return BinarySearch1( A, X, Mid + 1, High );
/*13*/        return Mid;                             /* X = A[ Mid ] */
/*14*/    }

/*15*/    int
/*16*/    BinarySearch( const char *A[ ], const char *X, int N )
/*17*/    {
/*18*/        return BinarySearch1( A, X, 0, N - 1 );
/*19*/    }
```

Figure 11.12:   Recursive implementation of binary search.

course, X is found. In Section 8.14.3 we wrote the binary search iteratively. Although it is not more efficient, it is instructive to rewrite the routine recursively. The straightforward implementation is shown in Figure 11.12 for strings.

The problem with the binary search is that insertions are not supported efficiently. The reason, of course, is that an array is used to store all the items, so inserting any element into the array would require pushing a large collection of other elements down a spot to make room. Thus we can avoid this problem by discarding the array and dynamically allocating a cell for each item. For reasons we'll see later, we call this structure a binary search tree. Then, as Figure 11.13 shows, we keep one cell, which in a binary search corresponds roughly to Mid, at the top of the tree. We call this the *root* of the tree. To access items that are smaller than the item stored at the root, we provide a pointer to a recursively defined subtree; similarly, to access items that are larger than the item stored at the root, we provide a pointer to another recursively defined subtree. We call these the left and right subtrees, reflecting the natural orientation. An empty tree is represented by a NULL Root pointer.

Without even looking at what kind of a structure this actually generates, we can write the type declarations and all the routines just by sticking with the recursive definition.

First, Figure 11.14 gives the type declarations. Because we are allowing arbitrary insertions, we have to allow for the possibility of duplicates. We keep a Count field for

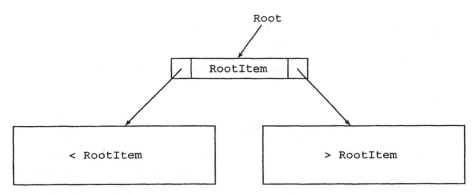

Figure 11.13:   Binary search tree.

```
/* 1*/    typedef struct TreeNode *Tree;

/* 2*/    typedef struct TreeNode
/* 3*/    {
/* 4*/        char *Item;        /* The Item */
/* 5*/        int Count;         /* Frequency Of Occurrence */
/* 6*/        Tree Left;         /* Left Tree,  Recursively Defined */
/* 7*/        Tree Right;        /* Right Tree, Recursively Defined */
/* 8*/    } TreeNode;
```

Figure 11.14:   Type declarations for the binary search tree.

that purpose. This will have the effect of simplifying the Remove operation, since we can just decrement the Count field corresponding to the deleted item. Following the pictorial description of Figure 11.13, we declare that a Tree is a pointer to a TreeNode and that a TreeNode has an item, a counter, and pointers to two other trees.

The close correspondence between the binary search and binary search tree, which is seen clearly by comparing Figures 11.11 and 11.13, suggests that the Find routine for the binary search tree should look like the recursive Find routine in Figure 11.12. Indeed, Figure 11.15 shows that there is a one-to-one correspondence between statements in the two routines. The binary search Find routine indicates the position where X is found by returning an array index or -1 if the search fails. For binary search trees, we return the position as a pointer to the node containing X, or NULL if X is not found. If the tree is empty, X is not found. Otherwise, if X is smaller than the item at the root, we return the position that is found recursively in the left tree. If X is larger than the item at the root, we return the position that is found by processing the right subtree recursively. Otherwise, we have a match, and we return the current position if the item has not been deleted. A comparison with Figure 11.11 shows that the logic is identical to the binary search logic.

Figure 11.16 illustrates deletion. Again we have four cases, and the code is very straightforward. The only tricky item is that these cases are mutually exclusive. In the Find routine, since each possibility was handled with a return, there was no need for the else clause. It is necessary here.

The Insert routine (Figure 11.17) is conceptually easy since, as before, there are four possibilities. Nevertheless, there are some dangers lurking. First, Insert must return

```
/* 1*/      /* Return A Pointer To Node Storing X if X Is Found */

/* 2*/      TreeNode *
/* 3*/      Find( const Tree Root, const char *X )
/* 4*/      {
/* 5*/          int Cmp;

/* 6*/          if( Root == NULL )                      /* Not Found */
/* 7*/              return NULL;
/* 8*/          if( ( Cmp = strcmp( X, Root->Item ) ) < 0 )
/* 9*/              return Find( Root->Left, X );   /* X < Root->Item */
/*10*/          if( Cmp > 0 )
/*11*/              return Find( Root->Right, X ); /* X > Root->Item */
/*12*/          return Root->Count ? Root : NULL;  /* X = Root->Item */
/*13*/      }
```

Figure 11.15:   Find for the binary search tree.

```
/* 1*/      void
/* 2*/      Remove( Tree Root, const char *X )
/* 3*/      {
/* 4*/          int Cmp;

/* 5*/          if( Root == NULL )                      /* Not Found */
/* 6*/              return;                             /* Do Nothing */
/* 7*/          else if( ( Cmp = strcmp( X, Root->Item ) ) < 0 )
/* 8*/              Remove( Root->Left, X );
/* 9*/          else if( Cmp > 0 )
/*10*/              Remove( Root->Right, X );
/*11*/          else if( Root->Count > 0 )
/*12*/              Root->Count--;
/*13*/      }
```

Figure 11.16:   Remove for the binary search tree.

a new tree, since the first insertion will change Root. Prior to the insertion, Root points at
NULL, but afterward it does not. As we mentioned in earlier chapters, it is a common error
to infer that since Root is a pointer, it is not subject to call-by value conventions. The rule
is that the object being pointed to by Root can change, but where Root points will not.
To Insert into an empty tree, we allocate a new cell, have Root point at it, and initialize
appropriately.

   Since Insert is recursive, at lines 15 and 18, we must "reattach" the recursively
formed subtree. If we do not, we lose parts of the tree. Line 20 handles duplicate items by
incrementing the count. Line 21 will return the resultant Root (which changes only if it
was NULL on entry). It is amazing how easy it is to forget this. Most but not all compilers
will detect the absence of a return statement. Strdup allocates enough memory to store
a copy of X (see Exercise 8.19).

   The final routine lists out all the elements in a binary search tree in sorted order. The
ability to do this quickly is what makes a binary search tree more useful than a hash table

```
/* 1*/    Tree
/* 2*/    Insert( Tree Root, const char *X )
/* 3*/    {
/* 4*/        int Cmp;

/* 5*/        if( Root == NULL )                          /* Spot Found */
/* 6*/        {
/* 7*/            Root = malloc( sizeof( struct TreeNode ) );
/* 8*/            if( Root == NULL || !( Root->Item = Strdup( X ) ) )
/* 9*/                Error( "Out of space!!" );
/*10*/            Root->Count = 1;
/*11*/            Root->Left = Root->Right = NULL;
/*12*/        }
/*13*/        else                                        /* X < Root->Item */
/*14*/        if( ( Cmp = strcmp( X, Root->Item ) ) < 0 )
/*15*/            Root->Left = Insert( Root->Left, X );
/*16*/        else
/*17*/        if( Cmp > 0 )                               /* X > Root->Item */
/*18*/            Root->Right = Insert( Root->Right, X );
/*19*/        else
/*20*/            Root->Count++;               /* X Was Previously Seen */

/*21*/        return Root;
/*22*/    }
```

Figure 11.17:   `Insert` **for the binary search tree.**

```
/* 1*/    void
/* 2*/    PrintInOrder( const Tree T )
/* 3*/    {
/* 4*/        if( T != NULL )
/* 5*/        {
/* 6*/            PrintInOrder( T->Left );
/* 7*/            if( T->Count )
/* 8*/                printf( "%s occurs %d times\n",
                                            T->Item, T->Count );
/* 9*/            PrintInOrder( T->Right );
/*10*/        }
/*11*/    }
```

Figure 11.18:   **Printing a binary search tree in sorted order.**

in some applications. Looking at Figure 11.12, we see that a recursive printing of the left subtree, followed by the root, followed by the right subtree will guarantee sorted order. This is implemented in Figure 11.18.

Although we have managed to implement everything recursively, it is still important to understand what the recursion is generating. Figure 11.19 shows a binary search tree (with count field omitted). Null pointers are not drawn. From the picture we can see why we call this data structure a tree.

Except for `PrintInOrder`, the operations we have described can be implemented rather easily without resorting to recursion. This is not surprising, since the binary search

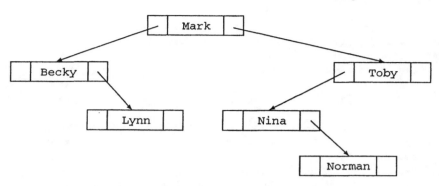

Figure 11.19:   Binary search tree expanded.

is also easily implemented nonrecursively. The searching operation starts at the root and branches down toward the bottom, depending on the result of a comparison. Insertions of new nodes is always at the bottom, at the point where a Find for the item would have failed. However, printing in sorted order is not so easy without recursion (it can be done using a stack, of course).

An important property that we see from Figure 11.19 is that the tree is not guaranteed to be perfectly balanced. In fact, if items are inserted in sorted order, the tree is very unbalanced and degenerates into a linked list of right pointers. The result is that the basic operations take linear time. This is an important limitation of binary search trees: they are not appropriate for large amounts of preordered input. Generalizations of the binary search tree, such as the AVL tree, red black tree, and splay tree can be used when the input sequence is not sufficiently random.

On the other hand, it is possible to show that with a random input sequence (which would be typical if we were scanning a document for a word-counting program), each basic searching or dynamic operation takes $O(\log N)$ time on average, and the PrintInOrder routine takes only $O(N)$ time. When that happens, the binary search tree is the choice for organizing data.

11.4.2   Quicksort

Perhaps the best general-purpose sorting algorithm is the aptly named *quicksort*. The basic algorithm is very simple to understand. Suppose we have a portion of an array that we want to sort. As with the binary search, we assume that this portion ranges from indices Low to High. In the basic binary search picture, we have one element in the position Mid; all elements to the left of position Mid are smaller than A[Mid], and all elements to the right are larger.

Suppose that as Figure 11.20 suggests, we can rearrange an arbitrarily arranged array so that there is some position PivotPos, and all elements to the left are smaller and all elements to right are larger. We do not require that this holds recursively or that PivotPos be halfway between Low and High. Thus there is a reasonable expectation that this rearrangement can be performed efficiently. If so, the entire array, from Low to High, can be sorted by performing this arrangement and then making two recursive calls. By recursively sorting the elements in the left group and then the elements in the right group, we will be guaranteed that the entire array, from Low to High, is sorted.

Low		PivotPos		High

```
| < Array[ PivotPos ] | Pivot | > Array[ PivotPos ] |
```

Figure 11.20:   Quicksort idea.

```
/* 1*/    static void
/* 2*/    QuickSort1( ElementType A[ ], int Low, int High )
/* 3*/    {
/* 4*/        int PivotPos;

/* 5*/        if( Low < High )
/* 6*/        {
/* 7*/            PivotPos = Partition( A, Low, High );
/* 8*/            QuickSort1( A, Low, PivotPos - 1 );
/* 9*/            QuickSort1( A, PivotPos + 1, High );
/*10*/        }
/*11*/    }


/* 1*/    void
/* 2*/    QuickSort( ElementType A[ ], unsigned int N )
/* 3*/    {
/* 4*/        QuickSort1( A, ( int ) 0, ( int ) N - 1 );
/* 5*/    }
```

Figure 11.21:   Basic recursive calls for Quicksort.

Figure 11.21 implements this algorithm. The driver routine calls QuickSort1 with Low=0 and High=N-1. If there are zero or one elements, there is nothing for QuickSort1 to do. Otherwise, we *partition* the array using some as yet unspecified method. The term *partition* reflects the fact that during the rearrangement, each element is classified as either a "small" or "large" element (including duplicates), depending on where it is placed. The element that is used for this decision is the Pivot, and thus the index where the Pivot winds up is termed PivotPos. When Partition returns, we are guaranteed that the conditions in Figure 11.20 hold, and thus two recursive calls complete the sort.

The only remaining detail is implementing the Partition routine. We will give a reasonably good implementation; the exercises and references provide information on further optimizations. The first thing we do is to select the pivot. Notice that we are choosing the element, not the position. The position will be determined once we have found out how many small and large elements there are. The simplest reasonable choice is to use the element in the middle position. (Using the element in position Low can lead to bad performance on already sorted input.) Once we do that we swap it immediately with the element in position High.

We then run two counters in opposite directions. i will search for "large" elements, starting at position Low. j will search for "small" elements, starting at position High-1 (skipping over A[High], which now contains the pivot). Eventually, i finds a "large" item and j finds a "small" item, and these items can be swapped if i is to the left of j. This process continues until i and j cross. Then i is at a "large" item, and this item can

	45	46	47	48	49	50	51	
	6	3	8	5	2	9	4	*Original input (Pivot=5)*
	6	3	8	4	2	9	5	*Swap A[Center] and A[High]*
	2	3	8	4	6	9	5	*After Swap using i=45, j=49*
	2	3	4	8	6	9	5	*After Swap using i=47, j=48*
	2	3	4	5	6	9	8	*After i≥j, Swap A[i] and A[High]*

Figure 11.22:   Illustration of the partitioning scheme.

be swapped with A[High]. As a result, the pivot is placed in position i, and thus i is the pivot position.

Figure 11.22 illustrates the algorithm for a small input. The pivot is chosen to be 5, since it is in the middle position. We then swap elements in the middle and High positions. The first "large" element that i sees is at position 45, and the first "small" element that j sees is at position 49. These elements are swapped. Similarly, elements at positions 47 and 48 are swapped. At this point we have the fourth array indicated in Figure 11.22. When i stops next, it stops at position 48, and j stops at position 47. Since i ≥ j, we do not perform a swap of the corresponding elements, and we can stop moving i and j. We finish by swapping elements in positions i and High.

The code for the Partition is shown in Figure 11.23. We define the macro SwapElements because the swap is the basic operation, and we do not want the overhead of a function call. Lines 9 and 22 implement the initial and final swaps involving the pivot. Lines 12 and 13 search for a "large" element, and lines 14 to 16 search for a "small" one. If i and j have not crossed, the elements are swapped.

We have to be careful that whenever i and j are used to index A, they are no smaller than Low or larger than High. Because both loops stop on equality with the pivot, we are guaranteed that i is never larger than High (because High stores the pivot). An explicit test is needed for j, however.[8]

11.5   Artificial Intelligence

As our last application, we show how to write a routine to have the computer select an optimal move in the game tic-tac-toe. In Section 7.6 we wrote many of the supporting routines that are needed. The only routine we need, besides those shown in Figures 7.18 and 7.19, is the function Terminal, which has the following prototype:

```
Score Terminal( const BoardType B );
```

Terminal returns either HumanWin, Draw, ComputerWin, or Unclear, depending on what the board B represents.

---

[8]The test is against zero because for Low > 0, A[Low-1] will be certain to stop j.

```
/* 1*/    #define SwapElements( i, j ) \
/* 2*/        { ElementType Tmp = A[ i ]; A[ i ] = A[ j ]; \
                                                  A[ j ] = Tmp; }

/* 3*/    static int
/* 4*/    Partition( ElementType A[ ], const int Low, const int High )
/* 5*/    {
/* 6*/        int Center = ( Low + High ) / 2;
/* 7*/        const ElementType Pivot = A[ Center ];
/* 8*/        int i = Low - 1, j = High;

/* 9*/        SwapElements( Center, High );
/*10*/        for( ; ; )
/*11*/        {
/*12*/            while( A[ ++i ] < Pivot ) /* Find "large" Element */
/*13*/                  ;                    /* i < High Is Guaranteed */
/*14*/            while( A[ --j ] > Pivot ) /* Find "small" Element */
/*15*/                if( j == 0 )           /* Don't Run Off The End! */
/*16*/                    break;

/*17*/            if( i >= j )
/*18*/                break;

/*19*/            /* i < j, A[ i ] >= Pivot, A[ j ] <= Pivot */
/*20*/            SwapElements( i, j );
/*21*/        }
/*22*/        SwapElements( i, High );

/*23*/        return i;
/*24*/    }
```

Figure 11.23:   Partition algorithm for Quicksort.

11.5.1   The Minimax Strategy

The idea we use is often referred to as a *minimax strategy*. The minimax strategy assumes optimal play by both players. The *value* of a position is a ComputerWin if optimal play implies that the computer can force a win. If the computer can force a draw but not a win, the value is Draw, and if the human player can force a win, the value is HumanWin. Since we want the computer to win, we have HumanWin < Draw < ComputerWin.

For the computer, the value of the position is the maximum of all the values of the positions that can result from making a move. Thus if one move leads to a winning position, two lead to a drawing position, and two lead to a losing position, the starting position is a winning position (because we can force the win). Moreover, the move that leads to the winning position is the move we want to make. For the human, we use the minimum instead of maximum.

This suggests a recursive algorithm to determine the value of a position. Keeping track of the best move is just a matter of bookkeeping. If the position is a terminal position (i.e., we can see right away that tic-tac-toe has been achieved or the board is full without tic-tac-toe), the position's value is immediate. Otherwise, we recursively try all moves, computing the value, and choose the maximum. The recursive call will then require that the human player evaluate the value of a position. For the human, the value is the minimum of all the possible next moves, since the human is trying to force the computer to lose. Thus the recursive function `ChooseMove` shown in Figure 11.24 takes a parameter S, which indicates whose turn it is to move.

Lines 13 and 14 handle the base case of the recursion. Otherwise, we set some values at lines 15 to 23, depending on which side is moving. The code in lines 29 to 39 is executed once for each available move. We try the move at line 29, recursively evaluate the move at line 30 (saving the value), and then undo the move at line 31. Lines 34 and 35 test to see if this is the best move seen so far, and if so, we adjust `Value` at line 37 and record the move at line 38. At line 41 we return the value of the position; the move is stored in the `BestRow` and `BestColumn` variables, which have been passed by reference.

11.5.2   Alpha Beta Pruning

Although the routine in Figure 11.24 optimally solves tic-tac-toe, it performs a lot of searching. Specifically, to choose the first move, it makes 549,946 recursive calls. One reason for this is that the algorithm does more searching than is needed. Suppose that the computer is considering five moves, C_1, C_2, C_3, C_4, and C_5. Suppose the recursive evaluation of C_1 reveals that C_1 forces a draw. Now C_2 is evaluated. At this stage, we have a position from which it would be the human's turn to move. Suppose that in response to C_2, the human can consider H_{2a}, H_{2b}, H_{2c}, and H_{2d}. Suppose that an evaluation of H_{2a} shows a forced draw. Automatically, C_2 is at best a draw, and possibly even a loss for the computer (because the human is assumed to play optimally). Because we need to *improve* on C_1, we do not have to evaluate any of H_{2b}, H_{2c}, H_{2d}. We say that H_{2a} is a *refutation*, meaning that it proves that C_2 is not a better move than what has already been seen. Thus we return that C_2 is a draw, and keep C_1 as the best move seen so far.

What this shows is that we do not need to evaluate each node completely; for some nodes, a refutation suffices. This means that some loops can terminate early. Specifically, when the human evaluates a position, such as C_2, a refutation, if found, is just as good as the absolute best move. The same logic applies to the computer also. At any point in the search, `Alpha` is the value that the human has to refute, and `Beta` is the value that the computer has to refute. When searching on the human side, any move less than `Alpha` is equivalent to `Alpha`, and on the computer side, any move greater than `Beta` is equivalent to `Beta`. This strategy is commonly known as alpha-beta pruning.

As Figure 11.25 shows, both `Alpha` and `Beta` are passed as additional parameters to the routine `Choose`. Initially, `Choose` is started with `Alpha` and `Beta` representing `HumanWin` and `ComputerWin`, respectively. Lines 18 and 22 reflect a change in the initialization of `Value`. The move evaluation is in lines 29 to 51 and is only slightly more complex. We have two symmetric cases which depend on whose turn it is to move. At line 32, we recursively process each move. `Value` represents the best move seen so far and is passed as `Alpha` to the human's evaluation routine. When the recursive call returns, if it has produced a better move, we adjust `Value` and record the move. If this move is a refutation, we can return immediately. This is shown at lines 34 to 39. The code for when the human moves is shown on lines 43 to 50.

It is important to understand that alpha-beta pruning computes exactly the same information. The only difference is that it does fewer recursive calls by being clever. In our

```
/* 1*/     /* Find The Best Move, And return Its Value */
/* 2*/     /* Assumes: Humanwin < Draw < Computerwin */

/* 3*/     int
/* 4*/     ChooseMove( BoardType B, Side S,
                           int *BestRow, int *BestColumn )
/* 5*/     {
/* 6*/         Side Opp;                                  /* The Opponent */
/* 7*/         int Reply;                  /* Value Of Opponent's Reply */
/* 8*/         int Value;                  /* Value Of Best Move, So Far */
/* 9*/         Piece Mypiece;         /* Piece Corresponding To Side S */
/*10*/         int Row, Column;                            /* Counters */
/*11*/         int Z;                                   /* Placeholder */
/*12*/         int SimpleEval;     /* Result Of A Simple Evaluation */

/*13*/         if( ( SimpleEval = Terminal( B ) ) != Unclear )
/*14*/             return SimpleEval;        /* Immediate Evaluation */

/*15*/             /* Set Some Variables Depending On Who S Is */
/*16*/         if( S == Me )
/*17*/         {
/*18*/             Opp = You; Value = HumanWin; Mypiece = Computer;
/*19*/         }
/*20*/         else
/*21*/         {
/*22*/             Opp = Me; Value = ComputerWin; Mypiece = Human;
/*23*/         }

/*24*/             /* Search for A Move */
/*25*/         for( Row = 0; Row < Bsize; Row++ )
/*26*/             for( Column = 0; Column < Bsize; Column++ )
/*27*/                 if( IsEmpty( B, Row, Column ) )
/*28*/                 {
/*29*/                     Place( B, Row, Column, Mypiece );
/*30*/                     Reply = ChooseMove( B, Opp, &Z, &Z );
/*31*/                     Unplace( B, Row, Column );

/*32*/                         /* Test if S Gets A Better Position */
/*33*/                         /* If So, Update */*
/*34*/                     if( S == Me && Reply > Value ||
/*35*/                         S == You && Reply < Value )
/*36*/                     {
/*37*/                         Value = Reply;
/*38*/                         *BestRow = Row; *BestColumn = Column;
/*39*/                     }
/*40*/                 }

/*41*/         return Value;
/*42*/     }
```

Figure 11.24:   **Routine to find an optimal tic-tac-toe move.**

```
/* 1*/    /* Same As ChooseMove, But Use Alpha Beta Pruning. */

/* 2*/    int
/* 3*/    Choose( BoardType B, Side S, int *BestRow, int *BestColumn,
/* 4*/            int Alpha, int Beta )
/* 5*/    {
/*14*/            /* Up To Here, Everything Is Identical... */
/*15*/            /* Set Some Variables Depending On Who S Is */
/*16*/        if( S == Me )
/*17*/        {
/*18*/            Opp = You; Value = Alpha; Mypiece = Computer;
/*19*/        }
/*20*/        else
/*21*/        {
/*22*/            Opp = Me; Value = Beta; Mypiece = Human;
/*23*/        }
/*24*/            /* Search For A Move */
/*25*/        for( Row = 0; Row < Bsize; Row++ )
/*26*/            for( Column = 0; Column < Bsize; Column++ )
/*27*/                if( IsEmpty( B, Row, Column ) )
/*28*/                {
/*29*/                    Place( B, Row, Column, Mypiece );
/*30*/                    if( S == Me )
/*31*/                    {
/*32*/                        Reply = Choose( B, Opp, &Z, &Z,
                                                  Value, Beta );
/*33*/                        Unplace( B, Row, Column );
/*34*/                        if( Reply > Value )
/*35*/                        {
/*36*/                            *BestRow = Row; *BestColumn = Column;
/*37*/                            if( ( Value = Reply ) >= Beta )
/*38*/                                return Value;  /* Refutation */
/*39*/                        }
/*40*/                    }
/*41*/                    else
/*42*/                    {
/*43*/                        Reply = Choose( B, Opp, &Z, &Z,
                                                  Alpha, Value );
/*44*/                        Unplace( B, Row, Column );
/*45*/                        if( Reply < Value )
/*46*/                        {
/*47*/                            *BestRow = Row; *BestColumn = Column;
/*48*/                            if( ( Value = Reply ) <= Alpha )
/*49*/                                return Value;  /* Refutation */
/*50*/                        }
/*51*/                    }
/*52*/                }

/*53*/        return Value;
/*54*/    }
```

Figure 11.25: Compute optimal tic-tac-toe move using alpha-beta pruning.

case, the first move is found in only 18,297 recursive calls, thus saving about a factor of 30.

This strategy can be used for more complex games; however, an obvious problem emerges: there will be too many positions for a complete evaluation. When this happens we terminate the search early at some unclear node and attempt to estimate a value for the position. The value will take the form of a number that is somewhere between the definitive win or loss and will be based on heuristic information that includes strategic principles. Programmers have applied this strategy successfully to complex games such as chess, checkers, and othello; the top computers can beat all but the best players in the world.

11.6   Summary

In this chapter we have examined *recursion* and seen that it is a powerful problem-solving tool. The fundamental rules, which you should never forget, are:

1. *BASE CASES*: Always have at least one case that can be solved without using recursion.

2. *DON'T GET STUCK*: Any recursive call must make progress toward a base case.

3. *YOU GOTTA BELIEVE*: Always assume that the recursive call works.

4. *COMPOUND INTEREST RULE*: Never duplicate work by solving the same instance of a problem in separate recursive calls.

We examined many interesting algorithms that are based on recursion. The textbooks [Cormen 90], [Sedgewick 90], and [Weiss 93] contain more details on these problems, as well as references for further reading. Information on the techniques used in computer games is described in a 1990 special issue of the journal *Artificial Intelligence*.

11.6.1   What Was Covered

- We cannot state it often enough: remember the four fundamental rules of recursion.

- Modular exponentiation, randomized primality testing, greatest common divisor, and multiplicative inverse problems can all be solved in time that is roughly proportional to the length of the input integers. These number-theoretical problems, once thought to have limited practicality, are central to the RSA cryptosystem.

- The binary search tree can be used to support `Find`, `Insert`, and `Remove` operations in time that is, on average, comparable to the binary search. However, in the worst case, which occurs for sorted insertion sequences, the binary search tree has poor performance. Items in a binary search tree can easily be output in sorted order. This is a property that hash tables do not share. Also, range searches (see Exercise 11) as well as maximum and minimum finding are supported.

- Quicksort is a recursive routine that yields the fastest general-purpose sorting algorithm.

- When combined with alpha-beta pruning, the minimax strategy can be used to solve quickly small games, such as tic-tac-toe. It can be extended, with other modifications, to produce expert play in games such as chess, checkers, and othello.

```
/* 1*/    /* Return Position Of X In A (DOES NOT WORK) */

/* 2*/    int
/* 3*/    BinarySearch1( const char *A[ ], const char *X,
                                            int Low, int High )
/* 4*/    {
/* 5*/        int Mid = ( Low + High ) / 2 ;
/* 6*/        int Cmp;

/* 7*/        if( Low > High )                        /* Not Found */
/* 8*/            return -1;
/* 9*/        if( ( Cmp = strcmp( X, A[ Mid ] ) ) < 0 )
/*10*/            return BinarySearch1( A, X, Low, Mid );
/*11*/        if( Cmp > 0 )                           /* X > A[ Mid ] */
/*12*/            return BinarySearch1( A, X, Mid, High );
/*13*/        return Mid;                             /* X = A[ Mid ] */
/*14*/    }

/*15*/    int
/*16*/    BinarySearch( const char *A[ ], const char *X, int N )
/*17*/    {
/*18*/        return BinarySearch1( A, X, 0, N - 1 );
/*19*/    }
```

Figure 11.26:   Incorrect binary search.

11.6.2   Friendly Reminders

- The most common error associated with recursion is the failure to make progress toward a base case. For example, consider the implementation of binary search shown in Figure 11.26. Here we have included the middle position in both recursive calls. Of course, this is inefficient, since it obviously does not need to be included, but is it an error? The answer is a subtle yes. Consider what happens when X is not found. Eventually, we reach the case where Low and High are identical. Thus Mid is also the same. When this happens, the recursive calls on lines 10 and 12 will both fail to make progress. Thus BinarySearch1 does not work for an unsuccessful search of a one-item array. However, because of recursion, that means that it does not work for any larger arrays, either.

- The other common error, as we saw earlier, is violating the compound interest rule. If you make redundant recursive calls, your program can literally take forever to run.

EXERCISES

1. Prove by induction the formula for the number of calls to the recursive function Fib.

2. Prove by induction the formula for F_N.

$$F_N = \frac{1}{\sqrt{5}} \left[\left(\frac{1+\sqrt{5}}{2} \right)^N - \left(\frac{1-\sqrt{5}}{2} \right)^N \right]$$

3. Prove the following identities relating to the Fibonacci numbers.

    (a) $F_1 + F_2 + \cdots + F_N = F_{N+2} - 1$

    (b) $F_1 + F_3 + \cdots + F_{2N-1} = F_{2N}$

    (c) $F_0 + F_2 + \cdots + F_{2N} = F_{2N+1} - 1$

    (d) $F_{N-1} F_{N+1} = (-1)^N + F_N{}^2$

    (e) $F_1 F_2 + F_2 F_3 + \cdots + F_{2N-1} F_{2N} = F_{2N}{}^2$

    (f) $F_1 F_2 + F_2 F_3 + \cdots + F_{2N} F_{2N+1} = F_{2N+1}{}^2 - 1$

    (g) $F_N{}^2 + F_{N+1}{}^2 = F_{2N+1}$

4. Write the routine

    ```
    void Permute( char *Str );
    ```

    which prints all the permutations of the characters in the string `Str`. If `Str` is `"abc"`, the strings that are output are `"abc"`, `"acb"`, `"bac"`, `"bca"`, `"cab"`, and `"cba"`. Use recursion.

5. Implement the `HugeInt` abstract data type.

6. Below are four alternatives for line 8 of the routine `Power`. Why are all of them wrong?

    ```
    /*8a*/      Tmp = Power( ( X * X ), N / 2, P );
    /*8b*/      Tmp = Power( Power( X, 2, P ), N / 2, P );
    /*8c*/      Tmp = Power( Power( X, N / 2, P ), 2, P );
    /*8d*/      Tmp = Power( X, N / 2, P ) * Power( X, N / 2, P ) % P;
    ```

7. Prove by induction that if $A > B \geq 0$ and the invocation `Gcd( A, B )` performs $k \geq 1$ recursive calls, then $A \geq F_{k+2}$ and $B \geq F_{k+1}$.

8. Prove by induction that in the extended gcd algorithm $|X| < B$ and $|Y| < A$.

9. Implement the binary search tree algorithms nonrecursively. `PrintInOrder` will require using a stack. The other routines are simple iterations.

10. Write routines `FindMin` and `FindMax` that return a pointer to the minimum and maximum items, respectively, in the binary search tree.

11. Write a routine to print out, in sorted order, only those items X in a binary search tree that satisfy the lexicographic ordering $Low \leq X \leq High$. Avoid recursive calls that are guaranteed not to print anything.

12. Write the routine `FreeTree` that takes a tree `T` as parameter and deallocates all memory associated with the tree.

13. Modify the tree routines to include a queue with each field. Then write a cross-reference generator, which reads the standard input and prints out each word alphabetically. Accompanying each word should be a list of line numbers on which the word occurs.

14. Implement a generic binary search tree by having each node store two tree pointers and a pointer to the generic item. You will need to pass a comparison function and item size to most of the tree routines.

15. The additional test at line 15 of `QuickSort1` is unnecessary if we can guarantee that `A[Low]` has an element that is at least as small as `Pivot`. This can be arranged by sorting `A[Low]`, `A[Mid]`, and `A[High]` prior to line 9. Of course, `Pivot` can no longer be a `const` and must be assigned `A[Center]` after the three-element sort. This is known as *median-of-three partitioning*, because the pivot is the median of three elements.

    (a) Does this algorithm work if there are fewer than three elements?

(b)   An additional benefit is that this rule makes it more likely that the pivot will partition the elements evenly, which leads to a slightly faster algorithm. Why?

(c)   Implement median-of-three partitioning.

(d)   Show that using median-of-three partitioning, we can swap `A[Center]` and `A[High-1]` and start `j` one more position to the left. What other changes are necessary? Implement them.

16.   The quicksort routine is inefficient for small subarrays. Experiment with the following modification: When `High-Low` is smaller than some `Cutoff` (typically 10), have `QuickSort1` terminate immediately. As a result, the array will be mostly sorted, but not completely. Have `QuickSort` perform an additional `InsertionSort` to finish up. For what value of `Cutoff` do you get the best performance?

17.   Implement a generic quicksort, as in Figures 9.17 and 9.18.

18.   Even if the computer has a move that gives an immediate win, it may not make it if it detects another move that is also guaranteed to win. Modify the tic-tac-toe algorithm so that when a winning position is found, the move that leads to the shortest win is always taken. You can do this by adding the number of empty squares to `ComputerWin`, so that a more empty board (i.e., quicker win) will give the highest value.

19.   Write a program that reads an integer K and then a sequence of numbers, and outputs the Kth smallest. The program should be significantly faster (on most inputs) than sorting. *Hint: Adjust* `Quicksort` *to make only one recursive call instead of two.*

20.   Write an alternative Gcd algorithm, based on the following observations (arrange that $A > B$):

(a) $gcd(A, B) = 2 * gcd(A/2, B/2)$ if A and B are both even.

(b) $gcd(A, B) = gcd(A/2, B)$ if A is even and B is odd.

(c) $gcd(A, B) = gcd(A, B/2)$ if A is odd and B is even.

(d) $gcd(A, B) = gcd((A + B)/2, (A - B)/2)$ if A and B are both odd.

Compare the performance of this algorithm with the algorithm in Figure 11.9.

21.   Let A be a sequence of N distinct sorted numbers $A_1, A_2, \ldots, A_N$, with $A_1 = 0$. Let B be a sequence of $N(N - 1)/2$ numbers, defined by $B_{i,j} = A_i - A_j$ ($i > j$). Let D be the sequence obtained by sorting B. Both B and D may contain duplicates. *Example: A = 0, 1, 5, 8. Then D = 1, 3, 4, 5, 7, 8.*

(a)   Write a program that constructs D from A. This part is easy.

(b)   Write a program that constructs some sequence A that corresponds to D. (Note that A is not unique.)

22.   A student needs to take a required group of major courses to graduate. Each course has some prerequisites. Write a program that reads a sequence of lines, each containing a required course and its prerequisites, and outputs a semester-by-semester plan that suggests which courses can be taken in each semester. The plan should not violate any prerequisites and should use the minimum number of semesters. You may assume no limit on the number of courses that can be scheduled in one semester. *Hint: For a course C, recursively compute the earliest semester that each of the prerequisites may be taken. Then C can be taken one semester after the latest of these prerequisites. Be careful to avoid redundant recursive calls.*

23.   Write a program that solves arbitrary addition or subtraction puzzles like the one in Exercise 3.19. Use a recursive algorithm that attempts to avoid a complete exhaustive search.

24.   Consider an N by N grid in which some squares are occupied. Two squares belong to the same group if they share a common edge. In Figure 11.27 there is one group of six squares, as well as two groups of three squares, one group of two squares, and ten single-square groups. Assume that the grid is represented by a two-dimensional array. Write a program that does the following:

(a) Computes the size of a group, given a square in the group

(b) Computes the number of different groups

(c) Lists all groups

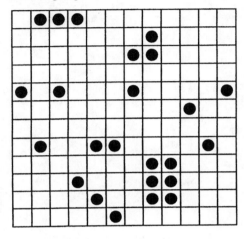

Figure 11.27:   **Example for Exercise 24.**

Part III

The Environment:
Files, UNIX, and C++

12

I/O

In this chapter we discuss input and output, applied to both the terminal and files. First, we give a detailed description of the `printf` and `scanf` functions, which we have already used. Then we discuss the routines that are used to access files. Although files are not part of the language proper, ANSI C specifies a set of routines that are required to be present on all C systems. In general, these routines are simple to use and do a fine job of hiding the onerous implementation details that used to come with files. On the other hand, the handling of files is an inherently machine-dependent chore. ANSI C attempts as much as possible to ensure some portability, but the underlying reality is that if you are not running under a UNIX system, you need to be careful. When appropriate, we'll point out possible portability issues; some are discussed in the exercises.

12.1 `printf`

`printf` is perhaps the most frequently used function in C. In this section we discuss its many features. As we have already seen, the first parameter to `printf` is the *control string*. It is possible, though unusual, for the control string to be a variable, which is constructed as the program runs. We almost always use a string constant.

The control string is written as output, except that parts of the control string that begin with the % character are interpreted as special fields. This part of the control string is known as the *conversion specification*. Each field is replaced by a corresponding additional parameter, which must be of the type indicated in the conversion specification. As an example, `%d` indicates that an `int` is expected; thus we have already seen that

```
printf( "Integer #1: %d\nInteger #2: %d\n", 37, 3737 );
```

writes

```
Integer #1: 37
Integer #2: 3737
```

`%f` indicates that a `double` is expected. Using `%d` but providing `5.0` does not produce 5.

Although this seems simple enough, several improvements come to mind. One improvement, from the example above, is that we may want to pad the output automatically with leading blanks so that a table lines up nicely. Of course, the question becomes: How much padding should be used? Sometimes, leading zeros work better than leading blanks, and sometimes we want to pad the output with trailing blanks. Also, there is the question of the sign bit. Since negative numbers begin with a -, perhaps positive numbers should begin with a +, since otherwise 37 and -37 do not line up in the case that they are left justified. Perhaps, as an alternative, a blank should be placed in lieu of a +. Another option would be to allow output in binary, octal, or hexadecimal, since C is used for systems work. For floating-point numbers, there is the additional problem of how many digits should be printed after the decimal point. If none, does 5.00000 get printed as 5. or 5? Also, when should floating-point numbers be represented using scientific notation?

All of these formats can be handled by `printf`, although the syntax can be confusing. We now discuss the integral and floating-point types separately.

12.1.1   Output for `int`

The conversion specifier for integral types ends in either d, i, u, o, x, or X, which indicate decimal, unsigned, octal, or hexadecimal. The i conversion (which is equivalent to the d conversion) is defined in ANSI C but is rarely used. Octal and hexadecimal numbers are treated as unsigned quantities. On a 32-bit machine, using the six formats, 37 is printed as

```
37 37 37 45 25 25,
```

while -37 is printed as

```
-37 -37 -37 37777777733 ffffffdb FFFFFFDB.
```

These specifiers may optionally be prefixed by h or l, indicating that the corresponding parameters are `short` or `long`. Do not use `%s` by accident, because this refers to a string, not a `short`. An easy pneumonic is that h stands for the second letter of `short`.[1] Note carefully that `unsigned long` is printed with `%lu` not `%ul`.

Prior to the conversion specifier, a minimum precision may be specified by using a period (.) followed by a decimal digit. This is typically used to specify how many decimal places are used in a floating-point output, but it also makes sense for integers. In this case, leading zeros are printed if needed. As an example, if a minimum precision of four digits is specified by `%.4`, then for 37, the output for our various integral types is

```
0037 0037 0037 0045 0025 0025,
```

and for -37 it is

```
-0037 -0037 -0037 37777777733 ffffffdb FFFFFFDB.
```

Prior to the minimum precision, we can specify the field length. By default the field is right justified, but by specifying a - immediately after the leading `%`, the field is left justified. Left-justified fields are padded with blanks automatically; right-justified fields are padded with blanks by default, but by specifying a 0 (zero) prior to the field width, we obtain padding with zeros. Before continuing with further rules, consult Figure 12.1 to see how various options affect the output. We are assuming four spaces between fields. Note that the field width includes the - sign.

---

[1] Actually, it stands for *half*.

```
   %d       37     -37
  %.4d      0037      -0037
 %11d               37                    -37
%11.4d             0037                  -0037
 %-11d     37                 -37
%-11.4d    0037               -0037
 %011d     00000000037        -0000000037
```

Figure 12.1: How different formats print 37 and -37.

```
   %d       37     -37
  %.4d      0037     -0037
 %11d               37                    -37
 %011d     00000000037        -0000000037
 % 011d     0000000037         -0000000037
 %+11d              +37                    -37
%+011d     +0000000037        -0000000037
 %-11d     37                 -37
 %- 11d     37                 -37
%-+11d     +37                 -37
%11.4d             0037                  -0037
%-11.4d    0037               -0037
%- 11.4d    0037               -0037
%-+11.4d   +0037               -0037
```

Figure 12.2: Previous table augmented with + and blank options.

The only other option that affects the conversion is how to handle the sign. Including a + option specifies that a leading + should be included if the output is positive. A blank space option specifies that a leading blank space should be included. By default, as we have seen, nothing is included. Because octal and hexadecimal numbers are treated as unsigned integers, this option is not applicable for them. However, so as not to leave them out of the action, the # option specifies a leading 0 for octal numbers and a leading 0x for hexadecimal numbers (capitalized if %X is used).[2] Figure 12.2 shows how the plus and space options affect output. Figure 12.3 shows how the # option affects output.

12.1.2 Run-Time Field Width Specification

Sometimes the field width is not known at compile time. ANSI C specifies that a * can be used in place of a field width. In this case a corresponding argument is used to determine the field width. This is also true for the minimum precision. The following statements correspond to lines 2 through 4 in Figure 12.1.

```
printf( "%.*d", 4, 37 );              /* %.4d   */
printf( "%*d", 11, 37 );              /* %11d   */
printf( "%*.*d", 11, 4, 37 );         /* %11.4d */
```

---

[2]Although Figure 12.3 shows the correct values, not all compilers get this right, especially when several options are combined. One of my compilers inserts two extra zeros for %#011x.

```
      %o            %x    45       fffffdb
     %.4o          %.4x   0045      fffffdb
     %11o          %11x              45          fffffdb
     %011o         %011x  00000000045  000fffffdb
     %#011o        %#011x 00000000045  0x0fffffdb
     %#11o         %#11x             045    0xfffffdb
     %-11o         %-11x  45            fffffdb
     %-#11o        %-#11x 045           0xfffffdb
     %11.4o        %11.4x            0045      fffffdb
    %-11.4o       %-11.4x 0045          fffffdb
    %-#11.4o      %-#11.4x 0045         0xfffffdb
```

Figure 12.3:   Options with octal and hexadecimals: 37 and -37, respectively.

12.1.3   Output for `double`

Floating-point numbers are printed using %f. This works for both float and double. For historical reasons, %lf has been used for double, but technically this use is undefined in ANSI C. For long double %Lf must be used. Watch out, because a lowercase l does not work. An alternative is to use e instead of f; this prints the output in scientific notation. Thus scientific notation can be used for float, double, and long double by specifying %e, %le, and %Le, respectively. A third possibility is to use g instead of f. This alternative allows the compiler to decide whether or not scientific notation is appropriate. ANSI C defines specific rules that are the basis for this decision.

For the %f conversion, most of what was said for %d applies, except that by default, the precision is 6 (places after the decimal point). No matter what the precision is, the result is supposed to be rounded to the closest floating-point number with appropriate precision. If the precision is 0, that raises the question of whether or not a decimal point should be output. By default the decimal point does not appear in this case but can be forced to appear by using the # option. Figure 12.4 shows the output of 37.3737 and -37.3737 for various control strings.

For output in scientific notation, which is performed with the %e conversion, a floating-point number X is represented as $D*10^P$, where $1 \leq D < 10$. For instance, 37.3737 is represented as $3.73737*10^1$. Except for the field width, all of the conversion specifiers are applied to D, which is then output, followed by the character e, and then P is output, with a sign and leading zeros. The total number of digits in the output of P depends on the implementation but is always at least 2.

Figure 12.5 shows some output using this conversion. Because four extra characters are added to represent the exponent, we have increased the field width to 15. If we keep the width at 11, those entries with six decimal places will not fit and thus will not line up with other entries of width 11. Just as hexadecimal numbers can be output in either upper or lower case, the %E conversion is identical to %e except that the e in the output string is written in upper case.

Finally, we discuss the %g conversion. A slight difference is that the minimum precision is 1, rather than zero. According to ANSI C, the number is printed in scientific notation only if the exponent would be at least as large as the precision, or smaller than -4. Trailing zeros are removed. %G prints the E in upper case rather than lower case.

```
        %f     37.373700      -37.373700
       %.3f    37.374      -37.374
       %11f        37.373700       -37.373700
      %011f    0037.373700     -037.373700
     % 011f     037.373700     -037.373700
      %+11f     +37.373700      -37.373700
     %+011f    +037.373700     -037.373700
      %-11f    37.373700       -37.373700
     %- 11f     37.373700       -37.373700
     %-+11f    +37.373700      -37.373700
     %11.3f         37.374          -37.374
     %11.0f             37              -37
    %#11.0f            37.             -37.
    %-11.3f    37.374          -37.374
   %- 11.3f     37.374          -37.374
   %-+11.3f    +37.374         -37.374
```

Figure 12.4:   **Options with** `%f`. **37.3737 and -37.3737, respectively.**

```
        %e     3.737370e+01    -3.737370e+01
       %.3e    3.737e+01      -3.737e+01
       %15e        3.737370e+01        -3.737370e+01
      %015e    0003.737370e+01    -003.737370e+01
     % 015e     003.737370e+01    -003.737370e+01
      %+15e     +3.737370e+01        -3.737370e+01
     %+015e    +003.737370e+01    -003.737370e+01
      %-15e    3.737370e+01        -3.737370e+01
     %- 15e     3.737370e+01        -3.737370e+01
     %-+15e    +3.737370e+01        -3.737370e+01
     %15.3e         3.737e+01           -3.737e+01
     %15.0e             4e+01               -4e+01
    %#15.0e            4.e+01              -4.e+01
    %-15.3e    3.737e+01        -3.737e+01
   %- 15.3e     3.737e+01        -3.737e+01
   %-+15.3e    +3.737e+01        -3.737e+01
```

Figure 12.5:   **Options with** `%e`. **37.3737 and -37.3737, respectively.**

12.1.4   Output for Characters and Strings

The `%c` and `%s` conversions are used for `char` and strings, respectively. This is discussed in Chapter 8 when characters and strings are introduced. The additional options apply to strings in the manner expected.

12.1.5   Special Characters

We have already seen that the *escape sequence* \n can be used to print out a newline. Figure 8.2 showed the other common escape sequences. Although these escape sequences are sufficient to allow representation of all possible strings, `printf` has a problem of its own: How does one print a % sign without having it confused as the start of a conversion? %% tells `printf` to output a %. Note that \% does not work, because output of % is not a string problem but a `printf` interpretation problem. \% is just interpreted as a %, which begins a conversion.

12.1.6   The `return` Value

You should understand that despite the huge variety of options available, `printf` is basically very stupid. If you do not supply the correct type and number of parameters to match the conversion specifier, `printf` will still output something. You do not get an automatic type conversion. Furthermore, if you provide an incorrect conversion specifier, such as %2D, `printf` will just output 2D. Unfortunately, although a return value is provided by `printf`, it will not report any of these errors. `printf` returns an int, which indicates the number of characters that were actually output. Note that a newline counts as one character.

If `printf` returns a negative value, nothing was written because of some error. Generally what this means is that the output was being redirected from the standard place, namely the terminal, into a file, or perhaps a printer, and that there was a problem. The most likely cause is a full disk or a lack of permission to write to the disk. Although the tendency is to ignore `printf`'s return value, for serious applications it needs to be checked to make sure that a disaster has not occurred.

12.2   `scanf`

The C function that reads formatted input is `scanf`. Ideally, we would like `scanf` to behave exactly like `printf`. Unfortunately, this is not true. One difference is that the conversion specifier for doubles is %1f for `scanf`, but %f for `printf`. The biggest difference, as we have seen, is that call by reference must be used for the additional parameters. Thus

```
scanf( "%d", X );
```

is incorrect:

```
scanf( "%d", &X );
```

must be used.

Another difference is that while `printf` has complicated expressions for specifying field length and how padding and sign bits are output, `scanf` is limited in this regard. The field width parameter, which is a minimum for `printf` (because padding is performed if necessary), is a maximum for `scanf`. Thus, as we will see, if the input is 12345 and the conversion specifier is %3d, only 123 is matched. There is also a difference in the way in which white space is handled. Even so, for casual users of `printf` and `scanf`, who tend simply to use unadorned %d-type converters, these differences are probably minor. There is, however, a very annoying problem: What do we do if the user provides bad input?

12.2.1   The Part That Is Similar to `printf`

The only real similarity between `printf` and `scanf` is that the basic conversions are almost the same.

```
/* 1*/     #include <stdio.h>

/* 2*/     main( void )
/* 3*/     {
/* 4*/         double X;

/* 5*/         scanf( "%f", &X );              /* 3 */
/* 6*/         printf( "%f\n", X );           /* 32.000000 */
/* 7*/         printf( "%lf\n", X );          /* Undefined */
/* 8*/         scanf( "%lf", &X );            /* 3 */
/* 9*/         printf( "%f\n", X );           /* 3.000000 */
/*10*/         printf( "%lf\n", X );          /* Undefined */

/*11*/         return 0;
/*12*/     }
```

Figure 12.6:   Effect of 1 for double-precision I/O.

ints

The basic conversions are still %d, %i, %u, %o, %x, and %X. In all cases the field matches a sequence of digits, which may be preceded (even for the unsigned case) by a + or -. However, 8 and 9 are not octal digits and thus terminate the scan, and abcdefABCDEF are allowed as valid hexadecimal digits.[3] The conversions may be preceded by h or l for short or long. Bugs that are difficult to track down can result from forgetting these qualifiers. Note carefully that unsigned long is read with %lu, not %ul. If the input that is read does not fit into the variable, the variable will be undefined, but the scan is successful. Thus the scan of 12345678901234 returns 1, indicating success.

doubles

scanf provides the %e, %f, %g, %E, and %G conversions, augmented with l or L. Unlike printf, however, all five conversions behave identically and recognize all forms of floating-point numbers. Of course, the usual truncation warnings apply. If the input that is read is too large or small, ANSI C specifies that the result is an appropriately signed HUGE_VAL, defined in <float.h>.

Forgetting the l or L qualifiers when specifying double or long double can lead to mistakes on machines where these types are longer than a float. This is a particularly common error because double is used so frequently and printf does not require the qualifier. Figure 12.6 shows the problems. The comments at the end of each line represent either the appropriate input or output value. Many programmers use %lf for printf, to get in the habit for scanf. Technically, however, this is wrong, though it always seems to work (because most libraries simply ignore the l).

char

Character types, which we discussed in Chapter 8, are read using the %c option. This is such a common operation that special routines exist for this purpose. Because of the high

---

[3]Consequently %x and %X are identical.

overhead of `scanf`'s function call, it is best to avoid using `scanf` to read one character repeatedly. Use `getchar` instead. Also, beware that the rules for white space, which we discuss below, can make the results different from what you expect.

Strings

The `%s` conversion is used to read an arbitrary sequence of non-white-space characters into a string. As we saw in Chapter 8, the variable that names the string is already an address, so the `&` is not required. You should always use a maximum-field-length qualifier with this option.

12.2.2   The `return` **Value, and Digestion**

Unlike `printf`, which returns the number of characters output, `scanf` returns the actual number of fields that are matched. If all goes well, this is the same as the number of extra parameters. Sometimes, only a partial match occurs. If

```
scanf( "%d %d", &X, &Y );
```

is applied to the input

```
5 junk
```

the return value would be 1, X would be 5, and Y would be unchanged. It is possible that no fields match, in which case zero is returned. It is also possible that the end of input has been reached prior to matching any input characters, and this is indicated by a return value of `EOF`.[4] A typical value of `EOF` is -1, which differentiates it from zero matches. However, ANSI C specifies only that `EOF` must be negative. An important point to know is that `scanf` gives up as soon as a match fails. Thus the previous `scanf` request when presented with input

```
junk 5
```

returns 0. X and Y are guaranteed to have unchanged values.

The most important point to realize is that input which is unmatched is considered unread. Therefore, a subsequent call to `scanf` will still see the input

```
junk 5
```

What this means, for instance, is that the routine in Figure 12.7 is incorrect, because it will never digest `junk`, and thus always report an error and enter an infinite loop. The fix, shown in Figure 12.8, is to make sure that on an error, some input is digested. The simplest way to do that is just to skip past the offending line of input. To do this we use the routine `SkipLine`, which we present later in this section.

12.2.3   **Differences from** `printf`

White Space

All consecutive white space characters in the control string are considered identical to just one. The effect is that any white space in the input stream is skipped. Note carefully that it is possible that there is no white space in the input stream—this is not an error. As an example, consider the request

---

[4]On UNIX, the end of input is signaled by typing a single line consisting of a `control d` character. Other operating systems typically accept `control z`.

```
/* 1*/    /* Read A Bunch Of Integers */
/* 2*/    /* Wrong Way To Check for Errors */

/* 3*/    #include <stdio.h>

/* 4*/    main( void )
/* 5*/    {
/* 6*/        int X, ArgsMatched;

/* 7*/        for( ; ; )
/* 8*/        {
/* 9*/            printf( "Enter an integer: " );
/*10*/            ArgsMatched = scanf( "%d", &X );
/*11*/            if( ArgsMatched == 0 )
/*12*/            {
/*13*/                printf( "You did not enter an integer... \n" );
/*14*/                continue;       /* Wrong: No Digestion Of Input */
/*15*/            }
/*16*/            else
/*17*/            if( ArgsMatched == 1 )
/*18*/                printf( "Read %d\n", X );
/*19*/            else
/*20*/                break; /* EOF */
/*21*/        }
/*22*/        return 0;
/*23*/    }
```

Figure 12.7: **Incorrect method for resolving** scanf **errors.**

```
/*11*/            if( ArgsMatched == 0 )
/*12*/            {
/*13*/                printf( "You did not enter an integer... \n" );
/*13a*/               SkipLine( );
/*14*/                continue;
/*15*/            }
```

Figure 12.8: **Correct method for resolving** scanf **errors.**

```
scanf( "%d %d\t%d\n", &X, &Y, &Z );
```

The use of the newline and tab sequence instead of a space is meaningless, because it is all white space. Three integers separated by any type and amount of white space will match. Notice that, unfortunately, this means that it is difficult to require that the three integers appear on the same input line. Without doing more work, this kind of error checking cannot be performed. We show below how this can be done. By the way, the newline sequence is bad because if white space follows the third integer, the scanf will not complete until some non-white space character, delimiting the end of the white space, is seen.

One might wonder what the following request does:

```
scanf( "%d%d%d", &X, &Y, &Z );
```

Clearly, if we want to assign 1, 2, and 3 to the three variables, they must be separated by white space. Otherwise, we'll read 123. Because of this, matches for most fields skip leading white space. The only exceptions are %c and the scanf only conversion % [. Thus the two previous scanf statements are functionally identical.

Ordinary Characters

One might think, then, that there is little difference in whether or not white space is used. If only simple conversion are used, this is true. Suppose, however, that the input line is of the form

```
A=35 B=42 C=21
```

Then the appropriate input statement is

```
scanf( "A=%d B=%d C=%d", &A, &B, &C );
```

The characters in the control string that are not part of a conversion and are not white space are called *ordinary characters*. Ordinary characters must be matched exactly, or the scanning of the input terminates. Note that to match a %, we must use %% in the conversion string, just as was done for printf. If we use

```
scanf( "A=%dB=%dC=%d", &A, &B, &C );
```

the matching input is

```
A=35B=42C=21
```

Not only does the white space make things more visible, but they could be required in some cases. For instance, if we are reading hexadecimal numbers instead of decimal numbers, 35B would be assigned to A and a mismatch in the input would be detected between the requested B and the actual =. Note also that the last input matches the scanf statement that contains white space. The white space in the control string merely instructs to skip white space *if it is present*.

Assignment Suppression

An immediate * following the % indicates that a field is to be parsed but that no object is there for it to be assigned to. This is known as *assignment suppression*. As an example, suppose that we only want to read every third integer. Then

```
scanf( "%*d %*d %d", &A );
```

reads three integers, assigning the last to A and discarding the other two. The return value is 1, the actual number of assignments performed.

As an example of assignment suppression, suppose that we want to read lines of the form

```
?=int ?=int ?=int
```

where ? represents some non-white-space character. We can do this with

```
scanf("%*1s=%d %*1s=%d %*1s=%d", &A, &B, &C );
```

In the control string, we look (three times) for a one-character string, which is ignored, an immediate =, and an integer. A space before the = in the control string would remove the immediacy requirement. Note carefully that if we replace %*1s with %*s, the string will match everything until white space is seen. This would include the =, making the subsequent search for = fail.

```
/* 1*/    void
/* 2*/    SkipLine( void )
/* 3*/    {
/* 4*/        scanf( "%*[^\n]" );    /* Skip To The End Of The Line */
/* 5*/        scanf( "%*1[\n]" );    /* Skip One Newline */
/* 6*/    }
```

Figure 12.9: **Using the** % [**conversion to implement** SkipLine.

The % [Conversion

The % [conversion fills a string, but the allowable characters can be restricted. Following the [is a list of allowable characters, known as the *scan set*, followed by a].[5] As an example, %5[abc] matches up to a five-character string composed entirely of a, b, or c. Any character not in the scan set signals that the matching string has ended.

An important point is that unlike the other formats, the % [converter does not skip over leading white space. Thus if there is some white space, and the particular type of white space is not in the scan set, a mismatch occurs. Thus you should either place the white space in the scan set or use white space before the start of the converter. In our case, of course, using white space before the converter would allow the newline to occur at an arbitrary place.

In addition to specifying a list of acceptable characters, two shorthands are sometimes available. First, a complete list such as % [abcdefg] can be specified by its range, and thus collapsed to % [a-g]. All lowercase letters except vowels can be given by

%[b-df-hj-np-tw-z]

Note that a – at the end of the scan set stands for itself, not a range. This range feature is not required by ANSI C and not all compilers support this option. For serious parsing applications, you should not use this feature of scanf, although in less demanding programs it can provide a convenient shorthand.

The second shorthand is guaranteed to be portable: by specifying ^, all of the remaining list becomes an unacceptable list of characters.[6] Thus % [^\n] specifies all characters but the newline. Note that if ^ does not appear as the first character but does appear later, it, as well as all the other characters in the scan set, are considered acceptable characters. This gives us an easy way to write SkipLine, which is shown in Figure 12.9.[7] First, we skip over the rest of the line. Then, we read exactly one newline character. Notice that we cannot combine the scanf directives, because in general we have to handle the case where we are already at the end of a line. Some sample scan sets are shown in Figure 12.10.

In Figure 12.9, if we remove the 1 from line 5, there will appear to be a delay because the scanf is not terminated until the next line of input is typed. This is because, until a non-newline character is seen, the scanf is not complete. In most circumstances, this requires that a nonblank line be typed. Of course, that line is read by the next scanf in a normal fashion—it is just the delay that is apparent. Consequently, including the newline

---

[5]] can be included by placing it first in the scan set.

[6]] can be excluded by placing it immediately after the ^.

[7] Of course using getchar is just as simple.

Scan Set	What It Means
%[abc]	Characters a, b, or c
%[a-z]	Lowercase alphabetic letters
%[A-Z]	Uppercase alphabetic letters
%[a-zA-Z]	All alphabetic letters
%[0-9]	Digits
%[^a-zA-Z]	Nonalphabetics
%[a-zA-Z^]	Alphabetics and ^
%[-^]	The ^ and −
%[^-]	All characters except −
%[^\n]	All characters except the newline
%[\t]	Blanks and tabs, but not newlines

Figure 12.10:   Some sample scan sets.

in a scan set can be a bad idea when input is coming from the terminal; it fools the user into thinking something is wrong.

The %n Conversion

One occasionally useful conversion that is applicable to both `printf` and `scanf` but has different meaning is the %n converter. For `printf`, when a %n is encountered, the number of characters that have thus far been output is assigned to an address specified by the next additional parameter. For `scanf`, a similar effect takes place, except that it is the number of matches that is assigned. In neither case is the actual number of output characters or matches affected.

As an example, unless disaster strikes, the `int CharCount` contains 4 after

```
printf( "This%n is a test\n", &CharCount );
```

 %n is not as useful as it appears. For instance, the statement

```
printf( "X has the value %d%n, "
        "and contains %d digits\n",
        X, &CharCount, CharCount - 16 );
```

cannot possibly do what is obviously intended: `CharCount-16` is evaluated *before* the call to `printf`. Thus you cannot use the value that is given by %n until after the statement is finished.

12.3   Extending Terminal I/O to Files

The most common use of files is the reading and writing of formatted data. We would like to be able to extend our terminal I/O routines, such as `printf`, `scanf`, `getchar`, and `putchar`, to work on files, and we would like to be able to work on many files at once.

`"r"`	Open text file for reading
`"w"`	Open text file for writing (truncate to zero length or create)
`"a"`	Open text file for appending
`"rb"`	Open binary file for reading
`"wb"`	Open binary file for writing (truncate to zero length or create)
`"ab"`	Open binary file for appending

Figure 12.11:   Basic modes for opening files.

12.3.1   The `FILE *` Type

To achieve the goals noted above, ANSI C implements a file abstract data type. This implementation is actually remarkably similar to the abstract data types that we described in Chapter 10. There, a stack abstract data type was implemented. We had routines for initializing a stack and also for recycling its memory when no longer need. We were also able to apply an operation such as `Push` by specifying the particular stack that was the target of the `Push`.

12.3.2   `fopen` and `fclose`

Just as the basic information associated with each stack was stored in a structure, for each file the basic information is stored in a structure of type `FILE`, which we refer to as a *stream*. This type is defined in the include file `<stdio.h>`. To perform any operations on a file, we must perform an initialization to obtain a stream. This is done by the function `fopen`. The complementary routine, `fclose`, allows the recycling of a stream when it is no longer needed. This is important because there is a predefined limit on the number of files open simultaneously, given by `FOPEN_MAX`, which could be as little as 8.

The prototypes are

```
FILE *fopen( const char *FileName, const char *Mode );
int fclose( FILE *Stream );
```

The parameters to `fopen` are the name of the file, and a string, called the *mode*, which represents the intended operations. Figure 12.11 lists the basic modes required by ANSI C. Compilers are free to add more. A common error is to use `'r'` as a mode instead of `"r"`.

The modes for text and binary files are identical except for the trailing b. UNIX does not distinguish between text and binary files, so it ignores the b. Most other systems, however, do distinguish between text and binary files. On those systems, a text file should consist only of printable characters. When an existing file is opened for writing, its contents are destroyed by truncating to zero length. Otherwise, if the file does not already exist, it is created. Opening a file for appending does not destroy its contents, and all writes occur at the end of the file.

It is possible to allow both reading and writing, by adding a + to the mode string. The positioning commands discussed in Section 12.5.3 must then be used to separate an input and output command. The mode `"r+"` allows both reading and arbitrary writing (by use of positioning commands). The mode `"w+"` allows reading and writing but first destroys the original file. The mode `"a+"` allows reading, but writes may occur only at the end of the file. Similar modes work for binary files, and in that case, the last two characters may be either +b or b+.

Because FILE is a structure, all the file routines pass and return a pointer to FILE. It would have been better to define FILE as a pointer to the structure, so the interface would have been somewhat clearer.

If something goes wrong, fopen returns a NULL pointer. This will occur if the mode is illegal, but the most common reason is an attempt to open a file that either does not exist (in the case of reading), or to which you have no permission to access. An error will also occur if you exceed the limit on files open simultaneously. Thus, before opening a file for writing with the "w" mode, it can first be opened for reading. By testing the return value of the fopen, we can warn the user if the file already exists (and would thus be overwritten). Then, if the user concurs, we can close the file and then reopen it for writing.

On many UNIX systems, the functions open and close deal with files at a lower, more direct level than fopen and fclose. The reason this is important is that it is a common programming error to use open and close instead of fopen and fclose; sometimes the compiler does not catch the error, and your program crashes.

12.3.3 getc, ungetc, **and** putc

The calls getc and putc provide single-character input and output for files, behaving just as getchar and putchar do for terminal I/O. Their prototypes are

```
int getc( FILE *Stream );
int putc( int Ch, FILE *Stream );
```

As with getchar and putchar, a single character is actually stored as an int, to allow EOF to be represented.

getc returns EOF if Stream is invalid or if the end of file is reached. One possible reason would be that the Stream is not opened for reading. putc returns EOF if a write error occurs. This can happen, for instance, if the device being written to is full.

A sometimes very helpful routine is ungetc. The prototype is

```
int ungetc( int Ch, FILE *Stream );
```

As a result of ungetc, Ch is pushed back onto the input stream as the next character to be read. The common use of this routine is to unread a character. As an example, when writing a compiler, the scanning routine does not know that a token has ended until another one begins. Thus although we have read the first character of the next token, we are not ready to use it until we have finished the work associated with recognizing the current token.

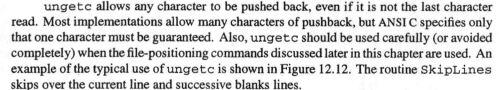

ungetc allows any character to be pushed back, even if it is not the last character read. Most implementations allow many characters of pushback, but ANSI C specifies only that one character must be guaranteed. Also, ungetc should be used carefully (or avoided completely) when the file-positioning commands discussed later in this chapter are used. An example of the typical use of ungetc is shown in Figure 12.12. The routine SkipLines skips over the current line and successive blanks lines.

ANSI C specifies two alternatives, fgetc and fputc. They are used in the extremely rare occasion in which a side effect is applied to Stream. Since that is almost certain to be poor programming practice, these routines are rarely used.

12.3.4 Example: Copying Text Files

Figure 12.13 shows the implementation of a function that copies files. The number of characters transferred is returned. The test at line 11 attempts to disallow copying a file

```
/* 1*/    /* Skip Over Current Line And Any Subsequent Blank Lines */

/* 2*/    void
/* 3*/    SkipLines( FILE *Fp )
/* 4*/    {
/* 5*/        int Ch;

/* 6*/        while( ( Ch = getc( Fp ) ) != EOF )
/* 7*/            if( Ch == '\n' )       /* End Of Current Line */
/* 8*/            {
/* 9*/                    /* Skip Over Newlines */
/*10*/                while( ( Ch = getc( Fp ) ) != EOF && Ch == '\n' )
/*11*/                    ;

/*12*/                    /* Push Back Non-Newline */
/*13*/                if( Ch != EOF )
/*14*/                    ungetc( Ch, Fp );

/*15*/                break;
/*16*/            }
/*17*/    }
```

Figure 12.12: `SkipLines` **for files.**

to itself, since once the file is opened for writing, its contents are destroyed. This test does not quite succeed, because, for example, a copy on UNIX from `junk` to `./junk` will not be caught.

The input file is opened at line 16, and the output file is opened at line 21. Because opening an output file may destroy a file, we open it after the input file. This prevents the unnecessary truncation of the output file in the case when the input file does not exist. Exercise 14 suggests an alternative method. Lines 26 to 33 copy the input to the output, much like a `getchar`/`putchar` combination. At line 27 we test the return value of `putc`, just in case the output device fills up prematurely. When we are done with the copy, we close the files at lines 34 and 35. Note that files are closed automatically when the program terminates. Even so, it is a good idea to use `fclose` for two reasons.

First, you may want to deal with lots of files, so you will run out of streams if you do not use `fclose`. Second, on some systems, files may be locked and other users may not be able to access a file until you declare that you have finished your access. Sometimes, access on a file is completed long before the program. In that case, there is no reason not to allow other users access to the file.

12.3.5 `fgets` **and** `fputs`

`fgets` and `fputs` are useful for inputting and outputting strings. The prototypes are

```
char *fgets( char *Str, int HowMany, FILE *Stream );
int fputs( const char *Str, FILE *Stream );
```

`fputs` is like `puts`, except that a terminating newline is not supplied unless it is already

```
/* 1*/    #include <stdio.h>
/* 2*/    #include <string.h>

/* 3*/    /* Copy From Sourcefile To Destfile And return The Number */
/* 4*/    /* Of Characters Copied; -1 for Errors */

/* 5*/    int
/* 6*/    Copy( const char *DestFile, const char *SourceFile )
/* 7*/    {
/* 8*/        int CharsCounted = 0;
/* 9*/        int Ch;
/*10*/        FILE *Sfp, *Dfp;

/*11*/        if( strcmp( SourceFile, DestFile ) == 0 )
/*12*/        {
/*13*/            printf( "Can not copy to self\n" );
/*14*/            return -1;
/*15*/        }

/*16*/        if( ( Sfp = fopen( SourceFile, "r" ) ) == NULL )
/*17*/        {
/*18*/            printf( "Can't open input file %s\n", SourceFile );
/*19*/            return -1;
/*20*/        }

/*21*/        if( ( Dfp = fopen( DestFile, "w" ) ) == NULL )
/*22*/        {
/*23*/            printf( "Can't open output file %s\n", DestFile );
/*24*/            fclose( Sfp ); return -1;
/*25*/        }

/*26*/        while( ( Ch = getc( Sfp ) ) != EOF )
/*27*/            if( putc( Ch, Dfp ) == EOF )
/*28*/            {
/*29*/                printf( "Unexpected error during write \n" );
/*30*/                break;
/*31*/            }
/*32*/            else
/*33*/                CharsCounted++;

/*34*/        fclose( Sfp );
/*35*/        fclose( Dfp );
/*36*/        return CharsCounted;
/*37*/    }
```

Figure 12.13: Copy routine.

present in Str. fgets reads characters from the input stream until one of three events occurs:

1. EOF is encountered.
2. A newline is encountered.
3. HowMany -1 characters are seen, before event 1 or 2 occurs.

After the characters are read, a null terminator is appended. A newline is stored only if it was encountered. `Str` is returned on success; if no characters were read because of an EOF or any other error, a NULL pointer is returned.

12.3.6   `feof`

The `feof` function can be used to see if the end-of-file condition **has been detected**. The prototype is

```
int feof( FILE *Stream );
```

 A typical use would be double-checking the cause of a NULL return value from `fgets`. A common misconception is that `feof` can be used to see if the end of file is about to occur. `feof` does not return true until after a read has failed.

12.3.7   `fprintf` **and** `fscanf`

The general formatting capabilities of `printf` and `scanf` are also available for files. The prototypes are

```
int fscanf ( FILE *Stream, const char *Format, ... );
int fprintf( FILE *Stream, const char *Format, ... );
```

The ellipses (...) indicate a variable number of arguments. Because the number of arguments is unknown, `Stream` is the first parameter to both `fscanf` and `fprintf`. This is in contrast to most of the other input and output routines.

 `fscanf` and `fprintf` have the same properties as those of the corresponding terminal I/O routines. A common error, which you are sure to make and which some compilers do not detect, is forgetting the stream. If the program compiles, the `Format` pointer will be used instead of the `Stream` pointer, and almost certainly result in a run-time crash.

12.3.8   `fflush`

Because output is an expensive operation, the routines that have been discussed perform *buffering*: writes are actually performed only when there is enough output to make it worthwhile. For data files, this generally means that the output is written in fixed-size blocks, such as 1024 bytes. The routine

```
int fflush( FILE *Stream );
```

forces a write-through. An example where this is important is a long-running program that writes only a small amount of data every hour. Since we want a record of the output as it becomes available (in case we need to restart the program due to a crash), we can place a `fflush` command after each output command.

12.4   `stdin`, `stdout`, **and** `stderr`

Our discussion has implied that file I/O is implemented in a manner similar to terminal I/O. This is somewhat misleading, because terminal I/O is actually implemented as a special case of file I/O. Specifically, when a program is invoked, three files are opened automatically and allocated the streams `stdin`, `stdout`, and `stderr`. These streams represent standard input, standard output, and standard error. Generally, these are all attached to the terminal, meaning that input, output, and error messages go to the terminal. Because they are usually implemented as `#define` statements, they cannot be used as an lvalue (i.e., in the left-hand side of an assignment operator). However, their meaning can be altered, either directly by the program (as we will see below) or indirectly (using the redirection facilities of a shell).

The routine `getchar(Ch)`, for example, is actually implemented by the call

```
getc( Ch, stdin );
```

Thus all the routines, such as `printf` and `scanf`, are just special cases of corresponding file routines, such as `fprintf` and `fscanf`. Notice, however, that while special routines exist to read and write from `stdin` and `stdout`, `stderr` is unique. Good programming practice dictates that all error messages be written to `stderr`, via `fprintf`. The reason is that if output is redirected, the error messages will still go to the screen.

Moreover, sometimes it is desirable to send all the error messages to a file rather than the screen. The function `freopen` can be used for this:

```
FILE *freopen( const char *FileName, const char *Mode, FILE *Stream );
```

`freopen` closes `Stream` and then opens `FileName`, assigning the result to `Stream`. A `NULL` pointer is returned if the new open fails. (Errors associated with closing the original file are ignored.) Thus

```
freopen( "error.log", "w", stderr );
```

will send error messages to `error.log` instead of the terminal, provided that all error messages are written to `stderr`.

Notice that `stdout` and `stderr` are different streams, so that if both are writing to the terminal (or the same file), they may be intermixed in an unpredictable way, depending on how the buffering is done. Another interesting item is that when the system determines that output is being sent to a terminal, buffering is done line by line rather than in blocks. Thus you may occasionally want to call `fflush(stdout)` to get output as it becomes available, especially if output lines are slow to fill.

 A common parsing technique is to call `fgets` on the `stdin` stream to read one line of input and then call `sscanf`. As an example, suppose that we want to read a line of input containing *exactly* three integers, separated by any amount of white space. We read one line via `fgets`, placing the result in `Str`. The expression

```
sscanf( Str, "%d%*[ \t]%d%*[ \t]%d%*[\n]", &A, &B, &C )
```

is then used. The control string requires that either blanks or tabs (in any amount) separate the three integers, and further, that a newline immediately follows the last integer. Thus a format error would be detected if `sscanf` did not return 3.

12.5   Binary Files

Although formatted input and output is nice, it is not always space efficient. For instance, writing out a 16-bit integer could require six characters (including the sign) when clearly two bytes will do. The binary file, therefore, is a sequence of characters, which need not be printable. Although UNIX systems do not distinguish between printable and non-

```
/* 1*/    struct utmp {
/* 2*/         char ut_line[ 8 ];   /* Tty Name */
/* 3*/         char ut_name[ 8 ];   /* User Id */
/* 4*/         char ut_host[ 16 ];  /* Host Name, if Remote */
/* 5*/         long ut_time;        /* Time On */
/* 6*/    };
```

Figure 12.14: UNIX (SVR2) `utmp` **structure in <utmp.h>.**

printable characters, most other systems do. If you intend to read or write a file that has nonprintable characters, you ought to be using binary mode.

Binary files can still be read and written via `fgetc` and `fputc`. However, the interpretation of a file as a sequence of characters allows unformatted block reads and writes and can thus be much faster than corresponding formatted writes, even if all the characters are printable. Additionally, the file is directly indexable: we can move to the *i*th character of a disk file in constant time, just as if it were a huge array.

12.5.1 `fread` and `fwrite`

The routines `fread` and `fwrite` are used to read and write chunks of binary data. The prototypes are

```
size_t fread ( void *Ptr, size_t ItemSz,
                    size_t NumItem, FILE *Stream );
size_t fwrite( const void *Ptr, size_t ItemSz,
                    size_t NumItem, FILE *Stream );
```

`fread` reads up to `NumItems`, each of size `ItemSz`, from `Stream`, placing the result at the address given by `Ptr`. It returns the number of items actually read; an error or premature end of file is indicated by a short count for the return value. `fwrite` is equivalent to `fread`, except that it performs output instead of input. The format of the data written by `fwrite` is machine (and perhaps even compiler) dependent, and thus binary files cannot safely be moved across systems.

12.5.2 Reading and Writing Login Information

As an example, we show how to read information from an accounting file that is typically present on UNIX. The only advantage of using UNIX in this example is that the structure declaration and data file are already present. You should be able to find or create a similar example on your system if you are not using UNIX. The accounting file on our system is named `/var/adm/wtmp` and consists of a sequence of `struct utmp` entries. This basic structure is shown in Figure 12.14 and is defined in the header `<utmp.h>`.

When a user logs on, an entry is added to the end of the accounting file. When a logoff occurs, another entry (with a blank name) is added; the accounting file also records reboots and crashes, and thus enough information is present to determine elapsed login time, although we will not attempt to do that much. Figure 12.15 shows a procedure that lists all the logins for a particular user.

At line 14 we open the accounting file as a binary file. Note that since this program works only on UNIX, and on a UNIX system there is no distinction between text and binary files, the mode `"r"` would have done just as well. But, of course, our purpose is to illustrate

```
/* 1*/    #include <stdio.h>
/* 2*/    #include <utmp.h>
/* 3*/    #include <time.h>

/* 4*/    static const char *Wtmp = "/var/adm/wtmp";
/* 5*/    static const UtmpSize = sizeof( struct utmp );

/* 6*/    #define NameLen       8
/* 7*/    #define LineLen       8

/* 8*/    int
/* 9*/    Logins( const char *SearchName )
/*10*/    {
/*11*/        int HowMany = 0;
/*12*/        struct utmp UtEntry;
/*13*/        FILE *Ufp;

/*14*/        if( ( Ufp = fopen( Wtmp, "rb" ) ) == NULL )
/*15*/        {
/*16*/            fprintf( stderr, "Can not open %s\n", Wtmp );
/*17*/            return -1;
/*18*/        }

/*19*/        while( fread( &UtEntry, UtmpSize, 1, Ufp ) == 1 )
/*20*/        {
/*21*/            char Name[ NameLen + 1] = "",
                      Line[ LineLen + 1] = "";

/*22*/            if( !strncmp( UtEntry.ut_name, SearchName, NameLen ) )
/*23*/            {
/*24*/                strncpy( Name, UtEntry.ut_name, NameLen );
/*25*/                strncpy( Line, UtEntry.ut_line, LineLen );
/*26*/                printf( "%-*s %-*s %26s", NameLen, Name, LineLen,
/*27*/                        Line, ctime( &UtEntry.ut_time ) );
/*28*/                HowMany++;
/*29*/            }
/*30*/        }

/*31*/        fclose( Ufp );
/*32*/        return HowMany;
/*33*/    }
```

Figure 12.15:   List logons for a given user.

binary files, so we have included the binary mode to make this explicit. The loop that begins at line 19 repeatedly reads one accounting structure. If we find a match, we print out the relevant information and increase our count of the number of logins.

    An important detail is that because the accounting file is not formatted, the concept of a null-terminated string is also no longer in effect. Therefore, eight-character names do not have the null terminator (although shorter ones do). We cannot just print UtEntry.ut_name, because when it is eight characters (e.g., operator), the lack of a null terminator will have `printf` include the `ut_line` field also (even if a field width is present). We use symbolic constants `NameLen` and `LineLen` to replace 8 and copy the name and line into a 9 byte array that can be null-terminated and printed. In this example we use the `*` option to specify a run-time field width.

Once again, some systems have lower-level routines named `read` and `write`. Be careful not to forget the `f`. This is also true of `fseek`, which is discussed below.

12.5.3 `fseek`, `ftell`, **and** `rewind`

Indexing in binary files is achieved with the `fseek` command. The prototype is

```
#define SEEK_SET 0
#define SEEK_CUR 1
#define SEEK_END 2

int fseek( FILE *Stream, long int Offset, int Whence );
```
As a result of `fseek`, the current position in the file is changed to either:

1. `Offset` characters from the beginning of the file, if `Whence` is SEEK_SET.
2. `Offset` characters from the current position in the file, if `Whence` is SEEK_CUR.
3. `Offset` characters from the end of the file, if `Whence` is SEEK_END.[8]

`fseek` also clears out any characters saved as a result of `ungetc`, and clears the end-of-file indicator. Notice that `Offset` may be negative.

As an example, the routine in Figure 12.16 prints the last `HowMany` characters in the (binary) file `FileName`. After opening the file for reading and allocating sufficient memory, we arrive at line 21. The first `fseek` takes us to the end, so the `ftell` tells us how large the file is (see below). A second `fseek` backs us up to `HowMany` bytes before the end of the file (or to the start if the file is short). We then read those bytes at line 27, and write the result out to the standard output at line 28. The rest of the routine cleans up.

The routine `rewind` sets the current position to the beginning of a stream by the call

```
fseek( Stream, 0L, SEEK_SET );
```
Generally, it is an error to attempt to `fseek` to before the beginning of a file. On some systems, notably UNIX, an `fseek` past the end of the file is supported by extending the file with undefined contents. This can create files with holes, which takes up much less space than their size would indicate. Many *core* files, for example, exhibit this property. Check your local manual pages for details on how your system handles these extreme cases.

`fseek` returns zero for success and nonzero for failure. An `fseek` can be applied to text files if `Offset` is equal to `0L` or if the `fseek` is to an offset in the file visited previously. The routine `ftell` returns the current offset; if this value is saved, it can be used for a subsequent `fseek`, even for text files. The prototype for `ftell` is

```
long int ftell( FILE *Stream );
```
`ftell` returns `-1L` on an error. This happens, for instance, if `Stream` is attached to a terminal. For files open for both input and output, there must be an `fseek`, `fsetpos`,

---

[8]ANSI C does not require "meaningful support" when `whence` is SEEK_END. Most libraries, however, do provide a good implementation.

```
/* 1*/    #include <stdio.h>
/* 2*/    #include <stdlib.h>

/* 3*/    /* Print Last HowMany Characters in FileName */

/* 4*/    void
/* 5*/    LastChars( const char *FileName, unsigned int HowMany )
/* 6*/    {
/* 7*/        FILE *Fp;
/* 8*/        char *Buffer;
/* 9*/        int CharsRead;
/*10*/        int FileSize;

/*11*/        if( ( Buffer = malloc( HowMany ) ) == NULL )
/*12*/        {
/*13*/            fprintf( stderr, "Out of space!!\n" );
/*14*/            return;
/*15*/        }

/*16*/        if( ( Fp = fopen( FileName, "rb" ) ) == NULL )
/*17*/            fprintf( stderr, "Can not open %s\n", FileName );
/*18*/        else
/*19*/        {
/*20*/                /* Get The Size Of The File */
/*21*/            fseek( Fp, 0, SEEK_END );
/*22*/            FileSize = ftell( Fp );
/*23*/            if( FileSize < HowMany )
/*24*/                HowMany = FileSize;

/*25*/                /* Copy Its End */
/*26*/            fseek( Fp, - HowMany, SEEK_END );
/*27*/            CharsRead = fread( Buffer, 1, HowMany, Fp );
/*28*/            fwrite( Buffer, 1, CharsRead, stdout );
/*29*/            fclose( Fp );
/*30*/        }

/*31*/        free( Buffer );
/*32*/    }
```

Figure 12.16:   Direct indexing in binary files.

or `rewind` separating an input and output command, (unless the input encounters an EOF) or the output function will fail. Between an output and an input command, a `fflush` can also (and should also) be used as a separator.

12.5.4 Example: The *last* Command

As a more complex example of direct indexing, we modify the program in Figure 12.15. Recall that new accounting records are placed at the end of the accounting file. Consequently, a sequential search of the accounting file produces the most recent login last. More typically, we would want to go back in time, listing recent logins first and distant logins last.

One way to do this is to use a stack, but this requires that the entire file be read before any information is produced. It is better to list the most recent logins immediately, because we might expect the user to terminate the program early, once enough information has been output. Moreover, if we want to extend the program to output all logins, we might not have enough memory to store the accounting file in the stack.

Figure 12.17 shows how direct indexing is used to search the accounting file. At line 19 we `fseek` to the last accounting structure, which naturally is located at one structure before the end. Lines 20 to 30 are unchanged from the corresponding code in Figure 12.15. At line 32 we back up to the previous structure. As a result of reading the current structure, we have advanced the current position by the size of an accounting structure. Thus we have to back up two accounting structures to read the previous one. If the `fseek` fails, something has gone wrong or, more likely, we have backed up to before the start of the file. In either case, we stop.

12.5.5 `fgetpos` **and** `fsetpos`

The `fseek` and `ftell` routines generally work well, but there is one limitation: because on most machines `Offset` is stored as a 32-bit integer, files larger than two gigabytes might not be representable. The routines `fgetpos` and `fsetpos` can be used to handle extraordinarily large files. The prototypes are

```
int fgetpos( FILE *Stream, fpos_t *Position );
int fsetpos( FILE *Stream, const fpos_t *Position );
```

12.6   `remove` **and** `rename`

In addition to the routines provided to support the relatively low-level file abstract data type, ANSI C specifies that two routines be provided to deal with files at a higher level. The prototypes for these two routines are

```
int remove( const char *Name );
int rename( const char *OldName, const char *NewName );
```

`remove` removes the file named `Name` (much like the UNIX command *rm* or the MS/DOS command *del*). If `Name` does not exist, you do not have permission to remove `Name`, or some other error occurs, a nonzero value is returned; otherwise, a zero is returned. If `Name` is already opened, behavior is implementation dependent.

`rename` changes the name of an already existing file `OldName` to `NewName`. The intent is to provide a mechanism by which a file's name can change, without a copy. Thus, even if `OldName` exists and `NewName` does not, the rename could fail, if, for instance, the two names imply different disks. In any event, `rename` returns zero on success and nonzero otherwise. If `NewName` exists, the result is implementation dependent (but likely to be an error).

12.7   Command Line Arguments

When we run a program such as *wc*, which is the UNIX program to count characters, lines, and words in a file, we can invoke it with arguments. For instance, the command

wc -w junk.c

```
/* 1*/    #include <stdio.h>
/* 2*/    #include <utmp.h>
/* 3*/    #include <time.h>

/* 4*/    static const char *Wtmp = "/var/adm/wtmp";
/* 5*/    static const UtmpSize = sizeof( struct utmp );

/* 6*/    #define NameLen        8
/* 7*/    #define LineLen        8

/* 8*/    int
/* 9*/    Logins( const char *SearchName )
/*10*/    {
/*11*/        int HowMany = 0;
/*12*/        struct utmp UtEntry;
/*13*/        FILE *Ufp;

/*14*/        if( ( Ufp = fopen( Wtmp, "rb" ) ) == NULL )
/*15*/        {
/*16*/            fprintf( stderr, "Can not open %s\n", Wtmp );
/*17*/            return -1;
/*18*/        }

/*19*/        fseek( Ufp, -UtmpSize, SEEK_END );
/*20*/        while( fread( &UtEntry, UtmpSize, 1, Ufp ) == 1 )
/*21*/        {
/*22*/            char Name[ NameLen +1] = "",
                      Line[ LineLen +1] = "";

/*23*/            if( !strncmp( UtEntry.ut_name, SearchName, NameLen ) )
/*24*/            {
/*25*/                strncpy( Name, UtEntry.ut_name, NameLen );
/*26*/                strncpy( Line, UtEntry.ut_line, LineLen );
/*27*/                printf( "%-*s %-*s %26s", NameLen, Name, LineLen,
/*28*/                            Line, ctime( &UtEntry.ut_time ) );
/*29*/                HowMany++;
/*30*/            }
/*31*/            /* Back Up Past Current Structure */
/*32*/            if( fseek( Ufp, -UtmpSize * 2, SEEK_CUR ) == -1 )
/*33*/                break;
/*34*/        }

/*35*/        fclose( Ufp );
/*36*/        return HowMany;
/*37*/    }
```

Figure 12.17:   Searching the accounting file from most recent entry.

prints the number of words in the file *junk.c*. This command consists of three arguments: the strings "wc", "-w", and "junk.c". These are known as the *command-line arguments*. ANSI C specifies that they can be made available through two parameters to main. These are a variable of type int and an array of strings. The conventional names for these parameters are `argc` and `argv`, so the prototype below shows a `main` that is prepared to handle command-line arguments.

```
main( int argc, char *argv[ ] )
```

In our example, `argc` would equal 3, `argv[0]` would be `"wc"`, `argv[1]` would be `"-w"`, and `argv[2]` would be `"junk.c"`. `argc` is meant to stand for *argument count*, while `argv` is meant to stand for *argument vector*.

Clearly, it is the type of the parameters, not their names, that is important. Sometimes the shorter names `c` and `v` are used. Note that not all systems support this implementation of command-line arguments; our VAX/VMS compiler does not.

12.7.1   Example: Implementing *wc*

To see how command line arguments are used, we write an almost complete implementation of the UNIX routine *wc*. As we have mentioned, *wc* prints a count of the number of characters, lines, and words in each file on the command line. (It also prints a total if there is more than one file, but we will not do that part of the program.) If the first parameter begins with a -, it is taken to be an option. In that case, only some subset of characters, lines, and words is printed. For instance, *-wl* specifies that words and lines are printed. If no input files are specified, the standard input is used. This is a standard practice in UNIX and MS/DOS, and allows pipes and I/O redirection.

Figure 12.18 illustrates the `main` routine for *wc*. At lines 3 to 5, we keep three global variables corresponding to whether or not character, line, and word counts are to be printed. By default, all three are. Line 8 skips over the command name, by lowering the argument count and incrementing the `argv` pointer. We traverse `argv` using pointer addition exclusively, even though we could also index it as an array. The reason is that pointer traversal is used more commonly, and thus it is important to become accustomed to the idiom.

At line 9 we check to see if an option is present. Since at this point `*argv` is the string representing the first argument, `**argv` is the zeroth character of that string. An alternative would be `(*argv)[0]`; the parentheses are necessary because postfix operators have higher precedence than prefix operators (although because the index is 0, both forms would access the same character!). If we see that an option is present, we call `SetOptions` at line 11 and then skip over the option via line 12.

If no files names are present, line 16 uses the standard input. Otherwise, a `do while` loop repeatedly processes each file name in turn. At line 20 we open the file represented by the current argument, and if successful, we process it at line 25 and then close it at line 26. `Wc` has printed whatever counts it has to, and at line 27 we print the file name. At line 30 we advance `argv` to the next argument, and at line 31 we decrement `argc` and continue the `do while` loop if there are more files to be processed.

The rest of the program has nothing to do with command line arguments and is just an exercise in string processing and file manipulation. `SetOptions`, shown in Figure 12.19, sets all the options to false, and then scans through the `Option` string which has been passed by `main`. The prefix operator at line 5 skips the leading `'-'`; the loop ends when a null terminator is encountered.

The `Wc` routine counts characters, lines, and words in a stream given by `Ifp` (Figure 12.20). The only tricky part is counting words. The variable `InWord` is either 1 or 0,

```
/* 1*/      #include <stdio.h>
/* 2*/      #include <ctype.h>

/* 3*/      int Cflag = 1;          /* Print Character Counts */
/* 4*/      int Lflag = 1;          /* Print Line Counts */
/* 5*/      int Wflag = 1;          /* Print Word Counts */

/* 6*/      main( int argc, char *argv[ ] )
/* 7*/      {
/* 8*/          argv++; argc--; /* Skip Command Name */

/* 9*/          if( argc > 0 && **argv == '-' )
/*10*/          {
/*11*/              SetOptions( *argv );
/*12*/              argv++; argc--;
/*13*/          }

/*14*/              /* If No Files, Use Standard Input */
/*15*/          if( argc == 0 )
/*16*/              Wc( stdin );
/*17*/          else
/*18*/          do
/*19*/          {
/*20*/              FILE *Ifp = fopen( *argv, "r" );

/*21*/              if( Ifp == NULL )
/*22*/                  fprintf( stderr, "Can not open %s\n", *argv );
/*23*/              else
/*24*/              {
/*25*/                  Wc( Ifp );
/*26*/                  fclose( Ifp );
/*27*/                  printf( " %s", *argv );
/*28*/              }
/*29*/              printf( "\n" );
/*30*/              argv++;
/*31*/          } while( --argc > 0 );

/*32*/          return 0;
/*33*/      }
```

Figure 12.18: main routine for *wc*.

depending on whether or not we are currently in the midst of processing a word. If we see non-white space and are not already in a word, then we have encountered a new word. This is handled in lines 12 to 17. Notice that in our implementation, the options control only what gets printed: we still count everything even if we do not use some of these counts. This is simpler and actually more efficient then testing the various flags in the middle of the routine.

```
/* 1*/   void
/* 2*/   SetOptions( const char *Option )
/* 3*/   {
/* 4*/        Lflag = Wflag = Cflag = 0;

/* 5*/        while( *++Option )
/* 6*/            switch( *Option )
/* 7*/            {
/* 8*/              case 'l':
/* 9*/                Lflag++; break;
/*10*/              case 'w':
/*11*/                Wflag++; break;
/*12*/              case 'c':
/*13*/                Cflag++; break;
/*14*/              default:
/*15*/                fprintf( stderr, "Bad option %c\n", *Option );
/*16*/            }
/*17*/   }
```

Figure 12.19:   Parse options for *wc*.

```
/* 1*/   void
/* 2*/   Wc( FILE *Ifp )
/* 3*/   {
/* 4*/        int Ch, InWord = 0, Words = 0, Lines = 0, Chars = 0;

/* 5*/        while( ( Ch = getc( Ifp ) ) != EOF )
/* 6*/        {
/* 7*/            Chars++;
/* 8*/            if( Ch == '\n' )
/* 9*/                Lines++;
/*10*/            if( isspace( Ch ) )
/*11*/                InWord = 0;
/*12*/            else if( !InWord )
/*13*/            {
/*14*/                /* New Word Seen */
/*15*/                InWord = 1;
/*16*/                Words++;
/*17*/            }
/*18*/        }

/*19*/        if( Lflag ) printf( "%8d", Lines );
/*20*/        if( Wflag ) printf( "%8d", Words );
/*21*/        if( Cflag ) printf( "%8d", Chars );
/*22*/   }
```

Figure 12.20:   Actual counting code for *wc*.

```
/* 1*/    #include <stdio.h>
/* 2*/    #include <stdlib.h>

/* 3*/    main( int argc, char *argv[ ], char *envp[ ] )
/* 4*/    {
/* 5*/        int i;

/* 6*/        for( i = 0; envp[ i ] != NULL; i++ )
/* 7*/            printf( "%s\n", envp[ i ] );

/* 8*/        printf( "TERMINAL TYPE IS: %s\n", getenv( "TERM" ) );

/* 9*/        return 0;
/*10*/    }
```

Figure 12.21:   Sample use of environment variables.

12.7.2   Environment Variables

In addition to command line arguments, some systems invoke C programs with *environment variables*. An environment variable can be used to indicate, for instance, the type of terminal that is currently being used. Environment variables are stored as a list of entries in the form name=value. The variable name is typically upper case. The getenv routine is provided by ANSI C to interface with environment variables. Its prototype is

```
char *getenv( const char *Name );
```

A pointer to the corresponding value in the environment list, or NULL, is returned. You should not attempt to use that pointer to change value because you may corrupt other environment variables.

Some systems provide the environment list as a third parameter to main. Like argv, the environment list is represented as a char *envp[ ]. The end of the environment list is marked with a NULL pointer. Figure 12.21 shows how environment variables are accessed. Lines 6 and 7 print out all of the environment variables. Line 8 uses getenv to get the value corresponding to the environment variable TERM. Note that getenv works even if envp is not declared as a third parameter to main. Also, some systems have the global variable environ, which is an equivalent representation of envp.

12.8   Summary

In this chapter we have examined the basic I/O routines scanf and printf. Similar routines named fscanf and fprintf are used for files. The scanf and printf *family* of routines, as we have seen, are feature-laden mechanisms. Also useful, but underused, are the routines sscanf and sprintf, which are discussed in Chapter 8. In this chapter we have also seen the interface that ANSI C provides for files. Although some of the details are system dependent, many but not all of the system dependencies are taken care of by the actual implementation. Below we list the important points, and also the pitfalls.

12.8.1   What Was Covered

- printf and scanf both work by examining the first parameter, which is known as the control string. Except in their most simple use the control strings perform different actions for printf and scanf.

- The % signals the beginning of a field. For both printf and scanf, the conversions %d, %i, %u, %o, and %x stand for decimal integer, decimal integer, unsigned decimal integer, unsigned octal integer, and unsigned hexadecimal integer. %X is also available.

- For printf, a minimum field length can be specified; for scanf, the specification represents a maximum field length.

- A run-time field width and/or minimum precision can be specified by using a * and supplying an additional parameter.

- To left-justify an output field, use -. Otherwise, it is right justified. To specify a leading +, use a +; otherwise, no sign is used for positive numbers. If you prefer a space, you can specify that, too.

- The # in the printf conversion specifies a special format for a field. For octal or hexadecimal, this means that a leading 0 or 0x is output; for floating-point numbers, it means that the decimal point is output even if nothing follows it.

- A . in a printf conversion specifier sets the precision. Most commonly this is used to determine the number of places after the decimal point in a floating-point number. For floating-point numbers, the default is six.

- In printf and scanf, use %% when you mean to use the % in a nonconversion context.

- printf and scanf return EOF when the end of output/input is reached. Otherwise, printf returns the number of characters output while scanf returns the number of parameters matched. You can see intermediate values of this quantity by using the %n conversion, but it is really a bad idea.

- For input, the scanning terminates on the first mismatch.

- White space encountered in the control string is output as it is when using printf. For scanf, however, any consecutive white space means that if there is any (not necessarily the same) amount of consecutive white space, including newlines, it is skipped.

- scanf allows matching to fixed characters. This can be used to require a rigid input format.

- By using the %[conversion, scanf can match strings with restricted alphabets.

- The * represents assignment suppression for scanf. The matched field is digested but not saved.

- Files are implemented as an abstract data type. The basic structure used to store this abstract data type is the *stream*, which is of type FILE. This structure, and the functions that can be applied to it are defined in the standard header file <stdio.h>.

- Prior to accessing a file, a stream must be assigned for it. This is done with fopen. When a file is no longer needed, the stream is freed by fclose.

- Files are closed automatically at program termination. However, since there is a limit on the number of files open simultaneously, it is a good idea to issue an fclose when a stream is no longer needed.

- `<stdio.h>` defines and opens three streams, `stdin`, `stdout`, and `stderr`, for normal input, output, and error messages.

- Parsing of complex input can be achieved by a combination of `fgets` and `sscanf`.

- Text files consists of printable characters. `getc`, `ungetc`, and `putc` can be used for single-character I/O. `fgets` and `fputs` can be used for string I/O. `fprintf` and `fscanf` can be used for elaborate formatted I/O.

- Binary files can contain nonprintable characters. `fread` and `fwrite` can be used for block I/O. `fseek`, `ftell`, and `rewind` can be used to access characters directly in a binary file, as if the file were an array of characters.

- Command-line arguments are accessible by the `argc` and `argv` parameters to `main`. Environment variables are accessible by the `getenv` function.

12.8.2   Friendly Reminders

- `scanf` requires the address of a variable, not the variable. Failure to use `&` for basic objects is the most common mistake when using `scanf`. Because `register` variables have no addresses, they cannot be the direct target of `scanf`.

- Always use `%h`, `%l`, and `%L` when appropriate. Otherwise, you may get errors. Be especially careful with `%lf`, which is needed to read in a `double`. `long double` requires `%Lf`, not just `%lf`.

- `%s` does not stand for short, but for a string. `%c` is used for characters.

- Octal and hexadecimal numbers are always unsigned on output.

- The combination of many `printf` features may not be handled correctly by your compiler.

- Incorrect specifiers such as `%2D` are treated as ordinary characters (after the `%` is ignored).

- Neither `printf` nor `scanf` will perform a type conversion. If the parameter type does not agree with the conversion specifier, you will get a bogus answer or a crash.

- When processing errors, you must make sure that some input is digested by `scanf` before reattempting a read. Otherwise, you will get an infinite loop.

- Most `scanf` conversions skip leading white space. The exceptions are `%c` and `%[`.

- The scan set range feature is not guaranteed in ANSI C.

- The most logical use of `%n` is illegal. It is better to avoid it.

- The mode for `fopen` is a string, not a character. Do not use `'r'`, for instance.

- Many of the file routines from `<stdio.h>` have similar, lower-level counterparts on some systems. Specifically, do not use `open`, `close`, `read`, `write`, or `seek`.

- Of course, do not mix `fprintf` and `printf` accidentally. Also, when using these file routines, it is easy to forget the stream as a parameter. Some compilers will not catch this.

- `feof` is not true until an attempted input operation has reached the end of file.

- Binary files are not portable across systems. Thus you cannot `fwrite` to a file, copy it to another system, and then expect `fread` to work.

- Boundary conditions for fseek such as seeking past the bounds of the file are handled in an implementation-specific manner.

EXERCISES

1. Write a program that computes the multiplication table for the first 15 numbers. Make it as pretty as possible and ensure that everything lines up correctly.

2. Write a statement, or statements, that scan for input lines containing exactly the following format:

   (a) Three integers, each separated by exactly one blank

   (b) Three integers, each separated by exactly one blank or tab

   (c) Three integers, each separated by exactly either eight blanks or one tab

   (d) Three integers representing X, Y, and Z. The format is

   ```
   X = int    Y = int    Z = int
   ```

   The variables may appear in any order but should only appear once. There should be exactly three per line. There may be space between any of the names, integers, and the =.

   (e) An integer followed by any of + - * / followed by an integer.

3. Repeat Exercise 2 for doubles.

4. Using only assignment suppression, write a program that counts:

   (a) The number of characters that are typed until an end-of-file marker

   (b) The number of lines that are typed until an end-of-file marker

   (c) Both the number of characters and lines that are typed until an end-of-file marker

5. For each of the modes "r", "w", "a", "r+", "w+", "a+", which of the following is true?

   (a) The file must already exist.

   (b) The file is truncated.

   (c) Reads are permitted.

   (d) Writes are permitted.

   (e) Writes are permitted only at the end of the stream.

6. Improve rename to copy and remove if the source and target files are on different file systems.

7. ungetc guarantees only one character of pushback. Write the routines NewFputc, NewFgetc, and NewUngetc, which provide unlimited pushback. *Hint: Routines in Chapter 10 make this trivial.*

8. What does fclose(stdin) do?

9. If the last line written to a text file does not terminate with a newline, your system is free to add a newline or not to write the partial last line. It may also complain when you read the file subsequently. What happens on your system?

10. On some systems, trailing blanks on a line are removed. Does this happen on your system?

11. ANSI C requires that text lines not exceeding 509 characters must be represented. What happens to longer lines on your system?

12. Some systems delete empty files. On your system, what happens if you issue an `fopen`, with mode `"w"`, followed immediately by an `fclose`?

13. Write a routine that provides complete login and logout information for a given user.

14. Modify the copy routine to prompt the user for confirmation if the destination file already exists.

15. Implement the copy routine by using `fread` and `fwrite` instead of character-by-character I/O. Does the choice of block size affect the speed of your program?

16. On UNIX the *tail* command is used to print out the end of a file. One form is

     tail -num file1 file2 ...

     which prints out the last num lines of each file. If no option is present, the default is 10 lines. If no files are present, the standard input is used.

     (a) Implement the *tail* command under the assumption that at most 4096 bytes need be output. Note to UNIX users: Check the return of `fseek` because they are illegal on pipes.

     (b) Implement the *tail* command without the previous assumption. *Hint: If a block of 4096 bytes does not produce the required number of newline characters, push the block onto a stack and read another block. Keep doing this as necessary.*

17. Experiment with `fseek`s past the end of the file. Can you `fseek` to `10000000L`? What does your directory listing program report for the file size? Can you tell how much space is really being used?

18. Let *M* be the maximum number of integers that can be sorted in main memory on your system. Write a routine that reads 10*M* integers from a binary file and sorts them. You will need to create temporary files and extend the merging idea shown in Chapter 10 to files.

19. Write a program that processes include statements. Since an included file may itself contain include statements, the basic inclusion function is recursive.

20. Write a program to reverse files specified as command-line arguments. Note that the files may be too large to fit in memory.

21. Write a program that maintains a database file. Each entry stores a structure consisting of a name, address, and phone number. The program should allow updates of the database and queries by name or phone number.

22. A file contains colon-separated fields. Write a program that sorts the file by any field requested by the user. Fields consisting only of digits should be sorted numerically, not lexicographically.

23. Write a *spelling checker*. To check a file's spelling, read a list of correctly spelled words (i.e. a *dictionary*) into a hash table and check each word in the input file. Note that the standard UNIX dictionary */usr/dict/words* is missing many words. Many systems have a more complete word listing in some directory under the name *web2*.

24. Modify the shortest path program in Section 10.4 to prompt the user for the name of the file that stores the connections database. After reading the file, prompt the user for requests.

25. Once again, assume the existence of an online dictionary. Read characters from the user until some subset of the characters can be arranged to form a nine-letter word (as verified by the dictionary). At that point print out the word formed. Make sure that your program is computationally efficient.

26. Modify the word search puzzle from Exercise 8.35 to search a dictionary, instead of a short word list, for matches. Words must be at least four characters long. Make sure that your program is computationally efficient.

13

UNIX Systems Programming

One of the most important uses of C is that it is the programming language used to implement anything of consequence on the UNIX operating system. In fact, except for a few lines of assembly language, almost all of the UNIX system is written in C, as is the C compiler. In this chapter we examine the use of C under the UNIX operating system. After nearly 20 years and a host of versions, UNIX remains one of the most popular and enduring operating systems ever written. Indeed, one can argue that C's success is a direct result of UNIX's success.

Its initial popularity was in the academic world, where UNIX systems were supplied complete with source code for virtually no charge. The original system ran on relatively inexpensive PDP11 minicomputers. The simplicity of the system, which was necessitated by the PDP11's limited memory, coupled with an easy-to-use shell that supported I/O redirection and pipes, more than made up for the terseness of the command syntax. The ability to add new programs easily and to alter the operating system (both for improved performance and to skirt security) made UNIX a hacker's paradise. In the years since, the UNIX operating system has undergone major changes in several directions, from several sources. The result is that UNIX performs well on the powerful machines of the 1990s, has some very unique bells and whistles (such as job control), and has many of the features that are needed for industrial applications.

One problem with the many improvements is that there are now many different versions of UNIX, which differ in subtle but sometimes very important ways. A detailed and complete description of programming in the UNIX environment, including specific information about the different implementations, can be found in [Stevens 92]. We presume that the user knows the basics of how to use UNIX, including the directory structure and the shell.

Our goal in this chapter is to provide a *general* overview of three facets of UNIX. First, we examine the basics of the UNIX file system. Although the details vary slightly from system to system, the differences are not significant in our discussion. We implement only slightly scaled-down versions of the *pwd* and *du* commands. Next we look at how processes work in UNIX. Specifically, we cover process creation and replication, pipes, and signals. A minimal shell that includes pipes and redirection will be written. Finally, we look at programs that help us use C, such as the profiler, archiver, and *make*. These programs are also more or less standard across different UNIX systems.

Throughout this chapter we see special functions known as *system calls*. These functions are used just like any other library routine, but are special because they provide a direct interface with the operating system. An important consequence is that system calls are expensive. Thus repeated calls to the operating system's I/O routines for single-character processing will be very time consuming. A second important consequence is that system calls are *atomic operations*: it is guaranteed that once the operating system agrees to begin processing a system call, it will not schedule any other intervening jobs before the system call returns.

13.1   The UNIX File System

We have already seen how to read, write, and create files using the standard library routines. In this section we first examine how to obtain information *about* a file. For instance, how does the *ls* routine know when a file was last accessed or modified, and how are the access privileges for a file determined?

One of the unique ideas in UNIX is that the concept of a file extends to include peripheral devices (such as printers) and directories. Consequently, the terminal is a file, and thus if we find out when it was last accessed, we can determine how long it has been idle. Under UNIX, this becomes a simple exercise once we know the terminal's corresponding file name.

Under UNIX, a directory is just a file that contains only a little more than a listing of the names of the files in the directory. We show how we can use that fact to implement both *pwd* and *du*. Finally, we look at the most basic I/O system calls. These are the routines that are used by `fopen`, for example, to implement the ANSI C file routines.

13.1.1   Getting File Information via `stat` and `lstat`

The UNIX file system records information for every file. Some of that information can be obtain by using the `stat` or `lstat` system call.[1] Both routines fill a variable of type `struct stat`, which is defined in `<sys/stat.h>`. Some of the important members of the structure are shown in Figure 13.1. The structure has other members, and the exact structure varies from system to system. Some systems do not support the `st_blocks` field, for instance.

Before we describe all the fields, we show how `lstat` is used to obtain information. Among other things, the *finger* command prints out the idle time for each user. We can find out who is currently on the system by examining the file */etc/utmp*, which stores data in the format given in `<utmp.h>` (see Section 12.5.2, where this was discussed). The idle time for a user is just the amount of time since the corresponding terminal was used.

As we mentioned above, peripheral devices such as terminals are treated as files by UNIX. A file corresponding to each terminal is located in the directory */dev*, along with files corresponding to other devices, such as printers, modems, disks, and tapes. Reads and

---

[1]The difference between `stat` and `lstat` has to do with how symbolic links are handled. We use `lstat` for our routines.

```
struct stat
{
    dev_t    st_dev;        /* Device number (file system) */
    ino_t    st_ino;        /* Inode number */
    mode_t   st_mode;       /* File type and permissions */
    short    st_nlink;      /* Number of hard links */
    uid_t    st_uid;        /* User ID of owner */
    gid_t    st_gid;        /* Group ID of owner */
    off_t    st_size;       /* Size in bytes */
    time_t   st_atime;      /* Last access time */
    time_t   st_mtime;      /* Last modified time */
    long     st_blocks;     /* Number of 512 byte blocks */
};
```

Figure 13.1:   Some fields in the `stat` **structure.**

writes to devices are treated differently by the operating system than are reads and writes to regular files: the operating system channels the data to and from the corresponding peripheral unit. Terminals are always considered *character devices*: reads and writes to character devices are done differently than to *block devices* such as disks.

The distinction between different types of devices and the method used to perform input and output is important for the system administrators, but for our purposes it is not relevant. Given a terminal such as `"console"`, we know that the corresponding device file will be `"/dev/console"`. If we call `lstat` on `"/dev/console"`, we can determine the last access time, and thus the idle time.

Figure 13.2 gives an implementation of `Idle`. We `#include` six standard headers. `<sys/types.h>` contains typedefs for `dev_t`, `ino_t`, and so on. `<stat.h>` contains the complete declaration of `struct stat`, as well as some macros that we will use. Note carefully that there is no `/` before `sys`. At line 17 we construct the name of the file in the */dev* directory corresponding to `Terminal`. We then call `lstat`, which fills the structure `StatBuf`, passed by reference, with information corresponding to `TerminalName`. `lstat` returns `-1` if something goes wrong: the most likely error is that `TerminalName` does not exist. Note that in some cases we can perform the `lstat` even if we have no permission to perform `fopen`. If the `lstat` fails, we call `perror` at line 19. `perror` will print `TerminalName` and then an error message that describes what may have gone wrong. This is done by examining the global variable `errno` which is always available in the UNIX environment. Many routines will set `errno` when an error occurs, and `perror` thus prints a message corresponding to the last error recorded.

Otherwise, the `lstat` succeeded. We doublecheck that `Terminal` represents a character device at line 21. The `st_mode` field contains information relating to the type of file. Some common possibilities are regular files, directories, symbolic links, character devices, and block devices. Figure 13.3 shows the macros that are available on our system. We will talk about the `st_mode` field in a minute, because it also determines access privileges. If we get to line 25, we are examining a character device. We then get the current time and return the difference using the routine `difftime`. On our system the `time_t` type is just an unsigned integer, so `difftime` is a simple subtraction. Since `time_t` could be a more exotic type, `difftime` is supplied for maximum portability.

We now describe the `stat` structure in more detail. Internally, each file is identified by the file system on which it resides (the `st_dev` field) and its inode number (`st_ino`).

```
/* 1*/    #include <errno.h>
/* 2*/    #include <stdio.h>
/* 3*/    #include <string.h>
/* 4*/    #include <sys/types.h>
/* 5*/    #include <sys/stat.h>
/* 6*/    #include <time.h>

/* 7*/    /* Return Number Of Seconds Terminal Has Been Idle */
/* 8*/    /* -1 Is Returned On Error */

/* 9*/    #define MaxLen 32
/*10*/    #define DevLen  6                    /* strlen( "/dev/" ) + 1 */

/*11*/    int
/*12*/    Idle( const char *Terminal )
/*13*/    {
/*14*/        struct stat StatBuf;
/*15*/        char TerminalName[ MaxLen ] = "/dev/";
/*16*/        time_t Now;

/*17*/        strncat( TerminalName, Terminal, MaxLen - DevLen );
/*18*/        if( lstat( TerminalName, &StatBuf ) < 0 )
/*19*/            perror( TerminalName );
/*20*/        else
/*21*/        if( !S_ISCHR( StatBuf.st_mode ) )
/*22*/            fprintf( stderr, "%s: Not a terminal\n",
                                            TerminalName );
/*23*/        else
/*24*/        {
/*25*/            time( &Now );
/*26*/            return ( int ) difftime( StatBuf.st_atime, Now );
/*27*/        }
/*28*/        return -1;                      /* Error Indicator */
/*29*/    }
```

Figure 13.2:   Print idle time for any terminal.

```
#define   S_ISBLK( M )                /* M is a block device */
#define   S_ISCHR( M )                /* M is a character device */
#define   S_ISDIR( M )                /* M is a directory */
#define   S_ISFIFO( M )               /* M is a pipe */
#define   S_ISREG( M )                /* M is a regular file */
#define   S_ISLNK( M )                /* M is a symbolic link */
#define   S_ISSOCK( M )               /* M is a socket */
```

Figure 13.3:   Macros to test for different types of files.

The st_nlink field indicates the number of names by which the file is known. On our system, for instance, all of the following files, located in the /bin directory, have the same file system and inode number: *chfn*, *chsh*, *ypchfn*, *ypchfn*. They are thus all the same files and are said to be *linked* together. The advantage of linking files is that by not storing four separate copies, space is saved. However, an alteration of *chfn* directly affects *chsh* (which may be good or bad). The `st_nlink` field records the number of links, which here is 4. If one of these files is deleted, the other three remain and the link count goes to 3.

Newer versions of UNIX have introduced another type of link, which is known as a symbolic link. A symbolic link is a file that contains the name of another file; it can be viewed as a pointer. For purposes of distinction, the links discussed in the preceding paragraph are called *hard links*. Symbolic links are useful because they can be made to directories and also between different file systems. Since all entries of a hard link share the `dev_t` field, they clearly must reside on the same file system. Further, hard links to a directory can be made only by privileged users (or specialized programs given such authority) because otherwise, difficult-to-fix inconsistencies (cycles in the directory structure) could be introduced into the file systems. Although cycles can also be introduced by symbolic links, using `lstat` it is easy to avoid following the trail of symbolic links. (`stat` does follow symbolic links, and thus can get stuck in cycles.) For our purposes, only knowledge of the existence of hard links and symbolic links is important.

Except for the `st_mode` field, all of the remaining fields are self-explanatory. The `st_mode` field is a collection of bits that combine to indicate the access privileges and type of file. Figure 13.4 shows the relevant fields (some systems have more). The `st_mode` field fits in 16 bits. The top 4 bits are used to indicate the type of file. A file is a directory if the `st_mode` bitwise anded with `_IFMT` yields `_IFDIR`. Thus the corresponding macro in Figure 13.3 is implemented as

```
#define  S_ISDIR( M )  ( ( ( M ) & _IFMT ) == _IFDIR )
```

The two bits `S_ISUID` and `S_ISGID` are the patented set-user and set-group id bits. When the file that is an executable image (not a shell program) runs, the effective user or group id is changed to match the owner or group of the file, as appropriate. The *passwd* program, for instance, uses this feature. When a user changes their password via *passwd*, the program must make an alteration to the system password file. Thus *passwd* runs as the privileged user *root* when executed. Needless to say, the set-user id bit, while being a great convenience, is also the source of virtually all security holes. On some systems, the feature is enabled only on the file systems containing the basic commands and is disabled on the user file systems.

The protection modes, shown in Figure 13.4, represent read, write, and execute permission for the owner of the file, group members of the file, and all others. Thus there are 9 bits, which are graphically visible as a result of an *ls -l* command. If the 9 bits are (octal) 0750, then assuming access to the directory that contains the file, the owner can read, write, and execute (0400, 0200, 0100), group members can read and execute (040, 010), and all others have no access. For directories, execute means search; thus a protection mode of 0700 allows only the owner access to files inside the directory, regardless of what the protection mode is on those files. In the next section we see what read and write access means for directories.

13.1.2   Directories

In the UNIX operating system, a directory is just a file that contains the names (and inode numbers) of the files in the directory. Unfortunately, the format of the directory file is system dependent. Originally, UNIX stored each entry in 16 bytes. Fourteen bytes

```
              /* Top four bits indicate file type */
#define  _IFMT      0170000           /* type of file */

#define  _IFDIR     0040000           /* directory */
#define  _IFCHR     0020000           /* character special */
#define  _IFBLK     0060000           /* block special */
#define  _IFREG     0100000           /* regular */
#define  _IFLNK     0120000           /* symbolic link */
#define  _IFSOCK    0140000           /* socket */
#define  _IFIFO     0010000           /* fifo */

              /* Set user id and group id bits */
#define  S_ISUID    0004000           /* set user id on execution */
#define  S_ISGID    0002000           /* set group id on execution */

              /* Protection bits */
#define  S_IRWXU    0000700           /* rwx, owner */
#define  S_IRWXG    0000070           /* rwx, group */
#define  S_IRWXO    0000007           /* rwx, other */

#define  S_IRUSR    0000400           /* read permission, owner */
#define  S_IWUSR    0000200           /* write permission, owner */
#define  S_IXUSR    0000100           /* execute/search permission, owner */
#define  S_IRGRP    0000040           /* read permission, group */
#define  S_IWGRP    0000020           /* write permission, group */
#define  S_IXGRP    0000010           /* execute/search permission, group */
#define  S_IROTH    0000004           /* read permission, other */
#define  S_IWOTH    0000002           /* write permission, other */
#define  S_IXOTH    0000001           /* execute/search permission, other */
```

Figure 13.4:   Protection modes.

represented a file name, and two bytes represented the inode number. This implied two limitations: 14 character filenames and 65,536 inodes per file system. This quickly became a problem. First, because disk capacities have increased so rapidly, the inode limitation became troublesome for some sites. Second, although users rarely use filenames longer than 14 characters, programs such as news readers like to generate meaningful, but usually long, filenames. Thus a more complex directory format came into existence to support variable-length filenames. Some systems still support the old-style 14 character filename, and still other systems allow the system administrator to choose which format to use, on a file system-by-file system basis. Because of this, a file system independent interface for directories was developed. It mimics the standard file package. Figure 13.5 shows the four important routines, and the header file which must be included.

The opendir routine opens a directory and returns a variable of type DIR *, much like fopen. We call this variable the *directory stream*. All subsequent access is through the directory stream. closedir and rewinddir mimic their fclose and rewind counterparts. It is especially important to closedir directories when they are no longer needed, as we will see.

The readdir routine provides the next entry in the directory stream, skipping entries that correspond to files deleted already. UNIX performs lazy deletion in this regard: in the

```
#include <dirent.h>

DIR *opendir(const char *dirname );
struct dirent *readdir( DIR *dirp );
int closedir( DIR *dirp );
void rewinddir( DIR *dirp );
```

Figure 13.5:   Routines to scan a directory.

directory, the file is marked deleted by changing its inode number to zero. This is preferable to a complete reorganization of the directory.[2] `readdir` returns NULL when the end of the directory has already been reached.

On any directory, `readdir` is guaranteed to find at least two entries. The first entry is for a file named " . ". The " . " entry is a link to the directory. The second entry is the file named " . . ", which is a link to the parent directory. When a directory is created, these links are guaranteed to be in place. Thus a directory always starts with a link count of 2: itself and its " . " entry. Furthermore, every time a subdirectory is created, its link count increases because the subdirectory's " . . " will link to it.

The " . . " entry is a convenience that allows easy traversal via the *cd* shell command. As we will see, it is also neeeded to implement certain commands. An important use of the " . " entry is to specify a default. When *ls* is called with no arguments, the directory listed is the current directory, namely " . ". We'll give two examples that use the directory routines.

13.1.3   Implementing the *pwd* Command

The UNIX command *pwd* prints the complete path name of the current directory.[3] Because of symbolic links, there are several possible answers. For instance, *pwd* and *echo $cwd* (which works for some shells) generally give different, though equivalent answers. Notice that except for the name, all other information about the current directory is easy to determine since we can perform an `lstat` on the directory " . ". However, the name is never known directly. To determine the complete path name, we have to examine every directory on the path from " / " to " . ".

Suppose that we have a routine

```
void PrintPath( char *DirName );
```

and the current directory is /usr1/nina/c. Thus we want the call

```
PrintPath( "." );
```

to output /usr1/nina/c. We can print this answer out in two steps. First, we can print /usr1/nina, by making a recursive call

```
PrintPath( "./.." );
```

---

[2]Of course, the disk blocks associated with the file are reclaimed by the operating system when an inode is no longer referenced by any directory entry. This is easily done by examining the `st_nlinks` field of the inode entry.

[3]As is typical of many UNIX commands, the meaning of *pwd* is not obvious: It abbreviates *print working directory*.

In general, the parameter of the recursive call will be the result of attaching `"/.."` to the end of `DirName`.

After the recursive call returns, we need only print out the last component of the path name. This is done by searching the parent directory for an entry matching the current directory: Unless the file system is inconsistent, we are guaranteed to find an entry in the parent directory that is a link to the current directory. In our case, for instance, in the directory `"./.."` (which is `/usr1/nina`) we are guaranteed to find an entry for `c` that is a link to `"."`.

Now that we have laid out the basic strategy, we are ready to write the code. The supporting routines are shown in Figure 13.6. First, we have six headers. `<dirent.h>` is needed for the directory searching routines. `<sys/param.h>` defines the constant `MAXPATHLEN`, which is the limit on the length of a path name. `Pwd1` is the basic recursive routine; we use `Pwd` as a driver to eliminate some base cases and print a trailing newline. Notice, by the way, that the strategy to print the full path name is identical to the strategy that was used in Chapter 11 to print the path resulting from a shortest path calculation. In computer science, many of the same ideas reoccur over and over.

We maintain a global variable `Slash` that will hold the result of an `lstat` on the root, `"/"`. The use of a global variable is justifiable here because it is written to only once. The alternative would be passing it to all the routines. Because the routines are recursive, we would have to incur the overhead repeatedly. The `main` routine merely fills `Slash` and calls `Pwd` with `"."` as a parameter.

The `IsMatch` function returns true if two `stat` structures, passed by reference, represent the same file. This is true if both the file systems and inode numbers match. The `Pwd` routine is a simple driver that handles the degenerate cases. We check to see if the current directory is `"/"`, and if so, we can print out a `"/"`. Otherwise, we call the recursive routine `Pwd1`. In either case, we print a trailing newline.

Figure 13.7 shows the routine `Pwd1`. We pass the name of a directory `Dir` and its corresponding `stat` structure. Clearly, `Dot` can be determined from `Dir` by an `lstat`; the only reason we pass it is that an `lstat` has already been done, and we prefer to avoid recomputing information. Lines 8 and 9 handle the base case. If `DirName` is synonymous with `"/"`, we return immediately. Otherwise, lines 10 to 17 do the recursion, which is the easy part. The `Parent` is formed by attaching a `"/.."` to `Dir`, and then we call `lstat` to get `DotDot`.[4]

If all is well, we make the recursive call at line 17. When it returns, all that is left is to print the last component. This is done by using the directory reading routines to search the parent directory for the name of the last component. Line 19 opens the directory using `opendir`, giving the directory stream `ParentDir`. At line 24 we continually read a directory entry. For each entry, at line 26, we form a path name by combining `Parent` and the name given by the current entry; if an `lstat` on this path name shows a match with `Dot`, we have found the name of the last component. We then print it, call `closedir`, and return. Unless the file system is corrupted, we are guaranteed eventually to find a match at line 27. Thus, if we reach line 34, a serious error outside our control has occurred.

---

[4]At lines 11 and 26, we should have tested that `Parent` and `FileName`, respectively, are large enough to store the resulting concatenation. We avoid this test to keep the routine short. Because each recursive call adds only three characters to `Parent`, this is unlikely to cause a problem.

```
/* 1*/    #include <stdio.h>
/* 2*/    #include <sys/types.h>
/* 3*/    #include <sys/stat.h>
/* 4*/    #include <sys/param.h>        /* For MAXPATHLEN */
/* 5*/    #include <dirent.h>
/* 6*/    #include <errno.h>

/* 7*/    struct stat Slash;       /* Stores Info for "/" */


/* 1*/    int
/* 2*/    main( void )
/* 3*/    {
/* 4*/        if( lstat( "/", &Slash ) < 0 )
/* 5*/            perror( "/" );
/* 6*/        else
/* 7*/            Pwd( "." );

/* 8*/        return 0;
/* 9*/    }


/* 1*/    int
/* 2*/    IsMatch( const struct stat *F1, const struct stat *F2 )
/* 3*/    {
/* 4*/        return F1->st_ino == F2->st_ino &&
                                  F1->st_dev == F2->st_dev;
/* 5*/    }


/* 1*/    void
/* 2*/    Pwd( const char *DirName )
/* 3*/    {
/* 4*/        struct stat Dot;

/* 5*/        if( lstat( DirName, &Dot ) < 0 )
/* 6*/            perror( DirName );
/* 7*/        else
/* 8*/        if( IsMatch( &Dot, &Slash ) )
/* 9*/            printf( "/" );
/*10*/        else
/*11*/            Pwd1( ".", &Dot );
/*12*/        printf( "\n" );
/*13*/    }
```

Figure 13.6: main **and supporting code for** *pwd*.

A deficiency of the routine is that we call lstat for every directory entry. Because lstat requires a response from the operating system, it is implemented as a *system call*, not a library routine. System calls are expensive, so it is worthwhile to do some extra work to avoid them. Also, our routines are a bit sloppy when errors (that theoretically should

```
/* 1*/    void
/* 2*/    Pwd1( const char *DirName, const struct stat *Dot )
/* 3*/    {
/* 4*/        struct stat DotDot, Buf;
/* 5*/        char FileName[ MAXPATHLEN ], Parent[ MAXPATHLEN ];
/* 6*/        DIR *ParentDir;
/* 7*/        struct dirent *Slot;

/* 8*/        if( IsMatch( Dot, &Slash ) )              /* Base Case */
/* 9*/            return;                               /* We Are At Slash */

/*10*/        /* First, Recursively Print Up To The Parent */
/*11*/        sprintf( Parent, "%s/..", DirName );
/*12*/        if( lstat( Parent, &DotDot ) < 0 )
/*13*/        {
/*14*/            perror( Parent );
/*15*/            return;
/*16*/        }
/*17*/        Pwd1( Parent, &DotDot );

/*18*/        /* Now, Print Last Component Of The Pathname */
/*19*/        if( ( ParentDir = opendir( Parent ) ) == NULL )
/*20*/        {
/*21*/            perror( Parent );
/*22*/            return;
/*23*/        }

/*24*/        while( ( Slot = readdir( ParentDir ) ) != NULL )
/*25*/        {
/*26*/            sprintf( FileName, "%s/%s", Parent, Slot->d_name );
/*27*/            if( !lstat( FileName, &Buf ) && IsMatch( &Buf, Dot ) )
/*28*/            {
/*29*/                printf( "/%s", Slot->d_name );
/*30*/                closedir( ParentDir );
/*31*/                return;
/*32*/            }
/*33*/        }
/*34*/        printf( "/???" );        /* This Should Never Occur */
/*35*/    }
```

Figure 13.7:   Recursive routine pwd1.

never happen) occur, because we will usually have a partial path printed before an error is detected. Exercise 1 suggests some improvements.

13.1.4   Implementing the *du* Command

The *du* command lists the total number of blocks used by the files in directories that are supplied as command-line arguments. The count includes totals for all subdirectories. The -*a* option lists each file encountered, along with its contribution to the block total. Of course,

```
/* 1*/    /* Simple du Program.  List Disk Usage.  Double */
/* 2*/    /* Counts Hard Links Or It Would Be The Same As du */

/* 3*/    #include <string.h>
/* 4*/    #include <errno.h>
/* 5*/    #include <stdio.h>
/* 6*/    #include <sys/types.h>
/* 7*/    #include <sys/stat.h>
/* 8*/    #include <sys/param.h>
/* 9*/    #include <dirent.h>

/*10*/    int aflag = 0;

/*11*/    long int du( const char *Dir );

/*12*/    int
/*13*/    main( int argc, char **argv )
/*14*/    {
/*15*/        if( argc > 1 )
/*16*/        {
/*17*/            if( strcmp( argv[ 1 ], "-a" ) == 0 )
/*18*/            {
/*19*/                argv++; argc--; aflag = 1;
/*20*/            }
/*21*/        }
/*22*/        if( argc == 1 )
/*23*/            du( "." );
/*24*/        else
/*25*/        while( --argc )
/*26*/            du( *++argv );

/*27*/        return 0;
/*28*/    }
```

Figure 13.8: main **and supporting code for** *du*.

if no directories are specified, the current directory is used as default. Because the number of blocks used by a file is given in the stat structure, the *du* command merely needs to perform an lstat on every file in the appropriate directory and keep a running count. Since we must examine subdirectories, it is natural that the entire function is once again recursive.

Figure 13.8 shows the include files and the main routine. The global variable aflag is used to indicate if the *-a* option is specified. main parses the arguments in the usual manner, calling du for each directory in argv. "." is used if no directories are specified. In Figure 13.9 we show the du routine. du will return the total number of blocks in DirName; a running count for the directory is kept in the local variable Blocks, which is initialized to zero at line 7.

We first attempt an opendir. If this is unsuccessful, we print an error message and return zero blocks. Otherwise, at lines 14 to 36 we process each entry in the directory.

```
/* 1*/    long
/* 2*/    du( const char *DirName )
/* 3*/    {
/* 4*/        DIR *DirPtr;              /* Pointer To Directory Stream */
/* 5*/        struct dirent *Slot;           /* Slot In Directory */
/* 6*/        struct stat StatBuf;
/* 7*/        long Blocks = 0L;
/* 8*/        char FileName[ MAXPATHLEN ];

/* 9*/        if( ( DirPtr = opendir( DirName ) ) == NULL )
/*10*/        {
/*11*/            perror( DirName );
/*12*/            return 0L;
/*13*/        }
/*14*/        while( ( Slot = readdir( DirPtr ) ) != NULL )
/*15*/        {
/*16*/            if( strcmp( Slot->d_name, ".." ) == 0 )
/*17*/                continue; /* Skip Parent */

/*18*/            sprintf( FileName, "%s/%s", DirName, Slot->d_name );
/*19*/            if( lstat( FileName, &StatBuf ) != 0 )
/*20*/            {
/*21*/                perror( FileName );
/*22*/                continue;
/*23*/            }
/*24*/            if ( S_ISDIR( StatBuf.st_mode ) )  /* Directories */
/*25*/            {
/*26*/                if( strcmp( Slot->d_name, "." ) == 0 )
/*27*/                    Blocks += StatBuf.st_blocks;
/*28*/                else
/*29*/                    Blocks += du( FileName );
/*30*/                continue;
/*31*/            }
/*32*/            /* Print In 1k Blocks, Not 512 Byte Blocks */
/*33*/            if( aflag )
/*34*/                printf( "%-8ld%s\n",
                                StatBuf.st_blocks/2, FileName );
/*35*/            Blocks += StatBuf.st_blocks;
/*36*/        }
/*37*/        if( Blocks )
/*38*/            printf( "%-8ld%s\n", Blocks/2, DirName );
/*39*/        closedir( DirPtr );
/*40*/        return Blocks;
/*41*/    }
```

Figure 13.9: **Recursive** du **routine.**

When that is done, we print a total (if it is nonzero), close the directory stream, and return the total number of blocks. In the main loop, we ignore the parent's entry. Everything else is a legitimate active file and needs to be added to the count of blocks. Thus at lines 18 to

23, we form a path name and call lstat to get the appropriate information. Once again, we should test that FileName is large enough to hold the entire path name, but we have omitted this in the interest of code compactness.

If we did not have to count subdirectories, we could completely eliminate lines 24 to 31, because lines 33 and 34 print the size of each individual file, and line 35 adds that size to the running total. When a directory is detected, via the macro call S_ISDIR at line 24, then instead of performing the actions at lines 33 to 35, we have to apply du recursively to the subdirectory. At line 29 we add the total number of blocks found in any subdirectory to our total for the current directory. However, " . " is not a subdirectory, so we do not want to process " . " recursively . If we did, we would not make progress in the recursion and eventually would crash. Thus we treat " . " like any other file, except that it is not subject to the -*a* option. We simply add its size to the running block count (just as is done at line 35). The continue statement at line 30 then sends us to the next entry in the current directory.

Our implementation of *du* is very similar to the actual implementation. One difference is in the handling of links. Blocks in files that are joined by a hard link are counted multiple times. The only way to avoid this is to keep a table that records (as file system, inode pairs) all files seen previously. Our program does avoid double-counting directories that are joined by symbolic links, because the lstat routine does not follow symbolic links. Thus lstat on a symbolic link reports how much space it takes to store the name of the pointed at file (i.e., one block).

If stat were used instead, the symbolic links would be followed, and the result would in many cases be a high overestimate. Worse, because symbolic links can create cycles in the directory structure, we would have to take precautions to avoid getting stuck in one. Storing previously visited directories, which would be necessitated to repair the overcounting, would be one solution.

Traversal of the directory structure is common among UNIX programs. *rm*, *ls*, and *cp* have the -*r* option to specify that all actions are to be applied to an entire directory recursively. The *find* command is a general program that traverses the directory structure looking for files that satisfy (possibly complex) properties. Some systems provide the functions ftw (*file tree walk*) and nftw (same, but do not follow symbolic links) to extend the general directory walking algorithm that we have shown to perform arbitrary actions for each file.

13.1.5 The UNIX File System Calls

For files, virtually all I/O can be performed using the ANSI C stream I/O package. Some applications, however, require an understanding of the low-level UNIX system calls on which the stream package is implemented. The basic system calls are open, close, read, write, and lseek, which, except for open, are almost identical to fopen, fclose, fread, fwrite, and fseek, respectively. Figure 13.10 shows their prototypes. Instead of the stream type FILE *, all access to a file is done via a *file descriptor*, which is a small nonnegative integer. File descriptors 0, 1, and 2 represent the standard input, standard output, and standard error. For maximum portability, the symbolic constants

STDIN_FILENO,   STDOUT_FILENO,   and   STDERR_FILENO

should be used.

```
#include <sys/types.h>
#include <sys/stat.h>
#include <fcntl.h>
#include <unistd.h>

int open( const char *FileName, int How, mode_t Permissions );
int close( int FileDes );
ssize_t read( int FileDes, void *DataBuffer, size_t NumBytes );
ssize_t write( int FileDes, const void *DataBuffer, size_t NumBytes );
off_t lseek( int FileDes, off_t Offset, int Whence );
```

Figure 13.10: Basic I/O system calls.

It is guaranteed that when an open succeeds, the lowest-available file descriptor is returned. Thus the standard input can be redirected by closing descriptor STDIN_FILENO and then opening another file for reading. Except for the use of the file descriptor instead of a stream, all the routines in Figure 13.10 except for open are identical to their stream counterparts. read and write should never be used for character at a time I/O, because the system call overhead is likely to be quite large. For block I/O, however, these calls will be faster than the standard I/O package. In Figure 13.11 we implement a copy routine using system calls.

Much like fopen, the second parameter to open determines which operations are allowable. A host of options, specified as bit patterns, are allowed. Multiple options are selected simultaneously by using a bitwise or. It is required that exactly one of O_RDONLY, O_WRONLY, and O_RDWR is specified. This allows reading, writing, or both reading and writing, respectively. Additional options, such as O_APPEND for writes restricted to the end of the file and the ones shown on line 16, are available. The options we have specified make this open equivalent to the older creat system call. When the O_CREAT option is specified, a mode specifying the access permissions must also be provided. The mode is formed using the bit patterns in <stat.h>. If a new file is created, its protection mode is determined by mode. The mode specified at line 17 indicates that everyone is granted read access, only the owner is granted write access, and nobody can execute. When a file is created, it will have access protections at least this restrictive, and possibly more, depending on the current setting of *umask*.

We conclude our discussion of UNIX files by mentioning the dup and dup2 system calls, whose prototypes are shown in Figure 13.12. dup returns a file descriptor that is synonymous with an already existing file descriptor FileDes. The new descriptor is the lowest-numbered available descriptor. dup2 forces the new descriptor to use NewFileDes. If NewFileDes is already in use, it is closed first; if FileDes equals NewFileDes, no opens or closes occur.

Figure 13.13 shows a sequence of dup operations that temporarily redirect the standard output. First we save a copy of the current standard output descriptor. Then we close the standard output and open an output file: assuming that descriptor 0 is already in use, we are guaranteed that the output file is opened as descriptor 1; thus all standard output goes to "output.log". If we then want to use the original standard output, we can duplicate the saved copy onto descriptor 1. When this is done, we no longer need the saved copy SaveStdout, and can close it.

```
/* 1*/    /* Copy From SrcFile To DestFile */
/* 2*/    /* Return Number Of Characters Copied, -1 for Errors */

/* 3*/    #include <stdio.h>
/* 4*/    #include <sys/stat.h>
/* 5*/    #include <fcntl.h>
/* 6*/    #include <sys/unistd.h>
/* 7*/    #include <string.h>
/* 8*/    #include <errno.h>

/* 9*/    #define BufSize 8192

/*10*/    long int
/*11*/    Copy( const char *DestFile, const char *SrcFile )
/*12*/    {
/*13*/        long int CharsRead, CharsCounted = 0L;
/*14*/        int SrcDesc, DestDesc;
/*15*/        char Buffer[ BufSize ];
/*16*/        const CreateFlag =  O_WRONLY | O_CREAT | O_TRUNC;
/*17*/        const Mode = S_IRUSR | S_IWUSR | S_IRGRP | S_IROTH;

/*18*/        if( strcmp( SrcFile, DestFile ) == 0 )
/*19*/        {
/*20*/            fprintf( stderr, "Can not copy to self\n" );
/*21*/            return -1L;
/*22*/        }

/*23*/        if( ( SrcDesc = open( SrcFile, O_RDONLY ) ) < 0 )
/*24*/        {
/*25*/            perror( SrcFile );
/*26*/            return -1L;
/*27*/        }
/*28*/        if( ( DestDesc = open( DestFile, CreateFlag, Mode ) )
                                                        < 0 )
/*29*/        {
/*30*/            perror( DestFile );
/*31*/            return -1L;
/*32*/        }

/*33*/        while( ( CharsRead = read( SrcDesc, Buffer, BufSize ) )
                                                        > 0 )
/*34*/            if( write( DestDesc, Buffer, CharsRead ) < CharsRead )
/*35*/            {
/*36*/                perror( DestFile );
/*37*/                break;
/*38*/            }
/*39*/            else
/*40*/                CharsCounted += CharsRead;

/*41*/        close( SrcDesc ); close( DestDesc );
/*42*/        return CharsCounted;
/*43*/    }
```

Figure 13.11:   Copy routine using system calls.

```
#include <unistd.h>

int dup( int FileDes );
int dup2( int FileDes, int NewFileDes );
```

Figure 13.12: dup **and** dup2 **system calls.**

```
SaveStdout = dup( STDOUT_FILENO );
close( STDOUT_FILENO );
open( "output.log", CreateFlag, Mode );
```

/ writes to standard output go to the file output.log */*

```
dup2( SaveStdout, STDOUT_FILENO );
close( SaveStdout );
```

/ writes to standard output are restored to original setting */*

Figure 13.13: **Using** dup **and** dup2.

13.2   Processes

UNIX is a *multiprocessing* system, which means that more than one program can be running at any point in time. Each instance of an executing program is called a *process*. The operating system scheduler creates an appearance of concurrency by systematically allowing each process to use resources such as the CPU or disk.

Under UNIX, a shell command such as

ls -l | wc

is implemented as two processes (one for *ls* and one for *wc*). Additional work is performed to synchronize these processes and to guarantee that the output from the *ls* process is used as the input to the *wc* process. We also know that an interrupt signal (such as a control-c) will terminate the *ls* and *wc* commands, but not the controlling shell. Thus the shell process is affected differently by interrupt signals.

In the remainder of the section we discuss the basics of processes. First, we will see how fork and exec are used to create processes to execute programs, and how the waitpid system call is used to achieve some synchronization between processes. Then we will look at the signal system call, which determines how processes deal with interrupts and other exceptional occurrences. Finally, we look at the pipe system call, which allows two related process to communicate easily with each other.

13.2.1   The Process Identifier

Each process is identified uniquely by a number, which is of type pid_t. Generally, this is a 16-bit integer. The routine getpid returns the process identifier for the current process. The routine getppid returns the process identifier for the parent of the current process. As you might suspect, processes are created by other processes. When we execute the command *a.out* from the terminal, the parent process is the shell.

One use of the process number is that we can terminate (runaway) jobs. The *kill* command (which also appears as a system call) can send a terminating signal to any process. Of course, most users can only terminate their own jobs.

Among other things, each process keeps track of its open files. Abstractly, this is done by storing an array of pointers into a global open file table that is maintained by the operating system. Each open file is given an entry in this *global file table*, where information such as the file system and inode number of the file, what operations are allowed (read, write, both, etc.) on the file, and the current offset in the file is maintained. Because each process may have several open files, an array of pointers into the global file table is maintained, and in fact a file descriptor is just an index into the process table. The maximum allowed number of files open simultaneously is just the size of the process's array of pointers into the global file table. Notice that as a consequence of this arrangement, a dup just duplicates the pointer: it means that the process now has two pointers to the same global file table, so either file descriptor provides access.

13.2.2   `fork` **and** `exec`

The `fork` system call is the only way to create a new process. The new process, which we call the *child*, is almost identical to the original process, which we call the parent. The only significant differences are that the two processes have different identifiers and different parent identifiers. Although `getpid` can thus be used to differentiate the parent and child, the return value from `fork` is a better mechanism.

If the `fork` fails to create a new process, usually because there are already too many, it returns -1. Otherwise, in the child, `fork` returns 0, and in the parent, `fork` returns the child's process id. This way, the parent and child have each other's process id, because the child can automatically determine the parent's process id via `getppid`.

Typical code would thus first test the `fork` for failure. If the `fork` has succeeded, there would generally be separate code for the parent and child processes. Control would continue onward from the `fork` call. Because the child is an identical copy of the parent, after the `fork`, all variables in the child have the same values as the parent. From then on, however, each process is independent: changes to variables in the child do not affect the parent. The important exception to (or consequence of, depending on your point of view) this rule is that files remain open across the `fork`. Thus both processes have pointers to the global file system table which are accessed by any file descriptors that happen to be open when the `fork` was made. We will explain the consequences of this after we look at an example in Figure 13.14.

Line 8 of the routine shown in Figure 13.14 creates a child process. If the return from the `fork` is -1, an error has occurred, and we exit after printing a message. Otherwise, we have two concurrently running processes. Since `fork` returns 0 for the child and a positive number for the parent, for each process, lines 14 and 16 identify the other process. A simple message in which each process identifies itself is printed, and then control reaches line 17, which is executed by both processes. Each process prints its id and then prints a message at line 23 three times before exiting.

Because the child and parent processes are not synchronized, the order in which output from the child and parent processes appear is nondeterministic and depends entirely on how the operating system schedules the processes. It is even possible that all of the output from the child process is performed before the identification output from the parent process.

```
/* 1*/     #include <stdio.h>
/* 2*/     #include <sys/types.h>
/* 3*/     #include <unistd.h>

/* 4*/     main( void )
/* 5*/     {
/* 6*/         pid_t Pid;
/* 7*/         long int i;

/* 8*/         if( ( Pid = fork( ) ) == -1 )
/* 9*/         {
/*10*/             perror( "" );
/*11*/             exit( -1 );
/*12*/         }

/*13*/         if( Pid == 0 )
/*14*/             printf( "I am the child; my parent is %d.",
                                                      getppid( ) );
/*15*/         else
/*16*/             printf( "I am the parent; my child is %d.", Pid );

/*17*/         /* Both Processes Execute Their Own Copies Of This */
/*18*/         printf( "  My process id is %d.\n", getpid( ) );
/*19*/         fflush( stdout );
/*20*/         for( i = 0; i < 3000000; i++ )
/*21*/             if( i % 1000000 == 0 )
/*22*/             {
/*23*/                 printf( "%s\n", Pid ? "Parent" : "Child" );
/*24*/                 fflush( stdout );
/*25*/             }

/*26*/         return 0;
/*27*/     }
```

Figure 13.14:   Process creation via `fork`.

The two calls to `fflush` at lines 19 and 24 are needed to ensure that the program behaves correctly when it is redirected to an output file. This is because when output commands are directed to a disk file, the standard I/O package does not actually make a call to `write` until it has a block's worth of data (typically 8192 bytes) or a call to `fflush` is reached. (Note that output to terminals is written when a newline is seen.) `fflush` is called automatically by `exit`, which itself is called automatically when `main` returns. Thus if the output is redirected, because there are so few data, each process actually makes only one call to `write`. Consequently, all of one process's output is written, followed by all of the other's, which is hardly the intended order. By calling `fflush`, we force the `writes`.

A direct consequence is that we need to be careful that all buffers, including the standard output and standard error, are empty prior to the `fork`, since otherwise the buffers, like all other variables, are duplicated, and each copy is emptied by the respective process. Figure 13.15 shows the simplest example of what can go wrong. The intention is that a

```
/* 1*/    #include <stdio.h>
/* 2*/    #include <unistd.h>

/* 3*/    main( void )
/* 4*/    {
/* 5*/        printf( "No flush because no newline" );
/* 6*/        fork( );                /* No Error Checks */
/* 7*/        return 0;               /* Call To exit( ) Is Implicit */
/* 8*/    }
```

Figure 13.15:   Double output because the `write` **is buffered until after the** `fork`.

message is printed once and then a `fork` is executed, with an immediate termination of both processes. But the message is printed twice, because each process calls `write` to flush the contents of its version of the buffer.

Because files remain open across a `fork`, we have to be careful when both processes access a file using the same shared descriptor. If `fd` represents a file open for reading, a `read` using `fd` in one process advances the notion of what has already been read for both processes. To avoid these problems, if a file is opened across a `fork`, one of the two processes will generally `close` it.

Although `fork` can be used to create a new process, by itself it is not sufficient to create a process that runs a different program. To do that, we need the `exec` function. Strictly speaking, there is no single `exec` function, but rather, a set of six `exec` functions that perform the same basic task but have slightly different interfaces.

The result of an `exec` is that the current process is completely replaced, or *overlaid*, with another program, and that program is run to termination. As a consequence, the `exec` family does not return, unless the *overlaying* failed. Typically, an `exec` is performed immediately after a `fork`. Because the `exec` does not create a new process but merely overwrites an existing process, the process id does not change. Files remain open across execs unless other arrangements are made. Consequently, if the standard input and output are redirected prior to an `exec`, the resulting program will also have its standard input and output redirected.

The simplest form of the `exec` is the `execl` command. The first parameter is the name of the program that is to be executed; subsequent parameters give the elements of the `argv` vector, followed by a `NULL` pointer. Figure 13.16, which implements a simplified version of the library routine `system`, illustrates a typical use of the combination of `fork` and `exec`. The `system` function takes a single string parameter and passes the string to `/bin/sh` for input, just as if it had been typed as a command from the terminal. Thus

`system( Command )`

is equivalent to the command

sh -c Command.

At line 11 we check that `Command` is not `NULL`; if it is, we return 1 immediately (as specified in the actual `system` semantics). Otherwise, we perform a `fork`. The child immediately performs an `execl`. Line 19 is executed only if the `execl` fails, in which case we terminate the process. As we saw earlier, if we use `exit`, any buffered data will be written twice. Thus we use `_exit`, which terminates without calling `fflush`. Notice that when the `execl` succeeds, the entire process is overwritten with a new image. This

```
/* 1*/      #include <stdio.h>
/* 2*/      #include <sys/types.h>
/* 3*/      #include <sys/wait.h>
/* 4*/      #include <unistd.h>
/* 5*/      #include <errno.h>

/* 6*/      int
/* 7*/      SimpleSystem( const char *Command )
/* 8*/      {
/* 9*/          pid_t Pid;
/*10*/          int Status;

/*11*/          if( Command == NULL )
/*12*/              return 1;

/*13*/          Pid = fork( );
/*14*/          if( Pid < 0 ) /* Error */
/*15*/              return -1;

/*16*/          if( Pid == 0 ) /* Child */
/*17*/          {
/*18*/              execl( "/bin/sh", "sh", "-c", Command, NULL );
/*19*/              _exit( 127 );  /* execl Failed; Give Up On Child */
/*20*/          }

/*21*/          /* else  Parent */
/*22*/          waitpid( Pid, &Status, 0 );
/*23*/          return Status;
/*24*/      }
```

Figure 13.16: **Simple implementation of** system.

means that all variables in the child process, including the buffered data, are overwritten, and that consequently, the buffer is not written twice.

The parent process does nothing but wait for the child to complete. This is done with the waitpid call: the parent will be inactive until the child with process id Pid terminates (either normally or abnormally).[5] The variable Status will contain the return value of the child. For instance, if the execl in the child failed, Status will contain 127. It is customary for main to exit with status 0 if there is no error, and with a nonzero value otherwise.

The waitpid is a generalization of the original wait commands. It is useful because a process can create several children. The waitpid call allows the process to wait for a specific child (as we have done here), or just some child. We will only use the form illustrated on line 22; for a full description, see the references. The exec command comes in several different flavors. execv replaces the second through last parameters with an array of char pointers (i.e., char **), much like main's argv. We will see this form in a later example.

----

[5]waitpid can also return -1 if it is terminated by a signal.

The `execlp` and `execvp` are like `execl` and `execv`, except that the first parameter does not have to be the explicit path name of the program that is executed. Instead, the usual search path is followed. The `execle` and `execve` allows an additional parameter, which is the equivalent of the `char **envp` parameter of `main` that was discussed in Section 12.7.2. By default, the global variable `environ` is used to initialize the environment.

Finally, we remark that the `fork` makes a complete copy of a process. If this copy calls an `exec` immediately, then by creating an immediately overwritten copy, the `fork` has done much more work than needed. Because of this, most systems provide `vfork`, which is identical to `fork` but makes only a partial copy of the process. An immediate `exec` is then required.

13.2.3 Signals

When an exceptional event such as a modem hangup, control-c, or illegal instruction occurs, a *signal* is generated. Unless arrangements are made, in most cases a signal will cause the termination of a process. Although this frequently may be a reasonable action, there are many cases where we would rather not terminate immediately. Consider, for example, the routine shown in Figure 13.16. An attempt to interrupt the child process will also interrupt the parent.

Since the parent is waiting for termination of the child, there is no reason why a termination of the child by an interrupt signal should be treated differently. Thus a more reasonable course of action is to allow the interrupt signal to terminate the child but not the parent. Then the `SimpleSystem` routine would return to its caller, with an indication that the child terminated due to an interrupt signal.

The most basic way of dealing with this is the `signal` function. `signal` used to be a system call but has been replaced with a more complex set of routines. The function is still present for compatibility, and also because the interface is simpler for the particular cases that we examine. As we will see, dealing with signals is a very complex task, which is easily mishandled in subtle ways. Figure 13.17 shows the header file `<signal.h>` that needs to be included. Currently, up to 31 different signals are recognized. We have listed some of the common signals.

The `kill` system call, which would be more correctly identified as `SendSignal`, can be used to generate and send a signal manually to *any* process (or group of processes). Note that interrupts cause the sending of a signal without an explicit call to `kill`. The prototype, which is not included in `<signal.h>`, is

```
int kill( pid_t Pid, int Sig );
```

`kill` returns -1 on error, which would occur, for instance, if you tried to `kill` somebody else's process.

The mysterious prototype for `signal` is shown in Figure 13.17. All it says is that the routine `signal` takes two parameters. The first is the signal number, which would be written portably by using one of the names given by the earlier sequence of `#define` statements. The second is the name of (or pointer to) a function that should be called when the signal is detected. Thus `Handler` represents how the signal is to be handled. `signal` returns the previous setting of `Handler`, so that a subsequent call to `signal` can restore the setting if necessary.

Three predefined signal handlers are provided. The first, `SIG_DFL`, represents the default handler, which is generally termination. The second, `SIG_IGN`, means that all

```
#define    SIGHUP    1   /* hangup */
#define    SIGINT    2   /* interrupt */
#define    SIGQUIT   3   /* quit */
#define    SIGILL    4   /* illegal instruction (not reset when caught) */
#define    SIGTRAP   5   /* trace trap (not reset when caught) */
#define    SIGABRT   6   /* used by abort, replace SIGIOT in the future */
#define    SIGFPE    8   /* floating point exception */
#define    SIGKILL   9   /* kill (cannot be caught or ignored) */
#define    SIGBUS    10  /* bus error */
#define    SIGSEGV   11  /* segmentation violation */
#define    SIGSYS    12  /* bad argument to system call */
#define    SIGPIPE   13  /* write on a pipe with no one to read it */
#define    SIGALRM   14  /* alarm clock */
#define    SIGSTOP   17  /* sendable stop signal not from tty */
#define    SIGTSTP   18  /* stop signal from tty */
#define    SIGCONT   19  /* continue a stopped process */
#define    SIGXCPU   24  /* exceeded CPU time limit */
#define    SIGXFSZ   25  /* exceeded file size limit */
#define    SIGUSR1   30  /* user defined signal 1 */
#define    SIGUSR2   31  /* user defined signal 2 */

/* signal() args & returns */
#define    SIG_ERR        ( void ( * )(   ) )-1
#define    SIG_DFL        ( void ( * )(   ) )0
#define    SIG_IGN        ( void ( * )(   ) )1

void ( *signal( int Sig, void ( *Handler )(   ) ) )(   );
```

Figure 13.17:   **Parts of** `<signal.h>`.

occurrences of a particular signal are to be ignored. The third, SIG_ERR, is not a real
handler but is returned if signal fails for some reason. An example of an error is the call

```
signal( SIGKILL, SIG_IGN )
```

because SIGKILL cannot be ignored. Thus sending a process a kill signal (rather than an
interrupt) is guaranteed to terminate it. The *disposition* of signals (i.e., the action to take for
each signal) remains intact across a fork. Furthermore, ignored signals remain ignored
across execs. All other signals are reset to their default action.

We now know enough to make SimpleSystem handle interrupts correctly. A
simple but unfortunately incorrect implementation is shown in Figure 13.18. After the
fork, the parent ignores both the interrupt and quit signals until the child returns. Then
the signal setting is reset to what it was when the call to WrongSystem began. Notice
that the signal routine is much easier to call than the prototype would indicate.

Although what we have done appears to be exactly what is needed, our implementation
has a subtle problem. Because the parent and child run independently, it is possible, for
instance, that the child will run first, perform the exec, and be subjected to an interrupt
before the parent has a chance to run and disable its interrupts. This is a so-called *race
condition*, whose outcome depends nondeterministically on how processes get scheduled.

Thus there is a small window of time during which the parent is not protected. On a
typical system, this may be an extremely short period of time, generally less than a second.

```
/* 1*/    #include <signal.h>        /* Other Omitted For Brevity */

/* 2*/    int
/* 3*/    WrongSystem( const char *Command )
/* 4*/    {
/* 5*/        pid_t Pid;
/* 6*/        int Status;
/* 7*/        void ( *SaveIntr )( ), ( *SaveQuit )( );

/* 8*/        if( Command == NULL )
/* 9*/            return 1;

/*10*/        Pid = fork( );
/*11*/        if( Pid < 0 )   /* Error */
/*12*/            return -1;

/*13*/        if( Pid == 0 ) /* Child */
/*14*/        {
/*15*/            execl( "/bin/sh", "sh", "-c", Command, NULL );
/*16*/            _exit( 127 );   /* execl Failed; Give Up On Child */
/*17*/        }
/*18*/          /* Parent */
/*19*/        SaveIntr = signal(  SIGINT, SIG_IGN );      /* Ignore */
/*20*/        SaveQuit = signal(  SIGQUIT, SIG_IGN );     /* Signals */

/*21*/        waitpid( Pid, &Status, 0 );

/*22*/        signal( SIGINT,  SaveIntr );                /* Restore */
/*23*/        signal( SIGQUIT, SaveQuit );                /* Signals */

/*24*/        return Status;
/*25*/    }
```

Figure 13.18:   system **with signal handles: INCORRECT VERSION.**

Thus it would be unlikely that this scenario would occur frequently. However, that does not diminish its importance, but rather, increases the difficulty of detecting and reproducing the error.

   The correct way to implement the system call is shown in Figure 13.19. We disable the appropriate interrupts *before* the fork. As before, the parent will reset its signals after the call to waitpid returns. The child will immediately reset its signal and then call exec. The RealSystem routine appears correct, but actually it is also slightly deficient. Later in this subsection we make a slight technical adjustment to line 23.

   In addition to the predefined SIG_IGN and SIG_DFL, it is possible to supply a user-defined handler function. The simplest use of this is shown in Figure 13.20. An interrupt normally causes the abrupt termination of a program without flushing of buffers. The interrupt handler Doexit makes an explicit call to exit (returning the symbolic constant SIGINT), to guarantee that the standard I/O buffers are flushed. Line 14 of main installs Doexit as the interrupt signal handler.

```
/* 1*/    #include <signal.h>        /* Others Omitted For Brevity */

/* 2*/    int
/* 3*/    RealSystem( const char *Command )
/* 4*/    {
/* 5*/        pid_t Pid;
/* 6*/        int Status;
/* 7*/        void ( *SaveIntr )( ), ( *SaveQuit )( );

/* 8*/        if( Command == NULL )
/* 9*/            return 1;

/*10*/        SaveIntr = signal(  SIGINT, SIG_IGN );        /* Ignore */
/*11*/        SaveQuit = signal(  SIGQUIT, SIG_IGN );      /* Signals */

/*12*/        Pid = fork( );
/*13*/        if( Pid < 0 )        /* Error */
/*14*/            return -1;

/*15*/        if( Pid == 0 )       /* Child */
/*16*/        {
/*17*/            signal( SIGINT, SaveIntr );              /* Restore */
/*18*/            signal( SIGQUIT, SaveQuit );            /* Signals */

/*19*/            execl( "/bin/sh", "sh", "-c", Command, NULL );
/*20*/            _exit( 127 );   /* execl Failed; Give Up On Child */
/*21*/        }
/*22*/          /* Parent */
/*23*/        waitpid( Pid, &Status, 0 );

/*24*/        signal( SIGINT,  SaveIntr );                /* Restore */
/*25*/        signal( SIGQUIT, SaveQuit );                /* Signals */

/*26*/        return Status;
/*27*/    }
```

Figure 13.19: system **with signal handlers.**

When a signal handler does not exit, but instead issues a return, execution continues at the point where the signal occurred, and generally speaking, the history is forgotten: unless a global variable is set explicitly by the exception handler, the program does not know that a signal occurred and was handled. In some cases this is perfectly appropriate, in others it is not.

Consider, for instance, the mail program. Sometimes, in the middle of replying to a mail message we realize that we would rather not send the letter. By typing two interrupts (rather than one, which could be accidental), the function that we are in terminates and control returns to the main part of the mail program. Implementing this requires that the signal handler be able to execute an arbitrary goto. Notice that the normal goto does not work, because a goto statement can transfer only within a function. The library contains

```
/* 1*/      /* Simple Demonstration Of signal Handling */
/* 2*/      /* Buffers Are Flushed On Interrupt */

/* 3*/      #include <signal.h>
/* 4*/      #include <stdio.h>
/* 5*/      #include <stdlib.h>
/* 6*/      #include <unistd.h>

/* 7*/      void
/* 8*/      Doexit( void )
/* 9*/      {
/*10*/          exit( SIGINT );        /* Flush Buffers */
/*11*/      }

/*12*/      main( void )
/*13*/      {
/*14*/          signal( SIGINT, Doexit );
/*15*/          for( ; ; )
/*16*/          {
/*17*/              sleep( 1 );
/*18*/              printf( "junk" );
/*19*/          }
/*20*/          return 0;
/*21*/      }
```

Figure 13.20:   Simple use of signal handler.

routines that can execute arbitrary jumps throughout the program. Figure 13.21 illustrates the technique.

In principle, the main routine is simply an infinite loop that calls DoCommands. We add interrupt-handling abilities as follows. First, at line 5 we declare a global variable RestartLoop of type jmp_buf, which is defined in <setjmp.h>. At line 20 we call setjmp, saving the current stack frame information in RestartLoop. Subsequent calls to longjmp which refer to RestartLoop will restore the stack frame, in effect implementing a goto. Thus we just need to enable the signal handler at line 21 and have the signal handler perform a longjmp. Our signal handler does a little more: It keeps track of how many times it has been called, and exits after three interrupts. Of course, by adjusting the code trivially, we can prompt the user for confirmation and implement other changes.

Inside the signal handler, the signal (being handled) is blocked temporarily. Otherwise, the signal handler might keep calling itself (and get confused) if a sequence of identical signals arrived. One might argue that because of the longjmp, the signal handler does not actually return, and thus the signal will continue to be blocked. Although our system does not share this interpretation, the exact semantics are not specified. Consequently there is a window of time during which the disposition of SIGINT is not guaranteed.

The routines siglongjmp, sigsetjmp, and the associated type sigjmp_buf can be used to guarantee either form of behavior. The only difference is that sigsetjmp takes a second parameter: If it is nonzero, then after the jump, we are guaranteed that the

```
/* 1*/    #include <stdio.h>
/* 2*/    #include <signal.h>
/* 3*/    #include <setjmp.h>
/* 4*/    #include <stdlib.h>

/* 5*/    static jmp_buf RestartLoop;

/* 6*/    static void
/* 7*/    IntrHandler( int SigNum )
/* 8*/    {
/* 9*/        static int NumCalls = 0;

/*10*/        if( ++NumCalls == 3 )    /* Allow Three Per Program */
/*11*/        {
/*12*/            fprintf( stderr, "Quitting...\n" );
/*13*/            exit( 0 );
/*14*/        }
/*15*/        fprintf( stderr, "Caught an interrupt: resetting\n" );
/*16*/        longjmp( RestartLoop, NumCalls );
/*17*/    }

/*18*/    main( void )
/*19*/    {
/*20*/        setjmp( RestartLoop );
/*21*/        signal( SIGINT, IntrHandler );
/*22*/        for( ; ; )
/*23*/            DoCommands( );

/*24*/        return 0;
/*25*/    }
```

Figure 13.21: `setjmp` and `longjmp`.

signal handler is in effect, whereas if the second parameter is zero, the signal that was just handled is blocked. This is illustrated in Figure 13.22. (There are quite a few details that have been left out here.)

Interrupt handlers that return from their calling point rather than exiting or returning to a neutral location via `longjmp` can make life difficult for the programmer. Let us revisit the `RealSystem` function in Figure 13.19. Recall that an interrupt or quit is ignored by the parent until the child returns. Suppose, however, that the child is ignoring `SIGHUP` (modem hangup signal), while the parent is (perhaps foolishly) catching it with an interrupt handler, which eventually returns. Because `waitpid` is a system call, and thus an *atomic* operation, the fact that control transfers from it to a signal handler implies that it must have returned. Thus receipt of a signal causes `waitpid` to return (with return code -1), and consequently, `RealSystem` will return even though the child is still running. The solution is to have line 23 stay in a loop if the return from `waitpid` and the `errno` variable both indicate that a signal was processed. Thus line 23 is rewritten as

```
/*23*/            while( waitpid( Pid, &Status, 0 ) == -1
                        && errno == EINTR );
```

```
/* 1*/    #include <stdio.h>
/* 2*/    #include <signal.h>
/* 3*/    #include <setjmp.h>
/* 4*/    #include <stdlib.h>

/* 5*/    static sigjmp_buf RestartLoop;

/* 6*/    static void
/* 7*/    IntrHandler( int SigNum )
/* 8*/    {
/* 9*/        static int NumCalls = 0;

/*10*/        if( ++NumCalls == 3 )    /* Allow Three Per Program */
/*11*/        {
/*12*/            fprintf( stderr, "Quitting...\n" );
/*13*/            exit( 0 );
/*14*/        }
/*15*/        fprintf( stderr, "Caught an interrupt: resetting\n" );
/*16*/        siglongjmp( RestartLoop, NumCalls );
/*17*/    }

/*18*/    main( void )
/*19*/    {
/*20*/        sigsetjmp( RestartLoop, 1 );
/*21*/        signal( SIGINT, IntrHandler );
/*22*/        for( ; ; )
/*23*/            DoCommands( );

/*24*/        return 0;
/*25*/    }
```

Figure 13.22: Using `siglongjmp` and `sigsetjmp`: **signal is not blocked**
after `siglongjmp`.

The original implementation of signals in UNIX was limited because the intention was either to ignore a signal or to terminate in almost all cases. Thus handling signals always led to race conditions. One problem was that when a signal was handled, the default was reinstated immediately. Thus the first statement in the handler typically reestablished the handler. However, there was always a window where a second signal would cause the default action, which would be termination. These unreliable semantics are no longer in effect for `signal`. Newer versions have greatly expanded the signal-handling capabilities, so if you intend to do any serious work with signals, you will need to know much more than what we have discussed here.

One limitation of `signal` is that it is impossible to determine directly how a signal is being handled. The indirect method requires making two calls to `signal`: the first sets the disposition to `SIG_IGN` but returns the original disposition, and the second call resets the original disposition. Besides making two calls instead of one, a signal may be lost in the time when `SIG_IGN` is in effect.

A second limitation of `signal` is that there is no mechanism to *block* signals. A signal must either be accepted or ignored, and thus discarded. We cannot postpone it. A third limitation is that a signal can terminate a system call. Generally, we would like to restart the system call, as was done with `waitpid`, although this is not always true and can vary depending on which signal was processed.

All of these improvements are handled by the `sigaction` routine, which replaces `signal` for any nontrivial application. See the references for more details.

13.2.4 Pipes

The last UNIX abstraction we discuss is the *pipe*. Like the queue abstract data type, the pipe allows reading from one end and writing to the other end. A pipe is created by calling the `pipe` function. The prototype is

```
int pipe( int FileDes[ 2 ] );
```

If the call succeeds, `pipe` returns zero, and the two file descriptors `FileDes[0]` and `FileDes[1]` will represent the read and write ends of the pipe. Otherwise, `pipe` will return -1. Because reads and writes of the pipe are implemented using file descriptors, the pipe is the basic mechanism used for communication between processes. The idea is that as a result of the `fork`, both the parent and child will have access to the pipe and can thus communicate by sending messages through the pipe.

Of course, just as with files, if both processes try to read from the pipe, we will have a race condition and the results will depend on which process performs the read first. Thus, typically, reads from the pipe will be performed by only one of the processes, and writes will be done only by the other. Figure 13.23 shows how we actually use pipes. In the first picture, we have performed the call `pipe(Fd)`. Assuming that the call succeeds, descriptor `Fd[0]` is open for reading from the pipe, and `Fd[1]` is open for writing to the pipe. `pipe` could fail if we have exceeded the limit on open file descriptors. We can also use either of `Fd[0]` or `Fd[1]` as we would any file descriptor that was obtained via an `open`, except that some operations, such as `lseek`, do not make sense. These descriptors can, and should, be closed when no longer needed, and they can also be duplicated by `dup` or `dup2`.

In a single process, a pipe is relatively useless. The same effect can be achieved with a queue, without the overhead (and limitations) of the system calls. In the second picture in Figure 13.23, we see the result of a `fork`. Either process can read or write to the pipe, using the normal `read` and `write` system calls. Typically, both processes close a different end of the pipe. In the third picture, we see that the child can write to the pipe and the parent can read from it. Thus we have one-way communication, which is typically sufficient. If two-way communication is needed, we can either use a second pipe, or try to use the original pipe, with both ends open in both processes. However, that generally requires that the programmer provide a fairly complex protocol.

Let us describe in broad terms how a pipe works. Because many users will want to use pipes and main memory is limited, we need to impose a limit on the number of characters that can be in the pipe. The constant `PIPE_BUF` in `<sys/config.h>` sets this limit, which is typically 8192 bytes. A `write` of `PIPE_BUF` bytes or less will not be interleaved with other writes to the pipe. Larger writes are written in chunks and may be interleaved. If a `write` is attempted to a pipe that is already full, the writing process will be suspended until the pipe is sufficiently empty. If a `read` is attempted to a pipe that is empty, the reading process is suspended until the pipe is sufficiently full. If the writing end

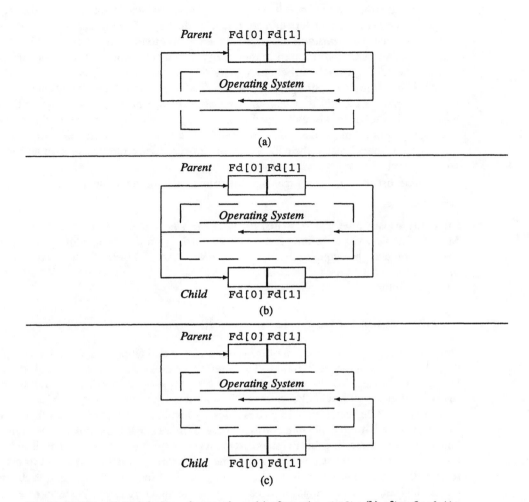

Figure 13.23:   Pictorial view of swapping: (a) after `Pipe(Fd)`; **(b) after** `fork()`;
(c) after parent and children close one end of the pipe.

of the pipe is already closed and the pipe is not full enough to satisfy the read request, the
`read` will return a short count. Writing to a file whose read end is closed will generate the
signal `SIGPIPE`.

The ability of processes to communicate via pipes is derived from the fact that file
descriptors are duplicated across `fork`s. Thus it should be evident that only processes that
share a common ancestor can share a pipe. Unrelated processes cannot communicate via
pipes, although newer versions of UNIX provide other mechanisms.

To appreciate the importance of pipes, it is worth considering how they could be
implemented if the operating system did not provide support. The obvious strategy would
be to use a disk file. We could write sequentially to the end of an initially empty file, and
read sequentially from the beginning. We could use wraparound, to avoid having the file
grow too large. The strategy has several limitations.

First, disk access is slow. The primary benefit of the pipe is that the operating system maintains a queue of characters in main memory, thus avoiding the overhead of accessing a disk. Second, the `read` will not wait for the `write` to deposit the required number of characters, but instead will return immediately, with a short count. We would then have to continue calling `read` until enough characters were written. This would be difficult to implement efficiently. Similarly, we would need to provide synchronization in the case where the pipe is too full to accept the `write`. Third, `read`s and `write`s to the pipe cannot be buffered, so we really need to access the disk every time we perform a write to the pipe. Furthermore, the typical wraparound strategy used to implement queues will complicate matters because the data are no longer stored sequentially as `read` and `write` would expect.

The most obvious use of pipes is by the command interpreter (the shell). The command

who | wc

implicitly uses a pipe that is shared by both the *who* command and the *wc* command. Specifically, *who* writes to the pipe, while *wc* reads from the pipe. Moreover, using the dup2 command, the output of the pipe replaces STDOUT_FILENO for the *who* command, and the input of the pipe replaces STDIN_FILENO for the *wc* command. We now know enough to implement a simple shell.

13.2.5 Implementing a Simple Shell

Our shell will support redirection of the standard input and output, pipes, and the & option, which puts a job in the background. This set of operations shows off almost all the basic UNIX system calls. We do not support much else, although it is simple enough to add as many features as you would like. Some of the additional features are suggested as exercises.

Figure 13.24 shows the `#include` files, symbolic constants, and types that are used by our program. A *full command* consists of one or more *simple commands* piped together, and possibly an indication that the standard input and output are redirected. This is indicated by the type declaration at lines 20 to 27. The `Background` field will be set to nonzero if the full command is to run as a background process. Line 19 indicates that each simple command is an array of strings, which corresponds to an `argv` array. We terminate the list of strings with a NULL pointer, to match the specification for `execv`.

We allow each simple command to have an `argc` of up to 10. A better but more complicated implementation would be to expand `SimpleCommand` as necessary to hold an arbitrarily long argument list.

`GetLine` is a macro that reads one line of input for processing as a command. `GetToken` returns the next symbol from `TheLine`, by setting the parameter `Token`, which is passed by reference. When `Token` is a word string, `Str` is filled with the corresponding word. Similarly, if an I/O redirection is seen, the name of the corresponding file is sent back via `Str`. `GetLine` returns a pointer to the position where subsequent scanning should continue. This is a straightforward, although somewhat lengthy routine that we leave as an exercise.

Figure 13.25 parses a line of input and fills a `FullComand` structure, which is passed by reference. The `Strdup` at line 35 is taken from Exercise 8.19. Because it makes a copy of the `Str`, this routine has a memory leak, which is easily fixed by clearing `Buf->Commands` in the segment before line 11. The lack of a `break` statement after

```
/* 1*/      #include <stdio.h>
/* 2*/      #include <string.h>
/* 3*/      #include <sys/types.h>
/* 4*/      #include <sys/stat.h>
/* 5*/      #include <fcntl.h>
/* 6*/      #include <sys/wait.h>
/* 7*/      #include <unistd.h>
/* 8*/      #include <errno.h>
/* 9*/      #include <signal.h>

/*10*/      /* Simple Shell */

/*11*/      /* A Simple Command Is An Array Of Up To MaxArgc+1 Strings */
/*12*/      /* The Last String Is NULL */
/*13*/      /* This Can Be Used Directly For execvp */
/*14*/      /* Very Limited Error Checking To Keep Code Short */

/*15*/      #define MaxArgc 10
/*16*/      #define MaxPipes 10
/*17*/      #define FileNameLen MaxLineLen
/*18*/      #define MaxLineLen 256

/*19*/      typedef char *SimpleCommand[ MaxArgc + 1  ];

/*20*/      typedef struct
/*21*/      {
/*22*/          char InFile[ FileNameLen ];
/*23*/          char OutFile[ FileNameLen ];
/*24*/          int NumPipes;
/*25*/          SimpleCommand Commands[ MaxPipes ];
/*26*/          int Background;
/*27*/      } FullCommand;

/*28*/      enum { Eoln, Error, From, To, Pipe, Word, Amper };

/*29*/      /* Read A Line, return NULL On EOF */
/*30*/      #define GetLine( S ) ( fgets( S, MaxLineLen, stdin ) )

/*31*/      /* Return Pointer Indicating Where To Begin Next Search */
/*32*/      /* Str Will Be Filled if *Token Is Word, From, Or To */
/*33*/      char *GetToken( char *TheLine, char *Str, int *Token );
```

Figure 13.24: Include files, types, and prototypes for simple shell.

the Pipe case is not accidental. When we see a pipe, or the end of a line, we are done processing the current simple command.

To keep the code simple, we skimp a bit on error checks. Each of the cases From, To, and Amper should never be executed more than once per call to Parse. Also, a production quality program would check that none of the routines that operates on strings overflows the array of characters. We get around that by using large strings in all cases. We should also check that the call to Strdup succeeds.

```
/* 1*/    /* Fill The Structure Referenced By Buf */

/* 2*/    int
/* 3*/    Parse( char *TheLine, FullCommand *Buf )
/* 4*/    {
/* 5*/        int CommandNum = 0, Token;
/* 6*/        char Str[ MaxLineLen ];
/* 7*/        int NumStr = 0;        /* # Of Strings In Current Command */

/* 8*/        Buf->NumPipes = Buf->Background = 0;
/* 9*/        strcpy( Buf->InFile, "" );
/*10*/        strcpy( Buf->OutFile, "" );

/*11*/        while( TheLine = GetToken( TheLine, Str, &Token ) )
/*12*/            switch( Token )
/*13*/            {
/*14*/              default:
/*15*/              case Error:
/*16*/                printf( "Syntax error\n" );
/*17*/                return -1;
/*18*/              case From:
/*19*/                strcpy( Buf->InFile, Str );
/*20*/                break;
/*21*/              case To:
/*22*/                strcpy( Buf->OutFile, Str );
/*23*/                break;
/*24*/              case Amper:
/*25*/                Buf->Background++;
/*26*/                break;
/*27*/              case Pipe:
/*28*/                Buf->NumPipes++;
/*29*/              case Eoln:
/*30*/                Buf->Commands[ CommandNum++ ][ NumStr ] = NULL;
/*31*/                NumStr = 0;
/*32*/                break;
/*33*/              case Word:
/*34*/                Buf->Commands[ CommandNum ][ NumStr++ ] =
/*35*/                    Strdup( Str );    /* This Is A Memory Leak */
/*36*/                break;
/*37*/            }
/*38*/        return 0;
/*39*/    }
```

Figure 13.25: `Parse` **function.**

The main routine is shown in Figure 13.26. Lines 16 and 17 instruct our shell to ignore the interrupt and quit signals. We then repeatedly prompt the user and read a line from the standard input. If the line is not empty, we parse it and run the resulting full command. We terminate when the end of input is detected. All that remains is an implementation of RunCommand.

```
/* 1*/    /* Print A Prompt */
/* 2*/    void
/* 3*/    Prompt( int Num )
/* 4*/    {
/* 5*/        printf( "[%d] ", Num );
/* 6*/        fflush( stdout );
/* 7*/    }

/* 8*/    /* Simple main */
/* 9*/    main( void )
/*10*/    {
/*11*/        FullCommand OneComm;
/*12*/        char OneLine[ MaxLineLen ];
/*13*/        int RetCode;
/*14*/        int CommandNum = 1;
/*15*/
/*16*/        signal( SIGINT, SIG_IGN );   /* Ignore Signals */
/*17*/        signal( SIGQUIT, SIG_IGN );

/*18*/        for( Prompt( CommandNum ); GetLine( OneLine ); )
/*19*/        {
/*20*/            if( OneLine[ 0 ] != '\n' )
/*21*/            {
/*22*/                CommandNum++;
/*23*/                Parse( OneLine, &OneComm );
/*24*/                RunCommand( &OneComm );
/*25*/            }
/*26*/            Prompt( CommandNum );
/*27*/        }

/*28*/        return 0;
/*29*/    }
```

Figure 13.26: main **procedure.**

Figure 13.27 shows two important routines. First, SetFiles is called to redirect the standard input and output. If the standard input is to be redirected, we call freopen to reset the standard input file. We do the same thing if necessary for the standard output. The routine UsePipe assumes that Fd represents an already established pipe. If WhichEnd is STDIN_FILENO, the read end of the pipe is duplicated as the standard input; otherwise, WhichEnd is STDOUT_FILENO, and the write end of the pipe is duplicated as the standard output. Since STDIN_FILENO and STDOUT_FILENO are 0 and 1, respectively, we arrive at the statement at line 4. We then close the original descriptors associated with the pipe. As we mentioned before, one process will call UsePipe with WhichEnd equal to STDIN_FILENO, and another process will call UsePipe with WhichEnd equal to STDOUT_FILENO. Once again, we have skimped on error checking. We should check that WhichEnd is not equal to Fd[WhichEnd], and that the call to dup2 succeeded.

The RunCommand routine is shown in Figure 13.28. Except for the handling of pipes, it is similar to the RealSystem routine in Figure 13.19. At line 7 we call fork to create a new process. The parent continues execution at line 36, and unless the command

```
/* 1*/    void
/* 2*/    SetFiles( FullCommand *Buf )
/* 3*/    {
/* 4*/        if( Buf->InFile[ 0 ] )
/* 5*/            if( freopen( Buf->InFile, "r", stdin ) == NULL )
/* 6*/            {
/* 7*/                perror( Buf->InFile );
/* 8*/                _exit( 127 );
/* 9*/            }

/*10*/        if( Buf->OutFile[ 0 ] )
/*11*/            if( freopen( Buf->OutFile, "w", stdout ) == NULL )
/*12*/            {
/*13*/                perror( Buf->OutFile );
/*14*/                _exit( 127 );
/*15*/            }
/*16*/    }

/* 1*/    void
/* 2*/    UsePipe( int Fd[ 2 ], int WhichEnd )
/* 3*/    {
/* 4*/        dup2( Fd[ WhichEnd ], WhichEnd );
/* 5*/        close( Fd[ 0 ] );
/* 6*/        close( Fd[ 1 ] );
/* 7*/    }
```

Figure 13.27:   Redirection and pipe routines.

is supposed to run in the background, it waits for the child to finish. In the child we redirect the standard input and output at line 11. If the process is not running in the background, we restore the signals to the default setting. Recall that prior to the `fork` both interrupt and quit were ignored. Lines 18 to 30 handle the pipes. Let us suppose for now that there are no pipes, and thus the `for` loop terminates immediately with `i==0`. Then line 31 calls `execvp` (using the current search path to track down the executable file). `Buf->Commands[i]` corresponds to the `argv` vector of the new process, and the zeroth component of that vector is the command name. Lines 32 and 33 are executed only if the `execvp` fails.

At this point, the only remaining detail is the handling of pipes. Suppose that we have the command

who | grep becky | wc

which lists the number of times the user `becky` is logged on. Figure 13.29 shows a sequence of processes that is created for this command. We now discuss the steps taken to reach this solution.

It should be clear that we need to create two more processes, and thus each pipe requires an *additional* `fork`. Thus we need a `for` loop, which is iterated once per pipe. Inside the `for` loop we execute a `fork`. The `fork` will create two processes. One process will need to execute a command, and the other will remain in the loop and `fork` again. The question is, then, who does what? After some thought, it becomes clear that in the

```
/* 1*/    int
/* 2*/    RunCommand( FullCommand *Buf )
/* 3*/    {
/* 4*/        pid_t Pid;
/* 5*/        int Fd[ 2 ];
/* 6*/        int i;

/* 7*/        if( ( Pid = fork( ) ) < 0 )  /* Error */
/* 8*/            return -1;

/* 9*/        if( Pid == 0 )  /* Child */
/*10*/        {
/*11*/            SetFiles( Buf );
/*12*/            if( !Buf->Background )
/*13*/            {
/*14*/                signal( SIGINT, SIG_DFL );   /* Restore Signals */
/*15*/                signal( SIGQUIT, SIG_DFL );  /* Before Exec */
/*16*/            }

/*17*/            /* For Each pipe, We Need An Additional Process */
/*18*/            for( i = Buf->NumPipes; i > 0; i-- )
/*19*/            {
/*20*/                if( pipe( Fd ) < 0 )
/*21*/                {
/*22*/                    perror( Buf->Commands[ 0 ][ 0 ] );
/*23*/                    _exit( 127 );
/*24*/                }
/*25*/                if( ( Pid = fork( ) ) < 0 )
/*26*/                    return -1;

/*27*/                UsePipe( Fd, Pid ? STDIN_FILENO : STDOUT_FILENO );
/*28*/                if( Pid != 0 )  /* Parent */
/*29*/                    break;
/*30*/            }
/*31*/            execvp( Buf->Commands[ i ][ 0 ], Buf->Commands[ i ] );
/*32*/            perror( Buf->Commands[ i ][ 0 ] );
/*33*/            _exit( 127 );       /* execl Failed; Give Up On Child */
/*34*/        }

/*35*/        /* Shell Process: Note Pid Is Last Command In Pipeline */
/*36*/        if( !Buf->Background )
/*37*/            waitpid( Pid, NULL, 0 );

/*38*/        return 0;
/*39*/    }
```

Figure 13.28: **Code to run a command: coordinates the** `forks` **and** `execs`**.**

first additional `fork`, the parent should execute the last command in the pipeline. This is because the output from the full command is printed by the last command, and thus if we do not wait for it, we might print a prompt before the full command is finished.

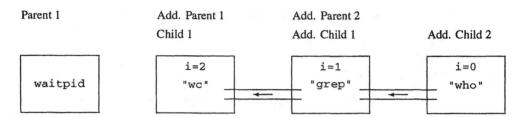

Figure 13.29: **How processes are created in** *who | grep becky | wc.*

Thus, for the first additional `fork`, the parent `exec`s the last command in the pipeline, and the child does a second additional `fork`. For that `fork` the parent should `exec` the next-to-last command. There are two reasons for this. First, consistency dictates that each iteration of the loop is identical. Thus each additional fork is just like the first: the parent runs a command, and the child continues the loop and `fork`s (at which point it becomes a parent, and runs). The second reason is that this scenario allows us to set up a pipe between commands in the pipeline.

At this point we can step through lines 17 to 31. The ith pipe connects command $i - 1$ and i. For each pipe right to left in the input line, we execute lines 20 to 29. At line 20, we attempt to establish a pipe. If it fails, we give up after reporting an error. Recall that `Buf->Commands[0][0]` is the name of the leftmost command in the pipeline. Otherwise, we perform a `fork`, creating a parent and a child process. The intent is that the parent will run the ith command, and the child will run the $(i - 1)$th command. Line 27 shows that the parent, which has nonzero `Pid`, will use the reading end of the pipe, and the child will use the writing end. At lines 28 and 29, the parent will exit the `for` loop and run the ith command by calling `execv`. The child stays in the loop for exactly one more iteration, decrements `i`, and creates a child of its own. This grandchild perpetuates the process, while the child performs an `exec` using the (decremented) value of `i` that corresponds to its place in `Buf->Commands`. We can see all this once again in Figure 13.29.

This example illustrates the remarkable power of the basic system calls. The exercises contain suggestions for additional features.

13.3   UNIX Program Development Tools

We conclude this chapter by examining some of the tools that UNIX provides to support program development. These tools are all relatively simple to use and not particularly fancy.

13.3.1   Making It Run: The *core* File and *dbx*

In the course of developing a program, you will almost always get one of the following run-time error messages, which we have referred to as a *program crash*:

```
Segmentation fault (core dumped)
Bus error (core dumped)
Illegal instruction (core dumped)
```

where	Print stack trace.
display exp, ...	Display the values of exp, ... after each *dbx* command.
dump	Print all variables local to current procedure.
list first, last	List source lines from first to last.
stop at line	Stop execution at line.
stop var	Stop execution when value of var changes.
run	Start execution.
step	Single step one line
help	Print help menu for *dbx*.
quit	Exit *dbx*

Figure 13.30:   Some common *dbx* **commands.**

A *segmentation fault* means that you have attempted to access an out-of-bounds memory location. Dereferencing a NULL pointer, for instance, will generate this type of error, and in many cases, dereferencing an undefined pointer will, too. A *bus error* is a less common form of an illegal memory access. Here it means that a pointer is misaligned. On many 32-bit machines, for instance, a pointer to an integer can only point at an address that is exactly divisible by 4. The most typical cause of a bus error is forgetting the & when using scanf. An *illegal instruction* invariably means that a runaway pointer has corrupted the part of memory that contains the instructions being executed.

All of these errors cause a signal to be sent to the running process. There are other signals that cause equivalent behavior, but they occur much less frequently. Some of these are shown in Figure 13.17. If a crashing signal is not caught, as is usually the case, the process terminates and writes an image in the form of a file named *core*. The shell, of course, ignores these signals, and when the child returns, it prints the appropriate error message shown above.

The core file is not written if the directory in which the program is started is not writable or if there is insufficient disk space. When no core file is generated, the message (core dumped) is omitted. The core file can be used by debuggers to determine more information about what went wrong. UNIX has several debuggers, which although not state of the art, can be very helpful in tracking down errors. *dbx* is invoked with the name of the executable file, and perhaps some options.

The simplest and most useful piece of information is a *stack trace*, which is obtained by popping activation records. Using *dbx*, the command where will list the functions that were started but were still pending when the program crashed.[6] *dbx* cannot extract more detailed information, such as line numbers, without extra help from the compiler. Specifically, it requires that source code be compiled with -g. This option will tell the compiler to generate extra information for use by the debugger. If the code has been compiled with -g, the debugger can be used to step through a program, stop at certain points, and print out current values of variables. Some of the commonly used commands are shown in Figure 13.30. Refer to the manual pages or the help inside *dbx* for options and more commands.

---

[6]This will not work if the executable file has been *stripped* of its symbol table. When that is the case, function addresses, rather than names, are printed.

13.3.2   Making It Run Fast: The Profiler *prof*

In Section 9.4 we saw that Shellsort operating on large objects takes considerably more time than Shellsort operating on integers. We were able to make the algorithm faster by using pointers to the objects, sorting the pointers, and then performing only a small number of object moves.

How did we know that the bottleneck of the sorting algorithm was the data movement? The answer is that a program called a *profiler* was used to determine how the sorting algorithm was spending its time. First, when we compile a program, we provide the *-p* (lowercase *p*) option. This option changes the function calling and exit sequence to keep track of time spent in each function. We then run the program as usual. When the program terminates, profiling information will be written to a file called *mon.out*, which is not human-readable. Finally, we run the command *prof*, supplying the name of the program as a command line argument. The result will be a table indicating how much time was spent in each procedure. The profiles of the sort procedures in Figures 9.13 and 9.16 are shown in Figure 13.31. Each profile represents 10 Shellsorts of 2000 objects. We use 10 sorts so that the overhead of generating the profile does not contribute significantly to the overall running time. The routine mcount is used to generate the mon.out file.

It is easy to see that in the original Shellsort, almost all of the running time is spent calling _memcpy. (Note that all C function names are preceded by an underscore, and assembler functions are not.) An average of 47,480 calls to _memcpy are made for each sort, accounting for a total of 0.7 second per sort. Only 0.02 second is charged to the rest of _Shellsort. _memcpy is the routine that is used to copy structures. In the indirect version of Shellsort, an average of only 2006 calls is made. The total time charged directly to _Shellsort and indirectly via _memcpy is only 0.08 second.

As we see in this example, the profiler is an easy-to-use mechanism that provides important information about a program's running time. Sometimes more detailed information is required. For instance, we might not want to count function call overhead. To do this, we need a function that returns the amount of CPU time that has been used so far. By calling this function twice—once before the segment of code that we want to time, and once after—and subtracting the return values, we obtain the elapsed time.

ANSI C specifies a function clock that measures CPU time. In Appendix D we discuss the clock function in more detail. Under UNIX, clock generally returns the sum of two types of time: *user* and *system*. The *system* time includes things such as system calls and any communal operating system charges, such as swapping and page faulting. The operating system overhead is divided among all processes. Thus the load of the system (i.e., number of active processes) will tend to increase the system time reported for a process. (Why?)

In many, though not all applications, we are concerned only with the *user* time. The getrusage system call can be used for this purpose, and in fact is the basis for an implementation of clock. Figure 13.32 shows getrusage and the related type declarations. If the first parameter to getrusage is RUSAGE_SELF then the request applies to the current process. The second parameter is a structure passed by reference. The rusage structure, declared in <sys/resource.h>, contains several fields, including two for the user and system time. The time is represented by the timeval structure, declared in <sys/time.h>. Note that this is not the same include file as <time.h>. Figure 13.33 shows the simple routine MilliElapsed, which returns the elapsed time, in milliseconds, since the previous call.

%time	cumsecs	#call	ms/call	name
94.6	7.03	474801	0.01	_memcpy
2.7	7.23	10	20.00	_Shellsort
2.2	7.39			mcount
0.3	7.41	20000	0.00	.mul
0.3	7.43	1	20.00	_main
0.0	7.43	1	0.00	_exit
0.0	7.43	2	0.00	_malloc
0.0	7.43	2	0.00	_on_exit
0.0	7.43	1	0.00	_profil
0.0	7.43	20000	0.00	_rand

%time	cumsecs	#call	ms/call	name
46.7	0.42	10	42.00	_Shellsort
42.2	0.80	20057	0.02	_memcpy
5.6	0.85	1	50.00	_main
4.4	0.89	20000	0.00	.mul
1.1	0.90			mcount
0.0	0.90	20000	0.00	.div
0.0	0.90	2	0.00	.udiv
0.0	0.90	2	0.00	.umul
0.0	0.90	22	0.00	_cfree
0.0	0.90	1	0.00	_exit
0.0	0.90	22	0.00	_free
0.0	0.90	22	0.00	_malloc
0.0	0.90	2	0.00	_on_exit
0.0	0.90	1	0.00	_profil
0.0	0.90	20000	0.00	_rand
0.0	0.90	2	0.00	_sbrk

Figure 13.31:   Output of *prof* for two versions of block Shellsort. Each run is for 10 random permutations of 2000 elements.

It is important to realize that although the type declaration in `<sys/time.h>` gives the appearance of a clock that is accurate to a microsecond, this is generally not the case. On some systems, the clock advances only 50 or 60 times per second. On our system, the clock advances only 100 times per second, or equivalently, once every 10 milliseconds. This means that on our system it is possible for a process to use 9.9 milliseconds and have an elapsed time of 0, and also for a process that uses only a microsecond to appear to have an elapsed time of 10 milliseconds. These anomalies are known as *quantization errors*; since prof obtains its timing information in the same manner, the accuracy of its timing data is also affected.

13.3.3   Making It Run for Others: The Archiver *ar*

`MilliElapsed` is an example of a function that is likely to be used by many different programs. As we have seen in Section 4.2.2, a source file, *MilliElapsed.c*, containing the `MilliElapsed` routine can be compiled once with the *-c* option to generate a *MilliElapsed.o* object file. The object file can then be passed as an additional argument to a subsequent *cc* compilation to indicate that it should be loaded.

```
struct timeval                          /* from sys/time.h */
{
    long tv_sec;                        /* seconds */
    long tv_usec;                       /* and microseconds */
};

struct rusage                           /* from sys/resource.h */
{
    struct timeval ru_utime;            /* user time used */
    struct timeval ru_stime;            /* system time used */
    /* Other fields omitted */
};


#include <sys/time.h>
#include <sys/resource.h>


enum { RUSAGE_SELF, RUSAGE_CHILDREN };      /* The Who parameter */


int getrusage( int Who, struct rusage *Buffer );
```

Figure 13.32: timeval **and** rusage **structures.**

```
/* 1*/    #include <sys/time.h>
/* 2*/    #include <sys/resource.h>

/* 3*/    #define Milli( X ) ( ( X.tv_sec * 1000 + X.tv_usec / 1000 ) )

/* 4*/    long int
/* 5*/    MilliElapsed( void )
/* 6*/    {
/* 7*/        struct Rusage Buf;
/* 8*/        static struct Timeval LastUtime;
/* 9*/        long int ElapsedTime;
/*10*/
/*11*/        getrusage( RUSAGE_SELF, &Buf );
/*12*/        ElapsedTime = Milli( Buf.ru_utime ) - Milli( LastUtime );
/*13*/        LastUtime = Buf.ru_utime;

/*14*/        return ElapsedTime;
/*15*/    }
```

Figure 13.33:   Routine to print elapsed time (in milliseconds) since last call to the routine.

The problem with that strategy is that if we have many different routines, we will have to provide many *.o* files to *cc*. A simple alternative is to create a library with all of our *.o* files. Libraries are maintained by the UNIX command *ar*. Many of the library routines that we have already used are found in */lib/libc.a*. This name reflects the convention that *.a* is the suffix used for libraries. The command

ar tv /lib/libc.a

lists all the routines contained in the library. (The *v* stands for *verbose* and causes a listing in a style similar to *ls -l*.)

When a library is provided as an argument to a *cc* command, it is scanned for functions that are needed but not defined in any of the other files. Thus, for the simple *Testing 123* program, `printf` is loaded but `scanf` is not. Also, any of the routines used by `printf`, either directly or indirectly, are also loaded. Consequently, libraries are listed last on the compilation command line.

The command

ar ruv $HOME/lib/my˙lib.a MilliElapsed.o

adds the `MilliElapsed` function to the library `my_lib.a`. The instruction *ru* means *replace and update*. Specifically, *MilliElapsed.o* is placed in the library only if it not already there, or if it is there, but is more recent. If the library does not exist, it is created.[7]

On some systems the *ranlib* command must be run after updating a library. As a result, a table of contents that indicates the location of each routine in the library is made at the start of the library. In our case we would type

ranlib $HOME/lib/my˙lib.a

Note that some systems perform *ranlib* as in implied part of the *ar* command.

We can then compile with

cc ... $HOME/lib/my˙lib.a

where ... represents the normal files and options.

Recall that when we use the standard library routines, we `#include` a file that contains constants, prototypes, and type declarations. It is reasonable to expect `#include` files will exist for our libraries, too. We can put the appropriate include files in a directory `$HOME/include`. The *-I* option can be used to add this directory to the include file search path. Then the compilation command becomes

cc -I$HOME/include ... $HOME/lib/my˙lib.a

We can avoid the extra typing by writing a simple shell script that calls the compiler with the library name and include search path. For large projects, however, a better solution is provided by the *make* command, which we discuss next.

13.3.4 Making It Easy to Compile: *make*

When a program consists of many source files, two problems surface. First there is the matter of deciding which files are compiled. It is not always true that *cc *.c* works. We may need additional options, and it might be the case that only some of the files are supposed to be compiled. For instance, there may be several `main` routines scattered in source files in the current directory.

The second problem is a matter of efficiency: if only one source file changes, it may be the case that only that file needs to be recompiled and then loaded with all the other *.o* files. The *make* utility attempts to automate this process. In this section we provide a very brief description.

---

[7]In our case, the directory `$HOME/lib` must, of course, already exist and be writable. Also, recall that the environment variable HOME is the full path name of the user's login directory.

```
# Makefile for following situation:
# tester.c and sub.c both include tester.h
# The source files may also use stuff from
# our library

tester: tester.o sub.o
        gcc -o tester tester.o sub.o $(HOME)/lib/my_lib.a

tester.o: tester.c tester.h
        gcc -O2 -I$(HOME)/include -c tester.c

sub.o: sub.c tester.h
        gcc -O2 -I$(HOME)/include -c sub.c
```

Figure 13.34:   Simple Makefile.

In the directory containing the source code we provide a file named Makefile. Although makefile is also an acceptable name, using the capitalized form allows the file to be easily visible when an *ls* command is used. The Makefile consists of a sequence of entries. A *dependency line* lists the name of a *target file* and all the other files that are needed to produce it. If any of those files change, the target file is recreated by applying the commands specified on the following line(s). These commands are indented by a tab stop (note that spaces will not do the trick).

In Figure 13.34 we show a simple Makefile. The global view is that source files tester.c and sub.c are used to compile tester. Both of the source files #include the file tester.h. The lines that begin with # are comments. tester depends directly on the object files tester.o and sub.o. *make* will recursively ensure that tester.o and sub.o are up to date. Once this is done, if tester is not up to date (relative to tester.o or sub.o), the object files are loaded by executing the gcc command.

tester.o depends on both the source file tester.c and the file tester.h. If either has been modified more recently than tester.o, tester.c is recompiled. A similar situation occurs for sub.o. Figure 13.35 shows a semantically equivalent Makefile that uses a few fancy features. First we see that macros can be defined. Thus we use macros to record the name of the C compiler, the options for the source code compilation, the include path, and libraries.

The first dependency states that the executable file tester depends on the two object files tester.o and sub.o. The action for this case is to invoke the compiler, with appropriate options, to load the object files and library. The second dependency is trickier. It says that each object file depends on the include file tester.h. But what about the fact that each object file depends on its corresponding .c source file? Because that is always true, it is an *implied dependency*, which *make* is always guaranteed to deduce. Thus it need not be listed explicitly. This is important, because otherwise we would need to write a dependency rule for each .c file. As it stands, one dependency rule suffices. The action is to compile the appropriate source file. $*.c is guaranteed to correspond to the out of date $*.o file that triggered the action. Though Figure 13.35 is lengthier than Figure 13.34, when there are many source files, Figure 13.35 does not get much longer. Thus it is the preferred style.

Any of the files that appear as a target can be brought up to date by *make*. In our case, we would issue the command *make tester*. By default *make* brings the first target up

```
# Makefile for following situation:
# tester.c and sub.c both include tester.h
# The source files may also use stuff from
# our library

CC      = gcc
CFLAGS  = -O2
INCLS   = -I$(HOME)/include
LIBS    = $(HOME)/lib/my_lib.a

OBJS    = tester.o sub.o
EFILE   = tester

$(EFILE): $(OBJS)
        $(CC) $(CFLAGS) -o $(EFILE) $(OBJS) $(LIBS)

$(OBJS): tester.h
        $(CC) $(CFLAGS) $(INCLS) -c $*.c
```

Figure 13.35: `Makefile` **that uses more** *make* **features.**

to date, and thus it is customary to put the ultimate target first. Our discussion illustrates only the most fundamental uses of *make*. A good UNIX book will give a more complete description.

13.3.5 Making It Pretty: Beautifiers *cb* and *indent*

UNIX systems provide programs that make source code look better. Typically, they indent and add white space in a consistent manner. The simplest such program is *cb*. It reads C source code and writes prettier code onto the standard output. *cb* provides few options, so you are stuck with one particular definition of "pretty." A more complex program is *indent*. Reading the manual pages is a must for this tool. *indent* allows you to specify a host of options that control the formatting. These options can also be placed in a file, to avoid repetitive typing. The most important rule is given in the *bugs* section of the manual pages. Do not say

indent *.c

It will overwrite the second *.c* file it finds with the beautified version of the first *.c* file.

13.4 Summary

In this chapter we have provided a quick tour of UNIX systems programming, as well as some the tools available for program development. Needless to say, we have left out many details. Specific information for all the commands is provided in Section 1 of the *UNIX Programmer's Manual*. This manual is accessible via the *man* command. Section 2 lists system calls, and Section 3 lists additional functions. The online manual pages are very terse and are not intended as a tutorial.

More information on using the UNIX commands can be found in [Abrahams 92] and [Sobell 89]. UNIX programming is covered in several books. The best of the bunch is probably [Stevens 92]. It is recent, covers all of the popular versions of UNIX, and is complete and detailed. It provides a host of examples and is very well written. Because UNIX keeps changing, many older books, such as [Kernighan 84], [Rochkind 85], and [Haviland 87], are somewhat dated. Even so, they all do a good job of explaining general principles.

13.4.1 What Was Covered

- UNIX treats peripheral devices and directories as files. As far as the user is concerned, the interface to devices and regular files is the same. The operating system hides the differences.

- The `stat` family can be used to obtain information *about* a file. This includes the type, owner, size, protection mode, and the time of last access or modification.

- A directory is just a file. It stores the names and inode numbers of the files in the directory. The `dir` family of routines can be used to read these entries portably.

- Each executing program is called a *process*.

- Processes are created by `fork`. The original process is the *parent*, and the new process is the *child*. Except for process ids and the return value from the `fork`, the parent and child are identical. An `exec` is used to overlay a process with a new program. It typically follows a `fork`.

- UNIX provides system calls to perform low-level I/O. A *file descriptor* is a small positive integer that indexes a table of pointers. Each of those pointers indexes a system-wide table that contains information for all files open currently. The `dup` system call duplicates an existing file descriptor; both file descriptors now point at the same entry in the system-wide table.

- A *pipe* is a pair of file descriptors. One end is the read end and the other is the write end. By judicious use of the `dup` and `fork`, two processes can communicate through the pipe.

- A *signal* is generated when an exceptional event, such as an interrupt, occurs. UNIX provides a mechanism for ignoring signals, handling signals specially, or blocking signals until they are ready to be handled. Unless arrangements are made, most signals cause program termination. Dealing with signals is complex and very system dependent; older versions of UNIX did not handle them well.

- When a program exits abnormally, a file named *core* is usually generated. The *dbx* debugger can be used to examine the remains.

- The *prof* command can be used to analyze where a program is spending its time. The program must be compiled with the *-p* option.

- The archiver *ar* can be used to create libraries.

- When a program consists of many source files, *make* should be used to avoid excessive recompilation.

13.4.2 Friendly Reminders

We do not provide the usual list of common errors because our intent is to provide a quick overview of UNIX programming. A list might imply that there are only a few details to consider. One warning that we mention is to remember that many of the include files needed for systems programming reside in the `sys` subdirectory.

Because there are so many different versions of UNIX, our best advice is to check the manual pages for specifics. If the pages are confusing, look at [Stevens 92].

EXERCISES

1. Our implementation of the *pwd* command makes a host of calls to `lstat`. By observing that inode numbers are available in the directory structure, modify the code to make fewer calls to `lstat`.

2. Implement the *du* routine so that double counting of links is avoided. This requires keeping a table of files seen previously. To make this efficient, you should use a hash table.

3. Write a program that gives exactly the same output as the command *ls -l*, without making direct or indirect calls to the *ls* command. To list the owner of a file, you need to look up the `getpwnam` family of commands.

4. Implement the command *localfinger*, which is the subset of *finger* that works only on the current machine.

5. If the disposition of a signal is to call a handler, it will be reset to the default mechanism (either ignore or do not ignore) when an `exec` is performed. Why is this a necessary action?

6. Suppose that signals are not ignored during the handler. Give a complete explanation of what can go wrong.

7. For the program depicted in Figure 13.36, state what gets printed if:

    (a) Signal handlers are reset to default when called (as is the old style).

    (b) Signals are blocked during execution of the handler.

    (c) Signals are ignored during execution of the handler.

    Verify your answers by learning more about `sigaction`. Based on your results, does the phrase *"execution of the handler"* include processing of another signal?

8. Rewrite the routine `SetFiles` in Figure 13.27. Have it call `close` and `open` instead of `freopen`. *Warning: You need to be careful to ensure that the files remain open across the* `exec`. *Read the manual pages for* `open` *carefully.*

9. Suppose that file descriptor 0 is already closed when the shell is invoked. What would happen if we try to run a command with the output redirected?

10. Many systems provide the functions `popen` and `pclose`, which have the following prototypes:

    ```
    FILE *popen( const char *Command, const char *Mode );
    int  pclose( FILE *Stream );
    ```

    `popen` executes `Command` and returns a stream. If `Mode` is `"r"`, we can read (the output of `Command`) from the stream, and if `Mode` is `"w"`, we can send input to the `Command` by writing to the stream. `pclose` closes the stream. The p in these two commands stands for the pipe that is set up. Write `popen` and `pclose`.

11. On your system, not including the command interpreter, how many processes can you have running simultaneously? Write a program to compute this number.

12. As we have mentioned, our shell is very lax on error checking. Identify all the places where an error check is in order, and modify the code appropriately.

```
/* 1*/    #include <stdio.h>
/* 2*/    #include <sys/types.h>
/* 3*/    #include <signal.h>

/* 4*/    pid_t Pid;

/* 5*/    void
/* 6*/    Handler1( void )
/* 7*/    {
/* 8*/        printf( "Entering Handler1\n" );
/* 9*/        kill( Pid, SIGUSR2 );
/*10*/        printf( "Leaving Handler1\n" );
/*11*/    }

/*12*/    void
/*13*/    Handler2( void )
/*14*/    {
/*15*/        printf( "Entering Handler2\n" );
/*16*/        kill( Pid, SIGUSR1 );
/*17*/        printf( "Leaving Handler2\n" );
/*18*/    }

/*19*/    main( void )
/*20*/    {
/*21*/        Pid = getpid( );
/*22*/        signal( SIGUSR1, Handler1 );
/*23*/        signal( SIGUSR2, Handler2 );
/*24*/        kill( Pid, SIGUSR1 );
/*25*/        return 0;
/*26*/    }
```

Figure 13.36:   Signal handlers that send other signals.

13. Extend the shell implementation to support the leading wild card (such as * or *.c) on the command line. When a leading * is seen, a search of the current directory is performed and all matching filenames are included in the command. If no files match, an error message is generated.

14. Why doesn't the *cd* command work in our shell? How would you make it work?

15. Incorporate a history mechanism into the shell.

16. Place all of the general-purpose routines that you have written thus far in a library. Place appropriate #include files in a single directory. Compile some programs that use these routines.

17. Write a program that accepts the names of input files and lists all the files that it #includes in a form similar to the *make* dependency line. Apply this recursively to the included files, to get a complete dependency chain.

Appendix A

Technical Issues

A.1 Scanning Order

An ANSI C compiler behaves as if the following phases occur, in the following order:

1. Trigraphs are expanded. Newline characters are introduced between lines of the source files should the operating system require it.

2. Each occurrence of the backslash character followed by a newline is deleted, thus creating logical source lines.

3. The resulting logical source file is decomposed into preprocessing tokens and sequences of white space. At each step, the next preprocessing token is the longest sequence of characters that could constitute a preprocessing token. Comments are replaced by a single space. Newlines are retained.

4. Preprocessing directives are executed and macros are expanded. If a `#include` is encountered, the named header file is processed recursively, beginning at step 1.

5. Escape sequences are processed.

6. String concatenation is performed.

7. White space is ignored. Each preprocessing token is converted to a token. The resulting token sequence is parsed.

A.2 Trigraphs

Figure A.1 shows the nine trigraph sequences that are recognized. No other sequences are allowed.

??<	{	??>	}	??/	\
??(	[	??)	]	??=	#
??!	|	??'	^	??-	~

Figure A.1:   Trigraph sequences.

Category	Examples	Associativity
Primary expression	*identifiers* *constants*	None
Postfix	Function( ) . -> [ ] ++ --	Left to right
Prefix and unary	sizeof * & ! ~ + - ++ --	Right to left
Type cast	(TypeName)	Right to left
Multiplicative	* / %	Left to right
Additive	+ -	Left to right
Shift	<< >>	Left to right
Relational	< <= > >=	Left to right
Equality	== !=	Left to right
Boolean AND	&	Left to right
Boolean XOR	^	Left to right
Boolean OR	|	Left to right
Logical AND	&&	Left to right
Logical OR	||	Left to right
Conditional	?:	Right to left
Assignment	= *= /= %= += -= &= |= ^= <<= >>=	Right to left
Comma	,	Left to right

Figure A.2:   Precedence and associativity of operators.

A.3   Precedence Rules

Figure A.2 lists the precedence of the C operators.

A.4   Sequence Points

Accessing a volatile object, modifying an object or file, or calling a function that does any of those operations indirectly is a *side effect*. ANSI C defines the sequence point. When a sequence point occurs, it is guaranteed that all side effects of the previous evaluation shall be complete and no side effects of subsequent evaluations have started. The most important consequence is that the result of modifying an object twice between sequence points is, strictly speaking, illegal. Specifically, an object may be altered at most once between sequence points, and if it is altered, the prior value may only be used to determine the value to be stored.

Sequence points are generated:

1.   At the end of the first operand of the logical *AND*, logical *OR*, conditional, and comma (`&&`, `||`, `?:`, and `,`) operators.

2.   After evaluation of the controlling expression of a `switch`, `if`, `while`, or `do`.

3.   After each evaluation of the three `for` statement expressions.

4.   After evaluation of the full expression in an expression statement.

5.   After evaluation of an initializer.

6.   After arguments have been evaluated prior to a function call.

7.   After the expression in a `return` is evaluated.

A.5   `const` **and** `volatile`

The `const` directive is used to specify that an object may not be modified by the programmer. Unless directed otherwise, the compiler may place `const` objects in read-only memory. Accessing a `const` type via a non-const type object results in undefined behavior. Many compilers will disallow it. (See Section 6.4 for more details.)

A `volatile` object may be modified externally, unbeknownst to the programmer. For example, a device driver might asynchronously set a memory location when data is ready to be read. In effect, we may assume that between each sequence point, it is possible for a `volatile` object to have its value changed. Consequently, code involving `volatile` objects may not be rearranged across sequence points by the optimizer. The compiler may not place `volatile` objects in read-only memory.

A.6   lvalues

An *lvalue* is an expression that designates an object. In K&R C, an lvalue was meant to imply something that could be assigned to. In ANSI C, these are *modifiable lvalues*. The following are lvalues:

1.   An identifier corresponding to an object

2.   A string literal

3. (lvalue)

4. lvalue.member

5. exp->member

6. *Ptr if Ptr points at an object

7. A[i] if *(A+i) is an lvalue

The following operators do not yield lvalues, even though it seems at first glance that they should.

1. The type cast

2. The conditional operator, even if the second and third expressions are lvalues

3. The comma operator, even if the second expression is an lvalue

A modifiable lvalue is an lvalue that

1. Is not a const qualified type

2. Is not an array type

3. Is not an incomplete type[1]

4. Is not a structure or union with a member that is a const-qualified type (*Note*: This rule is applied recursively.)

A.7   Difficult Function Prototypes

The declarations

```
int *Func( );          /* Func: function returning pointer to int */
int ( *Func )( );      /* Func: pointer to function returning int */
```

have different meanings because the postfix ( ) binds more tightly than the prefix *. This is the same general rule that we saw with operators. Thus to declare a pointer to a function returning an int, we need an extra set of parentheses.

Similarly, to declare a pointer to an array, we must parenthesize, or else we get an array of pointers.

```
int ( *PtrToArray )[ ];
```

It is quite easy to get carried away with the declarations, but by following these precedence rules carefully, you can declare just about anything. For instance, a pointer to a function returning a pointer to a double is declared as

```
double * ( *Func )( );
```

When declarations get this complex, it is time to use a typedef:

---

[1]An incomplete type is a type that lacks information to determine size. For instance, consider struct Node;

The full body of struct Node is declared elsewhere. Objects of type struct Node are modifiable lvalues only when the full declaration is visible (see Section 9.6).

```
typedef double *PtrDouble;
PtrDouble ( *Func )( );
```

As a final example, the declaration

```
int  ( * ( *X[3] )( ) )[ 5 ];
```

is parsed as follows

```
int  ( * ( *X[3] )( ) )[ 5 ];     /* X is an array[3] of A */
int  ( * ( *A )( ) )[ 5 ];        /* A is a ptr to func returning B */
int  ( * B )[ 5 ];                /* B is a pointer to C */
int  C[ 5 ];                      /* C is an array[5] of int */
```

Consequently, X is an array[3] of pointer to function returning pointer to array[5] of int. If we include the prototype list for functions, the declarations get considerably more complex, and it is difficult to express the English translation even if you know what it is!

Appendix B   **Grammar**

B.1   Lexical grammar

B.1.1   Tokens

(6.1) *token:*

> *keyword*
> *identifier*
> *constant*
> *string-literal*
> *operator*
> *punctuator*

(6.1) *preprocessing-token:*

> *header-name*
> *identifier*
> *pp-number*
> *character-constant*
> *string-literal*
> *operator*
> *punctuator*
> each non-white-space character that cannot be one of the above

B.1.2   Keywords

(6.1.1) *keyword:* one of

auto	double	int	struct
break	else	long	switch
case	enum	register	typedef
char	extern	return	union
const	float	short	unsigned
continue	for	signed	void
default	goto	sizeof	volatile
do	if	static	while

B.1.3   Identifiers

(6.1.2) *identifier:*

> *nondigit*
> *identifier nondigit*
> *identifier digit*

(6.1.2) *nondigit:* one of

> _ a b c d e f g h i j k l m
> n o p q r s t u v w x y z
> A B C D E F G H I J K L M
> N O P Q R S T U V W X Y Z

(6.1.2) *digit:* one of

> 0 1 2 3 4 5 6 7 8 9

B.1.4 Constants

(6.1.3) *constant:*

        floating-constant
        integer-constant
        enumeration-constant
        character-constant

(6.1.3.1) *floating-constant:*

        fractional-constant exponent-part$_{opt}$ floating-suffix$_{opt}$
        digit-sequence exponent-part floating-suffix$_{opt}$

(6.1.3.1) *fractional-constant:*

        digit-sequence$_{opt}$ **.** *digit-sequence*
        digit-sequence **.**

(6.1.3.1) *exponent-part:*

        e *sign$_{opt}$ digit-sequence*
        E *sign$_{opt}$ digit-sequence*

(6.1.3.1) *sign:* one of

        +   -

(6.1.3.1) *digit-sequence:*

        digit
        digit-sequence digit

(6.1.3.1) *floating-suffix:* one of

        f   l   F   L

(6.1.3.2) *integer-constant:*

        decimal-constant integer-suffix$_{opt}$
        octal-constant integer-suffix$_{opt}$
        hexadecimal-constant integer-suffix$_{opt}$

(6.1.3.2) *decimal-constant:*

        nonzero-digit
        decimal-constant digit

(6.1.3.2) *octal-constant:*

        0
        octal-constant octal-digit

(6.1.3.2) *hexadecimal-constant:*

        0x *hexadecimal-digit*
        0X *hexadecimal-digit*
        hexadecimal-constant hexadecimal-digit

(6.1.3.2) *nonzero-digit:* one of

        1   2   3   4   5   6   7   8   9

(6.1.3.2) *octal-digit:* one of

        0   1   2   3   4   5   6   7

(6.1.3.2) *hexadecimal-digit:* one of

    0 1 2 3 4 5 6 7 8 9

    a b c d e f

    A B C D E F

(6.1.3.2) *integer-suffix:*

    unsigned-suffix long-suffix$_{opt}$

    long-suffix unsigned-suffix$_{opt}$

(6.1.3.2) *unsigned-suffix:* one of

    u U

(6.1.3.2) *long-suffix:* one of

    l L

(6.1.3.3) *enumeration-constant:*

    identifier

(6.1.3.4) *character-constant:*

    ' c-char-sequence'

    L' c-char-sequence'

(6.1.3.4) *c-char-sequence:*

    c-char

    c-char-sequence c-char

(6.1.3.4) *c-char:*

    any member of the source character set except

        the single-quote ', backslash \, or new-line character

    escape-sequence

(6.1.3.4) *escape-sequence:*

    simple-escape-sequence

    octal-escape-sequence

    hexadecimal-escape-sequence

(6.1.3.4) *simple-escape-sequence:* one of

    \' \" \? \\

    \a \b \f \n \r \t \v

(6.1.3.4) *octal-escape-sequence:*

    \ *octal-digit*

    \ *octal-digit octal-digit*

    \ *octal-digit octal-digit octal-digit*

(6.1.3.4) *hexadecimal-escape-sequence:*

    \x *hexadecimal-digit*

    hexadecimal-escape-sequence hexadecimal-digit

B.1.5 String literals

(6.1.4) *string-literal:*

    "s-char-sequence$_{opt}$*"*

    L"s-char-sequence$_{opt}$*"*

(6.1.4) *s-char-sequence:*
> s-char
> s-char-sequence s-char

(6.1.4) *s-char:*
> any member of the source character set except
> > the double-quote ", backslash \, or new-line character
> *escape-sequence*

B.1.6 Operators

(6.1.5) *operator:* one of
> [ ] ( ) . ->
> ++ -- & * + - ~ ! sizeof
> / % << >> < > <= >= == != ^ | && ||
> ? :
> = *= /= %= += -= <<= >>= &= ^= |=
> , # ##

B.1.7 Punctuators

(6.1.6) *punctuator:* one of
> [ ] ( ) { } * , : = ; ... #

B.1.8 Header names

(6.1.7) *header-name:*
> <h-char-sequence>
> "q-char-sequence"

(6.1.7) *h-char-sequence:*
> h-char
> h-char-sequence h-char

(6.1.7) *h-char:*
> any member of the source character set except
> > the new-line character and >

(6.1.7) *q-char-sequence:*
> q-char
> q-char-sequence q-char

(6.1.7) *q-char:*
> any member of the source character set except
> > the new-line character and "

B.1.9 Preprocessing numbers

(6.1.8) *pp-number:*
> digit
> . digit
> pp-number digit
> pp-number nondigit
> pp-number e sign
> pp-number E sign
> pp-number .

B.2 Phrase structure grammar

B.2.1 Expressions

(6.3.1) *primary-expression:*
        identifier
        constant
        string-literal
        (*expression*)

(6.3.2) *postfix-expression:*
        primary-expression
        postfix-expression [*expression*]
        postfix-expression (*argument-expression-list*$_{opt}$)
        postfix-expression . *identifier*
        postfix-expression -> *identifier*
        postfix-expression ++
        postfix-expression --

(6.3.2) *argument-expression-list:*
        assignment-expression
        argument-expression-list , *assignment-expression*

(6.3.3) *unary-expression:*
        postfix-expression
        ++ *unary-expression*
        -- *unary-expression*
        unary-operator cast-expression
        sizeof *unary-expression*
        sizeof (*type-name*)

(6.3.3) *unary-operator:* one of
        & * + - ~ !

(6.3.4) *cast-expression:*
        unary-expression
        (*type-name*) *cast-expression*

(6.3.5) *multiplicative-expression:*
        cast-expression
        multiplicative-expression * *cast-expression*
        multiplicative-expression / *cast-expression*
        multiplicative-expression % *cast-expression*

(6.3.6) *additive-expression:*
        multiplicative-expression
        additive-expression + *multiplicative-expression*
        additive-expression - *multiplicative-expression*

(6.3.7) *shift-expression:*
        additive-expression
        shift-expression << *additive-expression*
        shift-expression >> *additive-expression*

(6.3.8) *relational-expression:*
>*shift-expression*
>*relational-expression* **<** *shift-expression*
>*relational-expression* **>** *shift-expression*
>*relational-expression* **<=** *shift-expression*
>*relational-expression* **>=** *shift-expression*

(6.3.9) *equality-expression:*
>*relational-expression*
>*equality-expression* **==** *relational-expression*
>*equality-expression* **!=** *relational-expression*

(6.3.10) *AND-expression:*
>*equality-expression*
>*AND-expression* **&** *equality-expression*

(6.3.11) *exclusive-OR-expression:*
>*AND-expression*
>*exclusive-OR-expression* **^** *AND-expression*

(6.3.12) *inclusive-OR-expression:*
>*exclusive-OR-expression*
>*inclusive-OR-expression* **|** *exclusive-OR-expression*

(6.3.13) *logical-AND-expression:*
>*inclusive-OR-expression*
>*logical-AND-expression* **&&** *inclusive-OR-expression*

(6.3.14) *logical-OR-expression:*
>*logical-AND-expression*
>*logical-OR-expression* **||** *logical-AND-expression*

(6.3.15) *conditional-expression:*
>*logical-OR-expression*
>*logical-OR-expression* **?** *expression* **:** *conditional-expression*

(6.3.16) *assignment-expression:*
>*conditional-expression*
>*unary-expression assignment-operator assignment-expression*

(6.3.16) *assignment-operator:* **one of**
>**=   *=   /=   %=   +=   -=   <<=   >>=   &=   ^= |=**

(6.3.17) *expression:*
>*assignment-expression*
>*expression* **,** *assignment-expression*

(6.4) *constant-expression:*
>*conditional-expression*

B.2.2 Declarations

(6.5) *declaration:*

           declaration-specifiers init-declarator-list$_{opt}$;

(6.5) *declaration-specifiers:*

           storage-class-specifier declaration-specifiers$_{opt}$

           type-specifier declaration-specifiers$_{opt}$

           type-qualifier declaration-specifiers$_{opt}$

(6.5) *init-declarator-list:*

           init-declarator

           init-declarator-list , init-declarator

(6.5) *init-declarator:*

           declarator

           declarator = initializer

(6.5.1) *storage-class-specifier:*

           typedef

           extern

           static

           auto

           register

(6.5.2) *type-specifier:*

           void

           char

           short

           int

           long

           float

           double

           signed

           unsigned

           struct-or-union-specifier

           enum-specifier

           typedef-name

(6.5.2.1) *struct-or-union-specifier:*

           struct-or-union identifier$_{opt}$ { struct-declaration-list }

           struct-or-union identifier

(6.5.2.1) *struct-or-union:*

           struct

           union

(6.5.2.1) *struct-declaration-list:*

           struct-declaration

           struct-declaration-list struct-declaration

(6.5.2.1) *struct-declaration:*

           specifier-qualifier-list struct-declarator-list ;

(6.5.2.1) *specifier-qualifier-list:*

> *type-specifier specifier-qualifier-list$_{opt}$*
> *type-qualifier specifier-qualifier-list$_{opt}$*

(6.5.2.1) *struct-declarator-list:*

> *struct-declarator*
> *struct-declarator-list , struct-declarator*

(6.5.2.1) *struct-declarator:*

> *declarator*
> *declarator$_{opt}$: constant-expression*

(6.5.2.2) *enum-specifier:*

> **enum** *identifier$_{opt}$ { enumerator-list }*
> **enum** *identifier*

(6.5.2.2) *enumerator-list:*

> *enumerator*
> *enumerator-list , enumerator*

(6.5.2.2) *enumerator:*

> *enumeration-constant*
> *enumeration-constant = constant-expression*

(6.5.3) *type-qualifier:*

> **const**
> **volatile**

(6.5.4) *declarator:*

> *pointer$_{opt}$ direct-declarator*

(6.5.4) *direct-declarator:*

> *identifier*
> *(declarator)*
> *direct-declarator [constant-expression$_{opt}$]*
> *direct-declarator (parameter-type-list)*
> *direct-declarator (identifier-list$_{opt}$)*

(6.5.4) *pointer:*

> * *type-qualifier-list$_{opt}$*
> * *type-qualifier-list$_{opt}$ pointer*

(6.5.4) *type-qualifier-list:*

> *type-qualifier*
> *type-qualifier-list type-qualifier*

(6.5.4) *parameter-type-list:*

> *parameter-list*
> *parameter-list , ...*

(6.5.4) *parameter-list:*

> *parameter-declaration*
> *parameter-list , parameter-declaration*

(6.5.4) *parameter-declaration:*

> *declaration-specifiers declarator*
> *declaration-specifiers abstract-declarator$_{opt}$*

(6.5.4) *identifier-list:*

> *identifier*
> *identifier-list , identifier*

(6.5.5) *type-name:*

> *specifier-qualifier-list abstract-declarator$_{opt}$*

(6.5.5) *abstract-declarator:*

> *pointer*
> *pointer$_{opt}$ direct-abstract-declarator*

(6.5.5) *direct-abstract-declarator:*

> *(abstract-declarator)*
> *direct-abstract-declarator$_{opt}$ [constant-expression$_{opt}$]*
> *direct-abstract-declarator$_{opt}$ (parameter-type-list$_{opt}$)*

(6.5.6) *typedef-name:*

> *identifier*

(6.5.7) *initializer:*

> *assignment-expression*
> *{ initializer-list }*
> *{ initializer-list , }*

(6.5.7) *initializer-list:*

> *initializer*
> *initializer-list , initializer*

B.2.3 Statements

(6.6) *statement:*

> *labeled-statement*
> *compound-statement*
> *expression-statement*
> *selection-statement*
> *iteration-statement*
> *jump-statement*

(6.6.1) *labeled-statement:*

> *identifier : statement*
> **case** *constant-expression : statement*
> **default** *: statement*

(6.6.2) *compound-statement:*

> *{ declaration-list$_{opt}$ statement-list$_{opt}$ }*

(6.6.2) *declaration-list:*

> *declaration*
> *declaration-list declaration*

(6.6.2) *statement-list:*

> *statement*
> *statement-list statement*

(6.6.3) *expression-statement:*

> *expression$_{opt}$;*

(6.6.4) *selection-statement:*

>   **if** (*expression*) *statement*
>   **if** (*expression*) *statement* **else** *statement*
>   **switch** (*expression*) *statement*

(6.6.5) *iteration-statement:*

>   **while** (*expression*) *statement*
>   **do** *statement* **while** (*expression*) ;
>   **for** (*expression*$_{opt}$; *expression*$_{opt}$; *expression*$_{opt}$) *statement*

(6.6.6) *jump-statement:*

>   **goto** *identifier* ;
>   **continue** ;
>   **break** ;
>   **return** *expression*$_{opt}$;

B.2.4 External definitions

(6.7) *translation-unit:*

>   *external-declaration*
>   *translation-unit external-declaration*

(6.7) *external-declaration:*

>   *function-definition*
>   *declaration*

(6.7.1) *function-definition:*

>   *declaration-specifiers*$_{opt}$ *declarator declaration-list*$_{opt}$ *compound-statement*

B.3 Preprocessing directives

(6.8) *preprocessing-file:*

>   *group*$_{opt}$

(6.8) *group:*

>   *group-part*
>   *group group-part*

(6.8) *group-part:*

>   *pp-tokens*$_{opt}$ *new-line*
>   *if-section* ;
>   *control-line*

(6.8.1) *if-section:*

>   *if-group elif-groups*$_{opt}$ *else-group*$_{opt}$ *endif-line*

(6.8.1) *if-group:*

>   **# if**   *constant-expression new-line group*$_{opt}$
>   **# ifdef**   *identifier new-line group*$_{opt}$
>   **# ifndef** *identifier new-line group*$_{opt}$

(6.8.1) *elif-groups:*
>   *elif-group*
>   *elif-groups elif-group*

(6.8.1) *elif-group:*
>   **# elif**   *constant-expression new-line group$_{opt}$*

(6.8.1) *else-group:*
>   **# else**   *new-line group$_{opt}$*

(6.8.1) *endif-line:*
>   **# endif**   *new-line*

control-line:

(6.8.2)	**# include**	*pp-tokens new-line*
(6.8.3)	**# define**	*identifier replacement-list new-line*
(6.8.3)	**# define**	*identifier lparen identifier-list$_{opt}$) replacement-list new-line*
(6.8.3)	**# undef**	*identifier new-line*
(6.8.4)	**# line**	*pp-tokens new-line*
(6.8.5)	**# error**	*pp-tokens$_{opt}$ new-line*
(6.8.6)	**# pragma**	*pp-tokens$_{opt}$ new-line*
(6.8.7)	**#**	*new-line*

(6.8.3) *lparen:*

>   the left-parenthesis character without preceding white space

(6.8.3) *replacement-list:*
>   *pp-tokens$_{opt}$*

(6.8) *pp-tokens:*
>   *preprocessing-token*
>   *pp-tokens preprocessing-token*

(6.8) *new-line:*

>   the new-line character

Appendix C

Minimums

Figure C.1 shows some of the minimum limits that a ANSI C compiler may place on the user. In addition, the `#include` files `<limits.h>` and `<floats.h>` contain the maximum and minimum values for the basic data types. In Appendix D we provide the minimums (in magnitude) that these values must have according to ANSI C.

Significant initial characters in an external identifier	6
Nesting levels of conditional inclusion	8
Nested `#include` statements	8
Nested `struct` or `union` definitions	15
Nested conditionals or loops	15
Significant initial characters in internal identifier or macro name	31
Formal parameters in a function or macro definition	31
Actual parameters in a function or macro definition	31
Nested levels of parentheses in an expression	32
Identifiers in single block scope	127
Members in a `struct` or `union`	127
Enumeration constants in an enumeration	127
`case` labels in a single `switch`	257
Characters in a logical source line	509
Characters in a constant string (after concatenation)	509
External identifiers	511
Macro identifiers simultaneously active	1024
Bytes in an object	32767

Figure C.1:   Some minimum limits.

Appendix D

The Library

In addition to the language proper, ANSI C defines a set of functions, known as the library. We have already discussed many of the library routines. Each library routine has a corresponding prototype in one of 15 header files. These header files also include macro definitions and `typedef` statements. This appendix provides a complete summary of the library. Each header file is discussed in its own section. First we list macros, types, and functions. For `typedef`s we provide a typical definition in some cases. Of course, each implementation is free to supply something different. We then provide descriptions of these functions. To avoid redundancy, we provide text references for those that have already been discussed.

A complete reference can, of course, be found in the ANSI C standard. Most systems provide complete online documentation of all library routines. A very good alternative, which discusses implementation of the library and all of the finer points, is [Plauger 92].

D.1 <assert.h>

```
#define assert( Expr )
```

`assert` must be a macro. If the macro `NDEBUG` is defined, calls to `assert` are ignored. Otherwise, if `Expr` is zero, an error message is printed and the program is aborted. This error message includes `Expr` as well as the source code file name and line number.

D.2   <ctype.h>

```
/* Typically macros */
int isalnum( int Ch );          /* nonzero if alphanumeric */
int isalpha( int Ch );          /* nonzero if alphabetic */
int iscntrl( int Ch );          /* nonzero if control char */
int isdigit( int Ch );          /* nonzero if [0-9]  */
int isgraph( int Ch );          /* nonzero if graphic */
int islower( int Ch );          /* nonzero if lower case */
int isprint( int Ch );          /* nonzero if printable */
int ispunct( int Ch );          /* nonzero if punctuation */
int isspace( int Ch );          /* nonzero if white space */
int isupper( int Ch );          /* nonzero if upper case */
int isxdigit( int Ch );         /* nonzero if [0-9a-fA-F] */

/* Typically functions */
int tolower( int Ch );          /* return lowercase equivalent */
int toupper( int Ch );          /* return uppercase equivalent */
```

The is... family of routines was discussed in Section 8.3. Recall that these routines are generally macros that index an array without checking that Ch is in the valid character set. The meanings of some functions can depend on the current locale (see Section D.6). Figure 8.4 shows the standard meanings.

tolower returns Ch if Ch is not an uppercase character; otherwise, it returns the corresponding lowercase character. toupper is similar.

D.3   <errno.h>

```
/* Macros */
#define EDOM
#define ERANGE

/* Modifiable lvalue; typically an int */
extern int errno;
```

errno is set by various routines to indicate an error. perror and strerror, whose prototypes are in <stdlib.h>, can be used to print error messages based on errno. EDOM and ERANGE are macros used by <math.h> routines for errno. Many systems define additional error codes.

D.4   <float.h>

```
/* Limits for floating types. */
/* Minimums are shown */

#define FLT_MAX          1E+37
#define DBL_MAX          1E+37
#define LDBL_MAX         1E+37

#define FLT_MIN          1E-37
#define DBL_MIN          1E-37
#define LDBL_MIN         1E-37

#define FLT_MAX_10_EXP   +37
#define DBL_MAX_10_EXP   +37
#define LDBL_MAX_10_EXP  +37

#define FLT_MIN_10_EXP   -37
#define DBL_MIN_10_EXP   -37
#define LDBL_MIN_10_EXP  -37

#define FLT_EPSILON      1E-5
#define DBL_EPSILON      1E-9
#define LDBL_EPSILON     1E-9

/* Representation Constants */
#define FLT_RADIX        2       /* Radix of exponent representation */
#define FLT_ROUNDS               /* -1, 0, 1, 2, or 3: see notes */

/* Number of (base FLT_RADIX) digits in the mantissa */
#define FLT_MANT_DIG
#define DBL_MANT_DIG
#define LDBL_MANT_DIG

/* Number of significant decimal digits */
#define FLT_DIG          6
#define DBL_DIG          10
#define LDBL_DIG         10

/* Minimums and maximums such that FLT_RADIX raised to 1 */
/* less than that power is a normalized floating-point number */
#define FLT_MIN_EXP
#define DBL_MIN_EXP
#define LDBL_MIN_EXP

#define FLT_MAX_EXP
#define DBL_MAX_EXP
#define LDBL_MAX_EXP
```

The header file contains macros that indicate the range of the floating-point types.

The minimum and maximum `float` values are given by `FLT_MIN` and `FLT_MAX`, respectively. The corresponding exponent limits are given by `FLT_MIN_10_EXP` and `FLT_MAX_10_EXP`. The constants shown above represent the minimum required by ANSI C. Similar macros are also defined for `double` and `long double`.

The largest `float` that is less than 1.0 is no larger than `1-FLT_EPSILON`. Thus `FLT_EPSILON` represents the granularity of the `float` type. Similar macros are defined for `double` and `long double`. Once again, the values specified are ANSI C minimums.

The model used is that a *normalized floating-point number* $x \neq 0$ is defined as

$$x = s * b^e * \sum_{k=1}^{p} f_k * b^{-k} \qquad \text{[D.1]}$$

where s is the sign (± 1), b is the base (radix of exponent representation), e is the exponent, p is the precision, and $\{f_k\}$ is a sequence of nonnegative integers less than b. `FLT_RADIX` is b; it must be at least 2. `FLT_ROUNDS` is the rounding method, given by:

-1 indeterminable

  0 toward zero

  1 to nearest representable

  2 toward positive infinity

  3 toward negative infinity

`FLT_MANT_DIG` is p, and `FLT_MIN_EXP` and `FLT_MAX_EXP` are the minimum and maximum allowable e. `FLT_DIG` represents the number of significant decimal digits; this is a function of the other parameters. All of these macros have counterparts for `double` and `long double`.

D.5 `<limits.h>`

```
#define CHAR_BIT      0x8       /* Bits per byte */
#define MB_LEN_MAX    1         /* Bytes per multibyte character */

/* Some limits for various types.  Each system sets its own, */
/* however, ANSI minimums (in magnitude) are shown. */

    /* Signed char, unsigned char, plain char */
#define SCHAR_MIN     -0x7F
#define SCHAR_MAX      0x7F
#define UCHAR_MAX      0xFF
#define CHAR_MIN     0 or SCHAR_MIN
#define CHAR_MAX     UCHAR_MAX or SCHAR_MAX

    /* short, unsigned short */
#define SHRT_MIN      -0x7FFF
#define SHRT_MAX       0x7FFF
#define USHRT_MAX      0xFFFF

    /* int, unsigned int */
#define INT_MIN       -0x7FFF
#define INT_MAX        0x7FFF
#define UINT_MAX       0xFFFF

    /* long, unsigned long */
#define LONG_MIN      -0x7FFFFFFF
#define LONG_MAX       0x7FFFFFFF
#define ULONG_MAX      0xFFFFFFFF
```

This file defines various system limits. These are self-explanatory.

D.6   <locale.h>

```
#define NULL                   /* Redefined to match stdio.h */

struct lconv
{
    char *decimal_point;    /* decimal point character */
    char *thousands_sep;    /* thousands separator character */
    char *grouping;         /* grouping of digits */

     /* For printing amount of money */
    char *mon_decimal_point; /* decimal point character */
    char *mon_thousands_sep; /* thousands separator */
    char *mon_grouping;     /* grouping of digits */

     /* For printing credits and debits */
    char *positive_sign;    /* credit symbol */
    char *negative_sign;    /* debit symbol */

     /* cs = currency symbol */
    char p_cs_precedes;     /* true if cs precedes credit */
    char p_sep_by_space;    /* true if space separates c.s. from credit */
    char n_cs_precedes;     /* true if cs precedes debit */
    char n_sep_by_space;    /* true if space separates c.s. from debit */

     /* Position codes are: */
     /* 0: Parentheses surround everything */
     /* 1: Sign string goes first */
     /* 2: Sign string goes last */
     /* 3: Sign string immediately precedes currency symbol */
     /* 4: Sign string immediately succeeds currency symbol */

    char p_sign_posn;       /* position of sign for credit */
    char n_sign_posn;       /* position of sign for debit */

     /* International money */
    char *int_curr_symbol;  /* currency symbol */
    char int_frac_digits;   /* number of fractional digits */

     /* Local money */
    char *currency_symbol;  /* currency symbol */
    char frac_digits;       /* number of fractional digits */
};

/* Used for setlocale.  Affected routines are indicated */
#define LC_ALL        /* Everything below */
#define LC_COLLATE    /* strcoll and strxfrm */
#define LC_CTYPE      /* character handling and multibyte functions */
#define LC_MONETARY   /* monetary quantities given by localeconv */
#define LC_NUMERIC    /* formatted I/O, string conv, and localeconv */
#define LC_TIME       /* strftime, and related routines */

/* Two functions */
char *setlocale( int Category, const char *Locale );
struct lconv *localeconv( void );
```

<locale.h> is an attempt to make C more easily usable internationally. It defines two functions, a structure, and a few macros for use with one of the functions. First, we examine setlocale. The widespread use of C in countries where English is not the native language has caused problems. Most European languages, for instance, have accented characters. Thus it is reasonable to expect that â has a character code. Since a char generally occupies 8 bits, we can usually store all characters, including accented ones. This is not true for Asian character sets; that is why the *multibyte character* was invented.

Now, of course, the usual character routines in <ctype.h> should work on these foreign character sets. So in other countries, these routines are altered. The problem is that routines written in one country no longer work in another country. Enter the locales. The idea is that the routines in <ctype.h> are written for a host of supported locales, such as France, Germany, and United States. By default, the traditional "C" locale is used. We can change to the "" locale, which represents the local environment, or we can change to some other locale (perhaps for testing before foreign shipment). What locales must be supported? Just "C" and "", and of course "" could be the same as "C". But it is possible that in the future, a host of locales will be standard.

The first parameter to setlocale is one of the categories given by the LC macros. Each category can affect some functions. LC_TIME is the most widely supported: by changing the locale for that category, you can affect the time zone used by the date printing routines. LC_ALL encompasses all of the categories. The second parameter is the locale, described above. As we have mentioned, "C" and "" are guaranteed to be acceptable locales, other locales may be errors. setlocale returns NULL on error, or the old setting (so it can be restored later, if needed).[1] The other function in <locale.h> is localeconv. The library maintains a struct lconv object; localeconv returns a pointer to that object. The user can then change fields of the object as desired.

The first three fields are strings representing the decimal point (by default " . "), the thousands separator (by default " "), and the grouping of digits (to determine where to place the separators). The printf family of routines is required to honor the decimal point convention; the other two fields might be ignored. Thus the output of the following code is 123,456.

```
struct lconv *Obj = localeconv( );
Obj->decimal_point = ",";
printf( "%f\n", 123.456 );
```

The remaining fields in the lconv structure dictate the form for output of monetary values. This is important, as C emerges as a system used for accounting software. Unfortunately, ANSI C does not provide a routine to output monetary values. Thus these remaining fields suggest a standard to be followed by those who would write monetary output routines.

---

[1]Consequently, NULL is also defined in <locale.h>.

D.7   <math.h>

```
/*Macro */
#define HUGE_VAL

/* Trigonometric functions -- all angles in radians */
double sin( double Theta );
double cos( double Theta );
double tan( double Theta) ;
double asin( double X );      /* Result is between +/- Pi/2 */
double acos( double X );      /* Result is between 0 and Pi */
double atan( double X );      /* Result is between +/- Pi/2 */
double atan2( double Y, double  X );  /* See notes */

/* Hyperbolic functions */
double sinh( double Theta );
double cosh( double Theta );
double tanh( double Theta );

/* Logarithms and exponents */
double exp( double X );       /* e^X */
double frexp( double Value, int *Exp );         /* See notes */
double ldexp( double Mantissa, int Exp );        /* See notes */
double log( double X );       /* Base e */
double log10( double X );     /* Base 10 */
double pow( double X, double Y );  /* X^Y */
double sqrt( double X );      /* Square root */

/* Useful stuff */
double modf( double Value, double *IntPart );  /* Get int and fraction */
double ceil( double X );      /* Ceiling function */
double floor( double X );     /* Floor function */
double fabs( double X );      /* Absolute value */
double fmod( double X, double Y );  /* Mod operation */
```

<math.h> provides routines for mathematical operations. On some UNIX machines, you must specify *-lm* as a last option to load these routines.

HUGE_VAL is the largest representable double. Either it or its negative is returned on overflow, as appropriate, and ERANGE is stored in errno (see Section D.3). For underflow (i.e., answers too small in magnitude), zero is returned. EDOM is stored in errno when a parameter to a math function is illegal (e.g., a negative number for sqrt).

Most of these functions do what you expect. All angles are in radians. For the inverse trigonometric function, there is always the question of which quadrant the returned angle should be in. This is indicated in the comments. For atan2, the quadrant of $\tan^{-1}(Y/X)$ is determined by the signs of Y and X. Note that either X or Y, but not both, may be zero.

frexp splits Value into a mantissa and exponent. The magnitude of the mantissa is either zero or resides in the half-open interval $[\frac{1}{2}, 1)$. The statement

```
Mantissa = frexp( Value, &Exp );
```

causes $Value = Mantissa * 2^{Exp}$ to hold. ldexp returns Value given the mantissa and exponent.

modf splits Value into an integer part (passed back by IntPart) and a fractional part that is returned. Both parts have the same sign as Value. fmod extends the mod operation to doubles.

D.8 <setjmp.h>

```
/* Typedef for jmp_buf -- typically an array */
typedef int jmp_buf[9];

/* Functions */
int setjmp( jmp_buf Environ );
void longjmp( jmp_buf Environ, int ReturnVal );
```

This header implements the nonlocal gotos that were seen in Section 13.2.3. Look there for further examples.

setjmp saves the current calling environment in Environ for later use by longjmp. It returns 0.

longjmp restores the environment, simulating a return from the previous setjmp. The return value simulated is either ReturnVal, or 1 if ReturnVal is 0. This way, we can tell if the statement after setjmp was reached as a result of a longjmp.

Both of these routines must be macros and are typically used in conjunction with signals.

D.9 <signal.h>

```
/* Minimum set of macros -- UNIX provides more */

   /* Types of signals */
#define SIGABRT     /* Abnormal termination. */
#define SIGFPE      /* Floating-point exception or divide by 0 */
#define SIGILL      /* Illegal instruction */
#define SIGINT      /* Interrupt signal */
#define SIGSEGV     /* Segment violation -- illegal memory access */
#define SIGTERM     /* Termination signal */

   /* How to handle signals */
#define SIG_DFL     /* Default handling of signal */
#define SIG_IGN     /* Ignore signal */
#define SIG_ERR     /* retuned if signal( ) fails */

void ( *signal( int SigNum, void ( *Handler )( int ) ) ) ( int SigNum )
int raise( int SigNum );

   /* Integer type accessible as an atomic unit */
typedef ... sig_atomic_t;
```

These routines are based on the signal handlers from early versions of UNIX. Signals are an inherently nonportable construct. All ANSI C specifies is a minimum interface. Most systems will provide more.

Section 13.2.3 shows how UNIX handles signals. There, raise is implemented by the kill system call. The type sig_atomic_t represents the largest integer type that is accessible as an atomic unit. For instance, on a 16-bit machine, a 32-bit-long int might be implemented as two pieces of data, and if a signal occurs between transmission of the halves, the second half could be lost. In that case, sig_atomic_t would be the int type.

D.10   <stdarg.h>

```
/* Macros to traverse variable argument lists */
/* Needless to say, this is highly machine dependent */
/* We give an implementation that works if parameters */
/* are stored consecutively */

typedef void *va_list;

#define va_start( ArgPointer, LastArg ) \
    ( ArgPointer = &LastArg + sizeof( LastArg ) )
#define va_arg( ArgPointer, Type ) \
    ( *( ( type * )( ArgPointer ) )++ )
#define va_end( ArgPointer ) \
    ( ArgPointer = NULL )
```

These macros are used to process a variable number of arguments. They work only on functions that are declared with ... to signify a variable number of parameters. va_end could be a function; the others must be macros.

A function must declare at least one fixed argument; the last one is passed to va_start, inside the function, to start things. The function must call va_end before returning.

Each call to va_arg returns the next argument. It requires the type of this argument. This type cannot be one that widens when passed as an argument; use double, int, or unsigned int in place of the shorter alternatives.

As an example, Figure D.1 shows a routine that prints an arbitrary number of strings, one per line. The calling routine terminates the parameter list with a NULL pointer.

D.11   <stddef.h>

```
/* Macro */
#define NULL
#define offsetof( StructType, StructMember )

/* Types; typical definitions are included */
typedef int ptrdiff_t;          /* Result of subtracting two pointers */
typedef unsigned int size_t;    /* Result of sizeof */
typedef char wchar_t;           /* Wide character */
```

```
/*  1*/    #include <stdio.h>
/*  2*/    #include <stdarg.h>

/*  3*/    void
/*  4*/    PrintStrings( const char *Str1, ... )
/*  5*/    {
/*  6*/        char *NextStr;
/*  7*/        va_list Argp;
/*  8*/
/*  9*/        puts( Str1 );
/*10*/        va_start( Argp, Str1 );
/*11*/        while( NextStr = va_arg( Argp, char * ) )
/*12*/            puts( NextStr );

/*13*/        va_end( Argp );
/*14*/    }

/*15*/    main( void )
/*16*/    {
/*17*/        PrintStrings( "This", "is", "a", "test", 0  );
/*18*/        return 0;
/*19*/    }
```

Figure D.1:   Using `<stdarg.h>`.

Two macros and three types are defined. `offsetof` is used to find out where in a structure a particular member is stored. `StructMember` cannot be a bit field; the return value is measured in bytes. Typical `typedefs` for the three types are shown. Of course, your system may be different.

D.12   <stdio.h>

```
/* Seen elsewhere */
#define NULL
typedef ... size_t;

/* Macros */
#define EOF                 /* End of file */

    /* Maximums */
#define FOPEN_MAX           /* Maximum # of files open simultaneously */
#define FILENAME_MAX        /* Longest filename allowed */
#define L_tmpnam            /* Longest filename generated by tmpnam */
#define TMP_MAX             /* # of unique filenames tmpnam generates */

    /* Standard input, output, and error */
#define stdin
#define stdout
#define stderr

    /* Use for fseek */
#define SEEK_CUR
#define SEEK_END
#define SEEK_SET

    /* Used by setbuf and setvbuf */
#define _IOFBF              /* Full buffering */
#define _IOLBF              /* Line buffering */
#define _IONBF              /* No buffering */
#define BUFSIZ              /* Size of setbuf's buffer */

/* Types */
typedef ... FILE ...;    /* Stream */
typedef ... fpos_t ...;  /* Used to specify offsets in large files */

/* And now ... the functions */
    /* High-level routines */
int remove( const char *FileName );
int rename( const char *OldName, const char *NewName );

    /* Temp files */
FILE *tmpfile( void )
char *tmpnam( char *Str );

    /* Typical file operations */
int fclose( FILE *Stream );
int fflush( FILE *Stream );
FILE *fopen( const char *FileName, const char *Mode );
FILE *freopen( const char *FileName, const char *Mode,
               FILE *Stream );
```

```
    /* Buffering */
void setbuf( FILE *Stream, char *Buffer );
int setvbuf( FILE *Stream, char *Buffer,
                int Mode, size_t BufferSize );

    /* printf and scanf */
int printf(  const char *Format, ... );
int vprintf( const char *Format, va_list ArgList );
int scanf(   const char *Format, ... );
int fprintf(  FILE *Stream, const char *Format, ... );
int vfprintf( FILE *Stream, const char *Format, va_list ArgList );
int fscanf(   FILE *Stream, const char *Format, ... );
int sprintf(  char *Str, const char *Format, ... );
int vsprintf( char *Str, const char *Format, va_list ArgList );
int sscanf( const char *Str, const char *Format, ... );

    /* Get/Put */
int fgetc( FILE *Stream );
char *fgets( char *Str, int HowMany, FILE *Stream );
int fputc( int Ch, FILE *Stream );
int fputs( const char *Str, FILE *Stream );
int getc( FILE *Stream );
int getchar( void );
char *gets( char *Str );            /* Removed from most libraries */
int putc( int Ch, FILE *Stream );
int putchar( int Ch );
int puts( const char *Str );
int ungetc( int Ch, FILE *Stream );

    /* Block and random I/O */
size_t fread( void *Ptr, size_t ItemSz,
                size_t NumItem, FILE *Stream );
size_t fwrite( const void *Ptr, size_t ItemSz,
                size_t NumItem, FILE *Stream );
int fgetpos( FILE *Stream, fpos_t *Position );
int fsetpos( FILE *Stream, const fpos_t *Position );
int fseek( FILE *Stream, long int Offset, int Whence );
long int ftell( FILE *Stream );
void rewind( FILE *Stream );

    /* Error checks */
void clearerr( FILE *Stream );
int feof( FILE *Stream );     /* True if EOF already seen */
int ferror( FILE *Stream );   /* True if error already detected */
void perror( const char *Str );
```

The macros and types defined in <stdio.h> are for the most part self-explanatory.

Like many of the functions in this header, remove and rename were discussed in Section 12.6.

`"r"`	Open text file for reading
`"w"`	Open text file for writing (truncate to zero length or create)
`"a"`	Open text file for appending
`"rb"`	Open binary file for reading
`"wb"`	Open binary file for writing (truncate to zero length or create)
`"ab"`	Open binary file for appending
`"r+"`	Open text file for update (reading and writing)
`"w+"`	Open text file for update (truncate to zero length or create)
`"a+"`	Open text file for update
`"rb+"` or `"r+b"`	Open binary file for update (reading and writing)
`"wb+"` or `"w+b"`	Open binary file for update (truncate to zero length or create)
`"ab+"` or `"a+b"`	Open binary file for update

Figure D.2:   **Modes for opening files.**

`tmpfile` creates a temporary binary file that is removed automatically when it is closed or `exit` is called at normal termination. The file is opened in `"wb+"` mode. A pointer to the stream, or NULL on error, is returned. `tmpnam` generates a string that is a valid, nonexisting filename. The first `TMP_MAX` calls are guaranteed to generate unique filenames. If `Str` is NULL, `tmpnam` returns a pointer to a static object (that is overwritten by subsequent calls). Otherwise, `Str` is assumed to point at an array of at least `L_tmpnam` characters that will store the resulting file name. In that case, `Str` is returned.

`fclose`, `fflush`, `fopen`, and `freopen` were all discussed in Chapter 12. Figure D.2 shows the allowable modes. `setvbuf` is called after `Stream` has been associated with an open file but before any other operation is performed. `Mode` determines buffering and is one of `_IOFBF`, `_IOLBF`, `_IONBF`. If `Buffer` is not NULL, the array it points at may be used to buffer I/O for `Stream`, instead of an internal buffer. The array size is given by `BufferSize`. Zero is returned on success; nonzero is returned otherwise. If `Buffer` is NULL, `setbuf` calls `setvbuf` with `_IONBF` for `Mode`. Otherwise, `setvbuf` is called with `_IOFBF` for `Mode` and `BUFSIZ` for `BufferSize`.

The formatted I/O routines were discussed in detail in Chapter 12. A summary of the conversion specifiers is shown in Figure D.3. The `vprintf` family of routines accept parameters in the form of `va_list` rather than `...`. Single character I/O, string I/O, and block I/O were all discussed at length in Chapter 12. The error routines are self-explanatory.

printf	*Symbol*	*scanf*
Run-time field width or precision	*	Assignment suppression
Left justified	-	
Include sign	+	
Prefix space if no sign	space	
Use alternate form	#	
Pad leading zeros	0	
Minimum Maximum	Field width Precision	Maximum
Short/long	h,l,L	Short/long
Decimal int.	d	Decimal int.
Decimal int.	i	Decimal int.
Octal	o	Octal
Unsigned	u	Unsigned
Hexadecimal	x,X	Hexadecimal
Floating point; f is double	e,f,g,E,G	Floating point; f is float
String	s	String with no white space
	[	String with scanset
Character	c	Character
Pointer	p	Pointer
Write num. characters	n	Write num. characters
%	%	%

Figure D.3: `printf` **and** `scanf` **conversions.**

D.13   <stdlib.h>

```c
/* Seen elsewhere */
#define NULL
typedef ... size_t ...;
typedef ... wchar_t ...;

/* Macros */
#define EXIT_FAILURE   /* Can be used by exit( ) to indicate failure */
#define EXIT_SUCCESS   /* Can be used by exit( ) to indicate success */
#define MB_CUR_MAX     /* Max number of bytes in active extended char set */
#define RAND_MAX       /* Max value returned by rand( ); at least 32767 */

/* Types for division.  Contain quot and rem fields */
typedef ... div_t ...;     /* Structure type returned by div function */
typedef ... ldiv_t ...;    /* Structure type returned by ldiv function */

/* Functions */
    /* Basic String to ... functions */
int atoi( const char *NumString );        /* String to int */
long int atol( const char *NumString );   /* String to long */
double atof( const char *NumString );     /* String to double */

    /* Fancier versions of String to ... functions */
double strtod( const char *NumStr, char **EndPtr );
long int strtol( const char *NumStr, char **EndPtr, int Base );
unsigned long int strtoul( const char *NumStr, char **EndPtr, int Base );

    /* Random numbers -- not too good */
int rand( void );                  /* Return next random number */
void srand( unsigned int Seed );   /* Initialize generator */

    /* Memory management */
void *malloc( size_t HowManyBytes );
void *calloc( size_t ItemSz, size_t NumItems );
void *realloc( void *Original, size_t NewBytes );
void free( void *Array );

    /* Program termination */
void abort( void );                     /* Terminate program with SIGABRT */
int atexit( void ( *Func )( void ) );   /* Call Func at normal termination */
void exit( int Status );                /* Exit program, flush buffers */

    /* Interact with system */
int system( const char *Command ); /* Execute Command */
char *getenv( const char *Name );  /* Find the environment variable */

    /* Binary search and quick sort: use at your own risk */
void *bsearch( const void *Key, const void *Base, size_t NumItems,
               size_t ItemSz, int( *Cmp )( const void *, const void * ) );
void qsort( void *Base, size_t NumItems,
            size_t ItemSz, int( *Cmp )( const void *, const void * ) );
```

```
    /* Integer math */
int abs( int X );
long int labs( long int X );
div_t div( int Numerator, int Denominator );
ldiv_t ldiv( long int Numerator, long int Denominator );

    /* Routines for multibyte characters -- see notes */
int mblen( const char *Mbc, size_t HowManyBytes );
int mbtowc( wchar_t *Pwc, const char *Mbc, size_t HowManyBytes );
int wctomb( char *Mbc, wchar_t Wchar );

    /* Routines for multibyte strings -- see notes */
size_t mbstowcs( wchar_t *PwStr, const char *MbStr, size_t HowManyBytes );
size_t wcstombs( char *MbStr, const wchar_t *PwStr, size_t HowManyBytes );
```

The `<stdlib.h>` header contains prototypes for a host of unrelated functions. There are nine basic groups, which we discuss separately.

D.13.1   `ato` Functions

The routines `atoi`, `atof`, and `atol` are present for compatibility with older libraries (see Section 8.7.5).

D.13.2   `strto` Functions

`strtod` attempts to convert the string `NumStr` to a `double`, which is returned. `strtod` skips leading white space. If successful, `EndPtr` is set to point at the first character in `NumStr` immediately following the converted part of the string. If no `double` is matched, `0.0` is returned and `*EndPtr` is set to `NumStr`. If an out-of-range `double` is matched, an appropriate `HUGE_VAL` is returned. In both cases, `errno` is set to `ERANGE`.

   `strtol` and `strtoul` have an additional parameter to specify the base. Base may range from 2 to 36; if base is 0, the base is deduced by examining the format to see if it is octal or hexadecimal. In any case, only digits corresponding to the base (except `x` and `X` for hexadecimal) may appear. On errors, either `LONG_MIN`, `LONG_MAX`, or `ULONG_MAX` is returned, as appropriate, and `errno` is set.

D.13.3   Random Numbers

The routines `srand` and `rand` are used to generate pseudorandom numbers between 0 and `RAND_MAX`. `rand` returns the next number, and `srand` is used to initialize the state of the random number generator. The routine suggested by ANSI C has known statistical deficiencies. Some systems provide alternates (e.g., `random` and `srandom` on UNIX).

D.13.4   Memory Management

These routines are discussed at length in Section 7.9.

D.13.5   Program Termination

`abort` causes the program to terminate by sending the signal `SIGABRT`. Unless arrangements are made, this is not considered "normal termination." The function `exit` terminates a program normally. It is called implicitly when `main` returns. As a result, functions registered with `atexit` are called in reverse order of their registration. Output streams are then flushed and closed. Files created by `tmpfile` are removed, and the program terminates with `Status` passed back to the calling environment.

D.13.6   Interacting with the System

The result of `system` is that `Command` is passed to the operating system's *command processor* and is run. How this is done is highly system dependent. `getenv` is used to search for environment variables. This is discussed in Section 12.7.2.

D.13.7   Binary Search and Quick Sort

`qsort` is a generic sorting routine, suitable for moderate amounts of random input. The interface is identical to the generic Shellsort we discussed in Section 9.5. `qsort` is not required to be efficient, and many library implementations are unsuitable for large amounts of input. You have been warned!

The `bsearch` routine is a generic binary search algorithm. It has the same interface as `qsort`, except that an additional `Key` parameter is added and a pointer to the found item (or `NULL` if not found) is returned. This is not as dangerous to use as `qsort`.

D.13.8   Integer Math

`abs` and `labs` are self-explanatory. The `div` and `ldiv` routines perform division and return a structure that stores a quotient and remainder. These structures are `div_t` and `ldiv_t`, defined earlier. If you need both quotient and remainder, you will generally save time by using these routines. Otherwise, just use `/` or `%`.

D.13.9   Multibyte Characters and Strings

In the `<locale.h>` description, we discussed how character sets might be extended to add local characters, such as â For most European languages, these new character sets can still be represented in 8-bit bytes. Many Asian character sets, however, are too large to fit in a byte. ANSI C provides an allowance for this possibility by defining the multibyte character.

Internally, a multibyte character is stored as a *wide character* of type `wchar_t`. One possibility is a 16-bit integer type, capable of holding 65,536 different characters. Externally, a single wide character maps into a sequence of nonextended characters. This is the *multibyte character* representation.

How all this is done is, of course, implementation specific and can depend on the `LC_CTYPE` locale. The maximum number of bytes in a multibyte character is given by `MB_CUR_MAX`. Although the null terminator is used to terminate an array of any type of characters, the multibyte character is typically not null terminated, because that could add an unacceptable space overhead.

The routine `mblen` returns the number of bytes that form the single multibyte character `Mbc`. `Mbc` is no more than `HowManyBytes` long. -1 is returned on error. `mbtowc` and `wctomb` convert between multibyte and wide-character formats. Corresponding routines are provided for strings composed of multibyte and wide characters.

These routines have many limitations and technicalities. It is best to consult your local documentation for details on using them.

D.14   `<string.h>`

```
/* Defined elsewhere */
#define NULL
typedef ... size_t;

    /* =, +=, ==, and length for strings */
char *strcpy( char *Lhs, const char *Rhs );
char *strcat( char *Lhs, const char *Rhs );
int strcmp( const char *Lhs, const char *Rhs );
size_t strlen( const char *Str );
int strcoll( const char *Lhs, const char *Rhs );  /* Extended strcmp */
size_t strxfrm( char *New, const char *Old, size_t N );

    /* Length limited versions of =, +=, == */
char *strncpy( char *Lhs, const char *Rhs, size_t N );
char *strncat( char *Lhs, const char *Rhs, size_t N );
int strncmp( const char *Lhs, const char *Rhs, size_t N );

    /* Find character Ch or string Pattern in Str */
char *strchr( const char *Str, int Ch );      /* First occurrence */
char *strrchr( const char *Str, int Ch );     /* Last occurrence */
char *strstr( const char *Str, const char *Pattern );

    /* String parsing routines -- see notes */
size_t strspn( const char *Str, const char *Set );
size_t strcspn( const char *Str, const char *Set );
char *strpbrk( const char *Str, const char *Set );
char *strtok( char *Str, const char *Set );
char *strerror( int Errnum );

    /* Memory copying and comparison routines */
void *memcpy( void *Lhs, const void *Rhs, size_t N );
void *memmove( void *Lhs, const void *Rhs, size_t N );
int memcmp( const void *Lhs, const void *Rhs, size_t N );
void *memchr( const void *Mem, int Ch, size_t N );
void *memset( void *Mem, int Ch, size_t N );
```

We discussed `strcpy`, `strcat`, `strcmp`, and `strlen` in Section 8.7. `strcoll` compares two strings using the locale-specific collating conventions. In the "C" locale, `strcoll` is identical to `strcmp`. However, in other locales, character Ch1 could be greater than Ch2, even if Ch1 appears earlier in the character set than Ch2. The category LC_COLLATE is used to change collating conventions. `strxfrm` transforms Old to New so that `strcmp` can be used on resultant strings to determine correct order.

`strncpy`, `strncat`, and `strncmp` are length-limited versions of the copy, concatenation, and comparison routines. These were discussed in Section 8.7.6. `strchr`, strrchr, and strstr are used to search Str for a pattern. See Section 8.9 for more details.

ANSI C provides routines that can be used to parse strings, without the overhead of the %[sscanf conversion. strspn scans Str for the first occurrence of a character that is not in the string Set, skipping over characters that are in Set. The number of skipped characters is returned. The null terminator always terminates the scan. strcspn scans for a character that is in the string Set. Otherwise, the behavior is identical to strspn. strpbrk is like strcspn, except that a pointer to the character in Str that stops the scan is returned. If no characters are found, a NULL pointer is returned.

strtok is used much like strpbrk, except that strtok remembers where the last nonmatch occurred, via an *internal state pointer*. If the internal state pointer is NULL, the end of Str has been seen. If Str is not NULL, strtok begins searching from Str. If all characters in Str are in Set, NULL is returned and the internal state is set to NULL. Otherwise, the internal state pointer points at the first character in Str that is not in Set. If Str and the internal state are both NULL, NULL is returned immediately. If Str is NULL and the internal state pointer is not NULL, strtok begins searching from the internal state pointer. If no nonmatches are found, the internal state pointer is returned and then set to NULL. Otherwise, the nonmatch is overwritten with a null terminator and the internal state pointer is returned and then set to the character immediately following the nonmatch.

memcpy and memmove copy N bytes from Rhs to Lhs. memmove, unlike memcpy, is safe even if the affected memory regions overlap. memcmp is like strncmp, except that it ignores null terminators. memchr searches N bytes starting from Mem for the character Ch. It returns a pointer to the first occurrence, or NULL if not found. It is similar to strchr, except that NULL terminators are ignored. memset copies the character Ch into each of N bytes, starting from Mem.

D.15 `<time.h>`

```
    /* Seen elsewhere */
#define NULL
typedef ... size_t;

    /* Macro */
#define CLOCKS_PER_SECOND      /* Divide clock( ) return by this */

    /* Types */
typedef ... clock_t ...;        /* Abstract clock type */
typedef ... time_t ...;         /* Abstract time type */
struct tm                       /* Broken down structure */
{
    int    tm_sec;      /* seconds after the minute (0- 61)  */
    int    tm_min;      /* minutes after the hour   (0- 59)  */
    int    tm_hour;     /* hours after midnight     (0- 23)  */
    int    tm_mday;     /* day of the month         (1- 31)  */
    int    tm_mon;      /* months since January     (0- 11)  */
    int    tm_year;     /* years since 1900         (0-   )  */
    int    tm_wday;     /* days since Sunday        (0-  6)  */
    int    tm_yday;     /* days since January 1     (0-365)  */
    int    tm_isdst;    /* daylight savings time flag        */
};

    /* Get time */
clock_t clock( void );          /* Return processor time used */
time_t time( time_t *Timer );   /* Return current time */

double difftime( time_t Now, time_t Then );   /* Return Now-Then */

    /* Convert between formats */
time_t mktime( struct tm *TimePtr );             /* struct tm => time_t */
struct tm *gmtime( const time_t *Timer );      /* time_t => struct tm */
struct tm *localtime( const time_t *Timer ); /* time_t => struct tm */

    /* Three routines to print time */
char *ctime( const time_t *Timer );
char *asctime( const struct tm *TimePtr );
size_t strftime( char *Str, size_t MaxSize, const char *Format,
                 const struct tm *TimePtr );
```

The amount of time used by the current process is reported by clock. The return value is a clock_t variable that must be divided by CLOCKS_PER_SECOND to convert to seconds. The library routine does not have to be particularly accurate.

Calendar times can be stored in one of two ways. The time_t type is an internal representation that typically counts the number of seconds since some beginning. The tm structure contains fields indicating month, day, and so on. The declaration shown represents the minimum subset of fields that are required by ANSI C.

Conversion	*Is replaced by the:*
`%a`	locale's abbreviated weekday name
`%A`	locale's full weekday name
`%b`	locale's abbreviated month name
`%B`	locale's full month name
`%c`	locale's appropriate date and time representation
`%d`	day of the month (01–31)
`%H`	hour (00–23)
`%I`	hour (01–12)
`%j`	day of the year (001–366)
`%m`	month (01–12)
`%M`	minute (00–59)
`%p`	locale's equivalent of AM/PM
`%S`	seconds (00–61—allows leap seconds)
`%U`	week number (00–53—first Sunday is week 1)
`%w`	week day (0–6—Sunday is 0)
`%W`	week number (00–53—first Monday is week 1)
`%x`	locale's appropriate date representation
`%X`	locale's appropriate time representation
`%y`	year without century (00–99)
`%Y`	year with century
`%Z`	time zone name or abbreviation
`%%`	% character

Figure D.4: Formats for `strftime`.

`time` returns the current time in a `time_t` variable. If `Timer` is not NULL, the current time is also filled in the structure that it points at. `difftime` subtracts two `time_t` times.

`mktime` converts from a `struct tm` to a `time_t` format. It also "normalizes" the broken-down structure by filling in the day of the week, day of year, and adjusting fields so that all values are in the standard range. Section 9.1.3 illustrated that use of `mktime`. `gmtime` and `localtime` convert in the other direction. The difference between the two routines is that `localtime` converts to local time, whereas `gmtime` converts to Greenwich Mean time.

Three routines are used to generate meaningful times for output. `asctime` expects a pointer to `tm` structure and returns a pointer to a 26-byte string that represents the local time. A typical result would be

```
Wed May 03 20:10:43 1995\n\0
```

Note carefully that the string is a static variable that is overwritten with each call to `asctime`.

`ctime` expects a `time_t` and returns a pointer to a string. It is equivalent to

```
asctime( localtime( Timer ) );
```

`strftime` places characters into the `Str` string. `Format` is meant to mimic `printf`. The format is copied into `Str`, except that the conversions in Figure D.4 are applied. Up to `MaxSize` characters are placed in `Str`.

D.16   Summary

Figure D.5 provides the location of the library's prototypes.

Routine	Header	Routine	Header	Routine	Header	Routine	Header
abort	stdlib.h	abs	stdlib.h	acos	math.h	asctime	time.h
asin	math.h	assert	assert.h	atan	math.h	atan2	math.h
atexit	stdlib.h	atof	stdlib.h	atoi	stdlib.h	atol	stdlib.h
bsearch	stdlib.h	calloc	stdlib.h	ceil	math.h	clearerr	stdio.h
clock	time.h	cos	math.h	cosh	math.h	ctime	time.h
difftime	time.h	div	stdlib.h	exit	stdlib.h	exp	math.h
fabs	math.h	fclose	stdio.h	feof	stdio.h	ferror	stdio.h
fflush	stdio.h	fgetc	stdio.h	fgetpos	setdio.h	fgets	stdio.h
floor	math.h	fmod	math.h	fopen	stdio.h	fprintf	stdio.h
fputc	stdio.h	fputs	stdio.h	fread	stdio.h	free	stdlib.h
freopen	stdio.h	frexp	math.h	fscanf	stdio.h	fseek	stdio.h
fsetpos	stdio.h	ftell	stdio.h	fwrite	stdio.h	getc	stdio.h
getchar	stdio.h	getenv	stdlib.h	gets	stdio.h	gmtime	time.h
isalnum	ctype.h	isalpha	ctype.h	iscntrl	ctype.h	isdigit	ctype.h
isgraph	ctype.h	islower	ctype.h	isprint	ctype.h	ispunct	ctype.h
isspace	ctype.h	isupper	ctype.h	isxdigit	ctype.h	labs	stdlib.h
ldexp	math.h	ldiv	stdlib.h	localeconv	locale.h	localtime	time.h
log	math.h	log10	math.h	longjmp	setjmp.h	malloc	stdlib.h
mblen	stdlib.h	mbstowcs	stdlib.h	mbtowc	stdlib.h	memchr	string.h
memcmp	string.h	memcpy	string.h	memmove	string.h	memset	string.h
mktime	time.h	modf	math.h	offsetof	stddef.h	perror	stdio.h
pow	math.h	printf	stdio.h	putc	stdio.h	putchar	stdio.h
puts	stdio.h	qsort	stdlib.h	raise	signal.h	rand	stdlib.h
realloc	stdlib.h	remove	stdio.h	rename	stdio.h	rewind	stdio.h
scanf	stdio.h	setbuf	stdio.h	setjmp	setjmp.h	setlocale	locale.h
setvbuf	stdio.h	signal	signal.h	sin	math.h	sinh	math.h
sprintf	stdio.h	sqrt	math.h	srand	stdlib.h	sscanf	stdio.h
strcat	string.h	strchr	string.h	strcmp	string.h	strcoll	string.h
strcpy	string.h	strcspn	string.h	strerror	string.h	strftime	time.h
strlen	string.h	strncat	string.h	strncmp	string.h	strncpy	string.h
strpbrk	string.h	strrchr	string.h	strspn	string.h	strstr	string.h
strtod	stdlib.h	strtok	string.h	strtol	stdlib.h	strtoul	stdlib.h
strxfrm	string.h	system	stdlib.h	tan	math.h	tanh	math.h
time	time.h	tmpfile	stdio.h	tmpnam	stdio.h	tolower	ctype.h
toupper	ctype.h	ungetc	stdio.h	va_arg	stdarg.h	va_end	stdarg.h
va_start	stdarg.h	vfprintf	stdio.h	vprintf	stdio.h	vsprintf	stdio.h
wcstombs	stdlib.h	wctomb	stdlib.h				

Figure D.5:   Location of library routines.

Index

Section

Two

Taken from
*Advanced
Unix® Programming*
by Warren W. Gay

CHAPTER 1

COMPILER NOTES AND OPTIONS

You are reading this book because you want to write software for UNIX. Perhaps you are interested in developing software to run on several UNIX platforms. Whether you must write for several platforms or a few, writing your software to compile successfully for each UNIX platform is a challenge. This chapter is aimed at reducing that challenge and improving your success rate. Additionally, you will find some valuable Internet resources in this chapter, along with some cross-platform examples and advice.

Online Manual Pages

Throughout this text, you will see references to online documents that exist on most UNIX systems. These online documents save the programmer a great deal of time when he is writing programs. Rather than fetch a book and look in the index for the correct page, you can pull up the information within seconds, instead. This electronic documentation can be brought into an editor, or segments of it can be cut and pasted using the normal X Window facilities. For this reason, this text places some emphasis on online manual page references for your convenience.

A document reference will appear in this text in the form `open(2)`, for example. To view the online document for that reference, you would normally enter

```
$ man 2 open
```

This causes the manual page for the **open** entry in section **2** to be displayed (the section is specified first). The section number is not always necessary, but it often is (otherwise, a manual entry from an earlier section will be presented instead).

A manual page section is a grouping of related documents. The following sections will be the sections of primary importance throughout this book:

User commands	1
System calls	2
Library calls	3

Most of this book will be focused on facilities documented in sections 2 and 3. Functions that interface to the UNIX kernel are grouped into section 2. Other function calls, which are documented in section 3, are those functions that perform commonly required services. These may or may not involve additional calls to the UNIX kernel. Commands such as the `man(1)` command are grouped in section 1.

If you don't know the name of the `man(1)` page you want, you can perform a keyword search. The following shows how you could search for information about changing owners of a file:

```
$ man -k owner
chown(2), fchown(2), lchown(2) - change owner and group of a file
chown(8)                - change file owner and group
$
```

This produces a number of references that have the keyword `owner` in them. Another way this can be done on most systems is to use the `apropos(1)` command:

```
$ apropos owner
chown(2), fchown(2), lchown(2) - change owner and group of a file
chown(8)                - change file owner and group
$
```

Both of these commands result in the same action being taken. If you have an unusual UNIX system and these don't work, then you might look up `man(1)` for additional insight.

Most sections are documented on most UNIX systems. For example, to find out what section **8** is all about under FreeBSD, you would enter

```
$ man 8 intro
```

A lookup of the man page `intro(x)`, where x is the section, will usually yield additional documentation about the section specified.

Manual Section Number Note

On some systems, you may have to specify the section number differently. For example, Solaris 8 supports the following syntax:

```
$ man -s 2 open
```

In this example, the section number follows the `-s` option. Some implementations of the `man(1)` command will work with or without the `-s` option for section numbers.

Manual References Used in This Book

References to `man(1)` pages will be used throughout this book when referring to functions and other programming entities. However, as you might expect, different UNIX platforms place the same information in different sections and sometimes under completely different headings.

An example of this problem is the function `strftime(3)`. For many UNIX implementations, including FreeBSD, the reference `strftime(3)` will provide the correct location of the online document for the `strftime()` function. However, UnixWare 7 uses the manual reference `strftime(3C)` instead. UnixWare has chosen to split some of its functions into a separate section **3C**.

Consequently, a choice in convention had to be made for this book. The manual page references used throughout this text are based on the FreeBSD (3.4 release) platform. This should provide a good reference for users of most UNIX systems. In places where it is important, the differences will be noted.

`man(1)` Resources on the Internet

If you must write code that is portable to many UNIX platforms, one valuable resource is the Internet. Table 1.1 lists a few Internet resources that can be used when you want to review manual pages for different UNIX platforms.

TABLE 1.1   Table of Internet `man(1)` Resources

URL	Description
`http://www.FreeBSD.org/cgi/man.cgi`	BSD
`http://docs.hp.com/index.html`	HPUX 10 & 11
`http://docs.sun.com/`	SunOS, Solaris
`http://www.ibm.com/servers/aix/`	IBM's AIX
`http://support.sgi.com/search/`	SGI IRIX/Linux
`http://doc.sco.com/`	UnixWare & SCO

There are probably many more resources available, in addition to those listed in Table 1.1. The `www.FreeBSD.org` reference is worth special mention because its Web site appears to have `man(1)` pages for a wealth of other releases listed next.

- 2.8 BSD, 2.9.1 BSD, 2.10 BSD, and 2.11 BSD
- 386BSD 0.0 and 386BSD 0.1
- 4.3BSD NET/2, 4.3BSD Reno, 4.4BSD Lite2
- FreeBSD 1.0-RELEASE to FreeBSD 4.0-RELEASE
- FreeBSD 5.0-current
- FreeBSD Ports
- Linux Slackware 3.1
- Minix 2.0
- NetBSD 1.2 to NetBSD 1.4

- OpenBSD 2.1 to OpenBSD 2.6
- Plan 9
- RedHat Linux/i386 4.2, 5.0, and 5.2
- SunOS 4.1.3, 5.5.1, 5.6, and 5.7
- ULTRIX 4.2
- UNIX Seventh Edition

There will likely be additions to this list by the time you read this.

Example Code in This Book

Even more challenging than having uniform `man` page references is the creation of example programs that would compile for all UNIX platforms. While this could be attempted, it has the danger that it would not be universally successful unless the code was tested on every platform. Even then, pitfalls abound, because there exist many different choices in compilers, libraries, and other customizable aspects of the UNIX platform.

The examples in this book have tried to be UNIX platform neutral. Practical considerations, however, made it necessary to pick one development platform for the examples. The major differences are addressed in the text as they come up. Look for additional tips, warnings, and notes for other UNIX differences that may be worth noting.

The challenges of supporting multiple UNIX platform differences include the following:

- Subtle differences in the different `make(1)` commands
- Differences in the feature set macros required to compile the programs
- Differences in location of the `include` files
- Differences in function prototype definitions
- Differences in C data types (`int` vs. `size_t`)

To deal with all of these problems would end up leaving the reader with a rat's nest of ugly source code to look at. Rather than give you difficult-to-read source code and complicated `make(1)` procedures, this book will simply use the FreeBSD Release 3.4 platform as the foundation for all program examples. Important differences in compilers and other areas will be noted along the way.

This approach provides the professional the advantage that learning can take place at home. FreeBSD is a stable and secure platform that can be loaded onto just about any reasonable Intel PC. Yet it remains very similar to many commercial UNIX platforms in the workplace.

> **FreeBSD/Linux Note**
>
> While FreeBSD can be installed with many useful Linux enhancements, the FreeBSD 3.4 Release used for the examples in this book did not have *any* Linux support installed. This was intentionally done to present a more traditional UNIX experience.

Compiling C Programs

This is an area in which there is considerable variation among the different UNIX platforms. The FreeBSD 3.4 Release of UNIX uses the very capable GNU compiler:

```
$ gcc --version
2.7.2.3
$
```

This is linked to the same command as the more commonly recognized UNIX command name cc, as demonstrated in the next FreeBSD session:

```
$ type cc
cc is a tracked alias for /usr/bin/cc
$ ls -li /usr/bin/cc
7951 -r-xr-xr-x  2 root  wheel  49680 Dec 20 00:46 /usr/bin/cc
$ type gcc
gcc is a tracked alias for /usr/bin/gcc
$ ls -li /usr/bin/gcc
7951 -r-xr-xr-x  2 root  wheel  49680 Dec 20 00:46 /usr/bin/gcc
$
```

Since both /usr/bin/cc and /usr/bin/gcc link to the same i-node **7951** in the example, you know that these two files are linked to the same executable file.

Other UNIX platforms that provide their own proprietary forms of C and C++ compilers differ substantially from the GNU compiler in the options they support, the warning messages they produce, and their optimizing capability. This chapter will look at some of the commonality between them and some of the differences.

The C Compile Command

Most UNIX platforms invoke their C compilers by the name cc. Linux and FreeBSD platforms support the **gcc** command name in addition to the standard cc name. Sometimes the GNU compiler will be installed as **gcc** on commercial platforms to distinguish it from the standard offering or in addition to the crippled (non-ANSI) one. For example, HP includes a non-ANSI compiler with the HPUX operating system, which is called the "bundled" compiler (this compiler is sufficient to rebuild a new HPUX kernel). The ANSI-capable compiler must be purchased separately and, when installed, replaces the bundled cc command.

However, within the same platform, there can also be choices. HPUX 10.2 supports

HP-UX C compiler	cc
HP-UX POSIX-conforming C	c89

The IBM AIX 4.3 platform supports:

C language "extended"	cc
ANSI C compiler	xlc or c89

The difference between the `xlc` and `c89` compilers under AIX is the configured defaults. In the following sections, the relatively standardized options will be examined.

The -c Compile Option

This option is probably the most universally standardized. The `-c` option indicates that the compiler should produce a translated object file (`*.o` file) but not attempt to link the translation into an executable. This option is used when compiling several separate source modules that will be linked together at a later stage by the linker. The following demonstrates a compile and link in one step:

```
$ cc hello.c
```

This all-in-one step command translates the C source file `hello.c` into the final output executable file `a.out`. The filename `a.out` is the default executable name for linker output. This practice dates back to at least 1970 when UNIX was written in assembler language on the PDP-11. Digital Equipment's (DEC) default linker output file name was `a.out`.

Alternatively, the object file can be produced separately and then linked as a separate step, as follows:

```
$ cc -c hello.c
$ cc hello.o
```

In this example, the first `cc` command with the `-c` option, produces the file `hello.o` as the result of the compile. Then the second `cc` command accepts the object file `hello.o` as input and produces the final executable file name `a.out`, which can then be run.

The -o Compile Option

This option is fairly standard also. The `-o` option allows the user to specify the name of the output file. For example, it could be explicit, as follows:

```
$ cc -c hello.c -o hello.o
```

The `-c` option indicates that an object file is being produced, and the `-o` option names the output object file as `hello.o`. The `-o` option can also be used to name the executable file, if that is the type of output requested:

```
$ cc hello.o -o my_hello_prog
```

The example shown indicates that the output executable file name will be named `my_hello_prog`.

The -g Option (Debug)

This standard option indicates to the compiler that debugging information should be generated in the output of the compile. This debugging information makes source code and variable name references possible in the debugger or when analyzing the `core` file after a program abort. Include this option whenever you need to debug the program interactively or perform a post-mortem on the `core` file. Be sure to use this option on all object modules that will be inspected by the debugger.

> **Optimization Warning**
>
> Most C compilers will not accept both the -g (debug) and -O (optimize) options at the same time. The GNU compiler will tolerate -g and first-level optimization (-O), but this may lead to a few surprises in the debugger.

The -D Option (Define)

This standard compiler option permits you to define a macro symbol from the compiler command line. It is most frequently done from a `Makefile` but is not limited to this practice. For example

```
$ cc -c -D_POSIX_C_SOURCE=199309L hello.c
```

defines the C macro constant `_POSIX_C_SOURCE` with a value of `199309L`. This macro definition has the effect of choosing a particular POSIX standard from the files included in the compile. Additional macros can be defined on the same command line:

```
$ cc -c -D_POSIX_C_SOURCE=199309L -DNDEBUG hello.c
```

In this example, the additional C macro `NDEBUG` was defined (with no value), in order to disable the code generation in the `assert(3)` macro invocations used within the program.

The -I Option (Include)

The standard `-I` compile option permits you to specify additional places to look for `include` files. For example, if you have additional `include` files located in an unusual place such as `/usr/local/include` for example, you could add the `-I` option as follows:

```
$ cc -c -I/usr/local/include -I/opt/include hello.c
```

Additional `-I` options can be added as shown, and the directories will be searched in the order given. Many UNIX compilers (non-GNU) will process the C statement

```
#include "file.h"
```

by looking in the current directory first, and then all of the directories given by the `-I` options, and then finally in the directory `/usr/include`.

The same (non-GNU) UNIX compilers will process the C language statement

```
#include <file.h>
```

by the same means, except that the current directory is *not* searched. However, the GNU compiler extends the -I option somewhat, as follows:

- -I directories preceding a -I- option are searched only for statements of the form `#include "file.h"` only.

- Directories provided with -I options following a -I- option are searched for both forms `#include "file.h"` and `#include <file.h>`.

- If no -I- option appears on the command line, then the behavior is the same as the non-GNU C compiler.

An example of this is provided in the following compile command:

```
$ gcc -c -I/usr/informix/include -I- -I/opt/oracle/include convutil.c
```

The example shown would allow the C language statement

```
#include "sqlca.h"
```

to include the file /usr/informix/include/sqlca.h. Another C language statement

```
#include <sqlca.h>
```

would include the file /opt/oracle/include/sqlca.h instead. This happens because the <file.h> form is not searched in the directories preceding the -I- separating option.

The -E Option (Expand)

This option is relatively standard among UNIX C compilers. It permits you to modify the command line to cause the compiler to emit the preprocessed C text to standard output without actually compiling the code.

This is useful when attempting to wade through C preprocessing directives and C macros. The output of a would-be compile can be directed to a file and then examined with an editor:

```
$ cc -c -E hello.c >cpp.out
```

In the example shown, the -E option causes the `include` files and the program to be preprocessed and redirected to the file `cpp.out`. You can then examine the file `cpp.out` with an editor or paging command and determine what the final C language code looks like. This is especially helpful when trying to debug new C macros that are causing compile errors that are difficult to diagnose.

The -O Option (Optimize)

This option is not standard among compilers. Some compilers require an argument to follow the -O, some don't, and some will optionally take an argument. FreeBSD accepts the following:

- -O and -O1 specify level 1 optimization.

- -O2 specifies level 2 optimization (increased optimization).

- -O3 specifies level 3 optimization (more than -O2).

- -O0 specifies no optimization.

For the GNU compiler, these options can be repeated, with the last appearing option establishing the final optimization level. For example

```
$ gcc -c -O3 -O0 hello.c
```

would compile with no optimization, because -O0 appears last.

Recall that the debug option (-g) is incompatible with optimization with most C compilers.

As a contrast to the GNU compiler, HP's compiler supports the following optimizing options in increasing levels of optimization:

Default optimization	+O0
Level 1 optimization	+O1
Level 2 optimization	+O2 (-O)
Level 3 optimization	+O3
Level 4 optimization	+O4

The -O (with no argument) option is equivalent to the HP option +O2 (note the plus sign).

The IBM AIX 4.3 compiler supports the options -O, -O2, and -O3 in increasing levels of optimization.

All of this emphasizes a need to review the compiler options in the cc(1) man page for the compiler you are using.

Warning Options

Warning messages is one area in which the GNU compiler excels. This compiler is so good at this that there is no need for a lint(1) command under FreeBSD or Linux. However, the warnings options for compilers vary considerably by platform and vendor.

The GNU compiler uses the -W option with an argument to indicate what is to be reported as warnings. In this book, the option -Wall will be used to cause the GNU compiler to report anything that looks suspicious.

It is also possible to specify individual warnings of interest. For example, -Wreturn-type can be specified to cause the compiler to report any return values that are missing or mismatched or a function that is defaulting to returning an int because no return type was declared for the function.

While the -Wreturn-type warning appears to be included with the specification of the -Wall option under FreeBSD, there were versions of the GNU compiler in which -Wreturn-type was not included under Linux. Since this is an important warning that can save you a lot of time, you may want to include it in addition to the -Wall option, just to be certain it is enabled.

ANSI C Compile Options

On some UNIX platforms you must indicate to your compiler that you are compiling ANSI C source code. HPUX UNIX compilers, for example, will assume the older K&R C code is being compiled instead, usually leading to a lot of compile errors. Therefore, for HPUX you will need to supply the option `-Aa` to compile any modern C source code. A few other commercial UNIX compilers have similar requirements.

Managing Compiler Warnings

The C compiler will often report messages. These messages can be divided into *error messages* and *warning messages*. Error messages indicate things that must be corrected in order for the compile to succeed. Warnings alert the programmer to bad practices and problems that might occur later when the program is run.

With the maximum compile warning level set, the compiler reports on the smallest of infractions, but it usually does so intelligently and diligently. Sometimes warnings are issued for valid C programming practices, and some developers disable these warnings with certain compiler options. By doing this, they prevent the C compiler from providing useful advice.

The best advice that can be provided here is to always use the maximum warning level available. This forces the developer to address all source code issues until the warnings disappear from the compilation. The only justifiable reason for going to a lower warning level is when you've inherited someone else's source code and you do not have the luxury of time to fix all the causes of warnings.

Compiler Warning Level Tip

Always compile with the maximum warning level turned on. Time spent eliminating causes of warning messages, can save a lot of time later while debugging your program.

With the GNU compiler under FreeBSD and Linux, this is done by adding the `-Wall` option.

The following shows how to use the GNU compiler under FreeBSD with the maximum warning level enabled:

```
bash$ gcc -Wall hello.c
```

The compile examples in this book will all use the `-Wall` option unless the example involves a non-GNU compiler.

Command Line Option Note

Most UNIX command-line options do not require a space to appear between the option letter and the option's argument. For example, the option may be specified as `-Wall` or `-W all`, since these are equivalent.

Working with Compiler Warning Messages

When a high warning level is used by the compiler, every possible warning message is reported. A low warning level will report only the most important messages and suppress the rest.

As noted earlier, there is one drawback to using a high warning level with your C compiler: Sometimes you'll receive warning messages for valid C language constructs. Well-designed compilers will help you cope with these problems, however, since they allow you to use tricks to convey your real intention.

Warnings About Assignments

A programmer often loves the economy of expression available in the C language. This means that the programmer will employ the smallest number of statements or operators to accomplish a task. Sometimes this involves doing an assignment and a test for non-zero all in one step. Consider the if statement in Listing 1.1.

LISTING 1.1   `asgn1.c`—Warnings About Value Assignment in the `if` Statement

```
 1:     #include <string.h>
 2:
 3:     char *
 4:     Basename(char *pathname) {
 5:         char *cp;                    /* Work Pointer */
 6:
 7:         if ( cp = strrchr(pathname,'/') )
 8:             return cp + 1;           /* Return basename pointer */
 9:         return pathname;             /* No directory component */
10:     }
```

Line Number Note

The program listings in this book include line numbers at the extreme left. Do not type these if you are entering the example programs manually. They are included only for ease of reference.

Here is the compile session for Listing 1.1:

```
$ cc -c -Wall asgn1.c
asgn1.c: In function `Basename':
asgn1.c:7: warning: suggest parentheses around assignment used as truth value
$
```

Notice the statement in line 7. The reason the compiler flags this statement as a possible error is that often the C programmer really intends to use the comparison operator == to compare values instead of assigning a value in an `if` statement. The compiler has no way of confirming whether the actual assignment is correct or whether a comparison was intended instead. The developer is left to decide the issue after the compiler has issued the warning.

Note that the statement is not incorrect, but neither is it certain that it reflects the programmer's true intention. Some might be tempted to argue that comparison is normal in an **if** statement and that the assignment in an **if** statement is unusual. The fact remains, however, that the C language is defined such that both are equally valid expressions.

Compiler writers have developed clever tricks for dealing with these thorny issues. This particular case can be resolved this way: If an assignment is coded as shown in Listing 1.1, it is flagged with a warning because it represents a possible error on the programmer's part. If this does represent an error, the programmer replaces the single equals symbol with a double equals symbol and recompiles. If the assignment is the intent, the programmer encloses the assignment with a set of brackets. When this is done, the compiler will assume that the programmer knows what he is doing.

Listings 1.2 and 1.3 show two different ways to resolve the warning issue in favor of the assignment.

LISTING 1.2 asgn2.c—Additional Parentheses Quiet an Assignment Warning

```
 1:  #include <string.h>
 2:
 3:  char *
 4:  Basename(char *pathname) {
 5:      char *cp;                   /* Work Pointer */
 6:
 7:      if ( (cp = strrchr(pathname,'/')) )
 8:          return cp + 1;          /* Return basename pointer */
 9:      return pathname;            /* No directory component */
10:  }
```

LISTING 1.3 asgn3.c—Parentheses and Comparison Quiet an Assignment Warning

```
 1:  #include <string.h>
 2:
 3:  char *
 4:  Basename(char *pathname) {
 5:      char *cp;                   /* Work Pointer */
 6:
 7:      if ( (cp = strrchr(pathname,'/')) != 0 )
 8:          return cp + 1;          /* Return basename pointer */
 9:      return pathname;            /* No directory component */
10:  }
```

Note the extra pair of parentheses around the assignment in line 7 of both Listings 1.2 and 1.3. The C syntax here did not require the parentheses, but the compiler took this as a cue from the developer that he knows what he is doing. While Listing 1.2 shows a solution acceptable to the GNU compiler, some other UNIX compilers will insist on the construct shown in Listing 1.3. For this reason, the solution in Listing 1.3 is preferred. It is clearer to the reader of the source code.

> **C/C++ Coding Tip**
>
> There is normally no longer a need to economize in C language expressions for the sake of optimization. Today's optimizing compilers are very effective at producing optimal code without any help from the programmer. For this reason it is better to make an expression easier to read than to reduce it to the fewest number of C operators.

This discussion has been presented using the C language `if` statement, but this issue applies to other statements as well. Warnings about assignments in the `switch` and `while` statements can be quieted in the same manner.

Warnings About Unused Arguments

Some compilers will complain about unused arguments. The thinking appears to be that if the argument is defined, then it was meant to be used. The truth of the matter is that the function arguments define an interface. There is no real requirement to fully use the interface that is defined, since an interface may also be intended for future use.

An example of the unused argument problem is the ubiquitous `main()` program. The main program interface is often defined as follows:

```
int main(int argc,char *argv[]);
```

If the program being written does not use the arguments that are present, it doesn't seem proper to remove the arguments simply because they are unused. This is what often is done by programmers to eliminate the compiler warnings.

Instead, it seems preferable to leave the arguments declared to indicate that the interface supports passing those values in that way. Listing 1.4 shows a simple way to avoid this problem.

LISTING 1.4 `uargs.c`—Quieting Unused Argument Warnings

```
1:    #include <stdio.h>
2:
3:    int
4:    main(int argc,char **argv) {
5:
6:        (void) argc;
7:        (void) argv;
8:
9:        puts("Hello World!");
10:       return 0;
11:   }
```

The C language permits a reference of a value in isolation, within a statement. Normally, this is not a useful construct, since there is no useful side effect in this case. However, it can be used as a useful compiler side effect, and this is exactly what is done with the `(void)` cast in lines 6 and 7 of Listing 1.4.

It should be noted that the GNU compiler in the FreeBSD 3.4 Release does not warn about unused arguments (`gcc` version 2.7.2.3). However, the compiler that you are using might.

Resolving Unused Variable Warnings

Sometimes the compiler will warn you about unused variables that you have declared in your code. These warnings create a strong temptation to remove the variables from your code immediately. You should exercise great care before doing so.

Program Cleanup Warning

Be extremely careful about removing unused variables and buffers. Make sure that you fully evaluate the C preprocessing directives of the source code before you assume that these values are never used. Sometimes compiling a program with different macro settings can cause these variable declarations to be needed. This is especially true when source code is compiled on different UNIX platforms.

The problem of unused variables often occurs in code that is designed to be portable to many different UNIX platforms. The specific problem is normally that the original developer never properly allowed for the unused declarations at the right time with the help of the correct C preprocessing directives. What often happens is that the source code is patched and modified by several people, and those changes never get fully retested on the other platforms on which it was meant to compile.

Listing 1.5 illustrates a program that, when compiled a certain way, will have unused variables. But are these variables truly unnecessary?

LISTING 1.5   `uvars.c`—An Example of Unused Variable Declarations

```
 1:    /* uvars.c */
 2:
 3:    #include <stdio.h>
 4:    #include <unistd.h>
 5:    #include <sys/types.h>
 6:
 7:    int
 8:    main(int argc,char **argv) {
 9:        pid_t PID;              /* Process ID */
10:
11:        (void) argc;
12:        (void) argv;
13:
14:    #ifdef SHOW_PID
15:        PID = getpid();         /* Get Process ID */
16:        printf("Hello World! Process ID is %d\n",(int)PID);
17:    #else
18:        puts("Hello World!");
19:    #endif
20:
21:        return 0;
22:    }
```

When Listing 1.5 is compiled without defining the C macro **SHOW_PID**, the result looks like this:

```
$ cc -Wall uvars.c
uvars.c: In function `main':
uvars.c:9: warning: unused variable `PID'
$
```

The compiler in this example has complained that the declared variable **PID** in line 9 is not used. This happens because the macro **SHOW_PID** is not defined, causing line 18 to be compiled in the place of lines 15 and 16. In this compile, the variable **PID** is unreferenced.

However, if you take this warning message at face value and remove the declaration of variable **PID** in line 9, then you will solve the immediate problem but create another, longer-term problem. If you define the macro **SHOW_PID** in the next compile, you find that it is necessary under different compile conditions:

```
$ cc -Wall -DSHOW_PID uvars.c
$ ./a.out
Hello World! Process ID is 73337
$
```

Adding the option **-DSHOW_PID** to the **cc** command line defined the **SHOW_PID** macro for this particular compile. As shown, you can see that the compile was successful and without any warning messages.

While this concept is obvious in this small example program, this same scenario often occurs in many real-life examples of UNIX code that are much more complex. The message here is to be careful about what you assume should be deleted from the source code when you get unused variable warnings.

Resolving Unreferenced String Warnings

Unreferenced string constants will also cause warnings to be generated. Sometimes programmers leave a string constant in a program so that it will become part of the final executable. A common practice is to define version strings in a program so that the executable file can be dumped and matched up with a particular version of a source module.

String Constant Tip
To eliminate compiler warnings about unreferenced string constants, simply declare the string constant as a constant using the C language **const** keyword.

The solution to these warnings is simply to define the string constant as a constant using the **const** keyword. The compiler does not complain about unreferenced constants. Listing 1.6 shows an example of an embedded CVS string that causes an unreferenced string warning to be issued by the compiler.

LISTING 1.6 ustring.c—Example of an Unreferenced CVS String

```
 1:   /* ustring.c */
 2:
 3:   #include <stdio.h>
 4:
 5:   static char cvsid[] =
 6:   "$Header: /home/cvs/prj/ustring.c,v 1.6 2010/03/30 01:59:34 uid Exp $";
 7:
 8:   int
 9:   main(int argc,char **argv) {
10:
11:           (void) argc;
12:           (void) argv;
13:
14:           puts("Hello World!");
15:           return 0;
16:   }
```

The compile session for Listing 1.6 is as follows:

```
$ cc -Wall ustring.c
ustring.c:5: warning: 'cvsid' defined but not used
$
```

Note lines 5 and 6 of Listing 1.6, where the string array **cvsid[]** is declared. The purpose of this declaration is simply to have the string constant appear in the final executable file. This allows you to identify the version of the source code that went into the executable program. It can be displayed with the **ident** command:

```
$ ident a.out
a.out:
     $Header: /home/cvs/prj/ustring.c,v 1.6 2010/03/30 01:59:34 uid Exp $
$
```

The **ident(1)** command locates the string constants that start with **$Header:** and end with the $ character. The problem is that the compiler complains about this string constant because the string itself is not used within the code.

Program Identification Tip

Some prefer to use the CVS/RCS identification string **Id** instead of **$Header$**, since the string is shorter (the directory path is not included). However, note that some versions of the **ident(1)** command will not report the **Id** string (for example, HPUX 10.2 and 11.0 will not report **Id**, but Linux and FreeBSD will).

Other UNIX platforms may not have the **ident(1)** command at all (AIX 4.3 and SunOS 5.6, for example). In that case you can use the **strings(1)** command and **grep(1)** for the string '**$Header:**' instead:

```
$ strings a.out | grep '$Header:'
```

The compiler is easily quieted about the unreferenced string by simply defining the string as a constant. The compiler does not require constants to be referenced. See Listing 1.7 for the corrected source code.

LISTING 1.7   `ustring2.c`—Eliminating the Unused String Constant Warning

```
 1:   /* ustring.c */
 2:
 3:   #include <stdio.h>
 4:
 5:   static const char cvsid[] =
 6:   "$Header: /home/cvs/prj/ustring.c,v 1.6 2010/03/30 01:59:34 uid Exp $";
 7:
 8:   int
 9:   main(int argc,char **argv) {
10:
11:           (void) argc;
12:           (void) argv;
13:
14:           puts("Hello World!");
15:           return 0;
16:   }
```

Line 5 of Listing 1.7 shows the added **const** keyword that is necessary to soothe the compiler. The compile session that follows confirms this:

```
$ cc -Wall ustring2.c
$
```

Unlike the other compile, there are no warning messages.

Compiling to Standards

Many UNIX platforms strive to adhere to various C and C++ standards where possible. Additionally, they all tend to support various enhancements that are not included in these standards. Most UNIX development environments will also support multiple C standards. So how does the programmer choose the standard to which he is compiling his source code?

Under UNIX, the choice of compile standard is established by a feature test macro that is defined. Generally, for any given platform, a standard is chosen by default. However, it is wiser to choose one explicitly to avoid difficulties compiling your project on the various UNIX platforms that you might be supporting. This may avoid other compile error surprises that might come about with newer releases of a vendor's UNIX platform.

FreeBSD 3.4-Release describes its standards support in **posix4(9)**. There you will find the following two feature test macros that will be used in this book:

- **_POSIX_SOURCE**

- **_POSIX_C_SOURCE**

The **_POSIX_SOURCE** feature macro is an older C macro that indicates that only POSIX and ANSI functionality should occur in the name space.

The one that will be used in this book is the **_POSIX_C_SOURCE** macro, because it allows you to choose a specific POSIX standard for compiling. The two FreeBSD documented values are

_POSIX_C_SOURCE=199009L	POSIX.1
_POSIX_C_SOURCE=199309L	POSIX.1B

Since the second selection allows the newer standard features to be compiled, it is preferred for new programs.

Listing 1.8 shows a simple feature macro test program. You can compile it in different ways and have it report information about standards to you.

LISTING 1.8   posix.c—Feature Macro Test Program

```
 1:    /* posix.c */
 2:
 3:    #include <stdio.h>
 4:    #include <unistd.h>
 5:
 6:    int
 7:    main(int argc,char **argv) {
 8:
 9:        (void) argc;
10:        (void) argv;
11:
12:    #ifdef _POSIX_SOURCE
13:        printf("_POSIX_SOURCE = %ld\n",(long)_POSIX_SOURCE);
14:    #endif
15:
16:    #ifdef _POSIX_C_SOURCE
17:        printf("_POSIX_C_SOURCE = %ld\n",(long)_POSIX_C_SOURCE);
18:    #endif
19:
20:    #ifdef _POSIX_VERSION
21:        printf("_POSIX_VERSION = %ld\n",(long)_POSIX_VERSION);
22:    #endif
23:
24:        return 0;
25:    }
```

Note that the `include` file `<unistd.h>` is necessary for this program to evaluate the various POSIX C feature macros. You will find that there is a considerable variety of responses to this test on different UNIX platforms.

FreeBSD 3.4-Release Feature Tests

When Listing 1.8 is compiled with various combinations of the `_POSIX_SOURCE` and `_POSIX_C_SOURCE` feature macros, you will see the following program responses:

```
$ cc posix.c && ./a.out
_POSIX_VERSION = 199009
$
```

In these examples, the `a.out` file is both compiled and invoked on the same command line for convenience (the shell `&&` operator will invoke the next command if the previous command was successful). In the above test, it is evident that FreeBSD defines the macro `_POSIX_VERSION` to indicate the version of the system for which the system is built. Here, it is reported that the default is the POSIX.1 standard (`199009`). It will be seen later, however, that not all UNIX environments will provide a `_POSIX_VERSION` value by default.

```
$ cc posix.c -D_POSIX_SOURCE && ./a.out
_POSIX_SOURCE = 1
_POSIX_VERSION = 199009
$
```

In this example, the compile explicitly defines the feature test macro `_POSIX_SOURCE`. It can be seen that the same macro is reassigned the value of `1` and that the `_POSIX_VERSION` macro is set to the value of `199009`.

```
$ cc posix.c -D_POSIX_C_SOURCE=199009L && ./a.out
_POSIX_C_SOURCE = 199009
_POSIX_VERSION = 199009
$
```

Here the standard is chosen by setting the feature macro `_POSIX_C_SOURCE` and specifically choosing POSIX.1 (`199009`). The `_POSIX_VERSION` macro is set to match in this example.

```
$ cc posix.c -D_POSIX_C_SOURCE=199309L && ./a.out
_POSIX_C_SOURCE = 199309
_POSIX_VERSION = 199009
$
```

This example chooses the POSIX.1B standard, but the feature test macro remains at the POSIX.1 value of `199009`. The FreeBSD `posix4(9)` documentation indicates that this tells your program that the operating system features are based on the POSIX.1 standard (even thought POSIX.1B was requested).

```
$ cc posix.c -D_POSIX_C_SOURCE=199506L && ./a.out
_POSIX_C_SOURCE = 199506
_POSIX_VERSION = 199009
$
```

This example is similar to the preceding one. A more recent standard is requested, but the `_POSIX_VERSION` macro suggests that only POSIX.1 (`199009`) is being supported.

HPUX 10.2 Feature Tests

For comparison, the `posix.c` module was tested under HPUX 10.2. With only the option `-Aa` specified to request a compile of ANSI C code, the following output was obtained from running `posix.c`:

```
$ cc -Aa posix.c && ./a.out
/usr/ccs/bin/ld: (Warning) At least one PA 2.0 object file (posix.o)
➥was detected. The linked output may not run on a PA 1.x system.
$
```

Even though `a.out` was invoked, there was no output. This indicates that none of the feature test macros were defined by default (unlike FreeBSD). The next example defines the macro `_POSIX_SOURCE`:

```
$ cc -Aa -D_POSIX_SOURCE posix.c && ./a.out
/usr/ccs/bin/ld: (Warning) At least one PA 2.0 object file (posix.o)
➥was detected. The linked output may not run on a PA 1.x system.
_POSIX_SOURCE = 1
_POSIX_VERSION = 199009
$
```

This is now identical to the FreeBSD output (with the exception of the pesky HP loader warning, which can be eliminated with several other options). Choosing the POSIX.1B standard yields the following results:

```
$ cc -Aa -D_POSIX_C_SOURCE=199309L posix.c && ./a.out
/usr/ccs/bin/ld: (Warning) At least one PA 2.0 object file (posix.o)
➥was detected. The linked output may not run on a PA 1.x system.
_POSIX_C_SOURCE = 199309
_POSIX_VERSION = 199309
$
```

This differs from the FreeBSD example in that the `_POSIX_VERSION` value shows support for POSIX.1B here (the value is `199309`).

AIX 4.3 Feature Tests

The AIX tests are presented here because of a few other wrinkles that were encountered. The next example shows the results of the default compile case:

```
$ cc posix.c && ./a.out
"posix.c", line 13.55: 1506-046 (S) Syntax error.
"posix.c", line 21.58: 1506-276 (S) Syntax error: possible missing ')'?
$
```

The error messages indicate that no defaults are established here. Defining the macro `_POSIX_SOURCE` helps and yields the following results:

```
$ cc -D_POSIX_SOURCE posix.c && ./a.out
_POSIX_SOURCE = 1
_POSIX_VERSION = 199506
$
```

Notice that `_POSIX_SOURCE` is redefined with the value 1, and the macro `_POSIX_VERSION` is given the value 199506, indicating the most recent POSIX standard value of all of the tests that are reported in this chapter. Specifically choosing an older standard is attempted next:

```
$ cc -D_POSIX_C_SOURCE=199309L posix.c && ./a.out
"posix.c", line 13.55: 1506-046 (S) Syntax error.
"posix.c", line 17.60: 1506-276 (S) Syntax error: possible missing ')'?
$
```

This just seems to buy trouble. Another attempt is made to specify the version that is apparently supported using the `_POSIX_C_SOURCE` feature test macro:

```
$ cc -D_POSIX_C_SOURCE=199506L posix.c && ./a.out
"posix.c", line 13.55: 1506-046 (S) Syntax error.
"posix.c", line 17.60: 1506-276 (S) Syntax error: possible missing ')'?
$
```

This seems to yield more compile errors. For AIX compiles, it would appear that you should only specify the `_POSIX_SOURCE` macro and avoid defining the `_POSIX_C_SOURCE` macro for a specific standard release.

SunOS 5.6 Feature Tests

The last example presented involves the reaction of the SunOS 5.6 release to various standards settings. The default case is attempted first:

```
$ cc posix.c && ./a.out
_POSIX_VERSION = 199506
$
```

Isn't this fun? In this case, the `_POSIX_VERSION` macro is set to the value of 199506, but no `_POSIX_SOURCE` macro is defined. In the next test, `_POSIX_SOURCE` is defined:

```
$ cc -D_POSIX_SOURCE posix.c && ./a.out
_POSIX_SOURCE = 1
_POSIX_C_SOURCE = 1
_POSIX_VERSION = 199506
$
```

This gets even more interesting. Now the `_POSIX_SOURCE` macro is redefined with the value of 1, which is what was expected. Here, the `_POSIX_C_SOURCE` macro now gets the value 1, which is interesting. Finally, the `_POSIX_VERSION` macro gives us the value of 199506, which indicates the level of support the C program can expect. The next test explicitly asks for this version of the standard:

```
$ cc -D_POSIX_C_SOURCE=199506 posix.c && ./a.out
_POSIX_C_SOURCE = 199506
_POSIX_VERSION = 199506
$
```

In this output, we lose the `_POSIX_SOURCE` macro, and the `_POSIX_VERSION` macro matches what was requested. One more test was conducted, this time requesting an older standard of POSIX.1B (`199309`):

```
$ cc -D_POSIX_C_SOURCE=199309L posix.c && ./a.out
_POSIX_C_SOURCE = 199309
_POSIX_VERSION = 199506
$
```

The `_POSIX_C_SOURCE` macro remains at the level that was requested, but the `_POSIX_VERSION` macro remains at the value `199506`. What does this tell you? It would seem that `_POSIX_VERSION` indicates what you have at your disposal, while `_POSIX_C_SOURCE` tells you what was requested.

Feature Test Summary

A writer of portable UNIX code must face a number of challenges to support multiple UNIX platforms. From the foregoing sections, it is plain that even just choosing the POSIX standard that you want to compile to is somewhat platform specific.

It would appear that the safest route with the platforms tested here is to specify the compile option. `-D_POSIX_SOURCE` is the most platform-neutral course to take, from a feature macro point of view. However, this is not a perfect solution, because it is evident that different POSIX standards were chosen on different UNIX platforms. This may cause other compile problems.

It seems that until UNIX vendors reach more agreement on the way that the feature test macros work, each UNIX platform will require its own special tweaking of feature test macros. You must first determine the lowest common denominator of the standard that your code is written for. Then determine how to select that standard on the UNIX platform chosen.

To simplify matters for this book, FreeBSD will be used for the program examples. The POSIX.1B standard will be requested in the example compiles (`_POSIX_C_SOURCE=199309L`), even though the FreeBSD 3.4-Release's `_POSIX_VERSION` macro indicates that only the POSIX.1 standard is supported.

Summary

This chapter has been a primer of sorts, to prepare you for all of those nasty compile issues that jump out at you when you begin a new project or port an old project on a new UNIX platform. The relatively standard compile options were covered to give you a quick start. You may find, however, that you still need to visit the vendor-specific options that were not discussed here. For example, HP has options that permit you to choose different instruction sets for the different PA-RISC platforms that are supported by the compiler.

You also learned (or reviewed) some tips on how to eliminate warning messages. This should enable you to keep the highest level of warnings enabled on your compiler and still accomplish tasks that the compiler might otherwise question.

Finally, you had an introduction to compiler feature test macros, which let you choose a standard to compile to. This treatment was by no means complete, since the other possibilities such as **_GNU_SOURCE** for Linux or **_HPUX_SOURCE** for HP were not tested. While these are not standards, they are often chosen to get the best combination of features for the specific platforms in question.

The next chapter will cover the subject of UNIX file system objects. For non-UNIX veterans, this is an essential foundation to build upon. Consequently, you are encouraged to absorb that chapter carefully. After an introduction to the various types of UNIX file system objects, the chapter will cover basic UNIX permissions as they affect the different objects. Then the core set of UNIX system calls as they affect the file system objects will be covered, giving you the core knowledge necessary for the remainder of this book.

CHAPTER 2

UNIX FILE SYSTEM OBJECTS

The early aspects of the UNIX file system design were conceived in the summer of 1969, largely by Ken Thompson at Bell Telephone Labs (BTL). An early version of the UNIX file system was loaded onto disk by paper tape. This allowed Ken Thompson and Dennis Ritchie to "drive the file system into the contortions that we wanted to measure," as Ken has been quoted.

Since this humble beginning, the basic ideas of the UNIX file system design have been copied in all other modern operating systems. This chapter will focus mostly on the objects that the UNIX file system presents to the users of the system. You will also examine some of the most basic operating system calls for working with file system objects from within your C program.

File System Objects

Modern UNIX file systems support the following types of file system objects:

- Regular Files (`S_IFREG`)
- Directories (`S_IFDIR`)
- Character Devices (`S_IFCHR`)
- Block Devices (`S_IFBLK`)
- Named Pipes (`S_IFIFO`)
- Sockets (`S_IFSOCK`)
- Symbolic Links (`S_IFLNK`)

The C macro names given within parentheses are provided by the include file `<sys/stat.h>` (see `stat(2)`). You'll see more of these in Chapter 6, "Managing Files and Their Properties."

Regular Files

A regular file is generally what is most important to users of a system. It stores the data that the user wants to retrieve and work with at a later time. The UNIX file system presents this data as a continuous stream of bytes.

A regular file consists of any number of data bytes, from zero to some maximum number. This is an important distinction to note, since many file systems, including CP/M and DOS, will present only multiples of a particular block size. This forces the DOS operating system to adopt the ^Z character as a marker for the end of a text file. Without this marker byte, it is otherwise impossible to have a file logically contain 3 bytes or 300 bytes, for example. However, UNIX has no such restriction, since it is logically able to present a file of any byte length.

Disk File Allocation Note

Although the UNIX file system is able to logically present a file of any size, it will still physically occupy a multiple of some block size. The precise nature of file allocation is hidden from the user and is determined by the type of file system in use.

Another feature of the UNIX file system is that the programmer can work with the file logically. There is no longer any need for the program to care about the block size in use by the underlying file. This permits the program to seek to any offset within the file and read any number of bytes, which may or may not span multiple disk blocks. For operating systems in 1969, this was a radical concept.

A regular file is identified by ls(1) as follows:

```
$ ls -l /etc/hosts
-rw-r--r--  1 root   wheel   112 Feb 19 11:07 /etc/hosts
$
```

The first character of the ls(1) output is a - (hyphen) to indicate that /etc/hosts is a regular file.

Directories

You cannot have more than one file in a file system without a directory. The first version of DOS created files only under the root directory. However, when a file was opened, this directory was searched to see if the file existed and where it was physically allocated.

The second step is important to the operating system in question.

UNIX supports a hierarchical file system, which allows directories to contain subdirectories. This allows the file system to be subdivided into logical groups of files and other file system objects. Can you imagine how difficult UNIX would be to use if the FreeBSD 3.4-Release contained all of its 60,014 (or more) files under the root directory?

Early releases of UNIX permitted directories to be read and written like regular files. Over time, several problems with this open concept emerged:

- Program errors or accidental writes to a directory could cause the loss of several files.

- New file systems supported different directory structure entries.

- Long filename support made it inconvenient to work directly with directory entries.

The first point illustrates one of the big weaknesses of early directory management. It was possible to lose the contents of an entire directory by accidentally overwriting the directory. The following command used to create havoc:

```
$ echo OOPS >directory
```

If *directory* was the name of a directory, this command would overwrite its contents, causing UNIX to lose track of all the files that it managed. Even worse, it usually meant that the space occupied by the files in that directory was lost, since the file system was not notified of any deletion. The following shows a modern response to this problem:

```
$ mkdir testdir
$ echo STUFF >testdir/file
$ ls -l testdir
total 1
-rw-r--r--  1 myid  megrp  5 Apr 15 15:16 file
$ echo OOPS >testdir
testdir: Is a directory.
$ ls -l testdir
total 1
-rw-r--r--  1 myid  megrp  5 Apr 15 15:16 file
$
```

The example creates a test directory and file and then attempts to overwrite the directory. The response from the UNIX kernel is that `testdir: Is a directory`.

When all file object names were limited to 14 characters, as they were in the earlier days, it was simple to work with the directories using direct file reads and writes. However, as different directory formats emerged and long filename support was introduced, this method proved to be unsafe and inconvenient.

For all of the reasons listed here, modern UNIX provides a set of library routines to search and manage directories. These will be covered in Chapter 7, "Directory Management."

A directory is identified by `ls(1)`, as the following example illustrates:

```
$ ls -dl /etc
drwxr-xr-x  14 root  wheel  2048 Apr  5 01:47 /etc
$
```

The first character shown by `ls(1)` is the letter `d`, indicating that `/etc` is a directory. Note especially the use of the `-d` option in the `ls(1)` command line. Without this option, `ls(1)` will attempt to list the contents of the directory, rather than the directory itself.

Block Devices

A block device is within a class of devices that work with fixed block sizes. A disk drive is a good example of this type of device. While the operating system permits you to logically read and write to your regular files using any transfer size, the operating system must read and write the disk device in terms of disk blocks of a fixed size.

Although disk devices get faster and larger each year, they are still slow when compared to the speed of the CPU. In addition to slow data transfer, disk rotation and head seek latencies add to the overall wait time involved in a disk I/O operation. Consequently, block devices are buffered with a disk cache by the UNIX kernel.

The disk cache will usually retain the most recently used disk blocks, but cache algorithms vary in order to achieve different performance goals. Because disk cache dramatically improves the performance of the file system, all file systems tend to be mounted using the block device.

Block devices can be readily identified by the `ls(1)` command as follows:

```
$ mount
/dev/wd0s2a on / (ufs, local, writes: sync 4505 async 92908)
/dev/wd0s2e on /usr (ufs, local, writes: sync 6924 async 118551)
procfs on /proc (procfs, local)
$ ls -l /dev/wd0s2a
brw-r-----  1 root   operator     0, 0x00030000 Feb 19 11:05 /dev/wd0s2a
$
```

The `mount(8)` (on many systems `mount(1M)`) command is used to find out what block devices have been used. Then the device `/dev/wd0s2a` was chosen in this example. The first character, shown by `ls(1)` in this example, is the letter **b**, indicating that `/dev/wd0s2a` is a block device.

Block devices are not necessarily representative of the entire disk. In most cases, these represent a disk partition so that an error in file system software cannot corrupt another partition. Additionally, each block device within the system usually has a corresponding character device as well. Block and character devices are also referred to as *block raw devices* and *character raw devices*, respectively.

When applied to a device, the word "raw" indicates that the disk space and structure are not managed. The raw device does not maintain a structure of files and directories within it. This is the job of file system software. Similarly, a database manages tables and rows within a raw device.

The cache feature of block devices may seem to suggest that a block device should be a good candidate for a database. This is usually not the case, however, since the database engine has its own custom cache algorithms that are tuned to the way that the database accesses the disk device. For this reason, database engines like Oracle, Sybase, and Informix usually perform better with the corresponding character device. This is one of the reasons that raw (character) device access to disks and partitions is being added to the Linux 2.4 kernel.

Character Devices

Character devices are a class of devices that work with various byte-sized inputs and outputs. These generally work with variable lengths of data, but not necessarily so (disks will insist on fixed block sizes). Your terminal (or pseudo-tty) is a special form of character device. As you type characters at your keyboard on the console, the operating system must read the characters and make them available to the program that is currently reading input from the terminal. This differs from the way that block devices work, in that the amount of data input is often small or variable in length.

QIC (Quarter-Inch Cartridge) tapes are another example of character devices. Tape devices will accept a program's idea of a record (within limits) and write a physical record to tape matching that size.

A character device is easily identified by the ls(1) command as shown below:

```
$ ls -l /dev/tty
crw-rw-rw-  1 root  wheel    1,   0 Apr 15 14:56 /dev/tty
$
```

The device /dev/tty is always known to the current session as your terminal device (the actual device name is different). The first character shown in the ls(1) output is c, telling you that this is a character device.

The mouse attached to the console is another example (FreeBSD):

```
$ ls -l /dev/sysmouse
crw-------  1 root  wheel   12, 128 Feb 19 11:05 /dev/sysmouse
$
```

Here again, you can see that the mouse is considered a character device.

Disks are also accessible using UNIX character devices. The same disks can be accessed using the corresponding block device that you read about earlier. However, character raw devices (for disks) are often provided to the database engines. Database engines manage the performance of disk I/O better than the block device cache because of their intimate knowledge of the data structures being used by the database.

By convention, the character raw device name of a block device usually has the letter r in front of it. See the following FreeBSD example:

```
$ mount
/dev/wd0s2a on / (ufs, local, writes: sync 4505 async 92982)
/dev/wd0s2e on /usr (ufs, local, writes: sync 6926 async 118585)
procfs on /proc (procfs, local)
$ ls -l /dev/rwd0s2a
crw-r-----  1 root  operator   3, 0x00030000 Feb 19 11:05 /dev/rwd0s2a
$
```

The mount(8) command was used to discover the block device names. Note that the ls(1) command adds the letter r to the device name to arrive at the character raw device name of /dev/rwd0s2a for the root mount. The first character of the ls(1) output shows the letter c, confirming that this is a character device.

Named Pipes (FIFOs)

In the period between 1970 and 1972, Doug McIlroy at BTL would sketch out how he would like to connect processes by saying "who into cat into grep." In 1972, Ken Thompson finally said, "I'm going to do it!" Overnight Ken worked to implement the pipe concept. Ken also had to rework many of the tools because, at the time, the tools did not support the idea of standard input—they read from files named on the command line instead. UNIX, starting with Third

Edition, was forever changed that night. The pipe feature was so well accepted that anyone who had seen it would not give it up.

Pipes are now routinely used on the command line under UNIX for all sorts of purposes, using the | pipe (vertical bar) symbol. These are anonymous pipes, since they exist only between the processes that are communicating with each other. They disappear from the system when both ends of the pipe become closed.

It is also possible to create a *named pipe* that exists in the file system. These are also known as FIFOs, since data that is written *first in* is *first out* of the pipe. The following shows a simple example:

```
$ mkfifo myFIFO
$ ls -l
total 0
prwxr-xr-x  1 myid   mygrp  0 Apr 15 16:55 myFIFO
$ ls -l >myFIFO &
$ tr '[a-z]' '[A-Z]' <myFIFO
TOTAL 0
PRWXR-XR-X  1 MYID   MYGRP  0 APR 15 16:55 MYFIFO
[1] 77637 Exit 0              ls -l >myFIFO
$
```

The example illustrates how the ls(1) command was able to redirect its output into the FIFO myFIFO (ls was placed into the background so that another command could be started in the same session). Then the tr(1) command was started to accept input from myFIFO, translating all lowercase letters into uppercase.

Notice also that the first letter of the ls(1) output is the letter p. This is how FIFO file system objects can be identified.

Sockets

The socket was a Berkeley University concept that found its way into 4.1BSD and 4.2BSD implementations of UNIX *circa* 1982. Sockets permit processes on one UNIX host to communicate over a network with processes on a remote host. Sockets can also be used to communicate with other processes within the same host. (The BSD lpr(1) command does this to accept output for spooling to a printer.)

Local sockets can also exist within the file system. This is the type of socket that can be used only between processes within the same host. If you have the PostgreSQL database installed on your FreeBSD system, you might have a socket like this one:

```
$ ls -l /tmp/.s.PGSQL.5432
srwxrwxrwx  1 postgres  wheel  0 Mar  7 04:43 /tmp/.s.PGSQL.5432
$
```

The example shows that the ls(1) command identifies the socket with the starting letter s.

Sockets that connect to remote systems, however, do not appear anywhere in the file system.

Symbolic Links

UNIX has supported linked files for quite some time. However, the symbolic link is a relatively new concept by UNIX standards. It was added to address the limitations of the normal link, sometimes now referred to as the "hard link."

Normally, files can be linked only when both links are contained on the same file system. On some systems, the /usr file system is different from other parts of the root file system. An attempt to create a link on a file system that is different from the file being linked will fail:

```
$ ln /etc/hosts /usr/me/work/my_link
ln: /home/me/work/my_link: Cross-device link
$
```

The UNIX kernel tells us that these two ends of a would-be link are on different devices. The symbolic link makes it possible to overcome this limitation:

```
$ ln -s /etc/hosts /usr/me/work/my_link
$ ls -dl my_link
lrwxr-xr-x  1 me    mygrp  10 Apr 15 17:22 my_link -> /etc/hosts
$
```

Note that the ln(1) command shown here uses the -s option to request a symbolic link, as if to say, "If you list the contents of my_link you will see the contents of your /etc/hosts file." The ls(1) command output for the symbolic link shows a starting letter l.

Symbolic links work around the original problem with hard links because they are actually a special kind of file that contains a pathname. When the UNIX kernel sees that it is a symbolic link, the kernel reads this special file to find out what the real pathname is. However, it is possible that the pathname listed is yet another symbolic link. The UNIX kernel will return the error ELOOP if the symbolic link is a circular reference or simply has too many indirect references. Chapter 6 will examine symbolic links further.

Symlink Recursion Note

The maximum symlink recursion in FreeBSD is defined by the macro MAXSYMLINKS. The macro is defined in the include file <sys/param.h>. For FreeBSD 3.4 Release, its value is 32. Other UNIX platforms may differ.

Special Files

While you may not have realized it, you already know about special files. These are file system objects that allow access to devices. Here are some of the examples that you have seen already:

/dev/tty	Terminal device
/dev/sysmouse	Mouse
/dev/wd0s2a	Block disk device
/dev/rwd0s2a	Character disk device

These are special files because they represent only the actual device in question (FreeBSD see `intro(4)`). It is only by convention that you tend to find these devices in the `/dev` directory. They could be placed in other directories.

Another important quality about special files is that their existence does not imply that the device or its driver support exists. For example, on a FreeBSD 3.4 Release system you might list a device:

```
$ ls -l /dev/da0
brw-r----- 1 root   operator    4, 0x00010002 Feb 19 11:05 /dev/da0
$ ls -l /dev/rda0
crw-r----- 1 root   operator   13, 0x00010002 Feb 19 11:05 /dev/rda0
$
```

The example shows a SCSI disk block and character device. Yet, if you were to switch to **root** to access this device, you would see the following:

```
# dd if=/dev/da0 of=/dev/null
dd: /dev/da0: Device not configured
#
```

The `dd(1)` command is told that the device is not configured (on the particular system on which it was tried). The file system object `/dev/da0` is just a placeholder that informs the kernel what device you want access to, if this special file is accessed.

Harking back to an earlier example

```
$ mount
/dev/wd0s2a on / (ufs, local, writes: sync 4505 async 92982)
/dev/wd0s2e on /usr (ufs, local, writes: sync 6926 async 118585)
procfs on /proc (procfs, local)
$ ls -l /dev/rwd0s2a
crw-r----- 1 root   operator    3, 0x00030000 Feb 19 11:05 /dev/rwd0s2a
$
```

The `/dev/rwd0s2a` device is listed as the disk device (partition) for use by the **root** file system. You can also access this same device with another special file, if you create one of your own:

```
$ mknod /usr/me/work/root c 3 0x30000
mknod: /usr/me/work/root: Operation not permitted
$ su -
Password:
# cd /usr/me/work
# mknod root c 3 0x30000
# ls -l root
crw-r--r-- 1 root   mygrp       3, 0x00030000 Apr 15 18:03 root
# rm root
# exit
$
```

The `mknod(1)` command requires **root** access (note the failed first attempt). As **root**, the `mknod(1)` command was used to create an entirely new special file `/usr/me/work/root`, which even used a different filename. Once that is created, you will find that you could access the same device by using either `/dev/rwd0s2a` or `/usr/me/work/root` (but I wouldn't advise that you do anything with your **root** file system!).

The special file `root` in the example was deleted also. Did that make the device disappear? No. Not only is the special file `/dev/rwd0s2a` still available, even if that entry was deleted, you could always re-create it with the `mknod(1)`.

The special file entry specifies three pieces of information:

- Block or character device (`b` or `c`)
- The major number for the device
- The minor number for the device

The major number (`3` in the example above) indicates what type of device it is (based upon the kernel configuration). The minor number can be as simple as the value zero, or it can reference a particular unit within a set. For example, a minor number of `2` might choose a second partition of the disk drive, and a minor number of `0` might reference the entire disk drive.

Minor numbers can also include bit flags. Some character devices such as tape drives have a bit set to indicate that the tape drive should be rewound upon close. In all cases, special file major and minor numbers are very kernel specific. You cannot use the same special files saved on an HPUX UNIX platform and restore them to an AIX 4.3 platform. This would be a recipe for disaster!

Special files are given attention here because they are important for those system programmers who want to take up daunting challenges such as writing database engines. The writer of any new device support must also be keenly interested in the special device entry for the hardware device.

Some device entries are pseudo devices. They don't actually represent hardware, but specialized kernel services. One pair of such devices under FreeBSD is the `/dev/kmem` and `/dev/mem` devices (see `mem(4)`). With the correct permissions, it is possible to inspect kernel memory through these special files. For example, a writer of a `ps(1)` command could choose to work through kernel structures this way (there are better ways).

Permissions

It is generally assumed in this book that the reader is already familiar with the UNIX access conventions that are applied. At the risk of stating the obvious, it is often useful at this stage to restate the precise way that permissions affect certain categories of file system objects. This is important because there are some minor semantic differences that depend on the file system object type.

Access of Regular Files

This is perhaps the simplest case to consider. Files can be controlled by

- Read access
- Write access
- Execute access

These are relatively simple concepts. However, a couple of interesting combinations exist:

- A file that has read and execute access
- A file that has execute-only access

The first case is necessary for shell scripts. In order for the shell interpreter to be started by the kernel with the !/bin/ksh hack, the UNIX kernel insists that the execute permission be given on the shell script. Additionally, the shell itself must interpret the file, so it must access enough to read the script. A shell script is unsuccessful if it has only one access permission or the other.

The execute permission is necessary to load and execute a binary executable as a process. This should be nothing new. However, an executable file, for instance /usr/local/bin/gzip, cannot be copied to your home directory with only execute permission. In this case, you are able only to execute gzip, but you are unable to ftp(1) it to your friends.

On older UNIX systems, there used to be a sticky bit available, which had meaning for executable files. When set on an executable file, this would cause the kernel to attempt to keep the program text (instructions) in its memory and swap other memory out instead. This optimization was often used on frequently accessed commands.

Access of Directories

Since directories are different from files, the semantics of directory access is a bit different also:

- *Read* grants permission to list the directory's contents.
- *Write* grants permission to modify the directory's contents.
- *Execute* grants permission to search the directory's contents and open a file or change to a subdirectory within it.

The read and execute permissions are similar, but distinct. You cannot list what files or subdirectories exist in a directory without read permission on that directory. However, if you already know the name of a file under that directory and you have execute access on the directory, then you can open that file (assuming the file grants read access).

You can also change to a subdirectory of a directory with execute-only access, if you already know the subdirectory's name (if the named subdirectory itself permits it with execute permission). A subdirectory without execute permission will not permit you to change to that directory, nor will it permit you to open files within it.

Many new UNIX users have difficulty understanding write access to directories. Write access permits users to create, rename, or delete files and other file system objects in that directory. Imagine a directory that contains a read-only file granting write access. That read-only file can be deleted because of the write permission available at the directory level. To disallow deleting of files, you must withdraw write permission on the directory containing the file. This also prevents the user from creating new files or renaming the existing ones in that directory.

Many UNIX systems allow a sticky bit to be set for directories. FreeBSD 3.4 Release describes this in its man page `sticky(8)`. This feature is necessary for dealing with shared directories such as the `/tmp` directory. Without the sticky bit, all users would have write access to the `/tmp` directory and be able to

- Rename another user's `temp` file

- Delete another user's `temp` file

- Move another user's `temp` file to another writable directory on the system

In short, there is room for a lot of mischief without any special treatment of the `/tmp` directory. Rather than customize the operating system to make special allowances for fixed directories, the sticky bit was permitted for directories. Look at your `/tmp` directory now. Under FreeBSD you would see:

```
$ ls -dl /tmp
drwxrwxrwt  2 root  wheel  512 Apr 15 03:33 /tmp
$
```

Notice the `t` where the `x` should go (last position in `drwxrwxrwt`). This indicates that both the execute bit (for others) and the sticky bit are present. The sticky bit (`S_ISVTX`) for directories imposes the rules that the file system object can be removed or renamed only when

- The user has write permission for the directory containing the object.

- The user is the owner of the file system object itself.

The only exception is for the `root` user, who is permitted to do anything. The sticky bit in this way permits only the user's own files in a given directory to be tampered with.

The sticky bit enables you to create a directory in which other users can create files of their own, but they cannot remove other users' files. Additionally, you can create read-only files for those users without worrying about those read-only files being renamed or deleted.

Working with Files Under UNIX

A file or device under UNIX is opened with the `open(2)` system call. Before `open(2)` is considered in detail, let's first examine the way UNIX references open files in general.

When you want to read from a file, such as `/etc/hosts`, you must indicate which file you want to read. However, if you had to name the path as a C string `"/etc/hosts"` each time you wanted to read part of the file, this would not only be tedious and inefficient, it would also be inflexible. How would you read from different parts of the same file? Obviously, a method by which the file can be opened more than once is much more flexible.

When you open a file under UNIX, you are given a reference to that file. You already know (since this is review) that it is a number. This is also known as a *file unit number* or a *file descriptor*. Conceptually, this number is a handle that refers back to the file that you named in the `open(2)` call.

File descriptors returned from an **open(2)** call allow you to name the path of the file system object once. After you have a file descriptor, you can read the **/etc/hosts** file one line at a time by providing the file descriptor to the **read(2)** function. The UNIX kernel then knows which file you mean, because it remembers it from the earlier **open(2)** call.

This provides flexibility also, since **open(2)** can be called a second (or *n*th) time for the same file. In this way, one part of your application can be reading one part of the file while another part is reading another. Neither read disturbs the other. The **read(2)** call can manage this because file state information is associated with each different file descriptor.

Finally, it should be apparent that an open file descriptor eventually needs to be closed. The **close(2)** function fills that need. When a process terminates because of a signal or for any other reason, including a normal exit, any file descriptors that are still open are closed by the UNIX kernel. If this were not done, the UNIX kernel would suffer from a serious memory leak, among other problems.

Less obvious is that, when an **execve(2)** is called to start a new program within a process, some file descriptors can be closed automatically, while others are left open. See **fcntl(2)** and the **F_SETFD** flag if this is of interest. The **execve(2)** call is covered in Chapter 19, "Forked Processes."

Opening and Closing Files

Files under UNIX are opened and closed with the following functions:

```
#include <sys/types.h>          /* for mode_t */
#include <sys/stat.h>           /* for mode_t */
#include <fcntl.h>              /* For open */

int open(const char *path, int flags, ... /* mode_t mode */);


#include <unistd.h>

int close(int d);
```

The **open(2)** call accepts a C string that represents the pathname of the file system object to be opened, some flags, and optionally some permission bits in the **mode** argument. The return value is either -1 (with **errno**) if the call fails or a file descriptor value that starts at the value zero.

Error Handling Note

The handling of **errno** is covered in Chapter 3, "Error Handling and Reporting," if you need to know more about this variable.

The returned file descriptor is always the lowest unused file descriptor number. If you have standard input already open (file unit **0**), standard output (file unit **1**), and standard error (file unit **2**), then the next successful **open(2)** call will return file unit **3**.

When you are finished with a file descriptor (an open file system object), you must close it with a call to `close(2)`.

Flags for `open(2)`

The second argument to `open(2)` can consist of several flag bits. These are given in Table 2.1.

TABLE 2.1 FreeBSD `open(2)` Flag Bits

Flag	Description
O_RDONLY	Open for read only
O_WRONLY	Open for write only
O_RDWR	Open for read and write
O_NONBLOCK	Do not block on open
O_APPEND	Append with each write
O_CREAT	Create file if necessary
O_TRUNC	Truncate file to 0 bytes
O_EXCL	Error if creating and the file already exists
O_SHLOCK	Atomically obtain a shared lock
O_EXLOCK	Atomically obtain an exclusive lock

The flag `O_NONBLOCK` causes the `open(2)` call not to block while waiting for the device to be ready. For example, opening a modem device can cause it to wait until a carrier is detected. On some UNIX platforms such as SGI's IRIX 6.5, there is also the `O_NDELAY` flag, which has special semantics when combined with the `O_NONBLOCK` flag.

The `O_APPEND` flag will cause each write to the file to be appended to the end of the file. This applies to all `write(2)` calls, not just the first one (intervening appends can be done by other processes).

The `O_CREATE` flag can be used to cause the file to be created, if necessary. However, when combined with the `O_EXCL` flag, if the file already exists, the `open(2)` call returns an error. A special case of this is when flags `O_CREATE` and `O_EXCL` are used and the pathname given is a symbolic link. The call will fail even if the pathname resolved by the symbolic link does not exist. Another way to state this is that if the *symbolic link* exists, the open call treats this as if the *file* already exists and returns an error.

When opening a file in order to overwrite it, you can specify the `O_TRUNC` flag. This causes the file to be emptied prior to `open(2)` returning successfully. Any prior content of the file is lost.

Flags O_SHLOCK and O_EXLOCK are permitted on FreeBSD 3.4 Release and cause certain flock(2) semantics to be applied. Chapter 5, "File Locking," will cover the topic of locking files under UNIX.

Closing Files Automatically

All files are closed when the current process terminates. However, by default they remain open across calls to the execve(2) function. If you need the open file descriptor to close prior to executing a new program (with execve(2)), then you should apply a call to fcntl(2) using the F_SETFD operation.

```
#include <fcntl.h>

int fcntl(int fd, int cmd, ...);
```

To change a file descriptor given by variable fd to close automatically before another executable is started by execve(2), perform the following:

```
int fd;                              /* Open file descriptor */
int b0;                              /* Original setting */

if ( (b0 = fcntl(fd,F_GETFD)) == -1 )  /* Get original setting */
    /* Error handling... */

if ( fcntl(fd,F_SETFD,1)) == -1 )      /* Set the flag TRUE */
    /* Error handling... */
```

Here both the fetching of the current setting and the setting of the close-on-exec flag are shown. Some platforms use a C macro to identify this bit. For example, SGI's IRIX 6.5 uses the FD_CLOEXEC macro instead of assuming it is the least significant bit.

Opening Special Files

There is actually nothing unusual about opening a special file. You open it as you would any other file. For example, if you have permission to open a disk partition, your program can use the open(2) call to open it for reading and writing. For example

```
int fd;

fd = open("/dev/wd0s2f",O_RDWR);
if ( fd == -1 )
    /* Error handling... */
```

From this point on, this sample program would have access to the entire disk or disk partition, assuming that the open call succeeded. File systems have their special files protected so that normal users cannot open them this way. If they could, they could seriously corrupt the file system.

The `open(2)` and `close(2)` functions can return the error `EINTR`. It is easy to overlook this fact for the `close(2)` function. See Chapter 15, "Signals," for a discussion of this error code.

Working with Sockets

Sockets require special treatment. They are not opened with the normal `open(2)` call. Instead, sockets are created with the `socket(2)` or `socketpair(2)` call. Other socket function calls are used to establish socket addresses and other operating modes. Socket programming is outside the scope of this book.

It should be noted, however, that once a socket is created and a connection is established (at least for connection-oriented protocols), reading and writing to a socket can occur like any open file, with calls to `read(2)` and `write(2)`. Sockets are like bi-directional pipes, and seeking is not permitted.

Duplicating File Descriptors

UNIX provides this unique capability to have one open file descriptor available as two (or more) separate file descriptors. Additionally, it is possible to take an open file descriptor and cause it to be available on a specific file unit number, provided the number is not already in use.

The function synopses for `dup(2)` and `dup2(2)` are as follows:

```
#include <unistd.h>

int dup(int oldfd);

int dup2(int oldfd, int newfd);
```

In the case of `dup(2)`, the returned file descriptor when successful is the lowest unused file unit number available in the current process. For `dup2(2)`, however, the new file descriptor value is specified in the argument `newfd`. When `dup2(2)` returns successfully, the `return` value should match `newfd`.

Interrupted System Call Warning

On some UNIX platforms, the `dup(2)` and `dup2(2)` calls can return the error `EINTR` (known to be documented for SGI's IRIX 6.5). See Chapter 15 for a discussion of this error code.

One situation in which `dup(2)` is helpful is in opening `FILE` streams to work with an existing socket. The following example takes the socket `s` and creates one input stream `rx` and another `tx` stream for writing:

```
int s;                          /* Open socket */
FILE *rx;                       /* Read stream */
FILE *tx;                       /* Write stream */

...
rx = fdopen(s,"r");             /* Open stream for reading on s */
tx = fdopen(dup(s),"w");        /* Open stream for writing on s */
```

Did you spot the dup(2) call? Why is it necessary? The dup(2) call is necessary because when the fclose(3) call is later made to close the rx stream, it will also close the file descriptor (socket) s. The dup(2) call ensures that the tx stream will have its own file descriptor to use, regardless of if stream rx is still open.

If the dup(2) were omitted from the example, the final data held in the buffers for tx would fail to be written to the socket when fclose(3) was called for tx (assuming rx has been closed first). The reason is that the underlying file descriptor will already have been closed. The dup(2) call solves an otherwise thorny problem.

Changing Standard Input

If you need to change your standard input, how is this accomplished? This may be necessary for the sort(1) command for example, since it processes the data presented on its standard input.

Assume that the input file to be sorted has been opened on unit 3 and held in variable fd. You can place this open file on standard input as follows:

```
int fd;                         /* Open input file for sort(1) */

close(0);                       /* Close my standard input */
if ( dup2(fd,0) == -1 )         /* Make fd available on 0 */
    /* Error handling... */
close(fd);                      /* This fd is no longer required */
```

The basic principle here is that once you close unit 0 (standard input), you can make the file that is open on unit 3 available as unit 0 by calling dup2(2). Once you have accomplished that, you can close unit 3, since it is not needed any longer.

You can apply this principle for standard output, standard error, or any other file unit you would like to control.

Interrupted System Call Warning

Note that the example avoided testing for errors for close(2), which should be done. Test for the error EINTR, and retry the close(2) call if the EINTR error occurs.

UNIX File I/O

Many C programming texts teach the reader how to do I/O using the `stdio(3)` functions `fopen(3)`, `fgets(3)`, `fread(3)`, `fwrite(3)`, and the rest. Because UNIX supports the `stdio(3)` interface, many new UNIX programmers think of this as UNIX file I/O. However, this interface is simply the `stdio(3)` set of routines, which is layered on top of the UNIX system calls. The underlying system calls perform the real UNIX file I/O.

There will be times where you'll need to use the "bare metal calls" such as `read(2)` and `write(2)` under UNIX. These and other UNIX I/O functions will be covered in Chapter 4, "UNIX Input and Output." These ultimately give you the most control and, in some cases, relief from bugs in `stdio(3)`.

Figure 2.1 illustrates how the `stdio(3)` functions call upon the section 2 functions. The `read(2)` and `write(2)` calls are serviced by the UNIX kernel, shown at the bottom of the figure.

FIGURE 2.1

The I/O software layers.

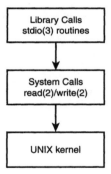

An example of a shortcoming of the `stdio(3)` routines is that they behave differently on different platforms. On some UNIX platforms, the error `EINTR` is returned when a signal handler returns, while on others this error is not returned at all. On still other UNIX platforms, the `stdio(3)` routines get confused dealing with `EINTR` and do not work correctly.

Sometimes you can live with the `stdio(3)` interface, but you'll want to perform a special control function on the open `FILE`. For example, you might need to issue an I/O control operation with `ioctl(2)` or set the close-on-exec flag using `fcntl(2)`. In these cases, you can gain access to the underlying file descriptor by using the `stdio(3)` macro `fileno(3)`. To set the close-on-exec flag on `FILE` stream `tx`, do the following:

```
FILE *tx;                              /* Opened by fopen(3) */

...
if ( fcntl(fileno(tx),F_SETFD,1)) == -1 )  /* Set the flag TRUE */
    /* Error handling... */
```

The example shows how the macro call `fileno(tx)` exposes the underlying UNIX file descriptor to the `fcntl(2)` function. This technique can sometimes be used with other functions such as `ioctl(2)`. However, be careful that what you are doing in this scenario does not upset what is being managed by the `stdio(3)` routines. For example, it might seem harmless to duplicate a file descriptor being used by `stdio(3)` and then call `lseek(2)` on the duplicated file descriptor. However, this will also change the file position for the original file descriptor. For some implementations of the `stdio(3)` library, this may cause you grief.

Summary

For many readers, this chapter has been a review. For those ramping up their knowledge to program in C under UNIX, this chapter will have exposed you to some important UNIX concepts. Perhaps you learned a few historical tidbits along the way.

Chapter 3 is another foundation-building chapter. Veterans can skip that chapter if they are in a hurry. If you are still building up your knowledge about UNIX programming, you will want to pay special attention to this chapter. It will help you master the material in the remainder of this book.

CHAPTER 3

ERROR HANDLING AND REPORTING

The UNIX operating system and its associated C libraries offer a rich set of system and function library calls, respectively. Within this set of calls there are very few functions, which cannot return an error. Reasons for errors include the incorrect use of parameters, inadequate buffer sizes, missing or misnamed file system objects, or simply a lack of access to a resource. A mechanism must exist to return an error indication to the caller of the function.

This chapter examines the error reporting mechanism used by the UNIX system and library function calls. This includes a discussion of the original error reporting mechanism that was used in the past and the implementation now in use. Additionally, it will be shown how UNIX error codes can be translated into meaningful text messages that can be reported to a user.

Determining Success or Failure

When a C function is called, the programmer is interested in two things upon its return:

- Did the function call succeed?
- If not, why did the call fail?

General Rules for Error Indication

The UNIX convention used by most system calls and library functions is that the return value indicates a general success or failure. Return values fall into two major categories:

- The return value is an integer value (`int` or `long`). Normally failure is indicated by a value of negative one (-1).
- The return value is a pointer type, such as pointers (`char *`), (`void *`) or a pointer to a structure. Failure is indicated by a null return pointer and success by a non-null pointer.

Exceptions to the General Rule

There are exceptions to the general rule just listed, but these are rare. When the functions `wait(2)`, `waitpid(2)`, `wait3(2)`, and `wait4(2)` return an error indication, they return the integer value `(pid_t)(-1)`. This is similar to the integer return case, except that the value `-1` is returned in a process ID data type.

An exception to the pointer rule is the `shmat(2)` function call. When it returns an error indication, it returns the pointer value `(void *)(-1)`.

Unusual exceptions to the general rule can be found in the functions `strtol(3)`, `strtoul(3)`, and `strtod(3)`, which return special values like `LONG_MIN`, `LONG_MAX`, `ULONG_MAX`, `+HUGE_VAL`, and `-HUGE_VAL`. These will be covered in detail in Chapter 10, "Conversion Functions."

Classifying Successful Return Values

For integer return values, a successful return value is normally anything other than `-1`. Often this is a value that is greater than or equal to zero. For example, the UNIX `open(2)` call returns a file descriptor number that can be zero or greater.

For pointer return values, a successful return value is normally a non-null pointer. An example is the `fopen(3)` function, which returns a pointer to a `FILE` object.

As noted previously, under unusual circumstances the null pointer can indicate a successful return from certain exceptional functions (recall `shmat(2)`). For this reason, the best programming practice is for the programmer to test for failure indication upon return from a function. Anything that does not classify as a failure should be considered a successful indication.

Other Return Indications

Before leaving the topic of function return indications, it is worth pointing out that some functions offer a third indication, in addition to the normal success or failure. These generally fall into two categories:

- No more information exists (examples include `waitpid(2)`, `wait3(2)`, `wait(4)`).
- A timeout has occurred without returning any "interesting" event (examples include `select(2)`, `poll(2)`).

In these examples, the designers of these functions have decided not to treat the "no information" or "timeout" case as an error. At the same time, these cases cannot be considered successful returns, since either no information is returned or a timeout has occurred.

This type of indication can be treated as an error by the programmer, with the exception that there will be no value provided in the global variable `errno`.

Determining the Reason for Failure

The foregoing discussion identifies most function calls as returning an indication of

- success
- failure
- in rare cases, no information

Once you have discovered that the function call has failed, you need to know why. For example, the UNIX `make(1)` command needs to know from `open(2)` when it fails that

- It was unable to open `makefile` because it did not exist.
- It lacked the permissions necessary to open `makefile` for reading.

The reason for the failure *might* have a bearing on the action taken by the command. For example, if it finds that file `makefile` does not exist, `make(1)` tries to open the file `Makefile` instead. However, when it discovers that it lacks permissions to open file `makefile`, some implementations of the `make(1)` command report this as an error to the user. See the following Note for variations on this theme by the different UNIX platforms tested.

Make Behavior Variation Note

The `make(1)` command's behavior varies on the different UNIX platforms tested. The following platforms report an error if they lack permission to read the file `makefile`:

Linux (GNU make 3.77)

SunOS 5.6 (reports a warning and tries to open `Makefile`)

The `make(1)` command on the following platforms ignores the file access error and proceeds to open `Makefile` instead:

FreeBSD 3.4 Release

HPUX 10.2 and HPUX 11.0

AIX 4.3

The nature of a failure is clearly important to the programmer of any software or utility program. The error-reporting mechanism that early developers of UNIX chose was the special external integer variable named `errno`. Whenever a function call returned a failure indication, it would first assign a reason code for the failure to the external `errno` variable. The calling program could then examine this external variable if it cared to know the reason for the failure. When the function returned a successful indication (or "no information" indication), the value of `errno` was left unchanged.

This mechanism was suitable for early versions of UNIX. However, this older method has limitations. To remove the inherent limitations of the `errno` variable, its definition has changed somewhat in modern versions of UNIX. If it is applied correctly, this change is transparent to you as a programmer.

The Old `errno` Value

The original method that the programmer used to gain access to the error code was to declare an external reference to the `int` value `errno`:

```
extern int errno;
```

When an attempt to open a file fails, a program can simply query the external variable `errno` to determine the reason for the failure. The following example shows how the `make(1)` command could be written using the old errno method:

```
#include <errno.h>                          /* Defines ENOENT */
extern int errno;                           /* Error code */
int fd;                                      /* File descriptor */

/* Attempt to open makefile */
if ( (fd = open("makefile",O_RDONLY)) == -1 ) { /* Fail to open? */
    if ( errno == ENOENT )                  /* File does not exist? */
        fd = open("Makefile",O_RDONLY);     /* No, so try Makefile instead */
}

if ( fd == -1 ) {                            /* Did either open(2) fail? */
    /* Yes, report the open failure... */
    ...
} else {
    /* makefile or Makefile is open on file unit fd */
}
```

The example shows that if `makefile` fails to open, with the error `ENOENT`, `Makefile` is opened. The example also illustrates that the reason for the error is never returned directly by the function, nor is it returned by an argument reference. Instead, using this older external variable methodology, the programmer queries this value when a function returns a failure indication.

Error Code Note

`ENOENT` means No Such File or Directory. This error code indicates that the requested file system object was not found (does not exist).

Referencing Error Codes by Name

Using the `errno` external variable convention for errors required that a series of error codes be agreed on in advance. Since numeric error codes might vary on different UNIX platforms, a set of C macros is defined to refer to these error codes (for example, error code `ENOMSG` is **83** for FreeBSD 3.4, **35** for HPUX, and **42** for Linux). The symbolic macro names can be used to refer to the same error codes on different UNIX platforms. These C macros are defined in the include file `errno.h`.

```
#include <errno.h>
```

Using symbolic macro references for error codes is important, since it allows your C programs to be portable to other UNIX platforms. Only a compile is required to reference the correct numeric value for these codes on a given platform.

UNIX `errno` codes are non-zero values and usually start at 1 and work up. Zero is sometimes used to indicate "no error" (this convention is used in rare cases with the functions `strtol(3)`, `strtoul(3)`, and `strtod(3)`, for example).

Applying `errno` Correctly

There is a temptation for novice programmers to use the `errno` value to test for success. However, it is incorrect to do so because the purpose of the `errno` value is to be a central place to which to post error codes. As a general policy, never expect the `errno` value to be cleared to zero for success. *Only errors (failures) are posted to this variable.*

There are special situations that require you to clear the `errno` value to zero before making a function call (some examples are `strtol(3)`, `strtoul(3)`, `strtod(3)`, and `getpwent(3)`). This is necessary because the function will not clear the `errno` value to zero when success is returned. Under these special circumstances, if the `errno` value remains as the value **0** (presuming it was cleared prior to the call), then this indicates a successful return. This technique must only be applied to *specially indicated* functions. This technique cannot be extended for use on other functions. The special cases will be carefully indicated within this book.

Application Warning

The `errno` value is updated by system and library functions only after an error indication is returned. This value is never cleared to zero for a successful operation. Always test the function's return value to determine if an error has been indicated. If so, then the value of `errno` has meaning.

Testing for Failure with Integer Return Values

Earlier it was shown how functions, which return integer results, use the value of -1 to indicate that a call has failed. The following `open(2)` example indicates when the value of `errno` is valid:

```
extern int errno;          /* Old way of gaining access to errno */
int fd;                    /* File descriptor */

if ( (fd = open("makefile",O_RDONLY)) == -1 ) {
    /* Failed: errno holds a valid error code */
    ...
} else {
    /* Success: fd holds file descriptor, and errno is meaningless here */
    ...
}
```

If the `open(2)` call returns a failed indication by a return value of -1, then we know that the error code will have been posted to the integer `errno`.

Testing for Failure with Pointer Results

Other functions that report their failure by returning a null pointer can identify when to use errno as follows:

```
FILE *fp = fopen("makefile","r");          /* Attempt to open makefile */

if ( fp == NULL ) {                        /* Failed? */
    /* Open Failed: the value of errno holds an error code */
    ...
} else {
    /* Open succeeded: the value of errno has no meaningful value */
    ...
}
```

Here the fopen(3) call indicates failure by returning a null pointer (which matches the C macro value NULL). Again, only when it is determined that the function has returned a failure indication is the value errno valid and does it contain an error code.

The New errno Value

If you've been a veteran of UNIX C/C++ code for some time, then you've probably noticed some changes in the declaration of the variable errno over the years. Modern UNIX platforms have undergone some changes in order to support threads.

While threads are a welcome addition to the UNIX platform, they have required a number of internal changes to the underlying C libraries and the way in which the errno variable is defined. A thread is a separate flow of instructions within one memory environment (all threads share one memory address space). Consequently, the traditional single global integer value of errno no longer suffices, since function calls in one thread would alter the errno values being referenced in another thread.

In order to support threads without requiring all existing software to be redesigned, a new declaration has been crafted for the errno value (usually a C macro). This new definition defines a separate copy of errno for each thread. Rather than have the programmer declare this variable, it is now done by the provided include file <errno.h> instead. This change in definition should be transparent to most UNIX source code. Note that there were older releases of the GNU libraries under Linux, where the extern int errno declaration was in conflict and required removal to compile successfully. The modern GNU libraries no longer suffer from this problem.

Declaring the New errno Variable

The new errno value is now defined in a platform-dependent manner. This means that you should let the system define it for you by including the file <errno.h>. You should no longer declare it as an external integer variable.

The <errno.h> include file will define errno in a manner that is appropriate for your specific UNIX platform. This also defines the errno macro constants for the error codes.

Using the New errno Variable

Once variable errno is appropriately declared for your platform, you can still use it as you did before. For example

```
int saved_errno;

saved_errno = errno;            /* Saving errno */
printf("errno = %d\n",errno);   /* Inspecting errno */
errno = ENOENT;                 /* Changing errno */
errno = 0;                      /* Clearing errno to zero */
```

You can obtain value of errno and change its value, just as before its definition changed. The change in the way errno is defined is meant to be transparent to you.

Reporting on errno Values

When an error occurs, it is simple for the program to test for a specific case and act upon it. The problem becomes more complex when all you want to do is report the error to the user. Users do not like to memorize error codes, so a method must exist to translate an errno code into a readable message.

Meaningful error messages can be reported by a UNIX program to the user, in the following ways:

- Use the perror(3) function to generate a message from the errno value and report it to stderr.

- Use the provided sys_errlist[] array of messages (on FreeBSD this is described by the man page strerror(3)).

- Use the strerror(3) function to return a message for the error code provided in the function argument.

Using the perror(3) Function

One function provided for reporting errors is the library function perror(3). This function takes one string argument and writes that string to stderr, followed by a colon and then a message for the current errno value. The function synopsis is as follows:

```
#include <stdio.h>

void perror(const char *s);
```

This function is easily tested by simply assigning an error of our choice to errno and calling perror(3). An example is provided in Listing 3.1.

LISTING 3.1   `perror.c`—A Test Program for `perror(3)`

```
1:   #include <stdio.h>
2:   #include <errno.h>
3:
4:   int
5:   main(int argc,char **argv) {
6:
7:       errno = EIO;
8:       perror("Test EIO Message");
9:       return 0;
10:  }
```

Line 7 shows how an I/O error was assigned to the `errno` variable (the error code was arbitrarily chosen to simulate an error). Line 8 calls upon the `perror(3)` function to report the error. The test session is shown below:

```
$ make perror
cc -c -D_POSIX_C_SOURCE=199309L -Wall perror.c
cc perror.o -o perror
$ ./perror
Test EIO Message: Input/output error
$
```

The session output shows the program-supplied message, which is followed by a colon and then by an interpretation of the error code that was assigned to variable `errno`. The value, `EIO` in this example, was translated to the message `Input/output error`.

Evaluating the `perror(3)` Function

At first sight, the `perror(3)` function might appear to be a good solution. In practice, however, this function is not very useful. The first problem is that the message must go to standard error. If the message must be

- Written to a log file

- Reported to an X Window pop-up

- Reported in a different format

- Stored as a string

then the function `perror(3)` is not able to help. Another problem that often occurs is this: What if the error code is not coming from `errno` but some other variable? The `perror(3)` function seems best left to academic examples because of its simplicity.

Using the `sys_errlist[]` Array

If you look up the `perror(3)` function in the FreeBSD `man(1)` pages (and on most UNIX platforms), you will also see that it describes the `sys_errlist[]` array. The synopsis of this array is this:

```
#include <stdio.h>      /* Defines sys_errlist[] and sys_nerr */

extern const char *sys_errlist[];
extern const int sys_nerr;
```

Variations:

```
#include <errno.h>      /* HPUX 10.2 & 11.0 */
/* None */              /* AIX 4.3 */
/* None */              /* SunOS 5.6, Solaris 8 */
/* None */              /* UnixWare 7 */
#include <errno.h>      /* SGI IRIX 6.5 */
```

The `sys_errlist[]` array is an external array of pointers to string constants. Each string describes a particular error that corresponds to an `errno` code. The array and the error codes are structured so that the error message can be obtained by using the `errno` value as the subscript into the array. For example

```
errno = EIO;                       /* Simulate an error */
printf("The EIO Message is '%s'\n",sys_errlist[errno]);
```

Having access to the error message text for each error code provides much more flexibility. When the `fopen(3)` call fails, you can report the reason for the failure, the pathname being opened, and whether it is being opened for reading or writing:

```
FILE *fp = fopen(pathname,"r");    /* Attempt to open a file */

if ( !fp ) {                       /* Did the open fail? */
    fprintf(stderr,"%s: Unable to open %s for read.\n",
        sys_errlist[errno],        /* The error message text */
        pathname);                 /* The file being opened */
    exit(13);
}
```

This example shows a typical format for error messages from UNIX programs. This typical format used can be summarized as

```
Explanation of error code: Explanation of the operation being attempted
```

Notice that this convention contradicts the format used by the `perror(3)` function.

Using `sys_nerr` to Range Check Errors

The largest error code that is provided for in the `sys_errlist[]` array is given by the external integer value of `sys_nerr` minus one. To be safe, you should technically always test the `errno` value before using it as a subscript:

```
int fd;                            /* File descriptor */

fd = open(pathname,O_RDONLY);      /* Attempt to open for read */
if ( fd == -1 ) {                  /* Did open(2) fail? */
    /* The open(2) call failed: */
    fprintf(stderr,"%s: opening %s for read\n",
        errno < sys_nerr ? sys_errlist[errno] : "?",
        pathname);
```

In the example shown, the C operator **?** is used to test **errno** to make sure that it is less than the value of **sys_nerr**. If it is, the value of **sys_errlist[errno]** can be safely supplied to **fprintf(3)**. If the errno value fails to be less than the **sys_nerr** value, the C string **"?"** is supplied instead, to prevent a program abort.

Evaluating the sys_errlist[] Array Method

While range-checking **errno** with the **sys_nerr** value is the correct thing to do, it is considered tedious and pedantic by many programmers. Therefore, many programmers ignore this test completely. Because programmers fail to apply this test, the practice of using the **sys_errlist[]** array has fallen out of favor, and another way has been subsequently provided.

Application Note

The **man(1)** pages provided by SGI for its IRIX 6.5 operating system state "Code using **sys_errlist**, and **sys_errlist** directly, will not be able to display any **errno** greater than 152." It is unclear from this text whether it is simply stating the SGI value of **sys_nerr** or whether this is a limitation of using the array on that platform.

The tone of the message suggests that the **sys_errlist[]** array falls short of **strerror(3)** and thus should be avoided in new code. A possible reason for this is that dynamic content could be provided by the **strerror(3)** function for errors with codes greater than 152.

The strerror(3) Function

This is the last of the error code conversion methods that will be examined. The synopsis of the **strerror(3)** function is as follows:

```
#include <string.h>

char *strerror(int errnum);
```

Include File Tip

A common mistake is to include the file **<errno.h>** instead of **<string.h>**. It is commonly assumed that the **strerror(3)** function is declared in the **<errno.h>** include file because it reports an error message. However, this function is grouped with the string functions, instead.

The **strerror(3)** function provides the flexibility afforded by the **sys_errlist[]** array, but it also performs the necessary range check on the error code being converted. If the error code is outside of the known list of error codes, an unknown error message is returned instead of a bad pointer.

Using the strerror(3) Function

Listing 3.2 shows a short program that we can use to test the **strerror(3)** function.

LISTING 3.2   `strerror.c`—Test Program for `strerror(3)`

```
 1:  #include <stdio.h>
 2:  #include <errno.h>
 3:  #include <string.h>
 4:
 5:  extern int sys_nerr;     /* Highest supported error code */
 6:
 7:  int
 8:  main(int argc,char **argv) {
 9:      int x;
10:      static int ecodes[] = { -1, EIO, 0 };
11:
12:      /* Get maximum code and add 4096 */
13:      ecodes[2] = sys_nerr + 4096;    /* A very high code */
14:
15:      for ( x=0; x<3; ++x ) {
16:          errno = ecodes[x];
17:          printf("%4d = '%s'\n",ecodes[x],strerror(errno));
18:      }
19:
20:      return 0;
21: }
```

This test program tries `strerror(3)` with a -1 value, `EIO`, and a very high error code, which should not exist.

Testing the Range Check in `strerror(3)`

When the program in Listing 3.2 is compiled and run, the following results are obtained under FreeBSD (3.4 Release):

```
$ make strerror
cc -c -D_POSIX_C_SOURCE=199309L -Wall strerror.c
cc strerror.o -o strerror
$ ./strerror
  -1 = 'Unknown error: -1'
   5 = 'Input/output error'
4183 = 'Unknown error: 4183'
$
```

This shows how well behaved the `strerror(3)` function is, despite the bad `errno` values that were provided to it. The error code **5** (`EIO`) correctly translated to the message `Input/output error`. The values **-1** and **4183** both provided a meaningful clue to a programming problem with a message of the form `Unknown error: 4183`. Had this program used the `sys_errlist[]` array instead, a program abort may have occurred.

Applying `strerror(3)` Correctly

One important thing to note about using the `strerror(3)` function is that the pointer returned by this function is only valid until the next call to the same function is made. The following code is incorrect:

```
char *eptr1 = strerror(EIO);
char *eptr2 = strerror(ENOENT); /*** value of eptr1 is now invalid ***/

printf("Msg1='%s', msg2='%s'\n",eptr1,eptr2);          /*** INCORRECT ***/
```

This code is not acceptable because by the time strerror(3) is called the second time and its return value is assigned to eptr2, the pointer value eptr1 is rubbish. Even if your experimentation proves this practice to be apparently safe, code should not be written to rely on this behavior. There is a possibility that someday (if not already), strerror(3) may return dynamic content and cause this to fail.

> **Application Warning**
>
> The value returned by strerror(3) is valid only until the next call to strerror(3).

Testing for Errors Using stdio(3)

One area that is often overlooked in various texts that describe the stdio(3) set of routines is the proper treatment of errors. You have already seen how to discriminate between an error return and a success return with the fopen(3) call. Immediately after a fopen(3) failure, the value of errno contains the reason for the open failure. However, the situation may not be so clear in other circumstances, which will be examined next.

Pitfalls of the ferror(3) Function

By way of review, examine the function synopsis for the ferror(3) function:

```
#include <stdio.h>

int ferror(FILE *stream);              /* Test stream for an error */
void clearerr(FILE *stream);           /* Clear an error indication */
```

The ferror(3) function returns a non-zero value (a logical True) when an error has occurred at some point on the FILE stream identified by the argument stream. This indicator remains True until the function clearerr(3) is called for the same stream. This in itself is not a problem.

What can be a problem is when ferror(3) is called to test for an error on a stream after several other stdio(3) calls have been made. If the value of errno is consulted at this later point, it may report incorrect results.

Only the indication of the occurrence of the error is saved within the stream object FILE by the stdio(3) set of routines. The errno value itself is valid only immediately after the stdio(3) call that failed (up to the point of the next errno modifying function call). Consequently, while ferror(3) can be useful in telling you that something went wrong on a FILE stream at some point in time, it will not provide you with the details of the error. This is because the value of errno may have been lost by other intervening calls.

Avoiding the `fclose(3)` Pitfall

When using `stdio(3)` function calls, you must check for errors immediately after the call that caused the error, when you want to consult `errno`. Errors can occur in surprising places when buffering is being used (see `setbuf(3)` for how to control this feature).

Data previously written by a call to `fwrite(3)` may have returned a successful indication earlier in the program. Later a failure can be reported by the `fclose(3)` function. To see why, look at the following example:

```
fwrite(buf,strlen(buf),1,fptr);    /* Write out a C string in buf[] */
if ( ferror(fptr) ) {              /* Write error occur? */
    /* Process write error */      /* Yes, process error.. */
}
if ( fclose(fptr) == EOF ) {       /* Did the close succeed? */
    /* errno = ENOSPC */           /* A failure during close occurred */
}
```

Some programmers are surprised to realize that `fclose(3)` can fail in the example provided. This can happen because the data written by `fwrite(3)` is still contained in a buffer provided by the stream `fptr`. When `fclose(3)` is finally called, it is first necessary to force the unwritten data in the buffer out to disk before closing the underlying file descriptor. If the disk is full, the `fclose(3)` call will fail and `errno` will report the error as code `ENOSPC`.

Note that in this scenario, `ferror(3)` cannot be used to test for an error because the `FILE` stream is destroyed by the `fclose(3)` call. Here it is essential to test the return value from `fclose(3)` and then report the reason contained within `errno` immediately upon detecting the failure.

Error Code Note

`ENOSPC` means No Space Left On Device. This error code is returned when there is insufficient disk space to enlarge a file. It frequently happens when `write(2)` is called and the size of the file would have increased as a result of the call, but no free space remained.

Delaying the Reporting of an Error

There are times when error reporting must wait until other steps are taken in the program to recover. Sometimes those steps can cause the value of `errno` to be lost. The following example illustrates this:

```
int z;                             /* status code */
int fd;                            /* open file descriptor */

z = write(fd,buf,n);               /* Write some data */
if ( z == -1 ) {                   /* Did this write fail? */
    unlink(pathname);              /* Yes, delete half baked file */
    fprintf(stderr,"%s: write error on %s\n",
        strerror(errno),
        pathname);
```

In this example, the program insists on calling unlink(2) first to remove the file that the write has failed to write to. It then reports the error, after the file has been deleted.

The problem is that by the time the error is reported by fprintf(3), the errno value for the failed write(2) call could be lost. The errno value may instead contain an error from the unlink(2) call (if it fails) that is more recent.

At the risk of stating the obvious, the value of errno can be saved in another variable and then reported later. Here is the modified example:

```
int z;                              /* status code */
int fd;                             /* open file descriptor */
int e;                              /* Saved errno value */

z = write(fd,buf,n);                /* Write some data */
if ( z == -1 ) {                    /* Did this write fail? */
    e = errno;                      /* Preserve the value of errno */
    unlink(pathname);               /* Delete this half baked file */
    fprintf(stderr,"%s: write error on %s\n",
        strerror(e),                /* Report e here (not errno) */
        pathname);
```

While it is true that you could simply move the fprintf(3) call to execute prior to the unlink(2) call, this is not always possible. If you must clean up something prior to opening a pop-up error message window, this might not be practical.

Summary

In this chapter, the general philosophy behind the UNIX C library method of reporting success and failure has been covered. You have studied the global variable errno and learned how to declare it and use it. Also very importantly, you learned when the value of errno is valid.

You have seen the different ways that error codes can be converted into a user-friendly message. Some of the pitfalls of error reporting were also examined, such as that of detecting an error too late with the function ferror(3).

While this chapter has been a review for seasoned programmers, this material is vitally important to those that are just starting out programming for UNIX. With this foundation, you are better equipped to tackle the upcoming chapters successfully.

CHAPTER 9

UNIX COMMAND-LINE PROCESSING

A nyone who has been using UNIX at the shell prompt for a time has unwittingly become acquainted with how UNIX commands work. Some of the most frequently used commands—`ls(1)`, `mv(1)`, `cp(1)`, `rm(1)`, and `ln(1)`, for example—use the same general command-line conventions.

This level of consistency is a result of a convention being adopted by UNIX developers and a library mechanism to make it easy to adhere to. In this chapter, you will look at

- UNIX command-line conventions
- Parsing command lines with `getopt(3)`
- Parsing suboptions with `getsubopt(3)`
- Parsing command lines with the GNU's `getopt_long(3)`

Command-Line Conventions

The general conventions used for most UNIX commands are as follows:

```
$ command_name [-options] [arg1 [arg2 [argn]]]
```

The square brackets indicate optional item zones on the command line. Options immediately follow the command name and begin with a hyphen. Each option consists of a single character—usually a letter but possibly a number or another character. When used, arguments follow the options. The number of valid arguments is determined by the command being invoked. An example of a typical UNIX command is as follows:

```
$ rm -f core
```

The option shown is specified by the hyphen and the letter `f`. The option `-f` is then followed by one argument, the filename `core` in this case.

Using Multiple Options

There can be several options used on a command line. An example using multiple options is

```
$ ls -l -u b*
```

The example uses the options `-l` and `-u`. In this case, the command argument is a wildcard filename.

Combining Multiple Options

Options can be grouped together behind a hyphen. The previous command is functionally equivalent to the following:

```
$ ls -lu b*
```

This `ls(1)` command demonstrates that option characters can be grouped following the initial hyphen character.

Using Options with Arguments

Some options accept arguments other than the command-line arguments already shown. Examine the following `tar(1)` command:

```
$ tar -cvf project.tar project
```

In this FreeBSD example, the options are grouped together as `-cvf`. However, the `tar(1)` `-f` option must be followed by a filename, which is given as `project.tar`. At the end of the command line is a command-line argument `project`, which is the directory name to be archived. The command could also have been written this way:

```
$ tar -cv -fproject.tar project
```

In this example, the argument immediately follows the option name. Options that take an argument can have the argument value immediately follow the option letter or specified next on the command line as in a regular argument.

Identifying Options or Arguments

You might wonder how to know if what follows the option letter is an option argument or more options. This can't be determined by the appearance of the command line. This behavior is defined by the option itself, which is declared within the program.

Arguments That Look Like Options

You may have encountered a situation in which you wanted to specify an argument that started with a hyphen, and your command complained about the improper options that were being used. For example, if `grep(1)` were used to search a source program for the string `--help`, you might experience the following under FreeBSD:

```
$ grep --help tempnam.c
grep: illegal option -- -
usage: grep [-[AB] <num>] [-CEFGLVXHPRSZabchilnqsvwxy]
       [-e <expr>] [-f file] [files ...]
$
```

The problem with this `grep(1)` command is that the command was confused about how to treat the text `--help`. The following technique shows how to avoid this little problem:

```
$ grep -- --help tempnam.c
$
```

The example shows that grep(1) understood the -- (double hyphen) on the command line to indicate that there were no further options. This permitted grep(1) to understand that --help was the text being searched for in the file tempnam.c.

The getopt(3) Function

What helps to make UNIX commands consistent in their syntax is that most commands use the library function getopt(3). Its synopsis is as follows:

```
#include <unistd.h>

extern char *optarg;
extern int optind;    /* initialized to 1 */
extern int optopt;
extern int opterr;    /* initialized to 1 */
extern int optreset;  /* extension to IEEE Std1003.2 "POSIX.2" */

int getopt(int argc, char * const *argv, const char *optstring);

extern void getoptreset(void);               /* SGI IRIX 6.5 only */
```

The getopt(3) function returns the option letter that is parsed. Alternatively, -1 is returned when the end of the options has been reached. The value ? is returned when an unrecognized option character has been encountered. If the argument optstring begins with a : character, then : is returned when an option expecting an argument does not have one given.

The getopt(3) External Values

Before you can use getopt(3), you need to be aware of how the external values are used by it. The two most important of these variables are the optarg and optind variables.

The optarg External Variable

The optarg external pointer variable is set to point at the argument supplied for the option being processed. However, this is only done for those options that take arguments (this will be expanded upon later). If getopt(3) were processing the option -fproject.tar or -f project.tar, then the variable optarg would point to the C string containing project.tar when getopt(3) is returned.

The optind External Variable

The external variable optind is initially set to the value 1. It is used by getopt(3) to point to the next argv[] value to be processed. This initial value causes getopt(3) to start processing options in argv[1]. When the end of the options is reached on the command line, the value of optind indicates where on the command line the first argument is located. For example, if the following command were to be processed by getopt(3)

```
$ rm -f core
```

then the optind value after all options are processed would be 2. This indicates that argv[2] has the first command-line argument following the options that were just processed.

The opterr External Variable

The external value opterr is initialized to the value of 1 (indicating true) and is used as input to the getopt(3) function. When it is true and an unrecognized option character is encountered, getopt(3) prints an error message to stderr indicating the unrecognized option. This behavior is suppressed when opterr is set to 0 (false). This is usually necessary when your program will be doing the error reporting itself or when the error message must go somewhere other than stderr.

The optreset External Variable

The FreeBSD platform exposes the external variable optreset. This is an extension to the IEEE Std1003.2 POSIX.2 standard and is not supported by other UNIX platforms. Setting this variable to 1 allows a new scan of options to be processed. This is normally accompanied by resetting the variable optind to 1.

To cause getopt(3) to rescan the command line a second time, the following procedure is used under FreeBSD:

```
optreset = 1;          /* Restart scan in getopt(3) */
optind = 1;            /* Restart scan with argv[1] */
```

This pair of assignments readies getopt(3) to start over. SGI's IRIX 6.5, for example, provides a getoptreset(3) function instead:

```
optind = 1;            /* Restart scan with argv[1] */
getoptreset();         /* Reset getopt(3) to start over */
```

Although the IRIX 6.5 documentation states that getoptreset(3) "can be used to reset all the internal state of getopt so that it may be used again on a different set of arguments," it might be wise to set optind=1 prior to making the call.

> **Documentation Note**
>
> The UNIX systems UnixWare 7, HPUX-11, Solaris 8, and AIX 4.3 do not document a formal way to reset the scanning of a command line.

The getopt(3) Function Call

The getopt(3) function returns an integer value that fits into one of the following categories:

- The option character just parsed.

- The character ?, indicating that an unrecognized option character was encountered.

- The character :, indicating that an option is missing its argument (this is supported only when the argument optstring begins with a colon character).

- The value -1, indicating that no more options exist (see the Note about EOF).

EOF Macro Application Note

Prior to the IEEE Std1003.2-1992 (POSIX.2) standard, the macro EOF was documented as the return value from getopt(3) when no more options remain to be processed. Now the standard documents that the value -1 is returned, and the use of the macro EOF in this context is discouraged.

The first argument `argc` for `getopt(3)` states how many argument values we have in the second array `argv[]`. This second argument is an array of C string pointers that point to each command-line argument. The values `argc` and `argv[]` are normally taken directly from the `main()` function interface.

The last argument to `getopt(3)` is the C string that drives the processing. It tells `getopt(3)` which options are supported and which options take arguments. This single string determines the whole personality of the command line.

Defining the `optstring` Argument

To support a few options such as the `tar(1)` example earlier, the `optstring` argument would be defined as follows:

```
int main(int argc,char **argv) {
    static char optstring[] = "cvf:";
```

Note how a colon (`:`) character follows the `f` character in the string `optstring`. The colon indicates that the option `-f` requires an argument. Option order is not significant in the `optstring`. The following would be equally acceptable:

```
int main(int argc,char **argv) {
    static char optstring[] = "vf:c";
```

Whenever `getopt(3)` processes an option, it searches the `optstring` argument. If the option character is not present in `optstring`, then it is not a supported option character, and it is treated as an error (a `?` is returned). When the option character is found within `optstring`, the `getopt(3)` function checks the next immediate character in the `optstring`. If it finds a colon, then it knows that it must extract an argument to go with this option.

`optstring` can be begun with a colon character, as shown:

```
int main(int argc,char **argv) {
    static char optstring[] = ":cvf:";
```

When the `optstring` is specified with a leading colon, `getopt(3)` will return a `:` character when a valid option was parsed but no argument was found following it. This allows your program to assume some other default for the option argument.

Defining an Option-Processing Loop

Listing 9.1 shows a typical option-processing loop using `getopt(3)`. The options supported in this program are the `-c`, `-v`, and `-f` options that were demonstrated by the earlier example using `tar(1)`.

LISTING 9.1 getopt.c—A Typical Option-Processing Loop Using getopt(3)

```
1:  /* getopt.c */
2:
3:  #include <stdio.h>
4:  #include <unistd.h>
5:
6:  int
7:  main(int argc,char **argv) {
8:      int rc;
9:      int optch;
10:     static char optstring[] = "cvf:";
11:
12:     while ( (optch = getopt(argc,argv,optstring)) != -1 )
13:         switch ( optch ) {
14:         case 'c' :
15:             puts("-c processed.");
16:             break;
17:         case 'v' :
18:             puts("-v processed.");
19:             break;
20:         case 'f' :
21:             printf("-f '%s' processed.\n",optarg);
22:             break;
23:         default :    /* '?' */
24:             rc = 1; /* Usage error has occurred */
25:         }
26:
27:     for ( ; optind < argc; ++optind )
28:         printf("argv[%d] = '%s'\n",optind,argv[optind]);
29:
30:     return rc;
31: }
```

When the program is compiled and run, the output should appear as follows:

```
$ make getopt
cc -c -D_POSIX_C_SOURCE=199309L -D_POSIX_SOURCE -Wall getopt.c
cc getopt.o -o getopt
$ ./getopt -cvf project.tar project_dir
-c processed.
-v processed.
-f 'project.tar' processed.
argv[3] = 'project_dir'
$
```

The session output shows how the various `case` statements in the program were exercised by the options -c, -v, and -f. Notice the use of the external variable `optarg` for the -f option case (lines 20–22). After all the options were processed, the `for` loop in lines 27–28 reported the remaining command-line arguments. This was shown to be the single argument `project_dir`.

The `getsubopt(3)` Function

Many UNIX platforms support suboptions. Suboptions are useful when your application has many possible parameter values and suboptions, which are best specified by name. SGI's IRIX 6.5 documents an example of suboptions using its `mount(1)` command:

```
# mount -o rw,hard,bg,wsize=1024 speed:/usr /usr
```

In this example, the `-o` represents the option, which is then followed by an argument consisting of suboptions. The argument `rw,hard,bg,wsize=1024` has several suboptions, which are separated by commas. As the example illustrates, some suboptions take arguments and others do not.

To make it easier for the application writer to parse suboptions, the function `getsubopt(3)` is provided. Its synopsis is as follows:

```
#include <stdlib.h>

extern char *suboptarg

int getsubopt(char **subopts_str, char *const *tokens, char **valuep);
```

The first argument `subopts_str` is a pointer to the string that is to be parsed. This pointer is updated with each call to the function.

The argument `tokens` is an array of token string pointers that represent valid suboption values. The last element of the array should be a null pointer, to mark the end of the array. Using the SGI `mount(1)` example shown earlier, the array could be declared and initialized as follows:

```
static char *tokens[] = {
    "rw",     /* [0] */
    "hard",   /* [1] */
    "bg",     /* [2] */
    "wsize",  /* [3] */
    NULL
};
```

The last argument, `valuep`, is a pointer to a character pointer. After the `getsubopt(3)` call returns the pointer to which it points, it will be null if there was no value for the parameter, or it will point to the value string. The following shows how the third argument is used:

```
char *valuep = NULL;

x = getsubopt(&optarg,&tokens[0],&valuep);

printf("The value = '%s'\n",valuep != NULL ? valuep : "<NULL>");
```

The return value from `getsubopt(3)` is the index into the `tokens[]` array if the value is a recognized suboption. The returned pointer for the `valuep` argument will contain a pointer to the value part of the **subopt=value** in the suboption or null if no value was provided. The index value `-1` is returned when the suboption is not recognized as an option in the `tokens[]` array.

Determining the End of Suboption Processing

The suboption parsing ends when the pointer being passed into the first argument of `getsubopt(3)` points to a null byte. An example will illustrate this best.

Assume that you must parse the option argument string found in the `getopt(3)` external variable `optarg`. Assume further that the `tokens[]` array was declared as shown earlier. The general loop used for `getsubopt(3)` then is as follows:

```
extern char *optarg;    /* getopt(3) */

char *valuep;
int x;

while ( *optarg != 0 )
    switch ( (x = getsubopt(&optarg,tokens,&valuep)) ) {
    case 3 :  /* wsize=arg */
        printf(" %s = '%s'\n",tokens[x],valuep ? valuep : "<NULL>");
```

When the suboption `wsize=1024` is parsed, the value for `x` that is returned by `getsubopt(3)` will be `3` (due to the `tokens[]` array). The pointer `optarg` is updated by `getsubopt(3)` to point to the next suboption. When no suboptions remain, the pointer `optarg` in this example will point to a null byte in the string.

Platform Support Note

Platforms that support `getsubopt(3)` include FreeBSD, Solaris 8, AIX 4.3, HPUX-11, and SGI IRIX 6.5. Linux (Red Hat 6.0) shows no support for this option.

A Full `getsubopt(3)` Example

The program shown in Listing 9.2 processes command-line arguments using both `getopt(3)` and `getsubopt(3)` in order to demonstrate how they work together. It implements a few options that might be used in a hypothetical tape transport control command `xmt`, similar to the `mt(1)` that is available on most UNIX platforms. The synopsis for this hypothetical command is as follows:

```
xmt [-f /dev/tape_device] [-c suboptions]
```

where `-f /dev/tape_device` specifies the tape device to use and `-c suboptions` specifies various tape commands:

   `rewind`   Rewind the tape drive

   `weof=n`   Write file mark(s)

   `fsf=n`   Forward space file(s)

   `bsf=n`   Backspace file(s)

The program presented in Listing 9.2 simply parses these options and suboptions and then lists the remaining command-line arguments.

LISTING 9.2   `xmt.c`—An Example Using `getsubopt(3)` and `getopt(3)`

```
1:    /* xmt.c */
2:
3:    #include <stdio.h>
4:    #include <stdlib.h>
5:    #include <unistd.h>
6:
7:    extern char *suboptarg;
8:    int getsubopt(char **optionp, char * const *tokens, char **valuep);
9:
10:   int
11:   main(int argc,char **argv) {
12:       int rc = 0;            /* Return code */
13:       int x;                 /* Arg index */
14:       int n;                 /* Int value */
15:       char *valuep;          /* Ptr to subopt value */
16:       int optch;             /* Option character */
17:       static char optstring[] = "f:c:";
18:
19:       /* Suboptions Table of Tokens : */
20:       static char *tokens[] = {
21:   #define _SO_WEOF     0
22:           "weof",            /* Write n EOF marks */

23:   #define _SO_FSF      1
24:           "fsf",             /* Forward space file */
25:   #define _SO_BSF      2
26:           "bsf",             /* Back space file */
27:   #define _SO_REWIND   3
28:           "rewind",          /* Rewind tape */
29:           NULL
30:       };
31:
32:       /*
33:        * Process all command line options :
34:        */
35:       while ( (optch = getopt(argc,argv,optstring)) != -1 )
36:           switch ( optch ) {
37:
38:           case 'f' :      /* -f device */
39:               printf("-f '%s' (tape device).\n",optarg);
40:               break;
41:
42:           case 'c' :      /* -c commands */
43:                   /*
```

continued from previous page

```
44:                      * Process all suboptions for -c :
45:                      */
46:                    while ( *optarg != 0 )
47:                        switch ( (x = getsubopt(&optarg,tokens,&valuep)) ) {
48:
49:                        case _SO_WEOF :
50:                            n = !valuep ? 1 : atoi(valuep);
51:                            printf("Write %d EOF marks (%s=%s)\n",
52:                                n,suboptarg,valuep);
53:                            break;
54:
55:                        case _SO_FSF :
56:                            n = !valuep ? 1 : atoi(valuep);
57:                            printf("Forward space %d file(s) (%s=%s)\n",
58:                                n,suboptarg,valuep);
59:                            break;
60:
61:                        case _SO_BSF :
62:                            n = !valuep ? 1 : atoi(valuep);
63:                            printf("Backspace %d file(s) (%s=%s)\n",
64:                                n,suboptarg,valuep);
65:                            break;
66:
67:                        case _SO_REWIND :
68:                            if ( valuep ) {
69:                                printf("Suboption %s does not take a arg\n",
70:                                    suboptarg);
71:                                rc = 1;      /* Flag usage error */
72:                            } else
73:                                printf("Rewind tape (%s)\n",suboptarg);
74:                            break;
75:
76:                        case -1 :
77:                            printf("Illegal suboption %s%s%s\n",
78:                                suboptarg,
79:                                valuep ? "=" : "",
80:                                valuep ? valuep : "");
81:                            break;
82:
83:                        default :
84:                            abort();     /* Should never get here */
85:                        }
86:                    break;
87:
88:            default :   /* '?' */
89:                rc = 1; /* Usage error has occurred */
90:            }
91:
92:        /*
93:         * Report all arguments :
94:         */
95:        for ( ; optind < argc; ++optind )
```

```
96:            printf("argv[%d] = '%s'\n",optind,argv[optind]);
97:
98:      return rc;
99:  }
```

Compiling and running this xmt command produces the following session output:

```
$ make xmt
cc -c -D_POSIX_C_SOURCE=199309L -D_POSIX_SOURCE -Wall -g xmt.c
cc xmt.o -o xmt
$ ./xmt -f /dev/tape -crewind,fsf=3,weof=2
-f '/dev/tape' (tape device).
Rewind tape (rewind)
Forward space 3 file(s) (fsf=3)
Write 2 EOF marks (weof=2)
$
```

From the example, you can see that the `rewind` suboption was processed first, followed by `fsf=3` and then `weof=2` to write two end-of-file marks on the tape.

GNU Long Options Extension

A number of GNU commands like the `gcc(1)` compiler for example have a large number of options to support. Besides the fact that you can exhaust all possible characters for those options, a user just cannot remember them all. The GNU solution to this problem is the convention of *long options*.

FreeBSD 3.4 Release includes `gcc(1)`, allowing the following demonstration of a long option:

```
$ gcc --version
2.7.2.3
$
```

Long options begin with two hyphens and must be followed by one or more characters. In order to process long options, the GNU function `getopt_long(3)` must be used.

The GNU `getopt_long(3)` Function

The `getopt_long(3)` function will process both the traditional short options and the newer GNU long options. The synopsis for `getopt_long(3)` is as follows:

```
#include <getopt.h>

int getopt_long(int argc, char * const argv[],
    const char *optstring,
    const struct option *longopts,
    int *longindex);
```

The function prototype is almost identical to `getopt(3)`, except for the two new arguments `longopts` and `longindex`. The argument `longindex` points to an integer, where an index value is returned.

Understanding the `option` Structure

The `longopts` structure pointer points to the array of `option` structure entries. The `option` structure is composed of four members:

- `name` points to a C string containing the name of the long option, without the leading hyphens.

- `has_arg` is defined as an integer but used as a Boolean value. It must be zero (false) if there is no argument or non-zero (true) if there is an argument for this option.

- `flag` either points to an integer or is null.

- `val` is used in different ways, depending upon how `flag` is initialized.

Setting Up the `option` Structure

The last array entry in the `option` structure array must be initialized with a null pointer for its `name` member, zero for the `has_arg` member, a null pointer for the `flag` member, and zero for the `val` member. This entry indicates to `getopt_long(3)` that there are no more entries in that array. Here is an example of two long options defined in the static `option` structure `long_opts[]`.

```
static struct option long_opts[] = {
    { "help", 0, 0, 'h' },     /* name, has_arg, flag, val */
    { "version", 0, 0, 'v' }, /* name, has_arg, flag, val */
    { 0, 0, 0, 0 }
};
```

Using a Null `option.flag` Pointer

The members `flag` and `val` of the `option` structure work together as a team. The easiest way to use these is through the following procedure:

1. Set `flag` to null.

2. Set the `int` member `val` to the value that you want `getopt_long(3)` to return. Often this is the ASCII character code for the equivalent short option letter.

Making a Long Option Look Short

A common practice is to set `val` to the short option letter equivalent of the long option. For example, if a command supports both `--help` and `-h`, then `option` member `flag` would be set to a null pointer, and `val` would be set to the ASCII value `'h'`. The structure would be initialized as follows:

```
static struct option long_opts[] = {
    { "help", 0, 0, 'h' }, /* name, has_arg, flag, val */
    { 0, 0, 0, 0 }
};
```

Processing when the `option.flag` Pointer Is Null

When processing the long option --`help`, the `getopt_long(3)` function performs the following basic steps:

1. The `getopt_long(3)` scans the `long_opts[]` array, using an index that we will call `x`. It will start with `x=0`.

2. A `strcmp(3)` is done to see if our option string `"help"` matches the entry in `long_opts[x].name` (`x` is currently the value zero). Note that the hyphens are already stripped off the option string.

3. The `strcmp(3)` function returns zero because the strings match.

4. Now `getopt_long(3)` knows the correct index value *x*. This is returned to the caller by using the integer pointer provided in the fifth argument (`longindex`).

5. The pointer in `long_opts[x].flag` is tested for a `null` pointer. If it is `null`, then processing proceeds to the next step.

6. The value of `long_opts[x].val` is used as the return value for `getopt_long(3)`.

A C code fragment illustrates the last three steps:

```
*longindex = x;              /* 4. Return array index */
if ( !long_opts[x].flag )    /* 5. if flag is null then */
    return long_opts[x].val; /* 6. return 'h' */
```

Your options loop within your program is now tricked into thinking the -`h` option was processed instead, because the value `'h'` was returned. This is the easiest way to use long options.

Using a Non-Null `option.flag` Pointer

When the structure `option` member `flag` is a non-null pointer, something different happens. First, examine Listing 9.3.

LISTING 9.3   A Non-Null `option.flag` Member

```
1:    static int cmdopt_v = 0;       /* Initialized to false */
2:    static struct option long_opts[] = {
3:        { "help", 0, 0, 'h' },     /* name, has_arg, flag, val */
4:        { "version", 0, &cmdopt_v, 1 },
5:        { 0, 0, 0, 0 }
6:    };
```

Listing 9.3 shows how the variables and the `long_opts[]` array are declared. The following points explain the reasoning behind this code:

1. Line 1 declares our -`v` option `flag` variable `cmdopt_v`. It is initialized to false (zero).

2. Array element `long_opts[1]` is initialized to accept the long option --`version` (line 4).

3. Member `long_opts[1].flag` (line 4) is initialized with a pointer to our variable `cmdopt_v` (in line 1).

4. Member `long_opts[1].val` (line 4) is initialized with the `int` value of 1.

5. Array element `long_opts[2]` has all members initialized to null or zero. This marks the end of the long options array.

With the declarations arranged as they are in Listing 9.3, the actions of `getopt_long(3)` when it processes the `--version` option can be explained.

1. Internally to `getopt_long(3)` an array index is initialized to zero. We will call this variable `x`.

2. A `strcmp(3)` is done to see if the option string version matches the entry in `long_opts[x].name` (x is currently the value zero).

3. The `strcmp(3)` function returns non-zero, because the strings do not match (`long_opts[0].name` points to C string `"help"`).

4. The `getopt_long(3)` function increments x to the value 1.

5. A `strcmp(3)` is done to see if our option string version matches the entry in `long_opts[x].name` (x=1).

6. The `strcmp(3)` function returns zero, because the option string version matches `long_opts[x].name`, which also points to a string `"version"`.

7. Now `getopt_long(3)` knows the correct index value x. This is returned to the caller by using the integer pointer provided in argument five (`longindex`) (x=1).

8. The pointer value `long_opts[1].flag` is tested to see if it is null. It is not null, so the processing moves on to the next step.

9. The integer value from `long_opts[1].val` is fetched and then stored at the location pointed to by `long_opts[1].flag`.

10. The `getopt_long(3)` function returns the value zero to indicate that this special long option has been processed.

Steps 9 and 10 are carried out when the `flag` member is not null. Step 6 in the list from the "Processing when `option.flag` Pointer Is Null" section is used when the `flag` member is null. Note again how `getopt_long(3)` returns zero in step 10.

The following code fragment summarizes steps 7 through 10 of the procedure:

```
*longindex = x;              /* 7. Return array index */
if ( !long_opts[x].flag )    /* 8. if flag is null */
    return long_opts[x].val; /*    return val */
/* Return val via flag ptr */
*(long_opts[x].flag) = long_opts[x].val; /* 9. Use ptr */
return 0;                    /* 10. Indicate flag use */
}
```

FreeBSD Linux Extensions Note

FreeBSD does not document or include development libraries for `getopt_long(3)` when Linux extensions are not installed.

Summary

This chapter has covered the operation of the `getopt(3)` and `getsubopt(3)` functions. Additionally, the `getopt_long(3)` function was included to cover the GNU/Linux method of parsing command lines. All of these functions help keep your applications smaller, simpler, and more reliable.

The next chapter covers the very important topic of performing numeric conversions.

CHAPTER 10

CONVERSION FUNCTIONS

The need for data conversions is always present within an application program. Arithmetic is performed using `int`, `float`, and `double` types because it is efficient and convenient. The same data must then be converted into ASCII strings in order for it to be displayed on a terminal. Data input also must undergo conversions.

In this chapter, you will examine

- The `atoi(3)`, `atol(3)`, and `atof(3)` family
- The `sscanf(3)` function
- The `strtol(3)` and `strtoul(3)` functions
- The `strtod(3)` function

All of these functions concern themselves with conversion from ASCII to a numeric C data type.

Simple Conversion Functions

These are the simplest functions for a C programmer to use, because they require no preparation or subsequent tests for conversion errors. With the exception of `atof(3)` on some UNIX platforms, the entire issue of conversion errors is ignored. For this reason, they are frequently not the best choice of conversion functions available.

Before the alternatives are explored, let's examine these traditional functions more closely.

Scrutinizing the Functions `atoi(3)` and `atol(3)`

The functions `atoi(3)` and `atol(3)` have the following synopsis:

```
#include <stdlib.h>

int atoi(const char *nptr);
long atol(const char *nptr);
```

These functions simply take the starting address of a C string and return the result as an `int` or a `long` data type value. Any leading whitespace characters, as defined by the C library function `isspace(3)`, are skipped before the conversion is begun. If the conversion fails, the functions `atoi(3)` and `atol(3)` simply give up and return zero.

Using the `atoi(3)` Function

The following is a simple example of using the `atoi(3)` function:

```
char buf[32];
int i;

strcpy(buf,"23");
i = atoi(buf);
```

In this example, the string `"23"` is converted to an integer value `23` and assigned to the variable i. However, had the input string contained bad input, the value of i would not contain a meaningful result (zero).

Understanding the Conversion Error Problem

As an example, consider the problem where the function `atoi(3)` is used. Assume that there is a debug command-line option of the form `-x n`, where n is the debug level between 0 and 9. Within the `getopt(3)` processing loop, the `optarg` value for `-x` must be converted to an integer value.

```
switch( optch ) {
case 'x' :
    cmdopt_x = atoi(optarg); /* Get debug level */
    break;
```

Assume that the user supplied the option as `-x high` on the command line because he didn't know any better. The `atoi(3)` function will glibly return the value `0` in this case because it cannot convert high to an integer numeric value. The program will be unaware that there should be a debug level set because the conversion value was `0` (due to the conversion error). Consequently, the program will run without any debug level at all. This results in a program action that is not user friendly.

Converting Garbled Data

A similar problem develops when the user supplies the debug option as `-x 5oops` because he is all thumbs on the keyboard. The program will glibly accept the value `5` that `atoi(3)` was able to convert successfully. The remaining part of the string `oops` is ignored.

The functions `atoi(3)`, `atol(3)`, and `atof(3)` all lack error return information. A better indication of when the conversion succeeded or failed is required.

Knowing Where the Conversion Ended

An additional limitation of the `atoi(3)` family of functions is that the caller is not given information about where the conversion ends in the input string. If it is necessary to write a function to extract the month, day, and year from a date string, you would have a challenge using the `atoi(3)` function. Consider the following variations in date strings that might be provided as input from a terminal:

- `01/01/2000`
- `1/2/2000`
- `12/1/2000`
- `1/ 9/2000`
- `1  / 31    /  2000`
- `6-31-2001`

The `atoi(3)` function can help only with the month extraction (assuming month/day/year format). After extracting the month, you are left with these questions: How many blanks were skipped over? How many digits were there? Were any trailing blanks present? Because no scan information is returned by `atoi(3)`, your code doesn't know where to start the extraction for the following day or year field.

The `atof(3)` Function

The `atof(3)` function is very similar to the `atoi(3)` function, except that it converts string values into floating point values. The synopsis for `atof(3)` is as follows:

```
#include <stdlib.h>

double atof(const char *nptr);
```

Its use is equally simple. The following is an example:

```
char buf[32];
double f;

strcpy(buf,"  -467.01E+02");
f = atof(buf);
```

The example shows some leading whitespace, a sign character, a decimal number, and a signed exponent. The `atof(3)` function skips over the leading whitespace and converts the remaining characters into a `double` C type value, which is assigned to variable `f`.

Again, the simplicity of this call woos many a C programmer into using this form of conversion. However, the problems that exist for `atoi(3)` and `atol(3)` also apply to the `atof(3)` function.

Most UNIX platforms implement the `atof(3)` function as a call to the function `strtod(3)`:

```
strtod(nptr, (char **)NULL);
```

The function `strtod(3)` does return the special values `+HUGE_VAL`, `-HUGE_VAL`, and `0` (zero), in conjunction with the external variable `errno` (see the section "Testing for Math Errors," later in this chapter). Since the implementation of `atof(3)` might not always be in terms of the `strtod(3)` function, you should use `strtod(3)` to test for errors.

Using `sscanf(3)` for Conversion and Validation

The function **sscanf(3)** is like a Swiss Army Knife for C input and conversion. While this mechanism is not a perfect solution for all conversions, it still enjoys simplicity of use and provides some measure of error detection.

Applying `sscanf(3)` to Numeric Conversion

Listing 10.1 shows a simple program that extracts the month, day, and year from a string. The input data has been deliberately made as messy as possible (lines 15–18) with lots of white-space.

LISTING 10.1   `sscanf.c`—Extracting Date Fields Using `sscanf(3)`

```
 1:   /* sscanf.c */
 2:
 3:   #include <stdio.h>
 4:   #include <stdlib.h>
 5:   #include <string.h>
 6:
 7:   int
 8:   main(int argc,char *argv[]) {
 9:       int x;
10:       char *datestr;        /* Date string to parse */
11:       int nf;               /* Number of fields converted */
12:       int n;                /* # of characters scanned */
13:       int mm, dd, yyyy;     /* Month, day and year */
14:
15:       static char *sdate[] = {
16:           "   1 /  2  /  2000  ",
17:           " 03 - 9-2001,etc."
18:       };
19:
20:       for ( x=0; x<2; ++x ) {
21:           datestr = sdate[x];      /* Parse this date */
22:           printf("Extracting from '%s'\n",datestr);
23:
24:           nf = sscanf(datestr,"%d %*[/-]%d %*[/-]%d%n",&mm,&dd,&yyyy,&n);
25:
26:           printf("%02d/%02d/%04d nf=%d, n=%d\n",mm,dd,yyyy,nf,n);
27:
28:           if ( nf >= 3 )
29:               printf("Remainder = '%s'\n",&datestr[n]);
30:       }
31:
32:       return 0;
33:   }
```

The variables used in this program are as follows:

- Variable **nf** receives the number of the conversions that **sscanf(3)** successfully accomplishes (line 11).

- Variable **n** receives the number of characters scanned so far (line 12).

- Variables **mm**, **dd**, and **yyyy** are the month, day, and year extracted values, respectively (line 13).

- The character pointer array **sdate[]** contains the two strings that are going to be used for extraction of the date components (lines 15–18).

Testing Numeric Conversions Using sscanf(3)

Compiling and running this program yields the following results under FreeBSD:

```
$ make sscanf
cc -c -D_POSIX_C_SOURCE=199309L -D_POSIX_SOURCE -Wall sscanf.c
cc sscanf.o -o sscanf
$ ./sscanf
Extracting from '  1 /  2 /  2000  '
01/02/2000 nf=3, n=18
Remainder = '  '
Extracting from ' 03 - 9-2001,etc.'
03/09/2001 nf=3, n=12
Remainder = ',etc.'
$
```

The first example shows how the date **01/02/2000** is successfully parsed. The second result **03/09/2001** is parsed out of the date string using hyphens instead. This is possible because the **sscanf(3)** **%[]** format feature was used to accept either a slash or a hyphen (line 24). The full format specifier used was **%*[/-]**. The asterisk indicates that the extracted value is not assigned to a variable (nor is it counted for the purposes of **%n**).

Notice that a space character precedes the **%*[/-]** format specification. This causes **sscanf(3)** to skip over preceding spaces prior to the slash or hyphen, if spaces are present.

The extracted results are reported in line 26, along with the values **nf** and **n**. Line 28 tests the value of **nf** before reporting the remainder string in line 29. This is necessary because the value of **n** is undefined if the **sscanf(3)** function did not work its way to the point of the **%n** specification (at the end of line 24).

The remainder strings show the points where the date extractions ended in both data examples. The last example shows the parse ending at the point **,etc.**.

Note that there are only three conversions present in the **sscanf(3)** call of line 24. This is because the **%n** specification does not count as a conversion.

Improving the sscanf(3) Conversion

One irritation that remains in our example in Listing 10.1 is that it does not skip over the trailing whitespace. This makes it difficult to test whether the entire input string was consumed when the date was extracted. Leftover data usually indicates that not all of it was valid.

This problem is remedied by altering the **sscanf(3)** statement on line 24 to read

```
nf = sscanf(datestr,"%d %*[/-]%d %*[/-]%d %n",&mm,&dd,&yyyy,&n);
```

If you look carefully at the format string, you will notice that one space was inserted before the %n specifier. This coaxes sscanf(3) into skipping over more whitespace before reporting how many characters were scanned. With the whitespace skipped, the test for leftovers is simple:

```
if ( datestr[n] != 0 ) {
    printf("EEK! Leftovers = '%s'\n",&datestr[n]);
```

If the expression datestr[n] points to a null byte after the conversion, then it is known that all the input string was valid for the conversion.

The Limitations of sscanf(3)

The sscanf(3) return count indicates whether or not the conversion(s) was successful. When the %n specifier is processed, the caller can also determine where the scanning ended. However, sscanf(3) still suffers from the limitation that it does not indicate to the caller where in the string the point of failure is when the conversion fails.

The strtol(3) and strtoul(3) Functions

The function sscanf(3) calls upon the functions strtol(3) and strtoul(3) to carry out its dirty work. You can go right to the source by calling them. The synopses for strtol(3) and strtoul(3) are as follows:

```
#include <stdlib.h>
#include <limits.h>

long strtol(const char *nptr, char **endptr, int base);

unsigned long strtoul(const char *nptr, char **endptr, int base);

Macros from <limits.h> :
    LONG_MAX
    LONG_MIN
    ULONG_MAX
    LONGLONG_MAX
    LONGLONG_MIN
    ULONGLONG_MAX
```

The function strtol(3) converts a possibly signed integer within a character string to a **long** integer data type value. The function strtoul(3) is functionally identical, except that no sign is permitted, and the returned conversion value is an **unsigned long** integer.

Within this section, only the strtol(3) function will be examined in detail, with the understanding that the same principles can be applied to the strtoul(3) function.

Using the strtol(3) Function

Listing 10.2 shows a short program that attempts to convert the first signed value in a character array named snum[]. Not only will it extract the integer value, but it will also indicate where the conversion ended.

LISTING 10.2   strtol.c—A Conversion Program Using strtol(3)

```
 1:   /* strtol.c */
 2:
 3:   #include <stdio.h>
 4:   #include <stdlib.h>
 5:
 6:   int
 7:   main(int argc,char *argv[]) {
 8:       long lval;
 9:       char *ep;
10:       static char snum[] = " -2567,45,39";
11:
12:       lval = strtol(snum,&ep,10);
13:
14:       printf("lval = %ld, ep = '%s'\n",lval,ep?ep:"<NULL>");
15:
16:       return 0;
17:   }
```

When the program is compiled and run, the following results are observed:

```
$ make strtol
cc -c -D_POSIX_C_SOURCE=199309L -D_POSIX_SOURCE -Wall strtol.c
cc strtol.o -o strtol
$ ./strtol
lval = -2567, ep = ',45,39'
$
```

From the output, you can see that the value lval was assigned the converted value. The character pointer ep pointed to the part of the string where the conversion stopped, namely ,45,39. Another parse could be continued after the comma is skipped, if the program were required to do this.

Testing for Errors

The strtol(3) and strtoul(3) functions return zero if the conversion fails completely. However, zero is a valid conversion value, and it should not be used as the only basis for concluding that an error took place.

If the returned pointer (variable ep in Listing 10.2) points to the starting point in the string, this indicates that a conversion error took place. This shows that no progress whatsoever was made in the conversion process. In Listing 10.2, you would test for the error in this manner:

```
if ( ep == snum ) {
    printf("Cannot convert value '%s'\n",snum);
```

This tests to see if the end pointer **ep** matches the starting point **snum**. If they are equal, then no progress was made in the conversion.

Testing the Conversion Pointer

It has already been demonstrated in Listing 10.2 that the return pointer **ep** shows where the conversion ended. This permits the caller to see if all of the input string was used to participate in the conversion. This can be tested as follows:

```
if ( *ep != 0 ) {
    printf("Conversion of '%s' failed near '%s'\n",snum,ep);
```

This not only tests that the conversion consumed all of the input, but it shows the point of failure if one occurs.

Performing Multiple Conversions

In Listing 10.2, three values separated by commas were used as input. A test for a successful field parse can be performed by testing for the delimiting comma:

```
if ( *ep != ',' )
    printf("Failed near '%s'\n",ep);
else {
    ++ep;    /* Skip comma */
    /* Parse next field */
```

In this example, it is known that the next character should be a comma. If it is not a comma, then an error has been encountered. Otherwise, the expected comma is skipped and the conversion proceeds with the next numeric value, using **strtol(3)**.

Using the base Argument for Radix Conversions

The **base** argument of the **strtol(3)** and **strtoul(3)** functions specifies the *radix value* of the number system. For the decimal number system, the radix value is 10.

The program shown in Listing 10.3 will allow you to run some tests with **strtol(3)** using different radix values.

LISTING 10.3 radix.c—Testing the **base** Argument of **strtol(3)**

```
1:   /* radix.c */
2:
3:   #include <stdio.h>
4:   #include <stdlib.h>
5:   #include <errno.h>
6:
7:   int
8:   main(int argc,char *argv[]) {
```

```
 9:        int i;              /* Iterator variable */
10:        char *ep;           /* End scan pointer */
11:        long base;          /* Conversion base */
12:        long lval;          /* Converted long value */
13:
14:        /*
15:         * Test for arguments :
16:         */
17:        if ( argc < 2 ) {
18:            printf("Usage: %s base 'string' [base 'string]...\n",argv[0]);
19:            return 1;
20:        }
21:
22:        /*
23:         * Process arguments :
24:         */
25:        for ( i=1; i<argc; ++i ) {
26:            /*
27:             * Get conversion base :
28:             */
29:            base = strtol(argv[i],&ep,10);
30:            if ( *ep != 0 ) {
31:                printf("Base error in '%s' near '%s'\n",argv[i],ep);
32:                return 1;
33:            } else if ( base > 36 || base < 0 ) {
34:                printf("Invalid base: %ld\n",base);
35:                return 1;
36:            }
37:            /*
38:             * Get conversion string :
39:             */
40:            if ( ++i >= argc ) {
41:                printf("Missing conversion string! Arg # %d\n",i);
42:                return 1;
43:            }
44:
45:            errno = 0;      /* Clear prior errors, if any */
46:
47:            lval = strtol(argv[i],&ep,(int)base);
48:
49:            printf("strtol('%s',&ep,%ld) => %ld; ep='%s', errno=%d\n",
50:                argv[i], base, lval, ep, errno);
51:        }
52:
53:        return 0;
54: }
```

This program is invoked with the radix (**base**) value as the first argument of a pair. The second argument of the pair is the input string that you want to convert. The following shows a compile-and-test run:

```
$ make radix
cc -c -D_POSIX_C_SOURCE=199309L -D_POSIX_SOURCE -Wall radix.c
cc radix.o -o radix
```

```
$ ./radix 10 '  +2345' 10 -456 10 '123  '
strtol('  +2345',&ep,10) => 2345; ep='', errno=0
strtol('-456',&ep,10) => -456; ep='', errno=0
strtol('123  ',&ep,10) => 123; ep='  ', errno=0
$
```

Three decimal conversions are attempted in the session shown. The first shows that the white-space was skipped successfully. The second shows that it was successful at converting a negative value. The third conversion shows how the variable ep points to the trailing whitespace.

Running Hexadecimal Tests

Setting the base to 16 will allow some hexadecimal conversions to be attempted:

```
$ ./radix 16 012 16 0x12 16 FFx
strtol('012',&ep,16) => 18; ep='', errno=0
strtol('0x12',&ep,16) => 18; ep='', errno=0
strtol('FFx',&ep,16) => 255; ep='x', errno=0
$
```

The first conversion converts the string 012 to 18 decimal, clearly a hexadecimal conversion. The second conversion demonstrates that the strtol(3) function will skip over the leading 0x characters when the base is 16. The third shows how FFx was properly converted, leaving a trailing unprocessed x.

Testing a Radix of Zero

When the radix is set to 0, the function strtol(3) will adapt to different number bases. Numbers are considered decimal unless they are prefixed by a leading zero (such as 017) or a leading zero and the letter x (such as 0xDEADBEEF or 0XDEADBEEF). The 0x notation introduces a hexadecimal number, for radix 16. If the leading zero is present without the letter x, then the conversion radix is set to 8, for octal.

The following demonstrates these types of conversions:

```
$ ./radix 0 '012' 0 '0x12' 0 '12'
strtol('012',&ep,0) => 10; ep='', errno=0
strtol('0x12',&ep,0) => 18; ep='', errno=0
strtol('12',&ep,0) => 12; ep='', errno=0
$
```

The session shown tests octal, hexadecimal, and decimal conversions, in that order.

Testing Binary Conversions

Even binary conversions are possible. The following session output shows some examples in which the radix is 2.

```
$ ./radix 2 '00001010' 2 '00010110'
strtol('00001010',&ep,2) => 10; ep='', errno=0
strtol('00010110',&ep,2) => 22; ep='', errno=0
$
```

Testing Radixes Above 16

Numbers can be represented in radixes above 16. These are not used very often, but they are available if you have the need:

```
$ ./radix 36 'BSD' 36 'FREEBSD' 36 'LINUX!' 36 'UNIX!' 36 'HPUX' 36 'SUN'
strtol('BSD',&ep,36) => 15277; ep='', errno=0
strtol('FREEBSD',&ep,36) => 2147483647; ep='', errno=34
strtol('LINUX!',&ep,36) => 36142665; ep='!', errno=0
strtol('UNIX!',&ep,36) => 1430169; ep='!', errno=0
strtol('HPUX',&ep,36) => 826665; ep='', errno=0
strtol('SUN',&ep,36) => 37391; ep='', errno=0
$
```

Above base 10, the conversion routines consider the letter A to be the digit 10, B to be the digit 11, and so on. Lowercase letters are treated the same as their uppercase counterparts. Radix 36 is the highest base supported and uses the letter Z defined as the value 35.

The radix 36 value of the string UNIX is 1430169. Others, including the value for the string FREEBSD, were reported. Could these be magic numbers in some contexts?

Testing for Overflows and Underflows

If an attempt is made to convert a very large value, the test program fails:

```
$ ./radix 10 '99999999999999999999'
strtol('99999999999999999999',&ep,10) => 2147483647; ep='', errno=34
$
```

Notice how the result 2147483647 was obtained instead of the correct decimal value of 99999999999999999999. Yet, the ep variable shows that the scan made it to the end of the string. The display of errno=34 provides a clue to the problem.

Interpreting LONG_MAX and ERANGE

Overflows are handled by a special return value LONG_MAX for strtol(3). When strtol(3) returns the value LONG_MAX, the value of errno must be tested as well. If it has the value ERANGE posted to it, then it can be concluded that an overflow has indeed occurred.

The overflow example tried in the previous section reported a return value of 2147483647. This is the value LONG_MAX (FreeBSD). Additionally, the value of errno=34 was reported. Under FreeBSD, this is the value ERANGE. Clearly, these two indications together conclude that an overflow has occurred.

The Overflow Test Procedure

Having strtol(3) return 2147483647 (LONG_MAX) whenever an overflow occurs would seem to preclude the function from ever being able to return this value normally. However, the overflow is further indicated by setting errno to ERANGE. This leads to the following procedure for testing for overflows and underflows:

1. Clear variable errno to zero. This is necessary because strtol(3) will not zero it.

2. Call strtol(3) to perform the conversion.

3. If the value returned is not LONG_MAX (and not LONG_MIN), then no overflow has occurred, and you are finished. Otherwise, proceed to step 4.

4. Test the value of errno. If it is still cleared to zero from step 1, then there was no overflow during the conversion, and the value returned truly represents the converted input value.

5. If the errno value is ERANGE, then an overflow during the conversion has occurred and the returned value LONG_MAX is not representative of the input value.

The same logic can be applied to testing for underflows when the value LONG_MIN is returned in step 3.

Proving the Overflow Test Procedure

You can prove this procedure with the test program from Listing 10.3:

```
$ ./radix 10 '99999999999999999999' 10 2147483647
strtol('99999999999999999999',&ep,10) => 2147483647; ep='', errno=34
strtol('2147483647',&ep,10) => 2147483647; ep='', errno=0
$
```

The first conversion fails and returns LONG_MAX (value 2147483647) and shows an errno value of 34, which is known to be the value ERANGE (under FreeBSD).

Notice that the second decimal conversion uses as input the maximum long value of 2147483647, and it converts successfully and returns LONG_MAX. This time, however, errno is not the value of ERANGE but remains as zero instead. This is due to line 45 in Listing 10.3, which reads

```
errno = 0;  /* Clear prior errors, if any */
```

Recall that the errno value is never cleared by a successful operation. It is only used to post errors. To allow differentiation between a successful conversion and an overflow, the value errno must be cleared before calling strtol(3). Otherwise, you will be testing a leftover error code if the conversion is successful.

Coding an Overflow/Underflow Test

If lval is assigned the strtol(3) return value, the overflow/underflow test should be written like this:

```
if ( lval == LONG_MAX || lval == LONG_MIN ) {
    /* Test for over / under flow */
    if ( errno == ERANGE ) {
        puts("Over/Under-flow occurred!");
```

This test only works if you clear errno to zero before calling the conversion function.

Testing for `strtoul(3)` Overflows

Function `strtoul(3)` does unsigned integer conversions. The maximum unsigned value is not the same as the maximum signed value. Consequently, the maximum value returned is `ULONG_MAX`. Otherwise, the general test procedure for overflow is quite similar to the one just covered.

1. Clear variable `errno` to zero.

2. Call `strtoul(3)` to perform the conversion.

3. If the value returned is not `ULONG_MAX`, then no overflow has occurred and you are finished. Otherwise, proceed to step 4.

4. Test the value of `errno`. If it is still cleared to zero from step 1, then there was no overflow during the conversion, and the value returned truly represents the input value.

5. If the `errno` value is `ERANGE` instead, then an overflow during conversion has occurred and the returned value `ULONG_MAX` is not truly representative of the input value.

Because `strtoul(3)` is an unsigned conversion, you have no minimum value to test like the `LONG_MIN` value for `strtol(3)`.

Large Integer Conversions

With the migration of UNIX systems to 64-bit CPUs, the C language now supports 64-bit integers. These data types are

*   `long long int`

*   `unsigned long long int`

or simply

*   `long long`

*   `unsigned long long`

With the appearance of these C data types comes the need to make conversions from strings to these 64-bit types.

Some UNIX platforms now support the `strtoll(3)` and `strtoull(3)` functions. Their synopsis is as follows:

```
#include <stdlib.h>

long long strtoll(const char *str, char **endptr, int base);

unsigned long long strtoull (const char *str, char **endptr, int base);
```

These functions work the same as their `strtol(3)` and `strtoul(3)` counterparts. The only difference is that you must use the macro `LONGLONG_MAX` or `LONGLONG_MIN` when testing for overflow/underflows for `strtoll(3)`. Use the macro `ULONGLONG_MAX` for `strtoull(3)`.

Data Type Note

Many UNIX systems of today define the C data type `long` to be the same size as the type `int`. As UNIX operating systems move to 64-bit CPU platforms, and as the application software migrates with it, the `long` data type will become 64 bits in length. When that happens, the `strtol(3)` and `strtoul(3)` functions will perform 64-bit conversions instead of the present 32-bit.

Consequently, some implementations such as HPUX-11 do not provide a `strtoll(3)` function. Instead, a 32- or 64-bit data model is chosen, and the correct implementation of `strtol(3)` and `strtoul(3)` is linked in to match the data model.

BSD `strtoq(3)` and `strtouq(3)` Functions

BSD is a little different in its large integer conversions. FreeBSD supports its `strtoq(3)` and `strtouq(3)` functional equivalents of the `strtoll(3)` and `strtoull(3)` functions. The 64-bit C data types that FreeBSD uses are

Signed 64-bit	quad_t
Unsigned 64-bit	u_quad_t

The function synopsis of the conversion routines for these data types is as follows:

```
#include <sys/types.h>
#include <stdlib.h>
#include <limits.h>

quad_t strtoq(const char *nptr, char **endptr, int base);

u_quad_t strtouq(const char *nptr, char **endptr, int base);
```

The C macros that you should use with `strtoq(3)` are `QUAD_MAX` and `QUAD_MIN`, when testing for overflow and underflow, respectively. For `strtouq(3)`, you must use the C macro `UQUAD_MAX` instead. Neither of these appears in the `man(1)` pages for these routines, but they can be found in the include file `<machine/limits.h>`.

64-bit Integer Note

It seems likely that FreeBSD will change its C data type `long` to be 64-bit in the future. This will result in the `strtol(3)` and `strtoul(3)` functions performing 64-bit conversion when that happens.

The `strtod(3)` Function

The `strtod(3)` function is used to perform string-to-floating point conversions. This function is quite similar in operation to the integer conversion functions just covered, but it has a few new wrinkles. The synopsis for `strtod(3)` is as follows:

```
#include <stdlib.h>
#include <math.h>

double strtod(const char *nptr, char **endptr);
```

Note that there is no **base** argument. No radix conversions are available for floating-point conversions other than base 10.

The input string **nptr** and the second argument **endptr** are used in precisely the same way they are used in the **strtol(3)** function.

Using the `strtod(3)` Function

The following shows how the **strtod(3)** function can be used to convert a floating-point value in a string buffer to the C **double** type:

```
static char buf[] = "-32000.009E+01";
char *ep;               /* Returned pointer */
double dval;            /* Converted value */

dval = strtod(buf,&ep); /* Convert buf to double */
```

The input string is converted and the floating-point result is returned and assigned to the variable **dval**. The point where the conversion ends is passed back to the caller by storing the pointer in pointer variable **ep**. In this example, **ep** should end up pointing to the null byte at the end of the **buf[]** array.

Testing for Math Errors

This function adds a new twist to overflow and underflow detection. In order to test for overflows and underflows, you must include the file **<math.h>**:

```
#include <math.h>
```

This include file defines the macro **HUGE_VAL**, which will be needed in the tests. Three return values from **strtod(3)** require further investigation by the program:

- +HUGE_VAL
- 0.0
- -HUGE_VAL

The test procedure will rely on the fact that the **errno** value is cleared before calling **strtod(3)**.

Testing for Overflow

When the value **+HUGE_VAL** is returned, you must check **errno** to see if the value **ERANGE** was posted there. If **errno** is set to **ERANGE**, then the conversion process had an overflow. If **errno** remains cleared to zero, then the value returned is a valid number.

Testing for Underflow

When the value -HUGE_VAL is returned, you must also check errno to see if the error ERANGE was posted there. If errno remains cleared to zero, then the returned value is a valid number.

Testing for Exponent Underflow

The function strtod(3) returns 0.0 when the converted value is extremely small in value fractionally—so small that the underlying data type cannot represent it. When zero is returned and ERANGE is posted to the errno variable, then it is known that the conversion failed because the input value was too small a fraction to represent. Another way to state this is that the exponent value underflowed.

Handling Exponent Underflow

In many cases, you might be happy just to round that small fractional value to zero and move on. However, this may not be suitable for all applications, especially scientific ones.

A scientific model may depend on the precision of that variable to represent a very small value. If precision is maintained, then that value might be later multiplied by a large value to compute a reasonable result.

However, if you simply allow the value to round to zero, then the multiplied result will be zero also—leading to an incorrect answer. Thus, it is better to abort the computation and point out that the value could not be contained with the necessary precision.

Precision Warning

Consider any computation that leads to a small result that does not quite underflow to be unstable. A significant loss of precision is likely when operating in this extreme exponent range.

Flowchart of Math Error Tests

The entire procedure for math error testing for strtod(3) is shown in Figure 10.1 as a flowchart. This should help summarize the overflow and underflow detection logic that should be used.

FIGURE 10.1

Testing for overflow and underflow after calling `strtod(3)`.

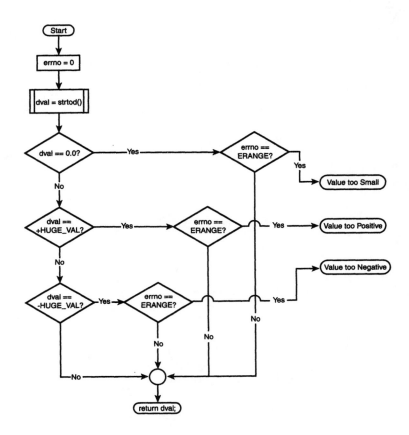

Summary

In this chapter, you learned about the limitations of the simple `atoi(3)` family of functions. The `sscanf(3)` function was discussed as a better replacement, and it was noted that some limitations remain with that approach. The remainder of the chapter covered the details of the `strtol(3)`, `strtoul(3)`, and `strtod(3)` functions.

The next chapter covers the UNIX library calls for working with dates and times. There you will learn how each user can manage his own concept of a time zone, and the system manages time for everyone. Conversions from strings to dates and dates to strings

CHAPTER 11

UNIX DATE AND TIME FACILITIES

D ate and time facilities are important to nearly everything you do in UNIX. When a process starts, the time is recorded in a kernel table. When you create a new file, the creation date and time are recorded. Modification times are recorded when you edit a file. Even when you just view a file, its access time is updated.

In this chapter, you will learn about date and time management functions that are available for your use in applications. This chapter covers

- UNIX Epoch Time
- Local, GMT, and UTC time zones
- The `localtime(3)` and `gmtime(3)` functions
- The `asctime(3)` function
- The `tzset(3)` function
- The `mktime(3)` function
- the `strftime(3)` function

UNIX Epoch Time

When reading the `man(1)` pages regarding time functions for UNIX, you will frequently encounter the term *Epoch Time*. This is the beginning of time for UNIX: January 1, 1970, at 00:00:00 GMT (Greenwich Mean Time). This coincides with the value of zero for the data type `time_t`.

Time Zones

Since the UNIX kernel bases its *Epoch Time* on the Greenwich Mean Time (GMT) time standard, it is instructive to do a review of time standards in general. Then, local time zones will be covered to provide a clear understanding of how they are related to the UNIX kernel clock.

Introducing World Time Standards

Originally, the GMT time standard was the world standard. Since then, a new world standard has emerged to coordinate the precise synchronization needed for distributed computer systems.

UNIX had its beginnings when GMT was the still the world standard. Consequently, much of the UNIX literature is steeped in the references to GMT today.

The GMT Time Standard

Greenwich Mean Time is based on the prime meridian of the Earth, which in 1884 was established as passing through Great Britain's Greenwich Observatory. Since then, the observatory has moved and been renamed the Royal Greenwich Observatory. However, its original location is still used to define the prime meridian.

The precise GMT time is determined by observations of the Sun. Due to variations in the Earth's rotation and its orbit around the Sun, small corrections are computed regularly and applied to arrive at the precise time.

The UTC Time Standard

UTC is the abbreviation for the time standard named Universelle Tempes Coordinaté in French, or Coordinated Universal Time in English. This standard is based on atomic clock measurements instead of solar observations, but it still uses the prime meridian. This standard replaced the GMT in 1986.

Choosing a World Time Standard

For many people, a fraction of a second is insignificant. They can set their UNIX system clocks according to the GMT time standard or the UTC time standard. The standards are so similar that they are sometimes used interchangeably.

The correct designation to use for the world time standard today is UTC. Consequently, new software should be written to display UTC instead of GMT.

Understanding Local Time Zones

UNIX allows for those people who do not live in the UTC time zone. This is done by taking your local time zone and adding an offset to arrive at UTC. In the Eastern time zone in North America, for example, UTC time is local time plus five hours. For much of Europe, it is the local time minus one hour.

Customizing Local Time Zones

Since UNIX is a multiuser operating system, it is designed to permit a user to define his own concept of local time. The `tzset(3)` function is used internally by a number of date and time functions to determine the local time zone. This function will be examined in more detail later in this chapter. The important thing to note is that it looks for an exported environment variable `TZ` to define your preference for local time. Your `TZ` value may be different from what other users on your system are using.

Setting the TZ Variable

When the environment variable TZ is found and has a properly defined value, the `tzset(3)` function will configure your local time zone. This will be used by the rest of the date and time functions where necessary. If the value TZ is not defined or is incorrectly set, the `tzset(3)` function falls back on the following zone information file (for FreeBSD):

```
/etc/localtime
```

Failing variable TZ and the zone information file, UTC time is assumed.

To configure your session for Eastern Standard Time and no daylight saving time, you can use

```
$ TZ=EST05
$ export TZ
```

This sets the time zone name to EST. Since it is west of the prime meridian, the offset is a positive 05 hours (think of this as local time + 5 hours = UTC). Eastern Daylight Saving Time can be configured as follows:

```
$ TZ=EST05EDT
$ export TZ
```

If you need more information on time zone configuration, a good place to start is the `man(1)` page for `tzset(3)`. More advanced information is found in the `tzfile(5)` man pages.

Defining the Date and Time Data Type

Originally, the UNIX time and date value was stored in the C data type `long`. As time passed, and as standardization efforts got underway, it was recognized that this was not good for long-range planning. The capacity of the `long` integer was going to run out someday (January 19, 2038, at 03:14:07 UTC, to be precise). The next second after that will cause the 31-bit positive number to roll over to a 32-bit value, making it a negative number.

Since the `long` integer data type was going to overflow in the near future, it was decided that date and time deserved its own special data type: `time_t`. This permits the underlying data type to be changed at a future date, requiring that applications only be recompiled.

To obtain the current system date and time from the UNIX kernel, you call upon the `time(3)` library function. Its synopsis is as follows:

```
#include <time.h>

time_t time(time_t *tloc);
```

The single argument provided to the `time(3)` function is optional (it must be null when not provided). When provided, it must point to a `time_t` variable that is to receive the current date and time. This will be the same value returned by the function. For example

```
time_t cur_time;

time(&cur_time);
```

If the pointer argument `cur_time` is invalid, the value `(time_t)-1` is returned and `errno` is set to the value `EFAULT`.

While the time since Epoch Time is useful to the UNIX kernel, it must be converted into various other forms to be displayed or to work with its components. The next section examines the library functions that are available for this.

Time Conversion Functions

All date and time functions in this section require the include file `<time.h>`. In the remainder of this chapter, the following conversions will be examined:

- `time_t` values to ASCII date/time strings
- `time_t` values to date/time components (second, minute, hour, day, month, year, and so on)
- Date/time components to ASCII strings
- Date/time components to `time_t` values

In addition to looking at the various conversion functions, a simple C++ class `DTime` will be built and illustrated. This object has been left as simple as possible to prevent obscuring the underlying functions being discussed. For this reason, the `DTime` class in its present form is not entirely suitable for use in production-mode programs. The include file and the class definition for `DTime` are shown in Listing 11.1.

LISTING 11.1 `dtime.h`—The Declaration of Class `DTime`

```
1:  // dtime.cc
2:
3:  #include <iostream.h>
4:  #include <stdlib.h>
5:  #include <unistd.h>
6:  #include <string.h>
7:  #include <errno.h>
8:  #include <time.h>
9:
10: extern "C" {
11: extern char *ctime_r(const time_t *clock, char *buf);
12: extern struct tm *localtime_r(const time_t *clock, struct tm *result);
13: extern struct tm *gmtime_r(const time_t *clock, struct tm *result);
14: extern char *asctime_r(const struct tm *tm, char *buf);
15: }
16:
17: /////////////////////////////////////////////////////////////
18: // Experimental DTime Class :
19: /////////////////////////////////////////////////////////////
20:
21: class DTime : public tm {
```

```
22:  private:
23:      time_t        dt;          // Date/time in epoch time
24:      char          buf[128];    // ctime(3)/strftime(3) buffer
25:  public:
26:      DTime();
27:      DTime &operator+=(long secs); // Add time
28:      DTime &operator-=(long secs); // Subtract time
29:      inline time_t time() { return dt; }
30:      time_t getTime();         // time(3)
31:      time_t putTime(time_t dt); // Put a time value into this->dt
32:      char *ctime();            // ctime(3)
33:      struct tm *localtime();   // localtime(3)
34:      struct tm *gmtime();      // gmtime(3)
35:      char *asctime();          // asctime(3)
36:      time_t mktime();          // mktime(3)
37:      char *strftime(const char *format); // strftime(3)
38:  };
39:
40:  extern ostream &operator<<(ostream &ostr,DTime &obj);
41:
42:  // End dtime.h
```

The class `DTime` inherits structure members from the `public tm` (line 21), which will be discussed later. Private member `dt` is the `time_t` data type that is required for several of the functions being discussed (line 23). A number of other functions require the use of a buffer. These use `buf[]` in line 24.

Listing 11.2 shows the constructor, the operators `+=` and `-=`, and the `getTime()` and `putTime()` methods.

LISTING 11.2   `gettime.cc`—The Constructor and `getTime()` Methods of `DTime`

```
 1:  // gettime.cc
 2:
 3:  #include "dtime.h"
 4:
 5:  /////////////////////////////////////////////////////////////
 6:  // Constructor:
 7:  /////////////////////////////////////////////////////////////
 8:
 9:  DTime::DTime() {
10:      dt = (time_t)(-1);        // No current time
11:  }
12:
13:  /////////////////////////////////////////////////////////////
14:  // Add seconds to the current time in this->dt :
15:  /////////////////////////////////////////////////////////////
16:
17:  DTime &
18:  DTime::operator+=(long secs) {
19:      dt += (time_t) secs;
20:      return *this;
```

continued from previous page

```
21:    }
22:
23:    //////////////////////////////////////////////////////////////
24:    // Subtract seconds to the current time in this->dt :
25:    //////////////////////////////////////////////////////////////
26:
27:    DTime &
28:    DTime::operator-=(long secs) {
29:        dt -= (time_t) secs;
30:        return *this;
31:    }
32:
33:    //////////////////////////////////////////////////////////////
34:    // Return current time :
35:    //////////////////////////////////////////////////////////////
36:
37:    time_t
38:    DTime::getTime() {
39:        return ::time(&dt);
40:    }
41:
42:    //////////////////////////////////////////////////////////////
43:    // Allow the caller to plug-in a time value :
44:    //////////////////////////////////////////////////////////////
45:
46:    time_t
47:    DTime::putTime(time_t dt) {
48:        return this->dt = dt;
49:    }
50:
51:    // End gettime.cc
```

The constructor initializes the member dt to the value (time_t)(-1) (lines 9–11). This is the error value that is returned by mktime(3), which is used here to indicate that no time is set.

The operators += and -= are overloaded for this class to allow the user to add or subtract time from the object (lines 17–31). This will be demonstrated later in the chapter.

The member getTime() retrieves the current time into member dt using the function time(3) that was discussed earlier (lines 37–40). The same value is returned.

The putTime() method is provided so that the user can supply a time_t value of his own choosing (lines 46–49).

Converting Time to String Form Using ctime(3)

This is perhaps the easiest of the date and time conversion functions to use. This function takes the time_t value as input and converts it to an ASCII string that can be displayed. The synopsis for ctime(3) is as follows:

```
#include <time.h>
```

```
char * ctime(const time_t *timep);
```

The `ctime(3)` function requires a pointer to the time variable that contains the time and date to be converted. The following example shows how to obtain the current system date and pass it to `ctime(3)`. The string returned is then displayed:

```
time_t td;      /* Time and Date */
```

```
time(&td);      /* Get current date */
printf("Today is %s", ctime(&td) );
```

The 26-byte string returned by `ctime(3)` is a date and time string of the form

```
Mon Jan 18 22:14:07 2038
```

The function returns a pointer to an internal static buffer, which is valid only until the next call. One annoying aspect of this returned date string is that a newline character is placed at the end.

The `ctime_r(3)` Function

The `ctime(3)` function returns a pointer to its internal static buffer. This makes it unsafe for threaded programs. A thread-safe version of this routine is available as `ctime_r(3)`:

```
#include <time.h>
```

```
char *ctime_r(const time_t *clock, char *buf);
```

The buffer supplied for argument `buf` must be at least 26 characters long. The pointer value returned is the same pointer supplied for `buf`.

The `DTime::ctime()` method is shown in Listing 11.3.

LISTING 11.3   `ctime.cc`—The Implementation of the `DTime::ctime()` Method

```
 1:   // ctime.cc
 2:
 3:   #include "dtime.h"
 4:
 5:   ////////////////////////////////////////////////////////////
 6:   // Returns the ctime(3) string for the current time_t
 7:   // value that is stored in this->dt. This routine assumes
 8:   // that this->getTime() has been previously called:
 9:   ////////////////////////////////////////////////////////////
10:
11:   char *
12:   DTime::ctime() {
13:       char *cp;
14:
15:       ::ctime_r(&dt,buf);      // Put ctime(3) string into buf[]
```

continued from previous page

```
16:        if ( (cp = strchr(buf,'\n')) != NULL )
17:            *cp = 0;            // Eliminate pesky newline character
18:        return buf;            // Return ptr to buffer
19:    }
20:
21:    // End ctime.cc
```

The `DTime::ctime()` method calls on the function `ctime_r(3)`. The function `ctime_r(3)` takes the time that is in the member `dt` and converts it to ASCII form in the private buffer `buf[]` (line 15). The annoying newline character is eliminated in lines 15 and 16. Line 18 returns the pointer to the private buffer containing the string.

The `localtime(3)` and `gmtime(3)` Functions

The programmer often needs direct access to the date and time components. The `time_t` data type may be convenient for math, but it is not always convenient for all forms of date arithmetic. To extract the date components from a `time_t` value, the function `localtime(3)` or `gmtime(3)` can be used:

```
#include <time.h>

struct tm *localtime(const time_t *timep);

struct tm *gmtime(const time_t *timep);

struct tm *localtime_r(const time_t *clock, struct tm *result);

struct tm *gmtime_r(const time_t *clock, struct tm *result);
```

The `localtime(3)` function returns time and date components according to the local time. To obtain time components according to the UTC time zone, use the `gmtime(3)` function. These functions both accept a pointer to a `time_t` value that is to be converted. The result from these functions is only valid until the next call.

The functions `localtime_r(3)` and `gmtime_r(3)` are thread-safe versions of the older `localtime(3)` and `gmtime(3)` functions, respectively. They have the additional pointer argument `result`, into which the results are written. This is different from returning the results in an internal static buffer as the older `localtime(3)` and `gmtime(3)` functions do.

The returned result is a pointer to a `struct tm`, which provides access to date and time components such as the day of the month and the year. The following example obtains the current date using `time(3)` and then calls on `localtime(3)`. The returned results are copied to the structure variable `dc` in this example:

```
time_t dt;           /* Current date */
struct tm dc;        /* Date components */

time(&td);           /* Get current date */
dc = *localtime(&dt); /* convert dt -> dc */
```

A better way to place the results into the dc structure is to use the new re-entrant counterpart of localtime(3):

```
time_t dt;              /* Current date */
struct tm dc;           /* Date components */

time(&td);              /* Get current date */
localtime_r(&dt,&dc);   /* convert dt -> dc */
```

In this manner, the results are placed into dc straightaway, rather than copying the results from one structure to another.

Listing 11.4 shows the implementation of DTime::localtime() and DTime::gmtime() methods using localtime_r(3) and gmtime_r(3), respectively.

LISTING 11.4   localtime.cc—The Implementation of DTime::localtime() and DTime::gmtime()

```
 1:  // localtime.cc
 2:
 3:  #include "dtime.h"
 4:
 5:  ///////////////////////////////////////////////////////////
 6:  // Return the local time components, based upon the
 7:  // current value of this->dt; assumes that a prior
 8:  // call to getTime() has been made:
 9:  ///////////////////////////////////////////////////////////
10:
11:  struct tm *
12:  DTime::localtime() {
13:      ::localtime_r(&dt,this);
14:      return this;
15:  }
16:
17:  ///////////////////////////////////////////////////////////
18:  // Return the UTC (GMT) time components, based upon the
19:  // current value of this->dt; assumes that a prior
20:  // call to getTime() has been made:
21:  ///////////////////////////////////////////////////////////
22:
23:  struct tm *
24:  DTime::gmtime() {
25:      ::gmtime_r(&dt,this);
26:      return this;
27:  }
28:
29:  // End localtime.cc
```

In both of these methods, the DTime class itself is used in the second argument because it inherits from struct tm. The pointer to the class is returned.

The Members of the `struct tm`

This is the structure that is used by several of the date/time functions, including `localtime(3)`, `gmtime(3)`, and `mktime(3)`. The structure is defined as follows:

```
struct tm {
    int    tm_sec;     /* seconds */
    int    tm_min;     /* minutes */
    int    tm_hour;    /* hours (0-23) */
    int    tm_mday;    /* day of the month (1-31) */
    int    tm_mon;     /* month (0-11) */
    int    tm_year;    /* year 2000=100 */
    int    tm_wday;    /* day of the week (0-6) */
    int    tm_yday;    /* day in the year (0-365) */
    int    tm_isdst;   /* daylight saving time */
};
```

This C structure is defined in the file `<time.h>`. The individual members of this structure are documented in Table 11.1.

Number Range Warnings

Note that member `tm_mon` starts at zero. To produce a month number 1–12, you must add 1 to this value.

Note also that you must add 1900 to member `tm_year` to arrive at the century.

`tm_isdst` Application Note

The member `tm_isdst` has three possible states:

When it is positive, daylight saving time is in effect.

When it is zero, daylight saving time is not in effect.

When it is negative, daylight saving time information is not known or is not available.

TABLE 11.1   The `struct tm` Structure Members

Member	Description
tm_sec	The number of seconds after the minute. Normally the range is 0 to 59, but this value can be as high as 61 to allow for leap seconds.
tm_min	The number of minutes after each hour; it ranges in value from 0 to 59.
tm_hour	The hour past midnight, from 0 to 23.
tm_mday	The day of the month, from 1 to 31.
tm_mon	The month of the year, from 0 to 11.

Member	Description
tm_year	The year, expressed as years since 1900. For example, the year 2010 is represented as 110.
tm_wday	The day of the week, in the range 0 to 6. Day 0 is Sunday, 1 is Monday, and so on.
tm_yday	The day of the year, in the range 0 to 365.
tm_isdst	This is a flag with three possible states. See the Note immediately prior to this table.

The class DTime that is developed in this chapter inherits from the struct tm. Consequently, the members are available to the programmer directly. (Its access is public; see line 21 of Listing 11.1.)

Conversion of Date/Time Components to Strings Using the asctime(3) Function

The asctime(3) function accepts the date and time components from the struct tm and composes an ASCII-formatted date string. Its synopsis is as follows:

```
#include <time.h>

char *asctime(const struct tm *tm_ptr);

char *asctime_r(const struct tm *tm, char *buf);
```

The single argument is a pointer to an input struct tm, which will be used to format a date string. The returned pointer from asctime(3) is to a static buffer that is valid only until the next call. Function asctime_r(3) is the re-entrant counterpart, which requires a destination buffer buf[] that is at least 26 bytes in size.

LISTING 11.5   asctime.cc—The Implementation of DTime::asctime()

```
 1:  // asctime.cc
 2:
 3:  #include "dtime.h"
 4:
 5:  //////////////////////////////////////////////////////////////
 6:  // This function returns the asctime(3) string, for the
 7:  // present members of this class (struct tm). This method
 8:  // assumes that the present struct tm members are valid.
 9:  //////////////////////////////////////////////////////////////
10:
11:  char *
12:  DTime::asctime() {
13:      return ::asctime_r(this,buf);
14:  }
15:
16:  // End asctime.cc
```

In the implementation of this `DTime` method, the function `asctime_r(3)` is used, passing the pointer `this` as input in the first argument. This works because the class inherits from the `struct tm`. The second argument is set as `buf` in line 13 to receive the ASCII result, which is then returned.

The `tzset(3)` Function

Previously, it was indicated that the `tzset(3)` function is responsible for establishing your definition of local time. This function looks for the exported `TZ` environment variable and falls back to the system-configured zone information file if it is not defined. The synopsis for `tzset(3)` is as follows:

```
#include <time.h>

extern long int timezone;      /* Not BSD */
extern char *tzname[2];
extern int daylight;           /* Not BSD */

void tzset(void);
```

The `tzset(3)` function is called on by any of the library date functions that need to know about the configured local time for this session. For example, after the function `localtime(3)` returns, it is known that the function `tzset(3)` has been called, because it must know about local time.

Once the function `tzset(3)` has been called, it does not need to be called again. However, if you aren't certain that it has been called, there is no harm in calling it again.

The `tzset(3)` External Variables

The side effect of calling function `tzset(3)` is that certain external variables are assigned values. These indicate to the date library routines what the local time zone is. These variables are

```
extern long int timezone;      /* Not BSD */
extern char *tzname[2];
extern int daylight;           /* Not BSD */
```

Understanding the `timezone` External Variable

The value `timezone` is the number of seconds you must add to your local time to arrive at UTC time. If you are in the Eastern Standard Time zone, then you need to add five hours to the local time to arrive at UTC time. To configure the external variable `timezone`, this value should be `+18000` (seconds).

BSD Support Note

FreeBSD, OpenBSD, and NetBSD do not appear to support the external variable `timezone`.

Understanding the `daylight` External Variable

The value of the **daylight** external variable indicates the following:

- When **daylight** is true (non-zero), daylight saving time is in effect.

- When **daylight** is false (zero), daylight saving time is not in effect.

BSD Support Note

FreeBSD, OpenBSD, and NetBSD do not appear to support the external variable **daylight**.

Understanding the `tzname[]` External Array

The **tzname[]** array of two-character strings provides the name strings of two time zones. The normal time zone string is provided in **tzname[0]**, and the daylight saving time zone is provided in **tzname[1]**. Examples might be **EST** and **EDT** for Eastern Standard Time and Eastern Daylight Saving Time, respectively.

When daylight saving time is not in effect, array elements **tzname[0]** and **tzname[1]** will point to the same C string.

Using the `tzname[]` External Array

To display the time zone currently in effect, use the following code on a non-BSD system:

```
tzset();                 /* Make sure externs are set */
printf("Zone is '%s'\n", tzname[daylight ? 1 : 0]);
```

---
daylight Variable Application Warning

Do not rely on the **daylight** external variable to be exactly one or zero. The documentation simply states that this value will be non-zero if daylight saving time is in effect.

Determining the Time Zone Under BSD

If you find that there is no support for the external variables **timezone** and **daylight**, the time zone can be determined by a more tedious procedure:

```
struct tm tmvals;                        /* Date/time components */
time_t td;                               /* Current time/date */
int x;                                   /* tmvals.is_dst */

time(&td);                               /* Get current time */
localtime_r(&td,&tmvals);                /* Populate tmvals */
x = tmvals.tm_isdst < 0 ? 0 : tmvals.tm_isdst;/* Assume not DST if unknown */
printf("Zone is '%s'\n",tzname[x ? 1 : 0]); /* Print time zone */
```

It must be noted that the assignment to x in the example was done because the value in **tmvals.tm_isdst** is a three-state flag. It can be negative, indicating that the time zone is not known. In the example, the code assumed that daylight saving time was not in effect, if it was not known.

Creating Epoch Time Values with the `mktime(3)` Function

If you want to construct a `time_t` value based on a specific date, you need the `mktime(3)` function. Its synopsis is as follows:

```
#include <time.h>

time_t mktime(struct tm *tm_ptr);
```

The `mktime(3)` function requires a pointer to a `struct tm`. This input/output structure contributes date and time components that are used to compute a `time_t` value, which is returned. Some values are also returned in this structure.

Testing for `mktime(3)` Errors

If the values in the `struct tm` are such that a date cannot be computed, the value `(time_t)` `(-1)` is returned. This happens when `tm_year` is set to a year before 1970 or when non-existent dates are supplied, such as February 30 or June 35.

Setting Input Members of `struct tm` for `mktime(3)`

Not all of the `struct tm` members are used for input when passed to the `mktime(3)` function. The following members are mandatory for input and are not altered by `mktime(3)`:

- `tm_sec` (seconds: 0 to 61)
- `tm_min` (minutes: 0 to 59)
- `tm_hour` (hours: 0 to 23)
- `tm_mday` (days of month: 1 to 31)
- `tm_mon` (months: 0 to 11)
- `tm_year` (years: year 2000 is value 100)
- `tm_isdst` (positive for daylight saving time, zero if no daylight saving time in effect)

Be sure to make the `tm_mon` member a zero-based month value (`0` to `11`).

Members of `struct tm` Altered by `mktime(3)`

The following members are ignored as input but are recomputed and altered before the `mktime(3)` function returns:

- `tm_wday` is ignored as input and is recomputed for output.
- `tm_yday` is ignored as input and is recomputed for output.

The fact that these two values are recomputed allows you to plug in a date and time and call `mktime(3)`. The returned values in the structure will tell you what the weekday and day of the year are.

Daylight Savings Tip

Do not forget to set `tm_isdst` before calling `mktime(3)`. This input value determines whether daylight saving time is in effect for the local date and time specified in the other members.

Failure to set this value correctly can allow the computed UTC `time_t` value to be incorrect by the amount of the daylight saving time difference.

Application Warning

Since the `tm_wday` and `tm_yday` values are replaced by recomputed values, never pass a constant or read-only structure to `mktime(3)`.

Implementing the `DTime::mktime()` Method

Listing 11.6 shows how the `DTime::mktime()` method was implemented. This method calls upon the C function `mktime(3)` to convert the current `struct tm` members that this class inherits into `time_t` values, which are returned. This method will be tested later in the chapter.

LISTING 11.6   `mktime.cc`—The Implementation of the `DTime::mktime()` Method

```
1:   // mktime.cc
2:
3:   #include "dtime.h"
4:
5:   //////////////////////////////////////////////////////////
6:   // This method assumes that the struct tm members of this
7:   // class already contain valid values (tm_wday and tm_yday
8:   // are ignored in this case):
9:   //////////////////////////////////////////////////////////
10:
11:  time_t
12:  DTime::mktime() {
13:      return dt = ::mktime(this);
14:  }
15:
16:  // End mktime.cc
```

Customizing Date and Time Formats with `strftime(3)`

The string format of the date and time can vary considerably with the preference of each user. The `strftime(3)` function makes it easier for the C programmer to implement custom date and time formats. Its synopsis is as follows:

```
#include <time.h>

size_t strftime(char *buf, size_t maxsize,
    const char *format, const struct tm *timeptr);
```

The arguments `buf` and `maxsize` specify the receiving buffer and its maximum size, respectively. The argument `format` specifies a `printf(3)`-like format string. The last argument, `timeptr`, points to a `struct tm` structure that will supply all of the input date and time values. The final output string size is returned, excluding the null byte.

If the output buffer is not large enough, the value `maxsize` is returned, indicating that `maxsize` characters were placed into the buffer. However, since there is no room for the null byte when this happens, do not expect one to be there.

The `strftime(3)` Format Specifiers

The format specifiers are quite different from the `sprintf(3)` variety. Table 11.2 lists the format specifiers that are supported. Notice that each specifier starts with the percent character (`%`) and is followed by a letter. All other text in the format string is copied verbatim, in the same way that `sprintf(3)` does. To include a percent character, use two successive percent characters.

TABLE 11.2 Format Specifiers for `strftime(3)`

Specifier	Description
%a	The abbreviated weekday name is substituted according to the locale.
%A	The full weekday name is substituted according to the locale.
%b	The abbreviated month name is substituted according to the locale.
%B	The full month name is substituted according to the locale.
%c	The preferred date and time representation for the current locale.
%d	The day of the month in decimal.
%H	The hour of the day in 24-hour form (00 to 23).
%I	The hour in 12-hour form (01 to 12).
%j	The day of the year as a decimal number (001 to 365).
%m	The month as a decimal number (01 to 12).
%M	The minute as a decimal number.
%p	The string AM or PM according to the time.
%S	The second as a decimal value.

Specifier	Description
%U	The week number of the current year, expressed as a decimal number. The first Sunday is considered the first day of the first week.
%W	The week number of the current year, expressed as a decimal number. The first Monday is considered the first day of the first week.
%w	The day of the week as a decimal number (0 to 6).
%x	The preferred date representation without time, for the current locale.
%X	The preferred time representation without date, for the current locale.
%y	The year without a century (00 to 99).
%Y	The year with the century.
%Z	The time zone or zone abbreviation.
%%	A single percent character (%).

Implementing the `DTime::strftime()` Method

To enable you to try out the `strftime(3)` C function, it has been included in the class `DTime` as the method `DTime::strftime()`. This is shown in Listing 11.7.

LISTING 11.7 strftime.cc—The Implementation of the `DTime::strftime()` Method

```
1:   // strftime.cc
2:
3:   #include "dtime.h"
4:
5:   /////////////////////////////////////////////////////////
6:   // Call strftime(3) to format a string, based upon the
7:   // current struct tm members. This method assumes that the
8:   // struct tm members contain valid values.
9:   /////////////////////////////////////////////////////////
10:
11:  char *
12:  DTime::strftime(const char *format) {
13:      size_t n = ::strftime(buf,sizeof buf-1,format,this);
14:      buf[n] = 0;              // Enforce a null byte
15:      return buf;              // Return formatted string
16:  }
17:
18:  /////////////////////////////////////////////////////////
19:  // Output operator for the DTime object :
20:  /////////////////////////////////////////////////////////
21:
22:  ostream &
```

continued from previous page

```
23:    operator<<(ostream &ostr,DTime &obj) {
24:
25:        if ( obj.time() == (time_t)(-1) )
26:            ostr << "[No current time]";
27:        else
28:            ostr << obj.ctime();
29:        return ostr;
30:    }
31:
32:    // End strftime.cc
```

A C++ function `operator<<()` was implemented in Listing 11.7 to make it possible to display this `DTime` class using the overloaded C++ `<<` operator. Line 25 checks to see if there is a current time for the object and, if so, the `DTime::ctime()` method is called to format a date/time string (line 28). This string is then sent to the output stream.

Testing Class `DTime`

Listing 11.8 shows a main program that will instantiate a `DTime` class and then invoke some operations on it.

LISTING 11.8 `main.cc`—The `main()` Program for Demonstrating the `DTime` Class

```
1:    // main.cc
2:
3:    #include "dtime.h"
4:
5:    int
6:    main(int argc,char **argv) {
7:        DTime obj;
8:
9:        (void) argc;
10:       (void) argv;
11:
12:       // Set and display epoch time in the local time zone :
13:       obj.putTime(0);          // Establish epoch time
14:       cout << "Local UNIX Epoch time is '" << obj << "'\n\n";
15:
16:       // Get and display the current time and date :
17:       obj.getTime();           // Get current date/time
18:       cout << "Current time is '" << obj << "'\n\n";
19:
20:       // Compute a date 30 days from today :
21:       obj += 30 * 24 * 60 * 60;
22:       cout << "30 days from now is '" << obj << "'\n";
23:
24:       // Get UTC values :
25:       obj.gmtime();            // Set struct tm values from time_t
26:       cout << "That date is " << obj.tm_mon + 1 << "/" << obj.tm_mday
27:            << "/" << obj.tm_year + 1900 << " "
```

```
28:              << obj.tm_hour << ":" << obj.tm_min << ":" << obj.tm_sec
29:              << " UTC\n\n";
30:
31:         // Reset to local time, and set to 1st of the month :
32:         obj.getTime();          // Get current time
33:         obj.localtime();        // In local time components
34:         obj.tm_mday = 1;        // Set to 1st of the month
35:         obj.tm_hour = obj.tm_min = obj.tm_sec = 0;
36:         obj.mktime();           // Now set the time_t value
37:         cout << "The 1st is '" << obj << "' in this month\n";
38:
39:         cout << "which is the same as "
40:              << obj.strftime("%A %B %d, %Y at %I:%M %p") << "\n";
41:
42:         return 0;
43:  }
```

Compiling and running this program yields output similar to the following:

```
$ make
cc -c -D_POSIX_C_SOURCE=199309L -D_POSIX_SOURCE -Wall gettime.cc
cc -c -D_POSIX_C_SOURCE=199309L -D_POSIX_SOURCE -Wall ctime.cc
cc -c -D_POSIX_C_SOURCE=199309L -D_POSIX_SOURCE -Wall asctime.cc
cc -c -D_POSIX_C_SOURCE=199309L -D_POSIX_SOURCE -Wall localtime.cc
cc -c -D_POSIX_C_SOURCE=199309L -D_POSIX_SOURCE -Wall mktime.cc
cc -c -D_POSIX_C_SOURCE=199309L -D_POSIX_SOURCE -Wall strftime.cc
cc -c -D_POSIX_C_SOURCE=199309L -D_POSIX_SOURCE -Wall main.cc
cc -o dtime gettime.o ctime.o asctime.o localtime.o mktime.o strftime.o main.o -
lstdc++
$ ./dtime
Local UNIX Epoch time is 'Wed Dec 31 19:00:00 1969'

Current time is 'Sun May  7 22:05:54 2000'

30 days from now is 'Tue Jun  6 22:05:54 2000'
That date is 6/7/2000 2:5:54 UTC

The 1st is 'Mon May  1 00:00:00 2000' in this month
which is the same as Monday May 01, 2000 at 12:00 AM
$
```

The first line of program output states your local time for UNIX Epoch Time. The example output was produced in the EST zone. Yours will differ if you are in a different time zone. This is accomplished in lines 13 and 14 of main.cc, shown in Listing 11.8. Line 13 sets the UNIX Epoch Time, which is the value (time_t)(0).

The next line of output beginning with Current time is is produced by lines 17 and 18. Line 17 sets the current date and time by calling obj.getTime().

Line 21 adds 30 days to the current time in obj using the overloaded += operator. Then the object is directed to cout in line 22 to display the date.

Line 25 establishes UTC values in the `struct tm` members that `DTime` inherits. Lines 26–29 access the structure members to send a manually formatted UTC time to `cout`.

Line 32 obtains the current time again for object `obj`. Lines 33–35 establish the first of the current month at midnight. Method `DTime::mktime()` is invoked at line 36, and then the object is sent to `cout` in line 37, displaying what the first of the current month is.

The last test in lines 39 and 40 tests the `strftime(3)` function by calling on the method `DTime::strftime()`.

Understanding the Effects of Locale

Some of the format specifiers that `strftime(3)` supports format according to a *locale*. An example of this is the `%A` specifier (the full weekday name).

In the UNIX context, the locale represents the language and cultural rules that are used on a particular host system. It defines the language used for certain messages and the lexicographic conventions for date and time. Locale also establishes the character set that is to be used.

The locale setting will determine whether, for example, your system uses the English names for the days of the week or French names. The names of the months are also affected by locale. Lexicographical conventions such as the `%X` specifier dictate whether the time should be shown in 12- or 24-hour format, for example.

For more information about locale, view the `man(1)` page for `mklocale(1)` under FreeBSD.

Summary

This chapter covered the UNIX time management and conversion functions. The next chapter covers the subject of converting user ID and group ID names into usernames and group names, and vice versa. These are useful functions when working with `stat(2)` and `fstat(2)`, for example. In addition, the password database routines will be covered.

## CHAPTER 20

PATTERN MATCHING

The UNIX shell must usually expand wildcard filenames for user or shell script commands. Under UNIX, this wildcard expansion is always performed before the command is executed. This simplifies the command, because it sees only the finalized arguments. It also helps to make all commands work consistently, because wildcard expansion is performed in one place only—the shell process.

However, the UNIX environment is a rich environment. If you don't like one shell, you usually can choose from other shell programs. Going a step further, you might choose to write your own. To assist in making these different shell programs behave in the same way for wildcard filenames, two groups of function calls are provided:

- Functions that match string patterns
- Functions that search directories with pattern matching applied

The function `fnmatch(3)` is provided under UNIX for matching strings in a shell-like manner.

Shell Patterns

While most users learn shell pattern matching behavior early in their exposure to UNIX, it is useful to review it here before introducing the functions that implement it.

A shell pattern can consist of normal characters and meta-characters. Normal characters represent themselves, and meta-characters have a special meaning for pattern matching. The set of meta-characters for shell patterns is relatively small. They are

*	Star (asterisk)
?	Question mark
[and]	Square brackets
!	Bang (in [])
-	Hypen (in [])
\	Backslash

Each meta-character is described in the subsections that follow.

The * Meta-Character

The * character can match zero or more characters. The following shell experiment on a FreeBSD system illustrates this meta-character at work:

```
$ cd /etc
$ ls -l hosts.*
-rw-r--r--  1 root  wheel  2278 Dec 20  1999 hosts.allow
-rw-r--r--  1 root  wheel   115 Dec 20  1999 hosts.equiv
-rw-r--r--  1 root  wheel   103 Dec 20  1999 hosts.lpd
$
```

The shell matches all files that begin with hosts. and are followed by zero or more characters. Consequently, the filenames hosts.allow, hosts.equiv, and hosts.lpd match on this particular system. The meta-character may be used in any position of the pattern, as the following example illustrates:

```
$ cd /etc
$ ls -l *lpd
-rw-r--r--  1 root  wheel   103 Dec 20  1999 hosts.lpd
$
```

This example matches any filename that is prefixed by zero or more characters and ends in the string lpd.

The ? Meta-Character

Unlike the *, the ? meta-character matches only one character. If there is no character in that position, there is no match. The following example shows how the ? meta-character can be used multiple times to effect a particular pattern match:

```
$ ls -l /etc/hosts.?????
-rw-r--r--  1 root  wheel  2278 Dec 20  1999 /etc/hosts.allow
-rw-r--r--  1 root  wheel   115 Dec 20  1999 /etc/hosts.equiv
$
```

In this example, only the filenames host.allow and hosts.equiv match. The filename hosts.lpd does not match because the last two ?? in the pattern did not have characters to match with.

The [and] Meta-Characters

The [and] meta-characters work together to specify a class of characters. The following example lists any file that has the letter x, y, or z within it:

```
$ ls -d *[xyz]*
exports          newsyslog.conf  skeykeys        ttys
gettytab         security        syslog.conf
$
```

The * meta-characters to the left and right of [xyz] permit zero or more characters to exist to the left and right of the middle pattern. However, the middle pattern [xyz] insists that a letter x, y, or z exist. In this case, there weren't any filenames with the letter z in them.

You can specify ranges of characters, as is shown in the following example:

```
$ ls -d *[x-z]*
exports          newsyslog.conf  skeykeys          ttys
gettytab         security        syslog.conf
$
```

The pattern [x-z] is equivalent to specifying the letters individually as [xyz]. Multiple ranges can also be specified: [x-za-c] allows any of the characters a, b, c, x, y, and z.

If you specify an unmatched pair of [and] characters, the character is taken literally, as the following example demonstrates:

```
$ >']'
$ ls -l ]
-rw-r-----  1 ehg   wheel   0 Jun 26 14:59 ]
$
```

The first command creates a file named] by using quotes. Then the file is listed using ls(1). This same behavior also exists for the closing square bracket:

```
$ >'['
$ ls -l [
-rw-r-----  1 ehg   wheel   0 Jun 26 14:59 [
$
```

The next example shows how [and] can be used in reverse order to cause them to be interpreted as they appear.

```
$ ls -l ] [
-rw-r-----  1 ehg   wheel   0 Jun 26 14:59 [
-rw-r-----  1 ehg   wheel   0 Jun 26 14:59 ]
$
```

The ! Meta-Character

The ! meta-character has special meaning only within the [and] meta-character pair, and only if it occurs as the first character within a range. It is known as the "not" character in this context. For example, compare the difference between the first ls(1) command and the second:

```
$ cd /tmp
$ ls *[0-9]
psql.edit.1001.13867    tmp-I53052      tmp-d53036      tmp-s52935
tmp-D52798              tmp-M53211      tmp-f53114      win98
tmp-G52945              tmp-d52925      tmp-o53048
$ ls *[!0-9]
c.t              dummy.file
$
```

The first ls(1) command lists only files and directories that end in a numeric digit (range [0-9]). The second ls(1) command, however, lists only those that do *not* end in a numeric digit (range [!0-9]).

In any other position within the range or outside of it, the ! character represents itself and is not special. The following example confirms this:

```
$ >'!'
$ ls -l !
-rw-r----- 1 ehg  wheel  0 Jun 26 15:10 !
$
```

Escaping Characters with \

There are times where meta-characters get in the way. To disable special treatment of meta-characters, you can escape them with the backslash character:

```
$ >'***FILE***'
$ ls
***FILE***              tmp-D52798          tmp-d52925          tmp-s52935
c.t                     tmp-G52945          tmp-d53036          win98
dummy.file              tmp-I53052          tmp-f53114
psql.edit.1001.13867    tmp-M53211          tmp-o53048
$ ls -l \*\*\*FILE\*\*\*
-rw-r----- 1 ehg  wheel  0 Jun 26 15:14 ***FILE***
$
```

The above example shows how a file with the unusual name of ***FILE*** was created. Then the ls(1) command is invoked to confirm its existence. Then another ls(1) command shows how the backslashes can be used to remove the special meaning from the * meta-character.

String Pattern Functions

To simplify program development of shells and other related functions that require this pattern matching capability, the function fnmatch(3) was developed. The function synopsis for it is as follows:

```
#include <fnmatch.h>

int fnmatch(const char *pattern, const char *string, int flags);
```

The argument **pattern** is the input pattern string, which is compared with the input argument **string**. The argument **pattern** contains the meta-characters, if any. The argument **string** is the string that you want to test for a match. The argument **flags** enables and disables certain features of the fnmatch(3) function.

The return value from fnmatch(3) is zero if a match is made. Otherwise, the value FNM_NOMATCH is returned instead.

Application Note

When the argument **pattern** is the C string "*" and the argument **string** is the null string "", function fnmatch(3) considers this to be a match.

The `flags` argument of the `fnmatch(3)` function accepts the following macros for various bit definitions, which may be ORed together:

FNM_NOESCAPE	Treat \ as a normal character (no quoting is performed).
FNM_PATHNAME	Slashes (/) in string must match slashes in pattern.
FNM_PERIOD	Leading periods (.) in string must only be matched by leading periods in pattern. This is affected by FNM_PATHNAME.
FNM_LEADING_DIR	Match the leading directory pattern, but ignore all text that follows the trailing slash (/) in pattern.
FNM_CASEFOLD	Ignore case distinctions in the pattern and string arguments.

Each of these option flags will be discussed in detail in the sections that follow. To aid in discussing and experimenting with these flags, the program in Listing 20.1 will be used.

LISTING 20.1   `fnmatch.c`—A Program to Exercise the `fnmatch(3)` Function

```
 1:  /* fnmatch.c */
 2:
 3:  #include <stdio.h>
 4:  #include <unistd.h>
 5:  #include <fnmatch.h>
 6:
 7:  /*
 8:   * Provide command usage instructions :
 9:   */
10:  static void
11:  usage(void) {
12:
13:      puts("Usage: fnmatch [options] <pattern> <strings>...");
14:      puts("\nOptions:");
15:      puts("\t-n\tShow non-matches");
16:      puts("\t-e\tFNM_NOESCAPE");
17:      puts("\t-p\tFNM_PATHNAME");
18:      puts("\t-P\tFNM_PERIOD");
19:      puts("\t-d\tFNM_LEADING_DIR");
20:      puts("\t-c\tFNM_CASEFOLD");
21:  }
22:
23:  /*
24:   * Report the flag bits in use as confirmation :
25:   */
26:  static void
27:  report_flags(int flags) {
28:
29:      fputs("Flags:",stdout);
30:      if ( flags & FNM_NOESCAPE )
31:          fputs(" FNM_NOESCAPE",stdout);
```

continued from previous page

```
32:        if ( flags & FNM_PATHNAME )
33:            fputs(" FNM_PATHNAME",stdout);
34:        if ( flags & FNM_PERIOD )
35:            fputs(" FNM_PERIOD",stdout);
36:        if ( flags & FNM_LEADING_DIR )
37:            fputs(" FNM_LEADING_DIR",stdout);
38:        if ( flags & FNM_CASEFOLD )
39:            fputs(" FNM_CASEFOLD",stdout);
40:        if ( !flags )
41:            puts(" NONE");
42:        else
43:            putchar('\n');
44:    }
45:
46:    /*
47:     * Main program :
48:     */
49:    int
50:    main(int argc,char **argv) {
51:        int x;                        /* Interator variable */
52:        int z;                        /* General status variable */
53:        int flags = 0;                /* fnmatch(3) flags argument */
54:        int cmdopt_n = 0;             /* When true, report non-matches */
55:        char *pattern;                /* Pattern string for fnmatch(3) */
56:        const char cmdopts[] = "epPdchn"; /* Supported command options */
57:
58:        /*
59:         * Process any command options :
60:         */
61:        while ( (z = getopt(argc,argv,cmdopts)) != -1 )
62:            switch ( z ) {
63:            case 'e' :
64:                flags |= FNM_NOESCAPE;        /* -e */
65:                break;
66:            case 'p' :
67:                flags |= FNM_PATHNAME;        /* -p */
68:                break;
69:            case 'P' :
70:                flags |= FNM_PERIOD;          /* -P */
71:                break;
72:            case 'd' :
73:                flags |= FNM_LEADING_DIR;     /* -d */
74:                break;
75:            case 'c' :
76:                flags |= FNM_CASEFOLD;        /* -c */
77:                break;
78:            case 'n' :
79:                cmdopt_n = 1;                 /* -n ; Show non-matches */
80:                break;
81:            case 'h' :
82:            default :
83:                usage();
84:                return 1;
```

```
85:              }
86:
87:         /*
88:          * We must have a pattern and at least one trial string :
89:          */
90:         if ( optind + 1 >= argc ) {
91:              usage();
92:              return 1;
93:         }
94:
95:         /*
96:          * Pick the pattern string and report the flags that
97:          * are in effect for this run :
98:          */
99:         pattern = argv[optind++];
100:        report_flags(flags);
101:
102:        /*
103:         * Now try pattern against all remaining command
104:         * line arguments :
105:         */
106:        for ( x=optind; x<argc; ++x ) {
107:             z = fnmatch(pattern,argv[x],flags);
108:             /*
109:              * Report matches, or report all, if -n
110:              * option was used :
111:              */
112:             if ( !z || cmdopt_n )
113:                 printf("%s: fnmatch('%s','%s',flags)\n",
114:                     !z ? "Matched" : "No match",
115:                     pattern,
116:                     argv[x]);
117:        }
118:
119:        return 0;
120: }
```

The first portion of the main program parses the command line for options (lines 58–93) and prepares for the test run (lines 99 and 100). The `report_flags()` function simply reports the flag option bits in effect as a confirmation.

The interesting code is in lines 106–117 where the function `fnmatch(3)` is called to test each command-line argument. By default, only the matches are reported unless the -n option has been supplied.

The following shows how to compile the program and provoke a usage display with the -h option:

```
$ make fnmatch
cc -c -Wall fnmatch.c
cc -o fnmatch fnmatch.o
```

```
$ ./fnmatch -h
Usage: fnmatch [options] <pattern> <strings>...

Options:
          -n       Show non-matches
          -e       FNM_NOESCAPE
          -p       FNM_PATHNAME
          -P       FNM_PERIOD
          -d       FNM_LEADING_DIR
          -c       FNM_CASEFOLD
$
```

From the output you can see that all options except -n apply additional fnmatch(3) flag bits. Initially no flags are in effect.

To make it simpler to perform some of the tests in this chapter, alter your PATH variable as follows:

```
$ PATH=$PWD:$PATH
```

Repeating one of the earlier tests, we can use our fnmatch command in place of ls(1):

```
$ cd /etc
$ fnmatch '*[xyz]*' *
Flags: NONE
Matched: fnmatch('*[xyz]*','exports',flags)
Matched: fnmatch('*[xyz]*','gettytab',flags)
Matched: fnmatch('*[xyz]*','newsyslog.conf',flags)
Matched: fnmatch('*[xyz]*','security',flags)
Matched: fnmatch('*[xyz]*','skeykeys',flags)
Matched: fnmatch('*[xyz]*','syslog.conf',flags)
Matched: fnmatch('*[xyz]*','ttys',flags)
$
```

Please notice two important things here:

- The pattern is in single quotes.

- The remaining arguments are expanded by the shell before our fnmatch command is executed.

If you add the option -n to the command line, you will list all of the entries that did not match the output. Only the command is shown here:

```
$ fnmatch -n '*[xyz]*' *
```

Any command-line options must appear before the pattern. After the options, the pattern must be the first command-line argument. All remaining arguments are tested against the pattern.

The FNM_NOESCAPE Flag

The FNM_NOESCAPE flag bit disables the fnmatch(3) capability to escape meta-characters. To test this, first change to the /tmp directory and create an empty test file named [file]:

```
$ cd /tmp
$ >'[file]'
```

Now test the `fnmatch` command using the escape characters:

```
$ fnmatch '\[file\]' *
Flags: NONE
Matched: fnmatch('\[file\]','[file]',flags)
$
```

From all of the files in the `/tmp` directory, it matched the pattern literally with filename
`[file]`. The pattern `\[file\]` matches because the escape characters indicate that the following meta-characters should be treated as normal characters. Adding the flag `FNM_NOESCAPE`
(option `-e`) changes things:

```
$ fnmatch -e '\[file\]' *
Flags: FNM_NOESCAPE
$
```

In this case, no match is attained. This happens because the leading backslash must now
match part of the string. The remainder of the pattern is now a range, since the backslashes are
not acting as escape characters when `FNM_NOESCAPE` is used.

The `FNM_CASEFOLD` Flag

The `FNM_CASEFOLD` allows the programmer to specify that `fnmatch(3)` ignore the case of the
letters when performing the pattern match. This is confirmed with the help of the test program
(option `-c` used):

```
$ cd /etc
$ fnmatch -c 'HOSTS*' *
Flags: FNM_CASEFOLD
Matched: fnmatch('HOSTS*','hosts',flags)
Matched: fnmatch('HOSTS*','hosts.allow',flags)
Matched: fnmatch('HOSTS*','hosts.equiv',flags)
Matched: fnmatch('HOSTS*','hosts.lpd',flags)
$
```

In this example, the pattern `HOSTS*` matches the file `hosts`, although the case differs.

Feature Warning

The `FNM_CASEFOLD` flag appears to be a GNU C library feature and is not available on other UNIX
platforms. This feature is supported by FreeBSD and Linux, however.

The `FNM_PATHNAME` Flag

The `FNM_PATHNAME` flag adds some pathname semantics to the `fnmatch(3)` function. This
option requires that slashes (`/`) occurring in patterns must match slashes in the supplied input
string. This makes it possible to perform directory and file pattern matches more intelligently.
To perform this test, first create a temporary directory in `/tmp` as follows:

```
$ make one
mkdir /tmp/one
mkdir /tmp/one/log
```

```
mkdir /tmp/one/two
mkdir /tmp/one/two/log
date >/tmp/one/log/date1.log
date >/tmp/one/log/.date3
date >/tmp/one/two/log/date2.log
$
```

From this, you can see that a number of subdirectories are created, and two log files were created with the **date(1)** command. Now perform the following:

```
$ fnmatch '/tmp/*/log/*.log' `find /tmp/one`
Flags: NONE
Matched: fnmatch('/tmp/*/log/*.log','/tmp/one/log/date1.log',flags)
Matched: fnmatch('/tmp/*/log/*.log','/tmp/one/two/log/date2.log',flags)
$
```

If you look at this output carefully, you will see that one match is not intended. The first match makes sense because the subdirectory **one** matches the first *, and the filename **date1** matches the second *.

In the second case, however, the first * actually matches the string **one/two**, and the second * matches the **date2** in **date2.log**. The spirit of this match suggests that there should have only been one directory level between **/tmp/** and **/log/*.log**.

To accomplish this, the **FNM_PATHNAME** flag (option **-p**) must be enabled:

```
$ fnmatch -p '/tmp/*/log/*.log' `find /tmp/one`
Flags: FNM_PATHNAME
Matched: fnmatch('/tmp/*/log/*.log','/tmp/one/log/date1.log',flags)
$
```

The results now agree with what was expected.

Macro Name Note

FNM_FILE_NAME is provided on some UNIX platforms as a synonym for FNM_PATHNAME.

The FNM_PERIOD Flag

This flag causes strings that have leading periods to match only when the pattern has leading periods. Another way to say this is that * and ?, for example, will not match a leading period in the string with the flag **FNM_PERIOD** enabled. This also applies to ranges.

Usually the **FNM_PERIOD** flag is used in combination with the **FNM_PATHNAME** flag. The **FNM_PATHNAME** flag causes a period to be considered a leading period, if it follows a slash (/) character. Assuming that you still have the directory **/tmp/one** from the last experiment, perform the following pattern test using only the **FNM_PATHNAME** (**-p**) option:

```
$ fnmatch -p '/tmp/*/log/*' `find /tmp/one`
Flags: FNM_PATHNAME
Matched: fnmatch('/tmp/*/log/*','/tmp/one/log/date1.log',flags)
```

```
Matched: fnmatch('/tmp/*/log/*','/tmp/one/log/.date3',flags)
$
```

Notice that in this experiment the pattern specifies * for the last filename component. Using this pattern, two files matched: **date1.log** and **.date3**. Adding the **FNM_PERIOD** flag (option -P), causes the following results to be displayed instead:

```
$ fnmatch -pP '/tmp/*/log/*' `find /tmp/one`
Flags: FNM_PATHNAME FNM_PERIOD
Matched: fnmatch('/tmp/*/log/*','/tmp/one/log/date1.log',flags)
$
```

In this output, fnmatch(3) does not permit the leading period in **.date3** to match with the * pattern character. If your object was the files prefixed with periods, then you would alter the match string:

```
$ fnmatch -pP '/tmp/*/log/.*' `find /tmp/one`
Flags: FNM_PATHNAME FNM_PERIOD
Matched: fnmatch('/tmp/*/log/.*','/tmp/one/log/.date3',flags)
$
```

In this example, the period (.) was added to the pattern string in order to effect a match to **.date3**.

The FNM_LEADING_DIR Flag

This option causes the pattern match to occur on a directory component level. After the pattern match, anything that follows starting with a slash (/) is ignored for pattern matching purposes.

```
$ cd /tmp
$ fnmatch -d 'on*' `find one`
Flags: FNM_LEADING_DIR
Matched: fnmatch('on*','one',flags)
Matched: fnmatch('on*','one/log',flags)
Matched: fnmatch('on*','one/log/date1.log',flags)
Matched: fnmatch('on*','one/log/.date3',flags)
Matched: fnmatch('on*','one/two',flags)
Matched: fnmatch('on*','one/two/log',flags)
Matched: fnmatch('on*','one/two/log/date2.log',flags)
$
```

The documentation does not suggest that **FNM_PATHNAME** is required. Experiments suggest that **FNM_LEADING_DIR** works with or without the **FNM_PATHNAME** flag.

Feature Warning

The **FNM_LEADING_DIR** flag appears to be a GNU C library feature and is not available on other UNIX platforms. This feature is supported by FreeBSD and Linux, however.

The glob(3) Function

The glob(3) function represents another way that a process can gather a list of file and directory name objects. Unlike the fnmatch(3) function, the glob(3) function actually performs directory searches. The function synopsis for glob(3) and globfree(3) is as follows:

```
#include <glob.h>

int glob(
    const char *pattern,
    int flags,
    int (*errfunc)(const char *, int),
    glob_t *pglob);

void globfree(glob_t *pglob);

typedef struct {
    int     gl_pathc;       /* count of total paths so far */
    int     gl_matchc;      /* count of paths matching pattern */
    int     gl_offs;        /* reserved at beginning of gl_pathv */
    int     gl_flags;       /* returned flags */
    char    **gl_pathv;     /* list of paths matching pattern */
} glob_t;
```

The first argument pattern for glob(3) is a shell pattern, like the patterns used by fnmatch(3). However, the argument flags uses a different set of flags that will be described shortly. Argument errfunc is an optional function pointer and must be a null pointer when it is not used. The final argument pglob is a pointer to a glob_t structure.

The function globfree(3) should be called after a successful call to glob(3) has been made, and the information contained in the structure glob_t is no longer required. This function releases memory occupied by the array member gl_pathv and perhaps other implementation-defined storage.

The glob_t structure member gl_pathv is a returned array of matching filenames. The member gl_pathc is a count of how many string pointers are contained in gl_pathv. When gl_pathc is zero, there is no gl_pathv array allocated, and it should not be referenced. When the gl_pathv array is allocated, the last member of the array is followed by a null pointer.

The member gl_flags is used by glob(3) to return flag bits. Flag bit GLOB_MAGCHAR is one flag that may be returned in this member to indicate that the pattern argument contained at least one meta-character.

The member gl_matchc contains the current number of matched pathnames for the current glob(3) call. Since glob(3) can be called to append to the gl_pathv array, gl_matchc is useful for determining how many paths were appending with the current function call.

The member gl_offs must be initialized prior to the first call to glob(3) for the given glob_t structure used, when the flag GLOB_DOOFFS is set. This member indicates how many initial gl_pathv array entries to reserve as null pointers. If you do not need to reserve any array entries, then initialize this value to zero (not using flag GLOB_DOOFFS also will work).

The flag GLOB_ERR causes glob(3) to stop the directory scan at the first sign of trouble. By default, glob(3) ignores directory scan errors and attempts to match as much as possible. Using flag GLOB_ERR changes this behavior so that glob(3) will exit with the first error encountered.

Multiple calls to glob(3) are permitted, to gather additional member entries. The GLOB_ERR flag applied in an earlier call will influence later calls when the same pglob argument is used. This is the result of the GLOB_ERR flag being saved in the gl_flags member of the glob_t structure.

Return Values for glob(3)

When glob(3) returns normally, the value zero is returned. However, when an error occurs, the value GLOB_NOSPACE or GLOB_ABEND is returned instead.

When GLOB_NOSPACE is returned, this indicates that glob(3) was unable to allocate or reallocate memory. This might be a sign that you are failing to call globfree(3).

The return value GLOB_ABEND indicates that the directory scan was stopped. An error may have occurred while scanning the directory and flag bit GLOB_ERR was set. Alternatively, the errfunc function may have returned non-zero to cause the scan to be stopped.

Before the individual glob(3) flags are discussed, an example program is presented in Listing 20.2. This program will permit you to experiment with the various glob(3) flags and patterns.

LISTING 20.2   glob.c—Exerciser for the glob(3) and globfree(3) Functions

```
 1:   /* glob.c */
 2:
 3:   #include <stdio.h>
 4:   #include <stdlib.h>
 5:   #include <unistd.h>
 6:   #include <errno.h>
 7:   #include <string.h>
 8:   #include <glob.h>
 9:
10:   /*
11:    * Provide command usage instructions :
12:    */
13:   static void
14:   usage(void) {
15:
16:       puts("Usage: glob [options] pattern...");
17:       puts("Options:");
18:       puts("\t-a\tGLOB_APPEND");
19:       puts("\t-c\tGLOB_NOCHECK");
20:       puts("\t-o n\tGLOB_DOOFFS");
21:       puts("\t-e\tGLOB_ERR");
22:       puts("\t-m\tGLOB_MARK");
23:       puts("\t-n\tGLOB_NOSORT");
```

continued from previous page

```
24:         puts("\t-B\tGLOB_BRACE");
25:         puts("\t-N\tGLOB_NOMAGIC");
26:         puts("\t-Q\tGLOB_QUOTE");
27:         puts("\t-T\tGLOB_TILDE");
28:     }
29:
30:     /*
31:      * Report the flag bits in use as confirmation :
32:      */
33:     static void
34:     report_flags(int flags) {
35:
36:         fputs("Flags:",stdout);
37:         if ( flags & GLOB_APPEND )
38:             fputs(" GLOB_APPEND",stdout);
39:         if ( flags & GLOB_DOOFFS )
40:             fputs(" GLOB_DOOFFS",stdout);
41:         if ( flags & GLOB_ERR )
42:             fputs(" GLOB_ERR",stdout);
43:         if ( flags & GLOB_MARK )
44:             fputs(" GLOB_MARK",stdout);
45:         if ( flags & GLOB_NOSORT )
46:             fputs(" GLOB_NOSORT",stdout);
47:         if ( flags & GLOB_NOCHECK )
48:             fputs(" GLOB_NOCHECK",stdout);
49:         if ( flags & GLOB_BRACE )
50:             fputs(" GLOB_BRACE",stdout);
51:         if ( flags & GLOB_MAGCHAR )
52:             fputs(" GLOB_MAGCHAR",stdout);
53:         if ( flags & GLOB_NOMAGIC )
54:             fputs(" GLOB_NOMAGIC",stdout);
55:         if ( flags & GLOB_QUOTE )
56:             fputs(" GLOB_QUOTE",stdout);
57:         if ( flags & GLOB_TILDE )
58:             fputs(" GLOB_TILDE",stdout);
59:         if ( !flags )
60:             puts(" NONE");
61:         else
62:             putchar('\n');
63:     }
64:
65:     /*
66:      * Error callback function :
67:      */
68:     static int
69:     errfunc(const char *path,int e) {
70:         printf("%s: %s\n",strerror(e),path);
71:         return 0;
72:     }
73:
74:     /*
75:      * Report the glob_t results :
76:      */
```

```
77:  static void
78:  report_glob(glob_t *gp) {
79:      int x;
80:      int g_offs = 0;                /* glob offset */
81:
82:      if ( gp->gl_pathc < 1 ) {
83:          puts("There are no glob results.");
84:          return;
85:      }
86:      printf("There were %d matches returned:\n",gp->gl_pathc);
87:
88:      if ( gp->gl_flags & GLOB_DOOFFS )
89:          g_offs = gp->gl_offs;     /* Allow for offset */
90:
91:      for ( x=0; x < gp->gl_pathc + g_offs; ++x )
92:          printf("%3d: %s\n",
93:              x,
94:              gp->gl_pathv[x] ? gp->gl_pathv[x] : "<NULL>");
95:
96:      report_flags(gp->gl_flags);
97:      putchar('\n');
98:  }
99:
100: /*
101:  * Main program :
102:  */
103: int
104: main(int argc,char **argv) {
105:     int z;                       /* General status */
106:     glob_t g;                    /* The glob area */
107:     int flags = 0;               /* All other flags */
108:     int a = 0;                   /* GLOB_APPEND flag */
109:     int offs = 0;                /* Offset */
110:     const char cmdopts[] = "aco:emnBNQTh";
111:
112:     /*
113:      * Process any command options :
114:      */
115:     while ( (z = getopt(argc,argv,cmdopts)) != -1 )
116:         switch ( z ) {
117:         case 'a' :
118:             a = GLOB_APPEND;
119:             break;
120:         case 'o' :
121:             flags |= GLOB_DOOFFS;
122:             offs = atoi(optarg);
123:             break;
124:         case 'e' :
125:             flags |= GLOB_ERR;
126:             break;
127:         case 'm' :
128:             flags |= GLOB_MARK;
129:             break;
```

continued from previous page

```
130:          case 'n' :
131:              flags |= GLOB_NOSORT;
132:              break;
133:          case 'c' :
134:              flags |= GLOB_NOCHECK;
135:              break;
136:          case 'B' :
137:              flags |= GLOB_BRACE;
138:              break;
139:          case 'N' :
140:              flags |= GLOB_NOMAGIC;
141:              break;
142:          case 'Q' :
143:              flags |= GLOB_QUOTE;
144:              break;
145:          case 'T' :
146:              flags |= GLOB_TILDE;
147:              break;
148:          case 'h' :
149:          default :
150:              usage();
151:              return 1;
152:          }
153:
154:      /*
155:       * We must have at least one pattern :
156:       */
157:      if ( optind >= argc ) {
158:          usage();
159:          return 1;
160:      }
161:
162:      /*
163:       * Pick the pattern string and report the flags that
164:       * are in effect for this run :
165:       */
166:      report_flags(flags|a);
167:
168:      /*
169:       * Now try pattern against all remaining command
170:       * line arguments :
171:       */
172:      for ( ; optind < argc; ++optind, flags |= a ) {
173:          /*
174:           * Invoke glob(3) to scan directories :
175:           */
176:          g.gl_offs = offs;         /* Offset, if any */
177:          z = glob(argv[optind],flags,errfunc,&g);
178:          if ( z ) {
179:              if ( z == GLOB_NOSPACE )
180:                  fputs("glob(3) ran out of memory\n",stderr);
181:              else if ( z == GLOB_ABEND )
182:                  fputs("glob(3): GLOB_ERR/errfunc\n",stderr);
```

```
183:            return 1;
184:        }
185:
186:        /*
187:         * Report glob(3) findings, unless GLOB_APPEND :
188:         */
189:        if ( !a ) {              /* If not GLOB_APPEND */
190:            report_glob(&g);     /* Report matches */
191:            globfree(&g);        /* Free gl_pathv[] etc. */
192:        } else {
193:            /*
194:             * GLOB_APPEND requested. Just accumulate
195:             * glob(3) results, but here we report the
196:             * number of matches made with each pattern:
197:             */
198:            printf("Pattern '%s' got %d matches\n",
199:                argv[optind],
200:                g.gl_matchc);
201:        }
202:    }
203:
204:    /*
205:     * If GLOB_APPEND used, then report everything at
206:     * the end :
207:     */
208:    if ( a ) {                  /* If GLOB_APPEND */
209:        report_glob(&g);        /* Report appended matches */
210:        globfree(&g);           /* Free gl_pathv[] etc. */
211:    }
212:
213:    return 0;
214: }
```

The program in Listing 20.2 is similar in many respects to Listing 20.1. Lines 115–160 have to do with parsing the command-line options, which enable various `glob(3)` flags. Note that option `-a` causes flag bit `GLOB_APPEND` to be stored into variable a, which is initialized as zero in line 108. This flag is kept separate from the other flags, which are stored as variable `flags` because `GLOB_APPEND` cannot be used the first time that `glob(3)` is called (line 177). However, the `for` loop causes a to be ORed to `flags` at the end of each loop, ensuring that `GLOB_APPEND` is used in successive iterations.

After all options are parsed from the command line, the flags in effect are reported in line 166 (note the input argument is `flags|a` so that `GLOB_APPEND` is included.

The `int` variable `optind` will point to the first non-option command-line argument after the `getopt(3)` loop has completed. These remaining command-line arguments are used as input patterns to `glob(3)` in the `for` loop of lines 172–202.

If the offset option `-o` is used, the variable `offs` contains this offset. Line 176 assigns this offset value to `g.gl_offs`. This assignment is significant only if the `GLOB_DOOFFS` flag is set in variable `flags`, when the `-o` option is processed from the command line.

The function `glob(3)` is called in line 177. The return value `z` is tested and reported in lines 178–184. Line 189 tests to see if variable `a` is zero. When `a` is zero, this indicates that no `GLOB_APPEND` is being used, and the report of each `glob(3)` pattern is reported immediately after each call (lines 190 and 191). Otherwise, when `GLOB_APPEND` has been requested, only the number of matches made for the current `glob(3)` call are reported in lines 198–200. The `GLOB_APPEND` results are reported at the end of the `for` loop in lines 209 and 210 instead.

Now examine the `report_glob()` function in lines 77–98. The `if` statement in line 82 is important, because if the `glob_t` member `gl_pathc` is zero, then `gl_pathv` is not allocated and should not be referenced. The program executes the `return` statement in line 84, when there are no results to report.

Note also in line 88 that the `if` statement tests for flag `GLOB_DOOFFS`. If it is present, you must allow for the offset when iterating through the `gl_pathv` array of pointers. Notice how the `for` loop allows for the offset `g_offs` in its test. This allowance is necessary because the loop starts at `x=0`.

To compile and provoke usage information from the program in Listing 20.2, perform the following:

```
$ make glob
cc -c  -Wall glob.c
cc -o glob glob.o
$ ./glob -h
Usage: glob [options] pattern...
Options:
        -a      GLOB_APPEND
        -o n    GLOB_DOOFFS
        -e      GLOB_ERR
        -m      GLOB_MARK
        -n      GLOB_NOSORT
        -B      GLOB_BRACE
        -N      GLOB_NOMAGIC
        -Q      GLOB_QUOTE
        -T      GLOB_TILDE
$
```

Lowercase option letters represent standard flags that are available for `glob(3)`. Uppercase options represent extension flags or non-universal ones. Option `-o` is the only option that takes an argument. It represents a numeric offset to be used with `GLOB_DOOFFS`. The `-e` option adds the `GLOB_ERR` flag, but this is not explored in the examples that follow. It is there for your own experimentation.

Flag `GLOB_DOOFFS`

This flag indicates that `glob_t` member `gl_offs` is being used to reserve a number of null pointers at the start of the `gl_pathv` array (allocated by `glob(3)`). When flag `GLOB_DOOFFS` is used, you must initialize `gl_offs` prior to calling `glob(3)`.

This sounds like a strange thing to do, but it makes a lot of sense when you are about to invoke execvp(2) to start a new command. The following prepares to execute the command cc -c -g *.c:

```
glob_t g;

g.gl_offs = 3;
glob("*.c",GLOB_DOOFFS,NULL,&g);

g.gl_pathv[0] = "cc";
g.gl_pathv[1] = "-c";
g.gl_pathv[2] = "-g";

execvp("cc",g.gl_pathv);
```

The variable g is the glob_t structure being used. Three entries are reserved in the g.gl_pathv array by assigning the value 3 to g.gl_offs (flag GLOB_DOOFFS is present in the flags argument). The call to glob(3) searches the directory for the pattern *.c.

The focus here is that g.gl_pathv[0] to g.gl_pathv[2] has been reserved for your own use. In this example, these reserved elements are used for the C compiler's first three arguments. This makes the result convenient to use with the system call execvp(2).

Try one experiment without using GLOB_DOOFFS so that you can then compare results with the next experiment. Make sure to enclose your patterns in single quotes to keep the shell from expanding them:

```
$ ./glob '*.c'
Flags: NONE
There were 2 matches returned:
  0: fnmatch.c
  1: glob.c
Flags: GLOB_MAGCHAR

$
```

This example uses no command-line options and provides one pattern '*.c'. In this result, you see two filenames were returned with the glob_t member gl_flags containing the flag GLOB_MAGCHAR. The GLOB_MAGCHAR flag, when returned, indicates that at least one meta-character was found in the pattern.

Now try the same experiment, but add an offset using the -o option. This experiment uses an offset of 3:

```
$ ./glob -o3 '*.c'
Flags: GLOB_DOOFFS
There were 2 matches returned:
  0: <NULL>
  1: <NULL>
  2: <NULL>
```

```
  3: fnmatch.c
  4: glob.c
Flags: GLOB_DOOFFS GLOB_MAGCHAR

$
```

Notice how three null pointers were reserved at the start of the **gl_pathv** array for your own use. The **gl_flags** member also reports the additional flag **GLOB_DOOFFS** that was supplied as input to **glob(3)**.

The GLOB_APPEND Flag

The flag **GLOB_APPEND** indicates that the **glob_t** structure is to have new matched pathnames appended to it instead of initializing it. The following example shows how this is done:

```
glob_t g;

g.gl_offs = 3;
glob("*.c",GLOB_DOOFFS,NULL,&g);
glob("*.C",GLOB_DOOFFS|GLOB_APPEND,NULL,&g);
```

The first call to **glob(3)** initializes the **glob_t** variable **g** and adds pathnames that match the pattern *.c. The second call with the flag **GLOB_APPEND** causes **glob(3)** to assume that **g** has already been initialized. Matches to *.C are then appended to the existing collection in **g.gl_pathv**.

Now test this feature as follows:

```
$ ./glob -a '*.c' '*.o'
Flags: GLOB_APPEND
Pattern '*.c' got 2 matches
Pattern '*.o' got 1 matches
There were 3 matches returned:
  0: fnmatch.c
  1: glob.c
  2: glob.o
Flags: GLOB_APPEND GLOB_MAGCHAR

$
```

The output shows how the first pattern '*.c' collected two matches, and the pattern '*.o' appended one more match. The result of all matches is reported at the end, and you can see that three final pathnames are reported.

The GlOB_MARK Flag

The **GLOB_MARK** flag marks directory entries by appending a slash (/) to them. Files are left as they are. The following example illustrates (note the **-m** option):

```
$ ./glob -am '/b*' '/etc/hosts'
Flags: GLOB_APPEND GLOB_MARK
Pattern '/b*' got 2 matches
Pattern '/etc/hosts' got 1 matches
There were 3 matches returned:
```

```
    0: /bin/
    1: /boot/
    2: /etc/hosts
Flags: GLOB_APPEND GLOB_MARK

$
```

Directories /bin and /boot were marked with a trailing slash. The filename /etc/hosts was not.

The GLOB_NOSORT Flag

The GLOB_NOSORT flag disables the sort feature of glob(3). The following example shows the default sorted result:

```
$ ./glob '/etc/h*'
Flags: NONE
There were 5 matches returned:
    0: /etc/host.conf
    1: /etc/hosts
    2: /etc/hosts.allow
    3: /etc/hosts.equiv
    4: /etc/hosts.lpd
Flags: GLOB_MAGCHAR

$
```

Adding the GLOB_NOSORT flag by using the -n option yields unsorted results:

```
$ ./glob -n '/etc/h*'
Flags: GLOB_NOSORT
There were 5 matches returned:
    0: /etc/hosts
    1: /etc/hosts.allow
    2: /etc/host.conf
    3: /etc/hosts.equiv
    4: /etc/hosts.lpd
Flags: GLOB_NOSORT GLOB_MAGCHAR

$
```

However, note that sorting and not sorting affect only the current glob(3) call when GLOB_APPEND is used. Consequently, while the default is to sort, appended results are not sorted ahead of earlier results. You can test this for yourself:

```
$ ./glob -a '/etc/h*' '/b*'
Flags: GLOB_APPEND
Pattern '/etc/h*' got 5 matches
Pattern '/b*' got 2 matches
There were 7 matches returned:
    0: /etc/host.conf
    1: /etc/hosts
    2: /etc/hosts.allow
    3: /etc/hosts.equiv
```

```
  4: /etc/hosts.lpd
  5: /bin
  6: /boot
Flags: GLOB_APPEND GLOB_MAGCHAR

$
```

Although the default suggests that the **gl_pathv** array should be sorted, it is sorted only within pattern groups. The first pattern matches for '**/etc/h***' are sorted, but the later matches for pattern '**/b***' are not sorted ahead of the earlier match set.

The GLOB_QUOTE Flag

By default, there is no quoting capability in **glob(3)**. Applying the flag **GLOB_QUOTE** allows **glob** to interpret a backslash (\) as a quote meta-character. The quote character causes the character following to be treated literally, even if it is a meta-character. The example illustrates this:

```
$ date >'*.c'
$ ./glob '*.c'
Flags: NONE
There were 3 matches returned:
  0: *.c
  1: fnmatch.c
  2: glob.c
Flags: GLOB_MAGCHAR

$
```

The example has carefully created a file named ***.c** that contains the current date and time. Without any special options, the **./glob** program picks up all files ending in the suffix **.c**. If you need quoting capability, to select only the file ***.c** you need **GLOB_QUOTE** (option **-Q**):

```
$ ./glob -Q '\*.c'
Flags: GLOB_QUOTE
There were 1 matches returned:
  0: *.c
Flags: GLOB_QUOTE

$
```

Here, **glob(3)** interprets the asterisk (*****) literally, because it is preceded by the quote character backslash (\) while the option **GLOB_QUOTE** is active.

The GLOB_NOCHECK Flag

Normally, when a pattern does not match, no results are returned. If you want to have the pattern returned as a result when no matches are found, add the **GLOB_NOCHECK** flag (option **-c** below):

```
$ ./glob '*.xyz'
Flags: NONE
There are no glob results.
```

```
$ ./glob -c '*.xyz'
Flags: GLOB_NOCHECK
There were 1 matches returned:
  0: *.xyz
Flags: GLOB_NOCHECK GLOB_MAGCHAR

$
```

In the first example, notice how no matches were found. Adding option -c causes the pattern itself (*.xyz) to be returned instead of no results.

The GLOB_ALTDIRFUNC Flag

This flag is documented by FreeBSD as an extension to glob(3) to enable programs such as restore(8) to provide globbing from directories stored on other media. The following additional glob_t members can be initialized with function pointers. When the flag GLOB_ALTDIRFUNC is used, these function pointers will be used in place of the glob(3) default functions for searching directories:

```
void *(*gl_opendir)(const char * name);
struct dirent *(*gl_readdir)(void *);
void (*gl_closedir)(void *);
int (*gl_lstat)(const char *name, struct stat *st);
int (*gl_stat)(const char *name, struct stat *st);
```

The program in Listing 20.2 does not support the GLOB_ALTDIRFUNC flag.

The GLOB_BRACE Flag

The GLOB_BRACE flag enables glob(3) to support csh(1) pattern groups that are specified between braces. The following example illustrates GLOB_BRACE (option -B):

```
$ ./glob -B '{*.c,*.o}'
Flags: GLOB_BRACE
There were 4 matches returned:
  0: fnmatch.c
  1: glob.c
  2: fnmatch.o
  3: glob.o
Flags: GLOB_BRACE GLOB_MAGCHAR

$
```

By using the GLOB_BRACE flag and the pattern '{*.c,*.o}', the glob(3) function was able to combine two patterns into one result. Notice that only the individual pattern results are sorted.

The GLOB_MAGCHAR Flag

The GLOB_MAGCHAR flag is never used as input to glob(3). However, it is returned in the glob_t member gl_flags when at least one meta-character exists in the pattern.

The GLOB_NOMAGIC Flag

The GLOB_NOMAGIC flag causes no results to be returned if the pattern did not make any matches and the pattern had meta-characters present. However, if no meta-characters exist in the pattern, then the pattern is returned in the same manner as GLOB_NOCHECK when no results are found. The following session shows the difference between GLOB_NOMAGIC (option -N) and GLOB_NOCHECK (option -c):

```
$ ./glob -N '*.z'
Flags: GLOB_NOMAGIC
There are no glob results.
$ ./glob -c '*.z'
Flags: GLOB_NOCHECK
There were 1 matches returned:
  0: *.z
Flags: GLOB_NOCHECK GLOB_MAGCHAR

$
```

The first command shows GLOB_NOMAGIC and a pattern with meta-characters present. The run with GLOB_NOMAGIC did not return any results, while the run with GLOB_NOCHECK returned the pattern *.z as a result. Now examine another experiment:

```
$ ./glob -N 'z.z'
Flags: GLOB_NOMAGIC
There were 1 matches returned:
  0: z.z
Flags: GLOB_NOMAGIC

$
```

In this experiment, flag GLOB_NOMAGIC causes pattern z.z to be returned, although this was not a match. The flag GLOB_NOCHECK would return the same result in this case.

The GLOB_TILDE Flag

This flag is used to enable glob(3) to interpret the Korn shell tilde (~) feature. The following illustrates (using option -T):

```
$ ./glob -T '~postgres/*'
Flags: GLOB_TILDE
There were 9 matches returned:
  0: /home/postgres/bin
  1: /home/postgres/data
  2: /home/postgres/errlog
  3: /home/postgres/include
  4: /home/postgres/lib
  5: /home/postgres/odbcinst.ini
  6: /home/postgres/pgsql-support.tar.gz
  7: /home/postgres/postgresql-7.0beta1.tar.gz
  8: /home/postgres/psqlodbc-025.tar.gz
Flags: GLOB_MAGCHAR GLOB_TILDE

$
```

In this example, the `glob(3)` function looked up the home directory for the `postgres` account and searched that home directory `/home/postgres`.

Summary

The pattern matching functions that were covered in this chapter are shell pattern matching functions. They provide the capability to expand wildcard filenames and perform `case` statement selection. When these are combined with the `fork(2)` and `exec(2)` functions of the last chapter, you have a good foundation for building a new shell.

The next chapter will delve into regular expressions. This is a more powerful pattern-matching tool that is well equipped to search for text within a file or a text editor's buffer.

CHAPTER 21

REGULAR EXPRESSIONS

T he patterns supported by the `fnmatch(3)` and `glob(3)` functions are useful for filename matches because they are simple and easily understood. Text searches, however, often require something more powerful. This chapter examines regular expressions and the support that exists for them.

Understanding Regular Expressions

While it is assumed that the reader is familiar with regular expressions, it is useful to review. This will ensure that the terminology is understood, and it may encourage you to use features that you've not been using.

Like shell patterns, regular expressions match on a character-by-character basis unless a meta-character is encountered in the pattern. Regular expressions have more meta-characters than shell patterns, which makes them more powerful. It also makes them more difficult to master.

Anchors

When searching for text within a file, it is often necessary to use anchors. An *anchor* is a meta-character that can cause a pattern to be attached to another entity. Regular expressions define two anchors:

The beginning	^
The end	$

The anchors may be attached to the beginning and end of a line or to the beginning and end of a string. The context of the anchor depends on the application.

The `egrep(1)` command uses regular expressions and can be used to illustrate. In the following example, only those lines that start with the letters `ftp` are displayed from the file `/etc/services`:

```
$ egrep '^ftp' /etc/services
ftp-data        20/tcp      #File Transfer [Default Data]
ftp-data        20/udp      #File Transfer [Default Data]
ftp             21/tcp      #File Transfer [Control]
ftp             21/udp      #File Transfer [Control]
```

```
ftp-agent        574/tcp    #FTP Software Agent System
ftp-agent        574/udp    #FTP Software Agent System
$
```

The egrep(1) pattern '^ftp' causes lines starting with ftp to be selected. The regular expression used here is ^ftp. The ^ anchor indicates that the pattern match can only succeed if ftp starts the text line. Without the anchor, other lines would have matched, including, for example, lines starting with tftp.

The next example matches lines ending with the text system:

```
$ egrep 'system$' /etc/services
#                24/tcp     any private mail system
#                24/udp     any private mail system
remotefs         556/tcp    rfs rfs_server        # Brunhoff remote filesystem
remotefs         556/udp    rfs rfs_server        # Brunhoff remote filesystem
mshnet           1989/tcp   #MHSnet system
mshnet           1989/udp   #MHSnet system
$
```

The $ anchor causes the pattern system$ to succeed only when the pattern ends at the end of the line. The anchors can also be used together:

```
$ egrep '^#$' /etc/services
#
#
#
#
$
```

In this example, the anchors in the pattern ^#$ were used to select only those lines in which # is the only character on the line. The ^ and $ anchors lose their special meaning when used in places other than the beginning and end of a pattern. For example, the pattern $#^ has no meta-characters in it.

Sets

A set is a collection of characters between the meta-characters [and]. Sets work the same as they do in shell patterns. The following egrep(1) command shows a set of two characters:

```
$ egrep '^™ftp' /etc/services
tftp             69/tcp     #Trivial File Transfer
tftp             69/udp     #Trivial File Transfer
mftp             349/tcp
mftp             349/udp
$
```

The first character on the line matches a t or m from the specified set [tm] in the regular expression.

When the character ^ occurs as the first character of the set, it becomes a meta-character. It reverses the sense of the set. For example the pattern [^tm] matches any character except t or m. If the ^ character occurs in any other place within the set, it is not special. For example, the pattern [tm^] matches the characters t, m, or ^.

To include the] character within the set, make it the first character of the set (or immediately following the ^ character). The following example searches for a line that starts with <abc> or [abc].

```
$ egrep '^[[<]abc[]>]' file
```

Range

A *range* is an extension of the set idea. A range is specified within the meta-characters [and] and has the hyphen character used between the extremes. For example, the range pattern [A-Z] specifies the set of all uppercase letters.

Ranges can be grouped together. For example, the range [A-Za-z] allows you to select any letter, without regard to case. They may also be combined with sets. The range pattern [A-Z01] will match any uppercase character or the digits 0 or 1.

Like sets, the ^ character reverses the sense of the set if it occurs as the first character. For example, the pattern [^A-Z] matches any character except uppercase alphabetic characters.

Character Classes

Regular expressions also include character classes. These use the meta-character pair [: and :]. An example of a character class is [:digit:], which represents any numeric digit. Valid class names are as follows and are listed in ctype(3):

alnum	digit	punct
alpha	graph	space
blank	lower	upper
cntrl	print	xdigit

These class names correspond to the ctype(3) macros isalnum(3), isdigit(3), ispunct(3), and so on.

The . Meta-Character

The . meta-character matches any single character. The following example shows a pattern in which any first character is accepted as a match:

```
$ egrep '^.ftp' /etc/services
tftp            69/tcp      #Trivial File Transfer
tftp            69/udp      #Trivial File Transfer
sftp            115/tcp     #Simple File Transfer Protocol
sftp            115/udp     #Simple File Transfer Protocol
bftp            152/tcp     #Background File Transfer Program
bftp            152/udp     #Background File Transfer Program
mftp            349/tcp
mftp            349/udp
$
```

Parenthesized Match Subexpression

A regular expression can be included within the parenthesis characters (and), which perform a grouping function. The following egrep(1) command illustrates a simple example:

```
$ egrep '^™(ftp)' /etc/services
tftp            69/tcp      #Trivial File Transfer
tftp            69/udp      #Trivial File Transfer
mftp           349/tcp
mftp           349/udp
$
```

Parenthesized matches cause substrings to be extracted from a matching operation. This and other uses of the parenthesis will become clearer as the chapter progresses.

Atoms

An *atom* is a unit that participates in pattern matching. The following are atoms within regular expressions:

- Any single non–meta-character
- A single anchor (^ or $)
- A set (such as [abc])
- A range (such as [A-Z])
- A character class (such as [:digit:])
- A parenthesized match (such as (abc[de]))

Atoms are important to understanding how a piece works in regular expressions.

Piece

A *piece* is an atom followed by the meta-character *, +, or ?. These meta-characters influence the matching process in the following ways:

*	Matches zero or more atoms
+	Matches one or more atoms
?	Matches zero or one atom

The pattern A* will match any of the following:

""	Null string
A	One A
AA	Two As
AAA	Three As

The pattern A+ insists that at least one A be matched. Alternatively, the pattern A? matches the null string or a single A character.

The pattern (abc)+ shows a parenthesized expression. This pattern matches any of the following:

abc	The + matches one () expression.
abcabc	The + matches two () expressions.
abcabcabc	The + matches any number of () expressions.

The possibilities are nearly endless when you include sets and ranges within the parentheses.

Branch

A *branch* of a regular expression is a pattern component that is separated by the pipe symbol |. It is used to specify alternative patterns to be matched. The following example shows two branches in the pattern:

```
$ egrep '^ftp|^telnet' /etc/services
ftp-data        20/tcp    #File Transfer [Default Data]
ftp-data        20/udp    #File Transfer [Default Data]
ftp             21/tcp    #File Transfer [Control]
ftp             21/udp    #File Transfer [Control]
telnet          23/tcp
telnet          23/udp
ftp-agent       574/tcp   #FTP Software Agent System
ftp-agent       574/udp   #FTP Software Agent System
telnets         992/tcp
$
```

The example selects those lines that begin with the text ftp or telnet. Branches can be used within parenthesized subexpressions:

```
$ egrep '^ftp(-agent)?' /etc/services
ftp-data        20/tcp    #File Transfer [Default Data]
ftp-data        20/udp    #File Transfer [Default Data]
ftp             21/tcp    #File Transfer [Control]
ftp             21/udp    #File Transfer [Control]
ftp-agent       574/tcp   #FTP Software Agent System
ftp-agent       574/udp   #FTP Software Agent System
$
```

In this example, the line must start with the letters ftp. The subexpression (-agent) indicates what the subexpression should match. This is modified, however, by the following ? operator, which says that zero or one of these subexpressions must match. Consequently, lines are selected that start with ftp, ftp-data, or ftp-agent.

Expression Bounds

You have already seen how the *, +, and the ? meta-characters affect the preceding atom. It is also possible to specify a bound instead. A *bound* consists of an opening brace character ({), an unsigned integer, a comma (,), another unsigned integer, and a closing brace (}). The fully specified bound {2,5} indicates that at least 2 atoms must match but no more than 5.

The second component of the bound is optional. For example, a bound of the form {3} indicates that exactly 3 matches must be made.

A bound may also be specified with a missing second count. For example, the bound {2,} specifies that 2 or more matches can be made.

The valid range for unsigned integers is between 0 and the value RE_DUP_MAX (which is 255 on most platforms). The following example demonstrates how to select those lines with a 6 followed by at least three zeros (the egrep(1) option -E is required to enable the bounds feature):

```
$ egrep -E '60{3,}' /etc/services
netviewdm1      729/tcp      #IBM NetView DM/6000 Server/Client
netviewdm1      729/udp      #IBM NetView DM/6000 Server/Client
netviewdm2      730/tcp      #IBM NetView DM/6000 send/tcp
netviewdm2      730/udp      #IBM NetView DM/6000 send/tcp
netviewdm3      731/tcp      #IBM NetView DM/6000 receive/tcp
netviewdm3      731/udp      #IBM NetView DM/6000 receive/tcp
#x11            6000-6063/tcp   X Window System
#x11            6000-6063/udp   X Window System
$
```

Quoted Characters

Given the number of meta-characters used in regular expressions, it is often necessary to quote meta-characters to remove their special meaning. The quote character used in regular expressions is the backslash (\) character. Any character that follows this backslash is interpreted literally; it is not treated as a meta character.

For example, if you want to match a pattern that includes parentheses, you need to quote the parenthesis characters. The expression \(abc\) matches the string (abc).

The Regular Expression Library

From the preceding discussion, you can appreciate that implementing regular expression searches on your own is less than trivial. However, regular expressions can be part of your programs with the help of the C library.

Compiling Regular Expressions

For efficiency, a regular expression is first compiled into an opaque data type `regex_t`. The function synopsis for compiling a regular expression is as follows:

```
#include <sys/types.h>
#include <regex.h>

int regcomp(regex_t *preg, const char *pattern, int cflags);

typedef struct {
    int         re_magic;
    size_t      re_nsub;    /* number of parenthesized subexpressions */
    const char *re_endp;    /* end pointer for REG_PEND */
    struct re_guts *re_g;   /* opaque */
} regex_t;
```

`pattern` is the string representing the regular expression that is to be compiled. The argument `preg` points to a data type declared as `regex_t`. This is where the compiled result is placed by the call. The argument `cflags` may have one or more of the following bitmasks ORed together:

REG_EXTENDED	Compile an extended regular expression, rather than the obsolete regular expression that is the default.
REG_NOSPEC	Disable all meta-characters. None of the pattern characters will be considered special when performing a match.
REG_ICASE	Ignore case when performing matching operations.
REG_NOSUB	Compile the pattern such that the matched expressions are not tracked. When matching is performed, only a success or failure will be reported.
REG_NEWLINE	Compile the pattern for newline sensitivity. Normally, when a newline appears in the string to be matched, it is not given special treatment.
REG_PEND	Compile the pattern such that the regular expression does not end with the first null byte encountered. The regular expression ends before the byte pointed to by `preg->re_endp`. This allows null bytes to be included in the regular expression.

An additional macro is defined as `REG_BASIC` (FreeBSD), which is declared as the value zero. You can use this macro when you have no other flags to specify.

Portability Note

FreeBSD 3.4 release and Linux support all of the flag options `REG_EXTENDED`, `REG_NOSPEC`, `REG_ICASE`, `REG_NOSUB`, `REG_NEWLINE`, and `REG_PEND`.

SGI IRIX 6.5, IBM AIX 4.3, UnixWare 7, and Solaris 8 do not support `REG_NOSPEC` and `REG_PEND`.

HPUX-11 does not support `REG_NOSPEC`, `REG_NOSUB`, and `REG_PEND`.

When successful, the `regcomp(3)` function returns zero, after filling the `preg` argument with the compiled result. Other return values represent error codes. These can be passed to the function `regerror(3)` to produce an error message.

Application Note

When the flag bit `REG_NOSUB` is not used, you can query the `re_nsub` member of the `regex_t` argument `preg` to find out how many subexpressions were present in the `pattern` argument.

The following demonstrates how to compile a regular expression:

```
int z;
regex_t reg;

z = regcomp(&reg,pattern,REG_EXTENDED);
if ( z != 0 )
    /* Report regcomp(3) error */
```

Once the `regcomp(3)` routine has returned successfully, the compiled expression in `reg` is ready for `regexec(3)` to use.

Reporting Errors

The function `regcomp(3)` and `regexec(3)` return different error codes from the rest of the UNIX library and system calls. FreeBSD documents these error codes, but you may find others on other UNIX platforms:

`REG_NOMATCH`	`regexec(3)` failed to match
`REG_BADPAT`	invalid regular expression
`REG_ECOLLATE`	invalid collating element
`REG_ECTYPE`	invalid character class
`REG_EESCAPE`	\ applied to unescapable character
`REG_ESUBREG`	invalid back-reference number
`REG_EBRACK`	brackets [ ] not balanced
`REG_EPAREN`	parentheses ( ) not balanced
`REG_EBRACE`	braces { } not balanced
`REG_BADBR`	invalid repetition count(s) in { }
`REG_ERANGE`	invalid character range in [ ]
`REG_ESPACE`	ran out of memory
`REG_BADRPT`	?, *, or + operand invalid

REG_EMPTY	empty (sub)expression
REG_ASSERT	you found a bug
REG_INVARG	invalid argument

To turn these error codes into a meaningful error message, call on the regerror(3) function:

```
#include <sys/types.h>
#include <regex.h>

size_t regerror(
    int errcode,
    const regex_t *preg,
    char *errbuf,
    size_t errbuf_size);
```

The regerror(3) function accepts the error code from regcomp(3) or regexec(3) in the argument errcode. The message is created in buffer errbuf for a maximum length of errbuf_size bytes. The length of the formatted message in bytes is returned. The function regerror(3) will return zero if the function is not implemented on some platforms.

The argument preg of type pointer to regex_t must be supplied. This will be the compiled result from a prior regcomp(3) call to provide the regerror(3) function with the necessary context it needs to format the message.

The following example shows how a regcomp(3) error can be reported using regerror(3):

```
int z;                              /* Error code */
regex_t reg;                        /* Compiled regexpr */
char ebuf[128];                     /* Error message buffer */

z = regcomp(&reg,pattern,REG_NOSUB|REG_EXTENDED);
if ( z != 0 ) {
    /* Report regcomp(3) error */
    regerror(z,&reg,ebuf,sizeof ebuf);
    printf("%s: regcomp(3)\n",ebuf);
    exit(1);
}
```

Freeing Regular Expressions

When you no longer require your compiled regular expression, you should use regfree(3) to free the storage it uses. The following shows the synopsis for regfree(3):

```
#include <sys/types.h>
#include <regex.h>

void regfree(regex_t *preg);
```

regfree(3) does not return a result. It accepts the argument preg, which must point to a compiled result in a data type regex_t. This will be a result previously established by regcomp(3). The last statement in the following example shows how regfree(3) is invoked:

```
int z;
regex_t reg;

z = regcomp(&reg,pattern,REG_EXTENDED);
if ( z != 0 )
    /* Report regcomp(3) error */

/* do stuff with regexec(3) here... */
regfree(&reg);                   /* Free compiled regexpr */
```

Matching Regular Expressions

Once you have successfully compiled your regular expression with the function regcomp(3), you are ready to perform some pattern matching with regexec(3):

```
#include <sys/types.h>
#include <regex.h>

int regexec(
    const regex_t *preg,
    const char *string,
    size_t nmatch,
    regmatch_t pmatch[],
    int eflags);

typedef struct {
    regoff_t  rm_so;        /* start of match offset */
    regoff_t  rm_eo;        /* end of match offset */
} regmatch_t;
```

The first argument preg is a pointer to the previously compiled regular expression, initialized by regcomp(3). The function returns 0 when successful, but it may return error codes such as REG_NOMATCH when unsuccessful. On platforms where regexec(3) is not implemented, the value REG_ENOSYS is returned (this macro is not always defined, however, for those systems that do support regexec(3)).

The argument string is the string that you want to match. The arguments nmatch and pmatch are used to return matched patterns to your calling program. This will be expanded upon later. Finally, the eflags argument may contain zero or an ORed combination of the following option flags:

REG_NOTBOL	The first character in string is not to be considered the start of the line. This prevents the anchor ^ from matching before the first string character. (This does not affect flag REG_NEWLINE; see regcomp(3).)
REG_NOTEOL	The null character that terminates the argument string is not to be considered the end of the line. This prevents anchor $ from matching at the end of string. (This does not affect flag REG_NEWLINE; see regcomp(3).)

REG_STARTEND	Process the argument `string` starting at byte offset `pmatch[0].rm_so` and consider the string ended before offset `pmatch[0].rm_eo`. The value of argument `nmatch` is ignored. FreeBSD documents that "this is an extension, compatible with but not specified POSIX 1003.2, and should be used with caution in software intended to be portable to other systems."

When the flag `REG_NOSUB` is not used in the call to `regcomp(3)`, the arguments `nmatch` and `pmatch` allow the caller to receive information about where the pattern matches occurred. There is a performance penalty associated with this, however and, if the pattern strings are not required, the `REG_NOSUB` flag is recommended for efficiency.

The `pmatch` argument points to an array of type `regmatch_t`. This defines an array of starting and ending offsets into the original `string` argument for each matched pattern. The argument `nmatch` specifies to `regexec(2)` how many array elements to fill in array `pmatch`.

Array element `pmatch[0]` identifies the starting and ending offsets of the pattern that was found in `string`. Offsets in `pmatch[1]` identify the starting and ending offsets for the first parenthesized subexpression found in the argument `string`. Element `pmatch[2]` contains the offsets for the second subexpression, and so on.

The following example shows how to define `nmatch` and a `pmatch` array to hold a maximum of 10 match strings.

```
const size_t nmatch = 10;    /* The size of array pm[] */
regmatch_t pm[10];           /* Pattern matches 0-9 */
```

Upon successful return from the `regexec(3)` function, the first character of the match is found at byte `string+pmatch[0].rm_so`. The last character of the match is found before the byte `string+pmatch[0].rm_eo`. The first byte of the first subexpression is found at `string+pmatch[1].rm_so` and ends before the byte `string+pmatch[1].rm_eo`.

Applying Regular Expressions

To give you some experience with the regular expression routines, the program in Listing 21.1 is provided:

LISTING 21.1   `regexpr.c`—A Program Using the `regexpr(3)` Routines

```
1:   /* regexpr.c */
2:
3:   #include <stdio.h>
4:   #include <stdlib.h>
5:   #include <unistd.h>
6:   #include <string.h>
7:   #include <sys/types.h>
8:   #include <regex.h>
9:
```

continued from previous page

```
10:  /*
11:   * Provide usage instructions :
12:   */
13:  static void
14:  usage(void) {
15:
16:      puts("Usage:\tregexpr [options] pattern <file");
17:      puts("Options:");
18:      puts("\t-e\tREG_EXTENDED");
19:      puts("\t-b\tREG_BASIC");
20:      puts("\t-n\tREG_NOSPEC");
21:      puts("\t-i\tREG_ICASE");
22:      puts("\t-s\tREG_NOSUB");
23:  }
24:
25:  /*
26:   * Perform a substring operation :
27:   */
28:  static char *
29:  substr(const char *str,unsigned start,unsigned end) {
30:      unsigned n = end - start;
31:      static char stbuf[256];      /* Local static buffer */
32:
33:      strncpy(stbuf,str+start,n); /* Copy substring */
34:      stbuf[n] = 0;                /* Null terminate */
35:      return stbuf;                /* Return static buffer */
36:  }
37:
38:  /*
39:   * Main program :
40:   */
41:  int
42:  main(int argc,char **argv) {
43:      int z;                       /* General status code */
44:      int x;                       /* Loop iterator */
45:      int lno = 0;                 /* Line number */
46:      int cmdopt_h = 0;            /* -h ; usage option */
47:      int cflags = 0;              /* Compile flags */
48:      regex_t reg;                 /* Compiled regular expression */
49:      char *pattern;               /* Regular expression */
50:      const size_t nmatch = 10;    /* The size of array pm[] */
51:      regmatch_t pm[10];           /* Pattern matches 0-9 */
52:      char ebuf[128];              /* Error message buffer */
53:      char lbuf[256];              /* Line buffer */
54:      const char cmdopts[] = "hebnis";
55:
56:      while ( (z = getopt(argc,argv,cmdopts)) != -1 )
57:          switch ( z ) {
58:          case 'b' :
59:              cflags |= REG_BASIC;
60:              break;
61:          case 'e' :
62:              cflags |= REG_EXTENDED;
```

```
63:                      break;
64:              case 'n' :
65:                  cflags |= REG_NOSPEC;
66:                  break;
67:              case 'i' :
68:                  cflags |= REG_ICASE;
69:                  break;
70:              case 's' :
71:                  cflags |= REG_NOSUB;
72:                  break;
73:              case 'h' :
74:              default  :
75:                  cmdopt_h = 1;
76:              }
77:
78:          if ( optind + 1 != argc || cmdopt_h ) {
79:              usage();
80:              return 1;
81:          }
82:
83:          /*
84:           * Compile the regular expression :
85:           */
86:          pattern = argv[optind];
87:
88:          z = regcomp(&reg,pattern,cflags);
89:
90:          if ( z != 0 ) {
91:              regerror(z,&reg,ebuf,sizeof ebuf);
92:              fprintf(stderr,"%s: pattern '%s'\n",ebuf,pattern);
93:              return 1;
94:          }
95:
96:          /*
97:           * Report the number of subexpressions :
98:           */
99:          if ( !(cflags & REG_NOSUB) )
100:             printf("There were %d subexpressions.\n",reg.re_nsub);
101:
102:         /*
103:          * Now process each line for matches :
104:          */
105:         while ( fgets(lbuf,sizeof lbuf,stdin) ) {
106:             ++lno;                          /* Increment the line number */
107:             if ( (z = strlen(lbuf)) > 0 && lbuf[z-1] == '\n' )
108:                 lbuf[z-1] = 0;              /* Eliminate newline character */
109:
110:             /*
111:              * Now apply regular expression matching to this line :
112:              */
113:             z = regexec(&reg,lbuf,nmatch,pm,0);
114:
115:             if ( z == REG_NOMATCH )
```

continued from previous page

```
116:            continue;
117:        else if ( z != 0 ) {
118:            regerror(z,&reg,ebuf,sizeof ebuf);
119:            fprintf(stderr,"%s: regcomp('%s')\n",ebuf,lbuf);
120:            return 2;
121:        }
122:
123:        for ( x=0; x<nmatch && pm[x].rm_so != -1; ++x ) {
124:            if ( !x )   /* Print the matching line number */
125:                printf("%04d: %s\n",lno,lbuf);
126:            printf("  $%d='%s'\n",
127:                x,                      /* Report substring $x */
128:                substr(lbuf,pm[x].rm_so,pm[x].rm_eo));
129:        }
130:    }
131:
132:    regfree(&reg);                      /* Free compiled regexpr */
133:    return 0;
134: }
```

This program is designed to accept command-line arguments to establish certain `regcomp(3)` option flags. After options, if any, the regular expression pattern string is taken from the command line. The pattern is then applied to data that is supplied to the program on standard input.

Compiling and invoking the usage information from the program are performed as follows:

```
$ make
cc -c  -Wall regexpr.c
cc -o regexpr regexpr.o
$ ./regexpr -h
Usage:  regexpr [options] pattern <file
Options:
        -e      REG_EXTENDED
        -b      REG_BASIC
        -n      REG_NOSPEC
        -i      REG_ICASE
        -s      REG_NOSUB
$
```

In lines 56–76 the program applies the various flags as the command-line options are parsed. The pattern string is established in line 86.

The pattern is compiled in line 88. If an error occurs, it is reported in lines 90–94. If the flag `REG_NOSUB` was not used, the value of `reg.re_nsub` is reported in line 100.

Standard input is read in the `while` loop at line 105. The newline character is removed in line 108 for convenience. The `recexec(3)` function is called in line 113. If no match is reported, the `continue` statement skips the remaining processing of the loop (line 116). Errors are reported in lines 117–121.

The for loop in lines 123–129 reports the matches returned from regexec(3). Line 125 reports the text line that brought about the match (when x=0 only). The match results are displayed as values $0 through $9 in lines 126–128. The $0 value is the match string, and $1 to $9 represent matched subexpressions, if any. However, if the starting offset is the value -1, the for loop exits (see line 123).

The following example uses the -e option for REG_EXTENDED and the -i option for REG_ICASE flags. Applying this to the source file regexpr.c, the following result was obtained:

```
$ ./regexpr -ei '([a-z]+)( *)\|= *REG_([a-z]+);' <regexpr.c
There were 3 subexpressions.
0059:            cflags  |= REG_BASIC;
  $0='cflags  |= REG_BASIC;'
  $1='cflags'
  $2='  '
  $3='BASIC'
0062:            cflags  |= REG_EXTENDED;
  $0='cflags  |= REG_EXTENDED;'
  $1='cflags'
  $2='  '
  $3='EXTENDED'
0065:            cflags  |= REG_NOSPEC;
  $0='cflags  |= REG_NOSPEC;'
  $1='cflags'
  $2='  '
  $3='NOSPEC'
0068:            cflags  |= REG_ICASE;
  $0='cflags  |= REG_ICASE;'
  $1='cflags'
  $2='  '
  $3='ICASE'
0071:            cflags  |= REG_NOSUB;
  $0='cflags  |= REG_NOSUB;'
  $1='cflags'
  $2='  '
  $3='NOSUB'
$
```

The subexpression was designed to capture the C variable and the flag name without the REG_ prefix, for the |= assignments. The $0 display for each line shows the extent of the entire match. The $1 match string shows the extracted C variable name cflags. The $2 subexpression was thrown in for good measure, to demonstrate the space characters that were matched by the subexpression (*). The $3 match string shows the extractions without the REG_ prefix.

The next example shows how a bound expression extracted a string constant with two or more leading spaces in it:

```
$ ./regexpr -e '" {2,}' <regexpr.c
There were 0 subexpressions.
0126:            printf("  $%d='%s'\n",
  $0='"  '
$
```

You are encouraged to apply other options and regular expressions to the `./regexpr` test program. Using this program as a testing tool, you can use regular expression routines in your application confidently.

Summary

This chapter has looked at regular expressions in depth. The `regexp(3)` set of routines truly enhances programs that need the flexible pattern matching that regular expressions provide.

The next chapter introduces interprocess communications. This will lead you into the topics of message queues, semaphores, and shared memory.

INDEX

E

G

S